BARRON'S

PSAT/ NMSQT*

19TH EDITION

Sharon Weiner Green, M.A.
Former Instructor in English
Merritt College
Oakland, California

Ira K. Wolf, Ph.D.
Former High School Teacher, College Professor, and
University Director of Mathematics Teacher Preparation

Brian W. Stewart, M.Ed.
Founder and President
BWS Education Consulting, Inc.

BARRON'S

ABOUT THE AUTHORS

Sharon Green started helping prepare students for the PSAT and SAT as a 13-year-old assistant at her father's college entrance tutoring course; she has never stopped since. A National Merit Scholar, she holds degrees from Harvard College, New York University School of Education, and the University of California at Berkeley. Her test preparation books, all published by Barron's, run the gamut from the California High School Proficiency Examination to the GRE. Whenever she can dig her way out from under multiple dictionaries, Sharon enjoys folk dancing, reading Jane Austen and science fiction, and watching Little League baseball.

Dr. Ira Wolf, who earned his bachelor's, master's, and doctoral degrees at Tufts, Yale, and Rutgers, respectively, has had a long career in math education. In addition to teaching math at the high school level for several years, he was a professor of mathematics at Brooklyn College and the Director of the Mathematics Teacher Preparation program at SUNY Stony Brook.

Dr. Wolf has been helping students prepare for college entrance exams, including the PSAT, SAT, ACT, and SAT Subject Tests, for more than 40 years. He is the founder of PowerPrep, Inc., a test preparation company on Long Island that has worked with more than 10,000 high school students since 2000.

Brian W. Stewart is the founder and president of BWS Education Consulting, Inc., a boutique tutoring and test preparation company based in Columbus, Ohio. His company has worked with thousands of students from all over the world to help them improve their test scores and earn admission to selective schools. Brian earned his A.B. in Philosophy at Princeton University and his Master's in Education at The Ohio State University. He is also the author of Barron's *ACT*, Barron's *Strategies and Practice for the PSAT/NMSQ*T, and Barron's *SAT Reading Workbook*. You can connect with Brian at *www.bwseducationconsulting.com*.

© Copyright 2018, 2016, 2014, 2012, 2010, 2008 by Barron's Educational Series, Inc.

Previous editions © copyright 2006, 2004, 2003, 1999, 1997, 1993, 1989, 1986, 1982, 1976, 1973, 1971, 1966, 1965 by Barron's Educational Series, Inc., under the title *How to Prepare for the PSAT/NMSQT*.

All inquiries should be addressed to:
Barron's Educational Series, Inc.
250 Wireless Boulevard
Hauppauge, NY 11788
www.barronseduc.com

International Standard Serial No.: 1941-7055

ISBN: 978-1-4380-1106-6

PRINTED IN THE UNITED STATES OF AMERICA
9 8 7 6 5 4 3 2 1

10%
POST-CONSUMER WASTE
Paper contains a minimum of 10% post-consumer waste (PCW). Paper used in this book was derived from certified, sustainable forestlands.

Contents

PART SIX: TEST YOURSELF

Preface

Welcome to the nineteenth edition of Barron's *PSAT/NMSQT*. If you are preparing for the PSAT, this is the book you need. This edition updates America's leading book focused on the PSAT. Along with the best of the time-tested features of earlier editions, today's nineteenth edition provides much, much more.

- It features three full-length sample tests modeled on the PSAT in length and difficulty, three crucial "dress rehearsals" for the day you walk into the examination room. In addition to the tests in this book, there are two full-length online practice tests.
- It clears up misconceptions you may have about the PSAT and gives you a brief rundown of the entire test.
- It prepares you for the Writing and Language section, teaching you how to spot errors and polish rough drafts so that you can shine on the PSAT and eventually on the SAT. **Note:** Although there's a Writing and Language section on the PSAT, you *don't* have to write an essay! The section contains reading passages with multiple-choice questions that test the mechanics of writing and expression of ideas.
- It briefs you on vocabulary-in-context and evidence-based reading questions, giving you key tips on how to tackle these important verbal question types.
- It takes you step by step through the double reading passages, showing you how to work your way through a pair of reading passages without wasting effort or time.
- It introduces you to the "grid-in" non-multiple-choice questions in the Math sections, teaching you shortcuts to solving problems and entering your own answers on a sample grid.
- It offers you advice on how (and when) to use a calculator in dealing with both multiple-choice and "grid-in" questions.
- It contains a separate chapter that reviews all math topics you need to know.
- It gives you the 300-word PSAT Power Word List, 300 vital words that are likely to occur on actual PSATs, plus Barron's PSAT Basic Word List, more than 1,300 words that you'll want to master as you work to build a college-level vocabulary. (For quick review, you can consult the list of Basic Word Parts.)

Most important, it teaches you the special tactics and strategies essential for scoring high on the PSAT.

No other book tells you as much about the test. No other book offers you as many questions modeled on the PSAT.

The PSAT is your chance to get yourself set for the all-important SAT. It's also your chance to qualify for some of the nation's most prestigious college scholarships. Go for your personal best; take the time to learn how to prepare for the PSAT.

This edition of Barron's *PSAT/NMSQT* is evidence of Barron's ongoing commitment to make this publication America's outstanding PSAT study guide.

PSAT/NMSQT Test Format		
Section 1 Reading	60 minutes	47 questions
1-Minute Break		
Section 2 Writing and Language	35 minutes	44 questions
5-Minute Break		
Section 3 Math—No Calculator	25 minutes	17 questions
1-Minute Break		
Section 4 Math—Calculator	45 minutes	31 questions

With the exception of four grid-in questions in each math section, all of the questions on the PSAT are multiple-choice.

Acknowledgments

The authors gratefully acknowledge all those sources who granted permission to use materials from their publications:

Pages 35–36: From *King Solomon's Ring* by Konrad Z. Lorenz, © 1952, Harper & Row, pp. 128–129.

Page 36: From "Social Behavior of the Jackdaw, *Corvus monedula*, in Relation to its Niche" by A. Röell, in *Behavior* vol. 64, no. 1/2 (1978), pp. 1–124.

Pages 38–39: From "The Tornado" by John T. Snow in *Scientific American Inc.*, April 1984, pp. 41–42. Reprinted with permission. Copyright © 1984 Scientific American, a division of Nature America, Inc. All rights reserved.

Pages 44–45: From *The Natural Wealth of Nations: Harnessing the Market for the Environment* (*The Worldwatch Environmental Alert Series*) by David Malin Roodman, Copyright © 1998, W. W. Norton & Company.

Pages 100, 103, 106, 108–109, 112–113: "The Spider and the Wasp." Reproduced with permission. Copyright © 1952 by Scientific American, a division of Nature America, Inc. All rights reserved.

Pages 114–116, 118–120: From *Chicano English in Context* by Carmen Fought, Copyright © 2003, Palgrave Macmillan, pp. 11–13.

Page 133: Excerpt from "Yonder Peasant, Who Is He?" in *Memories of a Catholic Girlhood*, copyright 1948 and renewed 1975 by Mary McCarthy, p. 57. Reprinted with permission by Houghton Mifflin Harcourt Publishing Company.

Pages 495–496: From "Huge Conservation Effort Aims to Save Vanishing Architect of the Savannah" by William K. Stevens, from *The New York Times* © 2/28/1989 The New York Times. All rights reserved. Used by permission and protected by the copyright laws of the United States. The printing, copying, redistribution, or retransmission of this Content without express written permission is prohibited.

Pages 501–502: From "Changing Climate: 10 years after *An Inconvenient Truth*" by Thomas Sumner, in *Science News*. Copyright © 2016. Reprinted with permission of Science News for Students.

Pages 504–505: From "These Journalists Dedicated Their Lives to Telling Other People's Stories. What Happens When No One Wants to Print Their Words Anymore?" from *The Nation* © 3/2/2016 The Nation. All rights reserved. Used by permission and protected by the copyright laws of the United States. The printing, copying, redistribution, or retransmission of this content without express written permission is prohibited.

ON THE ONLINE TESTS

> ### NOTE
> Link information for the two online practice tests can be found on the inside front cover of this book. Practice tests can be accessed on all mobile devices, including tablets and smartphones.

PART ONE
Introduction

Note the following icons, used throughout this book:

 Time saver

 Educated guess

 Did you notice?

 Look it up; math reference fact

 Prefixes, roots, and suffixes

 Positive or negative?

 Helpful Hint

 Caution!

 A calculator might be useful.

The PSAT/National Merit Scholarship Qualifying Test

Your plan to take the PSAT/NMSQT is perhaps your first concrete step toward planning a college career. The PSAT/NMSQT and the SAT—what do they mean to you? When do you take them? What sort of hurdles do you face? How do these tests differ from the tests you ordinarily face in school? In this section we answer these basic questions so that you will be able to move on to the following chapters and concentrate on preparing yourself for this test.

SOME BASIC QUESTIONS ANSWERED

What Is the PSAT/NMSQT?

Taking the PSAT/NMSQT is the first step in getting ready for the SAT. It is given each year in mid-October. Schools have the option of offering the exam on a Saturday or a Wednesday. You will take the PSAT on the day it is offered in your school.

The test has four sections:

- a 60-minute Reading section consisting of 47 multiple-choice questions.
- a 35-minute Writing and Language section consisting of 44 multiple-choice questions.
- a 25-minute Math section where calculators may not be used. This section consists of 17 questions: 13 multiple-choice questions and 4 grid-in questions.
- a 45-minute Math section where calculators may be used. This section consists of 31 questions: 27 multiple-choice questions and 4 grid-in questions.

Why Is the Test Called the PSAT/NMSQT?

The "P" in PSAT stands for "preliminary." So first and foremost the PSAT is the Preliminary SAT. As such, its function is to familiarize students with the types of questions that are on the SAT and to help students assess their strengths and weaknesses.

The PSAT also serves as the National Merit Scholarship Qualifying Test (NMSQT). Approximately 50,000 students nationally gain recognition in the NMSQT competition by earning high scores on the PSAT.

Who Takes the PSAT/NMSQT?

Essentially, all high school students who plan to take the SAT take the PSAT in October of their junior year. In addition, about 50 percent of sophomores and many freshmen take the

PSAT for practice, although many sophomores take the PSAT 10 (see below). **Note:** You can qualify for recognition in the National Merit Scholarship competition only as a junior. Even if you had perfect scores on the PSAT as a sophomore, you would have to take it again as a junior to receive a National Merit letter of commendation and/or to qualify as a semifinalist.

What Is the PSAT 10? How Will this Book Help Me Prepare for It?

The PSAT 10 is the same test as the PSAT/NMSQT. Thus, if you would like to prepare for the PSAT 10, this book is exactly what you need. Although the tests themselves are identical, there are three important differences between the PSAT 10 and the PSAT/NMSQT:

- The PSAT 10 is for tenth-grade students, while the PSAT/NMSQT is for eleventh-grade students (although many underclassmen take the PSAT/NMSQT).
- Sophomores, whether they take the PSAT 10 or the PSAT/NMSQT, cannot participate in the National Merit scholarship competition. Only juniors who take the PSAT/NMSQT can take part in this competition. Students who take either test will be considered for other scholarship programs through the Student Search Service®.
- The PSAT 10 is offered in the spring, while the PSAT/NMSQT is offered in the fall.

Some schools do not offer the PSAT 10. In that case, you may be able to take the PSAT/ NMSQT in your sophomore year. Check with your school. Some schools do not allow their sophomores to take the PSAT/NMSQT. Some schools that offer the PSAT 10 require their students to take it, whereas others leave the decision up to their students.

What Are Merit Scholarships?

Merit Scholarships are prestigious national awards that carry with them a chance for solid financial aid. Conducted by NMSC, an independent, nonprofit organization with offices at 1560 Sherman Avenue, Suite 200, Evanston, Illinois 60201-4897, the Merit Program today is supported by grants from more than 500 corporations, private foundations, colleges and universities, and other organizations. The top-scoring PSAT/NMSQT participants in every state are named Semifinalists. Those who advance to Finalist standing compete for one-time National Merit $2500 Scholarships and renewable, four-year Merit Scholarships, which may be worth as much as $10,000 a year for four years.

Check out Merit Scholarships at *www.nationalmerit.org.*

What Is the National Achievement Scholarship Program for Outstanding Black Students?

This program is aimed at honoring and assisting promising African-American high school students throughout the country. It is also administered by NMSC. Students who enter the Merit Program by taking the PSAT/NMSQT and who are also eligible to participate in the Achievement program mark a space on their test answer sheets asking to enter this competition as well. Top-scoring African-American students in each of the regions established for the competition compete for nonrenewable National Achievement $2500 Scholarships and for four-year Achievement Scholarships supported by many colleges and corporate organizations.

Note: To be considered for this program, you must mark the appropriate space on your answer sheet.

Check out the National Achievement Scholarship Program at *www.nationalmerit.org.*

How Can the PSAT/NMSQT Help Me?

If you are a high school junior, it will help you gauge your potential scores on the SAT that you will take in the spring. It will give you some idea of which colleges you should apply to in your senior year. It will give you access to scholarship competitions. It will definitely give you practice in answering multiple-choice questions, where timing is an important factor.

In addition, you may choose to take advantage of the College Board's Student Search Service. This service is free for students who fill out the biographical section of the PSAT/NMSQT. If you fill out this section, you will receive mail from colleges and search programs.

How Do I Sign Up for the PSAT?

You register for the PSAT through your school. Fees, when required, are collected by your school. Fee waivers are available for students whose families cannot afford the test fee; if this applies to you, talk to your counselor.

The test is given in October. In December the results are sent to your school and to the scholarship program that you indicated on your answer sheet in the examination room. Your school will send you your score report.

What if I Am a Home-Schooled Student?

If you are a home-schooler, you must make arrangements with the principal or counselor of a nearby high school to take the test. Do not wait until the school year starts to make your arrangements. If you want to take the test in October, start the process the previous June.

Because you are a home-schooler, your score report is supposed to be sent to your home address. When you fill out your answer sheet, you must enter the state's home-school code in the school code section of the answer sheet. This will ensure that you will receive your score report. You should be able to get this number from the exam proctor or supervisor.

How Is the PSAT Different from the SAT?

There are two differences between the tests.

1. **THE PSAT IS SHORTER THAN THE SAT.** The four sections of the PSAT consist of 129 questions and take a total of two hours and forty-five minutes to complete. The same four sections of the SAT consist of 144 questions and take a total of three hours to complete.
2. **UNLIKE ON THE SAT, THERE IS NO ESSAY-WRITING SECTION ON THE PSAT.** The SAT has an optional fifth section, which consists of a 50-minute essay. For students who choose to write the essay, the SAT takes three hours and fifty minutes to complete.

How Is the PSAT Scored?

The PSAT consists of four sections: Section 1 (Reading), Section 2 (Writing and Language), Section 3 (Non-calculator Math), and Section 4 (Calculator Math).

Sections 1 and 2 combined constitute the Evidence-Based Reading and Writing test, and Sections 3 and 4 combined constitute the Math test. For each test you will receive a score between 160 and 760. Your total PSAT score is the sum of those two test scores. For example, if John has a Reading and Writing score of 560 and a Math score of 610, his total PSAT score would be 560 + 610 = 1170. In addition to those scores, your score report will list an additional score called the Selection Index, which is used by the National Merit Scholarship Corporation to determine which students will receive recognition in the National Merit competition. Your selection index is determined by adding one-fifth of your Reading and Writing score to one-tenth of your Math score. So, John's Selection Index would be $\frac{1}{5}$ (560) + $\frac{1}{10}$ (610) = 112 + 61 = 173. John's score report would look something like the following.

Score Report

Reading and Writing	Math	Total Score	Selection Index
560	610	1170	173

For each of the scores reported to you, you will also receive a percentile ranking that shows how your scores compare with those of other students who have taken the PSAT.

Because the reading and math scores on the SAT range from 200 to 800, many students add 40 points to each of their scores to approximate what their SAT scores will be. So, for example, John might expect his reading SAT score to be about 600 and his math score to be about 650, for a total score of 1250. If he uses the Barron's SAT book to conscientiously prepare for the SAT, his scores might well be higher than that. On the other hand, if he doesn't prepare or prepares only minimally, his SAT scores might be no higher than his PSAT scores, and maybe even lower.

How Are the Results of Your PSAT/NMSQT Reported?

About six to eight weeks after the test, you will receive, from your school, the following:

1. an official score report that includes:

    a. the answer you gave for each question
    b. the correct answer for each question
    c. the difficulty level of each question
    d. a Selection Index, which is used to determine eligibility for NMSC programs

2. a copy of the original test booklet that you used in the examination room

You can also access your score report online. Create an account at *collegeboard.org* and you will have access to your score report, answer explanations, and target review suggestions.

Can I Do Anything if I Miss the Test but Still Want to Participate in Scholarship Competitions?

If you fail to take the PSAT/NMSQT because you were ill or involved in an emergency, you still may be able to qualify for a National Merit or National Achievement Scholarship. You need to contact the NMSC to find out about alternative testing arrangements that would enable you to take part in the National Merit competitions.

If you are of Hispanic descent, you need to contact the National Hispanic Scholar Recognition Program run by the College Board. You can arrange to be considered for this program by communicating with The College Board, Suite 600, 1233 20th Street NW, Washington, DC 20036.

HOW TO APPROACH THE PSAT/NMSQT

TEST-TAKING TACTICS

What Tactics Can Help Me When I Take the PSAT?

1. **MEMORIZE THE DIRECTIONS GIVEN IN THIS BOOK FOR EACH TYPE OF QUESTION.** These are only slightly different from the exact words you'll find on the PSAT you'll take. During the test, you won't have to waste even a few seconds reading any directions or looking at any sample questions.

2. **KNOW THE FORMAT OF THE TEST.** The test has four sections:

   ■ Section 1 is a 60-minute Reading section consisting of 47 multiple-choice questions.

   ■ Section 2 is a 35-minute Writing and Language section consisting of 44 multiple-choice questions.

   ■ Section 3 is a 25-minute Math section where calculators may not be used. This section consists of 17 questions: 13 multiple-choice questions and 4 grid-in questions.

   ■ Section 4 is a 45-minute Math section where calculators may be used. This section consists of 31 questions: 27 multiple-choice questions and 4 grid-in questions.

3. **ELIMINATE AS MANY WRONG ANSWERS AS YOU CAN AND THEN MAKE AN EDUCATED GUESS.** Deciding between two choices is easier than deciding among four. The more choices you eliminate, the better your chance of guessing correctly.

4. **BUBBLE IN AN ANSWER FOR EVERY QUESTION.** If you have no idea which answer choice is correct, *make a wild guess.* If you don't have enough time to answer every question in a particular section, *take your final ten seconds and make a wild guess on every question you haven't yet answered.*

5. **CHANGE ANSWERS** *ONLY* **IF YOU HAVE A GOOD REASON FOR DOING SO.** Don't give in to last-minute panic. It's usually better not to change your answers on a sudden hunch or whim.

6. **BE SURE TO BRING A CALCULATOR THAT YOU ARE COMFORTABLE USING.** In the first math section, calculators are not permitted. Even in the second math section, where calculators are permitted, many questions do not require you to use one. In the second math section, though, several questions cannot be answered without using a calculator, so you must bring one with you. **Note:** The test center will not have a calculator for you, you may not share a calculator with a friend, and you may not use the calculator on your phone.

7. **REMEMBER THAT YOU ARE ALLOWED TO WRITE ANYTHING YOU WANT IN YOUR TEST BOOKLET. MAKE GOOD USE OF IT.** Circle questions you skip, and put big question marks next to questions you answer but are unsure about. In reading passages, circle key words and underline or put a mark in the margin next to any major point. On math questions, mark up diagrams, adding lines when necessary. And, of course, use all the space provided to solve the problem. In short, write anything that will help you, using whatever symbols you like. But remember, the only thing that counts is what you enter on your answer sheet. No one will ever see anything that you write in your test booklet.

8. **BE CAREFUL NOT TO MAKE ANY STRAY MARKS ON YOUR ANSWER SHEET.** This test is graded by a machine, and a machine cannot tell the difference between an accidental mark and a filled-in answer. When the machine sees two marks instead of one, the answer is marked wrong.

9. **CHECK FREQUENTLY TO MAKE SURE YOU ARE ANSWERING THE QUESTIONS IN THE RIGHT SPOTS.** No machine is going to notice that you made a mistake early in the test, that you answered question 4 in the space for question 5, and that all your following answers are in the wrong place.

10. **BE PARTICULARLY CAREFUL IN MARKING THE STUDENT-PRODUCED RESPONSES ON THE MATH GRIDS.** Before you fill in the appropriate blanks in the grids, write your answer at the top of the columns. Then go down each column and make sure you fill in the right spaces. Be sure to answer every grid-in question.

11. **DON'T GET BOGGED DOWN ON ANY ONE QUESTION.** By the time you get to the actual PSAT, you should have a fair idea of how much time to spend on each question. If a question is taking too long, just guess and go on to the next question. This is no time to try to show the world that you can stick to a job no matter how long it takes. All the machine that grades the test will notice is that after a certain point you didn't have any correct answers. Just make a guess.

REDUCING ANXIETY

How Can I Prevent PSAT Anxiety from Setting In?

1. Use this book to prepare conscientiously. The better prepared you are, the less anxiety you will have.

2. Get a good night's sleep before the test so that you are well rested and alert, and be sure to eat a good breakfast. You have a full morning ahead of you; you should have a full stomach as well.

3. Allow plenty of time for getting to the test site. Taking a test is pressure enough. You don't need the extra tension that comes from worrying about whether you will get there on time.

4. Be aware of the amount of time the test is going to take. There are four sections. The four sections will take two hours and forty-five minutes total. Add to that a five-minute break after Section 2, one-minute breaks after Sections 1 and 3, plus at least thirty minutes for paper pushing. If the test starts at 8:00 A.M., don't make a dentist appointment for 11:30 A.M. You can't possibly get there on time, and you'll just spend the last half hour of the test worrying about it.

5. The College Board tells you to bring two sharpened No. 2 pencils to the test. Bring four. They don't weigh much, and this might be the one day in the decade when two pencil points decide to break. Bring full-size pencils, not little stubs. They are easier to write with, and you might as well be comfortable.

6. Speaking of being comfortable, wear comfortable clothes. This is a test, not a fashion show. Aim for the layered look. Wear something light, but bring a sweater. The test room may be hot, or it may be cold. You can't change the room, but you can put on the sweater.

7. Bring a watch or small travel clock, which you may keep on your desk. You need one. The room in which you take the test may not have a clock, and some proctors are not very good about posting the time on the blackboard. Don't depend on them. Each time you begin a test section, write down in your booklet the time according to your watch. That way you will always know how much time you have left. **Note:** The College Board does not permit you to bring any timer or watch with an audible alarm into the testing room. No beeps! And no cell phones!

8. Bring along some quick energy in your pocket—trail mix, raisins, a candy bar. Even if the proctors don't let you eat in the test room, you can still grab a bite en route to the restrooms during the five-minute break. Taking the test can leave you feeling drained and in need of a quick pickup—bring along your favorite comfort food.

9. There will be a break after the second section. Use this period to clear your thoughts. Take a few deep breaths. Stretch. Close your eyes and imagine yourself floating or sunbathing. In addition to being under mental pressure, you're under physical pressure from sitting so long in an uncomfortable seat with a No. 2 pencil clutched in your hand. Anything you can do to loosen up and get the kinks out will ease your body and help the oxygen get to your brain.

10. Most important of all, remember: very little is riding on the result of this test. If you do poorly, no one will know; your PSAT scores are not reported to the colleges to which you plan to apply. So relax!

SAMPLE PSAT QUESTIONS

The purpose of this section is to familiarize you with the kinds of questions that appear on the PSAT. Knowing what to expect when you take the examination is an important step in preparing for the test and succeeding in it.

If you wish, you can head straight for the diagnostic test that follows to learn about your strengths and weaknesses as a test taker and to get a sense of how well you might do on the PSAT. However, before you tackle the diagnostic test, we recommend that you take a few minutes to acquaint yourself with the kinds of questions you're going to encounter.

The directions that precede the various types of questions are similar to those on the PSAT. For all except the student-produced response questions, you are to choose the best answer and fill in the corresponding blank on the answer sheet.

EVIDENCE-BASED READING

You will encounter several types of questions in the evidence-based reading test. Among them are:

- main idea questions
- vocabulary-in-context questions
- command-of-evidence question pairs
- graphics questions

➡ Example 1 _____

Main Idea Question (based on a speech by Susan B. Anthony)

The primary purpose of the passage is to

(A) explain the logic behind giving women the right to vote.
(B) correct a misapprehension about voting rights.
(C) propose a constitutional amendment granting women the franchise.
(D) question whether women can receive equal protection under the law.

➡ Example 2 _____

Vocabulary-in-Context Question.
Note that the various answer choices are all *possible* meanings of the question word.

As used in line 12, "plain" most nearly means

(A) simple.
(B) obvious.
(C) intelligible.
(D) homely.

➡ Example 3 _____

Command-of-Evidence Question Pair.
The first question directly asks you about the content of the passage. The question immediately following asks you to point out exactly where in the passage you found evidence to support your answer.

Anthony makes which point about women's right to vote?

(A) The Federal Constitution guarantees the right to vote to both women and men.
(B) No state can deny voting rights to women, since women are citizens.
(C) It is unconstitutional to arrest and fine a woman for exercising her right to vote.
(D) Women have been fighting for the right to vote for over seventy years.

Which choice provides the best evidence for the answer to the previous question?

(A) Lines 12–15 ("Suffrage . . . voting rights")
(B) Lines 18–19 ("Anthony . . . indefatigable")
(C) Lines 24–28 ("The election . . . was arrested")
(D) Lines 32–34 ("Although . . . disenfranchised")

➡ **Example 4**_____

Graphics Question (based on an analysis of the passenger list of the Mayflower)

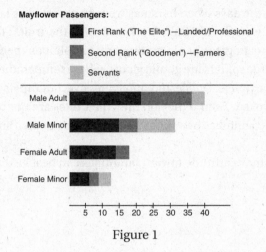

Figure 1

Which point from the passage is best supported by Figure 1?

(A) Lines 1–3 ("The preponderance . . . Pilgrims")
(B) Lines 8–11 ("Servants . . . the Compact")
(C) Lines 16–19 ("The death toll . . . ship")
(D) Lines 24–28 ("The majority . . . journey")

THE READING TEST

Your ability to read and understand the kind of material found in college texts and the more serious magazines is tested in the evidence-based reading section of the PSAT/NMSQT. There are four long reading passages on the test, ranging from 500 to 750 words, plus one pair of passages, also totaling 500 to 750 words.

Evidence-Based Reading Directions

The passages below are followed by questions on their content; questions following a pair of related passages may also be based on the relationship between the paired passages. Answer the questions on the basis of what is stated or implied in the passages and in any introductory material or accompanying graphics that may be provided.

Questions 1–6 are based on the following passages.

Passage 1

Spiders, and in particular hairy spiders, possess a highly developed sense of touch. Tarantulas, for example, perceive three distinct types of touch: a light whisper that flutters the sensitive leg hairs; a smooth rubbing of the body hair; a steady pressure
Line against the body wall. Press a pencil against the tarantula's body wall, and it will back
(5) away cautiously without reacting defensively. However, if the tarantula sees the pencil approaching from above, the motion will excite a defensive reaction: it will rear up, lifting its front legs and baring its fangs, maintaining this attack stance until the pencil stops moving.

Passage 2

"The eensy-weensy spider climbed up the waterspout . . ."

(10)   Tarantulas are the world's largest spiders. The very largest live in the jungles of South America, and, in the days when bananas were transported as large bunches on stalks, tarantulas often were accidentally imported with the fruit. Stout-bodied and hairy, tarantulas can create great panic among arachnophobes (people who fear spiders). Actually, these large spiders are gentle giants, whose temperaments do not match their

(15)   intimidating appearance. Docile and nonaggressive, tarantulas do not bite unless they are severely provoked. Even if they do bite, their bites are not particularly dangerous; they are about as painful as bee stings, and should be treated similarly.

1. In Passage 1, the author's attitude toward tarantulas can best be described as

    (A) apprehensive.
    (B) sentimental.
    (C) approving.
    (D) objective.

2. As used in line 6, "excite" most nearly means

    (A) irritate.
    (B) exhilarate.
    (C) stimulate.
    (D) discompose.

3. What does Passage 2 suggest about the usual reaction of an arachnophobe to tarantulas?

    (A) It is a voluntary reaction in response to the arachnophobe's surprise at the tarantula's sudden appearance.
    (B) It is an irrational reaction, for it fails to take into account the relative innocuousness of tarantula bites.
    (C) It is a nonaggressive reaction, in keeping with the timidity of the typical arachnophobe.
    (D) It is an unexpected reaction, since most people lack the arachnophobe's fear of large spiders.

4. Which choice provides the best evidence for the answer to the previous question?

    (A) Lines 10–12 ("The very largest . . . fruit")
    (B) Lines 12–13 ("Stout-bodied . . . spiders")
    (C) Lines 14–15 ("Actually . . . appearance")
    (D) Lines 16–17 ("Even . . . similarly")

5. Which statement best expresses the relationship between the two passages?

    (A) Passage 1 describes its subject by supplying details with which the author of Passage 2 would disagree.
    (B) Passage 1 provides scientific observations of the subject, while Passage 2 offers a popular introduction to the subject.
    (C) Passage 1 presents its subject in figurative terms, while Passage 2 is more technical in nature.
    (D) Both Passage 1 and Passage 2 assume readers will have an automatically negative response to the subject under discussion.

6. Which generalization about tarantulas is supported by both passages?

    (A) They have a marked degree of intelligence.
    (B) Their gentleness belies their frightening looks.
    (C) They have been unfairly maligned by arachnophobes.
    (D) They are capable of acting to defend themselves.

Questions 7–10 are based on the following passages.

Passage 1

Thomas Hobbes, who lived during the English Civil War (1642–1646), believed that a world without government would inevitably be a war of every man against every man. His view of human nature was so bleak that he could not imagine people living in
Line peace without an all-powerful government to constrain their actions. John Locke, writ-
(5) ing nearly forty years later, had a more optimistic impression of human nature. While he, like Hobbes, envisioned that a world without government would suffer disorder, he described this disorder as merely an "inconvenience."

Passage 2

What motivates a political philosopher? In the case of Thomas Hobbes, the driving force was fear. In his autobiography, Hobbes says as much, for it was fear that accom-
(10) panied him into the world. On Good Friday of 1588, Hobbes's mother heard that the Spanish Armada had set sail for England. Hobbes relates what ensued: "the rumour went everywhere through our towns that the last day for our nation was coming by fleet. At that point my mother was filled with such fear that she bore twins, me together with fear." In Hobbes's philosophy, fear, especially fear of war, plays a central role.

7. The first two sentences of Passage 1 (lines 1–4) primarily serve to

    (A) illustrate the physical damage done by the Civil War to Thomas Hobbes.
    (B) demonstrate the need for government to function as a restraining influence.
    (C) present the thinking of a political theorist.
    (D) argue in favor of the world view held by John Locke.

8. The author of Passage 1 does all of the following EXCEPT

    (A) establish a time frame.
    (B) contrast two differing viewpoints.
    (C) refute an argument.
    (D) quote a source.

9. Both passages support which of the following conclusions about Hobbes's world view?

    (A) It is more pragmatic than the world view expressed by John Locke.
    (B) It provides an insightful perspective despite its evident inconsistencies.
    (C) It met with little opposition in his lifetime.
    (D) It is inherently pessimistic in its outlook.

10. Which of the following best describes the relationship between the two passages?

    (A) Passage 1 draws a contrast that is weakened by examples in Passage 2.
    (B) Passage 2 presents a hypothesis that is disproved by Passage 1.
    (C) Passage 2 gives an anecdote that confirms a statement made in Passage 1.
    (D) Passage 1 poses a question that is explicitly answered in Passage 2.

Answers Explained

1. **(D)** The author's presentation about factual information about tarantulas is scientifically *objective*.

2. **(C)** To excite a defensive response is to *stimulate* or arouse that reaction.

3. **(B)** The arachnophobe's panicky reaction to the sight of a gentle tarantula is *irrational*. Nothing in the passage indicates that the arachnophobe's panicky reaction to a tarantula is *voluntary* (done of one's free will) or *nonaggressive*. It certainly is not an *unexpected* reaction; in fact, the arachnophobe's panicky reaction is actually quite predictable.

4. **(D)** It is irrational for someone to panic at the sight of a creature that is unlikely to bite and whose bite is neither particularly painful nor particularly dangerous.

5. **(B)** Passage 1 describes what you would see if you subjected a tarantula to various forms of stimuli (pressing a pencil against its body wall, holding a pencil above it, etc.). In other words, it *provides scientific observations of the subject* (the tarantula). Passage 2, in contrast, offers highly general, chatty information about tarantulas, providing *a popular introduction to the subject*.

6. **(D)** You can answer this question by using the process of elimination. Do both passages indicate that tarantulas have a marked degree of intelligence? Nothing in either passage suggests this. You can eliminate Choice A. Do both passages indicate that the tarantulas' gentleness belies (contradicts) their frightening looks? No. Although Passage 2 states that tarantulas are gentler creatures than their appearance suggests, Passage 1 says nothing about their being gentle. You can eliminate Choice B. Do both passages indicate that tarantulas have been maligned (slandered; bad-mouthed) by arachnophobes? No. Passage 1 says nothing at all about arachnophobes. You can eliminate Choice C. Do both passages indicate that tarantulas are capable of acting to defend themselves? Yes. Passage 1 portrays a tarantula's defensive reaction to a perceived threat: the spider immediately goes into its attack stance. Passage 2 indicates that tarantulas will bite if they are severely provoked; thus, they *are capable of acting to defend themselves*. The correct answer is Choice D.

7. **(C)** The opening sentences simply present Hobbes's thoughts on the nature of government.

8. **(C)** You can answer this question by using the process of elimination. Does the author establish a time frame? Yes. She states that the English Civil War took place between 1642 and 1646; she also states that Locke wrote 40 years after Hobbes did. You can eliminate Choice A. Does the author contrast two differing viewpoints? Definitely. You can eliminate Choice B. Does the author refute an argument? No. She merely states the arguments or beliefs of others. This is probably the correct answer. Just to be sure, check Choice D. Does the author quote a source? Yes. She quotes Locke, citing his description of the disorder created by the absence of government. You can eliminate Choice D. Only Choice C is left. It is the correct answer.

9. **(D)** Passage 1 describes Hobbes's view of human nature as "fearful and bleak." Passage 2 states that fear of war plays a central role in his philosophy. Both passages indicate that his world view *is inherently pessimistic.*

10. **(C)** The anecdote in Passage 1 about Hobbes's premature birth (which was brought on by his mother's fear of an attack by the Spanish fleet) *confirms the statement* in Passage 1 that his view of human nature was "fearful and bleak."

THE WRITING AND LANGUAGE TEST

The Writing and Language section consists of 44 questions to be answered in 35 minutes. A typical test has a variety of questions related to editing skills. What follows is a sample Writing and Language passage.

Questions 1–11 are based on the following passage.

Who Flew First?

Ask who piloted the first manned, powered, and controlled flight and you might be surprised at the answers. Most history classes teach that Wilbur and Orville Wright out of Dayton, Ohio operated the first successful airplane, ❶ <u>and</u> the truth is far more complicated. Gustaf Whitehead, Richard Pearse, Alberto Santos-Dumont, and Samuel Langley are among the ❷ <u>names that</u> pop up in the controversy surrounding aviation. While the Wright Brothers are credited with inventing the first airplane, ❸ <u>indications of the possible actuality exist</u> that they were not the first to fly.

(1) What seems more certain is that the Wright Brothers developed the three-axis ❹ <u>control system; known to pilots as roll, pitch, and yaw; still used</u> today to steer aircrafts. (2) So, if the brothers can't rightfully claim the first airplane, they continue to have dibs on the first "successful" airplane. (3) In 1903, at Kitty Hawk, NC, the Wright Brothers piloted an airplane up to 27 miles per hour and landed safely. (4) European papers seemed more eager to promote Wilbur and Orville's achievements. (5) When word finally did get out, the brothers attributed their interest in flight to a toy helicopter their father gave to them

1. (A) NO CHANGE
   (B) because
   (C) but
   (D) since

2. (A) NO CHANGE
   (B) names which
   (C) name that
   (D) name which

3. (A) NO CHANGE
   (B) observational data of people of the time exists
   (C) evidence exists
   (D) probable conformational substantiation exists

4. (A) NO CHANGE
   (B) control system known to pilots as roll, pitch, and yaw—still used
   (C) control system—known to pilots as roll, pitch, and yaw, still used
   (D) control system—known to pilots as roll, pitch, and yaw—still used

in childhood, **5** and its success gained by years of their experience from working in the bicycle shop. **6**

Gustaf Whitehead may be the greatest contender for the title. **7** He claims he flew several times before the Wright Brothers. The most notable instance of this was in Bridgeport, CT in 1901. While no conclusive photographs exist of his feat, a newspaper article claimed that his Number 21 aircraft flew at approximately 50 feet for a half a mile. A New Zealand farmer, Richard Pearse, is also said to have piloted and landed an airplane about nine months before the **8** Wright Brothers' debut at Kitty Hawk. Although it seems indisputable that Pearse did, in fact, fly, his aircraft was poorly controlled and he admitted that he had no success until 1904.

5. (A) NO CHANGE
   (B) and their success to years of experience gained in their bicycle shop.
   (C) and from their bicycle shop the gaining of experience that led them to success in the later years.
   (D) and by their experience in years of bicycle shop working for success.

6. The author would like to insert the following sentence into this paragraph.

   "The American media, however, initially did not take the brothers seriously, dismissing their flights as too brief for any real acknowledgement."

   Where would it most logically be placed?

   (A) Before sentence 1
   (B) Before sentence 2
   (C) Before sentence 4
   (D) Before sentence 5

7. The author wishes to combine the underlined sentences. Which would best accomplish the author's goal?

   (A) Since he claims he flew several times before the Wright Brothers, as a result he did his most notable instance in Bridgeport, CT in 1901.
   (B) He claims he flew several times before the Wright Brothers, most notably in Bridgeport, CT in 1901.
   (C) Claimed by him was the fact that before the Wright Brothers flew, he had flown, most notably in 1901 in Bridgeport, CT.
   (D) Claiming that he flew several times before the Wright Brothers, with the most notability in Bridgeport, CT in 1901.

8. (A) NO CHANGE
   (B) Wright Brother's debut
   (C) Wright Brothers debut
   (D) Wright Brother's debuts

In Brazil, the "father of flight" is Alberto Santos-Dumont, an aviation pioneer who flew hot air balloons until 1906 when he successfully piloted an airplane around the Eiffel Tower. ❾ With the flight being three years after that of Wilbur and Orville, many aviation scholars see Santos-Dumont as the first "official" inventor of the airplane. His aircraft flew at the impressive height of 197 feet for over 20 seconds covering a distance of more than 700 feet. ❿ Earlier than all other front-runners, Samuel Langley flew in 1896, but without landing gear, making his contribution to flight his powerful engine design rather than a fully operative aircraft. ⓫ Airplane technology has made significant strides in the past decade.

9. (A) NO CHANGE
   (B) From
   (C) Since
   (D) Despite

10. (A) NO CHANGE
    (B) Earlier then
    (C) Earliest than
    (D) Earliest then

11. Which of the following provides the most effective and relevant conclusion to the passage?

    (A) NO CHANGE
    (B) Depending on how you define "flight" and "airplane," the question of who flew first can become tricky indeed.
    (C) Clearly, the Wright Brothers have earned their rightful place in history as the true originators of human flight.
    (D) Despite these advances, the adverse consequences of jet flights on global warming need to be considered.

Answers Explained

1. **(C)** With transitions, it's important to analyze context and how the clauses interact. In this case, a contrasting transition is required, as the truth about the Wright Brothers, the passage states, is far more complicated than what is taught. "And" is incorrect, as the second clause does not build upon the first, but rather contradicts it. "Since" and "because" imply a causal relationship, which isn't the case.

2. **(A)** First, the passage refers to two people, so we need "names." Eliminate Choices C and D accordingly. As this is a *restrictive clause* rather than a *nonrestrictive clause*, it requires the use of "that." Choice B, therefore, can be eliminated, as well.

3. **(C)** The best way to view this question is in terms of concision. While all four choices express the same sentiment, Choice C is much more concise, while still managing to maintain the intended meaning. Choices A, B, and D are far too verbose in comparison to Choice C's concision.

4. **(D)** Notice how the phrase "known to pilots as roll, pitch, and yaw" is inconsequential to the integrity of the main clause; remove it, and our sentence still functions perfectly acceptably. That phrase, then, is what is known as a parenthetical. A parenthetical phrase can must be surrounded by commas or dashes to separate it from the main clause. Choice C is close, but it uses one comma and one dash, whereas the requirement is to pick either commas or dashes and then use two of that type.

5. **(B)** The verb used in the first part of the sentence is "attributed...to." The preposition is important, as we always attribute *to* something, rather than using another preposition. Choice B maintains that parallelism; their interest was attributed to a toy helicopter, and then their success was attributed to years of experience. Choices A, C, and D stray from *attributed to,* and therefore can be discounted.

6. **(C)** Recognize context here, specifically as it relates to sentence four. Paraphrased, our insertion says that the American media trivialized the Wright Brothers' accomplishment. Sentence four states that European media, however, was "more eager," and the implication is more eager than the American media. Therefore, this sentence must be inserted before sentence four to be most logical.

7. **(B)** Choice C is passive voice, and it can be eliminated. Choice A attempts to create a causal relationship between two events that are not cause and effect. Choice D is flawed in that it is actually a fragment, as we never establish a subject *or* a predicate. Choice B, however, combines the two effectively.

8. **(A)** We are attempting to phrase *the debut of the Wright Brothers* using possession. Recall that possession requires an apostrophe on a proper noun, so Choice C can be eliminated. Choices B and D can be eliminated because, by placing the apostrophe after "brother," it reads as the debut of *just one of the brothers.* As there are two brothers, the apostrophe must be placed *after* "brothers," as Choice A does correctly.

9. **(D)** It is important to discern the relationship between the two clauses, and it's probably easier to invert them and view the second clause first. Paraphrased then, it is, "Many scholars view Santos-Dumont as the "official" airplane inventor, *in spite of* the fact that his flight occurred three years *after* the Wright Brothers' flight." Notice the *in spite of,*

which is basically a twin of Choice D: "despite." *Even though* or *although* would also be acceptable here. "Despite" establishes an important qualification that Choices A, B, and C do not create.

10. **(A)** First, the appropriate word for comparisons is "than," while "then" is used to narrate a sequence. Eliminate Choices B and D, as a result. Also, when making comparisons using *than,* it is always better to use *-er* rather than *-est.* Select Choice A, accordingly.

11. **(B)** Choice A is flawed in that the passage was about the early history of aviation, rather than recent developments. Similarly, Choice D is completely off-topic. Choice C isn't logical, as the passage has, in fact, cast doubt on whether the Wright Brothers were first in aviation. Choice B, however, is both logical and relevant given the content of the passage.

THE MATH TEST

There are two types of questions on the Math portion of the PSAT:

1. multiple-choice questions
2. grid-in questions

The math questions are in Sections 3 and 4 of the PSAT.

- Section 3, the no-calculator section, is 25 minutes long and has 13 multiple-choice questions followed by 4 grid-in questions.
- Section 4, the calculator section, is 45 minutes long and has 27 questions followed by 4 grid-in questions. Note that even though you are permitted to use a calculator in Section 4, many of the questions do not require it.

Multiple-Choice Questions

Forty of the 48 mathematics questions on the PSAT are multiple-choice questions. Although you have certainly taken multiple-choice tests before, the PSAT uses a few different types of questions in these sections, and you must become familiar with all of them. By far, the most common type of question is one in which you are asked to solve a problem. The straightforward way to answer such a question is to do the necessary work, get the solution, then look at the choices and choose the one that corresponds to your answer. In Chapter 5 we will discuss other techniques for answering these questions, but for now let's look at a couple of examples.

➡ **Example 1**_____

What is the average (arithmetic mean) of –2, –1, 0, 1, 2, 3, and 4?

(A) 0

(B) $\frac{3}{7}$

(C) $\frac{4}{7}$

(D) 1

To solve this problem requires only that you know how to find the average of a set of numbers. Ignore the fact that this is a multiple-choice question. **Don't even look at the choices.**

- Calculate the average by adding the 7 numbers and dividing by 7.
- $\dfrac{-2 + -1 + 0 + 1 + 2 + 3 + 4}{7} = \dfrac{7}{7} = 1.$
- Now look at the four choices. Find 1, listed as Choice D, and blacken in D on your answer sheet.

In contrast to Example 1, some questions *require* you to look at all four choices in order to find the answers. Consider Example 2.

➡ Example 2 _____

If a and b are both odd integers, which of the following could be an odd integer?

(A) $a + b$

(B) $a^2 + b^2$

(C) $(a + 1)(b - 1)$

(D) $\dfrac{a+1}{b-1}$

The words *Which of the following* alert you to the fact that you will have to examine each of the four choices to determine which one satisfies the stated condition, in this case that the quantity *could* be odd. Check each choice.

- Could $a + b$ be odd? No, the sum of two odd integers is always even. Eliminate Choice A.
- Could $a^2 + b^2$ be odd? No, the square of an odd integer is odd. So, a^2 and b^2 are each odd, and their sum is even. Eliminate Choice B.
- Could $(a + 1)(b - 1)$ be odd? No, $(a + 1)$ and $(b - 1)$ are each even. The product of two even integers is even. Eliminate Choice C.
- Having eliminated Choices A, B, and C, you know that *the answer must be* Choice D. Check to be sure: $\dfrac{a+1}{b-1}$ need not even be an integer (e.g., if $a = 1$ and $b = 5$), but it *could be*. For example, if $a = 3$ and $b = 5$, then

$$\frac{a+1}{b-1} = \frac{3+1}{5-1} = \frac{4}{4} = 1$$

which is an odd integer. The answer is Choice D.

➡ Example 3 _____

In $\triangle ABC$, $AB = 3$ and $BC = 4$. Which of the following could be the perimeter of $\triangle ABC$?

I. 8

II. 10

III. 12

(A) II only

(B) III only

(C) II and III only

(D) I, II, and III

- Note that "I. 8" is simply an abbreviation of the statement, "The perimeter of $\triangle ABC$ could be 8." The same is true for "II. 10" and "III. 12." To answer this question, examine each of the three statements independently.

  I. Could the perimeter be 8? If it were, then the third side would be 1. In any triangle, though, the smallest side must be greater than the difference of the other two sides. So, the third side must be *greater* than $4 - 3 = 1$. It cannot equal 1. I is false.

  II. Could the perimeter be 10? That is, could the third side be 3? Yes, $\triangle ABC$ could be a 3-3-4 isosceles triangle. II is true.

  III. Could the perimeter be 12? That is, could the third side be 5? Yes. The three sides could be 3, 4, and 5. In fact, the most common right triangle to appear on the PSAT is a 3-4-5 right triangle. III is true.

- Only statements II and III are true. The answer is C.

Grid-In Questions

Eight of the 48 mathematics questions on the PSAT (four in each section) are what the College Board calls student-produced response questions. These are the only questions on the PSAT that are not multiple-choice. Since the answers to these questions are entered on a special grid, they are usually referred to as *grid-in* questions. Except for the method of entering your answer, this type of question is probably the one with which you are most familiar. In your math class, most test questions require you to determine an answer and write it down, and this is what you will do on the grid-in problems, except that on the PSAT, you must record your answer on a special grid, such as the one shown, so that it can be read by a computer.

Here is a typical grid-in question.

➡ **Example 4**_____

John has a rectangular garden. He decides to enlarge it by increasing its length by 20% and its width by 30%. If the area of the new garden is a times the area of the original garden, what is the value of a?

Solution. From the wording of the question, it is clear that the answer does not depend on the actual original dimensions. Therefore, pick an easy value. For example, assume that the original garden is a square whose sides are 10. Since 20% of 10 is 2 and 30% of 10 is 3, then the new garden is a 12 by 13 rectangle. Therefore, the area of the original garden is $10 \times 10 = 100$, and the area of the new garden is $12 \times 13 = 156$. So $156 = a(100)$, and $a = 1.56$.

To enter this answer, you write 1.56 in the four spaces at the top of the grid and blacken in the appropriate circle under each space. In the first column, under the 1, blacken the circle marked 1; in the second column, under the decimal point, blacken the circle with the decimal point; in the third column, under the 5, blacken the circle marked 5; and finally, in the fourth column, under the 6, blacken the circle marked 6.

Note that the only symbols that appear in the grid are the digits from 0 to 9, a decimal point, and a fraction bar (/). The grid does not have a minus sign, so *answers to grid-in problems can never be negative.* In Chapter 4, you will read suggestions for the best way to fill in grids. You will also learn the special rules concerning the proper way to grid-in fractions, mixed numbers, and decimals that won't fit in the grid's four columns. When you take the diagnostic test, just enter your answers exactly as was done in Example 4.

CALCULATOR TIPS

- You must bring a calculator to the test. Some, but not all, of the questions in the 45-minute section cannot be solved without using one.
- You should use a scientific calculator. A graphing calculator is acceptable but offers no real advantage.
- *Don't* buy a new calculator the night before the PSAT. If you need one, *buy one now* and become familiar with it. Do all the practice exams in this book with the calculator you plan to take to the test—probably the same calculator you use in school.
- Use your calculator when you *need* to; ignore it when you don't. Most students use calculators more than they should. You can solve many problems without doing *any* calculations—mental, written, or calculator-assisted.
- The College Board's position is that a "calculator is a tool" and that knowing when to use one and when not to use one is an important skill. Therefore, they intentionally include some questions in the calculator section on which it is better not to use your calculator.
- Throughout this book, the icon will be placed next to a problem where the use of a calculator is reasonable or recommended. As you will see, this judgment is subjective. Sometimes a question can be answered in a few seconds, with no calculations whatsoever, *if* you see the best approach. In that case, the use of a calculator is not recommended. If you don't see the easy way, however, and have to do some arithmetic, you may prefer to use a calculator.
- No PSAT problem ever requires a lot of tedious calculation. However, if you don't see how to avoid calculating, just do it—*don't spend a lot of time looking for a shortcut that will save you a little time!*

TACTICAL WRAP-UP

1. Memorize the directions given in this book for each type of question. That way, during the test you won't have to waste precious time reading the directions and sample questions.

2. Know the format of the test.

3. Eliminate as many wrong answers as you can and then make an educated guess.

4. If you can't eliminate any choices, just make a wild guess.

5. Be sure to bubble in an answer to every question.

6. Change answers *only* if you have a reason for doing so.

7. Calculators are permitted on one of the math sections of the test, so bring along a calculator that you are comfortable using.

8. Remember that you are allowed to write anything you want in your test booklet. Make good use of it.

9. Be careful not to make any stray marks on your answer sheet.

10. Check frequently to make sure you are answering the questions in the right spots.

11. Be particularly careful in marking the student-produced responses on the math grids.

12. Don't get bogged down on any one question. If a question has you dithering or bogged down, circle it in the test booklet and return to it only after you have answered all the questions you are sure of.

PRACTICE, PRACTICE, PRACTICE: ONLINE RESOURCES

Now that you know the tactics that will help you do well on the PSAT, be sure to use them whenever you do the exercises and model tests in this book and, of course, when you take your actual PSAT. In addition to all of the tests and practice questions in this book, you can get even more practice online at *http://barronsbooks.com/tp/psat19/* with two additional tests. (You will need your copy of PSAT, 19th edition handy to complete your online registration.)

PART TWO
A Diagnostic Test

Identify Your Weaknesses
Know Your Strengths

A Diagnostic Test

On the following pages, you will find a sample PSAT test. Take this test, following the directions below. Then score your answers and go over the answer explanation to each question. This should give you a fairly good sense of what your score would be if you didn't do any special preparation for the test.

Once you've done this, you'll be in good shape to come up with a review plan that meets your needs. You'll know which types of questions you have to practice, which topics in math you must review, which reading skills you have to concentrate on, and which writing skills you need to improve.

HERE'S WHAT YOU NEED TO KNOW

- Every question has the same value. Each correct answer is worth 1 raw score point.
- Except for 4 grid-in math questions in each math section, every question on the PSAT is multiple-choice.
- Bubble in an answer to every question.

SIMULATE TEST CONDITIONS (TAKE THIS DIAGNOSTIC PSAT AS IF IT WERE THE REAL THING)

Total Time: 2 hours, 45 minutes*

- Find a quiet place to work.
- Keep an accurate record of your time.
- If you finish a section early, do not start the next section. Use the remaining minutes to check your work.
- Read the questions closely.
- Work carefully, even if it means you don't get to all the questions.
- Do not spend too much time on questions that seem hard for you.
- If time permits, go back to any questions you left out.
- Whenever you can eliminate one or more answer choices, make an educated guess.
- When you can't eliminate any choices and when you are running out of time, make wild guesses.

> ### REMEMBER
>
> In addition to the diagnostic test and the two practice tests in this book, you have access to two online tests. You can find the link to the online tests on the inside front cover of this book.

*This does not count the short breaks between the sections (see page viii).

ANSWER SHEET
Diagnostic Test

Section 1: Reading

1. Ⓐ Ⓑ Ⓒ Ⓓ
2. Ⓐ Ⓑ Ⓒ Ⓓ
3. Ⓐ Ⓑ Ⓒ Ⓓ
4. Ⓐ Ⓑ Ⓒ Ⓓ
5. Ⓐ Ⓑ Ⓒ Ⓓ
6. Ⓐ Ⓑ Ⓒ Ⓓ
7. Ⓐ Ⓑ Ⓒ Ⓓ
8. Ⓐ Ⓑ Ⓒ Ⓓ
9. Ⓐ Ⓑ Ⓒ Ⓓ
10. Ⓐ Ⓑ Ⓒ Ⓓ
11. Ⓐ Ⓑ Ⓒ Ⓓ
12. Ⓐ Ⓑ Ⓒ Ⓓ
13. Ⓐ Ⓑ Ⓒ Ⓓ

14. Ⓐ Ⓑ Ⓒ Ⓓ
15. Ⓐ Ⓑ Ⓒ Ⓓ
16. Ⓐ Ⓑ Ⓒ Ⓓ
17. Ⓐ Ⓑ Ⓒ Ⓓ
18. Ⓐ Ⓑ Ⓒ Ⓓ
19. Ⓐ Ⓑ Ⓒ Ⓓ
20. Ⓐ Ⓑ Ⓒ Ⓓ
21. Ⓐ Ⓑ Ⓒ Ⓓ
22. Ⓐ Ⓑ Ⓒ Ⓓ
23. Ⓐ Ⓑ Ⓒ Ⓓ
24. Ⓐ Ⓑ Ⓒ Ⓓ
25. Ⓐ Ⓑ Ⓒ Ⓓ
26. Ⓐ Ⓑ Ⓒ Ⓓ

27. Ⓐ Ⓑ Ⓒ Ⓓ
28. Ⓐ Ⓑ Ⓒ Ⓓ
29. Ⓐ Ⓑ Ⓒ Ⓓ
30. Ⓐ Ⓑ Ⓒ Ⓓ
31. Ⓐ Ⓑ Ⓒ Ⓓ
32. Ⓐ Ⓑ Ⓒ Ⓓ
33. Ⓐ Ⓑ Ⓒ Ⓓ
34. Ⓐ Ⓑ Ⓒ Ⓓ
35. Ⓐ Ⓑ Ⓒ Ⓓ
36. Ⓐ Ⓑ Ⓒ Ⓓ
37. Ⓐ Ⓑ Ⓒ Ⓓ
38. Ⓐ Ⓑ Ⓒ Ⓓ
39. Ⓐ Ⓑ Ⓒ Ⓓ

40. Ⓐ Ⓑ Ⓒ Ⓓ
41. Ⓐ Ⓑ Ⓒ Ⓓ
42. Ⓐ Ⓑ Ⓒ Ⓓ
43. Ⓐ Ⓑ Ⓒ Ⓓ
44. Ⓐ Ⓑ Ⓒ Ⓓ
45. Ⓐ Ⓑ Ⓒ Ⓓ
46. Ⓐ Ⓑ Ⓒ Ⓓ
47. Ⓐ Ⓑ Ⓒ Ⓓ

Section 2: Writing and Language

1. Ⓐ Ⓑ Ⓒ Ⓓ
2. Ⓐ Ⓑ Ⓒ Ⓓ
3. Ⓐ Ⓑ Ⓒ Ⓓ
4. Ⓐ Ⓑ Ⓒ Ⓓ
5. Ⓐ Ⓑ Ⓒ Ⓓ
6. Ⓐ Ⓑ Ⓒ Ⓓ
7. Ⓐ Ⓑ Ⓒ Ⓓ
8. Ⓐ Ⓑ Ⓒ Ⓓ
9. Ⓐ Ⓑ Ⓒ Ⓓ
10. Ⓐ Ⓑ Ⓒ Ⓓ
11. Ⓐ Ⓑ Ⓒ Ⓓ

12. Ⓐ Ⓑ Ⓒ Ⓓ
13. Ⓐ Ⓑ Ⓒ Ⓓ
14. Ⓐ Ⓑ Ⓒ Ⓓ
15. Ⓐ Ⓑ Ⓒ Ⓓ
16. Ⓐ Ⓑ Ⓒ Ⓓ
17. Ⓐ Ⓑ Ⓒ Ⓓ
18. Ⓐ Ⓑ Ⓒ Ⓓ
19. Ⓐ Ⓑ Ⓒ Ⓓ
20. Ⓐ Ⓑ Ⓒ Ⓓ
21. Ⓐ Ⓑ Ⓒ Ⓓ
22. Ⓐ Ⓑ Ⓒ Ⓓ

23. Ⓐ Ⓑ Ⓒ Ⓓ
24. Ⓐ Ⓑ Ⓒ Ⓓ
25. Ⓐ Ⓑ Ⓒ Ⓓ
26. Ⓐ Ⓑ Ⓒ Ⓓ
27. Ⓐ Ⓑ Ⓒ Ⓓ
28. Ⓐ Ⓑ Ⓒ Ⓓ
29. Ⓐ Ⓑ Ⓒ Ⓓ
30. Ⓐ Ⓑ Ⓒ Ⓓ
31. Ⓐ Ⓑ Ⓒ Ⓓ
32. Ⓐ Ⓑ Ⓒ Ⓓ
33. Ⓐ Ⓑ Ⓒ Ⓓ

34. Ⓐ Ⓑ Ⓒ Ⓓ
35. Ⓐ Ⓑ Ⓒ Ⓓ
36. Ⓐ Ⓑ Ⓒ Ⓓ
37. Ⓐ Ⓑ Ⓒ Ⓓ
38. Ⓐ Ⓑ Ⓒ Ⓓ
39. Ⓐ Ⓑ Ⓒ Ⓓ
40. Ⓐ Ⓑ Ⓒ Ⓓ
41. Ⓐ Ⓑ Ⓒ Ⓓ
42. Ⓐ Ⓑ Ⓒ Ⓓ
43. Ⓐ Ⓑ Ⓒ Ⓓ
44. Ⓐ Ⓑ Ⓒ Ⓓ

ANSWER SHEET
Diagnostic Test

Section 3: Math (No Calculator)

1. Ⓐ Ⓑ Ⓒ Ⓓ   5. Ⓐ Ⓑ Ⓒ Ⓓ   9. Ⓐ Ⓑ Ⓒ Ⓓ   13. Ⓐ Ⓑ Ⓒ Ⓓ

2. Ⓐ Ⓑ Ⓒ Ⓓ   6. Ⓐ Ⓑ Ⓒ Ⓓ   10. Ⓐ Ⓑ Ⓒ Ⓓ

3. Ⓐ Ⓑ Ⓒ Ⓓ   7. Ⓐ Ⓑ Ⓒ Ⓓ   11. Ⓐ Ⓑ Ⓒ Ⓓ

4. Ⓐ Ⓑ Ⓒ Ⓓ   8. Ⓐ Ⓑ Ⓒ Ⓓ   12. Ⓐ Ⓑ Ⓒ Ⓓ

14.

15.

16.

17.

ANSWER SHEET
Diagnostic Test

Section 4: Math (Calculator)

1. Ⓐ Ⓑ Ⓒ Ⓓ
2. Ⓐ Ⓑ Ⓒ Ⓓ
3. Ⓐ Ⓑ Ⓒ Ⓓ
4. Ⓐ Ⓑ Ⓒ Ⓓ
5. Ⓐ Ⓑ Ⓒ Ⓓ
6. Ⓐ Ⓑ Ⓒ Ⓓ
7. Ⓐ Ⓑ Ⓒ Ⓓ
8. Ⓐ Ⓑ Ⓒ Ⓓ

9. Ⓐ Ⓑ Ⓒ Ⓓ
10. Ⓐ Ⓑ Ⓒ Ⓓ
11. Ⓐ Ⓑ Ⓒ Ⓓ
12. Ⓐ Ⓑ Ⓒ Ⓓ
13. Ⓐ Ⓑ Ⓒ Ⓓ
14. Ⓐ Ⓑ Ⓒ Ⓓ
15. Ⓐ Ⓑ Ⓒ Ⓓ
16. Ⓐ Ⓑ Ⓒ Ⓓ

17. Ⓐ Ⓑ Ⓒ Ⓓ
18. Ⓐ Ⓑ Ⓒ Ⓓ
19. Ⓐ Ⓑ Ⓒ Ⓓ
20. Ⓐ Ⓑ Ⓒ Ⓓ
21. Ⓐ Ⓑ Ⓒ Ⓓ
22. Ⓐ Ⓑ Ⓒ Ⓓ
23. Ⓐ Ⓑ Ⓒ Ⓓ
24. Ⓐ Ⓑ Ⓒ Ⓓ

25. Ⓐ Ⓑ Ⓒ Ⓓ
26. Ⓐ Ⓑ Ⓒ Ⓓ
27. Ⓐ Ⓑ Ⓒ Ⓓ

28. [grid-in response field]
29. [grid-in response field]
30. [grid-in response field]
31. [grid-in response field]

READING TEST

60 MINUTES, 47 QUESTIONS

Turn to Section 1 of your answer sheet to answer the questions in this section.

> **Directions:** Following each of the passages (or pairs of passages) below are questions about the passage (or passages). Read each passage carefully. Then, select the best answer for each question based on what is stated in the passage (or passages) and in any graphics that may accompany the passage.

Questions 1–9 are based on the following passage.

In the following passage from Jane Austen's novel Pride and Prejudice, *the heroine Elizabeth Bennet faces an unexpected encounter with her father's cousin (and prospective heir), the clergyman Mr. Collins.*

It was absolutely necessary to interrupt him now.

"You are too hasty. Sir," she cried. "You
Line forget that I have made no answer. Let me
(5) do it without further loss of time. Accept my
thanks for the compliment you are paying
me. I am very sensible of the honour of your
proposals, but it is impossible for me to do
otherwise than decline them."

(10)   "I am not now to learn," replied Mr.
Collins with a formal wave of the hand, "that
it is usual with young ladies to reject the
addresses of the man whom they secretly
mean to accept, when he first applies for
(15) their favour; and that sometimes the refusal
is repeated a second or even a third time. I
am therefore by no means discouraged by
what you have just said, and shall hope to
lead you to the altar ere long."

(20)   "Upon my word, Sir," cried Elizabeth,
"your hope is rather an extraordinary one
after my declaration. I do assure you that
I am not one of those young ladies (if such
young ladies there are) who are so daring as

(25) to risk their happiness on the chance of being
asked a second time. I am perfectly serious
in my refusal. You could not make me happy,
and I am convinced that I am the last woman
in the world who would make you so. Nay,
(30) were your friend Lady Catherine to know me,
I am persuaded she would find me in every
respect ill qualified for the situation."

"Were it certain that Lady Catherine would
think so," said Mr. Collins very gravely—"but
(35) I cannot imagine that her ladyship would
at all disapprove of you. And you may be
certain that when I have the honour of seeing
her again I shall speak in the highest terms of
your modesty, economy, and other amiable
(40) qualifications."

"Indeed, Mr. Collins, all praise of me will
be unnecessary. You must give me leave to
judge for myself, and pay me the compliment
of believing what I say. I wish you very happy
(45) and very rich, and by refusing your hand,
do all in my power to prevent your being
otherwise. In making me the offer, you must
have satisfied the delicacy of your feelings
with regard to my family, and may take
(50) possession of Longbourn estate whenever it
falls, without any self-reproach. This matter
may be considered, therefore, as finally
settled." And rising as she thus spoke, she
would have quitted the room, had not Mr.
(55) Collins thus addressed her.

GO ON TO THE NEXT PAGE

"When I do myself the honour of speaking to you next on this subject I shall hope to receive a more favourable answer than you have now given me; though I am far from (60) accusing you of cruelty at present, because I know it to be the established custom of your sex to reject a man on the first application, and perhaps you have even now said as much to encourage my suit as would be (65) consistent with the true delicacy of the female character."

"Really, Mr. Collins," cried Elizabeth with some warmth, "you puzzle me exceedingly. If what I have hitherto said can appear to you (70) in the form of encouragement, I know not how to express my refusal in such a way as may convince you of its being one."

1. It can be inferred that in the paragraphs immediately preceding this passage

   (A) Elizabeth and Mr. Collins quarreled.
   (B) Elizabeth met Mr. Collins for the first time.
   (C) Mr. Collins asked Elizabeth to marry him.
   (D) Mr. Collins gravely insulted Elizabeth.

2. As used in line 7, "sensible" most nearly means

   (A) logical.
   (B) appreciable.
   (C) sound in judgment.
   (D) keenly aware.

3. Instead of having the intended effect, Elizabeth's initial refusal of Mr. Collins (lines 7–9)

   (A) causes her to rethink rejecting him.
   (B) makes him less inclined to wed.
   (C) gives her the opportunity to consider other options.
   (D) fails to put an end to his suit.

4. Which choice provides the best evidence for the answer to the previous question?

   (A) Lines 3–5 ("You forget . . . time")
   (B) Lines 16–19 ("I am . . . long")
   (C) Lines 26–27 ("I am . . . refusal")
   (D) Lines 29–32 ("Nay, . . . situation")

5. It can be inferred from lines 33–36 that Mr. Collins

   (A) will take Elizabeth's words seriously.
   (B) admires Elizabeth's independence.
   (C) is very disappointed by her decision.
   (D) would accept Lady Catherine's opinion.

6. The reason Elizabeth insists all praise of her "will be unnecessary" (lines 41–42) is that she

   (A) feels sure Lady Catherine will learn to admire her in time.
   (B) is too shy to accept compliments readily.
   (C) has no intention of marrying Mr. Collins.
   (D) values her own worth excessively.

7. As used in line 42, "leave" most nearly means

   (A) holiday.
   (B) permission.
   (C) absence.
   (D) farewell.

GO ON TO THE NEXT PAGE

8. On the basis of his behavior in this passage, Mr. Collins may best be described as

   (A) malicious in intent.
   (B) both obtuse and obstinate.
   (C) unsure of his acceptance.
   (D) sensitive to Elizabeth's wishes.

9. Which choice provides the best evidence for the answer to the previous question?

   (A) Lines 33–36 ("Were it . . . you")
   (B) Lines 36–40 ("And . . . qualifications")
   (C) Lines 47–51 ("In making . . .
       self-reproach")
   (D) Lines 56–66 ("When . . . character")

Questions 10–19 are based on the following passages.

These passages present two perspectives on the behavior of European jackdaws, members of the crow family. Passage 1 was written by the Austrian naturalist Konrad Lorenz in 1949. Passage 2 was written by a Dutch colleague late in the twentieth century.

Passage 1

In the chimney the autumn wind sings the song of the elements, and the old firs before my study window wave excitedly with their
Line arms and sing so loudly in chorus that I can
(5) hear their sighing melody through the double panes.

Suddenly, from above, a dozen black, streamlined projectiles shoot across the piece of clouded sky for which my window
(10) forms a frame. Heavily as stones they fall, fall to the tops of the firs where they suddenly sprout wings, become birds and then light feather rags that the storm seizes and whirls out of my line of vision, more rapidly than
(15) they were borne into it.

I walk to the window to watch this extraordinary game that the jackdaws are playing with the wind. A game? Yes, indeed, it is a game, in the most literal sense of the
(20) word: practiced movements, indulged in and enjoyed for their own sake and not for the achievement of a special object. And rest assured, these are not merely inborn, purely instinctive actions, but movements that have
(25) been carefully learned. All these feats that the birds are performing, their wonderful exploitation of the wind, their amazingly exact assessment of distances and, above all, their understanding of local wind conditions,
(30) their knowledge of all the up-currents, air pockets and eddies—all this proficiency

GO ON TO THE NEXT PAGE

is no inheritance, but, for each bird, an individually acquired accomplishment.

(35) And look what they do with the wind! At first sight, you, poor human being, think that the storm is playing with the birds, like a cat with a mouse, but soon you see, with astonishment, that it is the fury of the

(40) elements that here plays the role of the mouse and that the jackdaws are treating the storm exactly as the cat its unfortunate victim. Nearly, but only nearly, do they give the storm its head, let it throw them high, high into the heavens, till they seem to fall

(45) upwards, then, with a casual flap of a wing, they turn themselves over, open their pinions for a fraction of a second from below against the wind, and dive—with an acceleration far greater than that of a falling stone—

(50) into the depths below. Another tiny jerk of the wing and they return to their normal position and, on close-reefed sails, shoot away with breathless speed into the teeth of the gale, hundreds of yards to the west: this

(55) all playfully and without effort, just to spite the stupid wind that tries to so drive them towards the east. The sightless monster itself must perform the work of propelling the birds through the air at a rate of well over

(60) 80 miles an hour; the jackdaws do nothing to help beyond a few lazy adjustments of their black wings. Sovereign control over the power of the elements, intoxicating triumph of the living organism over the pitiless

(65) strength of the inorganic!

Passage 2

In the Netherlands the jackdaw is a sedentary species. They breed in holes that they do not excavate themselves, and territorial defense is limited to the nest-hole.

(70) Both mates share the duties related to the

defense of the nest-site, the building of the nest, and the rearing of the young.

However, only the female incubates. During this time, she is fed by her mate. The

(75) mated pair remains together throughout the year and from year to year. Within the jackdaw population in the study area, two social categories can be distinguished, based on seasonal differences in nest-site defense:

(80) resident pairs and non-resident birds.

The resident pairs defend at least one nest-hole continuously from early fall (September) until the end of the breeding season (July), usually year after year. Only

(85) adult, mated jackdaws belong to this group.

Unlike the resident pairs, non-resident birds do not defend a nest-site in the winter. The non-resident component of the population is rather heterogeneous. It

(90) contains birds of all ages, mated and non-mated, breeders and non-breeders. During their first year of life, all jackdaws belong to the non-resident category. At the end of their first year of life, pairs are formed and

(95) some of these juvenile pairs obtain a nest-site, breed, and may become residents in fall. Adult jackdaws may belong to the non-resident category for several reasons. For instance, non-mated jackdaws do not defend

(100) a nest-site, and hence all non-mated birds, including residents remaining behind after their mate died or disappeared, become non-residents. Furthermore, jackdaws depend on natural holes for breeding. Hollow

(105) trees may fall, chimneys may be swept and provided with an "anti-jackdaw" cap, and church towers may be restored and made unavailable for jackdaw nesting. The loss of their nest-site probably is a common event in

(110) the life of a jackdaw pair.

GO ON TO THE NEXT PAGE

10. In Passage 1, the author's primary purpose is to

    (A) evoke an experience.
    (B) propose a hypothesis.
    (C) reconsider a theory.
    (D) explain an anomaly.

11. According to Passage 1, the bird's skill in adapting to wind conditions is

    (A) genetically determined.
    (B) limited by their understanding.
    (C) dependent on the power of the elements.
    (D) gained through repeated performance.

12. Which choice provides the best evidence for the answer to the previous question?

    (A) Lines 10–15 ("Heavily . . . it")
    (B) Lines 16–17 ("I . . . game")
    (C) Lines 25–33 ("All . . . accomplishment")
    (D) Lines 34–42 ("At first . . . victim")

13. As used in line 22, "rest" most nearly means

    (A) relax securely.
    (B) lie fallow.
    (C) are supported.
    (D) continue to be.

14. Throughout Passage 1, the author is most impressed by

    (A) the direction-finding skills employed by the birds.
    (B) the jackdaws' mastery of the forces of nature.
    (C) the fleeting nature of his encounter with the birds.
    (D) the jackdaws' phenomenal strength.

15. Which choice provides the best evidence for the answer to the previous question?

    (A) Lines 7–10 ("Suddenly . . . frame")
    (B) Lines 16–22 ("I walk . . . object")
    (C) Lines 22–25 ("And rest . . . learned")
    (D) Lines 62–65 ("Sovereign . . . inorganic")

16. The author of Passage 2 makes significant use of which of the following?

    (A) Observational data
    (B) Figurative language
    (C) Statistical correlations
    (D) Rhetorical questions

17. According to the author of Passage 2, jackdaws that fall into the non-resident category

    (A) by definition are less physically mature than resident pairs.
    (B) include resident pairs that have lost their nest-site.
    (C) never consist of mated pairs of adult birds.
    (D) cannot move from one category to the other.

18. As used in line 94, "formed" most nearly means

    (A) established.
    (B) molded.
    (C) educated.
    (D) articulated.

19. Compared to Passage 1, Passage 2 is

    (A) more detailed and less ambivalent.
    (B) more objective and less lyrical.
    (C) more metaphorical and less realistic.
    (D) more ambiguous and less literal.

GO ON TO THE NEXT PAGE

DIAGNOSTIC TEST 37

Questions 20–28 are based on the following passage.

Noted for their destructiveness, tornadoes have long fascinated both scientists and the public at large. The following passage is from a 1984 magazine article on tornadoes.

Tornadoes have long been enigmatic, for the very reason that it is important to understand them. They strike sporadically

Line and violently, generating the strongest of
(5) all surface winds and causing more deaths annually in the U.S. than any other weather phenomenon except lightning. This same behavior has made them inaccessible to planned observation. For example, it is now
(10) thought that the maximum wind speed possible in a tornado is on the order of 300 miles per hour, but this is only an estimate based on analysis of motion pictures and of damage to engineered structures. Estimates
(15) of atmospheric pressure changes, another crucial type of information, are available only for those few storms that happened to pass near weather stations. Meteorologists have thus had to build their sometimes elaborate
(20) models of tornado behavior on shaky observational foundations.

That is now changing. Since 1970 it has been possible to probe tornado-producing thunderstorms with Doppler radar and
(25) measure wind speeds within such storms from a safe distance. The result has been a vastly improved understanding of the updraft, the rising column of air at the heart of a thunderstorm, and of how it interacts
(30) with its environment. This has led to a much clearer picture of how a strong updraft begins to rotate and of how the spiraling winds intensify to the point where they give rise to a tornado.

(35) What is a tornado? A tornado is the product of a thunderstorm, specifically of the interaction of a strong thunderstorm with winds in the troposphere (the active layer of the atmosphere that extends nine
(40) to 17 kilometers up from the ground). The process by which a tornado is formed is one in which a small fraction of the tremendous energy of the thunderstorm, whose towering cumulonimbus cloud can
(45) be 10 to 20 kilometers across and more than 17 kilometers high, is concentrated in an area no more than several hundred meters in diameter. Before going into the process in detail let me first describe the phenomenon
(50) itself.

A tornado is a vortex; air rotates around the tornado's axis about as fast as it moves toward and along the axis. Drawn by greatly reduced atmospheric pressure in the central
(55) core, air streams into the base of the vortex from all directions through a shallow layer a few tens of meters deep near the ground. In the base the air turns abruptly to spiral upward around the core and finally merges,
(60) at the hidden upper end of the tornado, with the airflow in the parent cloud. The pressure within the core may be as much as 10 percent less than that of the surrounding atmosphere; about the same difference as
(65) that between sea level and an altitude of one kilometer. Winds in a tornado are almost always cyclonic, which in the Northern Hemisphere means counterclockwise.

The vortex frequently—not always—
(70) becomes visible as a funnel cloud hanging part or all of the way to the ground from the generating storm. A funnel cloud forms only if the pressure drop in the core exceeds a critical value that depends on
(75) the temperature and the humidity of the inflowing air. As air flows into the area

GO ON TO THE NEXT PAGE

of lower pressure, it expands and cools;
if it cools enough, the water vapor in it
condenses and forms droplets. The warmer
(80) and drier the inflowing air is, the greater the
pressure drop must be for condensation to
occur and a cloud to form. Sometimes no
condensation funnel forms, in which case the
tornado reveals itself only through the dust
(85) and debris it carries aloft.

    A funnel can be anywhere from tens of
meters to several kilometers long, and where
it meets the parent cloud its diameter ranges
from a few meters to hundreds of meters.
(90) Usually it is cone-shaped, but short, broad,
cylindrical pillars are formed by very strong
tornadoes, and long, ropelike tubes that trail
off horizontally are also common. Over a
tornado's brief lifetime (never more than a
(95) few hours) the size and shape of the funnel
may change markedly, reflecting changes in
the intensity of the winds or in the properties
of the inflowing air. Its color varies from a
dirty white to gray to dark blue gray when
(100) it consists mostly of water droplets, but if
the core fills with dust, the funnel may take
on a more exotic hue, such as the red of
west Oklahoma clay. Tornadoes can also be
noisy, often roaring like a freight train or a jet
(105) engine. This may result from the interaction
of the concentrated high winds with the
ground.

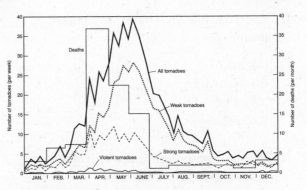

Figure 1. Weekly average of tornadoes recorded
in the U.S. from 1950 to 1982 shows that most
tornadoes (about 74 percent) strike between
March and July. Most violent tornadoes and most
deaths come in April, when the temperature
contrast across the polar front is sharpest.
Later the contrast is weaker, as are the resulting
thunderstorms and tornadoes. The death figures
are monthly averages for 1953 to 1982.

20. Tornadoes are characterized by which of the
following?

  I. Brevity of duration
 II. Intense concentration of energy
III. Uniformity of shape

(A) I only
(B) II only
(C) I and II only
(D) I, II, and III

21. The sentence in lines 48–50 ("Before . . .
itself") functions in the passage primarily as

(A) a transition.
(B) a concession.
(C) an apology.
(D) a refutation.

GO ON TO THE NEXT PAGE

DIAGNOSTIC TEST

22. As used in line 53, "Drawn" most nearly means

(A) traced.
(B) sketched.
(C) obtained.
(D) pulled.

23. The passage suggests that which of the following is true of a tornado?

(A) Its winds are invariably counterclockwise.
(B) It can last for days at a time.
(C) Its funnel cloud will not form if the air is cool and dry.
(D) It responds to changes in temperature and humidity.

24. According to the author, a direct relation may exist between the color a tornado takes on and

(A) the composition of the terrain it passes over.
(B) the intensity of the winds it concentrates.
(C) the particular shape of funnel it forms.
(D) the direction in which its winds rotate.

25. Which choice provides the best evidence for the answer to the previous question?

(A) Lines 79–82 ("The warmer . . . cloud to form")
(B) Lines 90–93 ("Usually . . . also common")
(C) Lines 98–103 ("Its . . . clay")
(D) Lines 103–107 ("Tornadoes . . . ground")

26. The primary purpose of the final paragraph is to

(A) propose the adoption of an observation technique.
(B) suggest a hypothesis about tornado dynamics.
(C) emphasize the need for further observations of tornado formation.
(D) provide a physical description of a phenomenon.

27. Which statement from the passage is best supported by Figure 1?

(A) Lines 3–7 ("They . . . lightning")
(B) Lines 30–34 ("This has led . . . tornado")
(C) Lines 61–66 ("The pressure . . . kilometer")
(D) Lines 82–85 ("Sometimes . . . aloft")

28. As used in line 11, "on the order of" most nearly means

(A) sequentially.
(B) approximately.
(C) at the command of.
(D) in the class of.

GO ON TO THE NEXT PAGE

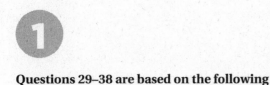

Questions 29–38 are based on the following passage.

This passage is adapted from Jane Addams, Twenty Years at Hull-House, *originally published in 1910.*

When Hull-House was established in
1889, the events of the Haymarket riot were
already two years old, but during that time
Line Chicago had apparently gone through the
(5) first period of repressive measures, and in
the winter of 1889–1890, by the advice and
with the active participation of its leading
citizens, the city had reached the conclusion
that the only cure for the acts of anarchy was
(10) free speech and an open discussion of the
ills of which the opponents of government
complained. Great open meetings were held
every Sunday evening in the recital hall of
the then new auditorium, and every possible
(15) shade of opinion was freely expressed. A
man who spoke constantly at these meetings
used to be pointed out to the visiting stranger
as one who had been involved with the
group of convicted anarchists, and who
(20) doubtless would have been arrested and
tried, but for the accident of his having been
in Milwaukee when the explosion occurred.
One cannot imagine such meetings being
held in Chicago today, nor that such a man
(25) should be encouraged to raise his voice
in a public assemblage presided over by a
leading banker. It is hard to tell just what
change has come over our philosophy or over
the minds of those citizens who were then
(30) convinced that if these conferences had been
established earlier, the Haymarket riot and
all its sensational results might have been
avoided.

At any rate, there seemed a further need
(35) for smaller clubs, where men who differed
widely in their social theories might meet

for discussion, where representatives of the
various economic schools might modify
each other, and at least learn tolerance
(40) and the futility of endeavoring to convince
all the world of the truth of one position.
Fanaticism is engendered only when men,
finding no contradiction to their theories,
believe that the very universe lends itself
(45) as an exemplification of one point of view.
"The Working People's Social Science Club"
was organized at Hull-House in the spring
of 1890, and for seven years it held a weekly
meeting. At eight o'clock every Wednesday
(50) night the secretary called to order from
forty to one hundred people; a chairman
for the evening was elected, a speaker was
introduced who was allowed to talk until
nine o'clock; his subject was then thrown
(55) open to discussion and a lively debate
ensued until ten o'clock, at which hour
the meeting was declared adjourned. The
enthusiasm of this club seldom lagged. Its
zest for discussion was unceasing, and any
(60) attempt to turn it into a study or reading club
always met with the strong disapprobation of
the members.

In these weekly discussions everything
was thrown back upon general principles
(65) and all discussion save that which "went
to the root of things" was impatiently
discarded as an unworthy, halfway measure.
I recall one evening in this club when
an exasperated member had thrown out
(70) the statement that "Mr. B. believes that
socialism will cure the toothache." Mr. B.
promptly rose to his feet and said that it
certainly would, that when every child's
teeth were systematically cared for from the
(75) beginning, the toothache would disappear
from the face of the earth, belonging, as
it did, to the extinct competitive order, as
the black plague had disappeared from the

GO ON TO THE NEXT PAGE

earth with the ill-regulated feudal regime
(80) of the Middle Ages. "But," he added, "why
do we spend time discussing trifles like the
toothache when great social changes are
to be considered which will of themselves
reform these minor ills?" Even the man who
(85) had been humorous fell into the solemn
tone of the gathering. It was, perhaps, here
that the socialist surpassed everyone else
in the fervor of economic discussion. He
was usually a German or a Russian, with a
(90) turn for logical presentation, who saw in
the concentration of capital and the growth
of monopolies an inevitable transition to
the socialist state. He pointed out that the
concentration of capital in fewer hands but
(95) increased the mass of those whose interests
were opposed to a maintenance of its power,
and vastly simplified its final absorption
by the community; that monopoly "when
it is finished doth bring forth socialism."
(100) Opposite to him, springing up in every
discussion was the individualist, or, as the
socialist called him, the anarchist, who
insisted that we shall never secure just
human relations until we have equality of
(105) opportunity; that the sole function of the
state is to maintain the freedom of each,
guarded by the like freedom of all, in order
that each man may be able to work out the
problems of his own existence.

29. As used in line 15, "shade" most nearly means

(A) slight amount.
(B) differing variation.
(C) protective covering.
(D) color gradation.

30. The reference in lines 15–27 to the man who
was involved with the group of anarchists
primarily serves to

(A) illustrate the danger of the ideas being
discussed at the meetings.
(B) emphasize the economic class of the
participants in the meetings.
(C) demonstrate that all peoples were
welcome to discuss their ideas in the
meetings.
(D) explain why limits had to be placed on
topics of discussion at the meetings.

31. It is reasonable to conclude that the main
goal of the individuals leading the meetings
described in the passage was to

(A) discourage extremism by encouraging
people to consider conflicting opinions.
(B) provide education about economics for
members of the working class.
(C) distract the participants from the misery
of their lives.
(D) promote a socialist system of
government.

32. As used in line 69, "thrown out" most nearly
means

(A) suggested.
(B) hurled.
(C) discarded.
(D) dismissed.

GO ON TO THE NEXT PAGE

33. The author indicates that, in comparison to the time at which she is writing, 1890 was remarkable for its

(A) upheaval and revolt.
(B) open debate and freedom of expression.
(C) focus on dental health.
(D) fear of monopolies and concentration of capital.

34. Which choice provides the best evidence for the answer to the previous question?

(A) Lines 23–27 ("One cannot . . . leading banker")
(B) Lines 42–45 ("Fanatacism is . . . point of view")
(C) Lines 63–67 ("In these . . . halfway measure")
(D) Lines 80–84 ("But . . . minor ills?")

35. Based on the passage, what was Addams's opinion of the debates sponsored by "The Working People's Social Science Club"?

(A) Addams believed that the participants' time would be better spent improving their vocational skills.
(B) Addams believed that the opinions of uneducated people were generally without merit.
(C) Addams believed that the debates would encourage a peaceful transition to socialism.
(D) Addams believed that the participants were passionate about debating.

36. Which choice provides the best evidence for the answer to the previous question?

(A) Lines 8–12 ("the city had . . . complained")
(B) Lines 34–41 ("At any rate . . . one position")
(C) Lines 58–62 ("Its zest for . . . the members")
(D) Lines 100–109 ("Opposite to him . . . existence")

37. Which choice best describes the structure of the first paragraph?

(A) A problem is described, examples are given, and a solution is suggested.
(B) A position is stated, historical context is given, and action is urged.
(C) A principle is stated, opposing principles are introduced, and a consensus is reached.
(D) A historical context is given, events are described, and an implied question is raised.

38. According to Addams, which statement about the debates in "The Working People's Social Science Club" is true?

(A) After bitter disagreement, the participants would reach consensus.
(B) The participants were so enthusiastic that the debates often became chaotic and disorderly.
(C) The speakers were so passionate that their speeches sometimes incited riots.
(D) The positions advocated by the debaters encompassed a wide range of political beliefs.

GO ON TO THE NEXT PAGE

Questions 39–47 are based on the following passage.

The following passage is adapted from The Natural Wealth of Nations *by David Malin Roodman.*

Many people accustomed to thinking of taxes as a necessary evil will be surprised to learn that some taxes can do economic good.
Line But when it comes to environmental harm, it
(5) is economically better to tax than not to tax.

Famed British economist Arthur Cecil Pigou was the first to advocate taxes on environmental harm. In his 1920's classic, *The Economics of Welfare,* he pointed to the
(10) hidden costs of smoke pouring from factories and fireplaces in Manchester, England. Costs of extra laundry cleaning, of artificial lighting necessitated by darkened air, and of repairs to corroded buildings had been estimated
(15) at £290,000 per year (about $10 million at today's prices). As a result, a steelmaker might have made £100 worth of steel with a furnaceful of coal, and done £200 in damage in the process—a gain for the company, but
(20) a net loss for the city. In effect, pollution victims were subsidizing pollution causers, and making society as a whole poorer.

Pigou's sensible prescription became received wisdom within economics, but most
(25) of the bricks in the environmental policy edifice built during the last 30 years have been fired from the stuff of regulations, not taxes. To be sure, regulations have scored important successes. In Western Europe, for
(30) example, regulators can point to a 47 percent reduction in sulfur emissions between 1970 and 1993, due substantially to rules requiring scrubbers in coal plants. In the United States, tightened tailpipe emissions standards for
(35) new cars and light trucks made catalytic converters universal over the same time span, cutting nitrogen oxide emissions 6 percent, carbon monoxide 33 percent, and volatile organic compounds 54 percent, all
(40) despite a 44 percent increase in driving. Nevertheless, regulations are increasingly being pushed beyond their limits. Because they often focus on means rather than ends—for example, by prescribing the use
(45) of particular kinds of water filters—they tend to discourage innovation. And though they often work well when there is a front-runner solution (such as catalytic converters for cars), they tend to break down in the
(50) face of complexity. A joint study by the U.S. Environmental Protection Agency (EPA) and Amoco Corporation documented one telling absurdity at the oil company's Yorktown, Virginia, refinery. Regulations required
(55) Amoco to spend $31 million on a wastewater treatment plant to stop airborne emissions of benzene, a carcinogen. Meanwhile, the rules failed to cover benzene emissions from a nearby loading dock—emissions that
(60) could have been reduced as much for just $6 million. As one exasperated refinery official put it, "Give us a goal to meet rather than all the regulations . . . That worked in the 1970s, when the pollution problems were much
(65) more visible and simpler. It's not working now."

The growing use of environmental taxes is one response to that plea. One of the best and earliest examples is the system of
(70) water pollution taxes in the Netherlands. Since 1970, gradually rising charges on emissions of organic material and heavy metals into canals, rivers, and lakes have spurred companies to cut emissions—
(75) without dictating how. Between 1976 and the mid-1990s, emissions of cadmium,

GO ON TO THE NEXT PAGE

chromium, copper, lead, mercury, nickel, and zinc into waters managed by regional governments (which adopted the charges (80) earliest) plummeted 72–99 percent—primarily because of the charges, according to statistical analyses. (See Figure 1.)

The Dutch example illustrates the strengths of environmental taxes at their (85) best. Companies that could prevent pollution most cheaply presumably did so most. Firms would also have passed part of the taxes on to their customers through higher prices, causing them to switch to (90) less-pollution-intensive products. And demand for pollution control equipment has spurred Dutch manufacturers to develop better models, triggering innovations that regulators could never have planned, (95) lowering costs, and turning the country into a global leader in the market. The taxes have in effect sought the path of least economic resistance—of least cost—in cleaning up the country's waters.

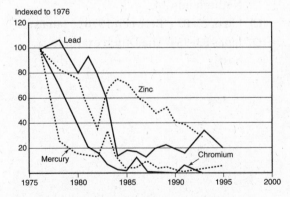

Figure 1. Industrial discharges of chromium and zinc, 1976 to 1993, and lead and mercury, 1976 to 1995, into regional surface waters, The Netherlands

39. The primary purpose of the passage is to

(A) refute critics of Pigou's classic economic theory.
(B) question the wisdom of using regulatory restrictions to combat environmental harm.
(C) point out the effectiveness of environmental taxes in reducing pollution.
(D) propose a novel approach to achieving a long-term economic goal.

40. According to the passage, environmental harm

(A) is an inevitable result of technological innovation.
(B) injures society, and therefore should be compensated for.
(C) provides subsidies for taxpayers who cannot afford them.
(D) is caused by the growing use of environmental taxes.

41. Which choice provides the best evidence for the answer to the previous question?

(A) Lines 6–11 ("Famed . . . England")
(B) Lines 16–22 ("As a result . . . poorer")
(C) Lines 23–28 ("Pigou's . . . taxes")
(D) Lines 50–54 ("A joint study . . . refinery")

GO ON TO THE NEXT PAGE

42. Which choice is an underlying assumption of the policies described in the passage?

  (A) Companies will find ways to reduce their negative impact on the environment if it is in their economic interest to do so.
  (B) Environmental taxation has a stifling effect on the adoption of innovative methods to reduce environmental harm.
  (C) The number of pollution problems rises as the number of regulatory restrictions increases.
  (D) It is easier and cheaper for firms to reduce water pollution than it is for them to curb air pollution.

43. The author most likely describes the situation at the Amoco refinery as a "telling absurdity" because

  (A) the company failed to meet its goals for reducing airborne emissions of benzene.
  (B) the imposition of environmental taxes on the company caused the price of oil to rise astronomically.
  (C) the company was forced to pursue a costly method of cutting pollution rather than a cheaper, more effective one.
  (D) the cost of cutting airborne emissions of benzene continues to rise despite the refinery's best efforts to economize.

44. As used in line 58, "cover" most nearly means

  (A) apply to.
  (B) stand in for.
  (C) stretch over.
  (D) report on.

45. As used in line 62, "meet" most nearly means

  (A) encounter.
  (B) convene.
  (C) converge.
  (D) satisfy.

46. The phrase "To be sure" in line 28 serves to

  (A) emphasize the need for certitude in economic policy making.
  (B) acknowledge that regulatory restrictions have been effective in reducing pollution.
  (C) convey the impression that regulatory restrictions are certain to eliminate environmental harm.
  (D) question whether regulations have been more effective than taxes in cutting harmful emissions.

47. Which statement from the passage is best supported by Figure 1?

  (A) Lines 57–66 ("Meanwhile, the rules . . . working now")
  (B) Lines 67–70 ("The growing use . . . Netherlands")
  (C) Lines 75–82 ("Between 1976 . . . analyses")
  (D) Lines 83–85 ("The Dutch example . . . best")

If there is still time remaining, you may review your answers.

WRITING AND LANGUAGE TEST

35 MINUTES, 44 QUESTIONS

Turn to Section 2 of your answer sheet to answer the questions in this section.

> **Directions:** Questions follow each of the passages below. Some questions ask you how the passage might be changed to improve the expression of ideas. Other questions ask you how the passage might be altered to correct errors in grammar, usage, and punctuation. One or more graphics accompany some passages. You will be required to consider these graphics as you answer questions about editing the passage.
>
> There are three types of questions. In the first type, a part of the passage is underlined. The second type is based on a certain part of the passage. The third type is based on the entire passage.
>
> Read each passage. Then, choose the answer to each question that changes the passage so that it is consistent with the conventions of standard written English. One of the answer choices for many questions is "NO CHANGE." Choosing this answer means that you believe the best answer is to make no change in the passage.

Questions 1–11 are based on the following passage.

Geronimo

(1)

The year is 1999. The day is ❶ without bearing hot. To escape the heat, my brother and I ask Mrs. Cleghorn if we can swim in her pool. When I leap into the six-feet-deep end, I yell out "Geronimo!" Mrs. Cleghorn laughs.

(2)

That stuffy afternoon, Mrs. Cleghorn relayed a wondrous tale about a brave but vicious Native American warrior who dodged bullets and evaporated mysteriously from caves. ❷ Geronimo defended his people and lands, for more than 25 years, as one of the very last natives to resist White colonization of the West.

1. (A) NO CHANGE
   (B) un-bare-ably
   (C) unbearably
   (D) non-bareingly

2. (A) NO CHANGE
   (B) Geronimo defended his people and lands for more than 25 years as one of the very last natives, to resist White colonization of the West.
   (C) Geronimo defended his people and lands for more than 25 years as one of the very last natives to resist White colonization of the West.
   (D) Geronimo defended his people and lands, for more than 25 years as one of the very last natives to resist White, colonization of the West.

GO ON TO THE NEXT PAGE

(3)

I still remember her warning: "Do not misunderstand. Geronimo, also known as Goyathlay, of the Bedonkohe Apache, was no hero. **❸** He was a man who had terrible things happen to him, and who, in turn, did terrible things to others."

(4)

For years, Geronimo flooded my imagination. He tiptoed soundlessly through the trees, disappeared effortlessly into the muddy river, and **❹** charging with violence at the most unsuspecting enemies. He was ruthless and, above all, fearless. I had all but forgotten Mrs. Cleghorn and her part in my **❺** infatuation with and interest in Native American history until four years later, when my seventh grade class watched a documentary on the Chiricahua Apache tribe.

(5)

Goyathlay was given his nickname in battle when he slashed ceaselessly at Mexican soldiers with a knife, **❻** casually ignoring the stream of bullets that slid right by him. Determined to kill and impossible to capture, Goyathlay seized the public's attention for decades. Born in June 1829 in modern-day New Mexico, Goyathlay, grandson of the chief, spent his childhood hunting. He had

3. The author is considering deleting the underlined sentence. Should it be deleted?

(A) Yes, because it repeats information from the previous sentence.

(B) Yes, because it is irrelevant to the focus of the paragraph.

(C) No, because it gives specific details of his misdeeds.

(D) No, because it provides a helpful elaboration on the previous sentence.

4. (A) NO CHANGE
   (B) charged violently
   (C) with the charge of violence
   (D) charging violently

5. (A) NO CHANGE
   (B) love for, passion for, and admiration of
   (C) infatuation with
   (D) DELETE the underlined portion

6. Which of the following phrases would provide a transition at this point in the sentence that is most consistent with the characterization of Goyathlay provided in the previous paragraph?

(A) NO CHANGE
(B) quickly fleeing
(C) timidly hiding from
(D) failing to understand

GO ON TO THE NEXT PAGE

married and had three children by the time his village was raided by Mexican soldiers. **❼** <u>A great misfortune befell him when he was but a young man</u>—a tragedy that embittered Goyathlay with a deep hatred for Mexicans and a lifelong bloodlust.

(6)

With 200 of his tribe's survivors, Goyathlay tracked down and killed the men who had brutally murdered his family. He quickly rose to the head military position in **❽** <u>their</u> tribe and became notorious for urging raids against Mexican, and later American, settlements in the Southwest. From the 1850s until 1886 when he surrendered, Goyathlay eluded the more than 5,000 U.S. troops assigned specifically to hunting him down. **❾** <u>Toward the end of his career as a warrior, he led a band</u> of 38 that pillaged villages and committed vicious, unprovoked murders of Mexicans and Americans alike.

(7)

Goyathlay formally surrendered in 1886 and was retained as a prisoner of war for **❿** <u>the remaining years of his life until he died.</u> He reached celebrity status in these later years and released an autobiography in 1905. On his deathbed, Goyathlay regretted his surrender, wishing instead that he had fought to the death. **⓫**

7. Given that all of the choices are true, which of the following would provide the most specific illustration of the tragedy that happened to Goyathlay, providing a logical explanation given the context of the paragraph?

  (A) NO CHANGE
  (B) His mother, wife, and children were among the dead
  (C) Goyathlay was greatly saddened by the destruction of the pristine environment
  (D) The raid came as quite a surprise

8. (A) NO CHANGE
  (B) there
  (C) his or her
  (D) his

9. (A) NO CHANGE
  (B) Toward the end, of his career as a warrior, he led a band
  (C) Toward the end of his career as a warrior he led a band
  (D) Toward the end of his career, as a warrior, he led a band

10. (A) NO CHANGE
  (B) what was left to be had of his lifetime.
  (C) the remainder of his life.
  (D) that time.

11. The author wishes to insert the following sentence as a stand-alone paragraph in the essay.

  "His name was Goyathlay," she amends, "but he too jumped without fear."

  Where would it most logically be placed?

  (A) Before paragraph 1
  (B) Before paragraph 2
  (C) Before paragraph 6
  (D) Before paragraph 7

GO ON TO THE NEXT PAGE

Questions 12–22 are based on the following passage and supplementary material.

Pop Stands for Popular

To many music connoisseurs, especially those of the Baby Boom and Generation X eras, pop music **12** doesn't really make economic sense. Generally speaking, the catchy, repetitive, digitally enhanced verse-chorus forms are dismissed as commercial rip-offs not worthy of the rock and roll that **13** preceded them. A tendency to prioritize beats and rhythmic elements—leaving decisions like lyrics and performing artists as a brief afterthought— **14** create a general distaste for pop music in an older audience. Not to mention, the shift from the album to the single in the digital age favors short, catchy recordings produced in a few hours of studio time rather than **15** a rapidly put-together piece of music that can make producers a quick dollar. But is this careless relegation appropriate?

The term "pop" music **16** originate in the 1920s, but took off in the 1950s and 1960s to describe the new, trendy alternative to rock and roll aimed at a young audience. Pop music gradually began to refer to spunky, dance music that borrows elements from several other styles.

12. The author wishes to express that the "music connoisseurs" in the sentence have a condescending attitude toward pop music. Which of the following would best accomplish this goal, given the context of the paragraph?

(A) NO CHANGE
(B) falls short of what constitutes "real" art.
(C) is mildly amusing to popular audiences.
(D) justifiably earns its name given its fame.

13. (A) NO CHANGE
(B) precedented
(C) proceeded
(D) preceding

14. (A) NO CHANGE
(B) creates
(C) creating
(D) creation

15. Which of the following options would create the most logical contrast in the sentence?

(A) NO CHANGE
(B) songs representing diverse nationalities and cultures, often sung in foreign tongues.
(C) musical compositions that prioritize poetic language over rhythmic aspects.
(D) the invested, personal relationship between singer and songwriter that invokes public nostalgia.

16. (A) NO CHANGE
(B) originates
(C) have originated
(D) originated

GO ON TO THE NEXT PAGE

As the genre took form and placed more and more emphasis on technical production, **⑰ it was further distanced from other genres.** Soon, pop music was demarcated from rock and roll completely and is now often seen as oppositional to the genre that inspired it. By the 1980s, music television, most notably MTV, boosted the demand for pop music with flashy stars like Michael Jackson, Madonna, and later heartthrobs like Britney Spears and Justin Timberlake. Where once these names would have grazed the same lists **⑱ as The Beatles, Elvis Presley, and Bruce Springsteen,** music lovers everywhere worked hard to separate pop from rock. Today, one affiliates pop with artists like Lady Gaga, Katy Perry, and Bruno Mars, distinguishable from their rock counterparts by their flamboyant costumes, animated dance moves, and foot-tapping, digitalized tunes.

But, with pop flourishing and reinventing the **⑲ music industry can one rightly assume, it unworthy or inferior?** One only has to look to the "King of Pop" to prove the genre is far from simplistic. Michael Jackson took the stage by storm for over four decades, breaking social barriers while he "moonwalked" across the world. He not only holds the record for the best-selling album of all time, but he was inducted into the Songwriters Hall of Fame, the Dance Hall of Fame, and **⑳ the Rock and Roll Hall of Fame not once, but twice.** Renowned dance moves like the "robot"

17. (A) NO CHANGE
    (B) distanced it was further from others genres.
    (C) genres distanced it further from others.
    (D) the distance of it from the others genres.

18. The narrator is considering deleting the underlined portion. Should it be deleted?

    (A) Yes, because it distracts from the message of the sentence.
    (B) Yes, because it is unnecessarily specific in detail.
    (C) No, because it clarifies the part of the sentence that precedes it.
    (D) No, because it specifies the authors of the aforementioned lists.

19. (A) NO CHANGE
    (B) music industry, can one rightly assume it unworthy or inferior?
    (C) music industry can one rightly assume it unworthy or inferior!
    (D) music industry can one rightly, assume it unworthy or inferior.

20. (A) NO CHANGE
    (B) the Rock and Roll, Hall of Fame not once but twice.
    (C) the, Rock and Roll Hall of Fame not once but twice.
    (D) the Rock and, Roll Hall of Fame, not once, but twice.

GO ON TO THE NEXT PAGE

credit Jackson's eminence as much as his thirteen Grammy awards. ㉑ Even if pop is not your cup of tea, you'll find it hard to deny its exceptional influence—in fact, in 2014 it was the ㉒ least popular major genre of streaming music.

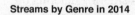

Streams by Genre in 2014

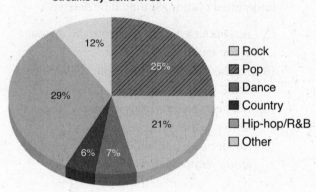

- Rock
- Pop
- Dance
- Country
- Hip-hop/R&B
- Other

25%
12%
29%
6% 7%
21%

Source: Nielsen

21. (A) NO CHANGE
    (B) So that
    (C) Because
    (D) Given

22. Which of the following is consistent with the graph that accompanies this passage?

    (A) NO CHANGE
    (B) second most popular
    (C) third most popular
    (D) most popular

GO ON TO THE NEXT PAGE

Questions 23–33 are based on the following passage.

Tierra del Fuego

If one **23** was to spin a globe and select a place to visit based simply on the exoticism of a name, the Tierra del Fuego archipelago in Argentina and Chile would be a wonderful candidate. Spanish for "Land of Fire," **24** Tierra del Fuego, lies at the, southernmost tip of South America and, despite its infernal name, actually is home to the closest city to the South Pole in the world. Due partly to this geographical remoteness, it is a region characterized by striking beauty and gorgeous terrain. **25** Yet, despite its otherworldly charm, Tierra del Fuego is victimized by something far too mundane: an invasive species of North American beaver.

An invasive species is a non-indigenous animal, fungus, or plant species introduced to an area **26** that have the potential to inflict harm upon the native ecosystem. In Tierra del Fuego, "invasive" describes the beaver perfectly. It was first introduced in 1946 by the Argentine government in an effort to catalyze a fur trading industry in the region. What started as a small influx of 50 beavers has since grown **27** to a number that can only be described as "out of sight." Unlike in North America where the beaver has several natural predators that help to maintain manageable population numbers, Tierra del Fuego has no such luxury; thus, what began with the **28** greatest and best of intentions has since fomented a veritable crisis

23. (A) NO CHANGE
   (B) had been
   (C) will be
   (D) were

24. (A) NO CHANGE
   (B) Tierra del Fuego lies at the southernmost tip of South America
   (C) Tierra del Fuego lies at the southernmost tip, of South America
   (D) Tierra del Fuego lies, at the southernmost tip of, South America

25. (A) NO CHANGE
   (B) Because of this fact
   (C) For this and other reasons
   (D) Moreover

26. (A) NO CHANGE
   (B) that has
   (C) which have
   (D) which has

27. Which of the following options would most logically complete the sentence with the specific detail?

   (A) NO CHANGE
   (B) to an overwhelming group of 30 mature beavers.
   (C) to a burgeoning population of more than 200,000.
   (D) to a burdensome number that taxes the natural resources of the region.

28. (A) NO CHANGE
   (B) best of thoughtful acts and intentions
   (C) best
   (D) best of intentions

GO ON TO THE NEXT PAGE

where beaver reproduction proceeds unimpeded and ㉙ without even a check.

Like most plans of mice, men, and beavers, this one went ㉚ indubitably awry; the fur industry never materialized as expected, and now the beavers have free rein to terrorize the region as they see fit. Therein lies the problem with the beaver: it isn't your standard animal. Beavers are destructive, ambitious, ㉛ and, dare I say—even maniacal. They gnaw through everything in their wake, and visitors to the area remark that the landscape is so destroyed that it appears as if a bulldozer or forest fire decimated the woodlands. Fifty percent of the forest, in fact, is critically damaged. Unlike many North American tree species that grow back once chewed by beavers, the trees in Tierra del Fuego aren't as resilient. At best, their recovery is decades away. ㉜ In contrast, beavers are mostly aquatic-dwelling animals.

㉝ Ultimately, there are two lessons to be learned from this. First, perhaps it is best not to interfere with the delicate harmony of an ecosystem. And second, "leaving it to beaver" was really a quite naive idea the entire time.

29. (A) NO CHANGE
    (B) with no checking.
    (C) unchecked.
    (D) non-checking.

30. Which phrase would provide the most logical transition at this point in the sentence?

    (A) NO CHANGE
    (B) surprisingly effectively
    (C) as expected
    (D) moderately successfully

31. (A) NO CHANGE
    (B) and—dare I say, even maniacal.
    (C) and dare I say even maniacal.
    (D) and—dare I say—even maniacal.

32. Which of the following would provide the most logical contrast with the previous sentence?

    (A) NO CHANGE
    (B) In consideration of the other side, some believe trees should be used as natural resources.
    (C) At worst, their destruction is irreparable.
    (D) Unfortunately, the beaver population continues to dwindle due to pollution.

33. Which of these sentences would provide the best introduction to the concluding paragraph?

    (A) NO CHANGE
    (B) Surprisingly, the expected destruction of this harmonious ecosystem has been held at bay.
    (C) In conclusion, even though a species may not be native to an environment, it can provide valuable contributions to it.
    (D) South American environmental destruction is unique in its utter devastation.

GO ON TO THE NEXT PAGE

Questions 34–44 are based on the following passage and supplementary material.

Nutrition Science

This time of year, clients come to me with one goal in mind: weight loss. I often have to explain to them that their goal is more likely *fat loss* than weight loss per se. Most of us have more stored body fat **34** than we prefer, but rarely do we want to lose muscle as well. Converting and burning fat while maintaining or building muscle is an art— **35** in contrast, it is my job.

(1) During high school, I went from puny and weak to fit and strong in one year, and my mother dropped 43 pounds and began an active lifestyle that prolonged her life. (2) We sought the help of a nutritionist. Weight lifting, resistance training, and cardiovascular exercise all greatly affected our progress, but I found the science behind a sound nutrition plan the most invigorating. (3) Time well spent in the kitchen made all the difference! **36**

What I love most about my job is that *everybody* benefits from healthy eating and supplemental nutrition—no matter your background or your goals, I can help you. Just a few of the benefits of fueling your body properly include **37** giving yourself the opportunity to make self-improvements—and that's to say nothing of dropping fat, building muscle, and **38** amplifying self-confidence. So, when clients show up at my office unhealthy, unhappy, or just in need of a little support, I am eager to show them what their own bodies can do with just a few dietary changes.

For many, "diet" refers to a short-term period of near-starvation that feels more like imprisonment than liberation. But, for the nutritionist, "diet" simply means a long-term nutritional plan customized to fit a client's needs and goals, and

34. (A) NO CHANGE
(B) then
(C) this
(D) those

35. (A) NO CHANGE
(B) nonetheless
(C) in fact
(D) them

36. The author wishes to place the following sentence in the previous paragraph:

"What was our secret?"

Where would it most logically be placed?

(A) Before Sentence 1
(B) After Sentence 1
(C) After Sentence 2
(D) After Sentence 3

37. Which of the following options provides the most effective and specific elaboration on the first part of the sentence?

(A) NO CHANGE
(B) feeling better today than you did the day beforehand
(C) better thinking, clearer mental processing, and improved intellectual activity
(D) increased cognition, energy, performance, and overall wellness

38. (A) NO CHANGE
(B) amplified
(C) amped
(D) amplification of

GO ON TO THE NEXT PAGE

ultimately working with exercise to promote a healthy, balanced lifestyle. **39** <u>However,</u> a diet plan should strive to make you feel *better*, not miserable; **40** <u>it should: be doable and sustainable.</u> Certainly, diets are not always easy—changing a lifestyle requires commitment, flexibility, and consistency—but a nutritionist works to build a manageable plan that makes gradual, lifelong improvements for every client.

Nutrition is a science. Nonetheless, for everybody, it **41** <u>comes</u> down to protein, carbohydrate, and fat intake. Protein supplies your body with essential building blocks for nearly every cell and tissue in your body; it boosts fat burn, stimulates lean muscle building, and discourages overeating. Carbohydrates, made up of sugars, fuel your body—simple sugars, however, should only comprise about **42** <u>8 percent</u> of your daily caloric intake. Fats have a bad reputation, but unfairly so; about **43** <u>2 out of every 5 calories</u> we consume daily should be in the form of fats. With just this minimal knowledge, you can start understanding your **44** <u>bodys</u> composition and what it needs for optimal health.

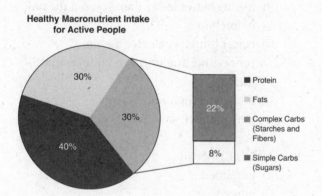

Healthy Macronutrient Intake for Active People

39. (A) NO CHANGE
    (B) Nevertheless
    (C) Unexpectedly
    (D) In essence

40. (A) NO CHANGE
    (B) it should, be doable and sustainable.
    (C) it should be doable and sustainable.
    (D) it should be doable, and sustainable.

41. (A) NO CHANGE
    (B) come
    (C) coming
    (D) had come

42. Which of the following is both consistent with the passage and supported by the data in the chart?

    (A) NO CHANGE
    (B) 22 percent
    (C) 30 percent
    (D) 40 percent

43. Which of the following is both consistent with the passage and supported by the data in the chart?

    (A) NO CHANGE
    (B) 4 out of every 10 calories
    (C) 3 out of every 5 calories
    (D) 3 out of every 10 calories

44. (A) NO CHANGE
    (B) body's
    (C) bodies
    (D) bodies'

If there is still time remaining, you may review your answers.

MATH TEST (NO CALCULATOR)

25 MINUTES, 17 QUESTIONS

Turn to Section 3 of your answer sheet to answer the questions in this section.

Directions: For questions 1–13, solve each problem and choose the best answer from the given choices. Fill in the corresponding circle on your answer sheet. For questions 14–17, solve each problem and enter your answer in the grid on your answer sheet.

Notes:
- Calculators are **NOT PERMITTED** in this section.
- All variables and expressions represent real numbers unless indicated otherwise.
- All figures are drawn to scale unless indicated otherwise.
- All figures are in a plane unless indicated otherwise.
- Unless indicated otherwise, the domain of a given function is the set of all real numbers x for which the function has real values.

REFERENCE INFORMATION

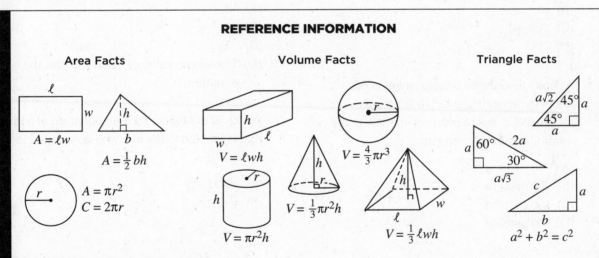

The arc of a circle contains 360°.
The arc of a circle contains 2π radians.
The sum of the measures of the angles in a triangle is 180°.

GO ON TO THE NEXT PAGE

1. If $4x = 12$, what is the value of $12x$?

   (A)   6
   (B)   24
   (C)   36
   (D)   48

2. Which of the following is the equation of a line that does not pass through Quadrant III?

   (A) $x - y - 1 = 0$
   (B) $x - y + 1 = 0$
   (C) $x + y - 1 = 0$
   (D) $x + y + 1 = 0$

3. If $f(x) = x^2 - 2^x$, what is the value of $f(3)$?

   (A) -1
   (B) 0
   (C) 1
   (D) 17

4. A bank raised the minimum payment on its charge accounts from $10 to $20 per month. What was the percent increase in the minimum monthly pament?

   (A)   10 percent
   (B)   50 percent
   (C)   100 percent
   (D)   200 percent

5. The formula for a team's winning percentage, P, for a season is $P = \dfrac{W}{W + L}$, where W and L are the numbers of games the team won and lost, respectively, during the season. Which of the following correctly expresses W in terms of P and L?

   (A) $W = \dfrac{PL}{1 - P}$

   (B) $W = \dfrac{PL}{P - 1}$

   (C) $W = \dfrac{L}{1 - P}$

   (D) $W = \dfrac{L}{P - 1}$

6. If $13 - 2\sqrt{x} = 7$, then what is the value of x?

   (A) -9
   (B) 6
   (C) 9
   (D)   There is no value of x that satisfies the equation.

7. Which of the following is an equation of a line that is parallel to the line whose equation is $y = 2x - 3$?

   (A) $y = 2x + 3$
   (B) $y = -2x - 3$

   (C) $y = \dfrac{1}{2}x - 3$

   (D) $y = -\dfrac{1}{2}x - 3$

GO ON TO THE NEXT PAGE

8. Leeds Central High School has an honor roll and a high honor roll. Students are placed on the honor roll if their average in the previous semester is between 88 and 94, inclusive. Students whose average is higher than 94 are instead placed on the high honor roll. Which of the following inequalities can be used to determine if a student whose average is A points will be placed on the honor roll?

(A) $|A - 94| \le 88$
(B) $|A - 88| \le 94$
(C) $|A - 88| \le 6$
(D) $|A - 91| \le 3$

9. If $A(3, -2)$ and $B(7, 2)$ are the endpoints of a diameter of a circle, what is the area of the circle?

(A) $2\sqrt{2}\,\pi$
(B) $4\sqrt{2}\,\pi$
(C) 8π
(D) 16π

10. Which of the following expressions is equivalent to $\dfrac{4n-3}{n+2}$?

(A) $\dfrac{4-3}{2}$
(B) $4 - \dfrac{3}{2}$
(C) $4 - \dfrac{11}{n+2}$
(D) $4 - \dfrac{3}{n+2}$

11. Which of the following are the solutions of the equation $3x^2 + 6x = 6$?

(A) $1 + \sqrt{2}$ and $1 - \sqrt{2}$
(B) $-1 + \sqrt{2}$ and $-1 - \sqrt{2}$
(C) $1 + \sqrt{3}$ and $1 - \sqrt{3}$
(D) $-1 + \sqrt{3}$ and $-1 - \sqrt{3}$

12. What is the volume, in cubic inches, of a cube whose surface area is 60 square inches?

(A) $10\sqrt{10}$
(B) $15\sqrt{15}$
(C) $60\sqrt{60}$
(D) 1,000

$$h(x) = x^3 + 2x^2 + cx + d$$

13. In the function above, c and d are constants. If $h(-1)$ and $h(1)$ are both equal to 5, what is the value of $h(2)$?

(A) 5
(B) 11
(C) 13
(D) 17

GO ON TO THE NEXT PAGE

Grid-in Response Directions

In questions 14–17, first solve the problem, and then enter your answer on the grid provided on the answer sheet. The instructions for entering your answers follow.

- First, write your answer in the boxes at the top of the grid.
- Second, grid your answer in the columns below the boxes.
- Use the fraction bar in the first row or the decimal point in the second row to enter fractions and decimals.

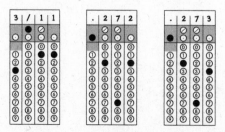

- Grid only one space in each column.
- Entering the answer in the boxes is recommended as an aid in gridding but is not required.
- The machine scoring your exam can read only what you grid, so you **must grid-in your answers correctly to get credit**.
- If a question has more than one correct answer, grid-in only one of them.
- The grid does not have a minus sign; so no answer can be negative.
- A mixed number *must* be converted to an improper fraction or a decimal before it is gridded.

  Enter $1\frac{1}{4}$ as 5/4 or 1.25; the machine will interpret 11/4 as $\frac{11}{4}$ and mark it wrong.

- **All decimals must be entered as accurately as possible.** Here are three acceptable ways of gridding

$$\frac{3}{11} = 0.272727\ldots$$

- Note that rounding to .273 is acceptable because you are using the full grid, but you would receive **no credit** for .3 or .27, because they are less accurate.

14. If $\frac{5}{8}x = \frac{7}{8}x$, what is the value of $\frac{11}{8}x$?

16. Evelyn's average (arithmetic mean) on her six math tests this marking period is 80. Fortunately for Evelyn, her teacher drops each student's lowest grade; doing so raises Evelyn's average to 90. What was her lowest grade?

$$g(x) = x^2 + bx + c$$

15. In the function above, b and c are constants. If $g(2) = 2$ and $g(3) = 5$, what is the value of $g(4)$?

17. What is the value of $\left(\sqrt{x} \cdot \sqrt[3]{x}\right)^6$ when $x = 2$?

STOP

If there is still time remaining, you may review your answers.

MATH TEST (CALCULATOR)

45 MINUTES, 31 QUESTIONS

Turn to Section 4 of your answer sheet to answer the questions in this section.

Directions: For questions 1–27, solve each problem and choose the best answer from the given choices. Fill in the corresponding circle on your answer sheet. For questions 28–31, solve each problem and enter your answer in the grid on your answer sheet.

Notes:
- Calculators **ARE PERMITTED** in this section.
- All variables and expressions represent real numbers unless indicated otherwise.
- All figures are drawn to scale unless indicated otherwise.
- All figures are in a plane unless indicated otherwise.
- Unless indicated otherwise, the domain of a given function is the set of all real numbers *x* for which the function has real values.

REFERENCE INFORMATION

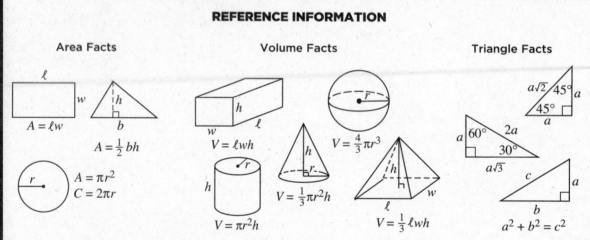

The arc of a circle contains 360°.

The arc of a circle contains 2π radians.

The sum of the measures of the angles in a triangle is 180°.

GO ON TO THE NEXT PAGE

1. If the ratio of the number of boys to girls in a club is 2:3, what percent of the club members are girls?

   (A) $33\frac{1}{3}$ percent

   (B) 40 percent

   (C) 60 percent

   (D) $66\frac{2}{3}$ percent

2. The Albertville Little League raised some money. They used 72 percent of the money to buy uniforms, 19 percent for equipment, and the remaining $243 for a team party. How much money did the team raise?

   (A) $2,400
   (B) $2,500
   (C) $2,600
   (D) $2,700

3. One day in North Central High School's cafeteria, the only sandwiches available were tuna fish salad, bologna, and grilled cheese. The table below, broken down by class, shows the types of sandwiches chosen by the students that day.

	Sophomores	Juniors	Seniors	Total
Tuna fish	170	200	190	560
Bologna	125	98	106	329
Grilled cheese	35	42	14	91
Totals	330	340	310	980

   Which of the following is closest to the percent of the juniors and seniors who did *not* choose tuna fish that day?

   (A) 33 percent
   (B) 40 percent
   (C) 50 percent
   (D) 67 percent

4. Al and Bob each have collections of rare 19th-century photographs. Al, who has just retired, plans to supplement his income by selling 25 of his photographs each year. Bob, who is a young, successful businessman, plans to add to his collection systematically by purchasing 20 photographs every year. If Al and Bob currently have 905 and 320 photographs in their collections, respectively, in how many years will they each have the same number of photographs?

   (A) 11
   (B) 13
   (C) 19
   (D) 23

5. Which of the following expressions is equivalent to

   $$\frac{(a+a+a)(a \cdot a \cdot a)(a^{\frac{1}{6}} \cdot a^{\frac{1}{3}} \cdot a^{\frac{1}{2}})}{a^{-1} \cdot a^{-2} \cdot a^{-3}}?$$

   (A) $3a^{-1}$
   (B) $3a^4$
   (C) $3a^{11}$
   (D) $3a^{14}$

6. In 2015, ABC Marketing Company had 31 employees. The mean annual salary was $82,000, and the median annual salary was $46,000. Which of the following statements could best explain the difference between the mean and the median in the company's payroll data?

   (A) A small number of employees earned less than $46,000.
   (B) A small number of employees earned more than $82,000.
   (C) The mode for this data was closer to $46,000 than to $82,000.
   (D) Most of the employees earned between $46,000 and $82,000.

GO ON TO THE NEXT PAGE

DIAGNOSTIC TEST

For questions 7 and 8, use the information in the graphs below.

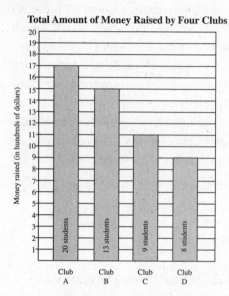

Total Amount of Money Raised by Four Clubs

Money raised (in hundreds of dollars)

20 students   13 students   9 students   8 students

Club A   Club B   Club C   Club D

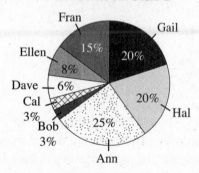

Percentage of Money Raised by the 8 Students in Club D

Fran 15%   Gail 20%   Ellen 8%   Dave 6%   Cal 3%   Bob 3%   Hal 20%   Ann 25%

7. In 2015, each Key Club member in the four high schools in Northampton County raised some money for a charity. The bar graph above shows the total amount of money raised by each club and the number of students who were members of the Key Club in each of those high schools. Which of the four Key Clubs had the highest average amount of money raised per member?

    (A) A
    (B) B
    (C) C
    (D) D

8. The student in Key Club D who raised the most money during 2015 raised, to the nearest tenth of one percent, what percent of the total amount of money raised in 2015 by the four Key Clubs shown in the bar graph?

    (A) 4.3 percent
    (B) 4.5 percent
    (C) 4.8 percent
    (D) 5.3 percent

9. The lengths of two sides of a right triangle are 5 and 9. Which of the following could be the length of the third side?

    I. $\sqrt{56}$

    II. $\sqrt{76}$

    III. $\sqrt{106}$

    (A) I only
    (B) III only
    (C) I and II only
    (D) I and III only

10. To go to a customer's house to do repair work, a plumber charges a flat fee of f dollars, which includes the first hour of her time. For her time in excess of one hour, she charges h dollars per hour. One day, she had two jobs. The first job took 3.5 hours, for which her charge was $290. The second job took 4.25 hours, for which her charge was $335. What is the value of $f + h$?

    (A) 60
    (B) 80
    (C) 140
    (D) 200

GO ON TO THE NEXT PAGE

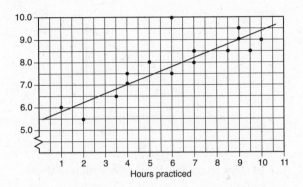

Hours practiced

11. At the Essex Conservatory, 15 piano students participated in a competition. Each student received a grade on a scale from 5 to 10 in increments of 0.5. The scatterplot above shows the relationship between the students' scores and the number of hours they practiced during the last two days before the competition. The line of best fit has also been drawn. If the equation of that line is written in the form $y = mx + b$, what is the value of $m + b$?

(A) 5.4
(B) 5.9
(C) 6.2
(D) 6.5

12. Each of the 15 members of a club owns a certain number of teddy bears. The following chart shows the number of teddy bears owned.

Number of Teddy Bears	Number of Members
6	2
8	5
10	4
12	4

What is the average (arithmetic mean) of the median, mode, and range of this set of data?

(A) 8
(B) 8.5
(C) 9
(D) 9.5

13. Larry bought Ava three gifts for their anniversary—a ring, perfume, and a book—for which he spent a total of $792. If the perfume cost three times as much as the book and the ring cost 10 times as much as the perfume and book combined, how much did he pay for the perfume?

(A) $18
(B) $36
(C) $48
(D) $54

GO ON TO THE NEXT PAGE

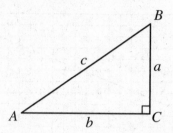

Questions 14 and 15 are based on the following information.

1,000 students at College A and 1,500 students at College B are taking a foreign language course. The table below shows the percent of students at each college who are taking courses in the six most popular foreign languages.

Subject	College A	College B
Arabic	11%	18%
Chinese	10%	17%
French	17%	14%
German	8%	11%
Italian	12%	8%
Spanish	24%	16%

14. How many more students at College B are taking a course in Arabic than at College A?

(A)   7
(B)   70
(C)   105
(D)   160

15. If one student is chosen at random from all the students at Colleges A and B who are taking a foreign language course, what is the probability, to the nearest thousandth, that he or she is not taking a course in one of the six languages listed in the chart?

(A) .144
(B) .168
(C) .170
(D) .830

16. In right triangle *ABC* above, which of the following is equal to $\sin A + \cos A$?

(A) $\dfrac{a+b}{c}$

(B) $\dfrac{a+b}{2c}$

(C) $\dfrac{ab}{c^2}$

(D) $\dfrac{a+b}{c^2}$

17. A parsec is a unit of length used by astronomers to measure extremely large distances to objects outside the solar system. One parsec is equal to 3.26 light years, the distance that light travels in one year. Given that the speed of light is approximately 300,000,000 meters per second, which of the following is closest to the number of meters in a parsec?

(A) 3×10^{12}
(B) 3×10^{14}
(C) 3×10^{16}
(D) 3×10^{18}

GO ON TO THE NEXT PAGE

The graphs below show the percentage of boys and girls at Meadowlands High School in 2010 and in 2015 who participated in the school's athletic programs.

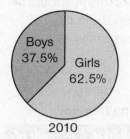
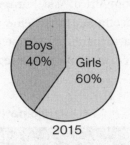

18. Compared with 2010, in 2015 there were six more boys and two more girls who participated in the school's athletic programs. How many students in total participated in 2015?

(A) 48
(B) 72
(C) 112
(D) 120

$$x - \frac{4}{5} > \frac{5}{4}$$

$$x - \frac{7}{10} < \frac{7}{5}$$

19. Which of the following is a solution of the system of inequalities above?

(A) 2.05
(B) 2.07
(C) 2.10
(D) 2.15

20. A bag contained 100 marbles—60 red ones, 30 white ones, and 10 blue ones. More white marbles were placed into the bag so that now 50 percent of the marbles are white. If n represents the number of white marbles that were added, which of the following equations could be used to find the value of n?

(A) $\dfrac{30+n}{100+n} = \dfrac{1}{2}$

(B) $\dfrac{30+n}{100} = \dfrac{1}{2}$

(C) $\dfrac{100+n}{30+n} = \dfrac{1}{2}$

(D) $\dfrac{100+n}{n} = \dfrac{1}{2}$

$$(ax^2 + bx + c)(dx + e) = x^3 + 6x^2 + 13x + 20$$

21. In the equation above, a, b, c, d, and e are constants. If the equation is true for all values of x, and if $c = 5$ and $d = 1$, what is the value of $a + b + e$?

(A) 4
(B) 6
(C) 7
(D) 9

GO ON TO THE NEXT PAGE

22. The road from Jack's house to Jill's house is exactly 10 kilometers. At different times, Jack and Jill each left home and walked toward the other's house. They walked at the same rate. They met at noon, 4 kilometers from Jill's house. If Jack left at 10:00, at what time did Jill leave?

    (A) 9:40
    (B) 10:40
    (C) 11:00
    (D) 11:20

23. Alice and Barbara each collect antique dolls. At the beginning of 2015, Alice had *a* dolls in her collection and Barbara had *b* dolls in hers. During 2015, Alice purchased a number of dolls, increasing the size of her collection by 25 percent. During that same year, Barbara sold a number of her dolls, decreasing the size of her collection by 25 percent. If at the end of 2015 Alice and Barbara had the same number of dolls, what is the ratio of *a* to *b*?

    (A) $\frac{3}{5}$

    (B) $\frac{3}{4}$

    (C) $\frac{4}{5}$

    (D) $\frac{5}{3}$

Questions 24 and 25 are based on the following information.

An international conference had participants from Africa, Asia, Europe, and the Americas. The incomplete table below shows the number of participants and the percentage of participants from each of the four regions.

Participation by Region

Region	Number of Participants	Percent of Participants
Africa	180	15
Asia	120	
Europe		40
The Americas		

24. What was the total number of participants at the conference?

    (A) 750
    (B) 1,200
    (C) 1,500
    (D) 1,800

25. How many of the participants were from the Americas?

    (A) 360
    (B) 420
    (C) 630
    (D) 720

GO ON TO THE NEXT PAGE

DIAGNOSTIC TEST

26. Sam's Sporting Goods sells baseballs and softballs in boxes of 10. The athletic director of a high school ordered 3 boxes of baseballs and 2 boxes of softballs. If the weight of a softball is 1.5 ounces more than the weight of a baseball and if the total weight of all the balls the director ordered was 17.5 pounds, what is the weight, in ounces, of a softball? (1 pound = 16 ounces)

(A) 5
(B) 5.5
(C) 6
(D) 6.5

27. All summer, Emily sells handmade bracelets in her crafts boutique for 60 percent more than she pays the jeweler who makes them. At the end of summer, she places everything in her shop on sale and sells her remaining bracelets for 20 percent less than her cost. The selling price during the end-of-summer sale represents a discount of what percent off the regular selling price that was in effect all summer?

(A) 40 percent
(B) 50 percent
(C) 60 percent
(D) 80 percent

GO ON TO THE NEXT PAGE

Grid-in Response Directions

In questions 28–31, first solve the problem, and then enter your answer on the grid provided on the answer sheet. The instructions for entering your answers follow.

- First, write your answer in the boxes at the top of the grid.
- Second, grid your answer in the columns below the boxes.
- Use the fraction bar in the first row or the decimal point in the second row to enter fractions and decimals.

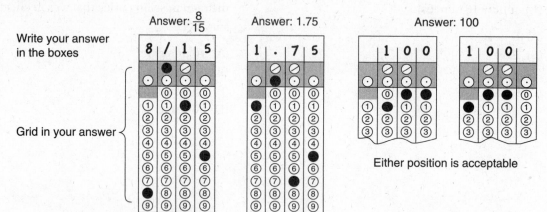

- Grid only one space in each column.
- Entering the answer in the boxes is recommended as an aid in gridding but is not required.
- The machine scoring your exam can read only what you grid, so you **must grid-in your answers correctly to get credit**.
- If a question has more than one correct answer, grid-in only one of them.
- The grid does not have a minus sign; so no answer can be negative.
- A mixed number *must* be converted to an improper fraction or a decimal before it is gridded.

  Enter $1\frac{1}{4}$ as 5/4 or 1.25; the machine will interpret 11/4 as $\frac{11}{4}$ and mark it wrong.

- **All decimals must be entered as accurately as possible.** Here are three acceptable ways of gridding

$$\frac{3}{11} = 0.272727\ldots$$

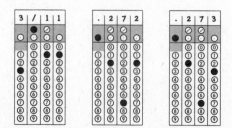

- Note that rounding to .273 is acceptable because you are using the full grid, but you would receive **no credit** for .3 or .27, because they are less accurate.

28. If $\left(\frac{1}{3}\right)^{-n} = 81$, what is the value of $\left(\frac{1}{4}\right)^{-n}$?

Questions 30 and 31 refer to the following information.

Every day to go to work, Adam drives the 6.5 miles between Exits 3 and 4 on Route 10, always at a constant rate of 50 miles per hour. At 50 miles per hour, Adam's car can go 24 miles on a gallon of gasoline. At 60 miles per hour, Adam's car can go only 20 miles on a gallon of gasoline.

29. What is the height, in feet, of a rectangular box whose width and length are 5 feet and 7 feet, respectively, and whose total surface area is 298 square feet?

30. How much less time, in seconds, would it take Adam to drive those 6.5 miles at 60 miles per hour instead of 50 miles per hour?

31. Last year, Adam drove the 6.5 miles from Exit 2 to Exit 3 a total of 240 times (always at 50 miles per hour). During last year, he paid an average of $3.60 per gallon for gasoline. How much more would gasoline have cost him if he had driven at 60 miles per hour each day? (Express your answer to the nearest dollar, and grid it in without the dollar sign.)

STOP

If there is still time remaining, you may review your answers.

ANSWER KEY
Diagnostic Test

Section 1: Reading

1.	C	14.	B	27.	A	40.	B
2.	D	15.	D	28.	B	41.	B
3.	D	16.	A	29.	B	42.	A
4.	B	17.	B	30.	C	43.	C
5.	D	18.	A	31.	A	44.	A
6.	C	19.	B	32.	A	45.	D
7.	B	20.	C	33.	B	46.	B
8.	B	21.	A	34.	A	47.	C
9.	D	22.	D	35.	D		
10.	A	23.	D	36.	C		
11.	D	24.	A	37.	D		
12.	C	25.	C	38.	D		
13.	D	26.	D	39.	C		

Number Correct   _____

Number Incorrect   _____

Section 2: Writing and Language

1.	C	12.	B	23.	D	34.	A
2.	C	13.	A	24.	B	35.	C
3.	D	14.	B	25.	A	36.	B
4.	B	15.	D	26.	B	37.	D
5.	C	16.	D	27.	C	38.	A
6.	A	17.	A	28.	D	39.	D
7.	B	18.	C	29.	C	40.	C
8.	D	19.	B	30.	A	41.	A
9.	A	20.	A	31.	D	42.	A
10.	C	21.	A	32.	C	43.	D
11.	B	22.	B	33.	A	44.	B

Number Correct   _____

Number Incorrect   _____

Section 3: Math (No Calculator)

1. **C**
2. **C**
3. **C**
4. **C**

5. **A**
6. **C**
7. **A**
8. **D**

9. **C**
10. **C**
11. **D**
12. **A**

13. **D**

14. **0**

15. **10**

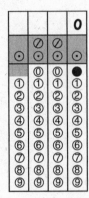

16. **30**

17. **32**

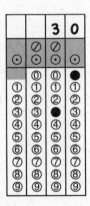

Number Correct   _____

Number Incorrect   _____

Section 4: Math (Calculator)

1. **C**	7. **C**	13. **D**	19. **B**	25. **B**
2. **D**	8. **A**	14. **D**	20. **A**	26. **D**
3. **B**	9. **D**	15. **B**	21. **C**	27. **B**
4. **B**	10. **D**	16. **A**	22. **B**	
5. **C**	11. **B**	17. **C**	23. **A**	
6. **B**	12. **A**	18. **D**	24. **B**	

28. **256**　　　　29. **9.5**

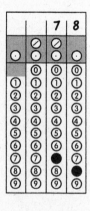

30. **78**　　　　31. **47**

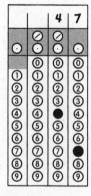

Number Correct _____

Number Incorrect _____

SCORE ANALYSIS

Reading and Writing Test

Section 1: Reading $\underline{\hspace{3cm}}$ = $\underline{\hspace{3cm}}$ (A)

                               # correct   raw score

Section 2: Writing $\underline{\hspace{3cm}}$ = $\underline{\hspace{3cm}}$ (B)

                               # correct   raw score

To find your Reading and Writing test scores, consult the chart below: find the ranges in which your raw scores lie and read across to find the ranges of your test scores.

$\underline{\hspace{4cm}}$ + $\underline{\hspace{4cm}}$ = $\underline{\hspace{4cm}}$ (C)

    range of reading   range of writing   range of reading + writing

      test scores   test scores   test scores

To find the range of your Reading and Writing Scaled Score, multiply (C) by 10.

Test Scores for the Reading and Writing Sections

Reading Raw Score	Writing Raw Score	Test Score
39–47	39–44	33–38
33–38	33–38	30–32
28–32	28–32	27–29
21–27	22–27	23–27
15–20	17–21	20–23
11–14	13–16	17–20
8–10	9–12	15–17
4–7	5–8	13–15
less than 4	less than 5	8–12

Math Test

Section 3: $\underline{\hspace{3cm}}$ = $\underline{\hspace{3cm}}$ (D)

              # correct   raw score

Section 4: $\underline{\hspace{3cm}}$ = $\underline{\hspace{3cm}}$ (E)

              # correct   raw score

Total Math raw score: (D) + (E) = $\underline{\hspace{3cm}}$

To find your Math Scaled Score, consult the chart below: find the range in which your raw score lies and read across to find the range for your scaled score.

Scaled Scores for the Math Test

Raw Score	Scaled Score	Raw Score	Scaled Score
39–48	700–760	16–19	450–490
35–38	650–690	12–15	400–440
31–34	600–640	9–11	350–390
25–30	550–590	6–9	300–340
20–24	500–540	less than 6	160–290

ANSWERS EXPLAINED

Section 1: Reading Test

1. **(C)** In the opening paragraph, Elizabeth interrupts Mr. Collins, saying that she has not answered a question he has just asked. She quickly gives her answer: she rejects his proposals. Mr. Collins responds by stating that he hopes to lead Elizabeth "to the altar ere long." This clearly suggests that Mr. Collins has just asked her to become his wife.

2. **(D)** Elizabeth is "sensible of the honour" Mr. Collins is paying her by proposing. She is all too *keenly aware* of his intentions and wants nothing to do with them.

3. **(D)** Elizabeth expects that by refusing Mr. Collins's proposal, she will put an end to his suit; that is the result she desires. However, her rejection fails to have this intended effect. Instead, Mr. Collins in his stubbornness and conceit continues to pursue her and even takes her refusal as an encouraging sign.

4. **(B)** Mr. Collins pompously states that he knows that young ladies customarily reject a suitor the first time he proposes. Thus, despite Elizabeth's clear refusal, he still hopes to lead her to the altar. Her initial refusal has failed *to put an end to his suit*.

5. **(D)** Mr. Collins breaks off in the middle of a sentence that begins, "Were it certain that Lady Catherine would think so—." He then finishes it awkwardly by saying, "but I cannot imagine that her ladyship would at all disapprove of you." By implication, his unspoken thought was that, if Lady Catherine didn't approve of Elizabeth, then Mr. Collins wouldn't want to marry her after all.

6. **(C)** Mr. Collins plans to praise Elizabeth to Lady Catherine in order to ensure Lady Catherine's approval of his bride. Elizabeth insists all such praise will be unnecessary because she has no intention of marrying Mr. Collins and thus there is no need of Lady Catherine's approval.

7. **(B)** To give oneself leave to do something is to give oneself permission to do it. Although "leave" can mean *holiday* (as in "maternity leave") or *departure* (as in *to take one's leave*) and often appears in the phrase "leave of absence," that is not the way it is used here.

8. **(B)** "Obtuse" means *thickheaded*, and "obstinate" means *stubborn*. Both apply to Mr. Collins, who can't seem to understand that Elizabeth is telling him "no."

9. **(D)** In these lines, Mr. Collins reiterates that he plans to bring up the topic of marriage with Elizabeth again despite everything she has said to him. Not only that: he considers everything negative she has said to him to be her way of encouraging him in his suit. Mr. Collins's speech clearly provides the reader with evidence that he is both stubborn and thickheaded.

10. **(A)** From the opening invocation of the song of the elements to the closing celebration of the birds' mastery of the power of the elements, Lorenz seeks to make his experience come alive for his readers. He is *evoking an experience*.

11. **(D)** The author of Passage 1 stresses that the birds' movements are "practiced movements," "movements that have been carefully learned." In other words, the birds' skill has been *gained through* practice or *repeated performance*.

12. **(C)** The author clearly states that the jackdaw's proficiency is not inherited or innate, but "an individually acquired accomplishment." It has been acquired or *gained through* repetition or *repeated performance.*

13. **(D)** The author is stressing that you can remain or continue to be sure of the truth of what he says. Although "rest" can mean *relax securely* ("I want to rest for a minute!"), *lie fallow* ("Let the fields rest this season"), or *are supported* ("Drivers' lower backs rest against lumbar cushions"), that is not how the word is used here.

14. **(B)** From the opening of the second paragraph through the passage's conclusion, Lorenz vividly describes the jackdaws' encounter with the storm. He first envisions the birds as the storm's prey: they are "seized" by the storm, whirled through the air by this force of nature. As the passage goes on, however, his view changes. The birds are playing with the storm. Even more: they have mastered this force of nature.

    Choices A and C are unsupported by the passage. Though Choice D may seem tempting, you can rule it out. Lorenz emphasizes the storm's strength ("the pitiless strength of the inorganic"), not the strength of the birds.

15. **(D)** The concluding sentence of the passage particularly celebrates the birds' "Sovereign control over the power of the elements," in other words, their mastery of the forces of nature.

16. **(A)** The author of Passage 2 neither makes use of figurative language such as metaphors and similes nor cites any statistics. He asks no rhetorical questions. However, he provides a great deal of *observational data* from his ongoing study of jackdaw behavior.

17. **(B)** Lines 86–88 state that "Unlike the resident pairs, non-resident birds do not defend a nest-site in the winter." The author of Passage 2 makes a special point of saying that nest-site loss is likely to be a common event in the life of a jackdaw pair. Without a nest-site to defend, a resident pair would automatically fall into the category of non-resident birds.

18. **(A)** The jackdaws formed or established mated pairs. Although "formed" can mean *molded* ("She formed the dough into a ball"), *educated* ("Professor Smith formed his graduate students into true scholars"), or *articulated* ("Trying not to stutter, Tim carefully formed each word he spoke"), that is not how the word is used here.

19. **(B)** Compared with Passage 1, Passage 2 is far *less lyrical* or poetic. As part of a scientific study, it is appropriately *more objective* (based on observable facts; impartial) than Lorenz's loving account of the jackdaws' flight.

20. **(C)** Use the process of elimination to arrive at the correct answer to this question.

    Statement I is true. The passage states that the tornado's lifetime is never more than a few hours. Therefore, you can eliminate Choice B.

    Statement II is true. The third paragraph indicates that a fraction of the thunderstorm's tremendous energy "is concentrated into an area no more than several hundred meters in diameter." A later portion of the passage refers to the tornado's "concentrated high winds." Therefore, you can eliminate Choice A.

    Statement III is untrue. The passage indicates that tornadoes may vary markedly in size and shape. Therefore, you can eliminate Choice D.

    Only Choice C is left. It is the correct answer.

21. **(A)** The third paragraph's concluding sentence serves as a *transition* or linking sentence connecting one part of the lengthy discussion to another. In this case, it introduces several paragraphs that describe tornadoes. The sentence is not a *concession* (acknowledgment; yielding a point in an argument). It is not an *apology* (expression of regret: formal defense). Neutral in tone, it is definitely not a *refutation* (disproof of an argument).

22. **(D)** Because the atmospheric pressure in the tornado's central core is so much lower than that of the surrounding atmosphere, air is drawn or *pulled* into the base of the tornado. Although "drawn" can mean *traced* ("a line drawn on the blackboard"), *sketched* ("the picture she had drawn"), or *obtained* ("contestants drawn from the audience"), that is not how the word is used here.

23. **(D)** Paragraph five states that the "warmer and drier the inflowing air is, the greater the pressure drop must be for condensation to occur and a cloud to form." This suggests that temperature and humidity affect the tornado and that *it responds to changes in temperature and humidity.*

24. **(A)** Scan the passage looking for the word "color" or one of its synonyms ("hue," "shade"). The hue or color of a tornado depends on what the soil in that region is made of.

25. **(C)** The sentence that begins with the words "Its color" provides the evidence for the answer to the previous question. In it, the author states, "if the core fills with dust, the funnel may take on a more exotic hue, such as the red of west Oklahoma clay."

26. **(D)** The author is giving a *physical description of* the tornado, a natural *phenomenon*. You can use the process of elimination to answer this question. Is the author proposing that scientists should adopt a particular technique for observing tornadoes? No, he makes no such proposal. You can eliminate Choice A. Is the author suggesting a hypothesis (tentative explanation made as a starting point for further investigation) about tornado dynamics? No, he appears to be describing tornado dynamics. You can eliminate Choice B. Is the author emphasizing a need for additional observations of the way tornadoes form? No. You can eliminate Choice C. Only Choice D is left. It is the correct answer.

27. **(A)** Look at the bottom line in Figure 1. It shows the number of violent tornadoes per week. Find the highest point in that line. It indicates the period with the greatest number of violent tornadoes per week. Now look at the line labeled "DEATHS," the one that resembles the outline of skyscraper, with steep, perpendicular sides. Find the highest point in that line. It indicates the period with the greatest number of deaths per week. Note the correlation between the period with the greatest number of violent tornadoes per week and the period with the greatest number of deaths per week. This supports the statement that tornadoes "strike sporadically and violently, with violent tornadoes generating the strongest of all surface winds and causing more deaths annually in the U.S. than any other weather phenomenon except lightning."

28. **(B)** In stating that the maximum wind speed possible in a tornado is on the order of 300 miles per hour, the author is making an estimate. He cannot give an exact maximum wind speed. He can say only that this maximum wind speed is approximately 300 miles

per hour. Although "order" can mean *sequence* ("in numerical order"), *command* ("the order to fire"), or *class* ("the order Carnivora"), that is not how the word is used here.

29. **(B)** A shade of opinion is a slightly *differing variation* of opinion. Although "shade" can mean *slight amount* ("just a shade of annoyance"), *protective covering* ("in the shade of the old oak tree"), or *color gradation* ("different shades of green"), that is not how it is used here.

30. **(C)** Choice C is the best answer. The passage as a whole argues for unfettered speech and argument as an antidote to extremism. In pointing out that anarchists were allowed to express their ideas in the meetings, Addams demonstrates the wide range of ideas discussed and the wide range of speakers who *were welcome to discuss their ideas in the meetings.*

    Choice A is incorrect. Although one might reasonably expect the anarchist's arguments to be extreme, Addams makes no mention of what he actually said in the meetings. Additionally, throughout the passage Addams presents the wide diversity of ideas discussed in a positive light. It is therefore unlikely that she would focus on the danger of those arguments. Choice B is incorrect. Although one might assume that the anarchist came from a poor or working class background, Addams makes no mention of his economic status in the passage. Choice D is incorrect. Although some might have wanted to place limits on the ideas to be discussed in the meetings, Addams does not do so in the passage.

31. **(A)** Choice A is the best answer because Addams states that the free speech in the meetings was seen as a "cure" for anarchy or *extremism.* Her argument is that open discussion of extreme ideas promotes moderation.

    Choice B is incorrect both because the passage makes no mention of economic education, and because Addams makes it clear that all ideas were welcome to the discussion. She does not indicate that any attempts were made to focus on a particular subject. Choice C is incorrect. Many of the arguments made focused on the misery of the participants' lives. Such arguments would make the participants more aware of their misery rather than less. Choice D is incorrect. The meetings were presided over by a prosperous banker, among others. It is unlikely that this capitalist would choose to use the discussions to promote a socialist government.

32. **(A)** In throwing out the statement that "Mr. B. believes that socialism will cure the toothache," the exasperated workingman has *suggested* (tentatively put forward a suggestion) that this statement should be a subject for the club's discussion. Although "thrown out" can mean *hurled* ("President Obama has just thrown out the first pitch"), *discarded* ("Bob has thrown out the trash"), or *dismissed* ("The judge has thrown out the charges"), that is not how it is used here.

33. **(B)** Addams looks back on the great open meetings and free speech of 1890 as noteworthy. Writing at a time when such free political discussions no longer occurred, she finds 1890 remarkable for its *open debate and freedom of expression.*

    Choice A is incorrect. Although Addams mentions the violent riots in 1890, she mentions no similar riots at the time in which she is writing. Thus, she is not making any comparison. Choice C is incorrect. Addams never suggests that there was any particular focus on dental health in 1890. Choice D is incorrect. Although Addams provides an example of discussions of monopolies and capitalism in 1890, she does not make any claims about the degree of concern regarding monopolies or capital accumulation at the time in which she is writing.

34. **(A)** Choice A is correct. In this sentence Addams contrasts the time at which she is writing with 1890 as she argues that public meetings in which holders of extreme views are encouraged to speak were common in 1890 but are now unimaginable. Choices B, C, and D are all incorrect; none of them compare the year 1890 with the time at which Addams is writing.

35. **(D)** Choice D is correct. Addams explicitly describes the participants' enthusiasm for debating the issues of the day.

   Choice A is incorrect. Addams's overall description of the meetings is favorable; she makes no mention of their being a waste of time. Choice B is incorrect. Addams makes no explicit value judgments about the quality of the arguments made. Additionally, her tone when describing arguments is positive rather than critical. Choice C is incorrect. Although Addams describes socialists making arguments at the meetings, she makes it clear that a wide variety of opinions were represented, and she does not indicate that any particular argument was more persuasive than the others.

36. **(C)** Choice C is correct. Addams's description of the "zest for discussion" of the participants, and their rejection of the suggestion to turn their debates into study sessions provide strong evidence that she *believed that the debates deeply engaged their participants*.

37. **(D)** Choice D is correct. In her opening sentence, Addams provides a historical context for the establishment of Hull-House, setting it two years after Chicago's Haymarket riot, after the first punitive reaction to the riot. She then goes on to describe certain events (the decision to create an open forum for discussing of society's ills; the inauguration of the Sunday evening open meetings), and to wonder how it has come to pass that people no longer believe in the effectiveness of public discussions and the free exchange of ideas in teaching tolerance and reducing civic conflict.

   Choice A is incorrect. The opening paragraph suggests no solution for a problem. Choice B is incorrect. The opening paragraph does not urge or exhort anyone to take any particular action. Choice C is incorrect. The opening paragraph neither states any principle, nor shows any consensus or general agreement being reached.

38. **(D)** Choice D is correct. The debaters advocated socialism, anarchism, and *a wide range of political beliefs*.

   Choice A is incorrect. According to Addams's reports of the discussions, the participants fail to reach consensus. Choice B is incorrect. Addams describes the debates as lively and enthusiastic, not as chaotic and disorderly. Choice C is incorrect. Addams does not regard the debaters' passionate speeches as a cause of riots; indeed, she presents the open debates as a possible remedy for the social ills that led to the Haymarket riot.

39. **(C)** Although the author spends some time discussing regulatory restrictions as a way of combating environmental harm, his main thrust is to *point out the effectiveness of environmental taxes in* combating such harm. In particular, he dwells on the effectiveness of such taxes in reducing pollution.

Choice A is incorrect. While the author discusses Pigou's theory, his primary purpose in writing is to educate his audience about the effectiveness of environmental taxes, not to refute Pigou's critics. Choice B is incorrect. Although the author makes some critical comments about the usefulness of regulatory restrictions, his main purpose is to argue in favor of the use of environmental taxes to protect the environment from harm. Choice D is incorrect. The author is not proposing a novel approach; the concept of environmental taxes goes back nearly one hundred years.

40. **(B)** Choice B is correct. Polluters harm society both physically, by the damage they do to the physical environment, and fiscally, in the financial burden that cleaning up pollution imposes on society. Environmental harm *injures society, and therefore should be compensated for.*

    Choice A is incorrect. Nothing in the passage suggests that environmental harm unavoidably results from technical innovation. Choice C is incorrect. Environmental harm provides no subsidies. Choice D is incorrect. Environmental harm is alleviated by the growing use of environmental taxes; it is not caused by their growing use.

41. **(B)** Lines 16–22 clarify the hidden costs to society of environmental harm. These costs financially injure society, which has to pay to repair the damage to the environment. Therefore, society needs to be financially compensated for these costs.

    Choices A and D are incorrect. Nothing in the passage suggests that environmental damage unavoidably results from technological innovation or is caused by the use of environmental taxation. Choice C makes no sense: environmental harm costs money to repair; it does not subsidize taxpayers.

42. **(A)** The assumption behind imposing environmental taxes is that companies will literally clean up their acts in order to get out of paying these taxes. In other words, they *will find ways to reduce their negative impact on the environment if it is in their economic interest to do so.*

    Choice B is incorrect. According to the passage, regulatory restrictions can stifle technological innovation; environmental taxes tend to stimulate innovation. Choices C and D are incorrect. Neither is supported by the passage.

43. **(C)** It is indeed absurd (foolishly nonsensical) to spend more money in order to achieve a less desirable result. The author describes this as "a telling absurdity" because the absurdity is so striking that it reveals just how ridiculous the situation is. Choices A, B, and D are incorrect. There is no evidence in the passage to support any of them.

44. **(A)** The rules failed to cover or apply to nearby benzene emissions that could have been cut for far less money than it took for Amoco to build a wastewater treatment plant. Although "cover" can mean *stand in for* ("Cover for me while I take a break"), *stretch over* ("the tent covers an area of one hundred square feet"), or *report on* ("Will the media cover the Sanders campaign?"), that is not how the word is used here.

45. **(D)** To meet a goal is to fulfill or *satisfy* that requirement. Although "meet" can mean *encounter* ("perhaps we'll meet them at the park"), *convene* ("the board will meet on Monday"), or *converge* ("the drapes won't meet"), that is not how the word is used here.

46. **(B)** The author has just stated that over the last thirty years most attempts to curb environmental harm have involved environmental regulations, not environmental taxes. He then catches himself, and *acknowledges that regulatory restrictions have been*

effective in reducing pollution. His goal is not to attack the use of regulatory restrictions; it is to advocate the use of environmental taxes.

47. **(C)** Figure 1 illustrates how dramatically the harmful emissions of chromium, zinc, lead, and mercury dropped between 1976 and the early 1990s. The graph allows the reader to trace the decrease of each separate industrial discharge and to visualize how immensely effective the Dutch campaign to reduce water pollution has been.

Section 2: Writing and Language Test

1. **(C)** The word that best fits this question is "unbearably." The sentence is communicating that it was so hot that the temperature was insufferable, which is a synonym for unbearable. Choices B and D are not words, and Choice A is nonsensical in this context.

2. **(C)** It is important to recognize that length alone does not necessarily make something a run-on sentence. Choice C, though lengthy, is perfectly correct without adding any commas to separate clauses. Choice B adds an unnecessary comma after "natives." Choice A adds two unnecessary commas after "lands" and "years." Choice D also adds two unnecessary commas.

3. **(D)** When deciding whether to delete a sentence, ask two things. First, is this information relevant? Second, have I already stated this information in some fashion before? In this instance, the information is both relevant and new and thus should be kept. Choice D is the right answer, as this information is a "helpful elaboration" on Goyathlay. Choice A is incorrect as this is new information. Choice B can be eliminated, as this information is indeed relevant. Choice C is incorrect, as the information is more general than "specific."

4. **(B)** Observe verb tense parallelism. Notice the other verbs in this sentence: "tiptoed" and "disappeared." We, therefore, want past tense verbs to match, and "charged" is our best option. With Choices A and D, "charging" breaks the parallelism. In Choice C, "with the charge" is simply a wordy way of saying "charged." Remember to maintain simplicity.

5. **(C)** In Choice A, it is unnecessary to use both "infatuation" and "interest," as "infatuation" already expressed a deep level of interest. Choice B behaves similarly, as "love," "passion," and "admiration" are superfluous when used together. Choice D is incorrect, as the deletion would give the impression that the narrator had a Native American lineage of her own. Choice C, "infatuation with," is our best option.

6. **(A)** It is imperative to find a choice here that fits the requirements of our question, which is to be consistent with the details describing Goyathlay in the previous paragraph. The key word in that paragraph was "fearless." Choice A, "casually ignoring" (bullets), is our best example of fearlessness. Choices B and C both express timidity and fear, instead. Choice D, "failing to understand," is not relevant in this context.

7. **(B)** Similar to the previous question, we must pay close attention to what is being asked of us. In this case, it is finding the best example of a "specific illustration of the tragedy that happened to Goyathlay" that is also logical in context. Choice A is not specific and, therefore, can be eliminated. Choice C is specific, but it is not logical in this context; it is

out of place with the information surrounding it. Choice D does not describe a tragedy, which leaves us with Choice B, "His mother, wife, and children were among the dead." It is certainly tragic and specific.

8. **(D)** Notice whom our possessive is describing: it's Goyathlay, who is a man. Thus, "his" is the proper possessive. "Their" is used as a possessive for multiple people, not one. "There" is not a possessive, at all. "His or her" refers to a single person of indeterminate gender. However, we know that Goyathlay is male, so Choice C can be eliminated as well.

9. **(A)** A comma is necessary to separate the dependent introductory clause from the independent clause that follows. Choices B and D are too choppy, and Choice C has no pauses whatsoever.

10. **(C)** Simpler is better as long as you maintain the original meaning. The correct answer is, "the remainder of his life." Choice A, "the remaining years of his life until he died," is simply a wordier version of Choice C. The concept is similar with Choice B, "what was left to be had of his lifetime." Choice D, "that time," is too simple; it eliminates relevant and important information.

11. **(B)** The line, "his name was Goyathlay," is our introduction to Goyathlay. Thus, it must be introduced before any other reference to Goyathlay, which preceded paragraphs 6 and 7, which are Choices C and D, respectively. Inserting it before paragraph 1, however, is too soon. This would, therefore, be the first sentence of the essay, and it is out of place in context.

12. **(B)** The question is looking for the answer that best expresses a "condescending attitude." Choices A, C, and D don't really express looking down upon something. Choice B, however, does.

13. **(A)** Choice B can be discounted because "precedent" is a noun rather than a verb. Using an -ing verb would not satisfy the rules for a complete sentence, so Choice D is incorrect. Recall that "preceded" signifies an event happening *before,* whereas *"proceeded"* means to take place *after.* As rock and roll came before pop, it *"preceded"* pop. Choice A is the correct answer.

14. **(B)** Diagnose what actually does the "creating" in this sentence, and that is our subject. In this case, that word is "tendency," which is a singular noun. To satisfy subject-verb agreement, we need a singular verb. "Creates" is the correct answer, rather than the plural verb "create." Choice C, "creating," would render the sentence a fragment instead.

15. **(D)** We are searching for the "most logical contrast." In this case, that contrast is with "short, catchy recordings produced in a few hours . . . ." A logical juxtaposition with something produced quickly is something created over a longer period of time. Choice D, featuring an "invested, personal relationship" among collaborators, implies a longitudinal effort rather than something done hastily. It is, therefore, our best option. Choice A would not be a contrast but rather a parallel concept. Choices B and C do not pertain to production time at all.

16. **(D)** First, diagnose the proper verb tense to use. The time frame is the 1920s. Furthermore, notice the other verbs in the paragraph like "began," "placed," and "was."

These are all past tense, so we should use a past tense verb to maintain parallelism. "Originated" is the only logical option for past tense.

17. **(A)** The current form of this phrase is the only option that puts the words in a logical sequence. The other options all unnecessarily shift the subject "it" to a later point in the sentence.

18. **(C)** The sentence says, "where once these names would have grazed the same lists as . . . ," and then we need to mention actual names of others on those lists. Thus, it is a necessary clarification and must be maintained. Choice D is incorrect as these are not the authors of the lists but are rather musical artists included on said lists.

19. **(B)** The principal clause of the sentence is, "can one rightly assume it unworthy or inferior?" Choices C and D can be eliminated due to the omission of the question mark. Choice A can be eliminated as it inserts an unnecessary comma in that principal clause.

20. **(A)** The best way to approach this question is to eliminate the obvious incorrect choices, and then evaluate what remains. Choices B, C, and D all place an unnecessary comma in "the Rock and Roll Hall of Fame." That is the title of the place, and no punctuation is necessary. Choice A, upon further evaluation, has no errors. It is our correct answer.

21. **(A)** This sentence requires a contrasting transition between pop "not being your cup of tea" on one hand, while still finding it "hard to deny its exceptional influence" on the other hand. "So that," "because," and "given" all address a cause-and-effect relationship, which is different from the contrasting relationship that we seek. "Even if" is the only viable answer.

22. **(B)** We must analyze the graph for this question, specifically looking for where pop ranked among our genre options. Hip-hop was first with 29 percent and pop is second at 25 percent. Thus, Choice B, "second most popular," is the correct answer.

23. **(D)** The subject is "one," but diagnosing the subject is not the difficult part of this question. The particular verb tense required here is the subjunctive mood, which is almost always incorrectly used both in spoken and written English. "Were" is the correct choice here, despite the fact that "one" is singular. Similarly, it is proper to say, "If I were you," or "if I were a doctor," for instance. Choice A is tempting, but it doesn't follow the subjunctive mood customs.

24. **(B)** It is important not to confuse length with a run-on sentence. "Tierra del Fuego lies at the southernmost tip of South America" is a single clause that requires no punctuation for separation; it is correctly fluid as is. Unnecessary commas are a tempting trap we must avoid.

25. **(A)** When determining the proper transition, analyze the relationship between this sentence and the previous one. Paraphrased, the sentences are saying, "Tierra del Fuego is gorgeous and exotic, but it is threatened by something as silly as the common beaver." We need a contrasting transition to achieve that "but." "Yet" is our only acceptable contrasting transition; the other choices all imply a cause-and-effect relationship.

26. **(B)** "That" versus "which" is a difficult battle. This sentence features a restrictive clause, as the wording after "that" is essential to the structure. In effect, the core of the sentence is: "An invasive species has the potential to inflict harm." "Which" is used in

nonrestrictive clauses where the wording isn't essential. Example: "That car, which is the newest model available, sells for $30,000." The core is "that car sells for $30,000," and the wording after "which" is inconsequential to the sentence's overall functioning. Seeing as we need "that," we can eliminate Choices C and D. As previously mentioned, the subject is "invasive species," which is a singular subject that will require the singular verb "has." Certainly, this was a difficult question, all things considered.

27. **(C)** This sentence requires both an answer that is logical and specific. We will begin with specificity. Choices A and D do not mention actual numbers, so they can be eliminated for being too general. Choice B is illogical, as 30 would in fact be a decrease, not an increase, from 50. Choice C, "200,000," is both logical and specific.

28. **(D)** Choices A, B, and D all express the same sentiment, but Choice D does it in a much more concise manner. Choice C, though concise, is too concise; it has eliminated so much information that the intended meaning of the sentence has been compromised.

29. **(C)** For one, following "unimpeded" with "unchecked" preserves syntactic parallelism. Second, it is much more concise than "without even a check" or "with no checking." Choice C is the best answer.

30. **(A)** Notice the context. The plan was for the beavers to create a flourishing fur trade. Instead, the beavers ended up eating the forest. "Indubitably awry" is the proper answer. Even if we weren't familiar with those words, we could eliminate the other choices as the plan certainly was not successful and did not go as expected.

31. **(D)** The phrase "dare I say" is unnecessary in that it could be eliminated and the sentence would still effectively function. It is, therefore, a parenthetical phrase and can be separated from the rest of the sentence with either commas or dashes—one both before and after. Choice C neglects both pauses. Choices A and B include the necessary pauses, but look more closely: they sacrifice parallelism by using one comma and one dash. Commas or dashes are acceptable, but we need to use the same one both times. Choice D uses two dashes and is, therefore, the best answer.

32. **(C)** We need the most logical contrast here. The previous sentence is, "At best, their recovery is decades away." The most effective contrast with "at best" would be "at worst," which is how Choice C functions. It is our best answer.

33. **(A)** When determining the best way to conclude the essay, recall the theme of the essay. Choice B is illogical, as the destruction has not been "held at bay." Choice C does not function, as the essay did not focus on beavers' "valuable contributions." Choices A and D are both appropriate to the theme, but notice how the paragraph proceeds by listing two lessons. Choice A, which mentions "two lessons," is more logical in context.

34. **(A)** Recall that "than" is used for comparisons, whereas "then" is used to narrate a sequence. In this case, we are making a comparison. Choice A is the correct answer.

35. **(C)** Transitions require analyzing the whole of the sentence to discover context. "Nonetheless" and "in contrast" are both contrasting transitions. A contrast here, though, isn't logical. Notice how the clauses fit together: the narrator says that nutrition is an art and that it is her job. "In fact" is the only choice that is logical, in context. It is as if the narrator is stating, "in fact, I am an artist."

36. **(B)** The proposed insertion is, "what was our secret?" Sentence 2, essentially, is that secret. Therefore, our insertion most logically fits right before sentence 2, or "after sentence 1," as Choice B states.

37. **(D)** The question calls for "the *most effective* and *specific* elaboration on the first part of the sentence," with the operative words being those that are italicized. The first part of the sentence mentions the "benefits" of proper nutrition. Choices A and B aren't very specific. Choice C is specific, but it describes cognitive rather than physical benefits, it isn't effective. Choice D is the best combination of specificity and effectiveness.

38. **(A)** Notice the context of the other terms in the list: "dropping fat" and "building muscle"—we will want an -ing verb to continue the parallelism of those terms. "Amplifying" is the only option that preserves that parallelism.

39. **(D)** "However" and "nevertheless" are both contrasting terms, and a contrast is not what we're searching for. Moreover, as the two words are practically twins, that should have been an indicator that neither was the correct answer. "Unexpectedly" doesn't function here, as it isn't a surprise that dieting should make you feel better. "In essence" is the only choice that functions in the context of the sentence.

40. **(C)** "It should be doable and sustainable" is one clause, and it should not be broken up by punctuation. Choice A incorrectly interprets this as a list; Choices B and D insert unnecessary commas that fracture the integrity of our clause.

41. **(A)** The subject is "it," and we will need a verb that agrees with "it," which is a singular noun. We can eliminate "come," which is a plural verb, and "coming," which is a gerund. Notice the other verbs in the paragraph, which are in present tense. Similarly, we need a present tense verb and can eliminate Choice D accordingly. "Comes" is singular and present tense and, therefore, is our correct answer.

42. **(A)** Analyze the chart. It states that simple carbohydrates should account for 8 percent of daily caloric intake.

43. **(D)** Analyze the chart. It states that 30 percent of daily caloric intake should be comprised of fats. The fraction for 30 percent is 3/10, or Choice D.

44. **(B)** Rephrased, the sentence is referring to the composition of your body, or your "body's composition," as Choice B states. "Body" must be singular, as we are discussing only the one body. Accordingly, eliminate Choices C and D, which are both plural. Choice A neglects the apostrophe that is necessary to demonstrate possession.

Section 3: Math Test (No Calculator)

1. **(C)** $4x = 12 \Rightarrow x = 3 \Rightarrow 12x = 36$

2. **(C)** The best way to answer this question is to rewrite each of the answer choices in slope-intercept form. Because the equations are so simple, you might be able to do this in your head, but it is safer to write them down:

   (A) $y = x - 1$ (B) $y = x + 1$ (C) $y = -x + 1$ (D) $y = -x - 1$

   If a line doesn't pass through Quadrant III, it cannot have a negative y-intercept. So, eliminate Choices A and D. Choices B and D both have y-intercepts of 1. Choice B slopes up and does pass through Quadrant III. Choice D slopes down, passing through Quadrants II, I, and IV but not III.

3. **(C)** $f(3) = 3^2 - 2^3 = 9 - 8 = 1$.

4. **(C)** The percent increase in the bank's charge is $\dfrac{\text{the actual increase}}{\text{the original amount}} \times 100\%$.

   The charge was originally $10, and the actual increase was $20 - $10 = $10. So, the percent increase is $\dfrac{10}{10} \times 100 = 100\%$.

5. **(A)** $P = \dfrac{W}{W+L} \Rightarrow P(W+L) = W \Rightarrow PW + PL = W \Rightarrow PL = W - PW \Rightarrow PL = W(1-P) \Rightarrow$

   $W = \dfrac{PL}{1-P}$

6. **(C)** $13 - 2\sqrt{x} = 7 \Rightarrow -2\sqrt{x} = -6 \Rightarrow \sqrt{x} = 3$. So, $x = 9$.
   On a question like this, you can always backsolve. Only Choice C works.

7. **(A)** The slope of the line $y = 2x - 3$ is 2, which is the coefficient of x. Parallel lines have equal slopes. Only Choice A, $y = 2x + 3$, also has a slope equal to 2.

8. **(D)** In questions such as these, first find the midpoint of the eligible values. A student whose average is A is eligible for the honor roll only if $88 \le A \le 94$. The midpoint of this interval is 91. All of the acceptable averages are within 3 points of 91—anywhere from 3 points less than 91 to 3 points greater than 91. The inequality that expresses this is $|A - 91| \le 3$.

9. **(C)** Use the distance forumula to calculate the length of diameter $\overline{AB}$:

$$AB = \sqrt{(7-3)^2 + (2-(-2))^2} = \sqrt{4^2 + 4^2} = \sqrt{32}$$

So the diameter is $\sqrt{32}$ and the radius is $\dfrac{\sqrt{32}}{2}$. The area is therefore

$$A = \pi r^2 = \pi \left(\dfrac{\sqrt{32}}{2} \right)^2 = \pi \left(\dfrac{32}{4} \right) = 8\pi$$

10. **(C)** An easy way to answer a question such as this is to plug in a number and test the answer choices. If $n = 0$, then the given expression is equal to $-\dfrac{3}{2}$. You should immediately see that neither Choice A nor Choice B is equal to $-\dfrac{3}{2}$. So, plug in 0 for n in Choices C and D. Only Choice C works: $4 - \dfrac{11}{n+2}$ becomes $\dfrac{8}{2} - \dfrac{11}{2} = -\dfrac{3}{2}$.

   Note that what you plug in is irrelevant. If $n = 1$, the given expression is equal to $\dfrac{1}{3}$ and only Choice C works. If $n = 8$, the given expression is equal to $\dfrac{29}{10}$ and again only Choice C works: $\dfrac{40}{10} - \dfrac{11}{10} = \dfrac{29}{10}$.

   **Alternatively, you can get the answer algebraically by dividing:

$$\begin{array}{r} 4 \\ n+2 \overline{\smash{\big)}\, 4n-3} \\ \underline{4n+8} \\ -11 \end{array}$$

So, $\dfrac{4n-3}{n+2} = 4 - \dfrac{11}{n+2}$.

11. **(D)** The first step, which isn't required but which keeps the numbers smaller and easier to work with, is to divide both sides of the given equation by 3:

$$3x^2 + 6x = 6 \Rightarrow x^2 + 2x = 2$$

Now subtract 2 from both sides to put the quadratic equation into standard form: $x^2 + 2x - 2 = 0$. Looking at the answer choices should make it clear that this equation cannot be solved by factoring. So use the quadratic formula:

$$x = \frac{-2 \pm \sqrt{4 - (-8)}}{2} = \frac{-2 \pm \sqrt{12}}{2} = \frac{-2 \pm 2\sqrt{3}}{2} = -1 \pm \sqrt{3}$$

So the two solutions are $-1 + \sqrt{3}$ and $-1 - \sqrt{3}$.

12. **(A)** If e is the edge of a cube, its surface area, A, is $6e^2$ and its volume, V, is e^3. Then

$$A = 6e^2 = 60 \Rightarrow e^2 = 10 \Rightarrow e = \sqrt{10} \Rightarrow$$
$$V = (\sqrt{10})^3 = (\sqrt{10})(\sqrt{10})(\sqrt{10}) = 10\sqrt{10}$$

13. **(D)** $h(1) = 5 \Rightarrow (1)^3 + 2(1)^2 + c(1) + d = 5 \Rightarrow 3 + c + d = 5 \Rightarrow c + d = 2$
$h(-1) = 5 \Rightarrow (-1)^3 + 2(-1)^2 + c(-1) + d = 5 \Rightarrow 1 - c + d = 5 \Rightarrow -c + d = 4$
By adding the two equations, we get that $2d = 4 + 2 = 6$, and so $d = 3$. Replacing d by 3 in the first equation gives $c + 3 = 2 \Rightarrow c = -1$. Finally,

$$h(2) = 2^3 + 2(2)^2 + -1(2) + 3 = 8 + 8 - 2 + 3 = 17$$

14. **0** Subtracting $\frac{5}{8}x$ from each side of the equation $\frac{5}{8}x = \frac{7}{8}x$ gives $0 = \frac{2}{8}x$. This implies that $x = 0$. So, $\frac{11}{8}x = 11(0) = 0$.

**Note that in general, if $ax = bx$ and if $a \neq b$, then $x = 0$.

Since $\frac{5}{8} \neq \frac{7}{8}$, $\frac{5}{8}x = \frac{7}{8}x \Rightarrow x = 0 \Rightarrow \frac{11}{8}x = 0$.

15. **10** $g(2) = 2 \Rightarrow 2^2 + 2b + c = 2 \Rightarrow 2b + c = -2$
$g(3) = 5 \Rightarrow 3^2 + 3b + c = 5 \Rightarrow 3b + c = -4$
By subtracting the first equation above from the second, we get $b = -4 - (-2) = -2$. Replacing b by -2 in the first equation gives $2(-2) + c = -2 \Rightarrow c = 2$. Finally,

$$g(4) = 4^2 + -2(4) + 2 = 16 - 8 + 2 = 10$$

16. **30** On her 6 tests combined, Evelyn earned a total of $6 \times 80 = 480$ points. The total of her 5 best grades is $5 \times 90 = 450$ points. So, her lowest grade was $480 - 450 = 30$.

17. **32** This question would be trivial if you could use a calculator. You would simply type in $\left(\sqrt{2} \cdot \sqrt[3]{2}\right)^6$ and hit the "enter" or "=" button. Since this question is in the noncalculator section, though, you have to use the laws of exponents to simplify the given expression.

$$\left(\sqrt{x} \cdot \sqrt[3]{x}\right)^6 = \left(x^{\frac{1}{2}} \cdot x^{\frac{1}{3}}\right)^6 = \left(x^{\frac{1}{2} + \frac{1}{3}}\right)^6 = \left(x^{\frac{5}{6}}\right)^6 = x^5$$

So, the answer is $2^5 = 2 \times 2 \times 2 \times 2 \times 2 = 32$.

Section 4: Math Test (Calculator)

1. **(C)** Since the ratio of the number of boys to girls is 2 : 3, let the number of boys be $2x$, and let the number of girls be $3x$. Then, the total number of members is $2x + 3x = 5x$. So the girls make up $\frac{3x}{5x} = \frac{3}{5} = 60$ percent of the members.

2. **(D)** Since 72% + 19% = 91%, the $243 spent on the party represents the other 9% of the money raised. If m represents the amount of money raised, then

    $$0.09m = 243 \Rightarrow m = 243 \div 0.09 = 2{,}700$$

3. **(B)** There are a total of 650 juniors and seniors (340 juniors and 310 seniors). Of those, 260 chose a sandwich other than tuna fish (98 + 42 + 106 + 14 = 260). So, the fraction of juniors and seniors who didn't choose tuna fish is $\frac{260}{650} = \frac{4}{10}$, which equals 40 percent.

4. **(B)** In y years, the number of photographs in Al's and Bob's collections will be $905 - 25y$ and $320 + 20y$, respectively. By solving the equation $905 - 25y = 320 + 20y$, we get that $45y = 585$ and so $y = 13$.

    **Note: you could answer this question just as easily without introducing a variable and solving an equation. Today, Al has $905 - 320 = 585$ more photographs than Bob. Each year, the difference in the size of their collections decreases by $20 + 25 = 45$ photographs. So it will take $585 \div 45 = 13$ years for the size of their collections to be the same.

5. **(C)** Start by calculating the numerator.

    $a + a + a = 3a$

    $a \cdot a \cdot a = a^3$

    $a^{\frac{1}{6}} \cdot a^{\frac{1}{3}} \cdot a^{\frac{1}{2}} = a^{\frac{1}{6} + \frac{1}{3} + \frac{1}{2}} = a^1 = a$

    So the numerator of the given expression is $(3a)(a^3)(a) = 3a^5$. Then calculate the denominator.

    $a^{-1} \cdot a^{-2} \cdot a^{-3} = a^{-6}$

    Finally, $\frac{3a^5}{a^{-6}} = 3a^5 \cdot a^6 = 3a^{11}$.

6. **(B)** Since the median is $46,000, half the employees earned less than $46,000. So Choices A and D are false. Nothing in the given information allows us to know the mode. Three employees might have earned $80,000, and no other annual salary might have been earned by more than one or two employees. So Choice C certainly would not be true. Even if it were, Choice C would not explain the difference between the mean and the median. So the answer must be Choice B. In fact, if 28 of the employees each earned about $46,000, but the president, vice president, and treasurer each earned about $500,000, then the mean salary of all 31 employees would have been well over $80,000.

7. **(C)** To calculate the average amount of money raised per member in each of the school's Key Clubs, divide the total amount of money raised by each club by the number of members of that club.

    - Key Club A: $1,700 \div 20 = \$85$
    - Key Club B: $1,500 \div 13 = \$115.38$
    - Key Club C: $1,100 \div 9 \approx \$122.22$
    - Key Club D: $900 \div 8 = \$112.50$

8. **(A)** Ann, the student who raised the most money in Key Club D, raised 25 percent of the $900 raised by her club. So the amount she raised was 25 percent of $900, which equals $225. The total amount raised by all the clubs was

$$\$1,700 + \$1,500 + \$1,100 + \$900 = \$5,200$$

So the amount Ann raised was $225 ÷ $5,200 = 0.04326. To the nearest tenth of one percent, she raised 4.3 percent of the total amount raised.

9. **(D)** Whenever we know two of the three sides of a right triangle, we can find the third side by using the Pythagorean theorem. There are only two possibilities. First, assume that the two given sides are both legs, and let x represent the hypotenuse. Then

$$x^2 = 5^2 + 9^2 = 25 + 81 = 106 \Rightarrow x = \sqrt{106}$$

and III is true. Now assume that one side is a leg and that the longer side is the hypotenuse; let y represent the other leg. Then

$$5^2 + y^2 = 9^2 \Rightarrow 25 + y^2 - 81 \Rightarrow$$
$$y^2 = 56 \Rightarrow y = \sqrt{56}$$

and I is true. Therefore, I and III only are true.

10. **(D)** The second job cost $335 – $290 = $45 dollars more than the first because it took $4.25 - 3.5 = 0.75$ hours longer. So the plumber's hourly rate, h, is $45 ÷ 0.75 hours = $60 per hour. Her charge of $290 for the first job consisted of her flat fee of f dollars plus $60 per hour for the 2.5 additional hours:

$$290 = f + 2.5(60) = f + 150 \Rightarrow f = 140$$

So, $f + h = 140 + 60 = 200$.

**Alternatively, to get the values of f and h, we could have solved the following system of equations:

$$335 = f + 3.25h \quad \text{and} \quad 290 = f + 2.5h$$

Subtracting the second equation from the first gives $45 = 0.75h$. Now proceed as above: $h = 45 ÷ 0.75 = 60$. Replacing h by 60 in either of the equations gives $f = 140$.

11. **(B)** The y-intercept can be read by looking at the line of best fit: $b = 5.5$. The slope of the line is obtained by using the slope formula. Since the line of best fit passes through the points (4, 7) and (9, 9), the slope of the line is $\frac{9-7}{9-4} = \frac{2}{5} = 0.4$. So $m = 0.4$ and $m + b = 0.4 + 5.5 = 5.9$.

12. **(A)** The mode is 8 since more people have 8 teddy bears than any other number. Since there are 15 members, the median is the eighth piece of data when arranged in increasing order; so the median is 10. The range is 6, the difference between the largest value (12) and the least value (6). Finally, the average of 6, 8, and 10 is 8.

13. **(D)** Let b represent the cost, in dollars of the book. Then $3b$ is the cost of the perfume and $10(b + 3b) = 10(4b) = 40b$ is the cost of the ring. So,

$$792 = 40b + 3b + b = 44b \Rightarrow b = 792 ÷ 44 = 18$$

Therefore, the book cost $18, the perfume cost $54, and the ring cost $720.

14. **(D)** At College A, 110 students (11 percent of 1,000) are taking a course in Arabic. At College B, 270 students (18 percent of 1,500) are taking a course in Arabic. This difference is $270 - 110 = 160$.

15. **(B)** At College A, 82 percent of the students who are taking a foreign language course are taking a course in one of the six languages listed in the chart

$$(11 + 10 + 17 + 8 + 12 + 24 = 82)$$

At College B, 84 percent of the students who are taking a foreign language course are taking a course in one of the six languages listed in the chart

$$(18 + 17 + 14 + 11 + 8 + 16 = 84)$$

Of the 2,500 students at Colleges A and B who are taking a foreign language course, the number who are taking a course in one of the six languages listed in the chart is

$$(82\% \text{ of } 1,000) + (84\% \text{ of } 1,500) = 820 + 1,260 = 2,080$$

So, the number who are not taking a course in one of those languages is

$$2,500 - 2,080 = 420$$

Finally, the probability that a student chosen at random from the students at Colleges A and B who are taking a foreign language course is not taking a course in one of the six languages listed in the chart is $420 \div 2,500 = 0.168$.

16. **(A)** $\sin A + \cos A = \dfrac{\text{opposite}}{\text{hypotenuse}} + \dfrac{\text{adjacent}}{\text{hypotenuse}} = \dfrac{a}{c} + \dfrac{b}{c} = \dfrac{a+b}{c}$

17. **(C)** Since there are 60 seconds in a minute, 60 minutes in an hour, 24 hours in a day, and 365 days in a year, the number of seconds in a year is $60 \times 60 \times 24 \times 365 = 31,536,000$. Since the speed of light is approximately 300,000,000 meters per second, a light year is approximately 31,536,000 seconds $\times$ 300,000,000 meters per seconds $= 9.46 \times 10^{15}$ meters, and one parsec is approximately $3.26 \times 9.46 \times 10^{15}$ meters $= 3.08 \times 10^{16}$ meters.

18. **(D)** Let x represent the number of students who participated in the school's athletic programs in 2010. Then the number of students who participated in 2015 was $x + 8$. The number of boys who participated in 2010 was $0.375x$. So, the number of boys who participated in 2015 could be expressed both as $0.375x + 6$ and as $0.4(x + 8)$. Therefore,

$$0.375x + 6 = 0.4(x + 8) \Rightarrow 0.375x + 6 = 0.4x + 3.2 \Rightarrow 2.8 = 0.025x \Rightarrow x = 112$$

So, in 2010, 112 students participated in the athletic programs. In 2015, $112 + 8 = 120$ students participated.

19. **(B)** $x - \dfrac{4}{5} > \dfrac{5}{4} \Rightarrow x > \dfrac{4}{5} + \dfrac{5}{4} = \dfrac{16}{20} + \dfrac{25}{20} = \dfrac{41}{20} = 2.05$

$x - \dfrac{7}{10} < \dfrac{7}{5} \Rightarrow x < \dfrac{7}{10} + \dfrac{7}{5} = \dfrac{7}{10} + \dfrac{14}{10} = \dfrac{21}{10} = 2.1$

Of the four choices, only 2.07, Choice B, is greater than 2.05 and less than 2.1.

20. **(A)** After n marbles were added to the bag, the number of marbles in the bag was $100 + n$, of which $30 + n$ were white. Therefore, the fraction of the marbles that were white is $\dfrac{30+n}{100+n}$. That fraction has to equal 50 percent, or $\dfrac{1}{2}$.

21. **(C)** Replace c by 5 and d by 1. Use the distributive property to multiply each term in the first polynomial by each term in the second polynomial:

$$(ax^2 + bx + 5)(x + e) = ax^3 + aex^2 + bx^2 + bex + 5x + 5e$$

Since the right side of the above equation is equal to $x^3 + 6x^2 + 13x + 20$ for all values of x, the coefficients of the corresponding powers of x must be equal. Since $5e = 20$, we have that $e = 4$. Since $ax^3 = x^3$, we have that $a = 1$. We know that $aex^2 + bx^2 = 6x^2$. From the above, $aex^2 = (1)(4)x^2 = 4x^2$. So, bx^2 has to equal $2x^2$, which means that $b = 2$. Finally, $a + b + e = 1 + 2 + 4 = 7$.

22. **(B)** Jill walked 4 kilometers and Jack walked 6 kilometers. So Jill walked $\frac{4}{6} = \frac{2}{3}$ the distance that Jack walked. Since their rates were the same, she did it in $\frac{2}{3}$ the time: $\frac{2}{3}$ of 2 hours is $\frac{4}{3}$ of an hour, or 1 hour and 20 minutes. She left at 10:40.

**Jack walked 6 kilometers in exactly 2 hours; so, he was walking at a rate of 3 kilometers per hour. Jill walked 4 kilometers, also at 3 kilometers per hour; so her walking time was $4 \div 3$ or $1\frac{1}{3}$ hours. Therefore, Jill left $1\frac{1}{3}$ hours, or 1 hour and 20 minutes, before noon—at 10:40.

23. **(A)** At the end of 2015, Alice had $a + 0.25a = 1.25a$ dolls and Barbara had $b - 0.25b = 0.75b$ dolls. Therefore, $1.25a = 0.75b \Rightarrow \frac{a}{b} = \frac{0.75}{1.25} = \frac{75}{125} = \frac{3}{5}$.

24. **(B)** The table says that the 180 participants from Africa made up 15 percent of the total number of participants. If T represents the total number of participants, $0.15T = 180$ and $T = 180 \div .15 = 1{,}200$.

25. **(B)** From the solution to question 24, we know that the total number of participants was 1,200. So the number of European participants was 480 (40 percent of 1,200). Therefore, the total number of participants *not* from the Americas was $180 + 120 + 480 = 780$. So, the total number of participants from the Americas was $1{,}200 - 780 = 420$.

26. **(D)** First, convert 17.5 pounds to ounces: 17.5×16 ounces $= 280$ ounces.

Let b and s represent the weight in ounces of a baseball and a softball, respectively. Then,

$$s = b + 1.5 \text{ and } 30b + 20s = 280$$

It's not necessary, but if you divide both sides of the second equation by 10, you will be working with smaller numbers: $3b + 2s = 28$

Replacing s in the second equation by $b + 1.5$ gives

$$3b + 2(b + 1.5) = 28 \Rightarrow 3b + 2b + 3 = 28 \Rightarrow$$
$$5b + 3 = 28 \Rightarrow 5b = 25 \Rightarrow b = 5 \Rightarrow s = 5 + 1.5 = 6.5$$

27. **(B)** In general, the easiest way to answer a question such as this one is to plug in an easy-to-use number. Assume that Emily purchases the bracelets from the jeweler for $100 each. Since 60 percent of $100 is $60, she sells them all summer for $160. Since 20 percent of $100 is $20, during the end-of-summer sale, she sells her remaining bracelets for $80, which represents a 50 percent reduction from the normal selling price of $160.

**In this case, finding the solution is just as easy if you use a variable. If Emily pays b dollars for each bracelet, all summer she sells them for $1.6b$. At the end of the summer, she sells them for $0.8b$, which is exactly half, or 50 percent, of $1.6b$.

28. **(256)** $\left(\frac{1}{3}\right)^{-n} = (3^{-1})^{-n} = 3^n$. So, $81 = 3^n$. You may simply recognize that $n = 4$. If not, then either use your calculator to take the fourth root of 81 or just multiply $3 \times 3 \times 3 \times \ldots$ until you reach the product of 81: $3^4 = 81$. Finally, $\left(\frac{1}{4}\right)^{-n} = (4^{-1})^{-n} = 4^n = 4^4 = 256$.

29. **(9.5)** The surface area of a rectangular box is given by $A = 2(\ell w + wh + \ell h)$. Replacing w by 5, ℓ by 7, and A by 298, we get $298 = 2(35 + 5h + 7h) = 70 + 24h$. Therefore, $24h = 228$ and $h = 9.5$.

30. **(78)** When Adam drives 60 miles per hour, he is traveling 60 miles per 60 minutes = 1 mile per 1 minute. While driving at 60 miles per hour, Adam takes 6.5 minutes to drive those 6.5 miles.

    If Adam drives 50 miles per hour, he is traveling 50 miles per 60 minutes = $\frac{5}{6}$ mile per 1 minute. While driving at 50 miles per hour, Adam takes $6.5 \div \frac{5}{6} = 6.5 \times \frac{6}{5} = \frac{39}{5} = 7.8$ minutes to drive those 6.5 miles.

    Adam would take $7.8 - 6.5 = 1.3$ minutes less to drive those 6.5 miles at 60 miles per hour instead of at 50 miles per hour. Finally, 1.3 minutes = 1.3×60 seconds = 78 seconds.

31. **(47)** Adam drove 6.5 miles per day $\times$ 240 days = 1,560 miles last year. At 60 miles per hour, Adam would have used $1,560 \div 20 = 78$ gallons of gasoline, which would have cost $78 \times \$3.60 = \$280.80$. At 50 miles per hour, Adam actually used $1,560 \div 24 = 65$ gallons of gasoline, which cost $65 \times \$3.60 = \$234$. So traveling at 60 miles per hour instead of at 50 miles per hour would have cost Adam $\$280.80 - \$234 = \$46.80$ more, which is \$47 to the nearest dollar.

PART THREE
The PSAT Reading Test

Chapter 1: The Evidence-Based Reading Test

Chapter 2: Building Your Vocabulary

The Evidence-Based Reading Test

1

Now more than ever, doing well on the evidence-based reading questions can make the difference between success and failure on the PSAT. These time-consuming questions are the ones most likely to bog you down. However, you can handle them, and this chapter will show you how.

FREQUENTLY ASKED QUESTIONS

1. HOW CAN I BECOME A BETTER READER?

READ, READ, READ!

Just do it.

There is no substitute for extensive reading to prepare you for the PSAT and for college work. The only way to build up your proficiency in reading is by reading books of all kinds. As you read, you will develop speed, stamina, and the ability to comprehend the printed page. But if you want to turn yourself into the kind of reader the colleges are looking for, you must develop the habit of reading—closely and critically—every day.

2. WHAT SORT OF MATERIAL SHOULD I READ?

Challenge yourself. Don't limit your reading to light fiction, graphic novels, and Xbox reviews. Branch out a bit. Try to develop an interest in as many fields as you can.

Check out some of these magazines:

- *The New Yorker*
- *Smithsonian*
- *The New York Review of Books*
- *The Economist*
- *Natural History*
- *Science News*

Explore popular encyclopedias on the Web. You'll find articles on anthropology, archaeoloogy, biology, ecology, geology, history, linguistics, psychology, sociology—the whole range of fields touched on by the PSAT. If you take time to sample these fields, you won't find the subject matter of the reading passages on the PSAT strange.

3. ON THE PSAT, IS IT BETTER TO READ THE PASSAGE FIRST OR THE QUESTIONS FIRST?

The answer is, it depends on the passage, and *it depends on you.* If you are a super fast reader, you may want to head for the questions first. It all depends on how good your visual memory is and on how good at scanning you are. If you're not a speed demon at reading, your best move may be to skim the whole passage before you read the questions. Only you can decide which method suits you best.

THE QUESTIONS-FIRST APPROACH

- As you read each question, be on the lookout for key words, either in the question itself or among the answer choices.
- Run your eye down the passage, looking for those key words or their synonyms. (That's called *scanning.*)
- When you spot a key word in a sentence, read that sentence and a couple of sentences around it.
- Decide whether you can confidently answer the question on the basis of just that part of the passage.
- Check to see whether your answer is correct.

GENERAL TIPS: WORKING YOUR WAY THROUGH THE READING SECTION

- **TACKLE PASSAGES WITH FAMILIAR SUBJECTS BEFORE PASSAGES WITH UNFAMILIAR ONES.** It's hard to concentrate when you read about something wholly unfamiliar to you. Give yourself a break. In each section, first tackle the reading passage that interests you or deals with the topic about which you have a clue. Then move on to the other passage. You'll do better that way.

- **IF YOU ARE STUMPED BY A TOUGH QUESTION, DO NOT SKIP THE OTHER QUESTIONS ON THAT PASSAGE.** Remember, the critical reading questions after each passage are not arranged in order of difficulty. They tend to be arranged sequentially: questions on Paragraph 1 come before questions on Paragraph 2. Try *all* the questions on the passage. That tough question may be just one question away from an easy one.

- **DO NOT ZIP BACK AND FORTH BETWEEN PASSAGES.** Stick with one passage until you feel sure you've answered all the questions you can on that passage. (If you don't, you'll probably have to waste time rereading the passage when you come back to it.) Before moving on to the next passage, be sure to go back over any questions you marked to come back to. In answering other questions on the passage, you may have acquired some information that will help you answer the questions you skipped.

- **READ AS FAST AS YOU CAN WITH UNDERSTANDING, BUT DON'T FORCE YOURSELF.** Do not worry about the time. If you worry about not finishing the test, you will start taking shortcuts and miss the correct answer in your rush.

- **TAKE NOTE OF ANY INTRODUCTORY MATERIAL AND FOOTNOTES.** There's a reason the test-makers included them.

- **TRY TO ANTICIPATE WHAT THE PASSAGE WILL BE ABOUT.** As you read the italicized introductory material and tackle the passage's opening sentences, ask yourself who or what the author is talking about.

- **READ WITH A PURPOSE.** Try to spot what kind of writing this is, what techniques are used, who its intended audience is, and how the author feels about the subject. Be on the lookout for names, dates, and places. In particular, try to remember where in the passage the author makes major points. Then, when you start looking for the phrase or sentence that will justify your answer choice, you may be able to save time by zipping back to that section of the passage without having to reread the whole thing.

- **WHEN YOU TACKLE THE QUESTIONS, GO BACK TO THE PASSAGE TO CHECK EACH ANSWER CHOICE.** Do not rely on your memory, and above all, do not ignore the passage and just answer questions based on other things you've read. Remember, the questions are asking you about what this author has to say about the subject, not about what some other author you once read said about it in another book.

- **USE THE LINE REFERENCES IN THE QUESTIONS TO BE SURE YOU'VE GONE BACK TO THE CORRECT SPOT IN THE PASSAGE.** It takes less time to locate a line number than to spot a word or phrase. Use the line numbers to orient yourself in the text.

- **WHEN DEALING WITH THE DOUBLE PASSAGES, IN GENERAL, TACKLE THEM ONE AT A TIME.** For the most part, the questions are organized sequentially: questions about Passage 1 come before questions about Passage 2. So, do things in order. First read Passage 1; then jump straight to the questions and answer all the questions on Passage 1. Next read Passage 2; then answer all the questions on Passage 2. Finally, tackle the two or three questions that refer to both passages. Go back to both passages as needed.

    Occasionally a couple of questions referring to both passages will come before the questions on Passage 1. Do not let this throw you. Use your common sense. You've just read the first passage. Skip the one or two questions on both passages, and head straight for the questions about Passage 1. Answer them. Then read Passage 2. Answer the questions on Passage 2. Finally, go back to the questions you skipped and answer them (plus any other questions at the end of the set that refer to both passages). This is not rocket science. One thing, though: whenever you skip from question to question or from passage to passage, *be sure you are filling in the right spaces on your answer sheet.*

- **BE ON THE LOOKOUT FOR WORDS OR PHRASES IN THE QUESTIONS THAT CAN CLUE YOU IN TO THE KIND OF QUESTION BEING ASKED.** If you can recognize just what a given question is asking for, you'll be better able to tell which particular reading tactic to apply.

Now that you have a general idea about how to work your way through the reading sections, it's time to think about how to handle the different reading question types.

- **VOCABULARY IN CONTEXT**—quick questions (you have to figure out which of several possible meanings of a familiar-looking word works in a particular context)

- **MAIN IDEA**—big picture questions (you have to figure out the central point the author is trying to make)

- **SPECIFIC DETAIL**—narrow focus questions (you have to zoom in on specific facts)

- **INFERENCE**—logic questions (you have to figure out what the author is suggesting or stating indirectly)

- **COMMAND-OF-EVIDENCE**—evidence questions (you have to locate the exact sentence, or sentences, that provides the best evidence in support of your answer to a previous question)

- **LITERARY TECHNIQUE**—technical questions (you have to know the meaning of literary terms)

- **GRAPHICS**—interpretation questions (you have to figure out how the information in a graph, table, or chart supports what is stated in the passage)

NOTE

Again, much depends on what kind of reader you are. How good is your memory? How fast do you read, and how well do you retain what you have read? Are you a detail-oriented reader, happiest going into material in depth, or are you a big picture reader, happy only after you have a general sense of everything going on? If you are a big picture reader, you may need to read both passages before you tackle the questions.

On the following pages you will find examples of these different question types. The questions are based on passages similar to ones on released PSAT tests. You may find the passages challenging, but you can take as much time as you need to figure them out.

The following passage is taken from a classic study of tarantulas published in Scientific American.

A fertilized female tarantula lays from 200 to 400 eggs at a time; thus it is possible for a single tarantula to produce several thousand young. She takes no care of them beyond weaving a cocoon of silk to enclose the eggs. After they hatch, the young walk
Line away, find convenient places in which to dig their burrows and spend the rest of their
(5) lives in solitude. Tarantulas feed mostly on insects and millipedes. Once their appetite is appeased, they digest the food for several days before eating again. Their sight is poor, being limited to sensing a change in the intensity of light and to the perception of moving objects. They apparently have little or no sense of hearing, for a hungry tarantula will pay no attention to a loudly chirping cricket placed in its cage unless the
(10) insect happens to touch one of its legs.

But all spiders, and especially hairy ones, have an extremely delicate sense of touch. Laboratory experiments prove that tarantulas can distinguish three types of touch: pressure against the body wall, stroking of the body hair, and riffling of certain very fine hairs on the legs called trichobothria. Pressure against the body, by a finger
(15) or the end of a pencil, causes the tarantula to move off slowly for a short distance. The touch excites no defensive response unless the approach is from above, where the spider can see the motion, in which case it rises on its hind legs, lifts its front legs, opens its fangs and holds this threatening posture as long as the object continues to move. When the motion stops, the spider drops back to the ground, remains quiet for
(20) a few seconds, and then moves slowly away.

The entire body of a tarantula, especially its legs, is thickly clothed with hair. Some of it is short and woolly, some long and stiff. Touching this body hair produces one of two distinct reactions. When the spider is hungry, it responds with an immediate and swift attack. At the touch of a cricket's antennae the tarantula seizes the insect
(25) so swiftly that a motion picture taken at the rate of 64 frames per second shows only the result and not the process of capture. But when the spider is not hungry, the stimulation of its hairs merely causes it to shake the touched limb. An insect can walk under its hairy belly unharmed.

The trichobothria, very fine hairs growing from disklike membranes on the legs,
(30) were once thought to be the spider's hearing organs, but we now know that they have nothing to do with sound. They are sensitive only to air movement. A light breeze makes them vibrate slowly without disturbing the common hair. When one blows gently on the trichobothria, the tarantula reacts with a quick jerk of its four front legs. If the front and hind legs are stimulated at the same time, the spider makes a sudden
(35) jump. This reaction is quite independent of the state of its appetite.

These three tactile responses—to pressure on the body wall, to moving of the common hair, and to flexing of the trichobothria—are so different from one another that there is no possibility of confusing them. They serve the tarantula adequately for most of its needs and enable it to avoid most annoyances and dangers. But they fail
(40) the spider completely when it meets its deadly enemy, the digger wasp *Pepsis.*

VOCABULARY-IN-CONTEXT QUESTIONS

Vocabulary-in-context questions are easy to spot. They look like this:

As used in line 13, "frabbledrab" most nearly means

(A) snipsnop.
(B) kangasplat.
(C) replix.
(D) oggitty.

TIP 1

Tackle vocabulary-in-context questions as if they were fill-in-the-blank questions. First, read the sentence, substituting *blank* for the word in quotes. Think of words you know that might make sense in the context. Then test each answer choice, substituting it in the sentence for the word in quotes. Ask yourself whether this particular answer choice makes sense in the specific context.

Vocabulary Power Practice

1. As used in line 16, "excites" most nearly means

   (A) enlivens.
   (B) inflames.
   (C) stimulates.
   (D) awakens.

2. As used in line 18, "holds" most nearly means

   (A) embraces.
   (B) maintains.
   (C) grasps.
   (D) contains.

> **WORDS HAVE MULTIPLE MEANINGS**
>
> A *run* in baseball is not the same thing as a *run* in your stocking.

3. As used in line 38, "serve" most nearly means

   (A) suffice.
   (B) perform.
   (C) distribute.
   (D) function as.

 Vocabulary-in-context questions take hardly any time to answer. If you're running out of time, answer them first.

CHECK YOUR ANSWERS

1. **(C)** The original sentence states that "The touch _____ no defensive response unless the approach is from above, where the spider can see the motion, in which case it rises on its hind legs, lifts its front legs, opens its fangs and holds this threatening posture as long as the object continues to move." To excite a defensive response is to *stimulate* that kind of reaction. *Excite* here is a technical physiological term, as in "exciting a nerve."

   Note that *many* of the answer choices could be substitutes for "excites" *in other contexts*. For example, if the sentence were "John is the least inquisitive person I know; nothing excites his curiosity," Choice D, *awakens*, would be the best word to substitute. Your job is to spot which meaning of the word works best this time.

2. **(B)** Again, look at the sentence, substituting *blank* for the keyword. "The touch excites no defensive response unless the approach is from above, where the spider can see the motion, in which case it rises on its hind legs, lifts its front legs, opens its fangs and *blanks* this threatening posture as long as the object continues to move." What word would make sense in the context? Summarize what's going on. The spider is performing an action *as long as* an object continues to move. It is holding or *maintaining* a defensive posture for as long as it perceives a threat. The correct answer is Choice B, *maintains*.

   Again, many of the answer choices could be substitutes for "holds" in other contexts. For example, if the sentence were "The gas tank holds 15 gallons of fuel," Choice D, *contains*, would be the best word to substitute.

3. **(A)** The three tactile responses are sufficient enough for or *suffice* the tarantula adequately to meet most of its needs and enable it to avoid most annoyances and dangers. Once again, you've found a word that makes sense in context. Even if *suffice* (meet the needs of; be enough for) is an unfamiliar word to you, you can use the process of elimination to rule out the other answer choices. Do the three tactile responses *perform* the tarantula adequately for most of its needs and enable it to avoid most annoyances and dangers? The sentence makes no sense. You can eliminate Choice B. Do the three tactile responses *distribute* the tarantula adequately for most of its needs and enable it to avoid most annoyances and dangers? Again, the sentence makes no sense. You can eliminate Choice C. Do the three tactile responses *function as* the tarantula adequately for most of its needs and enable it to avoid most annoyances and dangers? The sentence seems as if it should make sense, but it doesn't really. You can eliminate Choice D. Only Choice A is left. It is the correct answer.

   Note, by the way, that the three alternate answer choices were all possible synonyms for *serve*. "Serve" can mean *perform*, as in the question "Did you serve an apprenticeship?" It can mean *distribute*, as in the command "Serve the appetizers to the guests." It can also mean *function as*, as in the statement "Plates can serve as ashtrays." However, it has none of these meanings *in this particular context*.

The following passage is taken from a classic study of tarantulas published in Scientific American.

A fertilized female tarantula lays from 200 to 400 eggs at a time; thus it is possible for a single tarantula to produce several thousand young. She takes no care of them beyond weaving a cocoon of silk to enclose the eggs. After they hatch, the young walk

Line away, find convenient places in which to dig their burrows and spend the rest of their

(5) lives in solitude. Tarantulas feed mostly on insects and millipedes. Once their appetite is appeased, they digest the food for several days before eating again. Their sight is poor, being limited to sensing a change in the intensity of light and to the perception of moving objects. They apparently have little or no sense of hearing, for a hungry tarantula will pay no attention to a loudly chirping cricket placed in its cage unless the

(10) insect happens to touch one of its legs.

But all spiders, and especially hairy ones, have an extremely delicate sense of touch. Laboratory experiments prove that tarantulas can distinguish three types of touch: pressure against the body wall, stroking of the body hair and riffling of certain very fine hairs on the legs called trichobothria. Pressure against the body, by a finger

(15) or the end of a pencil, causes the tarantula to move off slowly for a short distance. The touch excites no defensive response unless the approach is from above, where the spider can see the motion, in which case it rises on its hind legs, lifts its front legs, opens its fangs and holds this threatening posture as long as the object continues to move. When the motion stops, the spider drops back to the ground, remains quiet for

(20) a few seconds, and then moves slowly away.

The entire body of a tarantula, especially its legs, is thickly clothed with hair. Some of it is short and woolly, some long and stiff. Touching this body hair produces one of two distinct reactions. When the spider is hungry, it responds with an immediate and swift attack. At the touch of a cricket's antennae the tarantula seizes the insect

(25) so swiftly that a motion picture taken at the rate of 64 frames per second shows only the result and not the process of capture. But when the spider is not hungry, the stimulation of its hairs merely causes it to shake the touched limb. An insect can walk under its hairy belly unharmed.

The trichobothria, very fine hairs growing from disklike membranes on the legs,

(30) were once thought to be the spider's hearing organs, but we now know that they have nothing to do with sound. They are sensitive only to air movement. A light breeze makes them vibrate slowly without disturbing the common hair. When one blows gently on the trichobothria, the tarantula reacts with a quick jerk of its four front legs. If the front and hind legs are stimulated at the same time, the spider makes a sudden

(35) jump. This reaction is quite independent of the state of its appetite.

These three tactile responses—to pressure on the body wall, to moving of the common hair, and to flexing of the trichobothria—are so different from one another that there is no possibility of confusing them. They serve the tarantula adequately for most of its needs and enable it to avoid most annoyances and dangers. But they fail

(40) the spider completely when it meets its deadly enemy, the digger wasp *Pepsis*.

MAIN IDEA QUESTIONS

Main idea questions look like this:

Which of the following best states the central thought of the passage?

The primary purpose of the passage is to . . .

In the second paragraph of the passage, the author primarily stresses that . . .

TIP 2

When asked to find a passage's main idea, be sure to check the opening and summary sentences of each paragraph. Authors often orient readers with a sentence that expresses a paragraph's main idea concisely. Although such topic sentences may appear anywhere in the paragraph, you can usually find them in the opening or closing sentences.

In PSAT reading passages, topic sentences are sometimes implied rather than stated directly. If you cannot find a topic sentence, ask yourself these questions:

- **Who or what is this passage about?**
- **What feature of this subject is the author talking about?**
- **What is the author trying to get across about this feature of the subject?**

You'll be on your way to locating the passage's main idea.

Main Idea Power Practice

1. The primary purpose of the passage is to

   (A) report on controversial new discoveries about spider behavior.
   (B) summarize what is known about the physical condition and reactions of tarantulas.
   (C) challenge the findings of historic laboratory experiments involving tarantulas.
   (D) discuss the physical adaptations that make tarantulas unique.

2. The main purpose of the third and fourth paragraphs is to

   (A) distinguish related phenomena.
   (B) propose alternative solutions.
   (C) indicate rival hypotheses.
   (D) question accepted theories.

CHECK YOUR ANSWERS

1. **(B)** Rather than covering new discoveries, challenging findings of historic experiments, or discussing tarantula adaptations, the passage *summarizes* general information about tarantulas.

   Go back to the passage and look at the opening sentences of the four paragraphs. (The shaded bits.) What are these sentences talking about? Tarantulas. What aspect of tarantulas are they talking about? They're talking about how tarantulas look—hairy, long-legged—and how they react when they observe a movement or sense a touch. They are summing up *what is known about the tarantula's physical condition and reactions.*

   Choice A is incorrect; the passage is not reporting controversial new discoveries; it is summing up what scientists already know about tarantulas. Choice C is incorrect: the passage does not challenge any findings of laboratory experiments; instead, it cites these findings. Choice D is incorrect; nothing in the passage supports it.

2. **(A)** Paragraph three describes how a tarantula reacts to a physical touch on its body hair, or common hair. Paragraph four describes how a tarantula reacts to a breath of air blowing gently against its trichobothria (very fine hairs growing from round membranes on its legs). The two paragraphs enable the reader to tell apart or *distinguish* these *related phenomena.* (A phenomenon is an observable fact or situation, in this case the spider's reaction to a type of light touch.)

The following passage is taken from a classic study of tarantulas published in Scientific American.

A fertilized female tarantula lays from 200 to 400 eggs at a time; thus it is possible for a single tarantula to produce several thousand young. She takes no care of them beyond weaving a cocoon of silk to enclose the eggs. After they hatch, the young walk
Line away, find convenient places in which to dig their burrows and spend the rest of their
(5) lives in solitude. Tarantulas feed mostly on insects and millipedes. Once their appetite is appeased, they digest the food for several days before eating again. Their sight is poor, being limited to sensing a change in the intensity of light and to the perception of moving objects. They apparently have little or no sense of hearing, for a hungry tarantula will pay no attention to a loudly chirping cricket placed in its cage unless the
(10) insect happens to touch one of its legs.

But all spiders, and especially hairy ones, have an extremely delicate sense of touch. Laboratory experiments prove that tarantulas can distinguish three types of touch: pressure against the body wall, stroking of the body hair, and riffling of certain very fine hairs on the legs called trichobothria. Pressure against the body, by a finger
(15) or the end of a pencil, causes the tarantula to move off slowly for a short distance. The touch excites no defensive response unless the approach is from above, where the spider can see the motion, in which case it rises on its hind legs, lifts its front legs, opens its fangs and holds this threatening posture as long as the object continues to move. When the motion stops, the spider drops back to the ground, remains quiet for
(20) a few seconds, and then moves slowly away.

The entire body of a tarantula, especially its legs, is thickly clothed with hair. Some of it is short and woolly, some long and stiff. Touching this body hair produces one of two distinct reactions. When the spider is hungry, it responds with an immediate and swift attack. At the touch of a cricket's antennae the tarantula seizes the insect
(25) so swiftly that a motion picture taken at the rate of 64 frames per second shows only the result and not the process of capture. But when the spider is not hungry, the stimulation of its hairs merely causes it to shake the touched limb. An insect can walk under its hairy belly unharmed.

The trichobothria, very fine hairs growing from disklike membranes on the legs,
(30) were once thought to be the spider's hearing organs, but we now know that they have nothing to do with sound. They are sensitive only to air movement. A light breeze makes them vibrate slowly without disturbing the common hair. When one blows gently on the trichobothria, the tarantula reacts with a quick jerk of its four front legs. If the front and hind legs are stimulated at the same time, the spider makes a sudden
(35) jump. This reaction is quite independent of the state of its appetite.

These three tactile responses—to pressure on the body wall, to moving of the common hair, and to flexing of the trichobothria—are so different from one another that there is no possibility of confusing them. They serve the tarantula adequately for most of its needs and enable it to avoid most annoyances and dangers. But they fail
(40) the spider completely when it meets its deadly enemy, the digger wasp *Pepsis*.

SPECIFIC DETAIL QUESTIONS

Specific detail questions often begin like this:

> According to the author, the reason for . . .
> The author makes which point about the . . .
> The author indicates that . . .

TIP 3

When you answer specific detail questions, point to the precise words in the passage that support your answer choice. You must be *sure* that the answer you select is in the passage. That means you must find a word or sentence or group of sentences that justifies your choice. Do *not* pick an answer just because it agrees with your personal opinions or with information on the subject that you've gotten from other sources.

Specific Detail Power Practice

1. According to the author, which of the following attributes is characteristic of female tarantulas?

   (A) Maternal instincts
   (B) Visual acuity
   (C) Sensitive hearing
   (D) High fertility

2. The author indicates that hunger in a tarantula

   (A) causes it to agitate a limb that has been touched.
   (B) diverts it from noticing pressure on its body wall.
   (C) intensifies its response to being touched.
   (D) requires it to digest its food for several days.

> **FACT VS. OPINION**
>
> **Fact:** A fertilized female tarantula lays from 200 to 400 eggs at a time. (You can verify this by checking encyclopedia articles or scientific studies on tarantulas or by directly observing tarantulas reproduce in a lab setting.)
>
> **Opinion:** Ben thinks that all tarantula bites are deadly. (Well, that's what *he* believes . . .)

CHECK YOUR ANSWERS

1. **(D)** The opening sentence provides the answer to this question. In laying 200 to 400 eggs at once, the female tarantula demonstrates her *high fertility* (ability to conceive and produce young).

   If you fail to spot the correct answer immediately, you can of course use the process of elimination to answer this question. Are female tarantulas noted for their *maternal instincts*? No. According to the passage, a female tarantula "takes no care of (her young) beyond weaving a cocoon of silk to enclose the eggs." You can eliminate Choice A. Are female tarantulas noted for their *visual acuity* (sharpness of sight)? No. The passage states that "(t)heir sight is poor, being limited to sensing a change in the intensity of light and to the perception of moving objects." You can eliminate Choice B. Are female tarantulas noted for their *sensitive hearing*? No. "They apparently have little or no sense of hearing"; it is their sense of touch that is sensitive. You can eliminate Choice C. Only Choice D is left. It is the correct answer.

2. **(C)** Paragraph three indicates that stroking or touching the body hair of a hungry tarantula causes it to immediately make a swift, fierce response. It also indicates that, when the tarantula is not hungry, touching its body hair causes it only to shake the affected limb. Thus, hunger in a tarantula clearly *intensifies its response to being touched*.

   Choice A is incorrect. When the spider is *not* hungry, then stroking its body hair causes it merely to shake or agitate the affected limb. When a spider *is* hungry, stroking its body hair stimulates it to react much more speedily and aggressively. Neither Choice B nor Choice D makes any sense in the context.

The following passage is taken from a classic study of tarantulas published in Scientific American.

A fertilized female tarantula lays from 200 to 400 eggs at a time; thus it is possible for a single tarantula to produce several thousand young. She takes no care of them beyond weaving a cocoon of silk to enclose the eggs. After they hatch, the young walk

Line away, find convenient places in which to dig their burrows and spend the rest of their

(5) lives in solitude. Tarantulas feed mostly on insects and millipedes. Once their appetite is appeased, they digest the food for several days before eating again. Their sight is poor, being limited to sensing a change in the intensity of light and to the perception of moving objects. They apparently have little or no sense of hearing, for a hungry tarantula will pay no attention to a loudly chirping cricket placed in its cage unless the

(10) insect happens to touch one of its legs.

But all spiders, and especially hairy ones, have an extremely delicate sense of touch. Laboratory experiments prove that tarantulas can distinguish three types of touch: pressure against the body wall, stroking of the body hair, and riffling of certain very fine hairs on the legs called trichobothria. Pressure against the body, by a finger

(15) or the end of a pencil, causes the tarantula to move off slowly for a short distance. The touch excites no defensive response unless the approach is from above, where the spider can see the motion, in which case it rises on its hind legs, lifts its front legs, opens its fangs and holds this threatening posture as long as the object continues to

move. When the motion stops, the spider drops back to the ground, remains quiet for
(20) a few seconds, and then moves slowly away.

The entire body of a tarantula, especially its legs, is thickly clothed with hair. Some
of it is short and woolly, some long and stiff. Touching this body hair produces one
of two distinct reactions. When the spider is hungry, it responds with an immediate
and swift attack. At the touch of a cricket's antennae the tarantula seizes the insect
(25) so swiftly that a motion picture taken at the rate of 64 frames per second shows only
the result and not the process of capture. But when the spider is not hungry, the
stimulation of its hairs merely causes it to shake the touched limb. An insect can walk
under its hairy belly unharmed.

The trichobothria, very fine hairs growing from disklike membranes on the legs,
(30) were once thought to be the spider's hearing organs, but we now know that they have
nothing to do with sound. They are sensitive only to air movement. A light breeze
makes them vibrate slowly without disturbing the common hair. When one blows
gently on the trichobothria, the tarantula reacts with a quick jerk of its four front legs.
If the front and hind legs are stimulated at the same time, the spider makes a sudden
(35) jump. This reaction is quite independent of the state of its appetite.

These three tactile responses—to pressure on the body wall, to moving of the
common hair, and to flexing of the trichobothria—are so different from one another
that there is no possibility of confusing them. They serve the tarantula adequately for
most of its needs and enable it to avoid most annoyances and dangers. But they fail
(40) the spider completely when it meets its deadly enemy, the digger wasp *Pepsis*.

INFERENCE QUESTIONS

Inference questions often begin like this:

The author implies that . . .
The passage suggests that . . .
It can be inferred from the passage that . . .
The author would most likely . . .
The author probably considers . . .

TIP 4

**When you answer inference questions, look for what the passage logically suggests but does
not directly state. Inference questions require you to use your judgment. You are drawing a
conclusion based on what you have read in the text. Think about what the passage suggests.
You must not take anything directly stated in the passage as an inference. Instead, you must
look for clues in the passage that you can use in coming up with your own conclusion. Then
you should choose as your answer a statement that logically follows from the information
the author has given you.**

Inference Power Practice

1. It can most reasonably be inferred from the opening paragraph that tarantulas

   (A) become apprehensive at sudden noises.
   (B) depend on their mothers for nourishment after hatching.
   (C) must consume insects or millipedes daily.
   (D) are reclusive by nature.

2. In the paragraphs immediately following this passage, the author most likely will

   (A) explain why scientists previously confused the tarantula's three tactile responses.
   (B) point out the weaknesses of the digger wasp that enable the tarantula to subdue it.
   (C) describe how the digger wasp goes about attacking tarantulas.
   (D) demonstrate how the tarantula's three tactile responses enable it to meet its needs.

BE ON THE LOOKOUT FOR QUALIFIERS

Little words like "somewhat," "often," and "almost" limit the meaning of other words. They are little words, but they can have a big impact. Which would you rather have the Terminator say, "No problem" or "Almost no problem"?

CHECK YOUR ANSWERS

1. **(D)** Since the passage states that female tarantulas abandon their offspring in cocoons to hatch on their own, and that young tarantulas go off to spend their lives in solitude, it follows that tarantulas must be *reclusive* or solitary by nature.

2. **(C)** The concluding sentence of the passage states that the tarantula's tactile responses do not help it when it meets (that is, is attacked by) its deadly enemy, the digger wasp. It follows that subsequent paragraphs will discuss *digger wasp attacks* in more detail.

   Choice B is incorrect. The concluding sentence of the passage indicates that the tarantula's usual tactile responses *fail* the spider when it meets the digger wasp. Thus, it is unlikely that the following few paragraphs will picture the tarantula subduing or overcoming the wasp.

COMMAND-OF-EVIDENCE QUESTIONS

Most command-of-evidence questions look like this:

Which choice provides the best evidence for the answer to the previous question?

(A) Line 5 ("Tarantulas . . . millipedes")
(B) Lines 8–10 ("They . . . legs")
(C) Lines 23–24 ("When . . . attack")
(D) Line 35 ("This reaction . . . appetite")

Others may look like this:

Which choice best supports the claim that . . .
Which choice provides the best support for the author's implication that . . .

Scan All the Questions on a Passage to Spot the Command-of-Evidence Questions Coming Up. Ten of the reading questions on your test will be questions that test how well you are able to identify which part of a passage provides the best support for a conclusion you reach. Thanks to the presence of the line numbers and parentheses in the answer choices, command-of-evidence questions are easy to spot. As you turn to the nine or ten questions on a particular passage, scan the group of questions quickly to spot the two questions on that passage that are command-of-evidence questions. In your booklet, circle the number of the question *immediately before* each command-of-evidence question. That's your cue to pay special attention as you answer this question. If you do it right, you'll be answering two questions, and not just one.

Here's what to do. As you answer the question *immediately before* a command-of-evidence question, note in your booklet what part of the passage helped you come up with your answer. Put a check mark in the margin next to the sentence that you think best supports the answer you chose. Next, move on to the command-of-evidence question. Look at the line numbers in the answer choices. Is the sentence you checked among the choices listed there? If it is, then that's most likely the correct answer. If not, then you need to reread the four sentences listed in the answer choices and think how each of them might back up one of the answers to the previous question.

Command-of-Evidence (COE) Power Practice

Each of the following command-of-evidence questions is paired with a content question that you have seen earlier. Note how the information in the answer to the COE question supports the correct answer to the preceding question.

(Specific Detail)

1. The author indicates that hunger in a tarantula

    (A) causes it to agitate a limb that has been touched.
    (B) diverts it from noticing pressure on its body wall.
    (C) intensifies its response to being touched.
    (D) requires it to digest its food for several days.

1A. Which choice provides the best evidence for the answer to the previous question?

    (A) Line 5 ("Tarantulas . . . millipedes")
    (B) Lines 8–10 ("They . . . legs")
    (C) Lines 23–26 ("When . . . capture")
    (D) Line 35 ("This reaction . . . appetite")

(Inference)

2. It can most reasonably be inferred from the opening paragraph that tarantulas

    (A) become apprehensive at sudden noises.

    (B) depend on their mothers for nourishment after hatching.

    (C) must consume insects or millipedes daily.

    (D) are reclusive by nature.

2A. Which choice provides the best evidence for the answer to the previous question?

    (A) Lines 1–2 ("A fertilized . . . young")

    (B) Lines 3–5 ("After they . . . solitude")

    (C) Lines 5–6 ("Once . . . eating again")

    (D) Lines 19–20 ("When . . . slowly away")

CHECK YOUR ANSWERS

1A. **(C)** Lines 23–26 paint a picture of what happens when the body hairs of a hungry tarantula are touched. The tarantula moves suddenly and fiercely, seizing its prey. This image supports the claim that hunger *intensifies* the tarantula's *response to being touched.*

2A. **(B)** The statement that "the young walk away, find convenient places in which to dig their burrows and spend the rest of their lives in solitude" clearly supports the claim that tarantulas are *reclusive* or solitary.

The following passage is taken from a classic study of tarantulas published in Scientific American.

    A fertilized female tarantula lays from 200 to 400 eggs at a time; thus it is possible for a single tarantula to produce several thousand young. She takes no care of them beyond weaving a cocoon of silk to enclose the eggs. After they hatch, the young walk
Line away, find convenient places in which to dig their burrows and spend the rest of their
(5) lives in solitude. Tarantulas feed mostly on insects and millipedes. Once their appetite is appeased, they digest the food for several days before eating again. Their sight is poor, being limited to sensing a change in the intensity of light and to the perception of moving objects. They apparently have little or no sense of hearing, for a hungry tarantula will pay no attention to a loudly chirping cricket placed in its cage unless the
(10) insect happens to touch one of its legs.
    But all spiders, and especially hairy ones, have an extremely delicate sense of touch. Laboratory experiments prove that tarantulas can distinguish three types of touch: pressure against the body wall, stroking of the body hair, and riffling of certain very fine hairs on the legs called trichobothria. Pressure against the body, by a finger
(15) or the end of a pencil, causes the tarantula to move off slowly for a short distance. The touch excites no defensive response unless the approach is from above, where the spider can see the motion, in which case it rises on its hind legs, lifts its front legs, opens its fangs and holds this threatening posture as long as the object continues to

move. When the motion stops, the spider drops back to the ground, remains quiet for
(20) a few seconds, and then moves slowly away.

The entire body of a tarantula, especially its legs, is thickly clothed with hair. Some
of it is short and woolly, some long and stiff. Touching this body hair produces one
of two distinct reactions. When the spider is hungry, it responds with an immediate
and swift attack. At the touch of a cricket's antennae the tarantula seizes the insect
(25) so swiftly that a motion picture taken at the rate of 64 frames per second shows only
the result and not the process of capture. But when the spider is not hungry, the
stimulation of its hairs merely causes it to shake the touched limb. An insect can walk
under its hairy belly unharmed.

The trichobothria, very fine hairs growing from disklike membranes on the legs,
(30) were once thought to be the spider's hearing organs, but we now know that they have
nothing to do with sound. They are sensitive only to air movement. A light breeze
makes them vibrate slowly without disturbing the common hair. When one blows
gently on the trichobothria, the tarantula reacts with a quick jerk of its four front legs.
If the front and hind legs are stimulated at the same time, the spider makes a sudden
(35) jump. This reaction is quite independent of the state of its appetite.

These three tactile responses—to pressure on the body wall, to moving of the
common hair, and to flexing of the trichobothria—are so different from one another
that there is no possibility of confusing them. They serve the tarantula adequately for
most of its needs and enable it to avoid most annoyances and dangers. But they fail
(40) the spider completely when it meets its deadly enemy, the digger wasp *Pepsis*.

ATTITUDE/TONE QUESTIONS

Attitude/tone questions often look like this:

Over the course of the passage, the narrator's attitude shifts from . . .
The author regards the idea that . . . with . . .
The author's attitude toward . . . is best described as one of . . .

TIP 6

When asked to figure out an author's attitude, mood, or tone, look for words that convey emotion, express values, or paint pictures. Note the author's choice of words. The presence of images and descriptive phrases can convey the author's attitude. So can the absence of images and of emotion-loaded vocabulary.

Attitude/Tone Questions Practice

1. The author's attitude toward tarantulas is best described as one of

   (A) skepticism.
   (B) indifference.
   (C) apprehension.
   (D) appreciation.

KNOW YOUR ATTITUDES

(If you don't know any of these words, look them up.)

😟	SAD	somber, melancholy, pessimistic, regretful
😊	HAPPY	optimistic, sanguine, amused, appreciative
😈	EVIL GRIN	mocking, sardonic, sarcastic, ironic, cynical, disdainful
😠	ANGRY	irate, outraged, incensed
😕	FOOLISH	baffled, puzzled, bemused, bewildered
😮	SURPRISED	astonished, astounded
😳	EMBARRASSED	discomfited, mortified
😐	WHATEVER	indifferent, ambivalent, equivocal

CHECK YOUR ANSWER

1. **(D)** Throughout the passage, the author presents a very balanced picture of the tarantula. The tarantula's poor vision and possibly nonexistent sense of hearing are balanced by its "extremely delicate sense of touch" and swiftness at capturing its prey. Its tactile responses "serve the tarantula adequately for most of its needs and enable it to avoid most annoyances and dangers." The author is objectively evaluating the tarantula. His attitude toward tarantulas is not *skeptical* (he is not doubtful or unconvinced by his observations of these spiders), nor is it *indifferent* (he is interested in tarantulas and in telling what he knows about them). He certainly does not view tarantulas with *apprehension* or fear. Instead, he values them, regarding them as fascinating creatures to study. His attitude is one of scholarly *appreciation*.

The following passage is excerpted from Chicano English in Context, *a 2003 sociolinguistic study by Carmen Fought.*

History of Mexican Immigration to Los Angeles

It needs to be strongly emphasized that as long as metropolitan Los Angeles (LA) has existed, there have been native speakers of dozens of different languages there; a large number of these are, of course, native speakers of Mexican Spanish.

Line California was a part of Mexico until 1848; before and since that time there has been

(5) a significant population movement between southern California and all parts of Mexico, particularly after World War II. At any given time, then, there are many recent

arrivals from Mexico, especially in the Latino neighborhoods, and still more who came to LA years ago. Many Californians of Latino ethnicity have lived in Southern California their whole lives, and so have their parents, and so on, for varying numbers (10) of generations. As a result, some Chicano English speakers come from families that have been in America as long as or longer than the Italian Americans on the Eastern seaboard or the Polish Americans in the Midwest.

The Latino Population of the United States

Latinos make up the fastest growing minority in the United States, and are now or soon will be the largest as well. Between 1999 and 2000, census figures show that the (15) US Latino population increased by more than 50 percent, from 22.4 million to 35.3 million. This represents 12.5 percent of the national population. The largest segment of this minority, people of Mexican origin, increased by 52.9 percent, from 13.5 million to 20.6 million. Because census questions relating to Latinos have changed over the decades, it is not easy to trace the long-term growth of this population in (20) detail. The Latino population also has a distinctive demographic profile; it is younger than other groups. Its median age in 2000 was 25.9 years, compared with 35.3 years for the entire population.

In recent decades, legal immigration from Mexico has been limited, averaging less than 100,000 per year during most of this period. There was a spike in the four years (25) from 1989 to 1992, however, with about 2.24 million immigrants arriving during that period. Illegal, undocumented immigration also occurs across the Mexican border. But numbers are naturally not known. Table 1.1 gives a breakdown of the Latino population by birthplace: native (US) born versus foreign born, based on available immigration and census enumerations.

Table 1.1. Latino population by birthplace

Year	Native Born (million)	Foreign Born (million) (%)	Total
1990	14.0	7.7 (35.8)	21.9
1980	10.4	4.2 (28.5)	14.6
1970	7.3	1.8 (19.9)	9.1
1940	1.4	0.4 (23.0)	1.8

(30) As can be seen from the figures in Table 1.1, native born Latinos have outnumbered immigrants historically by a large margin, a fact that would appear to have many social and linguistic implications. In 2000, 76.1 percent of Latinos in America (27.1 million) lived in seven states: California, Texas, New York, Florida, Illinois, Arizona and New Jersey. Just over half of them lived in either California (11.0 million, 31.1 (35) percent) or Texas (6.7 million, 18.9 percent) combined. Moreover, much of this population is concentrated in counties on or near the Mexican border, although there are also important enclaves in metropolitan areas elsewhere in the country.

Culver City

Culver City, the main location for my fieldwork, was developed by Harry H. Culver, a real-estate entrepreneur, between 1913 and its official founding in 1917, when it had
(40) a population of 550 and an area of 1.2 square miles. By 1940 its population had grown only to 8,976 (in an area of 3.2 square miles). Its population in 1980 was 38,189; this has changed little since then, reaching 38,816 in 2000. The demographic breakdown reported by the city is shown in Table 1.2.

The advantage of using Culver City, which is above the median of LA County in
(45) income, as a main location for fieldwork is that it includes Latino residents from a larger range of socio-economic categories, from very low income to middle class. This makes the area more representative in some ways of the Latino population as a whole.

Table 1.2. Population of Culver City, 2000

Ethnicity	%
White	52
Latino	23
Asian	13
African American	11
Other	1

The History of Chicano English

As noted above, Latinos in the USA are concentrated along the border with Mexico, in territory that was first explored and colonized by Spain, and was ceded to the
(50) USA by Mexico after the war of 1848. Thus, from the beginning of Anglo-American settlement in this region, Latino native speakers of English have been in close contact with native Spanish speakers, and with Anglo speakers of English as well.

Chicano English, therefore, is an important dialect to study because it is a contact dialect, one that emerged from the setting described above in which two languages,
(55) English and Spanish, were present. The early Mexican immigrants who arrived in Los Angeles learned English as a second language. Like adult learners of any language, they spoke a non-native variety that included phonological, syntactic and semantic patterns from their first language, in this case Spanish. But the children of these immigrants generally grew up using both Spanish and English (possibly in different
(60) settings or with different people). As the community began to stabilize, so did a new dialect of English.

LITERARY TECHNIQUE QUESTIONS

Literary technique questions often look like this:

Which of the following best describes the development of this passage?
In presenting the argument, the author does all of the following EXCEPT . . .
The statement in lines 00–00 is an example of . . .
In the passage, the author makes the central point primarily by . . .

Familiarize yourself with the common terms used to describe an author's technique. Even if you don't learn them all, once you've mastered a few, you'll be in a good position to eliminate incorrect answer choices and make an educated guess among the rest.

COMMON LITERARY TERMS

allusion	reference to something
analogy	comparison; similarity of functions or properties; likeness
anecdote	short account of an incident (often autobiographical)
antithesis	direct opposite
argumentative	presenting a logical argument
assertion	positive statement; declaration
cite	to refer to; to quote as an authority
euphemism	mild or indirect expression substituted for one felt offensive or harsh (Example: "Downsizing employees" is a euphemism for firing them.)
expository	concerned with explaining ideas, facts, etc.
generalization	simplification; general idea or principle
metaphor	an expression used to suggest a similarity between two things that are not literally equivalent (Example: "He's a tiger!")
narrative (adj.)	relating to telling a story
paradox	statement that contradicts itself (Example: "I always lie.")
rhetorical	relating to the effective use of language
thesis	the central idea in a piece of writing; a point to be defended

Literary Technique Power Practice

1. The author makes her point about her study's Culver City location through both

    (A) personal testimony and generalizations.
    (B) assertions and statistics.
    (C) comparisons and anecdotes.
    (D) observation and metaphor.

2. The final sentence of the sixth paragraph (lines 46–47) contains

    (A) an analogy.
    (B) a citation.
    (C) an allusion.
    (D) a qualification.

CHECK YOUR ANSWERS

1. **(B)** Throughout the passage the author makes significant use of both *assertions* (positive statements of fact or belief; claims) and *statistics* (numerical facts and data; the science of analyzing such data).

    Choice A is incorrect. Although the author makes some *generalizations* (general ideas or simplifications), she fails to include any *personal testimony* in her very impersonal account. Choice C is incorrect. Although the author makes some *comparisons* between native-born Latinos and immigrants, she tells no *anecdotes*. Choice D is incorrect. The author makes no use of *metaphor*; her writing is literal rather than figurative.

2. **(D)** Look closely at the sentence in question. "This makes the area more representative in some ways of the Latino population as a whole." What is the author's basic assertion? The inclusion of Latino residents from a larger range of socioeconomic categories makes Culver City more representative of the Latino population as a whole. Is this wholly true? Not entirely, for the author qualifies (adds a reservation to) her statement by saying it makes the area more representative *in some ways* of the Latino population as a whole. Thus, the sentence contains *a qualification* (modification or limitation).

The following passage is excerpted from Chicano English in Context, *a 2003 sociolinguistic study by Carmen Fought.*

History of Mexican Immigration to Los Angeles

It needs to be strongly emphasized that as long as metropolitan Los Angeles (LA) has existed, there have been native speakers of dozens of different languages there; a large number of these are, of course, native speakers of Mexican Spanish.
Line California was a part of Mexico until 1848; before and since that time there has been
(5) a significant population movement between southern California and all parts of Mexico, particularly after World War II. At any given time, then, there are many recent arrivals from Mexico, especially in the Latino neighborhoods, and still more who came to LA years ago. Many Californians of Latino ethnicity have lived in Southern California their whole lives, and so have their parents, and so on, for varying numbers
(10) of generations. As a result, some Chicano English speakers come from families that have been in America as long as or longer than the Italian Americans on the Eastern seaboard or the Polish Americans in the Midwest.

The Latino Population of the United States

Latinos make up the fastest growing minority in the United States, and are now or soon will be the largest as well. Between 1999 and 2000, census figures show that the
(15) US Latino population increased by more than 50 percent, from 22.4 million to 35.3 million. This represents 12.5 percent of the national population. The largest segment of this minority, people of Mexican origin, increased by 52.9 percent, from 13.5 million to 20.6 million. Because census questions relating to Latinos have changed

over the decades, it is not easy to trace the long-term growth of this population in
(20) detail. The Latino population also has a distinctive demographic profile; it is younger
than other groups. Its median age in 2000 was 25.9 years, compared with 35.3 years
for the entire population.

In recent decades, legal immigration from Mexico has been limited, averaging less
than 100,000 per year during most of this period. There was a spike in the four years
(25) from 1989 to 1992, however, with about 2.24 million immigrants arriving during that
period. Illegal, undocumented immigration also occurs across the Mexican border.
But numbers are naturally not known. Table 1.1 gives a breakdown of the Latino
population by birthplace: native (US) born versus foreign born, based on available
immigration and census enumerations.

Table 1.1. Latino population by birthplace

Year	Native Born (million)	Foreign Born (million) (%)	Total
1990	14.0	7.7 (35.8)	21.9
1980	10.4	4.2 (28.5)	14.6
1970	7.3	1.8 (19.9)	9.1
1940	1.4	0.4 (23.0)	1.8

(30)   As can be seen from the figures in Table 1.1, native born Latinos have outnumbered
immigrants historically by a large margin, a fact that would appear to have many
social and linguistic implications. In 2000, 76.1 percent of Latinos in America (27.1
million) lived in seven states: California, Texas, New York, Florida, Illinois, Arizona
and New Jersey. Just over half of them lived in either California (11.0 million, 31.1
(35) percent) or Texas (6.7 million, 18.9 percent) combined. Moreover, much of this
population is concentrated in counties on or near the Mexican border, although there
are also important enclaves in metropolitan areas elsewhere in the country.

Culver City

Culver City, the main location for my fieldwork, was developed by Harry H. Culver,
a real-estate entrepreneur, between 1913 and its official founding in 1917, when it had
(40) a population of 550 and an area of 1.2 square miles. By 1940 its population had grown
only to 8,976 (in an area of 3.2 square miles). Its population in 1980 was 38,189; this
has changed little since then, reaching 38,816 in 2000. The demographic breakdown
reported by the city is shown in Table 1.2.

The advantage of using Culver City, which is above the median of LA County in
(45) income, as a main location for fieldwork is that it includes Latino residents from a
larger range of socio-economic categories, from very low income to middle class. This
makes the area more representative in some ways of the Latino population as a whole.

Table 1.2. Population of Culver City, 2000

Ethnicity	%
White	52
Latino	23
Asian	13
African American	11
Other	1

The History of Chicano English

As noted above, Latinos in the USA are concentrated along the border with Mexico, in territory that was first explored and colonized by Spain, and was ceded to the
(50) USA by Mexico after the war of 1848. Thus, from the beginning of Anglo-American settlement in this region, Latino native speakers of English have been in close contact with native Spanish speakers, and with Anglo speakers of English as well.

Chicano English, therefore, is an important dialect to study because it is a contact dialect, one that emerged from the setting described above in which two languages,
(55) English and Spanish, were present. The early Mexican immigrants who arrived in Los Angeles learned English as a second language. Like adult learners of any language, they spoke a non-native variety that included phonological, syntactic and semantic patterns from their first language, in this case Spanish. But the children of these immigrants generally grew up using both Spanish and English (possibly in different
(60) settings or with different people). As the community began to stabilize, so did a new dialect of English.

GRAPHICS QUESTIONS

Graphics questions often begin like this:

Based on the information in Figure 1 . . .

Figure 1 provides support for which point made in the passage?

Which choice is best supported by the data in . . .

Taken together, the two figures suggest that . . .

TIP 8

When dealing with graph interpretation questions, use only the evidence in the figures and the passage. Graphic questions work both ways. Just as information in the graph or table throws light on what you read in the passage, so too information from the passage throws light on what you see in the graph or table supplementing what you read.

Graphics Power Practice

1. The large increase in the number of foreign-born Latinos in 1990 shown in Table 1.1 can most likely be attributed to

   (A) statistical error.
   (B) illegal, undocumented immigration.
   (C) the high birth rate among native-born Latinos.
   (D) the 1989–1992 spike in immigration.

CHECK YOUR ANSWER

1. **(D)** Between 1981 and 1990, the foreign born Latino population jumped from 4.2 million to 7.8 million, an increase of 3.6 million. The beginning of the paragraph states that, "In recent decades, legal immigration from Mexico has been limited, averaging less than 100,000 per year during most of this period." If this average had held true for the entire 1981–1990 decade, then the foreign-born Latino population should have increased from 4.2 million to about 5.2 million. However, between 1989 and 1992, 2.24 million foreign-born Latino immigrants gained legal admission to the United States, an average of roughly half a million per year. This strongly suggests that the large increase in the number of foreign-born Latinos in 1990 shown in Table 1.1 can most likely be attributed to the 1989–1992 spike in immigration.

   Choice A is incorrect. Nothing in the passage suggests that any statistical error took place in 1990. Choice B is incorrect. Illegal immigrants are not included in the figures shown in Table 1.1. Choice C is incorrect. The question asks about an increase in the number of foreign-born Latinos. This would be unaffected by a high birth rate among native-born Latinos.

Try these questions based on **short passages** in order to familiarize yourself with some common question types.

> **Directions:** Each of the passages below precedes one or two questions based on its content. Answer the questions following each passage on the basis of what is stated or implied in that passage.

Main Idea Questions

Question 1 is based on the following passage.

One of the world's most celebrated crusaders for social justice and peace is South Africa's Archbishop Desmond Tutu. Despite his prominence, however, Archbishop Tutu has always made time for his people. On the day in 1984 that he was named
Line winner of the Nobel Peace Prize, reporters and photographers mobbed the seminary
(5) where he was staying. A press conference was hastily set up. Just as it was to begin, the archbishop's student assistant entered the courtyard, returning from a family funeral. Leaving the microphones and cameras behind, the archbishop went to comfort her. The world press could wait; her grief could not.

1. The anecdote about Archbishop Tutu serves primarily to demonstrate his

    (A) celebrity.
    (B) sorrow.
    (C) compassion.
    (D) pacifism.

Question 2 is based on the following passage.

The following passage was written by a twentieth-century naturalist.

We were about a quarter mile away when quiet swept over the colony. A thousand or more heads periscoped. Two thousand eyes glared. Save for our wading, the world's business had stopped. A thousand avian personalities were concentrated
Line on us, and the psychological force of this was terrific. Contingents of home-coming
(5) feeders, suddenly aware of four strange specks moving across the lake, would bank violently and speed away. Then the chain reaction began. Every throat in that rookery let go with a concatenation of wild, raspy, terrorized trumpet bursts. With all wings now fully spread and churning, and quadrupling the color mass, the birds began to move as one, and the sky was filled with the sound of Judgment Day.

2. The author's primary purpose in this passage is to

    (A) explain a natural catastrophe.
    (B) criticize an expedition.
    (C) evoke an experience.
    (D) document an experiment.

Question 3 is based on the following passage.

How is a newborn star formed? For the answer to this question, we must look to the familiar physical concept of gravitational instability. It is a simple concept, long-known to scientists, having been first recognized by Isaac Newton in the late 1600s.

Line
(5) Let us envision a cloud of interstellar atoms and molecules, slightly admixed with dust. This cloud of interstellar gas is static and uniform. Suddenly, something occurs to disturb the gas, causing one small area within it to condense. As this small area increases in density, becoming slightly denser than the gas around it, its gravitational field likewise increases somewhat in strength. More matter now is attracted to the area, and its gravity becomes even stronger; as a result, it starts to contract, in
(10) process increasing in density even more. This in turn further increases its gravity, so that it accumulates still more matter and contracts further still. And so the process continues, until finally the small area of gas gives birth to a gravitationally bound object, a newborn star.

3. The primary purpose of the passage is to

   (A) illustrate a static condition.
   (B) support a theory considered obsolete.
   (C) demonstrate the evolution of the meaning of a term.
   (D) depict the successive stages of a phenomenon.

Question 4 is based on the following passage.

"The very first requirement in a hospital is that it should do the sick no harm." So wrote Florence Nightingale, nursing pioneer. Most people picture Nightingale as the brave "Lady with the Lamp" who journeyed to the Crimea to nurse British

Line soldiers wounded in the war. It was after the war, however, that Nightingale came
(5) into her own as the world's most renowned authority on hospital reform. In *Notes on Hospitals*, Nightingale addressed every aspect of hospital construction and management, from replacing wooden bedsteads with iron ones, to minimizing infection by dividing hospitals into airy, self-contained pavilions.

4. Which statement best expresses the author's central point about Florence Nightingale?

   (A) She deserved great praise for her work with wounded soldiers in the Crimea.
   (B) Her greatest accomplishments were in improving hospital planning and administration.
   (C) Her change of focus to hospital administration represented a loss to the nursing profession.
   (D) She was concerned about the effects of infection on mortality rates.

Question 5 is based on the following passage.

Although commonly held up as a cornerstone of American democracy, the Mayflower Compact had little impact on the growth of freedom in America. In fact, the compact limited its signers' liberty. That was its intent. Of the Mayflower's 100
Line emigrants, fewer than half were Pilgrims. The rest were "strangers," non-Pilgrims
(5) who, finding themselves hundreds of miles north of their planned destination in Virginia, believed themselves outside the bounds of governmental authority. Rather than respect the rules of the Pilgrims, these strangers wanted to go their own way. By signing the compact, both Pilgrims and non-Pilgrims agreed to accept whatever form of government was established after landing.

5. The primary purpose of the passage is to

   (A) demand a reevaluation of a political conflict.
   (B) propose an approach to analyzing historical documents.
   (C) describe the stages of a natural phenomenon.
   (D) correct a misapprehension about a historical event.

Question 6 is based on the following passage.

Critics call Edgar Allan Poe the father of detective fiction. If that is so, whom should we call detective fiction's mother? Agatha Christie, say some mystery readers. Dorothy Sayers, say others. Well before Christie and Sayers wrote their classic British
Line whodunits, however, an American named Anna Katharine Green wrote a best-seller
(5) about the murder of a Fifth Avenue millionaire. *The Leavenworth Case,* which sold over 150,000 copies, marked the initial appearance of Inspector Ebenezer Gryce, the first serial detective in genre history. Today, with two novels back in print after nearly a century, Gryce's long-neglected creator is finally beginning to receive the recognition she deserves.

6. The primary purpose of the passage is to

   (A) contrast the careers of Poe and Green.
   (B) introduce the concept of the serial detective.
   (C) dismiss the contributions of British mystery writers.
   (D) reclaim a forgotten literary pioneer.

Question 7 is based on the following passage.

What factors led to the decline of the armored knight? Although some scholars
have hypothesized that developing technology, in particular the invention of
firearms, rendered knights in armor obsolete, this suggestion seems unlikely.
Line On the contrary, throughout the Middle Ages and well into the fifteenth century,
(5) technological developments contributed to the effectiveness of the chivalry, enabling
them to consolidate their positions both politically and economically. Rather than
technological obsolescence spelling the doom of these mounted warriors, it seems
more likely that changes in basic army structure—the development of the modern
professional army, based on the Swiss model—and the high costs of outfitting
(10) themselves with steeds and armor led many knights to abandon their careers as
professional fighting men.

7. Which choice best reflects the overall sequence of events in the passage?

   (A) An explanation for a state of affairs is proposed but then rejected in favor of an
       alternative explanation.
   (B) An observation of a natural phenomenon is made, and a recent reinterpretation of
       that phenomenon is offered.
   (C) An abstract theory is formulated, and a practical application of that theory is
       described.
   (D) A theoretical question is raised, after which several areas in need of investigation
       are suggested.

Question 8 is based on the following passage.

The morning after the battle of Fredericksburg, the ground before the stone wall
was covered with wounded, dead, and dying Northerners. Hours passed by as soldiers
from both sides listened to the cries for water and pleas for help. Finally, Richard
Line Kirkland, a young Confederate sergeant, could bear it no more. Receiving permission
(5) from his general to help the wounded, he ventured over the wall. Under Northern
fire, he reached the nearest sufferer and gave him water. As soon as they understood
his intent, the enemy ceased fire, and for an hour and a half Kirkland tended the
wounded unharmed.

8. The primary purpose of the passage is to

   (A) establish that Kirkland sought his commander's approval before taking action.
   (B) indicate the young sergeant's eagerness to be seen as a hero.
   (C) dramatize the degree of suffering experienced during the Civil War.
   (D) depict an instance of heroism under fire.

Question 9 is based on the following passage.

To students today, continental drift is a commonplace. They cheerfully talk about supercontinents that break apart or about shifts in the earth's crust as if everyone has always known that this solid earth beneath our feet is seated on large, rigid plates
Line that float on a soft, partly molten layer of the earth's mantle. Not so. It was not quite
(5) a century ago that Alfred Wegener first proposed the theory that the components making up the supercontinent Pangaea had slowly moved thousands of miles apart over lengthy periods of geologic time.

9. The primary purpose of the passage is to

(A) explain the significance of a theory.
(B) contrast two opposing hypotheses.
(C) challenge a misconception.
(D) introduce a technical term.

Question 10 is based on the following passage.

In the 1880s, when the commercial theater had ceased to be regarded as a fit medium for serious writers, British intellectuals came to champion the plays of an obscure Norwegian dramatist. Hungry for a theater that spoke to their intellects,
Line they wholeheartedly embraced the social realist dramas of Henrik Ibsen. Eleanor
(5) Marx, daughter of Karl Marx, went so far as to teach herself Norwegian in order to translate Ibsen's *A Doll's House*, which she presented in an amateur performance in a Bloomsbury drawing room.

10. The passage serves mainly to

(A) rescue the plays of Henrik Ibsen from theatrical obscurity.
(B) explain the popularity of Ibsen's plays in Victorian England.
(C) deplore the lack of serious drama on the commercial stage.
(D) demonstrate the feasibility of teaching oneself Norwegian.

Vocabulary-in-Context Questions

Question 1 is based on the following passage.

One of the world's most celebrated crusaders for social justice and peace is South
Africa's Archbishop Desmond Tutu. Despite his prominence, however, Archbishop
Tutu has always made time for his people. On the day in 1984 that he was named
Line winner of the Nobel Peace Prize, reporters and photographers mobbed the seminary
(5) where he was staying. A press conference was hastily set up. Just as it was to begin, the
archbishop's student assistant entered the courtyard, returning from a family funeral.
Leaving the microphones and cameras behind, the archbishop went to comfort her.
The world press could wait; her grief could not.

1. In line 2, "prominence" most nearly means

   (A) projection.
   (B) protuberance.
   (C) conspicuousness.
   (D) renown.

Questions 2 and 3 are based on the following passage.

Although most of the world's active volcanoes are located along the edges of the
great shifting plates that make up Earth's surface, there are more than 100 isolated
areas of volcanic activity far from the nearest plate boundary. Geologists call these
Line volcanic areas hot spots. Lying deep in the interior of a plate, hot spots or intra-plate
(5) volcanoes are sources of magma, the red-hot, molten material within the earth's crust.
These intraplate volcanoes often form volcanic chains, trails of extinct volcanoes.
Such volcanic chains serve as landmarks signaling the slow but relentless passage of
the plates.

2. In line 6, "form" most nearly means

   (A) gradually appear.
   (B) influence.
   (C) make up.
   (D) enter into.

3. In line 7, "passage" most nearly means

   (A) ticket.
   (B) movement.
   (C) duct.
   (D) corridor.

Questions 4 and 5 are based on the following passage.

In this excerpt from Great Expectations, *the narrator, young Pip, has just had a frightening encounter in a graveyard with an escaped convict.*

The marshes were just a long black horizontal line then, as I stopped to look after him; and the river was just another horizontal line, not nearly so broad, nor yet so black; and the sky was just a row of long angry red lines and dense black lines
Line intermixed. On the edge of the river I could faintly make out the only two black things
(5) that seemed to be standing upright; one of these was the beacon by which the sailors steered,—like an unhooped cask upon a pole,—an ugly thing when you were near it; the other, a gibbet[1], with some chains hanging to it which had once held a pirate. The man was limping on towards this latter, as if he were the pirate come to life, and come down, and going back to hook himself up again. It gave me a terrible turn when
(10) I thought so; and as I saw the cattle lifting their heads to gaze after him, I wondered whether they thought so too. But now I was frightened again, and ran home without stopping

4. In line 5, "upright" most nearly means

   (A) honorably.
   (B) vertically.
   (C) correctly.
   (D) solidly.

5. In line 9, "turn" most nearly means

   (A) chance to perform.
   (B) change of direction.
   (C) bend.
   (D) shock.

Question 6 is based on the following passage.

What factors led to the decline of the armored knight? Although some scholars have hypothesized that developing technology, in particular the invention of firearms, rendered knights in armor obsolete, this suggestion seems unlikely.
Line On the contrary, throughout the Middle Ages and well into the fifteenth century,
(5) technological developments contributed to the effectiveness of the chivalry, enabling them to consolidate their positions both politically and economically. Rather than technological obsolescence spelling the doom of these mounted warriors, it seems more likely that changes in basic army structure—the development of the modern professional army, based on the Swiss model—and the high costs of outfitting
(10) themselves with steeds and armor led many knights to abandon their careers as professional fighting men.

---

[1]gallows

6. In line 6, "positions" most nearly means

(A) status.
(B) opinions.
(C) location.
(D) postures.

Question 7 is based on the following passage.

The following passage was written by a twentieth-century naturalist.

We were about a quarter mile away when quiet swept over the colony. A thousand or more heads periscoped. Two thousand eyes glared. Save for our wading, the world's business had stopped. A thousand avian personalities were concentrated
Line on us, and the psychological force of this was terrific. Contingents of home-coming
(5) feeders, suddenly aware of four strange specks moving across the lake, would bank violently and speed away. Then the chain reaction began. Every throat in that rookery let go with a concatenation of wild, raspy, terrorized trumpet bursts. With all wings now fully spread and churning, and quadrupling the color mass, the birds began to move as one, and the sky was filled with the sound of Judgment Day.

7. As used in line 5, "bank" most nearly means

(A) heap up.
(B) tilt sideways.
(C) deposit securely.
(D) count on.

Question 8 is based on the following passage.

How is a newborn star formed? For the answer to this question, we must look to the familiar physical concept of gravitational instability. It is a simple concept, long-known to scientists, having been first recognized by Isaac Newton in the late 1600's.
Line Let us envision a cloud of interstellar atoms and molecules, slightly admixed with
(5) dust. This cloud of interstellar gas is static and uniform. Suddenly, something occurs to disturb the gas, causing one small area within it to condense. As this small area increases in density, becoming slightly denser than the gas around it, its gravitational field likewise increases somewhat in strength. More matter now is attracted to the area, and its gravity becomes even stronger; as a result, it starts to contract, in
(10) process increasing in density even more. This in turn further increases its gravity, so that it accumulates still more matter and contracts further still. And so the process continues, until finally the small area of gas gives birth to a gravitationally bound object, a newborn star.

8. As used in line 6, "disturb" most nearly means

(A) worry.
(B) perplex.
(C) unsettle.
(D) harass.

Question 9 is based on the following passage.

"The very first requirement in a hospital is that it should do the sick no harm."
So wrote Florence Nightingale, nursing pioneer. Most people picture Nightingale
as the brave "Lady with the Lamp" who journeyed to the Crimea to nurse British
Line soldiers wounded in the war. It was after the war, however, that Nightingale came
(5) into her own as the world's most renowned authority on hospital reform. In *Notes
on Hospitals*, Nightingale addressed every aspect of hospital construction and
management, from replacing wooden bedsteads with iron ones, to minimizing
infection by dividing hospitals into airy, self-contained pavilions.

9. As used in line 6, "addressed" most nearly means

   (A) tackled.
   (B) lectured.
   (C) inscribed.
   (D) called.

Question 10 is based on the following passage.

Although commonly held up as a cornerstone of American democracy, the
Mayflower Compact had little impact on the growth of freedom in America. In fact,
the compact limited its signers' liberty. That was its intent. Of the Mayflower's 100
Line emigrants, fewer than half were Pilgrims. The rest were "strangers," non-Pilgrims
(5) who, finding themselves hundreds of miles north of their planned destination in
Virginia, believed themselves outside the bounds of governmental authority. Rather
than respect the rules of the Pilgrims, these strangers wanted to go their own way. By
signing the compact, both Pilgrims and non-Pilgrims agreed to accept whatever form
of government was established after landing.

10. As used in line 1, "held up" most nearly means

   (A) delayed.
   (B) cited.
   (C) supported.
   (D) waylaid.

Specific Detail Questions

Question 1 is based on the following passage.

Although most of the world's active volcanoes are located along the edges of the great shifting plates that make up Earth's surface, there are more than 100 isolated areas of volcanic activity far from the nearest plate boundary. Geologists call these
Line volcanic areas hot spots. Lying deep in the interior of a plate, hot spots or intra-plate
(5) volcanoes are sources of magma, the red-hot, molten material within the earth's crust. These intra-plate volcanoes often form volcanic chains, trails of extinct volcanoes. Such volcanic chains serve as landmarks signaling the slow but relentless passage of the plates.

1. According to the passage, hot spots differ from other areas of volcanic activity in their

   (A) temperature.
   (B) location.
   (C) composition.
   (D) volatility.

Question 2 is based on the following passage.

What factors led to the decline of the armored knight? Although some scholars have hypothesized that developing technology, in particular the invention of firearms, rendered knights in armor obsolete, this suggestion seems unlikely. On the contrary,
Line throughout the Middle Ages and well into the fifteenth century, technological
(5) developments contributed to the effectiveness of the chivalry, enabling them to consolidate their positions both politically and economically. Rather than technological obsolescence spelling the doom of these mounted warriors, it seems more likely that changes in basic army structure—the development of the modern professional army, based on the Swiss model—and the high costs of outfitting themselves with steeds and
(10) armor led many knights to abandon their careers as professional fighting men.

2. The passage makes the point that the institution of knighthood

   (A) glorified professional fighting men.
   (B) underwent significant change over time.
   (C) reached its high point in the fifteenth century.
   (D) died out in response to technological progress.

Question 3 is based on the following passage.

To students today, continental drift is a commonplace. They cheerfully talk about supercontinents that break apart or about shifts in the earth's crust as if everyone has always known that this solid earth beneath our feet is seated on large, rigid plates
Line that float on a soft, partly molten layer of the earth's mantle. Not so. It was not quite
(5) a century ago that Alfred Wegener first proposed the theory that the components making up the supercontinent Pangaea had slowly moved thousands of miles apart over lengthy periods of geologic time.

3. The author makes which point about the theory of continental drift?

   (A) It has taken a very long time to gain acceptance among young people.
   (B) It compares favorably with earlier theories about the formation of the continents.
   (C) It has been oversimplified since it was first proposed.
   (D) It is of relatively recent origin.

Question 4 is based on the following passage.

The following passage was written by a twentieth-century naturalist.

We were about a quarter mile away when quiet swept over the colony. A thousand or more heads periscoped. Two thousand eyes glared. Save for our wading, the world's business had stopped. A thousand avian personalities were concentrated
Line on us, and the psychological force of this was terrific. Contingents of home-coming
(5) feeders, suddenly aware of four strange specks moving across the lake, would bank violently and speed away. Then the chain reaction began. Every throat in that rookery let go with a concatenation of wild, raspy, terrorized trumpet bursts. With all wings now fully spread and churning, and quadrupling the color mass, the birds began to move as one, and the sky was filled with the sound of Judgment Day.

4. The "four strange specks" (line 5) are

   (A) wild birds.
   (B) animal predators.
   (C) intruding humans.
   (D) unusual cloud formations.

Question 5 is based on the following passage.

Many nonhuman primates live together in an organized troop or social group that includes members of all ages and both sexes. Such troops always move compactly together in a stable social unit. A typical primate troop characteristically exhibits
Line a ranking hierarchy among the males in the troop. This ranking hierarchy serves
(5) to alleviate conflict within the troop. The highest-ranking male or males defend, control, and lead the troop; the strong social bond among members and their safety is maintained.

5. The author of the passage indicates which of the following about the hierarchic structure within primate troops?

   (A) It lacks the flexibility to adapt to change.
   (B) It is a source of clashes within the troop.
   (C) It is uniquely a characteristic of nonhuman primates.
   (D) It fulfills a positive function for the social group.

Inference Questions

Question 1 is based on the following passage.

Luckily, I am writing a memoir and not a work of fiction, and therefore I do not have to account for my grandmother's unpleasing character and look for the Oedipal fixation or traumatic experience which would give her that clinical authenticity that is
Line nowadays so desirable in portraiture. I do not know how my grandmother got the way
(5) she was; I assume, from family photographs and the inflexibility of her habits, that she was always the same, and it seems as idle to inquire into her childhood as to ask what was ailing Iago or to look for the error in toilet-training that was responsible for Lady Macbeth. My grandmother's sexual history, bristling with infant mortality in the usual style of her period, was robust and decisive: three tall, handsome sons grew up,
(10) and one attentive daughter. Her husband treated her kindly. She had money, many grandchildren, and religion to sustain her. White hair, glasses, soft skin, wrinkles, needlework—all the paraphernalia of motherliness were hers; yet it was a cold, grudging, disputatious old woman who sat all day in her sunroom making tapestries from a pattern, scanning religious periodicals, and setting her iron jaw against any
(15) infractions of her ways.

1. Lines 1–4 suggest that the narrator views character portrayals in modern novels with

   (A) approbation.
   (B) outrage.
   (C) wistfulness.
   (D) disdain.

Question 2 is based on the following passage.

Little vegetation grows in the vast South African tableland known as the Nama Karroo. The open plateau, home to springboks and other members of the antelope family, seems a rocky, inhospitable place. Yet the springboks find sustenance,
Line searching among the rocks and pebbles, and coming up with mouthfuls of "stones"
(5) which they munch contentedly. These stones are in actuality plants, members of the genus Lithops, some of the strangest succulents in the world. Nature has camouflaged these stone plants so well that even trained botanists have trouble telling them apart from the rocks surrounding them.

2. The context suggests that a succulent (line 6) is most likely

   (A) an unusual rock form.
   (B) a method of camouflage.
   (C) a type of plant.
   (D) a species of antelope.

Question 3 is based on the following passage.

Outside in the neighborhoods, learning our way around the streets, we played among the enormous stone monuments of the millionaires—both those tireless Pittsburgh founders of the heavy industries from which the nation's wealth derived
Line (they told us in school) and the industrialists' couldn't-lose bankers and backers, all of
(5) whom began as canny boys, the stories of whose rises to riches adults still considered inspirational to children.

3. The passage suggests that the author regards the inspirational tales of the lives of the industrialists with a sense of

   (A) reverence.
   (B) irony.
   (C) envy.
   (D) nostalgia.

Question 4 is based on the following passage.

How is a newborn star formed? For the answer to this question, we must look to the familiar physical concept of gravitational instability. It is a simple concept, long-known to scientists, having been first recognized by Isaac Newton in the late 1600s.
Line   Let us envision a cloud of interstellar atoms and molecules, slightly admixed with
(5) dust. This cloud of interstellar gas is static and uniform. Suddenly, something occurs to disturb the gas, causing one small area within it to condense. As this small area increases in density, becoming slightly denser than the gas around it, its gravitational field likewise increases somewhat in strength. More matter now is attracted to the area, and its gravity becomes even stronger; as a result, it starts to contract, in
(10) process increasing in density even more. This in turn further increases its gravity, so that it accumulates still more matter and contracts further still. And so the process continues, until finally the small area of gas gives birth to a gravitationally bound object, a newborn star.

4. It can be inferred from the passage that the author views the information contained within it as

   (A) controversial, yet irrefutable.
   (B) commonly accepted and accurate.
   (C) speculative and untenable.
   (D) contradictory, yet compelling.

Question 5 is based on the following passage.

The following passage was written by a twentieth-century naturalist.

We were about a quarter mile away when quiet swept over the colony. A thousand
or more heads periscoped. Two thousand eyes glared. Save for our wading, the
world's business had stopped. A thousand avian personalities were concentrated
Line on us, and the psychological force of this was terrific. Contingents of home-coming
(5) feeders, suddenly aware of four strange specks moving across the lake, would bank
violently and speed away. Then the chain reaction began. Every throat in that rookery
let go with a concatenation of wild, raspy, terrorized trumpet bursts. With all wings
now fully spread and churning, and quadrupling the color mass, the birds began to
move as one, and the sky was filled with the sound of Judgment Day.

5. The visitors' response to the episode described above was most likely one of

(A) impatience.
(B) outrage.
(C) terror.
(D) awe.

Literary Technique and Style Questions

Question 1 is based on the following passage.

Although most of the world's active volcanoes are located along the edges of the
great shifting plates that make up Earth's surface, there are more than 100 isolated
areas of volcanic activity far from the nearest plate boundary. Geologists call these
Line volcanic areas hot spots. Lying deep in the interior of a plate, hot spots or intra-plate
(5) volcanoes are sources of magma, the red-hot, molten material within the earth's crust.
These intra-plate volcanoes often form volcanic chains, trails of extinct volcanoes.
Such volcanic chains serve as landmarks signaling the slow but relentless passage of
the plates.

1. The term "hot spot" is being used in the passage

(A) technically.
(B) colloquially.
(C) ambiguously.
(D) ironically.

Question 2 is based on the following passage.

How is a newborn star formed? For the answer to this question, we must look to the familiar physical concept of gravitational instability. It is a simple concept, long-known to scientists, having been first recognized by Isaac Newton in the late 1600s.

Line   Let us envision a cloud of interstellar atoms and molecules, slightly admixed with
(5) dust. This cloud of interstellar gas is static and uniform. Suddenly, something occurs to disturb the gas, causing one small area within it to condense. As this small area increases in density, becoming slightly denser than the gas around it, its gravitational field likewise increases somewhat in strength. More matter now is attracted to the area, and its gravity becomes even stronger; as a result, it starts to contract, in
(10) process increasing in density even more. This in turn further increases its gravity, so that it accumulates still more matter and contracts further still. And so the process continues, until finally the small area of gas gives birth to a gravitationally bound object, a newborn star.

2. Throughout the passage, the author's manner of presentation can best be described as

    (A) argumentative.
    (B) anecdotal.
    (C) expository.
    (D) hyperbolic.

Question 3 is based on the following passage.

Little vegetation grows in the vast South African tableland known as the Nama Karroo. The open plateau, home to springboks and other members of the antelope family, seems a rocky, inhospitable place. Yet the springboks find sustenance,
Line searching among the rocks and pebbles, and coming up with mouthfuls of "stones"
(5) which they munch contentedly. These stones are in actuality plants, members of the genus Lithops, some of the strangest succulents in the world. Nature has camouflaged these stone plants so well that even trained botanists have trouble telling them apart from the rocks surrounding them.

3. The quotation marks around the word "stones" (line 4) primarily serve to emphasize that the plants

    (A) are extraordinarily hard.
    (B) are not literally stones.
    (C) are inedible by humans.
    (D) can survive in an arid environment.

Question 4 is based on the following passage.

Recently a children's book about writing poetry came out. It was called *Poetry Matters*. In essence, that's the question poets face today. Does poetry matter? As Billy Collins wrote, "One of the ridiculous aspects of being a poet is the huge gulf between
Line how seriously we take ourselves and how generally we are ignored by everybody else."
(5) We think that what we write matters, but for the most part, in America no one cares. It may be different elsewhere on the globe—Osip Mandelstam once maintained that only in Russia was poetry respected, because there it got people killed. Here, we don't get killed, but we're dying anyway.

4. The assertion in the final sentence that "we're dying anyway" (line 8) is an example of

    (A) an apology.
    (B) a metaphor.
    (C) a euphemism.
    (D) an understatement.

Question 5 is based on the following passage.

Echoing leaders in the field such as Noam Chomsky, many linguists argue that the capacity for language is a uniquely human property. They contend that chimpanzees and related primates are incapable of using language because their brains lack the
Line human brain structures that make language. Other researchers, however, disagree,
(5) citing experiments in which apes have been taught to use symbolic communication systems, such as American Sign Language. In one study, for example, Georgia State professor E. Sue Savage-Rambaugh has worked with a "keyboard" consisting of 400 symbols to communicate with bonobos (also known as pygmy chimpanzees).

5. The quotation marks around the word "keyboard" (line 7) primarily serve to

    (A) indicate the word "keyboard" is being used in an unusual sense.
    (B) demonstrate the mechanical nature of human-chimpanzee communication.
    (C) illustrate the difficulty of teaching nonhuman primates to communicate.
    (D) convey the complexity of the bonobos' brain structure.

Paired Passage Questions

Questions 1–5 are based on the following passages.

Passage 1
True scientists are no strangers to hard work. To prove a hypothesis or confirm a discovery, they conduct test after test, examining their subject from every possible angle that might cast fresh light upon it. They never jump to conclusions, but inch by
Line methodical inch creep up upon them, slowly, unerringly, surely. This is the essence
(5) of modern scientific method, the method championed by Boyle and Hooke and other seventeenth-century experimental scientists.

Passage 2

According to the naturalist Donald Culross Peattie, many scientists reject the idea of scientific intuition. In Peattie's words, they "rely utterly on the celebrated inductive method of reasoning: the facts are to be exposed, and we have to conclude from them (10) only what we must." Peattie acknowledges the soundness of this rule for ordinary researchers (minds "that can do no better"), but nevertheless derides this step-by-step, fact-by-fact method as plodding. He points to Einstein, who, working in a patent office, suddenly, out of the blue, had his famous insight $e = mc^2$. "First he dreamed it; then he knew it; then, rather for others' sake, he proved it." This is how the really great (15) advances in science are made.

1. The author of Passage 1 characterizes true scientists as all of the following EXCEPT

   (A) analytic.
   (B) diligent.
   (C) accurate.
   (D) inspired.

2. As used in line 2, "conduct" most nearly means

   (A) carry out.
   (B) guide around.
   (C) transmit.
   (D) behave.

3. In Passage 1, the description of the way scientists work primarily serves to

   (A) emphasize the systematic and disciplined nature of the scientific method.
   (B) demonstrate the need to perform these routine tasks more efficiently.
   (C) encourage scientists to explore alternative methods to attain their goals.
   (D) raise questions about the validity of experiments performed outside a laboratory setting.

4. Unlike the author of Passage 1, the author of Passage 2 makes use of

   (A) scientific data.
   (B) direct citation.
   (C) historical references.
   (D) first person narration.

5. The author of Passage 1 would most likely respond to the first three sentences of Passage 2 (lines 7–12) by arguing that Peattie

   (A) refuses to acknowledge any contributions to scientific knowledge by ordinary researchers.
   (B) minimizes the value of intuition to the advancement of science.
   (C) fails to appreciate the virtues of the inductive method sufficiently.
   (D) misunderstands the way in which scientists apply the inductive method.

ANSWER KEY

Main Idea Questions

1. **C**	4. **B**	7. **A**	10. **B**
2. **C**	5. **D**	8. **D**	
3. **D**	6. **D**	9. **C**	

Vocabulary-in-Context Questions

1. **D**	4. **B**	7. **B**	10. **B**
2. **C**	5. **D**	8. **C**	
3. **B**	6. **A**	9. **A**	

Specific Detail Questions

1. **B**	3. **D**	5. **D**
2. **B**	4. **C**	

Inference Questions

1. **D**	3. **B**	5. **D**
2. **C**	4. **B**	

Literary Technique and Style Questions

1. **A**	3. **B**	5. **A**
2. **C**	4. **B**	

Paired Passage Questions

1. **D**	3. **A**	5. **C**
2. **A**	4. **B**	

ANSWERS EXPLAINED

Main Idea Questions

1. **(C)** The passage depicts Archbishop Tutu's *compassion*, his feeling for someone in need that leads him to ignore the persistent demands of the press. Choice B is incorrect: it is the distressed student assistant who feels grief or sorrow, not the archbishop.

2. **(C)** The author is *evoking* (imaginatively creating; producing a vivid impression of) *an experience* that a group of naturalists had when they visited a rookery (colony or breeding ground of wild birds).

    If you do not know the meaning of *evoke*, you can figure it out from its word parts. The prefix *e-* or *ex-* commonly means "out of." The root *voc* or *voke* means "call." To evoke an experience is to call it up or summon it so that others can share it.

3. **(D)** The entire second paragraph serves to describe or *depict the successive stages of* the formation of a gravitationally bound object. (Successive stages are steps that follow in order, one after another.) Key words that let you know that the passage is depicting the

successive stages of a phenomenon are "now," "even more," "further," "further still," and "finally."

4. **(B)** The passage contrasts the image of Nightingale, the night nurse carrying a lamp as she walked the wards, with the image of Nightingale, the hospital authority. What is more, it states that Nightingale "came into her own as the world's most renowned authority on hospital reform." To come into one's own is to achieve one's potential, to become fulfilled. According to the author, Nightingale did not reach her full potential until she became a recognized authority on hospital reform. To the author, therefore, *her greatest achievements were in improving hospital planning and administration.*

5. **(D)** The opening sentence states *a misapprehension* or misunderstanding *about a historical event.* Most people regard the Mayflower Compact "as a cornerstone of American democracy." This is a misunderstanding. The purpose of the passage is to *correct* that misunderstanding.

6. **(D)** Although the passage opens by mentioning Christie and Sayers as possible "mothers" of the genre detective fiction, it soon shifts its focus to American mystery writer Anna Katharine Green, who originated some of the genre's now familiar conventions. The passage concludes with the statement that today this long-neglected author "is finally beginning to receive the recognition she deserves." Clearly the passage's purpose is to *reclaim* (rescue) *a forgotten literary pioneer* from oblivion.

7. **(A)** What is this passage talking about? It is talking about possible causes of the decline and eventual disappearance of the armored knight. What factors caused this situation to come into being? The author first brings up an explanation that some scholars think possible: the invention of firearms wiped out knights in armor. Then the author shoots down that theory and proposes a different explanation in its place. In other words, "*(a)n explanation for a state of affairs is proposed but then rejected in favor of an alternative explanation.*"

8. **(D)** The passage serves simply to portray or *depict an instance of heroism under fire.*

9. **(C)** Although many people believe that the theory of tectonic drift has been around for aeons, the passage *challenges* that *misconception.*

10. **(B)** The heart of this passage is found not in its opening sentence or its concluding sentence but right smack in the middle: "Hungry for a theater that spoke to their intellects, they wholeheartedly embraced the social realist dramas of Henrik Ibsen." *Because* theatergoers in Victorian England were hungry for serious drama, they embraced (enthusiastically welcomed or adopted) Ibsen's plays. Thus, the passage serves mainly to *explain the popularity of Ibsen's plays in Victorian England.*

Vocabulary-in-Context Questions

1. **(D)** The archbishop's prominence is his fame or *renown.*

2. **(C)** To form a volcanic chain is to *make up* or constitute such a trail of extinct volcanoes.

3. **(B)** In line 1, the plates are described as "shifting." This suggests that the passage of the plates is their *movement* as they shift slowly but relentlessly.

4. **(B)** To be standing upright is to be standing *vertically*, that is, perpendicular.

5. **(D)** For a moment, the young narrator thinks he sees a dead pirate limping back to the gallows on which he was hanged, and the thought gives the boy a terrible *shock* or turn.

6. **(A)** For the knights to consolidate their political and economic positions is for them to strengthen or reinforce their *status* both politically and economically.

7. **(B)** Think how birds fly. They swoop, they wheel, they bank, that is, *tilt sideways*, tipping laterally as they go into a turn.

8. **(C)** The process of gravitational instability begins when something occurs to *unsettle* or disturb the static cloud of gas so that one small region becomes a little denser than the gas around it.

9. **(A)** When Nightingale addressed the various aspects of hospital construction and management, she *tackled* or dealt with them thoroughly and in great detail.

10. **(B)** The Pilgrims have traditionally been held up or *cited* as defenders of democracy.

Specific Detail Questions

1. **(B)** The opening sentence states that "most of the world's active volcanoes are located along the edges of the great shifting plates." However, there are "isolated areas of volcanic activity" that are located "far from the nearest plate boundary." These hot spots differ from other areas of volcanic activity in their *location*: they occur within the plates, not along the plates' edges.

2. **(B)** The passage's opening sentence asks the question, "What factors led to the decline of the armored knight?" To have the institution of knighthood suffer a decline is to have it undergo *significant change over time.* Choice D is incorrect. The passage states that technological progress "contributed to the effectiveness of the chivalry," not to knighthood's dying out or decline.

3. **(D)** The author stresses that "(i)t was not quite a century ago" that Wegener proposed the theory of continental drift." Thus, although people today may think the theory originated in the seventeenth century, the author makes the point that *it is of relatively recent origin.*

4. **(C)** The "four strange specks" of whom the birds become aware are the naturalists, the *intruding humans* who have invaded the birds' territory.

5. **(D)** In alleviating conflict within the troop and maintaining the safety of troop members, the troop's hierarchic structure *fulfills a positive function for the social group.*

Inference Questions

1. **(D)** McCarthy sneers at the need to look for Oedipal fixations and traumatic experiences in literary characters. She views such clinically authentic character portrayals in modern fiction with *disdain* (scorn).

2. **(C)** Examine the context. "These stones are in actuality *plants*, members of the genus Lithops, some of the strangest succulents in the world." A succulent is *a type of plant.*

3. **(B)** The author calls the industrialists and their "couldn't-lose" bankers and backers "canny boys" (shrewd fellows) and says the adults considered stories about these wheelers and dealers "inspirational to children." Clearly, she finds neither the stories nor the men inspirational: she looks on both with *irony*.

4. **(B)** To the author, the concept is both *commonly accepted* (it has been known since Newton's time) *and accurate* (correct in its details).

5. **(D)** The author describes the scene in vivid terms: trumpet bursts, churning wings, a sky "filled with the sound of judgment day." Clearly, the most likely response on the part of the visiting naturalists would have been *awe* (mixed reverence, fear, and wonder). Choice C is incorrect. The birds are wholly terrorized. The naturalists' fear, however, is mixed with reverence and wonder: they are *awed*.

Literary Technique and Style Questions

1. **(A)** The author uses the term "hot spot" to indicate a geological phenomenon; she uses the term *technically*, as it is used by geologists.

2. **(C)** The author's manner of presentation is *expository*: he is explaining a physical concept.

3. **(B)** The next sentence says that these stones in actuality are plants. Thus, the quotation marks around the word "stones" serve to underscore that these stonelike objects *are not literally stones*. (Quotation marks are sometimes used to indicate that a word is being used in a special sense.)

4. **(B)** The statement "we're dying anyway" is an example of a *metaphor* or implicit comparison. The author does not mean that he and his fellow poets are literally dying; they are dying metaphorically (figuratively), for their poetry does not matter to anyone, and to have their poetry ignored feels to them like death.

5. **(A)** A keyboard composed of 400 symbols would be far too unwieldy to manage. No actual keyboard is being used by Savage-Rambaugh in her research. The quotation marks here *indicated that the word "keyboard" is being used in an unusual sense*.

Paired Passage Questions

1. **(D)** You can arrive at the correct answer by the process of elimination.

   True scientists examine their subject from every possible angle. They are *analytic*. You can eliminate Choice A.

   True scientists are not strangers to hard work. Instead, they are *diligent* or hard-working. You can eliminate Choice B.

   True scientists work toward their conclusions unerringly, that is, without making errors. Therefore, they are *accurate*. You can eliminate Choice C.

   Only Choice D is left. It is the correct answer. The author never characterizes true scientists as *inspired* in their approach to science.

2. **(A)** To conduct test after test is to *carry out* or perform test after test.

3. **(A)** What is the effect of the description of the way scientists work? Each statement points out that true scientists do not jump to conclusions but methodically work their

way toward conclusions in a systematic and disciplined way. Thus, the cumulative effect of the description is to *emphasize the systematic and disciplined nature of the scientific method.*

4. **(B)** Unlike the author of Passage 1, the author of Passage 2 directly quotes a scientist, the naturalist Donald Culross Peattie. Thus, the author of Passage 2 makes use of *direct citation*. (Be on the lookout for quotation marks. They signal a direct quote or citation. While the author of Passage 1 refers to Boyle and Hooke by name, he does not quote them *directly*.)

5. **(C)** The author of Passage 1 wholeheartedly believes in the inductive method of reasoning, the modern scientific method advocated by Boyle and Hooke. Peattie, however, makes fun of this method and calls it plodding (poky and slow). It is therefore likely that the author of Passage 1 would respond to Peattie's mocking comments by arguing that Peattie *fails to appreciate the virtues of the inductive method sufficiently.*

READING WRAP-UP

1. Tackle passages with familiar subjects before passages with unfamiliar ones.

2. If you are stumped by a tough reading question, move on, but do not skip the other questions on that passage without giving them a shot.

3. Whenever you skip a question, *be sure you are filling in the right spaces on your answer sheet.*

4. Do not zip back and forth between passages.

5. Read as fast as you can with understanding, but don't force yourself.

6. Take note of any introductory material and footnotes.

7. Try to anticipate what the passage will be about.

8. Read with a purpose.

9. Read the footnotes.

10. When you tackle the questions, go back to the passage to check each answer choice.

11. Use the line references in the questions to be sure you've gone back to the correct spot in the passage.

12. When dealing with the double passages, *in general* tackle them one at a time.

13. Be on the lookout for words or phrases in the questions that can clue you in to the kind of question being asked.

14. Tackle vocabulary-in-context questions the same way you do fill-in-the-blank questions, substituting *blank* for the word in quotes.

15. When asked to find a passage's main idea, be sure to check the opening and summary sentences of each paragraph.

16. When you answer specific detail questions, point to the precise words in the passage that support your answer choice.

17. When you answer inference questions, look for what the passage logically suggests, but does *not* directly state.

18. Scan all the questions on a passage to spot the command-of-evidence questions coming up. Pay special attention as you answer the question immediately before a command-of-evidence question.

19. When asked to figure out an author's attitude, mood, or tone, look for words that convey emotion, express values, or paint pictures.

20. Familiarize yourself with the common terms used to describe an author's technique.

21. When dealing with graph interpretation questions, use only the evidence in the graphics and the passage.

Building Your Vocabulary 2

Recognizing the meaning of words is essential to comprehending what you read. The more you stumble over unfamiliar words in a text, the more you have to take time out to look up words in your dictionary, the more likely you are to wind up losing track of what the author has to say.

To succeed in college, you must develop a college-level vocabulary. You must familiarize yourself with technical words in a wide variety of fields, mastering each field's special vocabulary. You must learn to use these words, and reuse them until they become second nature to you. The time you put in now learning vocabulary-building techniques for the PSAT will pay off later on and not just on the PSAT.

LONG-RANGE STRATEGY

There is only one effective long-range strategy for vocabulary building: READ.

Read—widely and well. Sample different fields—physics, art history, political science, geology—and different styles. Extensive reading is the one sure way to make your vocabulary grow.

One of the major changes in the PSAT involves vocabulary. The PSAT has eliminated vocabulary questions involving esoteric words like, for example, esoteric. Instead, vocabulary questions on the PSAT involve common words used in uncommon ways, as well as words with multiple meanings whose specific meaning you can uncover by examining the context in which they occur.

Here is what the test makers say about the new vocabulary questions: "These words and phrases are neither highly obscure nor specific to any one domain. They are words and phrases whose specific meaning and rhetorical purpose are derived in large part through the context in which they are used." In other words, they are not technical jargon. They are words whose basic meaning you are likely to know, high-utility words likely to appear in many types of reading.

For this reason, in revising our Master Word List, we have eliminated many college-level vocabulary words that are unlikely to appear as question words on the PSAT and that are also unlikely to crop up in the reading passages you will find on the test. However, we have retained college-level vocabulary words that are likely to occur in the sorts of reading passages you will encounter. Even though these words will not be tested in the vocabulary-in-context questions on the test, they are important words, words you need to know on this PSAT and in your future college career.

A PLAN FOR USING THE WORD LIST

For those of you who wish to work your way through the word list and feel the need for a plan, we recommend that you follow the procedure described below in order to use the lists most profitably:

1. Set aside a definite time each day for the study of a list.
2. Devote at least one hour to each list.
3. First, go through the list looking at the short, simple-looking words (six letters at most). Mark those you don't know. In studying, pay particular attention to them.
4. Go through the list again looking at the longer words. Pay particular attention to words with more than one meaning and familiar-looking words that have unusual definitions that come as a surprise to you. Many tests make use of these secondary definitions.
5. List unusual words on index cards so that you can shuffle and review them from time to time. (Study no more than five cards at a time.)
6. Use the illustrative sentences in the list as models and make up new sentences of your own.

For each word, the following is provided:

- The word (printed in heavy type)
- Its part of speech (abbreviated)
- A brief definition
- A sentence illustrating the word's use

Whenever appropriate, related words are provided, together with their parts of speech. The forty-eight word lists are arranged in alphabetical order.

PSAT POWER WORD LIST

abstract	apathy	censor	consistency	derision
accessible	apprehension	chronic	consolidation	derivative
acclaim	apprenticeship	chronicle	convention	detachment
accommodate	appropriate	circumspect	conviction	determination
acknowledge	aristocracy	cite	corroborate	deterrent
acute	aspire	cliché	criterion	didactic
adversary	assert	coalesce	curtail	diffident
adverse	assumption	collaborate	dearth	digression
aesthetic	authentic	compliance	debilitate	discernible
affinity	autonomous	component	decry	disclose
alleviate	aversion	composure	deference	discord
altruistic	banal	compromise	defiance	discrepancy
ambiguous	beneficial	concentration	definition	discriminating
ambivalence	benign	concrete	definitive	disenfranchise
amenable	betray	condone	degenerate	disinterested
ample	brittle	confirm	demean	dismiss
analogy	buoyant	conformity	denounce	disparage
antagonism	candor	confront	depict	disperse
antipathy	capacity	conscientious	deplete	dissent

dissipate
distinction
distort
diverse
divulge
docile
doctrine
document
eclipse
economy
efficacy
elicit
elusive
embellish
embrace
endorse
engage
enhance
enigma
entice
enumerate
ephemeral
erode
erratic
erroneous
espouse
esteem
excerpt
execute
exemplary
expedite
exploit
facilitate
fallacious
farce
fastidious
feasible
fervor
figurative
flippant
forthright
frail

frivolous
generalization
generate
genre
gratify
gregarious
hackneyed
hamper
hinder
hostility
hyperbole
hypocritical
hypothetical
iconoclastic
immutable
impede
imperative
imperceptible
implausible
implement
implication
incongruity
inconsequential
inconsistency
incorporate
indicative
indifferent
indiscriminate
induce
industrious
inept
infallible
ingenious
ingenuous
inherent
initiate
innate
innocuous
inscrutable
insightful
intangible
integrity

intricacy
introspective
irony
judicious
loathe
magnitude
malice
material
medium
meticulous
misconception
misrepresent
mock
monarchy
monotony
mutability
naïveté
nonchalance
nostalgia
notorious
nuance
nurture
objective
obnoxious
obscure
opaque
optimist
orator
ostentatious
outmoded
pacifist
pacify
paradox
partial
patronize
pedantic
perpetual
pertinent
pervasive
pessimism
phenomena
plagiarize

plastic
potency
pragmatic
precedent
predator
premise
presumptuous
prevail
prey
problematic
profound
proliferation
prolific
prologue
prominent
promote
property
prosaic
prosperity
provocative
prudent
qualified
random
reflect
refute
relinquish
renown
reprehensible
reserved
resignation
resolution
resolve
restraint
retain
reticent
reverent
rigid
rudimentary
ruthless
satirize
scrutinize
serenity

sever
severity
singular
skeptical
solution
steadfast
stratagem
subdued
subversive
superficial
superfluous
suppress
surpass
susceptible
suspend
sustain
symmetry
synthesis
taciturn
tedious
temper
tentative
termination
thwart
toxic
transparent
trepidation
turbulence
urbane
utopia
vacillate
versatile
viable
volatile
wary
yield

The abridged Basic Word List follows. *Do not let this list overwhelm you.* You do not need to memorize every word. An entry preceded by a bullet (■) is a Power Word.

Word List 1   abate–accommodate

abate V. subside; decrease; lessen. Rather than leaving immediately, they waited for the storm to *abate*. abatement, N.

abdicate V. renounce; give up. When Edward VIII *abdicated* the British throne to marry the woman he loved, he surprised the entire world. When the painter Gauguin *abdicated* his family responsibilities to run off to Samoa, he surprised no one at all.

aberration N. deviation from the expected or the normal; mental irregularity or disorder. Survivors of a major catastrophe are likely to exhibit *aberrations* of behavior because of the trauma they have experienced. aberrant, ADJ. and N.

abet V. encourage; aid. She was accused of aiding and *abetting* the drug dealer by engaging in a money-laundering scheme to help him disguise his illegal income. abettor, N.

abrade V. wear away by friction; scrape; erode. The sharp rocks *abraded* the skin on her legs; so she put iodine on her *abrasions*.

abscond V. depart secretly to avoid capture. The teller who *absconded* with the bonds was not captured until someone recognized him from his photograph on *America's Most Wanted*.

absolute ADJ. complete; totally unlimited; certain. Although the king of Siam was an *absolute* monarch, he did not want to behead his unfaithful wife without *absolute* evidence of her infidelity.

absolve V. pardon (an offense); free from blame. The father confessor *absolved* him of his sins. absolution, N.

abstain V. refrain; hold oneself back voluntarily from an action or practice (especially one regarded as improper or unhealthy). After considering the effect of alcohol on his athletic performance, he decided to *abstain* from drinking while he trained for the race. abstinence, N. ; abstinent or abstemious, ADJ.

■ **abstract** ADJ. theoretical; not concrete; nonrepresentational. To him, hunger was an *abstract* concept; he had never missed a meal.

abstruse ADJ. obscure; profound; difficult to understand. She carries around *abstruse* works of philosophy, not because she understands them but because she wants her friends to think she does.

academic ADJ. related to education; not practical or directly useful. When Sharon applied for the faculty position, the department head inquired about her *academic* qualifications. Seismologists' studies about earthquakes are not of purely *academic* interest, for seismology is the major tool for assessing the danger of potential earthquakes.

accelerate V. move faster. In our science class, we learn how falling bodies *accelerate*.

■ **accessible** ADJ. easy to approach; obtainable. We asked our guide whether the ruins were *accessible* on foot.

accessory N. additional object; useful but not essential thing. The *accessories* she bought cost more than the dress. also ADJ.

■ **acclaim** V. applaud; announce with great approval. The NBC sportscasters *acclaimed* every American victory in the Olympics and lamented every American defeat. acclamation, acclaim, N.

accolade N. award of merit. In the world of public relations, a Clio is the highest *accolade* an advertising campaign can receive.

■ **accommodate** V. provide lodgings. Mary asked the room clerk whether the hotel would be able to *accommodate* the tour group on such short notice. accommodations, N.

■ **accommodate** V. oblige or help someone; adjust or bring into harmony; adapt. Mitch always did everything possible to *accommodate* his elderly relatives, from driving them to medical appointments to helping them with paperwork. accommodating, ADJ. (secondary meaning)

Word List 2   accomplice–alacrity

accomplice N. partner in crime. Because he had provided the criminal with the lethal weapon, he was arrested as an *accomplice* in the murder.

■ **acknowledge** V. recognize; admit. Although Ira *acknowledged* that the Beatles' tunes sounded pretty dated nowadays, he still preferred them to the hip-hop tunes his nephews played.

acquittal N. declaration of innocence; deliverance from a charge. His *acquittal* by the jury surprised those who had thought him guilty. acquit, V.

acumen N. mental keenness. His business *acumen* helped him to succeed where others had failed.

■ **acute** ADJ. quickly perceptive; keen; brief and severe. The *acute* young doctor realized immediately that the gradual deterioration of her patient's once *acute* hearing was due to a chronic illness, not an *acute* one.

adamant ADJ. hard; inflexible. Despite the entreaties of his constituents and the warnings of budget analysts, the senator was *adamant* that he intended to vote in favor of his party's tax plan. adamancy, N.

adapt V. alter; modify. Some species of animals have become extinct because they could not *adapt* to a changing environment.

addiction N. compulsive, habitual need. His *addiction* to drugs caused his friends much grief.

address V. direct a speech to; deal with or discuss. Due to *address* the convention in July, Brown planned to *address* the issue of low-income housing in his speech.

adept ADJ. expert at. She was *adept* at the fine art of irritating people. also N.

adhere V. stick fast to. I will *adhere* to this opinion until someone comes up with solid proof that I am wrong. adhesive, ADJ.

adjacent ADJ. adjoining; neighboring; close by. Philip's best friend Jason lived only four houses away, close but not immediately *adjacent*.

adjudicate V. pass legal judgment on; sit in judgment. Do you trust Judge Judy to *adjudicate* disputes impartially?

admonish V. warn; scold. The preacher *admonished* his listeners to change their wicked ways. admonition, N.

adopt V. legally take a child as one's own; choose to follow an approach or idea; assume a position or attitude; formally accept (a suggestion or report). Tom *adopted* a daughter, who told him about a new weight-loss plan that her foster mother had *adopted*. In response, Tom *adopted* a patronizing tone, saying that fad diets never worked. Was the committee's report *adopted* unanimously, or did anyone abstain?

adroit ADJ. skillful; nimble. The juggler's admirers particularly enjoyed his *adroit* handling of difficult balancing tricks.

adulterate V. make impure by adding inferior or tainted substances. It is a crime to *adulterate* foods without informing the buyer; when consumers learned that the manufacturer had *adulterated* its apple juice by mixing it with water, they protested vigorously.

■ **adversary** N. opponent. "Aha!" cried Holmes. "Watson, I suspect this delay is the work of my old *adversary* Professor Moriarty." adversarial, ADJ.

■ **adverse** ADJ. unfavorable; hostile. The recession had a highly *adverse* effect on Father's investment portfolio: he lost so much money that he could no longer afford the butler and the upstairs maid. adversity, N.

adversity N. unfavorable fortune; hardship; a calamitous event. According to the humorist Mark Twain, anyone can easily learn to endure *adversity*, as long as it is another man's.

advocate V. urge; plead for. Noted abolitionists such as Frederick Douglass and Sojourner Truth *advocated* the eradication of the Southern institution of slavery. also N.

■ **aesthetic** ADJ. artistic; dealing with or capable of appreciation of the beautiful. The beauty of Tiffany's stained glass appealed to Alice's *aesthetic* sense. aesthete, N.

affable ADJ. easily approachable; warmly friendly. Accustomed to cold, aloof supervisors, Nicholas was amazed by how *affable* his new employer was.

affected ADJ. artificial; pretended; assumed in order to impress. His *affected* mannerisms—his "Harvard" accent, his air of boredom, his flaunting of obscure foreign words—irritated many of us who had known him before he had gone away to school. affectation, N.

■ **affinity** N. kinship; attraction to. She felt an *affinity* with all who suffered; their pains were her pains. Her brother, in contrast, had an *affinity* for political wheeling and dealing; he manipulated people shamelessly, not caring who got hurt.

affirmation N. positive assertion; confirmation; solemn pledge by one who refuses to take an oath. Despite Tom's *affirmations* of innocence, Aunt Polly still suspected he had eaten the pie. affirm, V.

affluence N. wealth; prosperity; abundance. Galvanized by his sudden, unexpected *affluence*, the lottery winner dashed out to buy himself a brand new Ferrari. affluent, ADJ.

afford V. have enough money to pay for; provide. Although Phil is not sure he can *afford* a membership at the yoga studio, he wants to sign up because of the excellent training the studio *affords*.

aggregate V. gather; accumulate. America today is no country for working men and women: the poor grow poorer, while the rich greedily *aggregate* more and more wealth. aggregation, N.

agility N. nimbleness. The acrobat's *agility* amazed and thrilled the audience. agile, ADJ.

agitate V. stir up; disturb. Her fiery remarks further *agitated* the already angry mob.

alacrity N. cheerful promptness. Phil and Dave were eager to get off to the mountains; they packed up their ski gear and climbed into the van with *alacrity*.

Word List 3   alias–ancillary

alias N. an assumed name. John Smith's *alias* was Bob Jones. also ADV.

alienate V. make hostile; separate. Her attempts to *alienate* the two friends failed because they had complete faith in each other.

■ **alleviate** V. relieve; lessen. This should *alleviate* the pain; if it does not, we will use stronger drugs.

allude v. refer indirectly. Try not to mention divorce in John's presence because he will think you are *alluding* to his marital problems with Jill.

allure v. entice; attract. *Allured* by the song of the sirens, the helmsman steered the ship toward the reef. also N.

allusion N. indirect reference. When Amanda said to the ticket scalper, "Five hundred bucks? What do you want, a pound of flesh?," she was making an *allusion* to Shakespeare's *Merchant of Venice*.

aloft ADV. upward. The sailor climbed *aloft* into the rigging. To get into a loft bed, you have to climb *aloft*.

aloof ADJ. apart; reserved; standoffish. People thought James was a snob because he remained *aloof* while all the rest of the group conversed.

altercation N. noisy quarrel; heated dispute. In that hot-tempered household, no meal ever came to a peaceful conclusion; the inevitable *altercation* occasionally even ended in blows.

■ **altruistic** ADJ. unselfishly generous; concerned for others. The star received no fee for appearing at the benefit; it was a purely *altruistic* act. altruism, N.

amalgam N. mixture of different elements; alloy. In character, King Gustav was a strange *amalgam* of hard-headed practicality and religious zeal. amalgamate, V.

■ **ambiguous** ADJ. unclear or doubtful in meaning. The proctor's *ambiguous* instructions thoroughly confused us; we didn't know which columns we should mark and which we should leave blank. ambiguity, N.

■ **ambivalence** N. having contradictory or conflicting emotional attitudes. Torn between loving her parents one minute and hating them the next, she was upset by the *ambivalence* of her feelings. ambivalent, ADJ.

ameliorate v. improve; make more satisfactory. Carl became a union organizer because he wanted to join the fight to *ameliorate* working conditions in the factory.

■ **amenable** ADJ. readily managed; willing to give in; agreeable; submissive. A born snob, Wilbur was *amenable* to any suggestions from those he looked up to, but he resented advice from his supposed inferiors. Unfortunately, his incorrigible snobbery was not *amenable* to improvement.

amiable ADJ. agreeable; lovable; warmly friendly. In *Little Women*, Beth is the *amiable* daughter whose loving disposition endears her to all who have dealings with her.

amorous ADJ. moved by sexual love; loving. "Love them and leave them" was the motto of the *amorous* Don Juan.

amorphous ADJ. formless; lacking shape or definition. As soon as we have decided on our itinerary, we shall send you a copy; right now, our plans are still *amorphous*.

■ **ample** ADJ. abundant. Bond had *ample* opportunity to escape. Why did he let us catch him?

amplify v. broaden or clarify by expanding; intensify; make stronger. Charlie Brown tried to *amplify* his remarks, but he was drowned out by jeers from the audience. Lucy, however, used a loudspeaker to *amplify* her voice and drowned out all the hecklers.

anachronism N. something regarded as outmoded; something or someone misplaced in time. In today's world of personal copiers and fax machines, the old-fashioned mimeograph machine is clearly an *anachronism*; even the electric typewriter seems *anachronistic* next to a laptop PC.

■ **analogy** N. similarity; parallelism. A well-known *analogy* compares the body's immune system with an army whose defending troops are the lymphocytes or white blood cells. *Analogies* are useful, but you can't take them too far: cells, after all, are not soldiers; there is no boot camp for lymphocytes.

anarchist N. person who seeks to overturn the established government; advocate of abolishing authority. Denying she was an *anarchist,* Katya maintained she wished only to make changes in our government, not to destroy it entirely.

anarchy N. absence of governing body; state of disorder. For weeks China was in a state of *anarchy*, with soldiers shooting down civilians in the streets and rumors claiming that the premier was dead. Foreigners fleeing the country reported conditions were so *anarchic* that it was a miracle they escaped.

ancillary ADJ. serving as an aid or accessory; auxiliary. In an *ancillary* capacity Doctor Watson was helpful; however, Holmes could not trust the good doctor to solve a perplexing case on his own. also N.

Word List 4   animated–arrest

animated ADJ. lively; spirited. At first the teenager seemed bored, but his expression grew *animated* when the talk turned to rap music.

animosity N. active enmity. Mr. Fang incurred the *animosity* of the party's rulers because he advocated limitations of their power.

anomaly N. irregularity; something out of place or abnormal. A bird that cannot fly is an *anomaly*. A classical harpist in the middle of a heavy metal band is *anomalous;* she is also inaudible.

■ **antagonism** N. hostility; active resistance. Barry showed his *antagonism* toward his new stepmother by ignoring her whenever she tried talking to him. antagonistic, ADJ.

anticlimax N. letdown in thought or emotion. After the fine performance in the first act, the rest of the play was an *anticlimax*. anticlimactic, ADJ.

■ **antipathy** N. aversion; dislike. Tom's extreme *antipathy* for disputes keeps him from getting into arguments with his temperamental wife. Noise in any form is *antipathetic* to him. Among his particular *antipathies* are honking cars, boom boxes, and heavy metal rock.

antiquated ADJ. obsolete; outdated. Accustomed to editing his papers on word processors, Philip thought typewriters were too *antiquated* for him to use.

antiseptic N. substance that prevents infection. It is advisable to apply an *antiseptic* to any wound, no matter how slight or insignificant. also ADJ.

antithesis N. contrast; direct opposite of or to. Stagnation is the *antithesis* of growth.

■ **apathy** N. lack of caring; indifference. A firm believer in democratic government, she could not understand the *apathy* of people who never bothered to vote. She wondered whether they had ever cared or whether they had always been *apathetic.*

application N. request; act of putting something to use; diligent attention; relevance. Jill submitted her scholarship *application* to the financial aid office. Martha's research project is purely academic; it has no practical *application.* Pleased with how well Tom had whitewashed the fence, Aunt Polly praised him for his *application* to the task. Unfortunately, John's experience in book publishing had little or no *application* to the e-publishing industry.

appreciate V. be thankful for; increase in worth; be thoroughly conscious of. Little Orphan Annie truly *appreciated* the stocks Daddy Warbucks gave her, which *appreciated* in value considerably over the years. While I *appreciate* the skill and craftsmanship that went into Lucian Freud's paintings, I still dislike the paintings.

■ **apprehension** N. fear of future evil; understanding; arrest (of a criminal). Despite the *apprehension* many people feel about black bears, these bears are generally more afraid of humans than humans are of them. Our *apprehension* of the present inevitably is based on our understanding of the past. Inspector Javert's lifelong ambition was to bring about the *apprehension* and imprisonment of Jean Valjean.

■ **apprenticeship** N. time spent as a novice learning a trade from a skilled worker. As a child, Pip had thought it would be wonderful to work as Joe's *apprentice;* now he hated his *apprenticeship* and scorned the blacksmith's trade.

■ **appropriate** ADJ. fitting or suitable; pertinent. Madonna spent hours looking for a suit that would be *appropriate* to wear at a summer wedding.

■ **appropriate** V. acquire; take possession of for one's own use; set aside for a special purpose. The ranchers *appropriated* lands that had originally been intended for Indian use. In response, Congress *appropriated* additional funds for the Bureau of Indian Affairs.

arable ADJ. fit for growing crops. The first settlers wrote home glowing reports of the New World, praising its vast acres of *arable* land ready for the plow.

arbiter N. a person with power to decide a dispute; judge. As an *arbiter* in labor disputes, she is skillful: she balances the demands of both sides and hands down rulings with which everyone agrees. As an *arbiter* of style, however, she is worthless: she wears such unflattering outfits that no woman in her right mind would imitate her.

arbitrary ADJ. unreasonable or capricious; randomly selected without any reason; based solely on one's unrestricted will or judgment. The coach claimed the team lost because the umpire made some *arbitrary* calls.

arduous ADJ. hard; strenuous. Bob's *arduous* efforts had sapped his energy. Even using a chain saw, he found chopping down trees an *arduous,* time-consuming task.

arid ADJ. dry; barren. The cactus has adapted to survive in an *arid* environment.

■ **aristocracy** N. hereditary nobility; privileged class. Americans have mixed feelings about hereditary *aristocracy:* we say all men are created equal, but we describe people who bear themselves with grace and graciousness as natural *aristocrats.*

arrest V. stop or slow down; catch someone's attention. Slipping, the trapeze artist plunged from the heights until a safety net luckily *arrested* his fall. This near-disaster *arrested* the crowd's attention.

Word List 5   arrogance–authoritative

arrogance N. pride; haughtiness. Convinced that Emma thought she was better than anyone else in the class, Ed rebuked her for her *arrogance.*

articulate ADJ. effective; distinct. Her *articulate* presentation of the advertising campaign impressed her employers.

articulate V. express (an idea) clearly; pronounce distinctly. A skilled impromptu debater must be able to *articulate* her ideas clearly and fluently. A speech therapist helps patients *articulate* sounds.

ascendancy N. controlling influence; domination. Leaders of religious cults maintain *ascendancy* over their followers by methods that can verge on brainwashing.

ascetic ADJ. practicing self-denial; austere. The wealthy, self-indulgent young man felt oddly drawn to the strict, *ascetic* life led by members of some monastic orders. also N.

■ **aspire** V. seek to attain; long for. Because he *aspired* to a career in professional sports, Philip enrolled in a graduate program in sports management. aspiration, N.

assail v. assault. He was *assailed* with questions after his lecture.

■ **assert** v. state strongly or positively; insist on or demand recognition of (rights, claims, etc.). When Jill *asserted* that nobody else in the junior class had such an early curfew, her parents *asserted* themselves, telling her that if she didn't get home by nine o'clock, she would be grounded for the week. assertion, N.

assiduous ADJ. diligent. It took Rembrandt weeks of *assiduous* labor before he was satisfied with his self-portrait. assiduity, N.

assimilate v. absorb; cause to become homogeneous. The manner in which the United States was able to *assimilate* the hordes of immigrants during the nineteenth and early twentieth centuries should be a source of pride to Americans. The immigrants eagerly *assimilated* new ideas and customs; they soaked them up, the way plants soak up water.

assuage v. ease or lessen (pain); Jilted by Jane, Dick tried to *assuage* his heartache by indulging in ice cream.

■ **assumption** N. something taken for granted; taking over or taking possession of. The young princess made the foolish *assumption* that the regent would not object to her *assumption* of power. assume, v.

assurance N. promise or pledge; certainty; self-confidence. When Guthrie gave Guinness his *assurance* rehearsals were going well, he spoke with such *assurance* that Guinness felt relieved. assure, v.; assured, ADJ.

astute ADJ. wise; shrewd; keen. As tutor, she made *astute* observations about how to take multiple-choice tests. She was an *astute* observer: she noticed every tiny detail and knew exactly how important each one was.

asylum N. place of refuge; safety. Fleeing persecution, the political refugee sought *asylum* in the United States.

atrophy v. waste away. After three months in a cast, Stan's biceps had *atrophied* somewhat; however, he was sure that if he pumped iron for a while he would soon build it up.

attain v. reach or accomplish; gain. It took Bolingbroke years to *attain* his goal of gaining the throne.

attentive ADJ. watching carefully; considerate; thoughtful. Spellbound, the *attentive* audience watched the final game of the match, never taking their eyes from the ball. Stan's *attentive* daughter slipped a sweater over his shoulders without distracting his attention from the game.

attribute N. essential quality. His outstanding *attribute* was his kindness.

attribute v. ascribe or credit (to a cause); regard as characteristic of a person or thing. I *attribute* Andrea's success in science to the encouragement she received from her parents.

attrition N. gradual decrease in numbers; reduction in the work force without firing employees; wearing away of opposition by means of harassment. In the 1960s urban churches suffered from *attrition* as members moved from the cities to the suburbs. Rather than fire staff members, church leaders followed a policy of *attrition*, allowing elderly workers to retire without replacing them.

audacity N. boldness. Luke could not believe his own *audacity* in addressing the princess. Where did he get the nerve?

augment v. increase. Armies *augment* their forces by calling up reinforcements; teachers *augment* their salaries by taking odd jobs. Lexy *augments* her salary by working in a record store. Her *augmentation* of wealth has not been great; however, she has *augmented* her record collection considerably.

auspicious ADJ. favoring success; fortunate. With favorable weather conditions, it was an *auspicious* moment to set sail. Prospects for trade were good: under such promising *auspices* we were bound to thrive. Thomas, however, had doubts: a paranoid, he became suspicious whenever conditions seemed *auspicious*.

austere ADJ. forbiddingly stern; severely simple and unornamented. The headmaster's *austere* demeanor tended to scare off the more timid students, who never visited his study willingly. The room reflected the man, for it was *austere* and bare, like a monk's cell, with no touches of luxury to moderate its *austerity*.

■ **authentic** ADJ. genuine. The art expert was able to distinguish the *authentic* van Gogh painting from the forged copy. authenticate, v.

authoritative ADJ. having the weight of authority; overbearing and dictatorial. Impressed by the young researcher's well-documented presentation, we accepted her analysis of the experiment as *authoritative*.

Word List 6   autonomous–blasphemy

autonomous ADJ. self-governing. Although the University of California at Berkeley is just one part of the state university system, in many ways Cal Berkeley is *autonomous*, for it runs several programs that are not subject to outside control. autonomy, N.

avarice N. greediness for wealth. King Midas is a perfect example of *avarice*, for he was so greedy that he wished everything he touched would turn to gold.

averse ADJ. reluctant. The reporter was *averse* to revealing the sources of his information.

■ **aversion** N. firm dislike. Bert had an *aversion* to eggheads; Alex had an *aversion* to jocks. Their mutual *aversion* was so great that they refused to speak to one another.

avert V. prevent; turn aside. Hitting the brakes, the vigilant driver was able to *avert* what seemed like an inevitable collision. She *averted* her eyes from the dead opossum on the highway.

avid ADJ. greedy; eager for. Abner was *avid* for pleasure and partied with great *avidity*.

awe N. solemn wonder. The tourists gazed with *awe* at the tremendous expanse of the Grand Canyon.

axiomatic ADJ. self-evident; unquestionable. It is *axiomatic* that individuals differ; what stimulates some people will bore others. axiom, N.

baffle V. frustrate; perplex. The new code *baffled* the enemy agents.

balk V. foil or thwart; stop short; refuse to go on. When the warden learned that several inmates were planning to escape, he took steps to *balk* their attempt. However, he *balked* at punishing them by shackling them to the walls of their cells.

■ **banal** ADJ. hackneyed; commonplace; trite; lacking originality. The hack writer's worn-out clichés made his comic sketch seem *banal.* He even resorted to the *banality* of having someone slip on a banana peel!

bane N. cause of ruin; curse. Lucy's little brother was the *bane* of her existence: his attempts to make her life miserable worked so well that she could have fed him some ratsbane for having such a *baneful* effect.

barren ADJ. desolate; fruitless and unproductive. Looking out at the trackless, *barren* desert, Indiana Jones feared that his search for the missing expedition would prove *barren*.

begrudge V. resent. I *begrudge* every minute I have to spend attending meetings; they're a complete waste of time.

beguile V. mislead or delude; cheat; pass time. With flattery and big talk of easy money, the con men *beguiled* Kyle into betting his allowance on the shell game. Broke, Kyle *beguiled* himself during the long hours by playing solitaire.

belie V. contradict; give a false impression of. His coarse, hard-bitten exterior *belied* his underlying sensitivity.

belittle V. disparage or depreciate; put down. Parents should not *belittle* their children's early attempts at drawing, but should encourage their efforts. Barry was a put-down artist: he was a genius at *belittling* people and making them feel small.

benefactor N. gift giver; patron. In later years Scrooge became Tiny Tim's *benefactor* and gave him many gifts.

■ **beneficial** ADJ. helpful; advantageous; useful. Tiny Tim's cheerful good nature had a *beneficial* influence on Scrooge's disposition.

benevolent ADJ. generous; charitable. Mr. Fezziwig was a *benevolent* employer, who wished to make Christmas merrier for young Scrooge and his other employees.

■ **benign** ADJ. kindly; favorable; not malignant. Though her *benign* smile and gentle bearing made Miss Marple seem a sweet little old lady, in reality she was a tough-minded, shrewd observer of human nature. We were relieved that Tom's tumor turned out to be *benign*. benignity, N.

■ **betray** V. be unfaithful; reveal (unconsciously or unwillingly). The spy *betrayed* his country by selling military secrets to the enemy. When he was taken in for questioning, the tightness of his lips *betrayed* his fear of being caught.

biased ADJ. slanted; prejudiced. Because the judge played golf regularly with the district attorney's father, we feared he might be *biased* in the prosecution's favor. bias, N.

bizarre ADJ. fantastic; violently contrasting. The plot of the novel was too *bizarre* to be believed.

bland ADJ. soothing; mild; dull. Unless you want your stomach lining to be eaten away, stick to a *bland* diet. blandness, N.

blare N. loud, harsh roar; screech. I don't know which is worse: the steady *blare* of a teenager's boom box deafening your ears or a sudden blaze of flashbulbs dazzling your eyes.

blasphemy N. irreverence; sacrilege; cursing. In my father's house, the Dodgers were the holiest of holies; to cheer for another team was to utter words of *blasphemy*. blasphemous, ADJ.

Word List 7   blatant–candor

blatant ADJ. flagrant; conspicuously obvious; loudly offensive. To the unemployed youth from Dublin, the "No Irish Need Apply" placard in the shop window was a *blatant* mark of prejudice.

blithe ADJ. gay; joyous; carefree. Without a care in the world, Beth went her *blithe,* light-hearted way.

boisterous ADJ. rough and noisy; rowdy; stormy. The unruly crowd of demonstrators became even more *boisterous* when the mayor tried to quiet them.

bolster V. support; reinforce. The debaters amassed file boxes full of evidence to *bolster* their arguments.

boon N. blessing; benefit. The recent rains that filled our empty reservoirs were a *boon* to the whole community.

boundless ADJ. unlimited; vast. Mike's energy was *boundless:* the greater the challenge, the more vigorously he tackled the job.

bountiful ADJ. abundant; graciously generous. Thanks to the good harvest, we had a *bountiful* supply of food, and we could be as *bountiful* as we liked in distributing food to the needy.

bourgeois ADJ. middle class; selfishly materialistic; dully conventional. Technically, anyone who belongs to the middle class is *bourgeois,* but, given the word's connotations, most people resent it if you call them that.

boycott V. refrain from buying or using. In an effort to stop grape growers from using pesticides that harmed the farm workers' health, Cesar Chavez called for consumers to *boycott* grapes.

breach N. breaking of contract or duty; fissure; gap. Jill sued Jack for *breach* of promise, claiming he had broken his promise to marry her. The troops found a *breach* in the enemy's fortifications and penetrated their lines. also V.

brevity N. conciseness. Since you are charged for every transmitted word, *brevity* is essential when you send a telegram or cablegram.

■ **brittle** ADJ. easily broken; difficult. My employer's self-control was as *brittle* as an eggshell. Her *brittle* personality made it difficult for me to get along with her.

brusque ADJ. blunt; abrupt. Jill was offended by Jack's *brusque* reply; he had no right to be so impatient with her.

bungle V. mismanage; blunder. Don't botch this assignment, Bumstead; if you *bungle* the job, you're fired!

■ **buoyant** ADJ. able to float; cheerful and optimistic. When the boat capsized, her *buoyant* life jacket kept Jody afloat. Scrambling back on board, she was still in a *buoyant* mood, certain that despite the delay she'd win the race. buoyancy, N.

bureaucracy N. over-regulated administrative system marked by red tape. The Internal Revenue Service is the ultimate *bureaucracy*: taxpayers wasted so much paper filling out IRS forms that the IRS *bureaucrats* printed up a new set of rules that required taxpayers to comply with the Paperwork Reduction Act.

burgeon V. bloom; develop rapidly; flourish. From its start as a small Seattle coffeehouse, Starbucks seemed to *burgeon* almost overnight into a major national chain.

bustle V. move about energetically; teem. David and the children *bustled* about the house getting in each other's way as they tried to pack for the camping trip.

buttress V. support or prop up. Debaters collect huge files of evidence to *buttress* their arguments. The huge cathedral walls were supported by flying *buttresses.* also N.

cajole V. coax; wheedle. Jill tried to *cajole* Jack into buying her a fur coat, but no matter how much she coaxed him, he wouldn't give in to her *cajolery.*

calamity N. disaster; misery. As news of the *calamity* spread, offers of relief poured in to the stricken community. calamitous, ADJ.

calculated ADJ. deliberately planned; likely. Lexy's choice of clothes to wear to the debate tournament was carefully *calculated.* Her conventional suit was one *calculated* to appeal to the conservative judges.

callous ADJ. hardened; unfeeling. Carl had worked in the hospital for so many years that he was *callous* to the suffering in the wards. It was as if he had a *callus* on his soul.

■ **candor** N. frankness; open honesty. Jack can carry *candor* too far: when he told Jill his honest opinion of her, she nearly slapped his face. Instead of being so *candid,* try keeping your opinions to yourself.

Word List 8   capacity–choreography

capacity N. greatest amount or number that something can hold; amount that something can produce; power to understand or to perform; specified position or role. This thermos container has a one-liter *capacity.* Management has come up with a plan to double the factory's automobile production *capacity.* I wish I had the mental *capacity* to understand Einstein's theory of relativity. Rima traveled to Japan in her *capacity* as director of the Country Dance & Song Society.

capricious ADJ. unpredictable; fickle. The storm was *capricious:* it changed course constantly. Jill was *capricious,* too: she changed boyfriends almost as often as she changed clothes.

caption N. title; chapter heading; text under illustration. The capricious *captions* that accompany "The Far Side" cartoons are almost as funny as the pictures. also V.

captivate V. charm; fascinate. Although he was predisposed to dislike Elizabeth, Darcy found himself *captivated* by her charm and wit.

cardiac ADJ. pertaining to the heart. Since no one in his family had ever had *cardiac* problems, Bill was unconcerned about the possibility of a heart attack.

caricature N. exaggerated picture or description; distortion. The cartoonist's *caricature* of Senator Foghorn grossly exaggerated the size of the senator's nose and ears. also V.

carping ADJ. finding fault. A *carping* critic is a nitpicker, someone who loves to point out flaws. carp, V.

caste N. one of the hereditary classes in Hindu society; social stratification; prestige. She bore a mark on her forehead signifying she was a Brahmin, a member of the highest *caste.*

castigation V. punishment, severe criticism. Sensitive to even mild criticism, Virginia Woolf could not bear the *castigation* that she met in certain reviews. castigate, V.

casualty N. serious or fatal accident. The number of *casualties* on this holiday weekend was high.

catastrophe N. calamity; disaster. The 1906 San Francisco earthquake was a *catastrophe* that destroyed most of the city.

categorical ADJ. without exceptions; unqualified; absolute. Though the captain claimed he was never, never sick at sea, he finally had to qualify his *categorical* denial: he was "hardly ever" sick at sea.

catharsis N. release of repressed emotional tensions. She blurted out her feelings, but felt no *catharsis*, no flood of relief; instead, she merely felt embarrassed at having made a scene.

catholic ADJ. wide-ranging in interests. Her musical tastes are surprisingly *catholic*: she enjoys everything from the Anonymous Four to Lady Gaga.

caustic ADJ. burning; sarcastically biting. The critic's *caustic* review humiliated the actors, who resented his cutting remarks.

cede V. yield (title, territory) to; surrender formally. Eventually the descendants of England's Henry II were forced to *cede* their French territories to the King of France.

celebrated ADJ. Neil deGrasse Tyson is a *celebrated* American astrophysicist and popularizer of science. Director of the Hayden Planetarium, he gained fame as host of the radio show *Star Talk*.

■ **censor** N. inspector overseeing public morals; official who prevents publication of offensive material. Because certain passages in his novel *Ulysses* had been condemned by the *censor*, James Joyce was unable to publish the novel in England for many years.

censure V. blame; criticize. Though I don't blame Tony for leaving Tina, I do *censure* him for failing to pay child support.

cerebral ADJ. pertaining to the brain or intellect. The heroes of *Dumb and Dumber* were poorly equipped for *cerebral* pursuits.

cessation N. stopping. The airline workers threatened a *cessation* of all work if management failed to meet their demands. cease, V.

chagrin N. vexation (caused by humiliation or injured pride); disappointment. Embarrassed by his parents' shabby, working-class appearance, Doug felt their visit to his school would bring him nothing but *chagrin*. Someone filled with *chagrin* doesn't grin: he's too mortified.

chameleon N. lizard that changes color in different situations. Like the *chameleon*, the candidate assumed the political thinking of every group he met.

champion V. support militantly. Martin Luther King, Jr., won the Nobel Peace Prize because he *championed* the oppressed in their struggle for equality.

chaotic ADJ. in utter disorder. He tried to bring order into the *chaotic* state of affairs. chaos, N.

charismatic ADJ. compellingly charming; magnetic. The late Steve Jobs, former CEO of Apple, who commanded a rock-star-like following, was more than once called "the model of a *charismatic* leader."

charlatan N. quack; pretender to knowledge. When they realized that the Wizard didn't know how to get them back to Kansas, Dorothy and her friends were sure they'd been duped by a *charlatan*.

chary ADJ. cautious; sparing or restrained about giving. A prudent, thrifty, New Englander, DeWitt was as *chary* of investing money in junk bonds as he was *chary* of paying people unnecessary compliments.

chastise V. punish physically; scold verbally. "Spare the rod and spoil the child," Miss Watson said, grabbing her birch wand and proceeding to *chastise* poor Huck thoroughly.

chauvinist N. blindly devoted patriot. *Chauvinists* cannot recognize any faults in their country, no matter how flagrant they may be. Likewise, a male *chauvinist* cannot recognize his bias in favor of his own sex, no matter how flagrant that may be.

check V. stop motion; curb or restrain. Thrusting out her arm, Grandma *checked* Bobby's lunge at his sister. "Young man," she said, "you'd better *check* your temper."

chicanery N. trickery; deception. Those sneaky lawyers misrepresented what occurred, made up all sorts of implausible alternative scenarios to confuse the jurors, and in general depended on *chicanery* to win the case.

choreography N. art of representing dances in written symbols; arrangement of dances. Merce Cunningham used a computer in designing *choreography*: a software program allowed him to compose arrangements of possible moves and to view them immediately onscreen.

Word List 9   chronic–conception

■ **chronic** ADJ. long established (as a disease). The doctors were finally able to attribute his *chronic* headaches and nausea to traces of formaldehyde gas in his apartment.

■ **chronicle** V. report; record (in chronological order). The gossip columnist was paid to *chronicle* the latest escapades of the socially prominent celebrities. also N.

circumscribe V. limit; confine. School regulations *circumscribed* Elle's social life: she hated having to follow rules that limited her activities.

■ **circumspect** ADJ. prudent; cautious. As the trial date draws near, defendants and their lawyers become increasingly *circumspect* about their comments, for fear that reports of what they have said might prejudice the outcome.

cite v. refer to or quote, especially to justify a position; praise; summon someone before a court. When asked to support her position on the need to vaccinate children against polio, Rosemary *cited* several reports of dangerous new outbreaks of this once nearly eliminated disease. The mayor *cited* the volunteers of Hook & Ladder Company 1 for their heroism in extinguishing the recent fire. Although Terry was *cited* for contempt of court, he never went to jail.

clemency n. disposition to be lenient; mildness, as of the weather. The lawyer was pleased when the case was sent to Judge Smith's chambers because Smith was noted for her *clemency* toward first offenders. We decided to eat dinner in the garden to enjoy the unexpected *clemency* of the weather.

cliché n. phrase dulled in meaning by repetition; trite theme. In writing your SAT essay, avoid using *clichés* like "sadder but wiser" and "old as the hills." Once a novel item on restaurant menus, blackened seafood dishes are now just another gastronomic *cliché*.

climactic adj. relating to the highest point. When Jack reached the *climactic* portions of the book, he could not stop reading. climax, n.

clique n. small exclusive group. Fitzgerald wished that he belonged to the *clique* of popular athletes and big men on campus who seemed to run Princeton's social life.

coalesce v. combine; fuse. The brooks *coalesced* into one large river. When minor political parties *coalesce*, their *coalescence* may create a major coalition.

coalition n. association; union. Jesse Jackson's Rainbow *Coalition* brought together people of many different races and creeds.

cogitate v. think over. *Cogitate* on this problem; the solution will come.

cognitive adj. having to do with knowing or perceiving; related to the mental processes. Though Jack was emotionally immature, his *cognitive* development was admirable; he was very advanced intellectually.

cohere v. stick together. Solids have a greater tendency to *cohere* than do liquids.

cohesion n. tendency to keep together. A firm believer in the maxim "Divide and conquer," the evil emperor, by means of lies and trickery, sought to disrupt the *cohesion* of the federation of free nations.

coincidence n. two or more things occurring at the same time by chance. Was it just a *coincidence* that John and she had chanced to meet at the market for three days running, or was he deliberately trying to seek her out? coincident, adj.

collaborate v. work together. Three writers *collaborated* in preparing this book.

colossal adj. huge. Radio City Music Hall has a *colossal* stage.

collusion n. conspiring in a fraudulent scheme. The swindlers were found guilty of *collusion*. collude, v.

commiserate v. feel or express pity or sympathy for. Her friends *commiserated* with the widow.

compact adj. tightly packed; firm; brief. His short, *compact* body was better suited to wrestling than to basketball.

compact n. agreement; contract. The signers of the Mayflower *Compact* were establishing a form of government.

comparable adj. similar. People whose jobs are *comparable* in difficulty should receive *comparable* pay.

compatible adj. harmonious; in harmony with. They were *compatible* neighbors, never quarreling over unimportant matters. compatibility, n.

compile v. assemble; gather; accumulate. We planned to *compile* a list of the words most frequently used on SAT examinations. compilation, n.

complacent adj. self-satisfied; smug. Feeling *complacent* about his latest victories, he looked smugly at the row of trophies on his mantelpiece. complacency, n.

complement n. something that completes or fills up; number or quantity needed to make something complete. During the eighteenth century, fashionable accessories became an important *complement* to a lady's attire; without her proper fan and reticule, her outfit was incomplete. Gomer had the usual *complement* of eyes and ears, two of each.

complement v. complete; make perfect. The waiter recommended a glass of port to *complement* the cheese. also n.

compliance n. readiness to yield; conformity in fulfilling requirements. Bill was so bullheaded that we never expected his easy *compliance* to our requests. As an architect, however, Bill recognized that his design for the new school had to be in *compliance* with the local building code.

component n. element; ingredient. I wish all the *components* of my stereo system were working at the same time.

composure n. mental calmness. Even the latest work crisis failed to shake her *composure*.

compound n. something composed of the union of separate parts or elements; walled-in area containing separate buildings. As a chemical *compound*, a water molecule contains one oxygen atom and two hydrogen atoms linked by covalent bonds. The Kennedy *Compound* consists of three houses on six fenced-in acres of waterfront property on Cape Cod in Hyannis Port, Massachusetts.

compound v. make up into a whole; combine ingredients; make something bad worse. "The flavor of American life was *compounded* of risk, spontaneity, independence, initiative, drift, mobility, and opportunity." (Daniel Boorstin) Before pharmacies existed, doctors *compounded* their own medicines, using a mortar and pestle to grind the ingredients. Trying to run or hide away from your fears only *compounds* the problem; the only way to overcome fear is to tackle the problem head-on.

■ **compromise** V. adjust or settle by making mutual concessions; endanger the interests or reputation of. Sometimes the presence of a neutral third party can help adversaries *compromise* their differences. Unfortunately, your presence at the scene of the dispute *compromises* our claim to neutrality in this matter. also N.

compute V. reckon; calculate. He failed to *compute* the interest; so his bank balance was not accurate.

■ **concentration** N. action of focusing one's total attention; gathering of people or things close to one another; relative amount of a substance (in a mixture, solution, volume of space, etc.). As Ty filled in the bubbles on his answer sheet, he frowned in *concentration*. Oakland has one of the largest *concentrations* of Tagalog-speakers in California. Fertilizers contain high *concentrations* of nitrogen to help promote the growth of crops.

conception N. beginning; forming of an idea. From its *conception* in 2005, the research project ran into serious problems. I had no *conception* of how serious the problems had grown until I visited the project in 2015.

Word List 10 concerted–contention

concerted ADJ. mutually agreed on; done together. All the Girl Scouts made a *concerted* effort to raise funds for their annual outing. When the movie star appeared, his fans let out a *concerted* sigh.

concession N. something granted in response to a demand; acknowledgment; preferential rate; right granted to use land, property, and so on, for a specific purpose. Before they could reach an agreement, both sides had to make certain *concessions*. Signing up for marital counseling is not a *concession* of failure; it is a commitment to do your best to make the marriage a success. The government intended its recent tax *concessions* to help subsidize home owners through lower tax rates. California's Shell Oil Company was granted the parking *concession* for the 1915 World's Fair.

concise ADJ. brief but comprehensive. The instructions were *concise* and to the point: they included every necessary detail and not one word more. Precision indicates exactness; *concision* indicates compactness. To achieve *conciseness*, cut out unnecessary words.

concoct V. prepare by combining; make up in concert. How did the inventive chef ever *concoct* such a strange dish? concoction, N.

concrete ADJ. physical or material in nature, as opposed to abstract; real; specific. The word "boy" is *concrete*; the word "boyhood" is abstract. Unless the police turn up some *concrete* evidence of his guilt, we have no case against him. I don't have time to listen to vague pitches; come up with a *concrete* proposal, and then we can talk.

concur V. express agreement with an opinion; happen together. Justice Sotomayor wrote a minority opinion because she did not *concur* with the reasoning of her fellow justices. Sunday was both Mother's Day and Sally's graduation: it was a happy coincidence that the two events *concurred*.

condemn V. censure; sentence; force or limit to a particular state. In *My Cousin Vinnie*, Vinnie's fiancée *condemned* Vinnie for mishandling his cousin Tony's defense. If Vinnie didn't do a better job defending Tony, the judge would *condemn* Tony to death, and Vinnie would be *condemned* to cleaning toilets for a living.

condense V. make more compact or dense; shorten or abridge; reduce into a denser form. If you squeeze a slice of Wonder Bread, taking out the extra air, you can *condense* it into a pellet the size of a sugar cube. If you cut out the unnecessary words from your essay, you can *condense* it to a paragraph. As the bathroom cooled down, the steam from the shower *condensed* into droplets of water.

condescend V. act conscious of descending to a lower level; patronize. Though Jill was a star softball player in college, when she played a pickup game at the local park she never *condescended* to her teammates or acted as if she thought herself superior to them. condescension. N.

■ **condone** V. overlook voluntarily; forgive. Unlike the frail widow, who indulged her only son and *condoned* his mischievous behavior, the boy's stern uncle did nothing but scold.

■ **confine** V. shut in; restrict. The terrorists had *confined* their prisoner in a small room. However, they had not chained him to the wall or done anything else to *confine* his movements further. confinement, N.

■ **confirm** V. corroborate; verify; support. I have several witnesses who will *confirm* my account of what happened.

■ **conformity** N. agreement or compliance; actions in agreement with prevailing social customs. In *conformity* with the bylaws of the Country Dance and Song Society, I am submitting a petition nominating Susan Murrow as president of the society. Because Kate had always been a rebellious child, we were surprised by her *conformity* to the standards of behavior prevalent at her new school.

■ **confront** V. face someone or something; encounter, often in a hostile way. Fearing his wife's hot temper, Stanley was reluctant to *confront* her about her skyrocketing credit card bills.

congeal V. freeze; coagulate. His blood *congealed* in his veins as he saw the dreaded monster rush toward him.

congenial ADJ. pleasant; friendly. My father loved to go out for a meal with *congenial* companions.

conjecture V. surmise; guess. Although there was no official count, the organizers *conjectured* that more than 10,000 marchers took part in the March for Peace. also N.

connotation N. suggested or implied meaning of an expression. Foreigners frequently are unaware of the *connotations* of the words they use.

■ **conscientious** ADJ. scrupulous, careful. A *conscientious* editor, she checked every definition for its accuracy.

consensus N. general agreement. Every time the garden club members had nearly reached a *consensus* about what to plant, Mistress Mary, quite contrary, disagreed.

consequence N. result or outcome of an action; importance; self-importance. One *consequence* of the recent heavy downpour was a major mud slide that disrupted traffic for days. Like it or not, your score on the SAT may be of great *consequence* to you. Convinced of his own importance, the actor strutted about the dressing room with such an air of *consequence* that it was hard for his valet to keep a straight face. consequential, ADJ.

■ **consistency** N. absence of contradictions; dependability; degree of thickness. Sherlock Holmes judged puddings and explanations on their *consistency*: he liked his puddings without lumps and his explanations without improbabilities. Show up every day and do your job: *consistency* in performance is the mark of a good employee. If the pea soup is too thick, add some stock until it reaches the *consistency* you want. consistent, ADJ.

■ **consolidation** N. unification; process of becoming firmer or stronger. The recent *consolidation* of several small airlines into one major company has left observers of the industry wondering whether room still exists for the "little guy" in aviation. consolidate, V.

conspicuous ADJ. easily seen; noticeable; striking. Janet was *conspicuous* both for her red hair and for her height.

constituent N. resident of a district represented by an elected official. The congressman received hundreds of letters from angry *constituents* after he voted for cuts to Medicare.

constraint N. compulsion; repression of feelings. There was a feeling of *constraint* in the room because no one dared to criticize the speaker. constrain, V.

contagion N. infection. Fearing *contagion,* the health authorities took great steps to prevent the spread of the disease.

contempt N. scorn; disdain. The heavyweight boxer looked on ordinary people with *contempt,* scorning them as weaklings who couldn't hurt a fly. We thought it was *contemptible* of him to be *contemptuous* of people for being weak.

contend V. argue earnestly; struggle in rivalry. Sociologist Harry Edwards *contends* that some colleges exploit young African American athletes, supporting them as athletes *contending* against one another in sports, but failing to support them as students working toward a degree.

contention N. angry disagreement; point made in a debate or argument; competition. Some people are peacemakers; others seek out any excuse for quarrels and *contention*. It is our *contention* that if you follow our tactics, you will boost your score on the PSAT. Through his editor, Styron learned that he was in *contention* for the National Book Award.

Word List 11   contentious–curtail

contentious ADJ. quarrelsome. Disagreeing violently with the referees' ruling, the coach became so *contentious* that they threw him out of the game.

context N. writings preceding and following the passage quoted. Because these lines are taken out of *context,* they do not convey the message the author intended.

contingent ADJ. dependent on; conditional. Cher's father informed her that any increase in her allowance was *contingent* on the quality of her final grades. contingency, N.

contingent N. group that makes up part of a gathering. The New York *contingent* of delegates at the Democratic National Convention was a boisterous, sometimes rowdy lot.

contract V. compress or shrink; establish by agreement; incur an obligation; catch a disease. Warm metal expands; cold metal *contracts*. During World War II, Germany *contracted* an alliance with Italy and Japan. To pay for his college education, James *contracted* a debt of $20,000. If you think you have *contracted* an infectious disease, see your doctor.

■ **convention** N. social or moral custom; established practice. Flying in the face of *convention,* George Sand shocked society by taking lovers and wearing men's clothes.

converge V. approach; tend to meet; come together. African-American men from all over the United States *converged* on Washington to take part in the historic Million Man march.

convert N. one who has adopted a different religion or opinion. On his trip to Japan, though the president spoke at length about the merits of American automobiles, he made few *converts* to his beliefs. also V.

■ **conviction** N. judgment that someone is guilty of a crime; strongly held belief. Even her *conviction* for murder did not shake Peter's *conviction* that Harriet was innocent of the crime.

convoluted ADJ. complex and involved; intricate; winding; coiled. Talk about twisted! The new tax regulations are so *convoluted* that even my accountant can't unravel their mysteries.

■ **corroborate** V. confirm; support. Though Huck was quite willing to *corroborate* Tom's story, Aunt Polly knew better than to believe either of them.

corrosion N. destruction by chemical action. The *corrosion* of the girders supporting the bridge took place so gradually that no one suspected any danger until the bridge suddenly collapsed. corrode, V.

cosmopolitan ADJ. sophisticated. Her years in the capital had transformed her into a *cosmopolitan* young woman highly aware of international affairs.

countenance V. approve; tolerate. He refused to *countenance* such rude behavior on their part.

counterpart N. a thing that completes another; things very much alike. Night and day are *counterparts*, complementing one another.

covert ADJ. secret; hidden; implied. Investigations of the Central Intelligence Agency and other secret service networks reveal that such *covert* operations can get out of control.

credibility N. believability. Because the candidate had made some pretty unbelievable promises, we began to question the *credibility* of everything she said.

credulity N. belief on slight evidence; gullibility; naïveté. Con artists take advantage of the *credulity* of inexperienced investors to swindle them out of their savings. credulous, ADJ.

■ **criterion** N. standard used in judging. What *criterion* did you use when you selected this essay as the prizewinner? criteria, Pl.

cryptic ADJ. mysterious; hidden; secret. Thoroughly baffled by Holmes's *cryptic* remarks, Watson wondered whether Holmes was intentionally concealing his thoughts about the crime.

culmination N. attainment of highest point. Her inauguration as president of the United States marked the *culmination* of her political career. culminate, V.

culpable ADJ. deserving blame. Corrupt politicians who condone the illegal activities of gamblers are equally *culpable*.

cumulative ADJ. growing by addition. vocabulary building is a *cumulative* process: as you go through your flash cards, you will add new words to your vocabulary, one by one.

curb V. restrain. The overly generous philanthropist had to *curb* his beneficent impulses before he gave away all his money and left himself with nothing.

cursory ADJ. casual; hastily done. Because a *cursory* examination of the ruins indicates the possibility of arson, we believe the insurance agency should undertake a more extensive investigation of the fire's cause.

■ **curtail** V. shorten; reduce. When Elton asked Cher for a date, she said she was really sorry she couldn't go out with him, but her dad had ordered her to *curtail* her social life.

Word List 12   cynical–demolish

cynical ADJ. skeptical or distrustful of human motives. *Cynical* from birth, Sidney was suspicious whenever anyone give him a gift "with no strings attached." cynic, N.

daunt V. intimidate; frighten. "Boast all you like of your prowess. Mere words cannot *daunt* me," the *dauntless* hero answered the villain.

dawdle V. loiter; waste time. At the mall, Mother grew impatient with Jo and Amy because they tended to *dawdle* as they went from store to store.

■ **dearth** N. scarcity. The *dearth* of skilled labor compelled the employers to open trade schools.

■ **debilitate** V. weaken; enfeeble. Michael's severe bout of the flu *debilitated* him so much that he was too tired to go to work for a week.

decadence N. decay or decline, especially moral; self-indulgence. We named our best-selling ice cream flavor "chocolate *decadence*" because only truly self-indulgent people would treat themselves to something so calorific and cholesterol laden.

decipher V. decode. I could not *decipher* the doctor's handwriting.

decorous ADJ. proper. Prudence's *decorous* behavior was praised by her teachers, who wished they had a classroom full of such polite and proper little girls. decorum, N.

decoy N. lure or bait. The wild ducks were not fooled by the *decoy*. also V.

■ **decry** V. express strong disapproval of; disparage. The founder of the Children's Defense Fund, Marian Wright Edelman, strongly *decries* the lack of financial and moral support for children in America today.

deducible ADJ. derived by reasoning. If we accept your premise, your conclusions are easily *deducible*.

deface V. mar; disfigure. If you *deface* a library book, you will have to pay a hefty fine.

defamation N. harming a person's reputation. *Defamation* of character may result in a slander suit. If rival candidates persist in *defaming* one another, the voters may conclude that all politicians are crooks.

defeatist ADJ. attitude of one who is ready to accept defeat as a natural outcome. If you maintain your *defeatist* attitude, you will never succeed. also N.

- **deference** N. courteous regard for another's wishes; respect owed to a superior. In *deference* to the minister's request, please do not take photographs during the wedding service. As the Bishop's wife, Mrs. Proudie expected the wives of the lesser clergy to treat her with due *deference*.

- **defiance** N. opposition; willingness to resist. In learning to read and write in *defiance* of his master's orders, Frederick Douglass showed exceptional courage. defy, v.

- **definition** N. statement of a word's exact meaning; clarity of sound or image being reproduced; distinctness of outlines, boundaries. This word list gives three *definitions* for the word *definition*. The newest flat screen monitors have excellent resolution and amazing color *definition*. The gym's fitness program includes specific exercises to improve *definition* of the abdominal muscles.

- **definitive** ADJ. final; complete. Carl Sandburg's *Abraham Lincoln* may be regarded as the *definitive* work on the life of the Great Emancipator.

- **defunct** ADJ. dead; no longer in use or existence. The lawyers sought to examine the books of the *defunct* corporation.

- **degenerate** V. become worse; deteriorate. As the fight dragged on, the champion's style *degenerated* until he could barely keep on his feet.

- **delete** V. erase; strike out. Less is more: if you *delete* this paragraph, the composition will have more appeal.

- **deleterious** ADJ. harmful. If you believe that smoking is *deleterious* to your health (and the surgeon general certainly does), then quit!

- **deliberate** V. consider; ponder. Offered the new job, she asked for time to *deliberate* before she told them her decision.

- **delineate** V. portray; depict; sketch. Using only a few descriptive phrases, Jane Austen *delineates* the character of Mr. Collins so well that we can predict his every move. delineation, N.

- **delusion** N. false belief; hallucination. Don suffers from *delusions* of grandeur: he thinks he's a world-famous author when he's published just one paperback book.

- **demean** V. degrade; humiliate. Standing on his dignity, he refused to *demean* himself by replying to the offensive letter. If you truly believed in the dignity of labor, you would not think it would *demean* you to work as a janitor.

- **demeanor** N. behavior; bearing. His sober *demeanor* quieted the noisy revelers.

- **demolish** V. destroy; tear down. Before building a new hotel along the waterfront, the construction company had to *demolish* several rundown warehouses on that site. demolition, N.

demur V. object (because of doubts, scruples); hesitate. When offered a post on the board of directors, David *demurred*: he had doubts about taking on the job because he was unsure he could handle it in addition to his other responsibilities.

demystify V. clarify; free from mystery or obscurity. Helpful doctors *demystify* medical procedures by describing them in everyday language, explaining that a myringotomy, for example, is an operation involving making a small hole in one's eardrum.

- **denounce** V. condemn; criticize. The reform candidate *denounced* the corrupt city officials for having betrayed the public's trust. denunciation, N.

deny V. contradict; refuse. Do you *deny* his story, or do you support what he says? How could Pat *deny* the truth of the accusation that he'd been swiping the Oreos when he'd been caught with his hand in the cookie jar? denial, N.

- **depict** V. portray. In this sensational exposé, the author *depicts* John Lennon as a drug-crazed neurotic. Do you question the accuracy of this *depiction* of Lennon?

- **deplete** V. reduce; exhaust. We must wait until we *deplete* our present inventory before we order replacements.

deplore V. regret strongly; express grief over. Although Ann Landers *deplored* the disintegration of the modern family, she recognized that not every marriage could be saved.

deprecate V. express disapproval of; protest against. A firm believer in old-fashioned courtesy, Miss Post *deprecated* the unfortunate modern tendency to address new acquaintances by their first names. deprecatory, ADJ.

depreciate V. lessen in value. If you neglect this property, it will *depreciate*.

deprivation N. loss. In prison she faced the sudden *deprivation* of rights she had taken for granted: the right to stay up late reading a book, the right to privacy, the right to make a phone call to a friend.

derelict ADJ. abandoned; negligent. The *derelict* craft was a menace to navigation. Whoever abandoned it in mid harbor was *derelict* in living up to his or her responsibilities as a boat owner. dereliction, N.

- **derision** N. ridicule; mockery. Greeting his pretentious dialogue with *derision*, the critics refused to consider his play seriously. deride, V.

- **derivative** ADJ. unoriginal; derived from another source. Although her early poetry was clearly *derivative* in nature, the critics felt she had promise and eventually would find her own voice.

designation N. identifying name; appointment to a position or office. For years the president's home had no proper *designation*; eventually it was called the

White House. Given Gary's background in accounting, his *designation* as treasurer came as no surprise to his fellow board members.

despise V. look on with scorn; regard as worthless or distasteful. Mr. Bond, I *despise* spies; I look down on them as mean, *despicable*, honorless men, whom I would cheerfully wipe from the face of the earth.

despondent ADJ. depressed; gloomy. To the dismay of his parents, William became so seriously *despondent* after he broke up with Jan that they despaired of finding a cure for his gloom. despondency, N.

desultory ADJ. aimless; haphazard; digressing at random. In prison Malcolm X set himself the task of reading straight through the dictionary; to him, reading was purposeful, not *desultory*.

detachment N. emotional remoteness; group sent away (on a military mission, etc.); process of separation. Psychoanalysts must maintain their professional *detachment* and stay uninvolved with their patients' personal lives. The plane transported a *detachment* of Peace Corps volunteers heading for their first assignment abroad. Retinal *detachment*, in which the retina and optic nerve separate, causes severe vision loss.

■ **determination** N. resolve; measurement or calculation. Nothing could shake his *determination* that his children would get the best education that money could buy. Thanks to my pocket calculator, my *determination* of the answer to the problem took only seconds of my time.

■ **deterrent** N. something that discourages; hindrance. Does the threat of capital punishment serve as a *deterrent* to potential killers? deter, V.

detrimental ADJ. harmful; damaging. The candidate's acceptance of major financial contributions from a well-known racist ultimately proved *detrimental* to his campaign, for he lost the backing of many of his early grassroots supporters. detriment, N.

deviate V. turn away from (a principle, norm); depart; diverge. Richard never *deviated* from his daily routine: every day he set off for work at eight o'clock, had his sack lunch (peanut butter on whole wheat) at 12:15, and headed home at the stroke of five.

devious ADJ. roundabout; erratic; not straightforward. The Joker's plan was so *devious* that it was only with great difficulty we could follow its shifts and dodges.

devise V. think up; invent; plan. How clever he must be to have *devised* such a devious plan! What ingenious inventions might he have *devised* if he had turned his mind to science and not to crime.

dexterous ADJ. skillful. The magician was so *dexterous* that we could not follow him as he performed his tricks.

diagnosis N. art of identifying a disease; analysis of a condition. In medical school Margaret developed her skill at *diagnosis*, learning how to read volumes from

a rapid pulse or a hacking cough. diagnose, V.; diagnostic, ADJ.

dichotomy N. split; branching into two parts (especially contradictory ones). Willie didn't know how to resolve the *dichotomy* between his ambition to go to college and his childhood longing to run away to join the circus. Then he heard about Ringling Brothers Circus College, and he knew he'd found the perfect school.

Word List 14   didactic–disparate

■ **didactic** ADJ. teaching; instructional. Pope's lengthy poem *An Essay on Man* is too *didactic* for my taste: I dislike it when poets turn preachy and moralize.

differentiate V. distinguish; perceive a difference between. Tweedledum and Tweedledee were like two peas in a pod; not even Mother Tweedle could *differentiate* the one from the other.

■ **diffident** ADJ. shy; lacking confidence; reserved. Can a naturally *diffident* person become a fast-talking, successful used car salesman?

diffuse ADJ. both wordy and poorly organized; spread out (as opposed to concentrated). If you pay authors by the word, you're tempting them to produce *diffuse* books instead of concise ones. When a cloud covers the sun, the lighting is *diffuse*, or spread evenly across the entire sky overhead. diffusion, N.

■ **digression** N. wandering away from the subject. Nobody minded when Professor Renoir's lectures wandered away from their official theme; his *digressions* were always more fascinating than the topic of the day. digress, V.

dilemma N. problem; choice of two unsatisfactory alternatives. In this *dilemma*, he knew no one to whom he could turn for advice.

dilettante N. aimless follower of the arts; amateur; dabbler. He was not serious in his painting; he was rather a *dilettante*.

diligence N. steadiness of effort; persistent hard work. Her employers were greatly impressed by her *diligence* and offered her a partnership in the firm. diligent, ADJ.

dilute V. make less concentrated; reduce in strength. She preferred her coffee *diluted* with milk.

diminutive ADJ. small in size. Looking at the tiny gymnast, we were amazed that anyone so *diminutive* could perform with such power.

din N. continued loud noise. The *din* of the jackhammers outside the classroom window drowned out the lecturer's voice. also V.

■ **discernible** ADJ. distinguishable; perceivable. The ships in the harbor were not *discernible* in the fog.

discerning ADJ. mentally quick and observant; having insight. Though no genius, the star was sufficiently *discerning* to tell her true friends from the countless phonies who flattered her.

disclaimer N. denial of a legal claim or right; disavowal. Though reporter Joe Klein issued a *disclaimer* stating that he was *not* Anonymous, the author of *Primary Colors,* eventually he admitted that he had written the controversial novel. disclaim, V.

■ **disclose** V. reveal. Although competitors offered him bribes, he refused to *disclose* any information about his company's forthcoming product. disclosure, N.

disconcert V. confuse; upset; embarrass. The lawyer was *disconcerted* by the evidence produced by her adversary.

■ **discord** N. lack of harmony; conflict; Watching Tweedledum battle Tweedledee, Alice wondered what had caused this pointless *discord.*

discordant ADJ. disagreeable to the ear; not in harmony. Nothing is quite so *discordant* as the sound of a junior high school orchestra tuning up. Viewers disagree wildly about the merits of *Game of Thrones,* as the highly *discordant* comments on Facebook make obvious.

discount V. discredit; reduce in price. Be prepared to *discount* what he has to say about his ex-wife; he is still very bitter about the divorce. Sharon waited to buy a bathing suit until Macy's fall sale, when the department store *discounted* the summer fashions.

■ **discrepancy** N. lack of consistency; contradiction; difference. "Observe, Watson, the significant *discrepancies* between Sir Percy's original description of the crime and his most recent testimony. What do these contradictions suggest?"

■ **discriminating** ADJ. treating people of different classes unequally; able to see subtle differences. The firm was accused of *discriminating* hiring practices that were biased against women. A superb interpreter of Picasso, she was sufficiently *discriminating* to judge the most complex works of modern art. [secondary meaning] discrimination, N.

disdain V. view with scorn or contempt. In the film *Funny Face,* the bookish heroine *disdained* fashion models for their lack of intellectual interests. also N.

■ **disenfranchise** V. deprive of a civil right. The imposition of the poll tax effectively *disenfranchised* poor Southern blacks, who lost their right to vote.

disgruntled ADJ. discontented; sulky and dissatisfied. The numerous delays left the passengers feeling *disgruntled.* disgruntle, V.

■ **disinterested** ADJ. unprejudiced. Given the judge's political ambitions and the lawyers' financial interest in the case, the only *disinterested* person in the courtroom may have been the court reporter.

dismay V. discourage; frighten. The huge amount of work she had left to do *dismayed* her. also N.

■ **dismiss** V. let go from employment; refuse to accept or consider. To cut costs, the store manager *dismissed* all the full-time workers and replaced them with part-time employees at lower pay. Because Tina believed in Tony's fidelity, she *dismissed* the notion that he might be having an affair.

■ **disparage** V. belittle. A doting mother, Emma was more likely to praise her son's crude attempts at art than to *disparage* them.

disparate ADJ. basically different; unrelated. Unfortunately, Tony and Tina have *disparate* notions of marriage: Tony sees it as a carefree extended love affair, while Tina sees it as a solemn commitment to build a family and a home.

Word List 15   disparity–duplicity

disparity N. difference; condition of inequality. Their *disparity* in rank made no difference at all to the prince and Cinderella.

dispassionate ADJ. calm; impartial. Known in the company for his cool judgment, Bill could impartially examine the causes of a problem, giving a *dispassionate* analysis of what had gone wrong, and go on to suggest how to correct the mess.

dispatch N. speediness of execution; message sent with all due speed. Young Napoleon defeated the enemy with all possible *dispatch;* he then sent a *dispatch* to headquarters, informing his commander of the great victory. also V.

dispel V. scatter; cause to vanish. The bright sunlight eventually *dispelled* the morning mist.

■ **disperse** V. scatter. The police fired tear gas into the crowd to *disperse* the protesters.

disputatious ADJ. argumentative; fond of arguing. Convinced he knew more than his lawyers, Tom was a *disputatious* client, ready to argue about the best way to conduct the case.

dissemble V. disguise; pretend. Even though John tried to *dissemble* his motive for taking modern dance, we all knew he was there not to dance but to meet girls.

disseminate V. distribute; spread; scatter (like seeds). By their use of the Internet, propagandists have been able to *disseminate* their pet doctrines to new audiences around the globe.

■ **dissent** V. disagree. In the recent Supreme Court decision, Justice Sotomayor *dissented* from the majority opinion. also N.

dissertation N. formal essay. In order to earn a graduate degree from many of our universities, a candidate is frequently required to prepare a *dissertation* on some scholarly subject.

dissident ADJ. dissenting; rebellious. In the purge that followed the student demonstrations at Tiananmen

Square, the government hunted down the *dissident* students and their supporters. also N.

dissuade V. persuade not to do; discourage. Since Tom could not *dissuade* Huck from running away from home, he decided to run away with him. dissuasion, N.

■ **distinction** N. honor; contrast; discrimination. A holder of the Medal of Honor, George served with great *distinction* in World War II. He made a *distinction,* however, between World War II and Vietnam, which he considered an immoral conflict.

■ **distort** V. twist out of shape. It is difficult to believe the newspaper accounts of the riots because of the way some reports *distort* and exaggerate the actual events. distortion, N.

divergent ADJ. differing; deviating. Since graduating from medical school, the two doctors have taken *divergent* paths, the one going on to become a nationally prominent surgeon, the other dedicating himself to a small family practice in his hometown. divergence, N.

■ **diverse** ADJ. differing in some characteristics; various. The professor suggested *diverse* ways of approaching the assignment and recommended that we choose one of them. diversity, N.

diversion N. act of turning aside; pastime. After studying for several hours, he needed a *diversion* from work. divert, V.

■ **divulge** V. reveal. No lover of gossip, Charlotte would never *divulge* anything that a friend told her in confidence.

■ **docile** ADJ. obedient; easily managed. As *docile* as he seems today, that old lion was once a ferocious, snarling beast.

■ **doctrine** N. teachings, in general; particular principle (religious, legal, etc.) taught. He was so committed to the *doctrines* of his faith that he was unable to evaluate them impartially. The Monroe *Doctrine* declared the Western Hemisphere off-limits to European attempts at colonization.

■ **document** V. create a detailed record; provide written evidence to support statements. As a young photographer, Johnny Seal *documented* the Occupy Oakland demonstrations in his hometown. Sue kept all the receipts from her business trip in order to *document* her expenses for the Internal Revenue Service.

dogmatic ADJ. opinionated; arbitrary; doctrinal. We tried to discourage Doug from being so *dogmatic* but never could convince him that his opinions might be wrong.

dormant ADJ. sleeping; lethargic; latent. At fifty her long-*dormant* ambition to write flared up once more; within a year she had completed the first of her great historical novels.

doubtful ADJ. uncertain; undecided. From the outset, the outcome of the battle was *doubtful*: we had no certainty that we were going to win.

downcast ADJ. disheartened; sad. Cheerful and optimistic by nature, Beth was never *downcast* despite the difficulties she faced.

dubious ADJ. uncertain or suspicious; of doubtful quality. I am *dubious* about the value of the changes the College Board has made in the SAT. Many critics of the SAT contend that the test is of *dubious* worth: they doubt the test accurately predicts which students will succeed in college.

duplicity N. double-dealing; hypocrisy. When Tanya learned that Mark had been two-timing her, she was furious at his *duplicity.*

Word List 16   **duty–enhance**

duty N. tax on imported or exported goods. Because he was too stingy to pay the *duty* on the watch he'd bought in Switzerland, Rex foolishly tried to smuggle it through Customs.

dwindle V. shrink; reduce. The food in the lifeboat gradually *dwindled* away to nothing.

eccentric ADJ. irregular; odd or whimsical. The comet veered dangerously close to Earth in its *eccentric* orbit. People came up with some *eccentric* ideas for dealing with the emergency: someone even suggested tying a knot in the comet's tail! eccentricity, N.

eclectic ADJ. composed of elements drawn from disparate sources. His style of interior decoration was *eclectic*: bits and pieces of furnishings from widely divergent periods strikingly juxtaposed to create a unique decor. eclecticism, N.

■ **eclipse** V. darken; extinguish; surpass. The new stock market high *eclipsed* the previous record set in 1995.

■ **economy** N. national condition of monetary supply, goods production, etc.; prudent management of resources; efficiency or conciseness in use of words. The president favors tax cuts to stimulate the *economy*. I need to practice *economy* when I shop: no more impulse buying for me! Reading the epigrams of the pope, I admire the *economy* of his verse: in few words he conveys worlds of meaning.

ecstasy N. rapture; joy; any overpowering emotion. When Allison received her long-hoped-for letter of acceptance from Harvard, she was in *ecstasy*. ecstatic, ADJ.

effervescence N. inner excitement or exuberance; bubbling from fermentation or carbonation. Nothing depressed Sue for long; her natural *effervescence* soon reasserted itself. Soda that loses its *effervescence* goes flat. effervescent, ADJ. , effervesce, V.

■ **efficacy** N. power to produce desired effect. The *efficacy* of this drug depends on the regularity of the dosage. efficacious, adj.

egotistical ADJ. excessively self-centered; self-important; conceited. Typical *egotistical* remark: "But enough of this chit-chat about you and your little problems. Let's talk about what's really important: *Me!*"

egregious ADJ. notorious; gross; shocking. She was an *egregious* liar; we all knew better than to believe a word she said.

elated ADJ. overjoyed; in high spirits. Grinning from ear to ear, Carl Lewis was clearly *elated* by his ninth Olympic gold medal. elation, N.

■ **elicit** V. draw out (by discussion); call forth. The camp counselor's humorous remarks finally *elicited* a smile from the shy new camper.

eloquence N. expressiveness; persuasive speech. The crowds were stirred by Martin Luther King's *eloquence*. eloquent, ADJ.

elucidate V. explain; enlighten. He was called upon to *elucidate* the disputed points in his article.

elusive ADJ. evasive; baffling; hard to grasp. Trying to pin down exactly when the contractors would be done remodeling the house, Nancy was frustrated by their *elusive* replies. elude, V.

emancipate V. set free. At first, the attempts of the abolitionists to *emancipate* the slaves were unpopular in New England as well as in the South.

■ **embellish** V. make more beautiful; make a story more interesting by adding (generally fictitious) details. The costume designer *embellished* the leading lady's ball gown with yards and yards of ribbon and lace. We enjoyed my mother-inlaw's stories about how she came here from Russia, in part because she *embellished* the bare facts of the journey with humorous anecdotes and vivid descriptive details.

embrace V. hug; adopt or espouse; include. Clasping Maid Marian in his arms, Robin Hood *embraced* her lovingly. In joining the outlaws in Sherwood Forest, she had openly *embraced* their cause. The *Encyclopedia of the Middle Ages embraces* a wide variety of subjects, with articles on everything from agricultural implements to zodiac signs.

empathy N. ability to identify with another's feelings, ideas, etc. What made Ann such a fine counselor was her *empathy*, her ability to put herself in her client's place and feel his emotions as if they were her own. empathize, V.

empirical ADJ. based on experience. He distrusted hunches and intuitive flashes; he placed his reliance entirely on *empirical* data.

emulate V. imitate; rival. In a brief essay, describe a person you admire, someone whose virtues you would like to *emulate*.

encumber V. burden. Some people *encumber* themselves with too much luggage when they go for short trips.

■ **endorse** V. approve; support. Everyone waited to see which one of the rival candidates for the city council the mayor would *endorse*. endorsement, N. (secondary meaning).

enduring ADJ. lasting; surviving. Keats believed in the *enduring* power of great art, which would outlast its creators' brief lives. endure, V.

energize V. invigorate; make forceful and active. Rather than exhausting Maggie, dancing *energized* her.

enfranchise V. admit to the rights of citizenship (especially the right to vote). Although blacks were *enfranchised* shortly after the Civil War, women did not receive the right to vote until 1920.

■ **engage** V. pledge to do something (especially, to marry); hire someone to perform a service; attract and keep (attention); induce someone to participate; take part in; attack (an enemy). When Tom and Tina became *engaged*, they decided to *engage* a lawyer to write up a prenuptial agreement. Tom's job *engages* him completely. When he's focused on work, not even Tina can *engage* him in conversation. Instead, she *engages* in tennis matches, fiercely *engaging* her opponents.

engaging ADJ. charming; attractive. Everyone liked Nancy's pleasant manners and *engaging* personality.

engender V. cause; produce. To receive praise for real accomplishments *engenders* self-confidence in a child.

engross V. occupy fully. John was so *engrossed* in his studies that he did not hear his mother call.

■ **enhance** V. increase; improve. You can *enhance* your chances of being admitted to the college of your choice by learning to write well; an excellent essay can *enhance* any application.

Word List 17   enigma–explicate

■ **enigma** N. puzzle; mystery. "What *do* women want?" asked Dr. Sigmund Freud. Their behavior was an *enigma* to him. enigmatic, ADJ.

enmity N. ill will; hatred. At Camp David, President Carter labored to bring an end to the *enmity* that prevented the peaceful coexistence of Egypt and Israel.

enterprising ADJ. ready to undertake ambitious projects. An *enterprising* young man, Matt saw business opportunities on every side and was always eager to capitalize on them.

■ **enumerate** V. list; mention one by one. Huck hung his head in shame as Miss Watson *enumerated* his many flaws.

enunciate V. speak distinctly. Stop mumbling! How will people understand you if you do not *enunciate*?

- **ephemeral** ADJ. short-lived; fleeting. The mayfly is an *ephemeral* creature: its adult life lasts little more than a day.

epic N. long heroic poem, novel, or similar work of art. Kurosawa's film *Seven Samurai* is an *epic* portraying the struggle of seven warriors to destroy a band of robbers. also ADJ.

equivocal ADJ. ambiguous; intentionally misleading. Rejecting the candidate's *equivocal* comments on tax reform, the reporters pressed him to state clearly where he stood on the issue. equivocate, V.

- **erode** V. eat away. The limestone was *eroded* by the dripping water until only a thin shell remained. erosion, N.

- **erratic** ADJ. odd; unpredictable. Investors become anxious when the stock market appears *erratic.*

- **erroneous** ADJ. mistaken; wrong. I thought my answer was correct, but it was *erroneous.*

esoteric ADJ. hard to understand; known only to the chosen few. *New Yorker* short stories often included *esoteric* allusions to obscure people and events; the implication was, if you were in the in-crowd, you'd get the reference; if you came from Cleveland, you would not.

- **espouse** V. adopt; support. She was always ready to *espouse* a worthy cause.

- **esteem** V. respect; value; Jill *esteemed* Jack's taste in music, but she deplored his taste in clothes.

estranged ADJ. separated; alienated. The *estranged* wife sought a divorce. estrangement, N.

ethnic ADJ. relating to a population sub-group; relating to cultural and national origins. Germany now is home to more than two million Turks, who constitute the country's largest foreign *ethnic* group. America's Muslim community is made up of people from a wide variety of *ethnic* backgrounds and national origins.

evasive ADJ. not frank; eluding. The witness's *evasive* answers convinced the jury that he was withholding important evidence. evade, V.

evenhanded ADJ. impartial; fair. Do men and women receive *evenhanded* treatment from their teachers, or, as recent studies suggest, do teachers pay more attention to male students than to females?

eventuality N. possible occurrence. The government instituted new security procedures to prepare for the *eventuality* of a terrorist attack.

evocative ADJ. tending to call up (emotions, memories). Scent can be remarkably *evocative:* the aroma of pipe tobacco *evokes* the memory of my father; a whiff of talcum powder calls up images of my daughter as a child.

exacting ADJ. extremely demanding. Cleaning the ceiling of the Sistine Chapel was an *exacting* task, one that demanded extremely meticulous care on the part of the restorers. exaction, N.

- **excerpt** N. selected passage (written or musical). The cinematic equivalent of an *excerpt* from a novel is a clip from a film.

exclaim V. cry out suddenly. "Watson! Behind you!" Holmes *exclaimed*, seeing the assassin hurl himself at his friend.

- **execute** V. put into effect; carry out; put to death. The United States Agency for International Development is responsible for *executing* America's development policy and foreign assistance. The ballet master wanted to see how well Margaret could *execute* a pirouette. Captured by the British while gathering military intelligence, Nathan Hale was tried and *executed* on September 22, 1776. execution, N.

- **exemplary** ADJ. serving as a model; outstanding. At commencement the dean praised Ellen for her *exemplary* behavior as class president.

exemplify V. serve as an example of; embody. For a generation of balletgoers, Rudolf Nureyev *exemplified* the ideal of masculine grace.

exhaustive ADJ. thorough; comprehensive. We have made an *exhaustive* study of all published SAT tests and are happy to share our research with you.

exonerate V. acquit; exculpate. The defense team feverishly sought fresh evidence that might *exonerate* its client.

expansive ADJ. outgoing and sociable; broad and extensive; able to increase in size. Mr. Fezziwig was in an *expansive* humor, cheerfully urging his guests to join in the Christmas feast. Looking down on his *expansive* paunch, he sighed: if his belly *expanded* any further, his pants would need an *expansive* waistline.

expedient ADJ. suitable to achieve a particular end; practical; politic. A pragmatic politician, he was guided by what was *expedient* rather than by what was ethical. expediency, N.

- **expedite** V. hasten. Because we are on a tight schedule, we hope you will be able to *expedite* the delivery of our order. expeditious, ADJ.

expertise N. specialized knowledge; expert skill. Although she was knowledgeable in a number of fields, she was hired for her special *expertise* in computer programming.

explicate V. explain; interpret; clarify. Harry Levin *explicated* James Joyce's often bewildering novels with such clarity that even *Finnegan's Wake* seemed comprehensible to his students.

Word List 18   explicit–fleeting

explicit ADJ. totally clear; definite; outspoken. Don't just hint around that you're dissatisfied: be *explicit* about what's bugging you.

■ **exploit** N. deed or action, particularly a brave deed. Raoul Wallenberg was noted for his *exploits* in rescuing Jews from Hitler's forces.

exploit V. make use of, sometimes unjustly. Cesar Chavez fought attempts to *exploit* migrant farmworkers in California. exploitation, N.

expository ADJ. explanatory; serving to explain. The manual that came with my iPhone was no masterpiece of *expository* prose: its explanations were so garbled that I couldn't even figure out how to synchronize my contacts. exposition, N.

exposure N. risk, particularly of being exposed to disease or to the elements; unmasking. *Exposure* to sun and wind had dried out her hair and weathered her face. She looked so changed that she no longer feared *exposure* as the notorious Irene Adler, one-time antagonist of Sherlock Holmes.

expurgate V. clean; remove offensive parts of a book. The editors felt that certain passages in the book had to be *expurgated* before it could be used in the classroom.

extent N. degree; magnitude; scope. What is the *extent* of the patient's injuries? If they are not too *extensive*, we can treat him on an outpatient basis.

extraneous ADJ. not essential; superfluous. No wonder Ted can't think straight! His mind is so cluttered up with *extraneous* trivia, he can't concentrate on the essentials.

extrapolate V. infer; project from known data into the unknown; make a conjecture. On the basis of what they could *extrapolate* from the results of the primaries on Super Tuesday, the networks predicted that Hillary Clinton would be the Democratic candidate for the presidency.

extricate V. free; disentangle. Icebreakers were needed to *extricate* the trapped whales from the icy floes that closed them in.

extrinsic ADJ. external; not essential; extraneous. A critically acclaimed *extrinsic* feature of the Chrysler Building is its ornate spire. The judge would not admit the testimony, ruling that it was *extrinsic* to the matter at hand.

exuberant ADJ. joyfully enthusiastic; flamboyant; lavish; abundant. I was bowled over by Amy's *exuberant* welcome. What an enthusiastic greeting!

fabricate V. build; lie. If we *fabricate* the buildings in this project out of standardized sections, we can reduce construction cost considerably. Because of Jack's tendency to *fabricate,* Jill had trouble believing a word he said.

facile ADJ. easily accomplished; ready or fluent; superficial. Words came easily to Jonathan: he was a *facile* speaker and prided himself on being ready to make a speech at a moment's notice.

■ **facilitate** V. help bring about; make less difficult. Rest and proper nourishment should *facilitate* the patient's recovery.

facility N. natural ability to do something with ease; ease in performing; something (building, equipment) set up to perform a function. Morgan has always displayed a remarkable *facility* for playing basketball. Thanks to years of practice, he handles the ball with such *facility* that as a twelve-year-old he can outplay many students at the university's recreational *facility*.

faculty N. inherent mental or physical power; teaching staff. As he grew old, Professor Twiggly feared he might lose his *faculties* and become unfit to teach. Once he'd lost his *faculties*, he'd have no place on the *faculty*.

■ **fallacious** ADJ. false; misleading. Paradoxically, *fallacious* reasoning does not always yield erroneous results: even though your logic may be faulty, the answer you get may nevertheless be correct. fallacy, N.

fallible ADJ. liable to err. I know I am *fallible,* but I feel confident that I am right this time.

■ **farce** N. broad comedy; mockery. Nothing went right; the entire interview degenerated into a *farce*. farcical, ADJ.

■ **fastidious** ADJ. difficult to please; squeamish. Bobby was such a *fastidious* eater that he would eat a sandwich only if his mother first cut off every scrap of crust.

■ **feasible** ADJ. practical. Was it *feasible* to build a new stadium for the Yankees on New York's West Side? Without additional funding, the project was clearly unrealistic.

feint N. trick; shift; sham blow. Fooled by his opponent's *feint,* the boxer unwisely dropped his guard. also V.

ferment N. agitation; commotion. With the breakup of the Soviet Union, much of Eastern Europe was in a state of *ferment*.

■ **fervor** N. glowing ardor; intensity of feeling. At the protest rally, the students cheered the strikers and booed the dean with equal *fervor*. fervent, fervid, ADJ.

fester V. provoke keen irritation or resentment. Joe's insult *festered* in Anne's mind for days and made her too angry to speak to him.

fiasco N. total failure. Tanya's attempt to look sophisticated by smoking was a *fiasco:* she lit the wrong end of the cigarette, choked when she tried to inhale, and burned a hole in her boyfriend's couch.

fictitious ADJ. imaginary. Although this book purports to be a biography of George Washington, many of the incidents are *fictitious*.

fiery ADJ. easily provoked; passionate; burning. By reputation, redheads have *fiery* tempers; the least little thing can cause them to explode.

- **figurative** ADJ. not literal, but metaphorical; using a figure of speech. "To lose one's marbles" is a *figurative* expression; if you're told that Jack has lost his marbles, no one expects you to rush out to buy him a replacement set.

finesse N. delicate skill. The *finesse* and adroitness with which the surgeon wielded her scalpel impressed the observers in the operating theater.

finite ADJ. having an end; limited. Though Bill really wanted to win the pie-eating contest, the capacity of his stomach was *finite,* and he had to call it quits after eating only seven cherry pies.

fitful ADJ. spasmodic; intermittent. After several *fitful* attempts, he decided to postpone the start of the project until he felt more energetic.

flagrant ADJ. conspicuously wicked; blatant; outrageous. The governor's appointment of his brother-in-law to the State Supreme Court was a *flagrant* violation of the state laws against nepotism (favoritism based on kinship).

fleeting ADJ. transitory; vanishing quickly. The glory of a New England autumn is *fleeting*: the first gust of wind strips the trees of their colorful leaves.

Word List 19   flippant–garble

- **flippant** ADJ. lacking proper seriousness. When Mark told Mona he loved her, she dismissed his earnest declaration with a *flippant* "Oh, you say that to all the girls!" flippancy, N.

flout V. reject; mock. The headstrong youth *flouted* all authority; he refused to be curbed.

fluctuate V. waver; shift. The water pressure in our shower *fluctuates* wildly; you start rinsing yourself off with a trickle, and, two minutes later, a blast of water nearly knocks you down.

fluency N. smoothness of speech. He spoke French with *fluency* and ease.

foible N. weakness; slight fault. We can overlook the *foibles* of our friends; no one is perfect.

forbearance N. patience. We must use *forbearance* in dealing with him because he is still weak from his illness.

foreboding N. premonition of evil. Suspecting no conspiracies against him, Caesar gently ridiculed his wife's *forebodings* about the ides of March.

foreshadow V. give an indication beforehand; portend; prefigure. In retrospect, political analysts realized that Yeltsin's defiance of the attempted coup *foreshadowed* his emergence as the dominant figure of the new Russian republic.

foresight N. ability to foresee future happenings; careful provision for the future. A shrewd investor, she had the *foresight* to buy land just before the current real estate boom.

forestall V. prevent by taking action in advance. By setting up a prenuptial agreement, the prospective bride and groom hoped to *forestall* any potential arguments about money in the event of a divorce.

forfeit V. lose; surrender. Convicted murderers *forfeit* the right to inherit anything from their victims; the law does not allow them to benefit financially from their crimes.

forgo V. give up; do without. Determined to lose weight over the summer, Michelle decided to *forgo* dessert until she could fit into a size eight again.

formidable ADJ. inspiring fear or apprehension; difficult; awe inspiring. In the film *Meet the Parents,* the hero is understandably nervous about meeting his fiancée's father, a *formidable* CIA agent.

- **forthright** ADJ. outspoken; frank. Never afraid to call a spade a spade, she was perhaps too *forthright* to be a successful party politician.

fortuitous ADJ. accidental; by chance. Though he pretended their encounter was *fortuitous,* he'd actually been hanging around her usual haunts for the past two weeks, hoping she'd turn up.

foster V. rear; encourage. According to the legend, Romulus and Remus were *fostered* by a she-wolf who raised the abandoned infants as her own. also ADJ.

founder V. fail completely; sink. Unfortunately, the peace talks *foundered* when the two parties could not reach a compromise. After hitting the submerged iceberg, the *Titanic* started taking in water rapidly and soon *foundered*.

founder N. person who establishes (an organization, business). Among those drowned when the *Titanic* sank was the *founder* of the Abraham & Strauss department store.

- **frail** ADJ. weak. The delicate child seemed too *frail* to lift the heavy carton.

franchise N. right granted by authority; right to vote; business licensed to sell a product in a particular territory. The city issued a *franchise* to the company to operate surface transit lines on the streets for 99 years. For most of American history, women lacked the right to vote: not until the early twentieth century was the *franchise* granted to women. Stan owns a Carvel's ice cream *franchise* in Chinatown.

frantic ADJ. wild. At the time of the collision, many people became *frantic* with fear.

fraudulent ADJ. cheating; deceitful. The government seeks to prevent *fraudulent* and misleading advertising.

friction N. rubbing against; clash of wills. If it were not for the *friction* between the tires and the pavement, driving a car would be like sliding all over an ice rink. The *friction* between Aaron Burr and Alexander Hamilton intensified over time until it culminated in their famous duel.

frivolous ADJ. lacking in seriousness; self-indulgently carefree; relatively unimportant. Though Nancy enjoyed Bill's *frivolous,* lighthearted companionship, she sometimes wondered whether he could ever be serious. frivolity, N.

frustrate V. thwart; defeat. Constant partisan bickering *frustrated* the governor's efforts to convince the legislature to approve his proposed budget.

fugitive ADJ. fleeting or transient; elusive; fleeing. How can a painter capture on canvas the *fugitive* beauty of clouds moving across the sky? also N.

fundamental V. basic; primary; essential. The committee discussed all sorts of side issues without ever getting down to addressing the *fundamental* problem.

furtive ADJ. stealthy; sneaky. Noticing the *furtive* glance the customer gave the diamond bracelet on the counter, the jeweler wondered whether he had a potential shoplifter on his hands.

fusion N. uniting; blending; coalition. Rock and roll originally came into existence as a *fusion* of jazz, blues, and country music; it contains elements of all three musical genres.

futile ADJ. useless; hopeless; ineffectual. It is *futile* for me to try to get any work done around here while the telephone is ringing every thirty seconds. futility, N.

gainful ADJ. profitable. After having been out of work for six months, Brenda was excited by the prospect of *gainful* employment.

galvanize V. stimulate by shock; stir up; revitalize. News that the prince was almost at their door *galvanized* the ugly stepsisters into a frenzy of combing and primping.

garble V. mix up; jumble; distort. A favorite party game involves passing a whispered message from one person to another, till, by the time it reaches the last player, everyone has totally *garbled* the message.

Word List 20   garrulous–hazardous

■ **garrulous** ADJ. loquacious; wordy; talkative. My Uncle Henry can outtalk any three people I know. He is the most *garrulous* person in Cayuga County. garrulity, N.

■ **generalization** N. broad, general statement derived from specific instances; vague, indefinite statement. It is foolish to make *generalizations* based on insufficient evidence: that one woman defrauded the welfare system of thousands of dollars does not mean all welfare recipients are cheats. I would rather propose solutions to problems than make vague *generalizations*.

■ **generate** V. cause; produce; create. In his first days in office, President Obama managed to *generate* a new mood of optimism; we hoped he could *generate* a few new jobs.

generic ADJ. characteristic of an entire class or species. Sue knew so many computer programmers who spent their spare time playing fantasy games that she began to think that playing Dungeons & Dragons was a *generic* trait.

■ **genre** N. particular variety of art or literature. Both a short story writer and a poet, Langston Hughes proved himself equally skilled in either *genre*.

germane ADJ. pertinent; bearing upon the case at hand. The lawyer objected that the witness's testimony was not *germane* to the case and should be ignored by the jury.

gloss over V. explain away. No matter how hard he tried to talk around the issue, the president could not *gloss over* the fact that he had raised taxes after all.

grandeur N. impressiveness; stateliness; majesty. No matter how often he hiked through the mountains, David never failed to be struck by the *grandeur* of the Sierra Nevada range.

grandiose ADJ. pretentious; high-flown; ridiculously exaggerated; impressive. The aged matinee idol still had *grandiose* notions of his supposed importance in the theatrical world.

graphic ADJ. pertaining to visual art; relating to visual images; vividly portrayed. The illustrator Jody Lee studied the *graphic* arts at San Francisco's Academy of Art. In 2015 the PSAT began to include reading questions that required students to interpret *graphic* information from charts and diagrams. The description of the winter storm was so *graphic* that you could almost feel the hailstones..

■ **gratify** V. please. Amy's success in her new job *gratified* her parents.

gravity N. seriousness. We could tell we were in serious trouble from the *gravity* of the principal's expression.

grudging ADJ. unwilling; reluctant; stingy. We received only *grudging* support from the mayor despite his earlier promises of aid.

guile N. deceit; duplicity; wiliness; cunning. Iago uses considerate *guile* to trick Othello into believing that Desdemona has been unfaithful.

gullible ADJ. easily deceived. Overly *gullible* people have only themselves to blame if they fall for scams repeatedly. As the saying goes, "Fool me once, shame on you. Fool me twice, shame on me."

■ **hackneyed** ADJ. commonplace; trite. When the reviewer criticized the movie for its *hackneyed* plot, we agreed; we had seen similar stories hundreds of times before.

■ **halting** ADJ. hesitant; faltering. Novice extemporaneous speakers often talk in a *halting* fashion as they grope for the right words.

■ **hamper** V. obstruct. The new mother didn't realize how much the effort of caring for an infant would *hamper* her ability to keep an immaculate house.

harass V. to annoy by repeated attacks. When he could not pay his bills as quickly as he had promised, he was *harassed* by his creditors.

harbor V. provide a refuge for; hide. The church *harbored* illegal aliens who were political refugees.

haughtiness N. pride; arrogance. When she realized that Darcy believed himself too good to dance with his inferiors, Elizabeth took great offense at his *haughtiness.*

hazardous ADJ. dangerous. Your occupation is too *hazardous* for insurance companies to consider your application.

Word List 21   headstrong–imbalance

headstrong ADJ. stubborn; willful; unyielding. Because she refused to marry the man her parents had chosen for her, everyone scolded Minna and called her a foolish *headstrong* girl.

heckle V. harass; taunt; jeer at. The home team's fans mercilessly *heckled* the visiting pitcher, taunting him whenever he let anyone get on base.

heed V. pay attention to; consider. We hope you *heed* our advice and get a good night's sleep before the test. also N.

heresy N. opinion contrary to popular belief; opinion contrary to accepted religion. Galileo's assertion that Earth moved around the sun directly contradicted the religious teachings of his day; as a result, he was tried for *heresy.* heretic, N.

hiatus N. gap; pause. Except for a brief two-year *hiatus,* during which she enrolled in the Peace Corps, Ms. Clements has devoted herself to her medical career.

hierarchy N. arrangement by rank or standing; authoritarian body divided into ranks. To be low man on the totem pole is to have an inferior place in the *hierarchy.*

■ **hinder** V. slow down or make difficult (something); prevent. Although the operation was successful, an infection *hindered* the recovery of the patient, who remained hospitalized for an additional week. Gordon was determined not to let anyone *hinder* him from achieving his goal. hindrance, N.

■ **hostility** N. unfriendliness; hatred. Children who have been the sole objects of their parents' attention often feel *hostility* toward a new baby in the family, resenting the newcomer who has taken their place.

humane ADJ. marked by kindness or consideration. It is ironic that the *Humane* Society sometimes must show its compassion toward mistreated animals by killing them to put them out of their misery.

humble ADJ. modest; not proud. He spoke with great feeling of how much he loved his *humble* home, which he would not trade for a palace. humility, N.

husband V. use sparingly; conserve; save. Marathon runners must *husband* their energy so that they can keep going for the entire distance.

■ **hyperbole** N. exaggeration; overstatement. As far as I'm concerned, Apple's claims about the new computer are pure *hyperbole:* no machine is that good!

■ **hypocritical** ADJ. pretending to be virtuous; deceiving. It was *hypocritical* of Martha to say such nice things about my poetry to me and then make fun of my verses behind my back. hypocrisy, N.

■ **hypothetical** ADJ. based on assumptions or hypotheses; supposed. Suppose you are accepted by Harvard, Stanford, and Brown. Which one would you choose to attend? Remember, this is only a *hypothetical* situation. hypothesis, N.

■ **iconoclastic** ADJ. attacking cherished traditions. Deeply *iconoclastic,* Jean Genet deliberately set out to shock conventional theatergoers with his radical plays.

ideology N. system of ideas of a group. For people who had grown up believing in the communist *ideology,* it was hard to adjust to capitalism.

idiom N. expression whose meaning as a whole differs from the meanings of its individual words; distinctive style. The phrase "to lose one's marbles" is an *idiom:* if I say that Joe's lost his marbles, I'm not asking you to find some for him. I'm telling you *idiomatically* that he's crazy.

idiosyncrasy N. individual trait, usually odd in nature; eccentricity. One of Richard Nixon's little *idiosyncrasies* was his liking for ketchup on cottage cheese. One of Hannibal Lecter's little *idiosyncrasies* was his liking for human flesh.

ignoble ADJ. unworthy; base in nature; not noble. Sir Galahad was so pure in heart that he could never stoop to perform an *ignoble* deed.

illuminate V. brighten; clear up or make understandable; enlighten. Just as a lamp can *illuminate* a dark room, a perceptive comment can *illuminate* a knotty problem.

illusory ADJ. deceptive; not real. Unfortunately, the costs of running the lemonade stand were so high that Tom's profits proved *illusory.*

imbalance N. lack of balance or symmetry; disproportion. To correct racial *imbalance* in the schools, school boards have bussed black children into white neighborhoods and white children into black ones.

Word List 22   immaterial–incarcerate

immaterial ADJ. unimportant; irrelevant; intangible. Though Kit said it was wholly *immaterial* whether she had a birthday party or not, we wanted to throw her a party.

imminent ADJ. ; near at hand; impending. Rosa was such a last-minute worker that she could never start writing a paper till the deadline was *imminent*.

immobilize V. make unable to move. For a moment, Peter's fear of snakes *immobilized* him; then the use of his limbs returned to him and he bolted from the room.

immune ADJ. resistant to; free or exempt from. Fortunately, Florence had contracted chicken pox as a child and was *immune* to it when her baby broke out in spots.

■ **immutable** ADJ. unchangeable. All things change over time; nothing is *immutable*.

impair V. injure; hurt. Drinking alcohol can *impair* your ability to drive safely; if you're going to drink, don't drive.

impart V. give or convey; communicate. A born dancer, she *imparted* her love of movement to her audience with every step she took.

impartial ADJ. not biased; fair. Knowing she could not be *impartial* about her own child, Jo refused to judge any match in which Billy was competing.

impassable ADJ. not able to be traveled or crossed. A giant redwood had fallen across the highway, blocking all four lanes: the road was *impassable*.

impasse N. predicament offering no escape; deadlock; dead end. The negotiators reported they had reached an *impasse* in their talks and had little hope of resolving the deadlock swiftly.

impeccable ADJ. faultless. The uncrowned queen of the fashion industry, Diana was acclaimed for her *impeccable* taste.

■ **impede** V. hinder; block; delay. A series of accidents *impeded* the launching of the space shuttle.

impel V. drive or force onward. A strong feeling of urgency *impelled* her; if she failed to finish the project right then, she knew that she would never get it done.

■ **imperative** ADJ. absolutely necessary; critically important. It is *imperative* that you be extremely agreeable to Great-Aunt Maud when she comes to tea: otherwise she might not leave you that million dollars in her will. also N.

■ **imperceptible** ADJ. unnoticeable; undetectable. Fortunately, the stain on the blouse was *imperceptible* after the blouse had gone through the wash.

impetuous ADJ. violent; hasty; rash. "Leap before you look" was the motto suggested by one particularly *impetuous* young man.

impetus N. incentive; stimulus; moving force. A new federal highway program would create jobs and give added *impetus* to our economic recovery.

impiety N. irreverence; lack of respect for God. When members of the youth group draped the church in toilet paper one Halloween, the minister reprimanded them for their *impiety*. impious, ADJ.

implacable ADJ. incapable of being pacified. Relentlessly seeking revenge, Madame Defarge was the *implacable* enemy of the Evremonde family.

■ **implausible** ADJ. unlikely; unbelievable. Though her alibi seemed *implausible*, it in fact turned out to be true.

implement N. piece of equipment. We now own so many rakes, hoes, and hedge clippers that we need a tool shed in which to store all our gardening *implements*.

■ **implement** V. put into effect; supply with tools. The mayor was unwilling to *implement* the plan until she was sure it had the governor's backing.

implicate V. incriminate; show to be involved. Here's the deal: If you agree to take the witness stand and *implicate* your partners in crime, the prosecution will recommend that the judge go easy in sentencing you.

■ **implication** N. something hinted at or suggested; likely consequence; close involvement. When Miss Watson said that she hadn't seen her purse since the last time Jim was in the house, her *implication* was that Jim had taken it. This had potentially serious *implications* for Jim. If his *implication* in a theft were proved, he'd be thrown into jail. imply, V.

implicit ADJ. understood but not stated. Jack never told Jill he adored her; he believed his love was *implicit* in his deeds.

imply V. suggest a meaning not expressed; signify. When Aunt Millie said, "My! That's a big piece of pie, young man!" was she *implying* that Bobby was being a glutton in helping himself to such a huge piece?

import N. importance; meaning. To Miss Manners, proper etiquette was a matter of great *import*. Because Tom knew so little about medical matters, it took a while for the full *import* of the doctor's words to sink in.

impotent ADJ. weak; ineffective. Although he wished to break the nicotine habit, he found himself *impotent* to resist the craving for a cigarette.

impromptu ADJ. without previous preparation; off the cuff; on the spur of the moment. The judges were amazed that she could make such a thorough, well-supported presentation in an *impromptu* speech.

inadvertently ADV. unintentionally; by oversight; carelessly. Judy's great fear was that she might *inadvertently* omit a question on the exam and mismark her whole answer sheet.

inalienable ADJ. not to be taken away; nontransferable. The Declaration of Independence asserts that all people possess certain *inalienable* human rights that no powers on Earth can take away.

inane ADJ. silly; senseless. There's no point in what you're saying. Why are you bothering to make such *inane* remarks? inanity, N.

inarticulate ADJ. speechless; producing indistinct speech. A trained debater and the winner of trophies for extemporaneous speech, Lexy is far from *inarticulate*.

incapacitate V. disable. During the winter, many people were *incapacitated* by respiratory ailments.

incarcerate V. imprison. The civil rights workers were willing to be arrested and even *incarcerated* if by their imprisonment they could serve the cause.

Word List 23   incentive–infallible

incentive N. spur; motive. Mike's strong desire to outshine his big sister was all the *incentive* he needed to do well in school.

incessant ADJ. Don't you hate the *incessant* chirping noise the smoke detector makes when its battery runs down? That noise goes on and on nonstop.

incidental ADJ. not essential; minor. The scholarship covered his major expenses at college and some of his *incidental* expenses as well.

incipient ADJ. beginning; in an early stage. I will go to sleep early for I want to break an *incipient* cold.

incite V. arouse to action; goad; motivate; induce to exist. In a fiery speech, Mario *incited* his fellow students to go out on strike to protest the university's anti-affirmative-action stand.

inclusive ADJ. tending to include all. Our local dance works hard to be *inclusive* and welcoming to everyone who walks through the door.

incoherent ADJ. unintelligible; muddled; illogical. The excited fan blushed and stammered, her words becoming almost *incoherent* in the thrill of meeting her favorite rock star face to face. incoherence, N.

■ **incongruity** N. lack of harmony; absurdity. Everyone laughed at the *incongruity* of his wearing sneakers with formal attire. incongruous, ADJ.

■ **inconsequential** ADJ. insignificant; unimportant. Brushing off Ali's apologies for having broken the wine glass, Tamara said, "Don't worry about it; it's *inconsequential*."

■ **inconsistency** N. state of being self-contradictory; lack of uniformity or steadiness. How are lawyers different from agricultural inspectors? While lawyers check *inconsistencies* in witnesses' statements, agricultural inspectors check *inconsistencies* in Grade A eggs. inconsistent, ADJ.

■ **incorporate** V. introduce something into a larger whole; combine; unite. Breaking with precedent, President Truman ordered the military to *incorporate* blacks into every branch of the armed services. also ADJ.

incorrigible ADJ. uncorrectable. Though Widow Douglass hoped to reform Huck, Miss Watson pronounced him *incorrigible* and said he would come to no good end.

incredulous ADJ. unwilling or unable to believe; skeptical. When Marco claimed he hadn't eaten the jelly doughnut, Joyce took one *incredulous* look at his smeared face and laughed.

incumbent ADJ. obligatory; currently holding an office. It is *incumbent* upon all *incumbent* elected officials to keep accurate records of expenses incurred in office. also N.

indefatigable ADJ. tireless. Although the effort of taking out the garbage tired Wayne out for the entire morning, when it came to partying, he was *indefatigable*.

indelible ADJ. not able to be erased. The *indelible* ink left a permanent mark on my shirt. Young Bill Clinton's meeting with President Kennedy made an *indelible* impression on the youth.

■ **indicative** ADJ. suggestive; implying. A lack of appetite may be *indicative* of a major mental or physical disorder.

indict V. charge. The district attorney didn't want to *indict* the suspect until she was sure she had a strong enough case to convince a jury. indictment, N.

■ **indifferent** ADJ. unmoved or unconcerned by; mediocre. Because Consuela felt no desire to marry, she was *indifferent* to Edward's constant proposals. Not only was she *indifferent* to him personally, but she felt that, given his general silliness, he would make an *indifferent* husband.

indigenous ADJ. native. Cigarettes are made of tobacco, a plant *indigenous* to the New World.

■ **indiscriminate** ADJ. not marked by making careful distinctions; done at random. Mother disapproved of Junior's *indiscriminate* television viewing; she wished he'd be a little more discriminating in his choice of shows. The newspaper editorial denounced the terrorists for their *indiscriminate* killing of civilians.

indisputable ADJ. too certain to be disputed. In the face of these *indisputable* statements, I withdraw my complaint.

indomitable ADJ. unconquerable; unyielding. Focusing on her final vault despite her twisted ankle, gymnastics star Kerri Strug proved she had an *indomitable* will to win.

indubitable ADJ. unable to be doubted; unquestionable. Auditioning for the chorus line, Molly was an *indubitable* hit: the director fired the leading lady and hired Molly in her place!

■ **induce** V. move someone to do something by persuasion; bring about; conclude through inductive reasoning. After their quarrel, Tina said nothing could *induce* her to talk to Tony again. Drinking a glass of warm milk before bedtime can help *induce* sleep. Rather than indulging in vain speculation, Isaac Newton attempted to *induce* principles from observations. inducement, N.

indulgent ADJ. humoring; yielding; lenient. Jay's mom was excessively *indulgent:* she bought him every video game on the market. She *indulged* Jay so much, she spoiled him rotten.

■ **industrious** ADJ. diligent; hard-working. Look busy when the boss walks past your desk; it never hurts to appear *industrious.* industry, N.

■ **inept** ADJ. lacking skill; unsuited; incompetent. The *inept* glove maker was all thumbs. ineptitude, ineptness, N.

inequity N. unfairness. In demanding equal pay for equal work, women protest the basic *inequity* of a system that gives greater financial rewards to men.

inevitable ADJ. unavoidable. Though death and taxes are both supposedly *inevitable,* some people avoid paying taxes for years.

■ **inexorable** ADJ. relentless; unyielding; implacable. Despite the pleas for clemency, the judge was *inexorable* and gave the convicted man the maximum punishment allowed by law.

■ **infallible** ADJ. unerring; faultless. Jane refused to believe the pope was *infallible,* reasoning: "All human beings are capable of error. The pope is a human being. Therefore, the pope is capable of error."

Word List 24 infamous–insurmountable

infamous ADJ. notoriously bad. Charles Manson and Jeffrey Dahmer were both *infamous* killers.

infer v. deduce; conclude. From the students' glazed looks, it was easy for me to *infer* that they were bored out of their minds. inference, N.

infinitesimal ADJ. exceedingly small; so small as to be almost nonexistent. Making sure everyone was aware she was on an extremely strict diet, Melanie said she would have only an *infinitesimal* sliver of pie.

infraction N. violation (of a rule or regulation); breach. When Dennis Rodman butted heads with the referee, he committed a clear *infraction* of NBA rules.

■ **ingenious** ADJ. clever; resourceful. Franchising was an *ingenious* way to grow a new company in a new industry: rather than having the company pay the salesmen, the salesmen, as franchise owners, would pay the company. ingenuity, N.

■ **ingenuous** ADJ. naive and trusting; young; unsophisticated. The woodsman had not realized how *ingenuous* Little Red Riding Hood was until he heard that she had gone off for a walk in the woods with the Big Bad Wolf.

■ **inherent** ADJ. firmly established by nature or habit. Katya's *inherent* love of justice caused her to champion anyone she considered treated unfairly by society.

inhibit v. restrain; retard or prevent. Only two things *inhibited* him from taking a punch at Mike Tyson: Tyson's left hook and Tyson's right jab. The protective undercoating on my car *inhibits* the formation of rust.

■ **initiate** v. begin; originate; receive into a group. The college is about to *initiate* a program for reducing math anxiety among students.

inkling N. hint. "He was just an ordinary guy," his classmates said. "No one had the slightest *inkling* that he was a Russian spy."

■ **innate** ADJ. inborn. Mozart's parents soon recognized young Wolfgang's *innate* talent for music.

■ **innocuous** ADJ. harmless. An occasional glass of wine with dinner is relatively *innocuous* and should have no ill effect on you.

innovation N. change; introduction of something new. Although Richard liked to keep up with all the latest technological *innovations,* he didn't always abandon tried-and-true techniques in favor of something new. innovate, v.

inopportune ADJ. untimely; poorly chosen. A hip-hop concert is an *inopportune* setting for a quiet conversation.

inordinate ADJ. unrestrained; excessive. She had an *inordinate* fondness for candy, eating two or three boxes in a single day.

insatiable ADJ. not easily satisfied; greedy. Welty's thirst for knowledge was *insatiable;* she was in the library day and night.

■ **inscrutable** ADJ. impenetrable; not readily understood; mysterious. Experienced poker players try to keep their expressions *inscrutable,* hiding their reactions to the cards behind a so-called poker face.

■ **insightful** ADJ. discerning; perceptive. Sol thought he was very *insightful* about human behavior, but he was actually clueless as to why people acted the way they did.

insinuate v. hint; imply; creep in. When you say I look robust, do you mean to *insinuate* that I'm getting fat?

insipid ADJ. lacking in flavor; dull. Flat prose and flat ginger ale are equally *insipid*: both lack sparkle.

insolence N. impudent disrespect; haughtiness. How dare you treat me so rudely! The manager will hear of your *insolence.* insolent, ADJ.

insolvent ADJ. bankrupt; lacking money to pay. When rumors that he was *insolvent* reached his creditors, they began to press him to pay the money he owed them. insolvency, N.

instigate v. urge; start; provoke. Rumors of police corruption led the mayor to *instigate* an investigation into the department's activities.

insubordination N. disobedience; rebelliousness. At the slightest hint of *insubordination* from the sailors of the *Bounty*, Captain Bligh had them flogged; finally, they mutinied.

insubstantial ADJ. lacking substance; insignificant; frail. His hopes for a career in acting proved *insubstantial*; no one would cast him, even in an *insubstantial* role.

insurmountable ADJ. overwhelming; unbeatable; insuperable. Faced by almost *insurmountable* obstacles, the members of the underground maintained their courage and will to resist.

Word List 25   insurrection–jeopardize

insurrection N. rebellion; uprising. In retrospect, given how badly the British treated the American colonists, the eventual *insurrection* seems inevitable.

■ **intangible** ADJ. not able to be perceived by touch; vague. Though the financial benefits of his Oxford post were meager, Lewis was drawn to it by its *intangible* rewards: prestige, intellectual freedom, the fellowship of his peers.

integral ADJ. complete; necessary for completeness. Physical education is an *integral* part of our curriculum; a sound mind and a sound body are complementary.

integrate V. make whole; combine; make into one unit. We hope to *integrate* the French, Spanish, and Italian programs into a combined Romance languages department.

■ **integrity** N. uprightness; wholeness. Lincoln, whose personal *integrity* has inspired millions, fought a civil war to maintain the *integrity* of the Republic, that these United States might remain undivided for all time.

interminable ADJ. endless. Although his speech lasted for only twenty minutes, it seemed *interminable* to his bored audience.

intermittent ADJ. periodic; on and off. The outdoor wedding reception had to be moved indoors to avoid the *intermittent* showers that fell all afternoon.

interrogate V. question closely; cross-examine. Knowing that the Nazis would *interrogate* him about his background, the secret agent invented a cover story that would help him meet their questions.

intervene V. come between in order to prevent or alter; occur between (events, periods of time). If two good friends get into a fight, don't try to *intervene*: if you do, they may gang up on you. Spring break *intervened*, and Johnny headed to Fort Lauderdale for a short vacation before classes started again.

intimate V. hint or suggest; make known. Was Dick *intimating* that Jane had bad breath when he asked if she'd like a breath mint? We were taken by surprise when the principal *intimated* his decision to eliminate the after-school program.

intimidate V. frighten. I'll learn karate and then those big bullies won't be able to *intimidate* me any more.

intractable ADJ. unruly; stubborn; unyielding. Charlie Brown's friend Pigpen was *intractable*: he absolutely refused to take a bath.

intransigence N. refusal of any compromise; stubbornness. When I predicted that the strike would be over in a week, I didn't expect to encounter such *intransigence* from both sides. intransigent, ADJ.

■ **intricacy** N. complexity; knottiness. Philip spent many hours designing mazes of such great *intricacy* that none of his classmates could solve them. intricate, ADJ.

intrigue V. fascinate; interest. Holmes's air of reserve *intrigued* Irene Adler; she wanted to know just what made the great detective tick.

intrinsic ADJ. essential; inherent; built-in. Although my grandmother's china has little *intrinsic* value, I shall always cherish it for the memories it evokes.

■ **introspective** ADJ. looking within oneself. Though young Francis of Assisi led a wild and worldly life, even he had *introspective* moments during which he examined his soul.

intrude V. trespass; enter as an uninvited person. She hesitated to *intrude* on their conversation.

intuition N. immediate insight; power of knowing without reasoning. Even though Tony denied that anything was wrong, Tina trusted her *intuition* that something was bothering him. intuitive, ADJ.

inundate V. overwhelm; flood; submerge. This semester I am *inundated* with work: you should see the piles of paperwork flooding my desk. Until the great dam was built, the waters of the Nile used to *inundate* the river valley every year.

invalidate V. discredit; nullify. The relatives who received little or nothing sought to *invalidate* the will by claiming that the deceased had not been in his right mind when he signed the document.

irksome ADJ. annoying; tedious. The petty rules and regulations Bill had to follow at work irritated him: he found them uniformly *irksome*.

■ **irony** N. hidden sarcasm or satire; use of words that seem to mean the opposite of what they actually mean. Gradually his listeners began to realize that the excessive praise he was lavishing on his opponent was actually *irony*; he was in fact ridiculing the poor fool.

irrational ADJ. illogical; lacking reason; insane. Many people have such an *irrational* fear of snakes that they panic at the sight of a harmless garter snake.

irrefutable ADJ. indisputable; incontrovertible; undeniable. No matter how hard I tried to find a good comeback for her argument, I couldn't think of one: her logic was *irrefutable*.

irrelevant ADJ. not applicable; unrelated. No matter how *irrelevant* the patient's mumblings may seem, they give us some indications of what he has on his mind.

irrevocable ADJ. unalterable; irreversible. As Sue dropped the "Dear John" letter into the mailbox, she suddenly had second thoughts and wanted to take it back, but she could not: her action was *irrevocable*.

isolate V. keep apart; pinpoint; quarantine. The medical researchers *isolated* themselves in a remote village. Until they could *isolate* the cause of the plague and develop an effective vaccine, they had to avoid potential carriers of the disease. Anyone infected they *isolated* immediately.

jargon N. language used by a special group; technical terminology; gibberish. The computer salesmen at the store used a *jargon* of their own that we simply couldn't follow; we had no idea what they were jabbering about.

jeopardize V. endanger; imperil; put at risk. You can't give me a D in chemistry; you'll *jeopardize* my chances of getting into M.I.T. jeopardy, N.

Word List 26   jocular–lurk

jocular ADJ. said or done in jest. Although Bill knew the boss hated jokes, he couldn't resist making one *jocular* remark. jocularity, N.

■ **judicious** ADJ. sound in judgment; wise. At a key moment in his life, he made a *judicious* investment that was the foundation of his later wealth.

justification N. good or just reason; defense; excuse. The jury found him guilty of the more serious charge because they could see no possible *justification* for his actions.

juxtapose V. place side by side. You'll find it easier to compare the two paintings if you *juxtapose* them.

kindle V. start a fire; inspire. One of the first things Ben learned in the Boy Scouts was how to *kindle* a fire by rubbing two dry sticks together. Her teacher's praise for her poetry *kindled* a spark of hope inside Maya.

laborious ADJ. demanding much work or care; tedious. In putting together his dictionary of the English language, Doctor Johnson undertook a *laborious* task.

laconic ADJ. brief and to the point. Many of the characters portrayed by Clint Eastwood are *laconic* types, rugged men of few words.

lament V. grieve; express sorrow. Even advocates of the war *lamented* the loss of so many lives in combat. lamentation, N.

lampoon V. ridicule. This hilarious article *lampoons* the pretensions of some movie moguls. also N.

larceny N. theft. Because of the prisoner's long record of thefts, the district attorney refused to reduce the charge from grand *larceny* to petty *larceny*.

latent ADJ. potential but undeveloped; dormant. In the late twentieth century, Polaroid pictures were popular at parties, because you could see the *latent* photographic image gradually appear before your eyes. Sometimes *latent* tuberculosis becomes active years later.

laud V. praise. The NFL *lauded* Boomer Esiason's efforts to raise money to combat cystic fibrosis. laudable, laudatory, ADJ.

lenience N. mildness; permissiveness. Considering the gravity of the offense, we were surprised by the *lenience* of the sentence. also leniency; lenient, ADJ.

lethal ADJ. deadly. It is unwise to leave *lethal* weapons where children may find them.

lethargic ADJ. drowsy; dull. The stuffy room made her *lethargic*: she felt as if she was about to nod off.

levity N. lack of seriousness; lightness. Stop giggling and wiggling around in your seats: such *levity* is improper in church.

liability N. drawback; debts. Her lack of a college-level vocabulary was a *liability* that she was eventually able to overcome.

libel N. defamatory statement; act of writing something that smears a person's character. If Batman wrote that the Joker was a dirty, rotten, mass-murdering criminal, could the Joker sue Batman for *libel*?

likelihood N. state of being likely to happen. Mastering these vocabulary words increases the *likelihood* of your doing well on the PSAT.

linger V. loiter or dawdle; continue or persist. Hoping to see Juliet pass by, Romeo *lingered* outside the Capulet house for hours. Though Mother made stuffed cabbage on Monday, the smell *lingered* around the house for days.

loath ADJ. reluctant; disinclined. Fearing for her son's safety, the overprotective mother was *loath* to let him go on the class trip.

■ **loathe** V. detest. Booing and hissing, the audience showed how much they *loathed* the wicked villain.

lofty ADJ. very high. Though Barbara Jordan's fellow students used to tease her about her *lofty* ambitions, she rose to hold one of the highest positions in the land.

loquacious ADJ. talkative. Though our daughter barely says a word to us these days, put a phone in her hand and see how *loquacious* she can be: our phone bills are out of sight!

lucid ADJ. easily understood; clear; intelligible. Her explanation was *lucid* enough for a child to grasp.

lucrative ADJ. profitable. He turned his hobby into a *lucrative* profession.

lure v. entice; attract. Baiting his hook with the latest fly he had put together, Grandpa Joe swore that this new fly was so attractive that it could *lure* the wariest trout out of hiding.

lurk v. stealthily lie in waiting; slink; exist unperceived. "Who knows what evils *lurk* in the hearts of men? The Shadow knows!"

Word List 27 magnanimous–meticulous

magnanimous ADJ. generous. Philanthropists by definition are *magnanimous;* misers, by definition, are not. magnanimity, N.

■ **magnitude** N. greatness of extent; great importance; size. Seismologists use the Richter scale to measure the *magnitude* of earthquakes. Mexico's Bicentennial Celebration was an event of such *magnitude* that it had a lasting positive impact on the country's economy. When students work with very large numbers (millions and billions), they need to understand the *magnitude* of these numbers.

■ **malice** N. hatred; spite. Jealous of Cinderella's beauty, her wicked stepsisters expressed their *malice* by forcing her to do menial tasks.

malign v. speak evil of; bad-mouth; defame. Putting her hands over her ears, Rose refused to listen to Betty *malign* her friend Susan.

malignant ADJ. injurious; tending to cause death; aggressively malevolent. Though many tumors are benign, some are *malignant*, growing out of control and endangering the life of the patient.

malleable ADJ. capable of being shaped by pounding; impressionable. Gold is a *malleable* metal, easily shaped into bracelets and rings. Fagin hoped Oliver was a *malleable* lad, easily shaped into a thief.

manifest ADJ. evident; visible; obvious. Digby's embarrassment when he met Lady Gaga was *manifest:* his ears turned bright pink, he kept scuffing one shoe in the dirt, and he couldn't look her in the eye.

manipulate v. operate with one's hands; control or play upon (people, forces, etc.) artfully. Jim Henson understood how to *manipulate* the Muppets. Lady Gaga understands how to *manipulate* publicity.

marked ADJ. noticeable; targeted for vengeance. He walked with a *marked* limp, a souvenir of an old I.R.A. attack. As British ambassador, he knew he was a *marked* man.

marshal v. put in order. At a debate tournament, extemporaneous speakers have only a minute or two to *marshal* their thoughts before they address their audience.

massive ADJ. solid or heavy; large in scope; severe. The bust of Beethoven emphasizes his high forehead and *massive* brow. The composer suffered a *massive* hearing loss that left him unable to hear the music the orchestra played.

■ **material** ADJ. made of physical matter; unspiritual; important. Probing the mysteries of this *material* world has always fascinated physicist George Whitesides. Reporters nicknamed Madonna the *Material* Girl because, despite her name, she seemed wholly uninterested in spiritual values. Lexy's active participation made a *material* difference to the success of the fundraiser.

materialism N. preoccupation with physical comforts and things. By its nature, *materialism* is opposed to idealism, for where the *materialist* emphasizes the needs of the body, the idealist emphasizes the needs of the soul. materialistic, ADJ.

maverick N. rebel; nonconformist. To the masculine literary establishment, George Sand, with her insistence on wearing trousers and smoking cigars, was clearly a *maverick* who fought her proper womanly role.

maxim N. proverb; a truth pithily stated. Aesop's story of the hare and the tortoise illustrates the *maxim* "Slow and steady wins the race."

meager ADJ. scanty; inadequate. Still hungry after his *meager* serving of porridge, Oliver Twist asked for a second helping.

mediate v. settle a dispute through the services of an outsider. King Solomon was asked to *mediate* a dispute between two women, each of whom claimed to be the mother of the same child.

mediocre ADJ. ordinary; commonplace. We were disappointed because he gave a rather *mediocre* performance in this role.

meditation N. reflection; thought. She reached her decision only after much *meditation.*

■ **medium** N. means of doing something; substance in which an organism lives; form or material employed by an artist, author, or composer. M.I.T.'s use of the Internet as a *medium* of education has transformed the university into a global enterprise. Ty's experiment involved growing bacteria in a nutrient-rich *medium*. Johnny's favorite artistic *medium* is photography; he hopes to become a photojournalist.

melancholy ADJ. gloomy; morose; blue. To Eugene, stuck in his small town, a train whistle was a *melancholy* sound, for it made him think of all the places he would never get to see.

mentor N. counselor; teacher. During this very trying period, she could not have had a better *mentor,* for her adviser was sympathetic and understanding.

mercenary ADJ. interested in money or gain. Andy's every act was prompted by *mercenary* motives: his first question was always, "What's in it for me?"

mercurial ADJ. capricious; changing; fickle. Quick as quicksilver to change, he was *mercurial* in nature and therefore unreliable.

■ **meticulous** ADJ. excessively careful; painstaking; scrupulous. Martha Stewart, a *meticulous* housekeeper, fusses about each and every detail that goes into making up her perfect home.

Word List 28   migratory–nadir

migratory ADJ. wandering. The return of the *migratory* birds to the northern sections of this country is a harbinger of spring.

minute ADJ. extremely small. The twins resembled one another closely; only *minute* differences set them apart.

■ **misconception** N. misunderstanding; misinterpretation. I'm afraid you are suffering from a *misconception*, Mr. Collins: I do not want to marry you at all.

misconstrue V. interpret incorrectly; misjudge. She took the passage seriously rather than humorously because she *misconstrued* the author's ironic tone.

miserly ADJ. stingy; mean. The *miserly* old man greedily counted the gold coins he had hoarded over the years.

■ **misrepresent** V. give a false or incorrect impression, usually intentionally. The ad "Lovely Florida building site with water view" *misrepresented* the property, which was actually ten acres of bottomless swamp.

mitigate V. appease; moderate. Nothing Jason did could *mitigate* Medea's anger; she refused to forgive him for betraying her.

mobile ADJ. movable; not fixed. The *mobile* blood bank operated by the Red Cross visited our neighborhood today. mobility, N.

■ **mock** V. ridicule; imitate, often in derision. It is unkind to *mock* anyone; it is stupid to *mock* anyone significantly bigger than you. mockery, N.

mode N. prevailing style; manner; way of doing something. The rock star had to have her hair done in the latest *mode:* frizzed, with occasional moussed spikes for variety. Henry plans to adopt a simpler *mode* of life: he is going to become a mushroom hunter and live off the land.

mollify V. soothe. The airline customer service representative tried to *mollify* the angry passenger by offering her a seat in first class.

momentous ADJ. very important. When Marie and Pierre Curie discovered radium, they had no idea of the *momentous* impact their discovery would have upon society.

monarchy N. government under a single ruler. Though England today is a *monarchy*, there is some question whether it will be one in 20 years, given the present discontent at the prospect of Prince Charles as king.

■ **monotony** N. sameness leading to boredom. What could be more deadly dull than the *monotony* of punching numbers into a computer hour after hour?

monumental ADJ. massive; immense. Writing a dictionary is a *monumental* task; so is reading one.

mores N. conventions; moral standards; customs. In America, Benazir Bhutto dressed as Western women did; in Pakistan, however, she followed the *mores* of her people, dressing in traditional veil and robes.

motif N. theme. This simple *motif* runs throughout the entire score.

multifaceted ADJ. having many aspects. A *multifaceted* composer, Roger Davidson has recorded original pieces that range from ragtime tangos to choral masses.

mundane ADJ. worldly as opposed to spiritual; everyday. Uninterested in philosophical or spiritual discussions, Tom talked only of *mundane* matters such as the daily weather forecast or the latest basketball results.

muse V. ponder. For a moment he *mused* about the beauty of the scene, but his thoughts soon changed as he recalled his own personal problems. also N.

■ **mutability** N. ability to change in form; fickleness. Going from rags to riches and then back to rags again, the bankrupt financier was a victim of the *mutability* of fortune.

muted ADJ. silent; muffled; toned down. Thanks to the thick, sound-absorbing walls of the cathedral, only *muted* traffic noise reached the worshippers within.

myriad N. very large number. *Myriads* of mosquitoes from the swamps invaded our village every evening at twilight. also ADJ.

nadir N. lowest point. Although few people realized it, the Dow-Jones averages had reached their *nadir* and would soon begin an upward surge.

Word List 29   naïveté–obnoxious

■ **naïveté** N. quality of being unsophisticated; simplicity; artlessness; gullibility. Touched by the *naïveté* of sweet, convent-trained Cosette, Marius pledges himself to protect her innocence. naive, ADJ.

narrative ADJ. related to telling a story. A born teller of tales, Olsen used her impressive *narrative* skills to advantage in her story, "I Stand Here Ironing."

nebulous ADJ. vague; like a cloud. Phil and Dave tried to come up with a clear, intelligible business plan, not some hazy, *nebulous* proposal. A nebula is an interstellar cloud of dust, hydrogen, helium, and other ionized gases; such clouds are, by definition, *nebulous*.

negate V. cancel out or nullify; deny the truth of. A sudden surge of adrenalin can *negate* the effects of fatigue: there's nothing like a good shock to wake you up. I disagree with you strongly on many points, but I won't try to *negate* your viewpoint.

negligence N. neglect; failure to take reasonable care. Tommy failed to put back the cover on the well after he fetched his pail of water; because of his *negligence,* Kitty fell in.

negligible ADJ. so small, trifling, or unimportant that it may be easily disregarded. Because the damage to his car had been *negligible,* Michael decided he wouldn't bother to report the matter to his insurance company.

neophyte N. recent convert; beginner. This mountain slope contains slides that will challenge experts as well as *neophytes.*

■ **nonchalance** N. indifference; lack of concern; composure. Cool, calm, and collected under fire, James Bond shows remarkable *nonchalance* in the face of danger.

■ **nostalgia** N. homesickness; longing for the past. My grandfather seldom spoke of life in the old country; he had little patience with *nostalgia.* nostalgic, ADJ.

notable ADJ. conspicuous; important; distinguished. Normally *notable* for his calm in the kitchen, today the head cook was shaking, for the *notable* chef Bobby Flay was coming to dinner.

■ **notorious** ADJ. disreputable; widely known; scandalous. To the starlet, any publicity was good publicity: if she couldn't have a good reputation, she'd settle for being *notorious.* notoriety, N.

novelty N. something new; newness. First marketed in 1977, home computers were no longer a *novelty* by 1980. After the first couple of months at college, Johnny found that the *novelty* of living in a dormitory had worn off. novel, ADJ.

novice N. beginner. Even a *novice* at working with computers can install voice recognition software by following the easy steps outlined in the user's manual.

■ **nuance** N. shade of difference in meaning or color; subtle distinction. Jody gazed at the Monet landscape for an hour, appreciating every subtle *nuance* of color in the painting.

nucleus N. central point or core; component of protoplasm; central part of atom. Kathryn, Lexy, and Steven formed the *nucleus* of the debate team, which eventually grew to include most of the senior class.

nullify V. to make invalid; make null or void. Once the contract was *nullified,* it no longer had any legal force.

■ **nurture** V. nourish; educate; foster. The Head Start program attempts to *nurture* pre-kindergarten children so that they will do well when they enter public school. also N.

nutrient N. nourishing substance. As a budding nutritionist, Kim has learned to design diets that contain foods rich in important basic *nutrients.*

obdurate ADJ. stubborn. The manager was *obdurate* in refusing to discuss the workers' grievances.

■ **objective** ADJ. not influenced by personal feelings or prejudices; able to be perceived by the senses. Andrea loved her little son so much that it was impossible for her to be *objective* about his behavior. Nurses gather *objective* data about a patient by taking the patient's temperature or measuring the patient's height and weight.

objective N. goal; aim. Morgan's *objective* is to play basketball so well that he can be a starter on the varsity team.

obligatory ADJ. required; legally or morally binding. It is *obligatory* that books borrowed from the library be returned within two weeks.

obliterate V. destroy completely. In the film *Independence Day* the explosion *obliterated* the White House, vaporizing it completely.

oblivion N. obscurity; forgetfulness. After a brief period of popularity, Hurston's works fell into *oblivion;* no one bothered to reprint them or even to read them any more.

oblivious ADJ. inattentive or unmindful; wholly absorbed. Deep in her book, Nancy was *oblivious* of the noisy squabbles of her brother and his friends.

obnoxious ADJ. offensive; objectionable. A sneak and a tattletale, Sid was an *obnoxious* little brat.

Word List 30   obscure–painstaking

■ **obscure** ADJ. dark; vague; unclear. Even after I read the poem a fourth time, its meaning was still *obscure.* obscurity, N.

■ **obscure** V. make unclear; conceal. At times he seemed purposely to *obscure* his meaning, preferring mystery to clarity. We had hoped to see Mount Rainier, but Seattle's ever-present cloud cover *obscured* our view.

obsessive ADJ. related to thinking about something constantly; preoccupying. Ballet, which had been a hobby, began to dominate her life; her love of dancing became *obsessive.*

obsolescent ADJ. going out of use. Given how quickly computer technology changes, I've had to reconcile myself to the fact that, no matter how up-to-date a system I buy, it's practically *obsolescent* as soon as I've gotten it out of its box.

obsolete ADJ. no longer useful; outmoded; antiquated. The invention of the pocket calculator made the slide rule used by generations of engineers *obsolete.*

obstinate ADJ. stubborn; hard to control or treat. We tried to persuade him to give up smoking, but he was *obstinate* and refused to change. Blackberry stickers are the most *obstinate* weeds I know: once established in a yard, they're extremely hard to root out. obstinacy, N.

offensive ADJ. attacking; insulting; distasteful. Getting into street brawls is no minor matter for professional boxers, who are required by law to restrict their *offensive* impulses to the ring.

officious ADJ. meddlesome; excessively pushing in offering one's services. After her long flight, Jill just wanted to nap, but the *officious* bellboy was intent on showing her all the special features of the deluxe suite.

ominous ADJ. threatening. Those clouds are *ominous*; they suggest a severe storm is on the way.

omnivorous ADJ. eating both plant and animal food; devouring everything. Some animals, including man, are *omnivorous* and eat both meat and vegetables; others are either carnivorous or herbivorous.

■ **opaque** ADJ. not transparent; hard to understand or explain. The *opaque* window shade kept the sunlight out of the room. The language of the federal income tax forms was so *opaque* that I had to turn to an accountant for help. opacity, N.

opportunist N. individual who sacrifices principles for expediency by taking advantage of circumstances. Forget ethics! He's such an *opportunist* that he'll vote in favor of any deal that will give him a break.

opt V. decide in favor of; choose. Given the choice between the movie and the folk dance, Sharon *opted* to go to the dance.

■ **optimist** N. person who looks on the good side. The pessimist says the glass is half empty; the *optimist* says it is half full.

opulence N. extreme wealth; luxuriousness; abundance. The glitter and *opulence* of the ballroom took Cinderella's breath away. opulent, ADJ.

■ **orator** N. public speaker. The abolitionist Frederick Douglass was a brilliant *orator* whose speeches brought home to his audience the evils of slavery.

ordeal N. severe trial or affliction. June was so painfully shy that it was an *ordeal* for her to speak up when the teacher called on her in class.

ornate ADJ. excessively or elaborately decorated. The furnishings of homes that were shown on *Lifestyles of the Rich and Famous* tended to be highly *ornate*.

orthodox ADJ. traditional; conservative in belief. Faced with a problem, he preferred to take an *orthodox* approach rather than shock anyone. orthodoxy, N.

■ **ostentatious** ADJ. showy; pretentious; trying to attract attention. The latest casino in Atlantic City is the most *ostentatious* gambling palace in the East: it easily outglitters its competitors. ostentation, N.

■ **outmoded** ADJ. no longer stylish; old-fashioned. Unconcerned about keeping in style, Lenore was perfectly happy to wear *outmoded* clothes as long as they were clean and unfrayed.

outwit V. outsmart; trick. By disguising himself as an old woman, Holmes was able to *outwit* his pursuers and escape capture.

overbearing ADJ. bossy; arrogant; decisively important. Certain of her own importance and of the unimportance of everyone else, Lady Bracknell was intolerably *overbearing* in her manner. "In choosing a husband," she said, "good birth is of *overbearing* importance; compared to that, neither wealth nor talent signifies."

overt ADJ. open to view. According to the United States Constitution, a person must commit an *overt* act before he or she may be tried for treason.

■ **pacifist** N. one opposed to force; antimilitarist. Shooting his way through the jungle, Rambo was clearly not a *pacifist*.

■ **pacify** V. soothe; make calm or quiet; subdue. Dentists criticize the practice of giving fussy children sweets to *pacify* them.

painstaking ADJ. expending or showing diligent care and great effort. The new high-frequency word list is the result of *painstaking* efforts on the part of our research staff.

Word List 31   panacea–perjury

panacea N. cure-all; remedy for all diseases. Some people claim that vitamin C is a *panacea* that can cure everything from cancer to the common cold.

pandemonium N. wild tumult. When the ships collided in the harbor, *pandemonium* broke out among the passengers.

parable N. short tale illustrating a moral principle. In the *parable* of the good shepherd, Jesus encourages his followers to seek those who have strayed from the flock.

■ **paradox** N. something apparently contradictory in nature; statement that looks false but is actually correct. The therapist Carl Rogers once wrote, "The curious *paradox* is that when I accept myself just as I am, then I can change."

paragon N. model of perfection. The class disliked him because the teacher was always pointing him out as a *paragon* of virtue.

paramount ADJ. foremost in importance; supreme. Proper nutrition and hygiene are of *paramount* importance in adolescent development and growth.

parity N. equality in status or amount; close resemblance. Unfortunately, some doubt exists whether women's salaries will ever achieve *parity* with men's.

parochial ADJ. narrow in outlook; provincial; related to parishes. Although Jane Austen sets her novels in small rural communities, her concerns are universal, not *parochial*.

parody N. humorous imitation; spoof; takeoff; travesty. The show *Forbidden Broadway* presents *parodies* spoofing the year's new productions playing on Broadway.

■ **partial** ADJ. incomplete; having a liking for something. In this issue we have published only a *partial* list of contributors because we lack space to acknowledge everyone. I am extremely *partial* to chocolate eclairs.

partisan ADJ. one-sided; prejudiced; committed to a party. On certain issues of principle, she refused to take a *partisan* stand but let her conscience be her guide. also N.

passive ADJ. not active; acted upon. Mahatma Gandhi urged his followers to pursue a program of *passive* resistance rather than resort to violence and acts of terrorism.

patent ADJ. open for the public to read; obvious. It was *patent* to everyone that the witness spoke the truth. also N.

■ **patronize** V. support; act superior toward; be a customer of. Penniless artists hope to find some wealthy art lover who will *patronize* them. If a wine steward *patronized* me because he saw I knew nothing about fine wine, I'd refuse to *patronize* his restaurant.

■ **pedantic** ADJ. showing off learning; bookish. Leavening his decisions with humorous, down-to-earth anecdotes, Judge Walker was not at all the *pedantic* legal scholar. pedant, N.

pedestrian ADJ. ordinary; unimaginative. Unintentionally boring, he wrote page after page of *pedestrian* prose. (secondary meaning)

peerless ADJ. having no equal; incomparable. To his admirers, the reigning operatic tenor of his generation, Luciano Pavarotti, was *peerless*; no one could compare with him.

penitent ADJ. feeling regret or sorrow for one's offenses; repentant. When he realized the enormity of his crime, he became remorseful and *penitent*. also N.

perceptive ADJ. insightful; aware; wise. Although Maud was a generally *perceptive* critic, she had her blind spots: she could never see flaws in the work of her friends.

peremptory ADJ. demanding and leaving no choice. From Jack's *peremptory* knock on the door, Jill could tell he would not give up until she let him in.

perfunctory ADJ. superficial; not thorough; lacking interest, care, or enthusiasm. Giving the tabletop only a *perfunctory* swipe with her dust cloth, Betty promised herself she'd clean it more thoroughly tomorrow.

perjury N. false testimony while under oath. Rather than lie under oath and perhaps be indicted for *perjury*, the witness chose to take the Fifth Amendment, refusing to answer any questions on the grounds that he might incriminate himself.

Word List 32   **permutation–ponderous**

permutation N. transformation; rearrangement of elements. I'm pretty sure Ted's phone number ends in 5236 or some *permutation* of those digits.

pernicious ADJ. very destructive. Crack cocaine has had a *pernicious* effect on urban society: it has destroyed families, turned children into drug dealers, and increased the spread of violent crimes.

perpetrate V. commit an offense. Only an insane person could *perpetrate* such a horrible crime.

■ **perpetual** ADJ. everlasting. Ponce de León hoped to find the legendary fountain of *perpetual* youth. perpetuity, N.

perpetuate V. make something last; preserve from extinction. Some critics attack *The Adventures of Huckleberry Finn* because they believe Twain's book *perpetuates* a false image of blacks in this country. In environments where resources are unstable, large numbers of organisms are produced quickly on the chance that some will survive to *perpetuate* the species.

persevere V. persist; endure; strive. Despite the church's threats to excommunicate him for heresy, Galileo *persevered* in his belief that Earth moved around the Sun.

■ **pertinent** ADJ. to the point; relevant. Virginia Woolf's words on women's rights are as *pertinent* today as they were when she wrote them nearly a century ago.

peruse V. read with care. After the conflagration that burned down her house, Joan closely *perused* her home insurance policy to discover exactly what benefits her coverage provided her. perusal, N.

■ **pervasive** ADJ. pervading; spread throughout every part. Despite airing them for several hours, she could not rid her clothes of the *pervasive* odor of mothballs that clung to them. pervade, V.

perverse ADJ. stubbornly wrongheaded; wicked and perverted. When Jack was in a *perverse* mood, he would do the opposite of whatever Jill asked him. When Hannibal Lecter was in a *perverse* mood, he ate the flesh of his victims.

■ **pessimism** N. belief that life is basically bad or evil; gloominess. Considering how well you have done in the course so far, you have no real reason for such *pessimism* about your final grade.

petulant ADJ. touchy; peevish. If you'd had hardly any sleep for three nights and people kept on phoning and waking you up, you'd sound pretty *petulant*, too.

■ **phenomena** N. Pl. observable facts or events. We kept careful records of the *phenomena* we noted in the course of these experiments.

■ **philanthropist** N. lover of mankind; doer of good. In his role as *philanthropist* and public benefactor, John D. Rockefeller, Sr. donated millions to charity; as an individual, however, he was a tight-fisted old man.

phlegmatic ADJ. not easily excited to action or emotional displays; calm; sluggish. The nurse was a cheerful but *phlegmatic* person, untroubled by sudden emergencies.

pious ADJ. devout; religious. The challenge for church members today is how to be *pious* in the best sense, that is, to be devout without becoming hypocritical or sanctimonious. piety, N.

pique V. provoke or arouse; annoy. "I know something *you* don't know," said Lucy, trying to *pique* Ethel's interest.

pique N. irritation; resentment. She showed her *pique* at her loss by refusing to appear with the other contestants at the end of the competition.

pivotal ADJ. crucial; key; vital. The new "smart weapons" technology played a *pivotal* role in the quick resolution of the war with Iraq.

placate V. pacify; conciliate. The store manager, trying to *placate* the angry customer, offered to replace the damaged merchandise or to give back her money right away.

placid ADJ. calm; peaceful. Looking at the storm-tossed waters of the lake, Bob wondered why they ever called it Lake *Placid.*

■ **plagiarize** V. steal another's ideas and pass them off as one's own. The teacher could tell that the student had *plagiarized* parts of his essay; she could recognize whole paragraphs straight from *Barron's Book Notes.*

■ **plastic** ADJ. easily shaped; appearing artificial; offering possibilities for creativity; made out of plastic. As clay dries out, it becomes less and less *plastic,* until it can no longer be molded. Jody hated false friends, with their *plastic* smiles and fake concern for one's troubles. Writing is a wonderfully *plastic* medium: you can shape entire worlds with your words. The dumping of *plastic* trash has led to the formation of marine garbage patches in the Atlantic and Pacific Oceans.

platitude N. trite remark; commonplace statement. In giving advice to his son, old Polonius expressed himself only in *platitudes;* every word out of his mouth was commonplace.

plausible ADJ. having a show of truth but open to doubt; specious. Your mother made you stay home from school because she needed you to set up her new iPhone? I'm sorry, you'll have to come up with a more *plausible* excuse than that.

pliable ADJ. flexible; yielding; adaptable. In remodeling the bathroom, we have replaced all the old, rigid lead pipes with new, *pliable* copper tubing.

plight N. condition, state (especially a bad state or condition); predicament. Loggers, unmoved by the *plight* of the spotted owl, plan to keep on logging whether or not they ruin the owl's habitat.

polemical ADJ. aggressive in verbal attack; disputatious. Lexy was a master of *polemical* rhetoric; she should have worn a T-shirt with the slogan "Born to Debate."

ponderous ADJ. very heavy, and possibly awkward because of its heaviness; tedious and lacking fluency or grace. The elephant is *ponderous*, his trumpet call most thunderous. He cannot gallop, jump, or trot. The reason is he weighs a lot. (Do you think this rhyme is clever, or do you find it a bit *ponderous*?)

Word List 33   pore–preside

pore V. study deeply; stare. In doing research on the SAT, we *pored* over back issues of *Scientific American* to locate articles from which reading passages had been excerpted.

posterity N. descendants; future generations. We hope to leave a better world to *posterity.*

■ **potency** N. power; effectiveness; influence. Looking at the expiration date on the cough syrup bottle, we wondered whether the medication still retained its *potency.* potent, ADJ.

practical ADJ. based on experience; useful. Sharon gained *practical* experience in hospital work by acting as an emergency room volunteer.

■ **pragmatic** ADJ. practical (as opposed to idealistic); concerned with the practical worth or impact of something. This coming trip to France should provide me with a *pragmatic* test of the value of my conversational French class.

preamble N. introductory statement. In the *preamble* to the Constitution, the authors set forth the purpose of the document.

precarious ADJ. uncertain; risky. Saying the stock would be a *precarious* investment, the broker advised her client against purchasing it.

■ **precedent** N. something preceding in time that may be used as an authority or guide for future action. If I buy you a car for your sixteenth birthday, your brothers will want me to buy them cars when they turn sixteen, too; I can't afford to set such an expensive *precedent.*

precipitate ADJ. rash; premature; abrupt; hasty; sudden. Though I was angry enough to resign on the spot, I had enough sense to keep myself from quitting a job in such a *precipitate* fashion.

precipitate V. cause to happen suddenly; hurl or propel forcefully. The removal of American political support appears to have *precipitated* the downfall of the Marcos regime.

preclude V. make impossible; eliminate. Because the band was already booked to play in Hollywood on New Year's Eve, that booking *precluded* their accepting the New Year's Eve gig in London they were offered.

■ **predator** N. creature that seizes and devours another animal; person who robs or exploits others. Not just cats, but a wide variety of *predators*—owls, hawks, weasels, foxes—catch mice for dinner. A carnivore is by definition *predatory*, for it *preys* on weaker creatures.

predetermine v. predestine; settle or decide beforehand; influence markedly. Romeo and Juliet believed that Fate had *predetermined* their meeting. Bea gathered estimates from caterers, florists, and stationers so that she could *predetermine* the costs of holding a catered buffet. Philip's love of athletics *predetermined* his choice of a career in sports marketing.

predicament N. tricky or dangerous situation; dilemma. Tied to the railroad tracks by the villain, Pauline strained against her bonds. How would she escape from this terrible *predicament*?

predilection N. partiality; preference. Although my mother wrote all sorts of poetry over the years, she had a definite *predilection* for occasional verse.

preeminent ADJ. outstanding; superior. The king traveled to Boston because he wanted the *preeminent* surgeon in the field to perform the operation.

preempt v. head off; forestall by acting first; appropriate for oneself; supplant. Hoping to *preempt* any attempts by the opposition to make educational reform a hot political issue, the candidate set out her own plan to revitalize the public schools. preemptive, ADJ.

■ **premise** N. assumption; postulate. Acting on the *premise* that there's no fool like an old fool, P. T. Barnum hired a 90-year-old clown for his circus.

premonition N. forewarning. In horror movies, the hero often has a *premonition* of danger, yet he foolishly ignores it.

preposterous ADJ. absurd; ridiculous. When he tried to downplay his youthful experiments with marijuana by saying he hadn't inhaled, we all thought, "What a *preposterous* excuse!"

preside v. act as president or chairman; exercise control. When the club president cannot attend a meeting, the vice president will *preside* over that session.

Word List 34   prestige–prophetic

prestige N. impression produced by achievements or reputation. Many students want to go to Harvard College not for the education offered but for the *prestige* of Harvard's name.

presumptuous ADJ. taking liberties; overstepping bounds; nervy. I thought it was *presumptuous* of Mort to butt into Bishop Tutu's talk with Mrs. Clinton and ask them for their autographs; I wouldn't have had the nerve.

pretentious ADJ. ostentatious; pompous; making unjustified claims; overly ambitious. None of the other prizewinners are wearing their medals; isn't it a bit *pretentious* of you to wear yours?

■ **prevail** v. triumph; predominate; prove superior in strength, power, or influence; be current. A radical committed to social change, Reed had no patience with the conservative views that *prevailed* in the America of his day. prevalent, ADJ. ; prevailing, ADJ.

prevaricate v. lie. Some people believe that to *prevaricate* in a good cause is justifiable and regard their false statement as a "white lie."

■ **prey** N. target of a hunt; victim. In *Stalking the Wild Asparagus*, Euell Gibbons has as his *prey* not wild beasts but wild plants. also v.

pristine ADJ. unspoiled; spotless. Johnny kept his comic books in their original condition, as *pristine* as on the day he bought them. For his interview he wore a *pristine* white shirt and a brand-new tie.

privation N. hardship; want. In his youth, he knew hunger and *privation*.

■ **problematic** ADJ. doubtful; unsettled; questionable; perplexing. Given the way building costs have exceeded estimates for the job, whether the arena will ever be completed is *problematic*.

prodigal ADJ. wasteful; reckless with money. Don't be so *prodigal* spending my money; when you've earned some money, you can waste it as much as you want! also N.

prodigious ADJ. marvelous; enormous. Watching the champion weight lifter heave the weighty barbell to shoulder height and then boost it overhead, we marveled at his *prodigious* strength.

prodigy N. highly gifted child; extraordinary accomplishment or event. Menuhin was a *prodigy,* performing wonders on his violin when he was barely eight years old.

profane v. violate; desecrate; treat unworthily. The members of the mysterious Far Eastern cult sought to kill the British explorer because he had *profaned* the sanctity of their holy goblet by using it as an ashtray. also ADJ.

■ **profound** ADJ. deep; not superficial; complete. Freud's remarkable insights into human behavior caused his fellow scientists to honor him as a *profound* thinker. profundity, N.

profusion N. abundant quantity; lavish expenditure. Along the Mendocino coast, where there is enough moisture, wildflowers flourish in great *profusion*. Polly tried to win friends by her *profusion* in throwing extravagant parties.

■ **proliferation** N. rapid growth; spread; multiplication. Times of economic hardship inevitably encourage the *proliferation* of countless get-rich-quick schemes. proliferate, v.

■ **prolific** ADJ. abundantly fruitful. My editors must assume I'm a *prolific* writer: they expect me to revise six books this year!

■ **prologue** N. introduction (to a poem or play). In the *prologue* to *Romeo and Juliet*, Shakespeare introduces the audience to the feud between the Montagues and the Capulets.

prolong V. make longer; draw out; lengthen. In their determination to discover ways to *prolong* human life, doctors fail to take into account that longer lives are not always happier ones.

■ **prominent** ADJ. conspicuous; notable; sticking out. Have you ever noticed that Prince Charles's *prominent* ears make him resemble the big-eared character in *Mad* comics?

■ **promote** V. help to flourish; advance in rank; publicize. Founder of the Children's Defense Fund, Marian Wright Edelman ceaselessly *promotes* the welfare of young people everywhere.

prompt V. bring about or cause an action or feeling; cue someone to speak. Being cast as the lead in the school play *prompted* Dan to consider acting as a career. Unfortunately, he had trouble remembering his lines: the stage manager had to *prompt* him from the wings.

prone ADJ. inclined to; prostrate. She was *prone* to sudden fits of anger during which she would lie *prone* on the floor, screaming and kicking her heels.

propagate V. multiply; spread. Since bacteria *propagate* more quickly in unsanitary environments, it is important to keep hospital rooms clean.

propensity N. natural inclination. Convinced of his own talent, Sol has an unfortunate *propensity* to belittle the talents of others.

■ **property** N. quality or aspect; belongings; land. In science class we learned that each element has certain physical and chemical *properties*.

prophetic ADJ. foretelling the future. I have no magical *prophetic* powers; when I predict what will happen, I base my predictions on common sense. prophesy, V.

Word List 35　　proponent–qualified

proponent N. supporter; backer. In the Senate, *proponents* of the universal health care measure lobbied to gain additional support for the controversial legislation.

propriety N. fitness; correct conduct. Miss Manners counsels her readers so that they may behave with due *propriety* in any social situation and not embarrass themselves.

■ **prosaic** ADJ. dull and unimaginative; matter-of-fact; factual. Though the ad writers had come up with a wildly imaginative campaign to publicize the company's newest product, the head office rejected it for a more *prosaic,* down-to-earth approach.

■ **prosperity** N. good fortune; financial success; physical well-being. Promising to stay together "for richer, for poorer," the newlyweds vowed to be true to one another in *prosperity* and hardship alike.

protagonist N. principal character; leading actor. Emma, the *protagonist* of Jane Austen's novel, is an overindulged young woman convinced of her ability as a matchmaker.

prototype N. original work used as a model by others. The National Air and Space Museum displays the Wright brothers' first plane, the *prototype* of all the American aircraft that came after.

protract V. prolong. Seeking to delay the union members' vote, the management team tried to *protract* the negotiations endlessly, but the union representatives saw through their strategy.

provident ADJ. displaying foresight; thrifty; preparing for emergencies. In his usual *provident* manner, he had insured himself against this type of loss.

provincial ADJ. pertaining to a province; limited in outlook; unsophisticated. As *provincial* governor, Sir Henry administered the queen's law in his remote corner of Canada. Caught up in local problems, out of touch with London news, he became sadly *provincial.*

provisional ADJ. tentative. Kim's acceptance as an American Express cardholder was *provisional:* before issuing her a card, American Express wanted to check her employment record and credit history.

■ **provocative** ADJ. arousing anger or interest; annoying. In a typically *provocative* act, the bully kicked sand into the weaker man's face.

proximity N. nearness. Blind people sometimes develop a compensatory ability to sense the *proximity* of objects around them.

■ **prudent** ADJ. cautious; careful. A miser hoards money not because he is *prudent* but because he is greedy. prudence, N.

prune V. cut away; trim. With the help of her editor, she was able to *prune* her manuscript into publishable form.

pseudonym N. pen name. Samuel Clemens's *pseudonym* was Mark Twain.

puerile ADJ. childish; immature. Throwing tantrums? You should have outgrown such *puerile* behavior years ago.

puny ADJ. insignificant; tiny; weak. Our *puny* efforts to stop the flood were futile.

purge V. remove or get rid of something unwanted; free from blame or guilt; cleanse or purify. The Communist government *purged* the party to get rid of members suspected of capitalist sympathies. also N.

■ **qualified** ADJ. limited or restricted; certified. Unable to give the candidate full support, the mayor gave him only a *qualified* endorsement. The newly *qualified* nurse hoped to find a job in a neonatal intensive care unit.

Word List 36   quandary–reconcile

quandary N. dilemma. When both Harvard and Stanford accepted Lori, she was in a *quandary* as to which school she should attend.

quarry N. victim; object of a hunt. The police closed in on their *quarry*.

quarry V. dig into. They *quarried* blocks of marble out of the hillside. also N.

quell V. extinguish; put down; quiet. Miss Minchin's demeanor was so stern and forbidding that she could *quell* any unrest among her students with one intimidating glance.

quench V. douse or extinguish; assuage or satisfy. What's the favorite song of the fire department? "Baby, *Quench* My Fire!"

quibble N. minor objection or complaint. Aside from a few hundred teensy-weensy *quibbles* about the set, the script, the actors, the director, the costumes, the lighting, and the props, the hypercritical critic loved the play. also V.

quirk N. strange chance happening; odd habit; sudden twist. By a *quirk* of fate, he found himself working for the man whom he had fired years before. Photographing your food at restaurants seems like a harmless *quirk*, yet it annoys some people. Beth pretended that she was angry with the boys, but the slight *quirk* to her mouth betrayed her actual amusement.

quixotic ADJ. idealistic but impractical. Simon's head is in the clouds; he constantly comes up with *quixotic*, unworkable schemes.

rabid ADJ. like a fanatic; furious. He was a *rabid* follower of the Dodgers and watched them play whenever he could go to the ball park.

rally V. call up or summon (forces, vital powers, etc.); revive or recuperate. Washington quickly *rallied* his troops to fight off the British attack. The patient had been sinking throughout the night, but at dawn she *rallied* and made a complete recovery.

ramble V. wander aimlessly (physically or mentally). Listening to the teacher *ramble*, Shelby wondered whether he'd ever get to the point. also N.

rampant ADJ. growing in profusion; unrestrained. In the garden, the weeds were *rampant*: they killed all the flowers that had been planted in the spring. In the city, crime was *rampant*: the burglars and muggers were out of control.

rancor N. bitterness; deep-seated hatred. Thirty years after the war, she could not let go of the past but still felt an implacable *rancor* against the foe.

■ **random** ADJ. without definite purpose, plan, or aim; haphazard. Although the sponsor of the raffle claimed all winners were chosen at *random,* people had their suspicions when the grand prize went to the sponsor's brother-in-law.

rant V. rave; talk excitedly; scold; make a grandiloquent speech. When he heard that I'd totaled the family car, Dad began to *rant* at me like a complete madman.

ratify V. approve formally; confirm; verify. Party leaders doubted that they had enough votes in both houses of Congress to *ratify* the constitutional amendment.

rationale N. fundamental reason or justification; grounds for an action. Her need to have someplace to hang her earring collection was Dora's *rationale* for piercing fifteen holes in each ear.

rationalize V. give a plausible reason for an action in place of a true, less admirable one; offer an excuse. When David told gabby Gabrielle he couldn't give her a ride to the dance because he had no room in the car, he was *rationalizing*; actually, he couldn't stand being cooped up in a car with anyone who talked as much as she did.

raze V. destroy completely. Spelling is important: to raise a building is to put it up; to *raze* a building is to tear it down.

reactionary ADJ. recoiling from progress; politically ultraconservative. Opposing the use of English in worship services, *reactionary* forces in the church fought to reinstate the mass in Latin.

rebuff V. snub; beat back. She *rebuffed* his invitation so smoothly that he did not realize he had been snubbed.

rebuke V. scold harshly; criticize severely. NO matter how sharply Miss Watson *rebuked* Huck for his misconduct, he never talked back but just stood there like a stump. also N.

rebuttal N. refutation; response with contrary evidence. The defense lawyer confidently listened to the prosecutor sum up his case; she was sure that she could answer his arguments in her *rebuttal*.

recalcitrant ADJ. obstinately stubborn. Which animal do you think is more recalcitrant, a pig-headed pig or a stubborn mule?

recant V. disclaim or disavow; retract a previous statement; openly confess error. Those who can, keep true to their faith; those who can't, *recant*.

recapitulate V. summarize. Let us *recapitulate* what has been said thus far before going ahead.

receptive ADJ. quick or willing to receive ideas, suggestions, etc. Adventure-loving Huck Finn proved a *receptive* audience for Tom Sawyer's tales of buried treasure and piracy.

recession N. withdrawal; time of low economic activity. The slow *recession* of the floodwaters created problems for the crews working to restore power to the area.

reciprocate V. repay in kind. It was kind of Donna to have us over to dinner; I'd like us to *reciprocate* in some way, if we can.

reconcile V. correct inconsistencies; become friendly after a quarrel. Every time we try to *reconcile* our checkbook with the bank statement, we quarrel. However, despite these monthly lovers' quarrels, we always manage to *reconcile*.

Word List 37   recount–renovate

recount V. narrate or tell; count over again. About to *recount* the latest adventure of Sherlock Holmes, Watson lost track of exactly how many cases Holmes had solved and refused to begin his tale until he'd *recounted* them one by one.

rectify V. set right; correct. You had better send a check to *rectify* your account before American Express cancels your credit card.

rectitude N. uprightness; moral virtue; correctness of judgment. The Eagle Scout was a model of *rectitude*.

recuperate V. recover. The doctors were worried because the patient did not *recuperate* as rapidly as they had expected.

recurrent ADJ. occurring again and again. Because Phil suffered from *recurrent* ear infections, the doctors were concerned that these periodic attacks might eventually affect his hearing.

redundant ADJ. superfluous; repetitious; excessively wordy. The bottle of wine I brought to Bob's was certainly *redundant:* how was I to know Bob owned a winery? In your essay, you repeat several points unnecessarily; try to be less *redundant* in the future. redundancy, N.

refine V. free from impurities; perfect. Just as you can *refine* sugar by removing bits of cane and other unwanted material, you can *refine* verse by removing awkward metaphors and polishing rough rhymes. refinement, N.

■ **reflect** V. think seriously about; represent faithfully; show a physical image; create a good or bad impression. Mr. Collins *reflected* on Elizabeth's rejection of his proposal. Did it *reflect* her true feelings, he wondered. Looking at his image *reflected* in the mirror, he refused to believe that she could reject such a fine-looking man. Such behavior *reflected* badly upon her.

refrain V. abstain from; resist. Whenever he heard a song with a lively chorus, Sol could never *refrain* from joining in on the refrain.

refrain N. chorus. Whenever he heard a song with a lively chorus, Sol could never refrain from joining in on the *refrain*.

■ **refute** V. disprove. At his trial, Socrates attempted to *refute* the claims of those who accused him of corrupting the youth of Athens through his teachings.

regress V. move backward to an earlier, generally more primitive state. Although Timmy outgrew his need for a pacifier well over a year ago, occasionally when he's tired or nervous, he *regresses* and starts sucking his thumb.

reiterate V. repeat. He *reiterated* the warning to make sure that everyone understood it.

rejoinder N. retort; comeback; reply. When someone has been rude to me, I find it particularly satisfying to come up with a quick *rejoinder*.

rejuvenate V. make young again. The charlatan claimed that his elixir would *rejuvenate* the aged and weary.

relegate V. banish to an inferior position; delegate; assign. After Ralph dropped his second tray of drinks that week, the manager swiftly *relegated* him to a minor post cleaning up behind the bar.

relevant ADJ. pertinent; referring to the case in hand. How *relevant* Virginia Woolf's essays are to women writers today; it's as if Woolf in the 1930s foresaw our current literary struggles. relevancy, N.

relic N. surviving remnant; memento. Egypt's Department of Antiquities prohibits tourists from taking mummies and other ancient *relics* out of the country. Mike keeps his photos of his trip to Egypt in a box with other *relics* of his travels.

■ **relinquish** V. give up something with reluctance; yield. Once you get used to fringe benefits like expense account meals and a company car, it's very hard to *relinquish* them.

relish V. savor; enjoy. Watching Peter enthusiastically chow down, I thought, "Now there's a man who *relishes* a good dinner!" also N.

reminiscence N. recollection. Her *reminiscences* of her experiences are so fascinating that she ought to write a book.

remiss ADJ. negligent. The prison guard was accused of being *remiss* in his duty when the prisoner escaped.

remnant N. remainder. I suggest that you wait until the store places the *remnants* of these goods on sale.

remorse N. guilt; self-reproach. The murderer felt no *remorse* for his crime.

remunerative ADJ. lucrative; rewarding. Because work as an insurance agent was far more *remunerative* than work as a church organist, Ives eventually resigned from his church job. remuneration, N.

renegade N. deserter; traitor. Because he had abandoned his post and joined forces with the Indians, his fellow officers considered the hero of *Dances with Wolves* a *renegade*. also ADJ.

renounce V. abandon; disown; repudiate. Even though she knew she would be burned at the stake as a witch, Joan of Arc refused to *renounce* her belief that her voices came from God. renunciation, N.

renovate V. restore to good condition; renew. We *renovated* our kitchen, replacing the old cabinets and countertop and installing new appliances.

Word List 38   renown–reticent

■ **renown** N. fame. For many years an unheralded researcher, Barbara McClintock gained international *renown* when she won the Nobel Prize in physiology and medicine.

repeal V. revoke; annul. What would the effect on our society be if we decriminalized drug use by *repealing* the laws against the possession and sale of narcotics?

repel V. drive away; disgust. In the game *Zombie Attack*, your goal is to *repel* the zombie hordes, driving them away from Gotham City. At first, the Beast's ferocious appearance *repelled* Beauty, but she came to love the tender heart hidden behind that beastly exterior.

repercussion N. result or impact (of an event, etc.); rebound; reverberation. The brothers' quarrel had serious *repercussions*, for it led to their estrangement.

repertoire N. list of works of music, drama, etc., a performer is prepared to present. The opera company decided to include *Madame Butterfly* in its *repertoire* for the following season.

replenish V. fill up again. Before she could take another backpacking trip, Carla had to *replenish* her stock of freeze-dried foods.

■ **reprehensible** ADJ. deserving blame. Shocked by the viciousness of the bombing, politicians of every party uniformly condemned the terrorists' *reprehensible* deed.

repress V. restrain; hold back; crush; suppress. Anne's parents tried to curb her impetuosity without *repressing* her boundless high spirits.

reprieve N. temporary stay. During the twenty-four-hour *reprieve*, the lawyers sought to make the stay of execution permanent. also V.

reprimand V. reprove severely; rebuke. Every time Ermengarde made a mistake in class, she was afraid that Miss Minchin would *reprimand* her and tell her father how badly she was doing in school. also N.

reproachful ADJ. expressing disapproval. He never could do anything wrong without imagining the *reproachful* look in his mother's eye.

reprove V. censure; rebuke. Though Aunt Bea at times would *reprove* Opie for inattention in church, she believed he was at heart a God-fearing lad.

repudiate V. refuse to have anything to do with; reject as untrue or unauthorized; refuse to pay. Angered by Cordelia's refusal to express her love for him in flattering words, King Lear *repudiates* his daughter, disinheriting her. The lawyer maintained that this new evidence would *repudiate* the allegations against her client. On separating from Tony, Tina announced that she would *repudiate* all debts incurred by her soon-to-be ex-husband.

reputable ADJ. respectable. If you want to buy antiques, look for a *reputable* dealer; far too many dealers today pass off fakes as genuine antiques.

rescind V. cancel. Because of the public outcry against the new taxes, the senator proposed a bill to *rescind* the unpopular financial measure.

reserve N. backup supply; body of troops not part of the regular military forces; place set aside for specific purpose; formal but distant manner. Australia supplies much of the world's uranium from its abundant uranium *reserves*. Reluctant to enlist in the regular army, Don considered joining the *reserves*. On their African safari, Tom and Susan visited some fascinating big game *reserves*. Although Mark's air of *reserve* attracted some girls, it put off Judy, who felt his aloofness showed a lack of warmth.

■ **reserved** ADJ. self-controlled; careful in expressing oneself. They made an odd couple: she was outspoken and uninhibited; he was cautious and *reserved*. (secondary meaning)

■ **resignation** N. patient submissiveness; statement that one is quitting a job. If Bob Cratchit had not accepted Scrooge's bullying with such *resignation*, he might have gotten up the nerve to hand in his *resignation*. resigned, ADJ.

resilient ADJ. elastic; having the power of springing back. Highly *resilient*, steel makes excellent bedsprings. resilience, N.

■ **resolution** N. firmness of purpose; formal expression of intent; solving of a problem. Nothing could shake Philip's *resolution* that his children would get the best education that money could buy. The symphony board passed a *resolution* to ban cell phone use during concerts. Friar Laurence hoped for a peaceful *resolution* of the conflict between the feuding Montagues and Capulets. resolute, ADJ.

■ **resolve** V. decide; settle; solve. "I have *resolved*, Watson, to travel to Bohemia to *resolve* the dispute between Irene Adler and the King. In my absence, do your best to *resolve* any mysteries that arise."

■ **restraint** N. moderation or self-control; controlling force; restriction. Control yourself, young lady! Show some *restraint!*

resumption N. taking up again; recommencement. During summer break, Don had not realized how much he missed university life; at the *resumption* of classes, however, he felt marked excitement and pleasure. resume, V.

■ **retain** V. keep; employ. Fighting to *retain* his seat in Congress, Senator Foghorn *retained* a new manager to head his reelection campaign.

retaliation N. repayment in kind (usually for bad treatment). Because everyone knew the Princeton Band had stolen Brown's mascot, the whole Princeton student body expected some sort of *retaliation* from Brown. retaliate, v.

- **reticent** ADJ. reserved; uncommunicative; inclined to be silent. Fearing his competitors might get advance word about his plans from talkative staff members, Hughes preferred *reticent* employees to loquacious ones.

Word List 39   retract–saturate

retract V. withdraw; take back. When I saw how Fred and his fraternity brothers had trashed the frat house, I decided to *retract* my offer to let them use our summer cottage for the weekend. Startled, the crab *retracts* its claws; then, scuttling backward, it withdraws. retraction, N.

retrieve V. recover; find and bring in. The dog was intelligent and quickly learned to *retrieve* the game killed by the hunter.

retroactive ADJ. taking effect prior to its enactment (as a law) or imposition (as a tax). Because the new pension law was *retroactive* to the first of the year, even though Martha had retired in February, she was eligible for the pension.

- **reverent** ADJ. respectful; worshipful. Though I bow my head in church and recite the prayers, sometimes I don't feel properly *reverent*. revere, v.

revoke V. cancel; retract. Repeat offenders who continue to drive under the influence of alcohol face having their driver's license permanently *revoked*.

rift N. opening made by splitting; open space; break in friendly relations. After the recent earthquake, geologists observed several fresh *rifts* in the Hayward hills. Through a *rift* in the dense clouds the pilot glimpsed a beacon light far below. Unsure how he had offended Jo, Laurie tried to think of some way to mend the *rift* in their friendship.

- **rigid** ADJ. unable to bend; not easily changed; unwilling to change (beliefs, opinions). Deacon Dobbs wore a *rigid* white plastic collar that chafed his neck. His church maintained *rigid* rules concerning women's roles within the congregation, and Dobbs was far too *rigid* in his beliefs to challenge the church's teachings.

rigor N. severity. Many settlers could not stand the *rigors* of the New England winters.

rousing ADJ. lively; stirring. "And now, let's have a *rousing* welcome for Lady Gaga, who'll lead us in a *rousing* rendition of 'The Star Spangled Banner.'"

- **rudimentary** ADJ. limited to the basics; imperfectly developed. Although my grandmother's English vocabulary was limited to a few *rudimentary* phrases, she always could make herself understood. Echidnas lack external ears; their tails are, at best, *rudimentary*. They dine on a diet of termites and ants, with beetle larvae supplementary.

rupture N. act of breaking; fracture; break in harmony or peaceful relations. The *rupture* of gas lines caused by the earthquake contributed greatly to the fire that ensued.

ruse N. trick; stratagem. Because they wanted to decorate the living room for their mother's surprise birthday party, the girls tried to think of some good *ruse* to lure her out of the house for a couple of hours.

- **ruthless** ADJ. pitiless; cruel. Captain Hook was a dangerous, *ruthless* villain who would stop at nothing to destroy Peter Pan.

sagacious ADJ. keen; shrewd; having insight. Holmes is far too *sagacious* to be fooled by a simple trick like that. sagacity, N.

salutary ADJ. tending to improve; beneficial; wholesome. The punishment had a *salutary* effect on the boy, for he became a model student.

sanction V. approve; impose a penalty on. Nothing will convince me to *sanction* the engagement of my daughter to such a worthless young man. The board has no legal authority to *sanction* members as a way to enforce the ethics code.

sap V. diminish; undermine. The element kryptonite has an unhealthy effect on Superman: it *saps* his strength.

sarcasm N. scornful remarks; stinging rebuke. Though Ralph tried to ignore the mocking comments of his supposed friends, their *sarcasm* wounded him deeply.

- **satirize** V. mock. Cartoonist Gary Trudeau often *satirizes* contemporary politicians; through the comments of the *Doonesbury* characters, Trudeau ridicules political corruption and folly. satirical, ADJ.

saturate V. soak thoroughly. Thorough watering is the key to lawn care: you must *saturate* your new lawn well to encourage its growth.

Word List 40   savory–shun

savory ADJ. tasty; pleasing, attractive, or agreeable. The Smitten Kitchen's recipes enable amateur chefs to create *savory* delicacies for their guests.

scamper V. run about playfully. Looking forward to the game of hide-and-seek, the children *scampered* off to find good spots in which to hide.

scanty ADJ. meager or insufficient; revealing (of clothing). Thinking his helping of food was *scanty*, Oliver Twist asked for more. A *scanty* bikini top may be all right for the beach, but not for the office.

scapegoat N. someone who bears the blame for others. After the *Challenger* disaster, NASA searched for *scapegoats* on whom they could cast the blame.

scavenge V. hunt through discarded materials for usable items; search, especially for food. If you need parts for an old car that the dealers no longer have in stock, try *scavenging* for odd bits and pieces at the auto wreckers' yards. scavenger, N.

schematic ADJ. relating to an outline or diagram; using a system of symbols. In working out the solution to this logic puzzle, you may find it helpful to construct a simple *schematic* diagram outlining the order of events.

schism N. division, split. His reforms led to a *schism* in the church and the establishment of a new sect opposing the old order.

scrupulous ADJ. conscientious and extremely thorough; careful to behave in an ethical and morally right way. Although Alfred is *scrupulous* in fulfilling his duties at work, he is less conscientious about his obligations to his family and friends at home. Betsy was far too *scrupulous* to try to steal away another girl's boyfriend. scruple, V.

■ **scrutinize** V. examine closely and critically. Searching for flaws, the sergeant *scrutinized* every detail of the private's uniform.

seasoned ADJ. experienced. Though pleased with her new batch of rookies, the basketball coach wished she had a few more *seasoned* players on the team. (secondary meaning)

seclusion N. isolation; solitude. One moment she loved crowds; the next, she sought *seclusion.*

sect N. separate religious body; faction. As university chaplain, she sought to address universal religious issues and not limit herself to concerns of any one *sect.*

secular ADJ. worldly; not pertaining to church matters. The church leaders decided not to interfere in *secular* matters.

sedate ADJ. calm and composed; grave. To calm the agitated pony, we teamed him with a *sedate* mare that easily accepted the harness.

sedition N. resistance to authority; insubordination; rebellion. Her words, though not treasonous in themselves, were calculated to arouse thoughts of *sedition.* seditious, ADJ.

sensory ADJ. pertaining to the physical senses. Blasted by sound waves, dazzled by flashing lights, jostled by crowds, a newcomer to rock concerts can suffer from *sensory* overload.

■ **serenity** N. calmness; placidity. The *serenity* of the sleepy town was shattered by a tremendous explosion.

servile ADJ. slavishly submissive; fawning; cringing. Constantly fawning over his employer, Uriah Heep was a *servile* creature.

servitude N. slavery; compulsory labor. Born a slave, Frederick Douglass resented his life of *servitude* and plotted to escape to the North.

■ **sever** V. cut; separate. The released prisoner wanted to begin a new life and *sever* all connections with his criminal past. Dr. Guillotin invented a machine that could neatly *sever* an aristocratic head from its equally aristocratic body.

■ **severity** N. harshness; intensity; austerity; rigidity. The *severity* of Jane's migraine attack was so great that she took to her bed for a week.

sham V. pretend. He *shammed* sickness to get out of going to school. also N.

shortcomings N. failures; deficiencies. Aware of his own *shortcomings* as a public speaker, the candidate worked closely with debate coaches to prepare for the coming campaign.

shrewd ADJ. clever; astute. A *shrewd* investor, he took clever advantage of the fluctuations of the stock market.

shun V. keep away from. Cherishing his solitude, the recluse *shunned* the company of other human beings.

Word List 41 simile–splendor

simile N. comparison of one thing with another, using the word *like* or *as*. "My love is like a red, red rose" is a *simile.*

simplistic ADJ. oversimplified. Though Jack's solution dealt adequately with one aspect of the problem, it was *simplistic* in failing to consider various complications that might arise.

simulate V. feign; pretend. The judge ruled that the accused racketeer had *simulated* insanity and was in fact sane enough to stand trial.

■ **singular** ADJ. unique; extraordinary; odd. Though the young man tried to understand Father William's *singular* behavior, he still found it odd that the old man incessantly stood on his head. singularity, N.

sinister ADJ. evil; conveying a sense of ill omen. Aware of the Penguin's *sinister* purpose, Batman wondered how he could save Gotham City from the ravages of his evil enemy.

■ **skeptical** ADJ. doubting; suspending judgment until having examined the evidence supporting a point of view. I am *skeptical* about this project; I want some proof that it can work. skepticism, N.

slacken V. slow up; loosen. As they passed the finish line, the runners *slackened* their pace.

sneer V. smile or laugh contemptuously; make an insulting comment or face. "I could paint better than that with both hands tied behind my back," *sneered* Marvin.

sobriety N. moderation (especially regarding indulgence in alcohol); seriousness. Neither falling-down drunks nor stand-up comics are noted for *sobriety.* sober, ADJ.

solemnity N. seriousness; gravity. The minister was concerned that nothing should disturb the *solemnity* of the marriage service.

solicit V. request earnestly; seek. Knowing she needed to have a solid majority for the budget to pass, the mayor telephoned all the members of the city council to *solicit* their votes.

soliloquy N. talking to oneself. Dramatists use the *soliloquy* as a device to reveal a character's innermost thoughts and emotions.

soluble ADJ. able to be dissolved; able to be explained. Sugar is *soluble* in water; put a sugar cube in water, and it will quickly dissolve. Thanks to Sherlock Holmes, the Mystery of the Missing Sugar Cube proved to be *soluble* after all.

■ **solution** N. act of solving (a problem, difficult situation, etc.); liquid mixture whose components are uniformly distributed. If you get a foreign object in your eye, one possible *solution* to the problem is to try to flush the object out of your eye with clean water or a saline *solution*.

solvent ADJ. able to dissolve; able to pay all debts. Sol was perpetually broke until he invented Glu-Off, whose *solvent* power was strong enough to dissolve Crazy Glue. It proved so popular that Sol is finally *solvent*. also N.

somber ADJ. gloomy and depressing; dark and drab. From the doctor's grim expression, I could tell he had *somber* news. Dull brown and charcoal gray are pretty *somber* colors; can't you wear something bright?

sophisticated ADJ. worldly-wise and urbane; complex. When Sophie makes wisecracks, she thinks she sounds *sophisticated*, but instead she sounds sophomoric. A few years ago, the new IBM laptop with the butterfly keyboard and the built-in quad-speed fax modem seemed the height of computer *sophistication*.

specious ADJ. seemingly reasonable but incorrect; misleading (often intentionally). To claim that, because houses and birds both have wings, both can fly, is extremely *specious* reasoning.

speculate V. theorize or ponder; assume a financial risk; gamble. Students of the stock market *speculate* that the seeds of the financier's downfall were planted when he *speculated* heavily in junk bonds.

spendthrift N. someone who wastes money. Easy access to credit encourages people to turn into *spendthrifts* who shop till they drop.

splendor N. magnificence; grandeur; brilliance. Awed by the glittering chandeliers and finely costumed courtiers, Cinderella was overwhelmed by the *splendor* of the ball.

Word List 42   spontaneity–subsequent

spontaneity N. lack of premeditation; naturalness; freedom from constraint. When Betty and Jennifer met, Jen impulsively hugged her roommate-to-be, but Betty drew back, unprepared for such *spontaneity*. spontaneous, ADJ.

sporadic ADJ. occurring irregularly. Although you can still hear *sporadic* outbursts of laughter and singing outside, the big Halloween parade has passed; the party's over till next year.

spurious ADJ. false; counterfeit; forged; illogical. The hero of Jonathan Gash's mystery novels is an antique dealer who gives the reader advice on how to tell *spurious* antiques from the real thing.

squander V. waste. If you *squander* your allowance on candy and comic books, you won't have any money left to buy the new box of crayons you want.

stagnant ADJ. motionless; not advancing. Mosquitoes commonly breed in ponds of *stagnant* water. Mike's career was *stagnant*; it wasn't going anywhere, and neither was he! stagnate, V.

stalemate N. deadlock. Negotiations between the union and the employers have reached a *stalemate*: neither side is willing to budge from its previously stated position.

stamina N. strength; staying power. I doubt that she has the *stamina* to run the full distance of the marathon race.

stanza N. division of a poem. We all know the first *stanza* of the "The Star Spangled Banner." Does anyone know the last?

static ADJ. unchanging; lacking development. Why watch chess on TV? I like watching a game with action, not something *static* where nothing seems to be going on. stasis, N.

statute N. law enacted by the legislature. The *statute* of limitations sets the limits on how long you have to take legal action in specific cases.

■ **steadfast** ADJ. loyal; unswerving. Penelope was *steadfast* in her affections, faithfully waiting for Ulysses to return from his wanderings.

stem V. check the flow. The paramedic used a tourniquet to *stem* the bleeding from the slashed artery.

stem from V. arise from. Morton's problems in school *stemmed from* his poor study habits.

stereotyped ADJ. oversimplified; lacking individuality; seen as a type. My chief objection to the book is that the characters are *stereotyped*; they don't come across as real people with individual quirks, fears, and dreams. stereotype, N., V.

stifle V. suppress; extinguish; inhibit. Halfway through the boring lecture, Laura gave up trying to *stifle* her yawns.

stipulate V. make express conditions; specify. Before agreeing to reduce American military forces in Europe, the president *stipulated* that NATO inspection teams be allowed to inspect Soviet bases.

stock ADJ.   regularly available for sale at a store; used so regularly that it becomes trite; indicating a conventional character type. Rather than ordering custom-made cabinets, Sharon saved money by purchasing *stock* units. In your college interview, avoid giving *stock* answers to the interviewer's questions: you don't want to bore her to tears. The characters of the *commedia dell' arte* usually represent fixed social types, *stock* characters, such as foolish old men, sneaky servants, and boastful military officers.

■ **stoic** ADJ. impassive; unmoved by joy or grief. I wasn't particularly *stoic* when I had my flu shot; I squealed like a stuck pig. also N.

stolid ADJ. unruffled; impassive; dull. Marianne wanted a romantic, passionate suitor like Willoughby, not a *stolid*, unimaginative one like Colonel Brandon.

■ **stratagem** N. deceptive scheme. Though Wellington's forces seemed to be in full retreat, in reality their withdrawal was a *stratagem* intended to lure the enemy away from its sheltered position.

stratify V. divide into classes; be arranged into strata. As the economic gap between the rich and the poor increased, Roman society grew increasingly *stratified*.

strident ADJ. loud and harsh; insistent. Whenever Sue became angry, she tried not to raise her voice; she had no desire to appear *strident*.

stringent ADJ. binding; rigid; strict. Protesting that the school dress code was too *stringent*, Katya campaigned to have the rules relaxed.

studied ADJ. not spontaneous; deliberate; thoughtful. Given Jill's previous slights, Jack felt that the omission of his name from the guest list was a *studied* insult.

stupefy V. make numb; stun; amaze. Disapproving of drugs in general, Laura refused to take sleeping pills or any other medicine that might *stupefy* her. stupefaction, N.

■ **subdued** ADJ. less intense; quieter. Bob liked the *subdued* lighting at the restaurant because he thought it was romantic. I just thought it was dimly lit.

subjective ADJ. existing in the mind, rather than in the object itself; opposite of objective; personal. Your analysis is highly *subjective*; you have permitted your emotions and your opinions to color your thinking.

sublime ADJ. exalted; noble and uplifting; utter. Lucy was in awe of Desi's *sublime* musicianship, while he was in awe of her *sublime* naïveté.

subordinate ADJ. occupying a lower rank; inferior; submissive. Bishop Proudie's wife expected all the *subordinate* clergy to behave with great deference to the wife of their superior.

subsequent ADJ. following; later. In *subsequent* lessons, we shall take up more difficult problems.

Word List 43   subside–tantalize

subside V. settle down; sink to a lower level. The doctor assured Johnny's parents that their son's fever would eventually *subside*. Once the floodwaters sub-

sided, the Greens set about assessing the damage to their waterlogged house.

substantial ADJ. ample; solid; in essentials. The scholarship represented a *substantial* sum of money.

substantiate V. establish by evidence; verify; support. You should provide all documentation you have available to *substantiate* your claim that you were the victim of identity theft, as well as copies of all bills, invoices, and other correspondence establishing the losses you are claiming.

substantive ADJ. real, as opposed to imaginary; essential; solidly based; substantial. Bishop Tutu received the Nobel Peace Prize in recognition of his *substantive* contributions to the peace movement in South Africa.

subtlety N. perceptiveness; ingenuity; delicacy. Never obvious, she expressed herself with such *subtlety* that her remarks went right over the heads of most of her audience. subtle, ADJ.

■ **subversive** ADJ. tending to overthrow or destroy. At first glance, the notion that styrofoam cups may actually be more ecologically sound than paper cups strikes most environmentalists as *subversive*.

succinct ADJ. brief; terse; compact. Don't bore your audience with excess verbiage: be *succinct*.

suffragist N. advocate of voting rights (for women). In recognition of her efforts to win the vote for women, Congress authorized coining a silver dollar honoring the *suffragist* Susan B. Anthony.

■ **superficial** ADJ. on the surface; not thorough. Justin's fall left him with *superficial* scrapes and bruises that healed quickly. To revise a textbook properly, you must do more than make a few *superficial* changes to the manuscript.

■ **superfluous** ADJ. unnecessary, especially in being excessive. Betsy lacked the heart to tell June that the wedding present she brought was *superfluous*; she and Bob had already received five toasters. Please try not to include so many *superfluous* details in your report; just give me the facts.

■ **suppress** V. crush; subdue; inhibit. Too polite to laugh in anyone's face, Roy did his best to *suppress* his amusement at Ed's inane remark.

surmount V. overcome. Could Helen Keller, blind and deaf since childhood, *surmount* her physical disabilities and lead a productive life?

■ **surpass** V. exceed. Her PSAT scores *surpassed* our expectations.

■ **susceptible** ADJ. impressionable or easily influenced; having little resistance, as to a disease. Said the patent medicine man to the extremely *susceptible* customer, "Buy this new miracle drug, and you will no longer be *susceptible* to the common cold."

■ **suspend** V. defer or postpone; expel or eject; halt or discontinue; hang from above. When the judge *suspended* his sentence, Bill breathed a sigh of relief. When the principal *suspended* her from school, Wanda tried to look as if she didn't care. When the trapeze artist broke her arm, she had to *suspend* her activities: she no longer could be *suspended* from her trapeze.

■ **sustain** v. live through; keep up. Stuart *sustained* such heavy losses in the stock market that he could no longer *sustain* his jet-setting lifestyle.

symbiosis N. interdependent relationship (between groups, species), often mutually beneficial. Both the crocodile bird and the crocodile derive benefit from their *symbiosis*: pecking away at food particles embedded in the crocodile's teeth, the bird receives nourishment; the crocodile, meanwhile, receives proper dental hygiene. symbiotic, ADJ.

■ **symmetry** N. arrangement of parts so that balance is obtained; state of having pleasing proportions. Something lopsided by definition lacks *symmetry*. In choreographing, we strive for *symmetry*, so that a movement performed by one couple will balance a similar movement performed by another pair.

■ **synthesis** N. combination of different parts (ideas, styles, genres) to create a connected whole; chemical production of a more complex substance from simpler ones; electronic production of sounds. Combining their owners' Catholicism with their own West African beliefs, Haitian slaves created a *synthesis* now known as Voodoo. The *synthesis* of aspirin involves the reaction of salicylic acid and acetic anhydride in the presence of a catalyst. Using digital tools, musicians mix sounds from different instruments, creating a *synthesis* of new musical sounds. synthesize, v.

synthetic ADJ. made by combining different substances; (of an action or emotion) not genuine. Tires, once manufactured from rubber plants, today are made from *synthetic* materials produced from crude oil. Although the dean strongly condemned the actions of the campus police, we felt his outrage was *synthetic*: he took no action against the police for their brutal treatment of the demonstrators.

■ **taciturn** ADJ. habitually silent; talking little. The stereotypical cowboy is a *taciturn* soul, answering lengthy questions with "Yep" or "Nope."

tactile ADJ. pertaining to the organs or sense of touch. His callused hands had lost their *tactile* sensitivity.

taint v. contaminate; cause to lose purity; modify with a trace of something bad. One speck of dirt on your utensils may contain enough germs to *taint* an entire batch of preserves.

tangential ADJ. peripheral; only slightly connected; digressing. Despite Clark's attempts to distract her with *tangential* remarks, Lois kept on coming back to her main question: why couldn't he come out to dinner with Superman and her?

tangible ADJ. able to be touched; real; palpable. Although Tom did not own a house, he had several *tangible* assets—a car, a television, a PC—that he could sell if he needed cash.

tantalize v. tease; torture with disappointment. Tom *tantalized* his younger brother, holding the ball just too high for Jimmy to reach.

Word List 44   tedious–transcendent

■ **tedious** ADJ. boring; tiring. The repetitious nature of work on the assembly line made Martin's job very *tedious*. tedium, N.

■ **temper** v. make something less intense or extreme; toughen (steel, glass) by heating and then cooling. Not even her supervisor's grumpiness could *temper* Nancy's enthusiasm for her new job. Heated in a forge and then *tempered*, stainless steel blades hold an edge well.

temperament N. characteristic frame of mind or disposition; emotional excess. Although the twins look alike, they differ markedly in *temperament*: Todd is calm, but Rod is excitable. Racket-throwing tennis star John McEnroe was famed for his displays of *temperament*.

temperate ADJ. restrained; self-controlled; moderate in respect to temperature. Try to be *temperate* in your eating this holiday season; if you control your appetite, you won't gain too much weight.

tenacity N. firmness; persistence. Jean Valjean could not believe the *tenacity* of Inspector Javert. Here all Valjean had done was to steal a loaf of bread, and the inspector had pursued him doggedly for twenty years!

tenet N. doctrine; dogma. The agnostic did not accept the *tenets* of their faith.

tentative ADJ. hesitant; not fully worked out or developed. Unsure of his welcome at the Christmas party, Scrooge took a *tentative* step into his nephew's drawing room. Phil had a *tentative* plan for organizing the camping trip; he just needed to think through a few more details before he was ready to share his ideas.

tenuous ADJ. thin; weak; unsubstantial. Napoleon's alliance with Russia quickly proved *tenuous*: it disintegrated altogether in 1812.

■ **termination** N. end. Though the time for *termination* of the project was near, we still had a lot of work to finish before we shut up shop.

terrestrial ADJ. earthly (as opposed to celestial); pertaining to the land. In many science fiction films, alien invaders from outer space plan to destroy all *terrestrial* life.

terse ADJ. concise; abrupt; pithy. There is a fine line between speech that is *terse* and to the point and speech that is too abrupt.

theoretical ADJ. not practical or applied; hypothetical. Bob was better at applied engineering and computer programming than he was at *theoretical* physics and math. While I can still think of some *theoretical* objections to your plan, you've convinced me of its basic soundness.

therapeutic ADJ. curative. Now better known for its racetrack, Saratoga Springs first gained attention for the *therapeutic* qualities of its famous "healing waters."

thesis N. statement advanced as a premise to be supported; long essay. In her speech, Lexy made a convincing argument, supporting her *thesis* with statistics as well as anecdotal evidence. In graduate school, she wrote a doctoral *thesis*, which was later published to great reviews.

thrifty ADJ. careful about money; economical. A *thrifty* shopper compares prices before making major purchases.

thrive V. prosper; flourish. Despite the impact of the recession on the restaurant trade, Philip's cafe *thrived.*

■ **thwart** V. baffle; frustrate. Batman searched for a way to *thwart* the Joker's evil plan to destroy Gotham City.

timidity N. lack of self-confidence or courage. If you are to succeed as a salesman, you must first lose your *timidity* and fear of failure.

tirade N. extended scolding; denunciation; harangue. Every time the boss holds a meeting, he goes into a lengthy *tirade,* scolding us for everything from tardiness to padding our expenses.

titanic ADJ. gigantic. *Titanic* waves beat against the majestic S.S. *Titanic,* driving it against the concealed iceberg.

title N. right or claim to possession; mark of rank; name (of a book, film, etc.). Though the penniless Duke of Ragwort no longer had *title* to the family estate, he still retained his *title* as head of one of England's oldest families. The *title* of his autobiography was *From Riches to Rags.*

torpor N. lethargy; sluggishness; dormancy. Throughout the winter, nothing aroused the bear from his *torpor:* he would not emerge from hibernation until spring. torpid, ADJ.

■ **toxic** ADJ. poisonous. Caution: poison! Manufacturers put the skull and crossbones on bottles of iodine to warn purchasers that iodine is *toxic* if taken internally. toxicity, N.

tractable ADJ. docile; easily managed. Although Susan seemed a *tractable* young woman, she had a stubborn streak of independence that occasionally led her to defy the powers-that-be when she felt they were in the wrong.

transcendent ADJ. surpassing; exceeding ordinary limits; superior. Standing on the hillside watching the sunset through the Golden Gate was a *transcendent* experience for Lise: it was so beautiful it surpassed her wildest dreams.

Word List 45   transcribe–unfeasible

transcribe V. copy. It took hours for the secretary to *transcribe* his shorthand notes of the conference into a form others could read.

transgression N. violation of a law; sin. Forgive us our *transgressions;* we know not what we do. transgress, V.

transient ADJ. momentary; temporary; staying for a short time. Lexy's joy at finding the perfect Christmas gift for Phil was *transient;* she still had to find presents for Roger, Laura, Allison, and Uncle Bob. Located near the airport, this hotel caters to a largely *transient* trade.

transition N. going from one state of action to another. During the period of *transition* from oil heat to gas heat, the furnace will have to be shut off.

transitory ADJ. impermanent; fleeting. Fame is *transitory*: today's rising star is all too soon tomorrow's washed-up has-been. transitoriness, N.

translucent ADJ. partly transparent. We could not recognize the people in the next room because of the *translucent* curtains that separated us.

■ **transparent** ADJ. permitting light to pass through freely; easily detected. The blue Caribbean waters were so *transparent* that we could clearly see the colorful tropical fish darting through the coral reefs. John's pride in his son is *transparent*; no one who sees the two of them together can miss it.

travail N. painful physical or mental labor; drudgery; torment. Like every other high school student she knew, Sherry detested the yearlong *travail* of cramming for the SAT.

trenchant ADJ. cutting; keen. With *trenchant* wit, Frank Rich made some highly cutting remarks as he panned another dreadful play.

■ **trepidation** N. fear; nervous apprehension. As she entered the office of the dean of admissions, Sharon felt some *trepidation* about how she would do in her interview.

trifling ADJ. trivial; unimportant. Why bother going to see a doctor for such a *trifling,* everyday cold?

trigger V. set off. John is touchy today; say one word wrong and you'll *trigger* an explosion.

trite ADJ. hackneyed; commonplace. The *trite* and predictable situations on many television programs turn off viewers, who respond by turning off their sets.

trivial ADJ. trifling; unimportant. Too many magazines ignore newsworthy subjects and feature *trivial* gossip about celebrities.

■ **turbulence** N. state of violent agitation. Warned of approaching *turbulence* in the atmosphere, the pilot told the passengers to fasten their seat belts.

turmoil N. great commotion and confusion. Lydia running off with a soldier! Mother fainting at the news! The Bennet household was in *turmoil.*

tyranny N. oppression; cruel government. Frederick Douglass fought against the *tyranny* of slavery throughout his entire life. tyrant, N.

ubiquitous ADJ. being everywhere; omnipresent. That Christmas "The Little Drummer Boy" seemed *ubiquitous*: Justin heard the tune everywhere he went.

ultimate ADJ. final; not susceptible to further analysis. Scientists are searching for the *ultimate* truths.

unanimity N. complete agreement. We were surprised by the *unanimity* with which members of both parties accepted our proposals. unanimous, ADJ.

unbecoming ADJ. unattractive; improper. What an *unbecoming* dress Mona is wearing! That girl has no color sense. At the court martial the captain was charged with conduct *unbecoming* an officer.

underlying ADJ. fundamental; lying below. The *underlying* cause of the student riot was not the strict curfew rule but the moldy cafeteria food. Miss Marple seems like a sweet little old lady at first, but there's an iron will *underlying* that soft and fluffy facade.

undermine V. weaken; sap. The recent corruption scandals have *undermined* many people's faith in the city government. The recent torrential rains have washed away much of the cliff side; the deluge threatens to *undermine* the pillars supporting several houses at the edge of the cliff.

underscore V. emphasize. Addressing the jogging class, Kim *underscored* the importance to runners of good nutrition.

undulating ADJ. moving with a wavelike motion. The Hilo Hula Festival was an *undulating* sea of grass skirts.

unequivocal ADJ. plain; obvious. My answer to your proposal is an *unequivocal* and absolute "No."

unfeasible ADJ. not practical or workable. Roy's plan to enlarge the living room by knocking down a couple of internal walls proved *unfeasible* when he discovered that those walls were holding up the roof.

Word List 46   unfounded-vent

unfounded ADJ. baseless; not based on fact. Cher feared that her boyfriend was unfaithful; fortunately, her suspicions proved to be *unfounded*.

uniformity N. sameness; monotony. At *Persons Magazine*, we strive for *uniformity* of style; as a result, all of our writers wind up sounding exactly alike.

unique ADJ. without an equal; single in kind. You have the *unique* distinction of being the only student whom I have had to fail in this course.

universal ADJ. characterizing or affecting all; present everywhere. At first, no one shared Christopher's opinions; his theory that the world was round was met with *universal* disbelief.

unmitigated ADJ. unrelieved or immoderate; absolute. After four days of *unmitigated* heat, I was ready to collapse from heat prostration. The congresswoman's husband was an *unmitigated* jerk: not only did he abandon her, he took her campaign funds, too!

unobtrusive ADJ. inconspicuous; not blatant. Reluctant to attract notice, the governess took a chair in a far corner of the room and tried to be as *unobtrusive* as possible.

unprecedented ADJ. novel; unparalleled. Margaret Mitchell's book *Gone with the Wind* was an *unprecedented* success.

unravel V. disentangle; solve. With equal ease Miss Marple *unraveled* tangled balls of yarn and baffling murder mysteries.

unrequited ADJ. not reciprocated. Suffering the pangs of *unrequited* love, Olivia rebukes Cesario for his hard-heartedness.

unseemly ADJ. unbecoming; indecent; in poor taste. When he put whoopie cushions on all the seats in the funeral parlor, Seymour's conduct was most *unseemly.*

untenable ADJ. indefensible; not able to be maintained. Wayne is so contrary that, the more *untenable* a position is, the harder he'll try to defend it.

unwarranted ADJ. unjustified or groundless; undeserved. Your assumption that I would accept your proposal is *unwarranted*, sir; I do not want to marry you at all. We could not understand Martin's *unwarranted* rudeness to his mother's guests.

uphold V. give support; keep from sinking; lift up. Bold Sir Robin was ready to fight to the death to *uphold* the honor of his lady.

upright ADJ. honest; ethical; erect; perpendicular. An *upright* person acts straight: he does not cheat. An *upright* post stands straight: it does not lean.

■ **urbane** ADJ. suave; refined; elegant. Country-bred and naïve, Anna felt out of place among her *urbane* and sophisticated new classmates. urbanity, N.

usurp V. seize another's power or rank. The revolution ended when the victorious rebel general succeeded in *usurping* the throne.

■ **utopia** N. ideal place, state, or society. Fed up with this imperfect universe, Don would have liked to run off to Shangri-la or some other fictitious *utopia.* utopian, ADJ.

■ **vacillate** V. waver; fluctuate. Uncertain which suitor she ought to marry, the princess *vacillated,* saying now one, now the other. vacillation, N.

validate V. confirm; ratify. I will not publish my findings until I *validate* my results.

vantage N. position giving an advantage. They fired upon the enemy from behind the trees, walls, and any other point of *vantage* they could find.

vapid ADJ. dull and unimaginative; insipid and flavorless. "*Bor*-ing!" said Cheryl, as she suffered through yet another *vapid* lecture about Dead White Male Poets.

vehement ADJ. forceful; intensely emotional; with marked vigor. Alfred became so *vehement* in describing what was wrong with the Internal Revenue Service that he began jumping up and down and frothing at the mouth. vehemence, N.

venerate V. revere. In Tibet today, the common people still *venerate* their traditional spiritual leader, the Dalai Lama.

vent V. make known (opinions, feelings); give off; give emotional release to. At the city council meeting, homeowners *vented* their opinions about the proposed new factory in their residential neighborhood. The homeowners claimed that the factory would *vent* gases into the air, creating unpleasant smells. Exasperated, the factory owner *vented* his anger, ranting at his critics.

Word List 47 venturesome–weather

venturesome ADJ. bold. A group of *venturesome* women were the first to scale Mt. Annapurna.

veracity N. truthfulness. Asserting his *veracity,* young George Washington proclaimed, "Father, I cannot tell a lie!"

verbose ADJ. wordy. Someone mute can't talk; someone *verbose* can hardly stop talking.

■ **versatile** ADJ. having many talents; capable of working in many fields. She was a *versatile* athlete, earning varsity letters in basketball, hockey, and track.

viable ADJ. having a reasonable chance of success; capable of living or growing into something living. The plan to build a new stadium, though lacking a few details, is *viable* and stands a good chance of winning popular support. By definition, a fetus is *viable* once it has reached the stage of being capable of living, under normal conditions, outside the uterus or womb.

vicarious ADJ. acting as a substitute; done by a deputy. Though Maud was too meek to talk back to anyone, she got a *vicarious* kick out of Rita's sharp retorts.

vie V. contend; compete. Politicians *vie* with one another, competing for donations and votes.

vigor N. active strength. Although he was over 70 years old, Jack had the *vigor* of a man in his prime. vigorous, ADJ.

vindicate V. clear from blame; exonerate; justify or support. The lawyer's goal was to *vindicate* her client and prove him innocent on all charges. The critics' extremely favorable reviews *vindicate* my opinion that *The Madness of King George* is a brilliant movie.

vindictive ADJ. out for revenge; malicious. Divorce sometimes brings out a *vindictive* streak in people; when Tony told Tina he wanted a divorce, she poured green Jello into the aquarium and turned his tropical fish into dessert.

virulent ADJ. extremely poisonous; hostile; bitter. Laid up with a *virulent* case of measles, Vera blamed her doctors because her recovery took so long. In fact, she became quite *virulent* on the subject of the quality of modern medical care.

vital ADJ. vibrant and lively; critical; living, breathing. The *vital,* highly energetic first aid instructor stressed that it was *vital* in examining accident victims to note their *vital* signs.

vivacious ADJ. animated; lively. The hostess on *The Morning News* was a bit too bubbly and *vivacious* for me to take before I'd had my first cup of coffee.

■ **volatile** ADJ. changeable; explosive; evaporating rapidly. The political climate today is extremely *volatile*: no one can predict what the electorate will do next. Maria Callas's temper was extremely *volatile*: the only thing you could predict was that she was sure to blow up. Ethyl chloride is an extremely *volatile* liquid: it evaporates instantly.

voluble ADJ. fluent; glib; talkative. Excessively *voluble* speakers suffer from logorrhea: they run off at the mouth a lot!

voluminous ADJ. extensive; bulky or large. Despite her family burdens, she kept up a *voluminous* correspondence with her friends. A caftan is a *voluminous* garment; most people wearing one look as if they're draped in a small tent.

vulnerable ADJ. susceptible to wounds. His opponents could not harm Achilles, who was *vulnerable* only in his heel.

waive V. give up a claim or right voluntarily; refrain from enforcing; postpone considering. Although technically prospective students had to live in Piedmont to attend high school there, occasionally the school *waived* the residence requirement in order to enroll promising athletes.

wane V. decrease in size or strength; draw gradually to an end. When lit, does a wax candle *wane*?

wanton ADJ. unrestrained; willfully malicious; unchaste. Pointing to the stack of bills, Sheldon criticized Sarah for her *wanton* expenditures. In response, Sarah accused Sheldon of making an unfounded, *wanton* attack.

warrant V. give adequate grounds for; give a warranty for a product. No matter how irritated Warren was, that did not *warrant* his rudeness to his mother's guests. The Honda dealership *warranted* the condition of our new van.

■ **wary** ADJ. very cautious. The spies grew *wary* as they approached the sentry.

wayward ADJ. ungovernable; unpredictable; contrary. Miss Watson warned Huck that if he didn't mend his ways she would ship him off to a school for *wayward* youths.

weather V. endure the effects of weather or other forces. Reporters wondered whether Governor Gray Davis would *weather* his latest political challenge and remain in office or whether he would be California's first governor to be recalled.

Word List 48   whimsical–zeal

whimsical N. capricious; fanciful. In *Mrs. Doubtfire*, the hero is a playful, *whimsical* man who takes a notion to dress up as a woman so that he can look after his children, who are in the custody of his ex-wife. whimsy, N.

wile N. trick intended to deceive; stratagem. At the end of the movie, the hero sees through the temptress's *wiles* and returns to his sweetheart back home.

willful ADJ. intentional; headstrong. Donald had planned to kill his wife for months; clearly, her death was a case of deliberate, *willful* murder, not a crime of passion committed by a hasty, *willful* youth unable to foresee the consequences of his deeds.

wily ADJ. cunning; artful. If coyotes are supposed to be such sneaky, *wily* creatures, how does Road Runner always manage to outwit Wile E. Coyote?

withdrawn ADJ. introverted; remote. Rebuffed by his colleagues, the initially outgoing young researcher became increasingly *withdrawn*.

wither V. shrivel; decay. Cut flowers are beautiful for a day, but all too soon they *wither*.

withhold V. hold back; desist from giving; keep possession of. The tenants decided to *withhold* a portion of the rent until the landlord kept his promise to renovate the building.

withstand V. stand up against; successfully resist. If you can *withstand* all the peer pressure in high school to cut classes and goof off, you should survive college just fine.

wrath N. anger; fury. She turned to him, full of *wrath*, and said, "What makes you think I'll accept lower pay for this job than you get?"

wry ADJ. twisted; with a humorous twist. We enjoy Dorothy Parker's verse for its *wry* wit.

■ **yield** V. give in; surrender. The wounded knight refused to *yield* to his foe.

■ **yield** V. produce; deliver. Along the riverbanks in Nairobi, the fertile soil *yields* potatoes, vegetables, and barley. Although the two researchers used somewhat different methods, both methods *yielded* similar results.

yield N. amount produced; crop; income on investment. An experienced farmer can estimate the annual *yield* of his acres with surprising accuracy.

zeal N. eager enthusiasm. Wang's *zeal* was contagious; soon all his fellow students were busily making posters, inspired by his ardent enthusiasm for the cause. zealous, ADJ.

Directions: Briefly review the power words in each boldfaced grouping. Then tackle the ten sentence completion questions on that group of words. Answer key and explanations are located on page 206.

abstract–aversion

1. In the course of the competition, Morgan developed a real respect for the determination and skill of his ---- .

   (A) assumption
   (B) adversary
   (C) apprenticeship
   (D) analogy
   (E) ambivalence

2. John preferred working on real-life engineering problems to tackling ---- questions in his theoretical physics class.

   (A) accessible
   (B) autonomous
   (C) altruistic
   (D) adverse
   (E) abstract

3. It was entirely ---- of Marisa to make an anonymous donation to the Mayor's Disaster Relief Fund; she refused to take credit for her generous act.

   (A) ambiguous
   (B) aesthetic
   (C) acute
   (D) altruistic
   (E) autonomous

4. The boys' ---- toward one another was so obvious that we feared they might get into a fight.

   (A) affinity
   (B) antagonism
   (C) assumption
   (D) apathy
   (E) aristocracy

5. Use an ice pack on your swollen knee: it can help ---- the pain and reduce the swelling.

   (A) alleviate
   (B) acknowledge
   (C) appropriate
   (D) acclaim
   (E) assert

6. Let us take a moment to ---- the contributions of everyone who helped make this festival such a great event.

   (A) aspire
   (B) accommodate
   (C) alleviate
   (D) abstract
   (E) acknowledge

7. Something that can be easily reached is by definition ---- .

   (A) abstract
   (B) accessible
   (C) aesthetic
   (D) ambiguous
   (E) ample

8. Before becoming a master woodworker, Karl had to serve an ---- with a member of the woodworkers' guild.

   (A) antipathy
   (B) affinity
   (C) ambivalence
   (D) apprenticeship
   (E) assumption

9. Tweedledum could not explain the ---- he felt for Tweedledee. Why did he dislike his brother so intensely?

(A) affinity
(B) apathy
(C) apprehension
(D) assumption
(E) aversion

10. The harvest had been plentiful; the farmers were pleased to have an ---- supply of grain stored for the winter.

(A) acute
(B) amenable
(C) ample
(D) authentic
(E) autonomous

banal–convention

11. When Bonnie spilled the coffee all over the tablecloth, her bright red blush ---- how embarrassed she felt.

(A) betrayed
(B) compromised
(C) confronted
(D) coalesced
(E) condoned

12. While some doctors assert that taking large doses of vitamin C can be ---- to patients, other medical experts maintain such megadoses are worthless.

(A) banal
(B) beneficial
(C) buoyant
(D) circumspect
(E) concrete

13. Barbara had such ---- hearing that she could easily overhear whispered conversations on the other side of the room.

(A) accessible
(B) acute
(C) aesthetic
(D) ambiguous
(E) authentic

14. We were relieved when the disputing parties finally agreed to ---- ; the conflict had gone on far too long, and it was time they reached a settlement.

(A) condone
(B) confront
(C) cite
(D) confirm
(E) compromise

15. "Strong as an ox" is an example of a ---- , a sadly overused sentence or phrase that has lost its original force.

(A) caricature
(B) chronicle
(C) cliché
(D) component
(E) conformity

16. When we remodeled our house, we had to rewire the building to be in ---- with the current building code.

(A) compliance
(B) composure
(C) component
(D) consolidation
(E) convention

17. Most bars of soap sink to the bottom of the bathtub. Ivory soap, however, is ---- : it floats.

(A) banal
(B) beneficial
(C) benign
(D) brittle
(E) buoyant

18. In his diary, Samuel Pepys attempted to ----
    the daily events of his life, faithfully recording
    them in great detail.

    (A) condone
    (B) chronicle
    (C) collaborate
    (D) coalesce
    (E) compromise

19. Beat the butter and sugar together until the
    resulting liquid has the ---- of heavy cream.

    (A) candor
    (B) composure
    (C) compromise
    (D) consistency
    (E) convention

20. John was very ---- about locking up the store
    when he left work; I never worried that he
    would forget and leave things unlocked.

    (A) banal
    (B) benign
    (C) brittle
    (D) conscientious
    (E) concrete

conviction–disenfranchise

21. The hack writer hadn't had a fresh idea in
    years. Even the titles of his books were ---- .

    (A) convoluted
    (B) derivative
    (C) detached
    (D) diffident
    (E) definitive

22. Pneumonia ---- Tom so badly that he felt
    unable to go hiking until he had fully regained
    his strength.

    (A) debilitated
    (B) depicted
    (C) disclosed
    (D) denounced
    (E) decried

23. Many educators ---- the over-emphasis on
    standardized tests today and wish that less
    importance could be given to the SAT and
    ACT.

    (A) demean
    (B) depict
    (C) deplete
    (D) decry
    (E) digress

24. Although the teacher encouraged everyone to
    participate in class discussions, Martin was
    too ---- to speak up.

    (A) derivative
    (B) didactic
    (C) diffident
    (D) discernible
    (E) discordant

25. When you make a stupid remark, people are
    likely to respond to it with ---- .

    (A) corrosion
    (B) deference
    (C) derision
    (D) deterrent
    (E) discrepancy

26. A psychologist cannot afford to get
    emotionally involved with her patients; she
    must maintain her ---- .

    (A) dearth
    (B) digression
    (C) discord
    (D) detachment
    (E) derision

27. The ---- of good jobs in rural Arizona
    convinced Meg to move to Phoenix, where
    she hoped to find more opportunities of
    employment.

    (A) dearth
    (B) defamation
    (C) defiance
    (D) digression
    (E) disclaimer

28. The night was so dark that the path to the house was not easily ----.

   (A) discernible
   (B) derivative
   (C) didactic
   (D) diffident
   (E) discriminating

29. The speaker strayed away from the topic from time to time, but nobody minded his ---- .

   (A) defiances
   (B) defamations
   (C) derisions
   (D) deterrents
   (E) digressions

30. If you do not ---- your uncontrolled shopping sprees, you will be broke in less than a month.

   (A) curtail
   (B) debilitate
   (C) demean
   (D) depict
   (E) disclose

disinterested–erroneous

31. It can damage a child's self-esteem if you ---- his first attempts to perform a complex task.

   (A) divulge
   (B) disparage
   (C) dissipate
   (D) endorse
   (E) entice

32. Juanita enjoyed riding spirited horses, but Eva preferred her mounts to be more ---- .

   (A) disinterested
   (B) docile
   (C) diverse
   (D) ephemeral
   (E) erratic

33. Is there a clear ---- between the graphic novel and the conventional comic book? Both are similar in appearance.

   (A) dispatch
   (B) dissent
   (C) distinction
   (D) doctrine
   (E) enigma

34. Because John lacked the data he needed to come up with the correct answer, he leaped to an ---- conclusion.

   (A) elated
   (B) elusive
   (C) ephemeral
   (D) enigmatic
   (E) erroneous

35. Monica would never ---- anything that a friend told her in confidence. She was good at keeping secrets.

   (A) dismiss
   (B) disparage
   (C) disperse
   (D) dissipate
   (E) divulge

36. When Alan ---- in vigorous physical exercise, he sweats profusely.

   (A) disparages
   (B) distorts
   (C) embellishes
   (D) engages
   (E) entices

37. Marilyn tried to trap the mouse under a wastebasket, but the small rodent proved too ---- for her to capture.

   (A) docile
   (B) disinterested
   (C) elusive
   (D) erroneous
   (E) esoteric

38. Supreme Court Justice Ruth Bader Ginsburg would frequently ---- from majority decisions of the court and express her open disagreement with the court's rulings.

   (A) disparage
   (B) elicit
   (C) disperse
   (D) dissent
   (E) endorse

39. In the months before Christmas, television ads try to ---- viewers to buy lavish gifts for the whole family.

   (A) disparage
   (B) embellish
   (C) enhance
   (D) entice
   (E) enumerate

40. By definition, something ---- does not last very long.

   (A) disinterested
   (B) docile
   (C) diverse
   (D) ephemeral
   (E) erroneous

espouse–hypothetical

41. Tim was always friendly and ---- , happily striking up conversations with strangers on the bus.

   (A) fastidious
   (B) figurative
   (C) gregarious
   (D) hackneyed
   (E) hypocritical

42. Although Georgette Heyer wrote several mystery novels, the majority of her works fall under the ---- of historical fiction.

   (A) farce
   (B) fervor
   (C) excerpt
   (D) genre
   (E) hostility

43. The slender youth looked ---- and vulnerable compared to his robust, muscular opponent.

   (A) fastidious
   (B) flippant
   (C) frail
   (D) frivolous
   (E) hypocritical

44. William Lloyd Garrison left the American Anti-Slavery Society (which he had helped found) because its leaders refused to ---- the cause of women's rights.

   (A) espouse
   (B) excerpt
   (C) exploit
   (D) generate
   (E) gratify

45. Because of her ---- behavior during her enlistment, Maya was awarded the Army Good Conduct Medal.

   (A) exemplary
   (B) fastidious
   (C) feasible
   (D) frivolous
   (E) hypothetical

46. Hoping to speed up the delivery of his team's new uniforms, the coach asked the manufacturer to ---- the order.

   (A) esteem
   (B) gratify
   (C) expedite
   (D) exploit
   (E) hamper

47. In the movie *The Odd Couple*, one roommate is a slob, while the other is a ---- soul, extremely particular about how neat the apartment should be.

(A) fallacious
(B) fastidious
(C) figurative
(D) flippant
(E) gregarious

48. Before I purchase a book on Kindle, I like to read the free sample ---- taken from it, so that I can decide whether the book will be worth its purchase price.

(A) excerpt
(B) exploit
(C) farce
(D) fervor
(E) genre·

49. Is it possible to build a suspension bridge across this river? We need to determine whether such a project is ---- .

(A) exemplary
(B) fastidious
(C) feasible
(D) forthright
(E) hypocritical

50. "I hate oatmeal," exclaimed Bobby, viewing his cereal bowl with ---- .

(A) esteem
(B) excerpt
(C) farce
(D) generalization
(E) hostility

iconoclastic–integrity

51. Morgan came up with an excuse that was so ---- that no one could believe it.

(A) impartial
(B) iconoclastic
(C) indicative
(D) implausible
(E) imperative

52. Because George was extremely afraid of heights, nothing could ---- him to ride on the Ferris wheel.

(A) impede
(B) implicate
(C) incorporate
(D) implement
(E) induce

53. I cannot trust Edmund: there is an ---- between what he says and what he does.

(A) implement
(B) inconsistency
(C) ineptness
(D) imperative
(E) integrity

54. Although Diane seldom spoke at board meetings, everyone paid attention when she did because her comments were so ---- .

(A) immutable
(B) inexorable
(C) inconsequential
(D) insightful
(E) intangible

55. The state of California fines people who ---- traffic by driving too slowly, thereby creating hazardous conditions for other drivers.

(A) impede
(B) initiate
(C) incorporate
(D) implement
(E) induce

56. The counselor warned Brian that his ----
attitude toward his homework assignments
would have a negative effect on his chances of
graduating from high school.

(A) imperceptible
(B) indifferent
(C) industrious
(D) ingenious
(E) innocuous

57. Inspector Javert's pursuit of Jean Valjean was
---- ; he was determined to recapture Valjean
and send him back to prison.

(A) iconoclastic
(B) imperceptible
(C) inexorable
(D) inconsequential
(E) ingenuous

58. We called him "Fumblefingers" because he
was particularly ---- at tasks that required
manual dexterity.

(A) iconclastic
(B) industrious
(C) inept
(D) inherent
(E) insightful

59. She was true to her principles and would
never compromise them. In other words, she
was a model of ---- .

(A) incongruity
(B) inconsistency
(C) implication
(D) inscrutability
(E) integrity

60. We all make mistakes: no one is ---- .

(A) iconoclastic
(B) imperceptible
(C) infallible
(D) ingenuous
(E) inherent

intricacy–outmoded

61. Bernice bought only the latest, most trendy
fashions; she refused to buy anything the least
bit ---- .

(A) outmoded
(B) ostentatious
(C) opaque
(D) nocturnal
(E) meticulous

62. Bored by the dull routine of his assembly line
job, Mario wished something exciting would
happen to break the ---- .

(A) intricacy
(B) magnitude
(C) malice
(D) monotony
(E) mutability

63. The music department has designed a
scholarship program to ---- student musicians
by providing them with opportunities to play
in the local community orchestra.

(A) loathe
(B) misrepresent
(C) mock
(D) nurture
(E) obscure

64. Wanting to try her hand at a new artistic
----, Julie switched from oil-painting to
photography.

(A) magnitude
(B) mutability
(C) nostalgia
(D) misconception
(E) medium

65. Michael looked back on his days in the Peace Corps with ---- and longed to visit Malaysia again.

   (A) intricacy
   (B) malice
   (C) monotony
   (D) nonchalance
   (E) nostalgia

66. A seismometer is an instrument used to measure and record the ---- of earthquakes.

   (A) magnitude
   (B) monotony
   (C) irony
   (D) nonchalance
   (E) malice

67. "Beets!" exclaimed Susan. "I ---- beets. Can't you ever cook a vegetable I like?"

   (A) loathe
   (B) misrepresent
   (C) mock
   (D) nurture
   (E) obscure

68. Frederick Douglass was a famous ---- whose speeches about his days as a slave deeply moved audiences throughout the North.

   (A) misconception
   (B) monarch
   (C) medium
   (D) optimist
   (E) orator

69. Spoiled rotten by his parents, Willy was an ---- little brat.

   (A) introspective
   (B) obnoxious
   (C) opaque
   (D) optimistic
   (E) outmoded

70. Luck comes and goes: that's what we mean when we speak of the ---- of fortune.

   (A) magnitude
   (B) monarchy
   (C) monotony
   (D) mutability
   (E) nonchalance

pacifist–prosperity

71. Someone who always expects things to turn out badly is a ---- .

   (A) pacifist
   (B) paradox
   (C) pessimist
   (D) pedant
   (E) predator

72. Sharon was so ---- to sweets that she had a difficult time sticking to her diet.

   (A) presumptuous
   (B) pertinent
   (C) pervasive
   (D) partial
   (E) pragmatic

73. Mercedes Lackey is a ---- author, turning out three or four novels every year.

   (A) pedantic
   (B) partial
   (C) presumptuous
   (D) prolific
   (E) plastic

74. I used to shop at Walmart, but when I learned how little they paid their workers, I decided not to ---- their stores anymore.

   (A) pacify
   (B) patronize
   (C) plagiarize
   (D) prevail
   (E) proliferate

75. Stan's life held little drama or excitement; generally he followed a ----, everyday routine.

    (A) prolific
    (B) prosaic
    (C) pervasive
    (D) prominent
    (E) presumptuous

76. Because medications lose strength when they are stored in hot, humid environments, try storing your medications in a dry place to maintain their ---- .

    (A) paradox
    (B) pessimism
    (C) phenomena
    (D) potency
    (E) proliferation

77. Science fiction stories often are based on a puzzling aspect of time travel, in which someone traveling in the past performs an action that would have made the trip back in time impossible (for example, by killing her grandfather at a time before she was born). This is known as the grandfather ---- .

    (A) paradox
    (B) philanthropist
    (C) potency
    (D) proliferation
    (E) prologue

78. Bribery of city officials was so ---- that it was accepted as the normal cost of doing business in Chicago.

    (A) pedantic
    (B) pervasive
    (C) pessimistic
    (D) plastic
    (E) partial

79. An "invalid argument" is an argument that cannot reach any logical or sensible conclusion because the argument's basic assumption or ---- is not based upon real evidence or facts.

    (A) potency
    (B) phenomena
    (C) premise
    (D) prologue
    (E) proliferation

80. The hungry lion prowled the grassland in search of ---- .

    (A) prologue
    (B) predator
    (C) premise
    (D) proliferation
    (E) prey

provocative–stoic

81. The housekeeper closely ---- each piece of silverware to make sure that the maids had removed every speck of tarnish.

    (A) refuted
    (B) relinquished
    (C) satirized
    (D) repudiated
    (E) scrutinized

82. Nothing could disturb the monk's ---- ; no matter what happened, he remained calm and undisturbed.

    (A) severity
    (B) serenity
    (C) renown
    (D) prudence
    (E) solution

83. Josie was too ---- to believe the used car salesman's claim that the automobile had been owned by a little old lady who drove it only once a week to church.

(A) provocative
(B) random
(C) reprehensible
(D) reverent
(E) skeptical

84. The poet Seamus Heaney gained worldwide ---- when he received the 1995 Nobel Prize in Literature.

(A) renown
(B) resignation
(C) resolution
(D) restraint
(E) severity

85. Because seeing violent acts can negatively affect children's behavior, it is ---- to limit young people's exposure to such violence on television.

(A) provocative
(B) prudent
(C) reprehensible
(D) reticent
(E) singular

86. The pirate captain was a ---- killer, showing no mercy as he condemned victim after victim to walk the plank.

(A) random
(B) reserved
(C) reticent
(D) reverent
(E) ruthless

87. Wanting to win the debate, Kathryn searched for new evidence that might help ---- her opponent's argument.

(A) reflect
(B) refute
(C) sever
(D) relinquish
(E) retain

88. Nothing could shake Maria's ---- to rebuild her home after the flood had destroyed it.

(A) restraint
(B) renown
(C) resolution
(D) reticence
(E) severity

89. Susan had ---- success growing produce this season; she canned so many tomatoes, carrots, and green beans that she ran out of room in her pantry.

(A) reprehensible
(B) reticent
(C) singular
(D) skeptical
(E) stoic

90. When I began posting daily quotes on Facebook, I didn't have any particular plan in mind; I just made a ---- selection of quotations.

(A) random
(B) reticent
(C) reverent
(D) reprehensible
(E) ruthless

stratagem–yield

91. Stacy found proofreading a ---- job and wished she had more exciting work to do.

(A) subversive
(B) susceptible
(C) tedious
(D) transparent
(E) volatile

92. Someone cautious and on the lookout for trouble is by definition ---- .

    (A) taciturn
    (B) urbane
    (C) versatile
    (D) volatile
    (E) wary

93. Martin's ambition was to ---- his big brother's athletic achievements by setting a new school record for the half-mile.

    (A) surpass
    (B) sustain
    (C) temper
    (D) vacillate
    (E) synthesize

94. Warning of severe ---- ahead, the pilot advised the passengers to strap in and prepare for a bumpy ride.

    (A) stratagem
    (B) symmetry
    (C) synthesis
    (D) termination
    (E) turbulence

95. No matter how hard Juan tried to strike up a conversation with the fellow in the next seat, he could not get a word out of the ---- young man.

    (A) subversive
    (B) superfluous
    (C) susceptible
    (D) taciturn
    (E) viable

96. Fortunately, the wound was only ---- ; the knife failed to cut deep enough to do major damage.

    (A) subversive
    (B) superficial
    (C) superfluous
    (D) susceptible
    (E) synthetic

97. In biology, the modern ---- consolidated the results of various early twentieth-century lines of investigation that supported and reconciled the Darwinian theory of evolution and the Mendelian laws of inheritance.

    (A) synthesis
    (B) toxicity
    (C) termination
    (D) trepidation
    (E) turbulence

98. The paint thinner called acetone is a ---- solvent; if you don't keep the container tightly sealed, liquid acetone will evaporate rapidly.

    (A) superficial
    (B) tedious
    (C) toxic
    (D) versatile
    (E) volatile

99. The windstorm had knocked down some of the lampposts lining the avenue, shattering the perfect ---- of the pairs of matched pillars.

    (A) stratagem
    (B) symmetry
    (C) turbulence
    (D) termination
    (E) trepidation

100. Make up your mind where you want to go on vacation. Don't just ---- !

    (A) surpass
    (B) sustain
    (C) temper
    (D) vacillate
    (E) subdue

Answer Key

1.	**B**	21.	**B**	41.	**C**	61.	**A**	81.	**E**
2.	**E**	22.	**A**	42.	**D**	62.	**D**	82.	**B**
3.	**D**	23.	**D**	43.	**C**	63.	**D**	83.	**E**
4.	**B**	24.	**C**	44.	**A**	64.	**E**	84.	**A**
5.	**A**	25.	**C**	45.	**A**	65.	**E**	85.	**B**
6.	**E**	26.	**D**	46.	**C**	66.	**A**	86.	**E**
7.	**B**	27.	**A**	47.	**B**	67.	**A**	87.	**B**
8.	**D**	28.	**A**	48.	**A**	68.	**E**	88.	**C**
9.	**E**	29.	**E**	49.	**C**	69.	**B**	89.	**C**
10.	**C**	30.	**A**	50.	**E**	70.	**D**	90.	**A**
11.	**A**	31.	**B**	51.	**D**	71.	**C**	91.	**C**
12.	**B**	32.	**B**	52.	**E**	72.	**D**	92.	**E**
13.	**B**	33.	**C**	53.	**B**	73.	**D**	93.	**A**
14.	**E**	34.	**E**	54.	**D**	74.	**B**	94.	**E**
15.	**C**	35.	**E**	55.	**A**	75.	**B**	95.	**D**
16.	**A**	36.	**D**	56.	**B**	76.	**D**	96.	**B**
17.	**E**	37.	**C**	57.	**C**	77.	**A**	97.	**A**
18.	**B**	38.	**D**	58.	**C**	78.	**B**	98.	**E**
19.	**D**	39.	**D**	59.	**E**	79.	**C**	99.	**B**
20.	**D**	40.	**D**	60.	**C**	80.	**E**	100.	**D**

Answer Explanations

abstract–aversion

1. **(B)** *Adversary* means opponent. Morgan respected his opponent, the person competing against him.

2. **(E)** *Abstract* means theoretical, as opposed to applied or practical. John liked working on practical problems, not theoretical or abstract ones.

3. **(D)** *Altruistic* means unselfishly generous. Because Marisa took no credit for her donation, her generosity was wholly unselfish.

4. **(B)** *Antagonism* means hostility. The boys' obvious hostility made it seem likely that they would get into a fight.

5. **(A)** *Alleviate* means relieve or lessen. The ice pack helps relieve pain and lessen swelling.

6. **(E)** *Acknowledge* means express recognition or appreciation. We recognize people's contributions and thank them.

7. **(B)** *Accessible* means easy to approach, or obtainable.

8. **(D)** An *apprenticeship* is time spent as a novice learning a trade from a skilled worker.

9. **(E)** *Aversion* means strong dislike.

10. **(C)** *Ample* means abundant or plentiful. Thanks to the plentiful harvest, the farmers have ample stores of grain.

banal–convention

11. **(A)** *Betray* here means reveal unconsciously or unintentionally. Bonnie's blush reveals or gives away her embarrassment.

12. **(B)** *Beneficial* means helpful or useful. The signal word "While" is your clue that the missing word is an antonym for *worthless*.

13. **(B)** *Acute* means sharp or keen. Someone with acute hearing could easily eavesdrop on others' conversations.

14. **(E)** To *compromise* is to settle a disagreement by both sides adjusting their demands.

15. **(C)** A *cliché* is by definition a phrase dulled by overuse.

16. **(A)** *Compliance* means the state of being in accordance with requirements. If you follow the requirements of the building code exactly, then your renovation will be in *compliance* with the building code.

17. **(E)** By definition, something *buoyant* is able to float.

18. **(B)** *Chronicle* means to report or record in chronological order. Note the root *chron* here: *chron* means time.

19. **(D)** *Consistency* here means degree of thickness. It can also mean uniformity or dependability.

20. **(D)** *Conscientious* means careful or scrupulous. There's little need to worry about doors being left unlocked if the person in charge of locking up is very careful.

conviction–disenfranchise

21. **(B)** *Derivative* means unoriginal. A writer without fresh ideas is apt to be unoriginal in his choice of titles.

22. **(A)** *Debilitated* means weakened or incapacitated. Pneumonia leaves its victims weak and enfeebled for some time.

23. **(D)** *Decry* means denounce or condemn. The educators criticize that standardized tests are overemphasized today.

24. **(C)** *Diffident* means shy or lacking in confidence. Someone so modest would find it difficult to speak up in class.

25. **(C)** *Derision* means mockery or ridicule. People often make fun of stupid remarks.

26. **(D)** *Detachment* means emotional distance and objectivity. Psychologists need to maintain their detachment.

27. **(A)** A *dearth* is a scarcity or lack. The lack of good jobs in her area motivated Meg to move.

28. **(A)** *Discernible* means able to be perceived or observed. At night a path might well be harder to see or discern.

29. **(E)** *Digressions* by definition are off-topic remarks, comments that wander away from the main subject.

30. **(A)** *Curtail* means cut short or reduce. The shopaholic needs to cut short those shopping sprees.

disinterested–erroneous

31. **(B)** *Disparage* means belittle or speak mockingly about. Children need encouragement, not disparagement.

32. **(B)** *Docile* means easily managed and obedient. It is an antonym for *spirited* or vigorous and lively.

33. **(C)** A *distinction* is a difference.

34. **(E)** *Erroneous* means mistaken or wrong. If you lack the information you need to come up with a right answer, you are likely to come up with a wrong one.

35. **(E)** *Divulge* means reveal. Someone who is good at keeping secrets is unlikely to divulge something told to her in confidence.

36. **(D)** One meaning of *engage* is participate or take part in. Participating in vigorous physical exercise often makes people sweat.

37. **(C)** *Elusive* means evasive or hard to grasp. The mouse was too slippery and tricky for her to catch.

38. **(D)** *Dissent* means disagree. Because Justice Ginsburg disagreed with the decision, she expressed her dissent in a minority opinion.

39. **(D)** *Entice* means attract or tempt. The ads tempt viewers to spend more than they possibly should.

40. **(D)** *Ephemeral* means short-lived or fleeting.

espouse–hypothetical

41. **(C)** *Gregarious* means sociable. Someone who is comfortable chatting with strangers on the bus is by definition gregarious.

42. **(D)** A *genre* is a particular variety of art or literature. Most of Heyer's novels belong to the genre of historical fiction.

43. **(C)** *Frail* means weak. Someone who is slender and who appears easy to wound (vulnerable) might well be described as frail.

44. **(A)** *Espouse* means support or adopt. Garrison left the Anti-Slavery Society because the group would not support the cause of women's rights.

45. **(A)** *Exemplary* means outstandingly good and worth imitating. Maya's exemplary behavior earned her the Good Conduct Medal.

46. **(C)** *Expedite* means hasten or speed up some action. The coach wishes to hasten the delivery of his order.

47. **(B)** *Fastidious* means hard to please or excessively demanding. Felix was fastidious about how neat the apartment should be.

48. **(A)** An *excerpt* is a selected passage taken from a longer work.

49. **(C)** *Feasible* means practical or capable of being done. Major projects often require a preliminary feasibility study.

50. **(E)** *Hostility* means hatred. Bobby hates oatmeal.

iconoclastic–integrity

51. **(D)** *Impromptu* means off the cuff or unprepared. Uncle Fred had to speak spontaneously without any time for preparation.

52. **(E)** *Induce* means persuade. Ferris wheels take riders high above the ground. Nothing could persuade acrophobic George to ride on one.

53. **(B)** *Inconsistency* is the state of being self-contradictory. What Edmund does contradicts what he says he's going to do.

54. **(D)** *Insightful* means perceptive, full of insights. It makes sense that people would pay attention to insightful comments.

55. **(A)** *Impede* means hinder or delay. Excessively slow drivers impede the flow of traffic.

56. **(B)** *Indifferent* here means unconcerned. Brian is unconcerned about doing his homework; if he doesn't put a little more care and effort into doing his work, he may not graduate.

57. **(C)** *Inexorable* means relentless and implacable. An inexorable pursuit is unstoppable; nothing can make Javert give up the chase.

58. **(C)** *Inept* means lacking skill. Someone called "Fumblefingers" is likely to be physically inept.

59. **(E)** *Integrity* means uprightness and honesty. Someone who remains true to her principles shows integrity.

60. **(C)** *Infallible* means faultless, not capable of making errors.

intricacy–outmoded

61. **(A)** *Outmoded* means no longer stylish. Bernice refused to buy last year's outmoded fashions.

62. **(D)** *Monotony* means a boring constancy or lack of variety. The dull routine of Mario's assembly line job was sadly monotonous.

63. **(D)** *Nurture* means nourish or foster. The scholarship program fosters or promotes the development of student musicians.

64. **(E)** A *medium* is a form or material of artistic expression.

65. **(E)** *Nostalgia* is a longing for the past. Michael longs for the good old days in the Peace Corps.

66. **(A)** *Magnitude* means size or greatness of extent. Seismometers measure the size or greatness of earthquakes.

67. **(A)** *Loathe* means detest or dislike intensely. What vegetables do you loathe?

68. **(E)** An *orator* is a public speaker.

69. **(B)** *Obnoxious* means highly objectionable or annoying. By definition, brats are obnoxious.

70. **(D)** *Mutability* means fickleness or changeableness. The only sure thing about luck is that it's bound to change.

pacifist–prosperity

71. **(C)** A *pessimist* is by definition someone whose outlook on life is gloomy.

72. **(D)** To be *partial* to sweets is to be fond of them. Someone fond of eating sweets would have trouble sticking to a diet.

73. **(D)** *Prolific* means highly productive or fruitful. An author who produces three or four novels every year is definitely productive.

74. **(B)** *Patronize* means support or be a customer of. If you disapprove of a business's policies, refuse to patronize that firm.

75. **(B)** *Prosaic* means dull and commonplace. An everyday, unexciting routine would strike most people as prosaic.

76. **(D)** *Potency* means power or effectiveness. When medications lose their potency, they become ineffective.

77. **(A)** A *paradox* is a self-contradictory situation or statement.

78. **(B)** *Pervasive* means widespread or prevalent. Corruption that is so widespread that it is accepted as normal is definitely pervasive.

79. **(C)** A *premise* by definition is a fundamental assumption upon which one bases an argument.

80. **(E)** *Prey* is, in this case, an animal being hunted by a predator, the carnivorous lion seeking food. *Prey* can also be any victim of muggers, swindlers, and so on.

provocative–stoic

81. **(E)** *Scrutinized* means examined closely and critically. The housekeeper was making sure the maids had done a good job.

82. **(B)** *Serenity* means calmness and peacefulness. The key words here are "calm and undisturbed."

83. **(E)** *Skeptical* means disbelieving or having doubts. A skeptical buyer would have doubts about a used car salesman's claims.

84. **(A)** *Renown* means fame. Winning the Nobel Prize in Literature earned Heaney great renown.

85. **(B)** *Prudent* means judicious and sensible, cautiously using good judgment. It is prudent to avoid exposing children to influences that can have a bad effect on their behavior.

86. **(E)** *Ruthless* means merciless. The key words here are "showing no mercy."

87. **(B)** *Refute* means disprove. Kathryn hopes to refute the opposing debater's argument.

88. **(C)** *Resolution* means determination. Maria is determined or resolved to rebuild.

89. **(C)** *Singular* means extraordinary, possibly even unique. Susan's bumper crop of vegetables was extraordinary.

90. **(A)** *Random* means haphazard, without a definite plan or purpose. No plan dictated my choice of quotes; I left it to chance.

stratagem–yield

91. **(C)** *Tedious* means boring or tiring. It is the opposite of exciting.

92. **(E)** *Wary* means very cautious. If you are wary, you know you need to beware of danger.

93. **(A)** *Surpass* means exceed or do better than.

94. **(E)** *Turbulence* is a state of violent agitation. Turbulent winds often cause plane rides to be bumpy.

95. **(D)** *Taciturn* means habitually silent. It is hard to get someone naturally taciturn to chat.

96. **(B)** *Superficial* means shallow or trivial. A superficial wound cuts the surface of the skin but does not pierce dangerously deep.

97. **(A)** A *synthesis* brings together different, simple parts, combining them into a complex, unified whole.

98. **(E)** *Volatile* means evaporating rapidly, possibly even explosively.

99. **(B)** *Symmetry* is the arrangement of parts to achieve balance among them. When the parts are out of order, the symmetry is destroyed.

100. **(D)** *Vacillate* means waver in mind or dither.

In addition to reviewing the Power Word List, what other quick vocabulary-building tactics can you follow when you face a test deadline?

One good approach is to learn how to build up (and tear apart) words. You know that words are made up of other words: the room in which you store things is the storeroom; the person whose job is to keep the books is the bookkeeper.

Just as words are made up of other words, words are also made up of word parts: prefixes, suffixes, and roots. A knowledge of these word parts and their meanings can help you determine the meanings of unfamiliar words.

Most modern English words are derived from Anglo-Saxon (Old English), Latin, and Greek. Because few students nowadays study Latin and Greek (and even fewer study Anglo-Saxon!), the majority of high school juniors and seniors lack a vital tool for unlocking the meaning of unfamiliar words.

Build your vocabulary by mastering basic word parts. Learning thirty key word parts can help you unlock the meaning of over 10,000 words. Learning fifty key word parts can help you unlock the meaning of over 100,000!

COMMON PREFIXES

Prefixes are syllables that precede the root or stem and change or refine its meaning.

Prefix	Meaning	Illustration
ab, abs	from, away from	*abduct* lead away, kidnap *abjure* renounce *abject* degraded, cast down
ad, ac, af, ag, an, ap, as, as, at	to, forward	*adit* entrance *adjure* request earnestly *admit* allow entrance *accord* agreement, harmony *affliction* distress *aggregation* collection *annexation* add to *apparition* ghost *arraignment* indictment *assumption* arrogance, the taking for granted *attendance* presence, the persons present
ambi	both	*ambidextrous* skilled with both hands *ambiguous* of double meaning *ambivalent* having two conflicting emotions
an, a	without	*anarchy* lack of government *anemia* lack of blood *amoral* without moral sense
ante	before	*antecedent* preceding event or word *antediluvian* ancient (before the flood) *antenuptial* before the wedding

Prefix	Meaning	Illustration
anti	against, opposite	*antipathy* hatred
		antiseptic against infection
		antithetical exactly opposite
arch	chief, first	*archetype* original
		archbishop chief bishop
		archaeology study of first or ancient times
be	over, thoroughly	*bedaub* smear over
		befuddle confuse thoroughly
		beguile deceive, charm thoroughly
bi	two	*bicameral* composed of two houses (Congress)
		biennial every two years
		bicycle two-wheeled vehicle
cata	down	*catastrophe* disaster
		cataract waterfall
		catapult hurl (throw down)
circum	around	*circumnavigate* sail around (the globe)
		circumspect cautious (looking around)
		circumscribe limit (place a circle around)
com, co, col, con, cor	with, together	*combine* merge with
		commerce trade with
		communicate correspond with
		coeditor joint editor
		collateral subordinate, connected
		conference meeting
		corroborate confirm
contra, contro	against	*contravene* conflict with
		controversy dispute
de	down, away	*debase* lower in value
		decadence deterioration
		decant pour off
demi	partly, half	*demigod* partly divine being
di	two	*dichotomy* division into two parts
		dilemma choice between two bad alternatives
dia	across	*diagonal* across a figure
		diameter distance across a circle
		diagram outline drawing
dis, dif	not, apart	*discord* lack of harmony
		differ disagree (carry apart)
		disparity condition of inequality; difference
dys	faulty, bad	*dyslexia* faulty ability to read
		dyspepsia indigestion

Prefix	Meaning	Illustration
ex, e	out	*expel* drive out
		extirpate root out
		eject throw out
extra, extro	beyond, outside	*extracurricular* beyond the curriculum
		extraterritorial beyond a nation's bounds
		extrovert person interested chiefly in external objects and actions
hyper	above; excessively	*hyperbole* exaggeration
		hyperventilate breathe at an excessive rate
hypo	beneath; lower	*hypoglycemia* low blood sugar
in, il, im, ir	not	*inefficient* not efficient
		inarticulate not clear or distinct
		illegible not readable
		impeccable not capable of sinning; flawless
		irrevocable not able to be called back
in, il, im, ir	in, on, upon	*invite* call in
		illustration something that makes clear
		impression effect upon mind or feelings
		irradiate shine upon
inter	between, among	*intervene* come between
		international between nations
		interjection a statement thrown in
intra, intro	within	*intramural* within a school
		introvert person who turns within himself
macro	large, long	*macrobiotic* tending to prolong life
		macrocosm the great world (the entire universe)
mega	great, million	*megalomania* delusions of grandeur
		megaton explosive force of a million tons of TNT
meta	involving change	*metamorphosis* change of form
micro	small	*microcosm* miniature universe
		microbe minute organism
		microscopic extremely small
mis	bad, improper	*misdemeanor* minor crime; bad conduct
		mischance unfortunate accident
		misnomer wrong name
mis	hatred	*misanthrope* person who hates mankind
		misogynist woman-hater

Prefix	Meaning	Illustration
mono	one	*monarchy* government by one ruler *monotheism* belief in one god
multi	many	*multifarious* having many parts *multitudinous* numerous
neo	new	*neologism* newly coined word *neophyte* beginner; novice
non	not	*noncommittal* undecided *nonentity* person of no importance
ob, oc, of, op	against	*obloquy* infamy; disgrace *obtrude* push into prominence *occlude* close; block out *offend* insult *opponent* someone who struggles against; foe
olig	few	*oligarchy* government by a few
pan	all, every	*panacea* cure-all *panorama* unobstructed view in all directions
para	beyond, related	*parallel* similar *paraphrase* restate; translate
per	through, completely	*permeable* allowing passage through *pervade* spread throughout
peri	around, near	*perimeter* outer boundary *periphery* edge *periphrastic* stated in a roundabout way
poly	many	*polygamist* person with several spouses *polyglot* speaking several languages
post	after	*postpone* delay *posterity* generations that follow *posthumous* after death
pre	before	*preamble* introductory statement *prefix* word part placed before a root/stem *premonition* forewarning
prim	first	*primordial* existing at the dawn of time *primogeniture* state of being the first born
pro	forward, in favor of	*propulsive* driving forward *proponent* supporter
proto	first	*prototype* first of its kind
pseudo	false	*pseudonym* pen name
re	again, back	*reiterate* repeat *reimburse* pay back

Prefix	Meaning	Illustration
retro	backward	*retrospect* looking back *retroactive* effective as of a past date
se	away, aside	*secede* withdraw *seclude* shut away *seduce* lead astray
semi	half, partly	*semiannual* every six months *semiconscious* partly conscious
sub, suc, suf, sug, sup, sus	under, less	*subway* underground road *subjugate* bring under control *succumb* yield; cease to resist *suffuse* spread through *suggest* hint *suppress* put down by force *suspend* delay
super, sur	over, above	*supernatural* above natural things *supervise* oversee *surtax* additional tax
syn, sym, syl, sys	with, together	*synchronize* time together *synthesize* combine together *sympathize* pity; identify with *syllogism* explanation of how ideas relate *system* network
tele	far	*telemetry* measurement from a distance *telegraphic* communicated over a distance
trans	across	*transport* carry across *transpose* reverse, move across
ultra	beyond, excessive	*ultramodern* excessively modern *ultracritical* exceedingly critical
un	not	*unfeigned* not pretended; real *unkempt* not combed; disheveled *unwitting* not knowing; unintentional
under	below	*undergird* strengthen underneath *underling* someone inferior
uni	one	*unison* oneness of pitch; complete accord *unicycle* one-wheeled vehicle
vice	in place of	*vicarious* acting as a substitute *viceroy* governor acting in place of a king
with	away, against	*withhold* hold back; keep *withstand* stand up against; resist

COMMON ROOTS AND STEMS

Roots are basic words that have been carried over into modern English from an earlier form of English or from another language. Stems are variations of roots brought about by changes in declension or conjugation.

Root or Stem	Meaning	Illustration
ac, acr	sharp	*acrimonious* bitter; caustic *acerbity* bitterness of temper *acidulate* to make somewhat acid or sour
aev, ev	age, era	*primeval* of the first age *coeval* of the same age or era *medieval* or *mediaeval* of the middle ages
ag, act	do	*act* deed *agent* doer
agog	leader	*demagogue* false leader of people *pedagogue* teacher (leader of children)
agri, agrari	field	*agrarian* one who works in the field *agriculture* cultivation of fields *peregrination* wandering (through fields)
ali	another	*alias* assumed (another) name *alienate* estrange (turn away from another)
alt	high	*altitude* height *altimeter* instrument for measuring height
alter	other	*altruistic* unselfish, considering others *alter ego* a second self
am	love	*amorous* loving, especially sexually *amity* friendship *amicable* friendly
anim	mind, soul	*animadvert* cast criticism upon *unanimous* of one mind *magnanimity* greatness of mind or spirit
ann, enn	year	*annuity* yearly remittance *biennial* every two years *perennial* present all year; persisting for several years
anthrop	man	*anthropology* study of man *misanthrope* hater of mankind *philanthropy* love of mankind; charity
apt	fit	*aptitude* skill *adapt* make suitable or fit

Root or Stem	Meaning	Illustration
aqua	water	*aqueduct* passageway for conducting water *aquatic* living in water *aqua fortis* nitric acid (strong water)
arch	ruler, first	*archaeology* study of antiquities (study of first things) *monarch* sole ruler *anarchy* lack of government
aster	star	*astronomy* study of the stars *asterisk* starlike type character (*) *disaster* catastrophe (contrary star)
aud, audit	hear	*audible* able to be heard *auditorium* place where people may be heard *audience* hearers
auto	self	*autocracy* rule by one person (self) *automobile* vehicle that moves by itself *autobiography* story of one's own life
belli	war	*bellicose* inclined to fight *belligerent* inclined to wage war *rebellious* resisting authority
ben, bon	good	*benefactor* one who does good deeds *benevolence* charity (wishing good) *bonus* something extra above regular pay
biblio	book	*bibliography* list of books *bibliophile* lover of books *Bible* The Book
bio	life	*biography* writing about a person's life *biology* study of living things *biochemist* student of the chemistry of living things
breve	short	*brevity* briefness *abbreviate* shorten *breviloquent* marked by brevity of speech
cad, cas	to fall	*decadent* deteriorating *cadence* intonation, musical movement *cascade* waterfall
cap, capt, cept, cip	to take	*capture* seize *participate* take part *precept* wise saying (originally a command)
capit, capt	head	*decapitate* remove (cut off) someone's head *captain* chief

Root or Stem	Meaning	Illustration
carn	flesh	*carnivorous* flesh-eating *carnage* destruction of life *carnal* fleshly
ced, cess	to yield, to go	*recede* go back, withdraw *antecedent* that which goes before *process* go forward
celer	swift	*celerity* swiftness *decelerate* reduce swiftness *accelerate* increase swiftness
cent	one hundred	*century* one hundred years *centennial* hundredth anniversary *centipede* many-footed, wingless animal
chron	time	*chronology* timetable of events *anachronism* a thing out of time sequence *chronicle* register events in order of time
cid, cis	to cut, to kill	*incision* a cut (surgical) *homicide* killing of a man *fratricide* killing of a brother
cit, citat	to call, to start	*incite* stir up, start up *excite* stir up *recitation* a recalling (or repeating) aloud
civi	citizen	*civilization* society of citizens, culture *civilian* member of community *civil* courteous
clam, clamat	to cry out	*clamorous* loud *declamation* speech *acclamation* shouted approval
claud, claus, clos, clud	to close	*claustrophobia* fear of close places *enclose* close in *conclude* finish
cognosc, cognit	to learn	*agnostic* lacking knowledge, skeptical *incognito* traveling under assumed name *cognition* knowledge
compl	to fill	*complete* filled out *complement* that which completes something *comply* fulfill
cord	heart	*accord* agreement (from the heart) *cordial* friendly *discord* lack of harmony

Root or Stem	Meaning	Illustration
corpor	body	*incorporate* organize into a body *corporeal* pertaining to the body, fleshly *corpse* dead body
cred, credit	to believe	*incredulous* not believing, skeptical *credulity* gullibility *credence* belief
cur	to care	*curator* person who has the care of something *sinecure* position without responsibility *secure* safe
curr, curs	to run	*excursion* journey *cursory* brief *precursor* forerunner
da, dat	to give	*data* facts, statistics *mandate* command *date* given time
deb, debit	to owe	*debt* something owed *indebtedness* debt *debenture* bond
dem	people	*democracy* rule of the people *demagogue* (false) leader of the people *epidemic* widespread (among the people)
derm	skin	*epidermis* skin *pachyderm* thick-skinned quadruped *dermatology* study of skin and its disorders
di, diurn	day	*diary* a daily record of activities, feelings, etc. *diurnal* pertaining to daytime
dic, dict	to say	*abdicate* renounce *diction* speech *verdict* statement of jury
doc, doct	to teach	*docile* obedient; easily taught *document* something that provides evidence *doctor* learned person (originally, teacher)
domin	to rule	*dominate* have power over *domain* land under rule *dominant* prevailing
duc, duct	to lead	*viaduct* arched roadway *aqueduct* artificial waterway
dynam	power, strength	*dynamic* powerful *dynamite* powerful explosive *dynamo* engine making electrical power

Root or Stem	Meaning	Illustration
ego	I	*egoist* person who is self-interested *egotist* selfish person *egocentric* revolving about self
erg, urg	work	*energy* power *ergatocracy* rule of the workers *metallurgy* science and technology of metals
err	to wander	*error* mistake *erratic* not reliable, wandering *knight-errant* wandering knight
eu	good, well, beautiful	*eupeptic* having good digestion *eulogize* praise *euphemism* substitution of pleasant way of saying something blunt
fac, fic, fec, fect	to make, to do	*factory* place where things are made *fiction* manufactured story *affect* cause to change
fall, fals	to deceive	*fallacious* misleading *infallible* not prone to error, perfect *falsify* lie
fer, lat	to bring, to bear	*transfer* bring from one place to another *translate* bring from one language to another *conifer* bearing cones, as pine trees
fid	belief, faith	*infidel* nonbeliever, heathen *confidence* assurance, belief
fin	end, limit	*confine* keep within limits *finite* having definite limits
flect, flex	bend	*flexible* able to bend *deflect* bend away, turn aside
fort	luck, chance	*fortuitous* accidental, occurring by chance *fortunate* lucky
fort	strong	*fortitude* strength, firmness of mind *fortification* strengthening *fortress* stronghold
frag, fract	break	*fragile* easily broken *infraction* breaking of a rule *fractious* unruly, tending to break rules
fug	flee	*fugitive* someone who flees *refuge* shelter, home for someone fleeing

Root or Stem	Meaning	Illustration
fus	pour	*effusive* gushing, pouring out *diffuse* widespread (poured in many directions)
gam	marriage	*monogamy* marriage to one person *bigamy* marriage to two people at the same time *polygamy* having many wives or husbands at the same time
gen, gener	class, race	*genus* group of animals with similar traits *generic* characteristic of a class *gender* class organized by sex
grad, gress	go, step	*digress* go astray (from the main point) *regress* go backwards *gradual* step by step, by degrees
graph, gram	writing	*epigram* pithy statement *telegram* instantaneous message over great distance *stenography* shorthand (writing narrowly)
greg	flock, herd	*gregarious* tending to group together, as in a herd *aggregate* group, total *egregious* conspicuously bad; shocking
helio	sun	*heliotrope* flower that faces the sun *heliograph* instrument that uses the sun's rays to send signals
it, itiner	journey, road	*exit* way out *itinerary* plan of journey
jac, jact, jec	to throw	*projectile* missile; something thrown forward *trajectory* path taken by thrown object *ejaculatory* casting or throwing out
jur, jurat	to swear	*perjure* testify falsely *jury* group of men and women sworn to seek the truth *adjuration* solemn urging
labor, laborat	to work	*laboratory* place where work is done *collaborate* work together with others *laborious* difficult
leg, lect, lig	to choose, to read	*election* choice *legible* able to be read *eligible* able to be selected

Root or Stem	Meaning	Illustration
leg	law	*legislature* law-making body *legitimate* lawful *legal* lawful
liber, libr	book	*library* collection of books *libretto* the "book" of a musical play *libel* slander (originally found in a little book)
liber	free	*liberation* the act of setting free *liberal* generous (giving freely); tolerant
log	word, study	*entomology* study of insects *etymology* study of word parts and derivations *monologue* speech by one person
loqu, locut	to talk	*soliloquy* speech by one individual *loquacious* talkative *elocution* speech
luc	light	*elucidate* enlighten *lucid* clear *translucent* allowing some light to pass through
magn	great	*magnify* enlarge *magnanimity* generosity, greatness of soul *magnitude* greatness, extent
mal	bad	*malevolent* wishing evil *malediction* curse *malefactor* evildoer
man	hand	*manufacture* create (make by hand) *manuscript* written by hand *emancipate* free (let go from the hand)
mar	sea	*maritime* connected with seafaring *submarine* undersea craft *mariner* seaman
mater, matr	mother	*maternal* pertaining to motherhood *matriarch* female ruler of a family, group, or state *matrilineal* descended on the mother's side
mit, miss	to send	*missile* projectile *dismiss* send away *transmit* send across
mob, mot, mov	move	*mobilize* cause to move *motility* ability to move *immovable* not able to be moved

Root or Stem	Meaning	Illustration
mon, monit	to warn	*admonish* warn *premonition* foreboding *monitor* watcher (warner)
mori, mort	to die	*mortuary* funeral parlor *moribund* dying *immortal* not dying
morph	shape, form	*amorphous* formless, lacking shape *metamorphosis* change of shape *anthropomorphic* in the shape of man
mut	change	*immutable* not able to be changed *mutate* undergo a great change *mutability* changeableness, inconstancy
nat	born	*innate* from birth *prenatal* before birth *nativity* birth
nav	ship	*navigate* sail a ship *circumnavigate* sail around the world *naval* pertaining to ships
neg	deny	*negation* denial *renege* deny, go back on one's word *renegade* turncoat, traitor
nomen	name	*nomenclature* act of naming, terminology *nominal* in name only (as opposed to actual) *cognomen* surname, distinguishing nickname
nov	new	*novice* beginner *renovate* make new again *novelty* newness
omni	all	*omniscient* all-knowing *omnipotent* all-powerful *omnivorous* eating everything
oper	to work	*operate* work *cooperation* working together
pac	peace	*pacify* make peaceful *pacific* peaceful *pacifist* person opposed to war
pass	feel	*dispassionate* free of emotion *impassioned* emotion-filled *impassive* showing no feeling

Root or Stem	Meaning	Illustration
pater, patr	father	*patriotism* love of one's country (fatherland) *patriarch* male ruler of a family, group, or state *paternity* fatherhood
path	disease, feeling	*pathology* study of diseased tissue *apathetic* lacking feeling; indifferent *antipathy* hostile feeling
ped, pod	foot	*impediment* stumbling block; hindrance *tripod* three-footed stand *quadruped* four-footed animal
ped	child	*pedagogue* teacher of children *pediatrician* children's doctor
pel, puls	to drive	*compulsion* a forcing to do *repel* drive back *expel* drive out, banish
pet, petit	to seek	*petition* request *appetite* craving, desire *compete* vie with others
phil	love	*philanthropist* benefactor, lover of humanity *Anglophile* lover of everything English *philanderer* one involved in brief love affairs
pon, posit	to place	*postpone* place after *positive* definite, unquestioned (definitely placed)
port, portat	to carry	*portable* able to be carried *transport* carry across *export* carry out (of country)
poten	able, powerful	*omnipotent* all-powerful *potentate* powerful person *impotent* powerless
psych	mind	*psychology* study of the mind *psychosis* mental disorder *psychopath* mentally ill person
put, putat	to trim, to calculate	*putative* supposed (calculated) *computation* calculation *amputate* cut off
quer, ques, quir, quis	to ask	*inquiry* investigation *inquisitive* questioning *query* question

Root or Stem	Meaning	Illustration
reg, rect	rule	*regicide* murder of a ruler *regent* ruler *insurrection* rebellion; overthrow of a ruler
rid, ris	to laugh	*derision* scorn *risibility* inclination to laughter *ridiculous* deserving to be laughed at
rog, rogat	to ask	*interrogate* question *prerogative* privilege
rupt	to break	*interrupt* break into *bankrupt* insolvent *rupture* a break
sacr	holy	*sacred* holy *sacrilegious* impious, violating something holy *sacrament* religious act
sci	to know	*science* knowledge *omniscient* knowing all *conscious* aware
scop	watch, see	*periscope* device for seeing around corners *microscope* device for seeing small objects
scrib, script	to write	*transcribe* make a written copy *script* written text *circumscribe* write around, limit
sect	cut	*dissect* cut apart *bisect* cut into two pieces
sed, sess	to sit	*sedentary* inactive (sitting) *session* meeting
sent, sens	to think, to feel	*consent* agree *resent* show indignation *sensitive* showing feeling
sequi, secut, seque	to follow	*consecutive* following in order *sequence* arrangement *sequel* that which follows *non sequitur* something that does not follow logically
solv, solut	to loosen	*absolve* free from blame *dissolute* morally lax *absolute* complete (not loosened)

Root or Stem	Meaning	Illustration
somn	sleep	*insomnia* inability to sleep *somnolent* sleepy *somnambulist* sleepwalker
soph	wisdom	*philosopher* lover of wisdom *sophisticated* worldly wise
spec, spect	to look at	*spectator* observer *aspect* appearance *circumspect* cautious (looking around)
spir	breathe	*respiratory* pertaining to breathing *spirited* full of life (breath)
string, strict	bind	*stringent* strict *constrict* become tight *stricture* limit, something that restrains
stru, struct	build	*constructive* helping to build *construe* analyze (how something is built)
tang, tact, ting	to touch	*tangent* touching *contact* touching with, meeting *contingent* depending upon
tempor	time	*contemporary* at same time *extemporaneous* impromptu *temporize* delay
ten, tent	to hold	*tenable* able to be held *tenure* holding of office *retentive* holding; having a good memory
term	end	*interminable* endless *terminate* end
terr	land	*terrestrial* pertaining to earth *subterranean* underground
therm	heat	*thermostat* instrument that regulates heat *diathermy* sending heat through body tissues
tors, tort	twist	*distort* twist out of true shape or meaning *torsion* act of twisting *tortuous* twisting
tract	drag, pull	*distract* pull (one's attention) away *intractable* stubborn, unable to be dragged *attraction* pull, drawing quality
trud, trus	push, shove	*intrude* push one's way in *protrusion* something sticking out

Root or Stem	Meaning	Illustration
urb	city	*urban* pertaining to a city *urbane* polished, sophisticated (pertaining to a city dweller) *suburban* outside of a city
vac	empty	*vacuous* lacking content, empty-headed *evacuate* compel to empty an area
vad, vas	go	*invade* enter in a hostile fashion *evasive* not frank; eluding
veni, vent, ven	to come	*intervene* come between *prevent* stop *convention* meeting
ver	true	*veracious* truthful *verify* check the truth *verisimilitude* appearance of truth
verb	word	*verbose* wordy *verbiage* excessive use of words *verbatim* word for word
vers, vert	turn	*vertigo* turning dizzy *revert* turn back (to an earlier state) *diversion* something causing one to turn aside
via	way	*deviation* departure from the way *viaduct* roadway (arched) *trivial* trifling (small talk at crossroads)
vid, vis	to see	*vision* sight *evidence* things seen *vista* view
vinc, vict, vanq	to conquer	*invincible* unconquerable *victory* winning *vanquish* defeat
viv, vit	alive	*vivisection* operating on living animals *vivacious* full of life *vitality* liveliness
voc, vocat	to call	*avocation* calling, minor occupation *provocation* calling or rousing the anger of *invocation* calling in prayer
vol	wish	*malevolent* wishing someone ill *voluntary* of one's own will
volv, volut	to roll	*revolve* roll around *evolve* roll out, develop *convolution* coiled state

COMMON SUFFIXES

Suffixes are syllables that are added to a word. Occasionally, they change the meaning of the word; more frequently, they serve to change the grammatical form of the word (noun to adjective, adjective to noun, noun to verb).

Suffix	Meaning	Illustration
able, ible	capable of (adjective suffix)	*portable* able to be carried *interminable* not able to be limited *legible* able to be read
ac, ic	like, pertaining to (adjective suffix)	*cardiac* pertaining to the heart *aquatic* pertaining to the water *dramatic* pertaining to the drama
acious, icious	full of (adjective suffix)	*audacious* full of daring *perspicacious* full of mental perception *avaricious* full of greed
al	pertaining to (adjective or noun suffix)	*maniacal* insane *final* pertaining to the end *logical* pertaining to logic
ant, ent	full of (adjective or noun suffix)	*eloquent* pertaining to fluid, effective speech *suppliant* pleader (person full of requests) *verdant* green
ary	like, connected with (adjective or noun suffix)	*dictionary* book connected with words *honorary* with honor *luminary* celestial body
ate	to make (verb suffix)	*consecrate* to make holy *enervate* to make weary *mitigate* to make less severe
ation	that which is (noun suffix)	*exasperation* irritation *irritation* annoyance
cy	state of being (noun suffix)	*democracy* government ruled by the people *obstinacy* stubbornness *accuracy* correctness
eer, er, or	person who (noun suffix)	*mutineer* person who rebels *lecher* person who lusts *censor* person who deletes improper remarks
escent	becoming (adjective suffix)	*evanescent* tending to vanish *pubescent* arriving at puberty

Suffix	Meaning	Illustration
fic	making, doing (adjective suffix)	*terrific* arousing great fear *soporific* causing sleep
fy	to make (verb suffix)	*magnify* enlarge *petrify* turn to stone *beautify* make beautiful
iferous	producing, bearing (adjective suffix)	*pestiferous* carrying disease *vociferous* bearing a loud voice
il, ile	pertaining to, capable of (adjective suffix)	*puerile* pertaining to a boy or child *ductile* capable of being hammered or drawn *civil* polite
ism	doctrine, belief (noun suffix)	*monotheism* belief in one god *fanaticism* excessive zeal; extreme belief
ist	dealer, doer (noun suffix)	*fascist* one who believes in a fascist state *realist* one who is realistic *artist* one who deals with art
ity	state of being (noun suffix)	*annuity* yearly grant *credulity* state of being unduly willing to believe *sagacity* wisdom
ive	like (adjective suffix)	*expensive* costly *quantitative* concerned with quantity *effusive* gushing
ize, ise	make (verb suffix)	*victimize* make a victim of *rationalize* make rational *harmonize* make harmonious *enfranchise* make free or set free
oid	resembling, like (adjective suffix)	*ovoid* like an egg *anthropoid* resembling man *spheroid* resembling a sphere
ose	full of (adjective suffix)	*verbose* full of words *lachrymose* full of tears
osis	condition (noun suffix)	*psychosis* diseased mental condition *neurosis* nervous condition *hypnosis* condition of induced sleep
ous	full of (adjective suffix)	*nauseous* full of nausea *ludicrous* foolish
tude	state of (noun suffix)	*fortitude* state of strength *beatitude* state of blessedness *certitude* state of sureness

PART FOUR
The PSAT Writing and Language Test

Chapter 3: The Evidence-Based Writing and Language Test

The Evidence-Based Writing and Language Test 3

The PSAT Writing and Language section tests your command of English grammar and editing skills. This chapter comprehensively reviews the concepts that you will need on test day.

FREQUENTLY ASKED QUESTIONS

How Is the Writing and Language Section Structured?

- It is the second section of the PSAT, following Reading.
- There are 44 questions.
- There is a time limit of 35 minutes.
- There are 4 passages.
- Questions are in a random order of difficulty.

What Is Tested on the Writing and Language Section?

The Writing and Language section tests the fundamentals of English grammar and essential editing skills. More specifically, the following are overviews of the concepts assessed:

IDEA DEVELOPMENT: Is the writing well developed, clear, well supported, and focused? Can the student integrate information from quantitative graphs into the passage?

ORGANIZATION: Does the writing follow a logical sequence? Are the transitions, introductions, and conclusions effective?

LANGUAGE USE: Is the writing appropriately precise and concise? Is the style and tone consistent? Is proper syntax used?

SENTENCE STRUCTURE: Are sentences complete? Is parallel structure and proper word order used?

USAGE RULES: Is the verb tense and number use (singular and plural) consistent? Is the language consistent with conventional expressions?

PUNCTUATION: Does the student know how to properly use commas, semicolons, colons, and dashes?

What Are the Most Important Things I Can Do to Be Successful?

CAREFULLY REVIEW THIS CHAPTER. It comprehensively covers the major grammar and editing concepts you will need to know for the PSAT.

WORK THROUGH THE WRITING AND LANGUAGE PRACTICE TESTS IN THIS BOOK. They are carefully designed to align with what you will face on test day and are based on careful analysis of the released PSATs from College Board.

READ WIDELY! The more familiar you are with what good writing should look like, the easier it will be for you to spot the best options on this section.

PRACTICE WITH OTHER MATERIALS IF NEEDED. The PSAT Writing and Language section is virtually identical to the SAT Writing and Language section. So, if you run out of practice materials in this book, check out *Barron's SAT* or any of the other Barron's books for the SAT. You can find further practice at *KhanAcademy.org*, the official College Board practice website. Also, since the PSAT Writing and Language section closely mirrors the content covered by the ACT English section, you can improve your PSAT Writing and Language performance by practicing ACT English passages.

GENERAL TIPS

Working Your Way Through the Writing and Language Questions

1. **USE THE FULL AMOUNT OF TIME.** The PSAT Writing and Language section is typically easy to finish for most students. With 35 minutes and 4 passages, you should take about *9 minutes per passage* to finish. You are much more likely to make careless errors if you rush through the questions. Instead, do the questions one time well so that you do not miss the subtle issues that many questions test. Even though with many tests it makes sense to finish early so that you have time to check your work, it is advisable with the PSAT Writing and Language test to pace yourself to finish right on time. You are more likely to avoid careless errors if you catch them the first time, rather than if you go through the test quickly and then quickly scan over your answers to check. If you find that you are able to comfortably finish the PSAT Writing and Language text with time to spare, you may consider reading through the passages before doing the questions so that you have a better understanding of the meaning and flow of the essay. Although this is not necessary to perform well, it can sometimes be advisable for those students who would otherwise simply waste this time just sitting there during the last few minutes of the test.

2. **WRITE ON THE TEST BOOKLET.** With many school tests, teachers require students to avoid marking on the test booklets—this makes sense, as they want to reuse the booklets for other classes. No one is going to use your PSAT booklet but you. So, write on it whenever and wherever you find it helpful. Here are a couple of common cases where writing can make a difference:

   You can carefully underline and circle key words in the questions. If a question asks you about "specific" information and you miss this word, you will miss the question. If you underline the key words as you read, you are much less likely to make careless reading mistakes.

You can write down possible placements for reordering sentences and paragraphs. It is not necessary to keep all of the possible placements of a sentence straight in your head. Write down where Choice A should go in the paragraph, where Choice B should go, and so on. The less you have to keep track of in your head, the more mental power you will free up to think through the questions.

3. **MOUTH IT OUT AS YOU READ.** "Hear" the passage in your head and test out the sound of the different options. You don't have to know the exact rules for misplaced modifiers and proper sentence construction to recognize that this sounds wrong: "Excited was I the brand new science fiction movie to see." When you are doing the PSAT Writing and Language test, you must answer the questions correctly—you do not need to write out a justification for each answer. This chapter comprehensively covers the grammar rules you will need to know—study them, and you will be much more confident and decisive. Coupled with this knowledge, you will put yourself in the best position to succeed if you filter the questions not just through your eyes but through your ears as well.

4. **MAKE SURE THAT EVERYTHING MAKES SENSE GIVEN THE CONTEXT.** To determine if a sentence provides an effective introduction, you must understand the paragraph as a whole. To see if a verb has the correct tense, you must see how the verbs in nearby sentences are used. Some questions will require that you look only at the sentence that the underlined portion is in, whereas other questions will require a couple of paragraphs of context. When you have any doubt about how much of the surrounding context to consider, err on the side of reading *too much* rather than *too little*. Since the Writing and Language section is relatively easy to finish, you should take the necessary time to be certain everything is consistent and logical.

5. **UNDERSTAND THAT THERE WILL NOT BE GRAMMAR GIMMICKS—JUST GRAMMAR RULES.** The PSAT will only test you on topics where there are clearly defined grammar rules. Topics on which there is disagreement on proper English usage (using the Oxford comma, using "but" or "because" to start a sentence, and whether it is OK to use the first person "I" or second person "you" in formal papers) will not be tested. In addition, you do not need to worry about if there will be two right answers—the PSAT is an extremely well-crafted test, and it is a virtual certainty that it will be free of errors. So, instead of wasting your time trying to determine the "tricks" of the test, boost your grammar knowledge and go in with confidence.

6. **GUESS SMART, NOT JUST RANDOMLY.** Remember—there is no penalty for guessing on the PSAT. Thus, be certain that you answer every single test question. If you do feel unconfident about a question, here are some tips that can help you make an educated guess:

If two or three of the answers are extremely similar, it is highly unlikely that one of those will be the correct option. For example, if a question has these options—(A) but, (B) however, (C) nevertheless, and (D) consequently—the answer is most likely (D) because the other options are all synonymous.

NO CHANGE has just as much of a chance of being correct as any other answer. Many students unfairly dismiss this as a possibility, believing that questions *must* have some kind of a change.

Come back to questions if you do not feel confident. Doing this will allow you to reexamine the question with fresh eyes after you've given your mind a chance to subconsciously process what the question was asking.

IDEA DEVELOPMENT QUESTIONS

Big Picture Idea Questions

Big picture idea questions require you to consider how the writer's message and structure can be clarified. You may need to consider *thesis statements* (which express the primary argument of the passage), *topic sentences* (which are usually the first sentence of a paragraph and state its overall message), and *claims* and *counterclaims* (statements in favor of or against the author's argument).

 TACTIC 1

Put the general meaning of the passage or paragraph into your own words. Then think about what would be the most logical choice.

If you approach these types of questions by looking at a limited amount of context, you will likely choose an incorrect answer. Take the time necessary to paraphrase the meaning of as much of the passage as is relevant. Also, be certain that you carefully read the question to be clear on what is being asked.

SAMPLE QUESTION

❶ Students will not be prepared for the real world if they cannot do simple mental math. This is true not just for those who are in science and math fields but for anyone who needs to approximate discounts for sales and calculate the appropriate tip at a restaurant. Schools should give students the tools they need to succeed by, ironically, taking away the tool of a calculator on occasion.

1. Which sentence, if inserted at the beginning of the paragraph, would provide the best introduction to what follows?

(A) Scientific careers give students the best opportunity for high-paying jobs.
(B) Many students are far too dependent on their calculators for basic computations.
(C) I, for one, do not see the relevance of learning calculus if I am going to be a humanities major.
(D) The funding for mathematical education across all age groups needs to be increased.

Start a question like this by carefully reading what is asked—we need a good introductory topic sentence. Before reading the choices, go ahead and read the paragraph that follows and put its general meaning into your own words. For example, this paragraph could be paraphrased as "No matter what profession students have later in life, they will need to be able to do basic math calculations." Now that we have an idea of what the paragraph is about, we can look at the choices one by one. Choice B is correct because it gives a clear statement of the argument that the remainder of the paragraph will support. The other choices all go on loosely related but ultimately irrelevant tangents.

BIG PICTURE IDEA DRILL

Write an introductory sentence to this paragraph. A sample good introduction follows.

_____

_____

First, without a good night's sleep, teens will be more likely to fall asleep in class, falling behind in their studies. Second, if teenagers who are of driving age are tired, they will be more susceptible to automotive accidents. Third, teens who do not have adequate rest are far more vulnerable to illness—both physical and mental. In conclusion, teens should make it a priority to get the recommended nine hours of nightly rest.

Sample Introductory Sentence: Teenagers need to make a good night's sleep a top priority for several key reasons.

Support Questions

In contrast to the previous question type, support questions are more focused on how to develop more specific ideas. You will need to consider how to use details and examples to give support to the author's argument.

TACTIC

Think *specific*, not *vague*, when it comes to supporting main ideas.

If someone is making a convincing argument, he or she will use specific and relevant facts and figures instead of vague generalities. Suppose you are trying to convince your parent to extend your curfew from 10 P.M. to midnight. Which of these statements would be more convincing to your parent?

- I would really like to stay out later because I think I'll act really well and not get into trouble. You don't have anything to worry about after all. You really should let me for the reasons I just discussed.
- I have demonstrated increased responsibility these past few months by making sure my room is kept tidy, keeping my GPA at its highest level ever, and becoming the president of two clubs at school. With my improved maturity, it is time for an extended curfew.

Clearly, the second one is more persuasive—it gives three specific and relevant reasons as to why you have earned the right to an extended curfew.

SAMPLE QUESTION

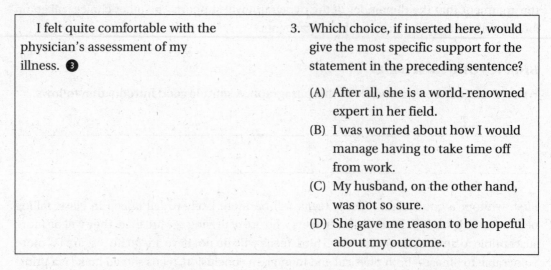

I felt quite comfortable with the physician's assessment of my illness. **3**

3. Which choice, if inserted here, would give the most specific support for the statement in the preceding sentence?

(A) After all, she is a world-renowned expert in her field.

(B) I was worried about how I would manage having to take time off from work.

(C) My husband, on the other hand, was not so sure.

(D) She gave me reason to be hopeful about my outcome.

To support the previous sentence, we need something that would demonstrate why the narrator feels comfortable in the physician's ability to accurately diagnose the illness. Choices B and C are irrelevant, and Choice D is far too vague. Choice A gives a concrete reason why the narrator would be confident in the doctor's assessment—if someone is a world-renowned expert, she is likely the best at what she does.

SUPPORT DRILL

Create a sentence at the underlined point in the paragraph that provides excellent support for the surrounding context.

The once-in-a-lifetime snowstorm was among the worst storms ever recorded in my city.

_____

_____

_____

With ice and snowfall like that, I hope that such a storm never occurs again as long as I live.

Sample Supporting Sentence: It left an inch of freezing rain coating all the roads and over a foot of snow on all surfaces, causing some roofs to collapse under the immense weight.

Focus Questions

When writing papers for school, you may be tempted to expand your word count by inserting unnecessary wording that *seems* relevant but actually is not. The PSAT will evaluate your skill in determining whether statements are closely tied to the purpose of the essay, or if they go on tangents.

Make sure the wording is actually relevant, not just superficially related.

The incorrect choices on questions like these will often look connected to the given context, but upon closer examination, you can see that they are off topic. Be sure to take your time in carefully thinking through these types of questions.

SAMPLE QUESTION

When making pasta from scratch, start with fresh ingredients— **12** eating this type of food is delicious.

12. Which choice best maintains the focus of the sentence?

(A) NO CHANGE

(B) pasta-making can be a labor-intensive project.

(C) trust your instincts, not hearsay.

(D) the best flour and eggs you can find.

Do not worry about whether the choices are true—the only thing you need to consider is if the choice best accomplishes the author's goal. The first sentence tells the reader to "start with fresh ingredients." Choice D is the only one that does this, giving the specific examples of "flour and eggs." Choices A and B are somewhat related to the topic but are unfocused. If you were rushing through this question, these two choices would be quite tempting. Choice C is far too off topic.

FOCUS DRILL

Which numbered selections should be removed from the paragraph because they are irrelevant?

Apartment hunting in a large city is an involved process. **1** Large cities can be found in many countries around the globe. While it would be nice if there were one comprehensive list of apartments that met your needs **2** for location, price, and amenities, such a list doesn't exist. **3** Lists can be found, however, for popular restaurants and coffee shops. Instead, you must do extensive searching yourself; you will become quite proficient at combing through online listings, tips on social media, and newspaper advertisements. **4** The time you will devote to your apartment search will approach the time spent on a part-time job. When it comes to selecting a residence, this investment of time is well worth it. **5** One day, you may have time to go on the vacation of a lifetime.

Answer

Keep sentences 2 and 4 because they maintain focus on the paragraph's topic of apartment hunting. Remove sentences 1, 3, and 5 because of irrelevance.

Quantitative Information Questions

The PSAT has questions that require you to analyze quantitative graphics and integrate statements about them into the passage. You will need to be sure that the statement is both supported by the graph and connected to the passage.

Carefully examine the axes and labels of the graphs to be clear on the data presented.

The graphs can come in all sorts of forms: tables, charts, maps, diagrams, and more. Even though you won't have to have any background knowledge on the data to understand it, it is easy, given the sheer variety of graphics you may find, to make careless errors. So, take time to fully grasp the information presented before you jump to the accompanying questions.

SAMPLE QUESTION

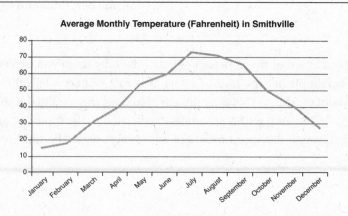

21. Which choice provides an accurate interpretation of the data in this chart?

    (A) The warmest day of the year was found in July.
    (B) A randomly selected day in June is going to be warmer than a randomly selected day in March.
    (C) The average temperature in Smithville generally decreases between August and January.
    (D) The months of December and January have the most inhospitable weather out of any of the months in Smithville.

It is critical that you come to conclusions based *only on the evidence given.* Choice C gives the only correct option, since the graph provides information about the average temperature during these months only. Choice A is incorrect because we do not have detailed information about the temperatures on each day. Choice B is incorrect because a randomly selected day could be quite hot or cool—we only have information about the *average* temperature for the entire month. Choice D is incorrect because temperature is not the sole factor determining how nice the weather is; air pressure, precipitation, wind, and pollution can all play major roles.

QUANTITATIVE INFORMATION DRILL

Consider the following graph. Which of the five statements that follow is/are justifiable based on the graph?

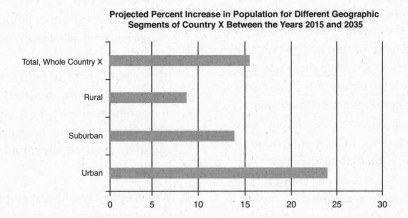

Projected Percent Increase in Population for Different Geographic Segments of Country X Between the Years 2015 and 2035

1. In 2035, there will be at least twice as many residents in urban areas of country X as in rural areas of country X.

2. The projected rate of increase in the urban population of country X is nearly three times the projected rate of increase in the rural population of country X over the twenty-year period starting in 2015.

3. The rate of increase in the suburban population of country X between the years 2020 and 2030 will be greater than the rate of increase in the rural population of country X during the same time period.

4. The majority of the residents of country X reside in urban and suburban areas.

5. The projected rate of growth in the rural population during the years 2015 through 2035 is less than the projected rate of growth for the population of country X as a whole.

Answers
1. Not justifiable
2. Justifiable
3. Not justifiable
4. Not justifiable
5. Justifiable

The eternal question about careers is ❶ "how do I decide which career I would like to do when I'm out of school?" This is a concern that haunts young people as they decide upon a college major and older people as they confront mid-life crises. ❷ While there is not a clear answer to this question, there are several things that merit consideration.

It is important to realize that not all of your time is going to be spent working. If you have a job that pays well and requires only a reasonable amount of time, you can treat the job as a "means to an end." ❸ Some of the wealthiest billionaires in the world have net worths in excess of the gross domestic products of small countries.

1. Which choice would most effectively introduce the major theme of the essay?

   (A) NO CHANGE
   (B) "how can I go about finding a job given the challenges in today's economy?"
   (C) "should I prioritize enjoyment of my job or my monetary compensation?"
   (D) "what is it that makes some careers more intellectually stimulating than others?"

2. Which option would best emphasize the uncertainty and complexity surrounding the essay's topic while leading into the rest of the sentence?

   (A) NO CHANGE
   (B) While many have successfully chosen their career paths,
   (C) Since competition for high-paying jobs is a fierce as ever,
   (D) Because advanced machines are rapidly replacing many jobs that have been done by humans,

3. Which option provides the most focused and relevant elaboration on the previous sentence?

   (A) NO CHANGE
   (B) Many people will never successfully sort out the intractable dilemma of how to prioritize the demands of their supervisors with the demands of their customers.
   (C) The social welfare programs in many Scandinavian countries enable both mothers and fathers to spend significant time at home with their kids.
   (D) In other words, if the job provides you the money and time that you need to enjoy hobbies and spend quality time with your family outside of work, it can be worth pursuing.

If it is possible to have a career that you truly enjoy, then it probably will not feel like work. The time you spend there will not feel like a drain on your other interests. **❹** Most people can determine the most appropriate careers based on which subjects they enjoy the most in school. If you are like most people, try to find a less dreamy niche at which you excel and that you enjoy.

You should excel at your chosen profession to the point where you are making enough money to live "comfortably" for your needs and lifestyle. If you are **❺** terrified due to financial concerns, it will be challenging to enjoy your work, no matter how fun it is. When you come home each day from a job that pays decently and that you find stimulating, you will feel fulfilled and rejuvenated instead of **❻** frustrated and drained.

4. Which option sets up the most relevant contrast with the sentence that follows?

(A) NO CHANGE
(B) Some careers involve long hours and great demands, with workers expected to be "on-call" 24 hours a day, and 7 days a week.
(C) If you are so talented that you can pursue a fantasy job as a professional athlete or musician, go for it.
(D) Instead, have your work be the equivalent of play, and you'll never "work" a day in your life.

5. Which phrasing would best express a degree of moderate concern?

(A) NO CHANGE
(B) preoccupied with
(C) optimistic about
(D) despondent over

6. Which choice of words would most consistently complete the contrast in the sentence?

(A) NO CHANGE
(B) saddened and unhappy.
(C) exhausted and disloyal.
(D) burdened and morose.

To summarize, **7** make sure you have a profession that commands the respect of your peers. Try to find a balance between work and non-work interests, and be sure the expected compensation will be sufficient to meet your needs. And be open to changing your mind about your priorities— **8** according to current research, people are mostly consistent throughout their lives as to their major career priorities.

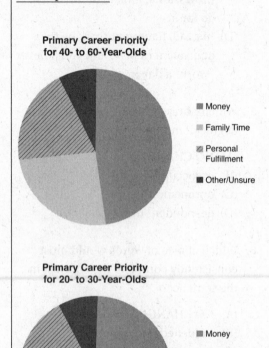

Primary Career Priority for 40- to 60-Year-Olds

- Money
- Family Time
- Personal Fulfillment
- Other/Unsure

Primary Career Priority for 20- to 30-Year-Olds

- Money
- Family Time
- Personal Fulfillment
- Other/Unsure

Surveys of 100 randomly selected 40- to 60-year-olds and 100 randomly selected 20- to 30-year-olds about their primary career priorities.

7. Which option most effectively introduces the concluding paragraph?

(A) NO CHANGE
(B) do not look at choosing a career as an "either-or" decision.
(C) realize that ultimately, family must come first.
(D) be certain your job will not be subject to lay-offs and unexpected shifts in the economy.

8. Which option uses the most relevant and justifiable conclusion based on the data in the graphs to build on the point made in the first part of the sentence?

(A) NO CHANGE
(B) Based on current surveys, monetary compensation is consistently the most important factor in making a career choice, regardless of age.
(C) According to recent surveys, as people age, they tend to prefer spending more time with family to having a satisfying profession.
(D) Based on the latest research, age is a more important factor in choosing a career than race or other demographics.

Answers

1. **(C)** Since this questions asks about the major theme of the essay, it is helpful to quickly read through the essay, or at a minimum, read the topic sentences of each paragraph. Doing so will help you paraphrase the overall topic and message of the passage. Throughout the essay, the narrator focuses on how to prioritize money or enjoyment in a career. Accordingly, Choice C makes the most sense because it addresses these two themes. It is not Choice A or D because these themes are too narrow. It is not Choice B because the author does not focus on job-finding prospects.

2. **(A)** Focus on the key words in the question: "emphasize the uncertainty and complexity." Choices B, C, and D all assert a great deal of certainty. Choice A stands out as being much less certain and emphatic.

3. **(D)** The question requires an elaboration on the previous sentence—the previous sentence states that it is possible to consider a job to be tolerable if it gives you the financial means to enjoy non-work activities. Choice D is the only option that elaborates on this theme. The other options are all loosely related to the topic of the essay, but none directly elaborates on the sentence that comes before.

4. **(C)** The question requires that we set up a contrast with the sentence that comes immediately afterward. The sentence that follows states that people should have less lofty and more realistic expectations for what type of job they should pursue. Choice C sets up the most logical contrast with the sentence that follows because it acknowledges that if someone can actually obtain a position in a "dream-job," it is a no-brainer to do so. Choices A, B, and D all are related to the essay's focus on the workplace but fail to offer a clear contrast with the sentence that follows.

5. **(B)** The question asks for "moderate concern," making it important to avoid an answer that uses emotionally extreme language. Choices A and D both convey extreme negativity, whereas Choice C conveys a positive emotion. Choice B is correct because to be "preoccupied" is consistent with feeling moderately concerned about something.

6. **(A)** The words with which a contrast needs to be made are "fulfilled and rejuvenated." Choice A sets up the most logical contrast, since "frustrated and drained" express a negative attitude and a lack of energy. Choices B, C, and D all express negativity, but not in a way that provides a logical contrast with the preceding language.

7. **(B)** The paragraph goes on to state that balance and flexibility in choosing a career are critically important. Choice B provides a logical introduction to this theme, asserting that the choice of a career should not be an all-or-nothing proposition. All of the other options express extremes, making them inconsistent with the balanced attitude advocated in this paragraph.

8. **(C)** The first part of the sentence encourages readers to have an open mind. It is most logical to go with Choice C because it gives statistical evidence that having an open mind is important because career priorities can change quite a bit as people age. Choices A and B do not logically build off the first part of the sentence, and Choice D focuses on irrelevant information.

ORGANIZATION QUESTIONS

Logical Sequence Questions

These questions assess your ability to put sentences and ideas in the most logical sequence. The PSAT will generally prefer events to be in the order in which they happened, and for the ideas to be clear as the passage unfolds. The writer should not confuse the reader as to how things unfold.

TACTIC 5

Try labeling the possible placements of sentences in the passage, making it easier to visualize the potential options.

You are able to write on the PSAT, so take advantage of this and physically write down where the different choices would be in the passage. This will make you less likely to make careless errors than if you try to keep track of everything in your head.

SAMPLE QUESTION

[1] Online discussion is both a blessing and a curse for politeness. [2] It is a blessing when participants feel comfortable openly sharing their views. [3] As a general rule, online discourse is best when there is transparency among those posting commentary. [4] It is a curse when participants can hide behind the shroud of anonymity to bully and intimidate. [5] That way, commenters will be more inclined to be fair and polite when they present their views. **11**

11. What would be the most logical placement of sentence 3?

(A) Where it is now
(B) Before sentence 1
(C) After sentence 4
(D) After sentence 5

Sometimes the proper order of sentences becomes clear based on what *follows* the sentence, not just what comes before. In this case, sentence 3 leads into the topic of sentence 5—mentioning that there should be "transparency" (i.e., openness) in online discourse would logically justify the message of sentence 5 that commenters will be more inclined to be fair and polite. After all, if everyone knew who was talking, the participants would not be able to say hurtful things without fear of reprisal. Therefore, the answer is C. The other placements are illogical because they would not logically connect to statements about the need for openness with personal identity.

LOGICAL SEQUENCE DRILL

Put these sentences into a paragraph in the most logical order:

[1] On the one hand, there are teenagers who are inclined to use and trust what they find online.

[2] There need not be such a conflict if teachers are willing to see how far online resources have come in their quality, and students are willing to see the ease with which they can use printed materials.

[3] There is a fundamental conflict when it comes to high school research projects.

[4] Ultimately, good librarians are needed to help bridge the gap between teens and their teachers.

[5] On the other hand, there are teachers who encourage students to use time-tested printed material for their sources.

Answer

[3] There is a fundamental conflict when it comes to high school research projects. [1] On the one hand, there are teenagers who are inclined to use and trust what they find online. [5] On the other hand, there are teachers who encourage students to use time-tested printed material for their sources. [2] There need not be such a conflict if teachers are willing to see how far online resources have come in their quality, and students are willing to see the ease with which they can use printed materials. [4] Ultimately, good librarians are needed to help bridge the gap between teens and their teachers.

Introductions, Conclusions, and Transitions Questions

Questions about the best connections between different parts of the passage *are among the most frequent question types on the PSAT*. These questions require you to consider what wording would make the flow of the passage most logical and meaningful. Be sure you know the "big three" transitional words—"but," "also," and "because"—and some of their common synonyms.

BUT: however, on the other hand, in contrast to, yet, still, nevertheless, conversely, in spite of, despite, unlike, besides, although, instead, rather, otherwise, regardless, notwithstanding

ALSO: additionally, moreover, further, as well, besides, likewise, what is more, furthermore, in addition, similarly

BECAUSE: consequently, so, therefore, as a result, thus, hence, in order to, if . . . then, since, so that, due to, whenever

Treat the transitional wording as a blank, and then consider what type of transition is needed given what comes before and after it.

What comes before and after the transitional wording could be in contrast to one another, be in support of one another, or have some other relationship. Look at as much of the passage as needed—sometimes just a couple of sentences, sometimes a couple of paragraphs—to determine what wording is needed.

SAMPLE QUESTION

Those not accustomed to the effects of caffeine may experience jitteriness upon initial consumption. Despite this, many students try caffeine for the first time the morning of the PSAT in an effort to be alert. ❼ As a result, they should rely on a good night's sleep and natural adrenaline to maximize performance.

7. Which choice provides the most logical transition at this point in the paragraph?

(A) NO CHANGE
(B) Instead,
(C) Consequently,
(D) Moreover,

The sentence that precedes the question states that students try caffeine in order to improve their test performance. The sentence that follows states that students should rely on more natural solutions to improve performance. Choice B is the only option that shows the needed contrast between these two ideas. "As a result" and "consequently" both show cause and effect, and "moreover" is synonymous with "also."

TRANSITIONAL WORDING DRILL

Write appropriate transitional words in the underlined portions. Use the "word bank" of transitions—each word will be used only once.

Word Bank

while	and	in fact
but	since	perhaps

_____ it is unusual that I enjoy waiting in line for hours on the opening night of a big movie, _____ I am not alone. _____, dozens of other moviegoers wait along with me, _____ we enjoy passing the time speculating on the movie's potential plot twists. _____ it could be expected that tempers would be short as people stood patiently in line, the truth is that people are extremely polite. _____ we are all full of hopeful anticipation, everyone is in a fairly good mood.

Answer

Perhaps it is unusual that I enjoy waiting in line for hours on the opening night of a big movie, but I am not alone. In fact, dozens of other moviegoers wait along with me, and we enjoy passing the time speculating on the movie's potential plot twists. While it could be expected that tempers would be short as people stood patiently in line, the truth is that people are extremely polite. Since we are all full of hopeful anticipation, everyone is in a fairly good mood.

ORGANIZATION PRACTICE

❶ When I was young, I could not put down books. I read all the Harry Potter books several times over and was a big fan of other fantasy and science fiction texts. Once I entered middle school, I lost much of the joy of reading. ❷ Since I loved reading for fun, I had to read certain books for summer reading. Not only did I have to read them, I had to take careful notes on the texts ❸ from when school started again, there would inevitably be a major reading test. I suppose it is like going to see a movie— ❹ if you had to take notes for a quiz while watching the film, you would probably just stay out in the lobby!

{1} Fortunately, my new English teacher helped reawaken my love of reading. {2} Not surprisingly, when you can read a book that actually interests you, you tend to do much better when it comes to recall. {3} ❺ In contrast, I don't even mind taking a few notes or highlighting key phrases if it helps

1. Which choice provides the best introduction to the paragraph?

   (A) NO CHANGE
   (B) Books have always fascinated me.
   (C) Some of the best books are ones you would not expect.
   (D) Some of my happiest memories come from my childhood travel.

2. (A) NO CHANGE
   (B) As a result of
   (C) In addition to
   (D) Instead of

3. (A) NO CHANGE
   (B) until
   (C) because
   (D) by

4. Which choice best concludes the sentence with a logical explanation?

   (A) NO CHANGE
   (B) Who has the money to see a movie in a crowded theater when you can enjoy it much more comfortably at home?
   (C) Both movies and books have plot lines, character development, and metaphorical imagery.
   (D) Nobody enjoys a movie when it is interrupted by delinquents who talk and text through its entirety.

5. (A) NO CHANGE
   (B) In fact,
   (C) Without equivocation,
   (D) Unfortunately,

me understand a well-written story's plot. ❻ Rather than forcing us to read certain books, she gave us considerable leeway in choosing which books most interested us.

My newfound attitude toward reading comes at just the right time. I am about to take some much more challenging AP courses, and ❼ you surely cannot believe what happened, there will be some material in the classes that will be rather dry. If I still had my middle-school mentality toward reading, I would likely surf the web for book summaries instead of actually reading the texts. ❽ On the other hand, I am able to find interesting articles and blogs to divert my attention from studying.

6. What is the most logical placement of the underlined sentence in this paragraph?

(A) Where it is now
(B) Before sentence 1
(C) Before sentence 2
(D) Before sentence 3

7. Which choice provides the best transition at this point in the sentence?

(A) NO CHANGE
(B) the classes will take place in my school
(C) despite my misgivings about the teachers
(D) let's face it

8. Which option would provide the best conclusion to the paragraph?

(A) NO CHANGE
(B) Instead, I am able to buckle down when I need to read an antiquated historical document or a chapter about balancing chemical equations.
(C) Middle school was a tough time for me in general—it was difficult for me to figure out to which group I really belonged.
(D) After all, online videos are far more interesting than the boring films our teachers force upon us in school.

Answers

1. **(A)** The paragraph shows a shift in the narrator's attitude toward reading—as a young child, she enjoyed reading, and as she progressed in school, she lost her joy in reading. Choice A best introduces this paragraph because it is the only option that previews this transition in attitude. Choices B and D are simply positive, and Choice C is too loosely related to what follows.

2. **(D)** The previous sentence establishes that the narrator has lost joy in reading. The current sentence serves to explain how this shift in attitude came about—namely, rather than reading recreationally, the narrator was required to read certain texts. Choice D is the only option that shows this contrast. Choices A and B both show cause and effect, and Choice C indicates a list.

3. **(C)** A cause-and-effect transition is needed here because the narrator is stating that she has to take notes so that she could be prepared for the test upon her return from vacation—Choice C is the only option that provides a cause-and-effect transition.

4. **(A)** The paragraph as a whole states that the narrator became progressively less interested in reading as it became something she was required to do, instead of something she chose to do. Choice A makes sense in this context because it provides an analogy that shows how being forced to watch a movie for school makes the experience much less enjoyable. Choices B, C, and D are somewhat connected to the sentence but are not relevant to the paragraph.

5. **(B)** The sentence that comes before this makes the general point that it is easier to read books that are interesting to you. The remainder of the current sentence states that the narrator is fine with taking notes and highlighting words if doing so will help her better understand a story she finds interesting. Choice B is the best option because it provides a transition indicating a clarification. None of the other options indicates a clarification is taking place—Choices A and D show contrast, and Choice C shows certainty.

6. **(C)** This sentence should be placed before sentence 2 because it provides a logical transition after sentence 1, which states that the English teacher helped the narrator become interested once again in reading. Without having this sentence moved to this place, the paragraph would not have a clear elaboration on how the teacher accomplished this shift in the narrator's attitude. All of the other options would prevent this clear elaboration from taking place.

7. **(D)** "Let's face it" uses concise language that matches the relatively informal tone of the essay. Choice A is too wordy and extreme, Choice B is illogical and irrelevant, and Choice C changes the emphasis from the reading requirements to the teachers themselves.

8. **(B)** This paragraph states that the narrator now has a mindset that enables her to read material that is academic and dry. Choice B concludes this paragraph well because it concretely illustrates how being able to read less entertaining texts can be helpful. Choice A confuses the intended meaning, and Choices C and D are too disconnected from the topic of the paragraph.

EFFECTIVE LANGUAGE USE

Precision Questions

Choosing the appropriate word for a given situation is extremely important to effective writing. Consider the following words:

dishonest	grumpy	careless
lazy	confrontational	

All of the above words could reasonably be used to express a "bad" attitude. A writer should use the most *precise* word to express his or her intended idea—if the author's subject is "bad" because of constant fibbing, then "dishonest" would be correct; if the subject is "bad" because of violent disrespect, "confrontational" would be correct. The PSAT will have questions where you will need to choose the most precise wording to express the intended meaning.

Go beyond the simple dictionary definitions of words. Instead, consider the subtle ways that word meaning can change depending on context.

Many of the incorrect options on precision questions will probably be loosely synonymous with the correct option. Be careful that your choice truly is the best way to express the author's message.

SAMPLE QUESTION

> An eagle can spot its prey from a great distance, since it has an extremely **❹** acute sense of sight.
>
> 4. (A) NO CHANGE
>   (B) interesting
>   (C) good
>   (D) rigorous

All of the options are adjectives that generally mean positive characteristics. Choice A is correct because "acute" means *very perceptive*, which is appropriate given that the eagle has an excellent sense of sight. "Good" could work, but it is too vague. "Interesting" and "rigorous" are illogical given the context.

PRECISION DRILL

Choose which of the two words is more appropriate, given the context of the sentence.

1. Down by 30 points near the end of the game, the team was clearly (finished or completed).

2. John was (emotional or passionate) about his career choice, believing he had finally found his calling.

3. I hope the servers are not too (conservative or conservationist) with the portion sizes—I am really hungry!

4. The e-mail demonstrated significant (disrespect or negativity) by addressing the professor so informally.

5. Your hotel room is quite (luxurious or expensive); the linens are really soft, the bathroom is capacious, and the view is magnificent.

Answers

1. finished
2. passionate
3. conservative
4. disrespect
5. luxurious

Concision Questions

When you write your college application essay, you will face what is likely an unusual situation—you will have a *word maximum* instead of a word minimum for your essay. Teachers often give students general guidance on the word count of a paper, and many students respond by being overly repetitive and wordy so that their papers meet the word count requirement. If you are accustomed to inflating your paper word count, be very careful when it comes to questions about concision. These questions require you to determine what phrasing expresses the author's meaning in the most concise way possible while preserving descriptive ideas. This concept is among the most commonly tested on the PSAT Writing and Language section.

TACTIC

8

Shorter is not necessarily sweeter—consider which choice expresses all the intended meaning while not being repetitive.

SAMPLE QUESTION

He has been the preeminent expert on the subject for ⓰ the duration of the past twenty years.

16. (A) NO CHANGE
    (B) the past.
    (C) the past two decades.
    (D) for the time that has passed in the previous two decades.

The original wording is unnecessarily repetitive—readers will understand that "years" are units that have duration. Choice B removes the descriptive language about the length of time that has passed. Choice D is far too wordy. Choice C correctly preserves the meaning about the twenty years that have passed, but it does so using far fewer words than Choices A and D.

CONCISION DRILL

Cross out any part of the sentence that is needlessly repetitive or irrelevant, but leave in descriptive wording.

1. Blue Dog Democrats—Democrats who side with Republicans on some issues—have become more rare in the increasingly polarized political climate.

2. My boss received my e-mail that I wrote to her late last night.

3. Trucks that drive on the roadway cause more wear on roads than do cars.

4. The winner of the 2014 Miss America Pageant was excited to use her newfound fame to advocate for underrepresented groups.

5. Choose the book you most want to read from the teacher's list—make sure you make a decision that aligns with what the teacher has selected.

Answers

1. Fine as is.
2. My boss received my e-mail ~~that I wrote to her~~ late last night.
3. Trucks ~~that drive on the roadways~~ cause more wear on roads than do cars.
4. Fine as is.
5. Choose the book you most want to read from the teacher's list. ~~make sure you make a decision that aligns with what the teacher has selected.~~

Style and Tone Questions

There is nothing inherently wrong with more formal or informal language. As long as a writer has a consistent "voice," it is perfectly fine. Suppose you are hanging out with your friends. Which statement would be more appropriate?

> **"My, it was most serendipitous that my colleague shared the magnificent portraiture that was bequeathed to him by his associate."**

> **"It was cool that my friend shared the picture his buddy took."**

Obviously, the second choice would be preferable. Your job on questions about style and tone is to determine what choice expresses a given idea in a way that "fits" with the voice of the passage.

TACTIC

9 **Look at enough context to determine how the writer is expressing him- or herself.**

Do not assume that a writer will avoid using "you" or has to use technical language. Analyze enough of the passage so you can make a good judgment.

SAMPLE QUESTION

> When you enter the theme park, you will be too excited to think clearly, so be sure to have a plan ahead of time. First, know which rides you want to ride the most. Second, be aware of the height requirements. Finally, determine a meeting place for your party.

12. Which option most closely matches the stylistic pattern used in the paragraph?

(A) NO CHANGE
(B) it would be great to know of a meeting place for you and your party beforehand.
(C) a place to meet with your party should be known.
(D) a meeting place for you and your party it is vital to determine.

If we look at the two sentences that precede the question, the stylistic pattern becomes clear: the author is giving a series of general recommendations. Choice A is the only option that follows the structure of the previous two sentences. The other options use convoluted wording that does not match the voice of what comes before.

STYLE AND TONE DRILL

Choose which of the two words or phrases is more stylistically appropriate, given the context of the sentence.

1. The Chief of Staff to the President strongly agreed with the President's (spin or stance).

2. It is incumbent upon the newly elected club officers to (build rapport with or be comfy with) their fellow club members.

3. The lethal parasitic infection was (invading or flocking to) the countryside.

4. Whenever you're feeling blue, be sure to (chronicle your contentment or count your blessings).

5. Upon hearing the tragic news of the building collapse, the building owner felt (despondent or unenthusiastic).

Answers

1. stance
2. build rapport with
3. invading
4. count your blessings
5. despondent

Combining Sentences Questions

The PSAT will assess your understanding of syntax by asking you sentence combination questions. You will need to pick the option that best joins two sentences in a way that improves the flow and organization of the words.

TACTIC 10 Join the sentences in the clearest way that preserves the original meaning.

SAMPLE QUESTION

32 Surprisingly, the man had a difficult time in making a decision. He had to make a choice between accepting a harsh sentence and a much milder one.

32. Which option most effectively joins the underlined sentences?

(A) Surprisingly, the man had a difficult time in making a decision between the options of first, a harsh sentence, and second, a much milder one.

(B) Surprisingly, a difficult time was had by the man between the acceptance of a harsh sentence and a much milder one.

(C) Surprisingly, the man had a difficult time deciding between accepting a harsh sentence and a much milder one.

(D) A choice between a much milder sentence and a harsh one presented difficulty for the man when he had to make a decision on the matter.

Option C is correct because it preserves the original meaning of the two separate sentences, while joining them in a way that is concise and consistent. Choices A and D are unnecessarily wordy, and Choice B uses the passive voice.

SENTENCE COMBINATION DRILL

Write a combined version of the following pairs of sentences or phrases. There are a variety of ways this can be done—sample answers follow.

1. My dog was interested in going for a walk. However, he was more interested in having his dinner.

2. It is critical that we spend frugally. It is also vitally important that we save for a rainy day.

3. My telescope needs batteries. Due to this fact, I am unable to use it.

4. While he should not be considered a good friend. In fact, he is one of my greatest enemies.

5. During those moments of time when you take out the trash, here is another thing you should do. Be sure to also take out the recycling.

Sample Answers

1. While my dog was interested in going for a walk, he was more interested in having his dinner.
2. It is critical that we both spend frugally and save for a rainy day.
3. Since my telescope needs batteries, I am unable to use it.
4. Far from being a good friend, he is one of my greatest enemies.
5. Whenever you take out the trash, also take out the recycling.

Test anxiety has become an increasingly **❶** prevalent and widespread problem among standardized test-takers. **❷** While some measure of anxiety is to be expected. For it is in fact welcome in order to sharpen one's focus, so many students today find that their anxiety hinders their ability to perform on high-stakes tests. What are some things that can be done to alleviate test anxiety?

1. (A) NO CHANGE
   (B) prevalent
   (C) spread from near to far
   (D) wide-ranging and quite impactful

2. How could the two sentences most effectively be combined?

   (A) While some measure of anxiety is to be expected, for the reason that it is in fact welcome in order to sharpen one's focus because many students today find that their anxiety hinders their ability to perform on high-stakes tests.

   (B) While some measure of anxiety is to be expected and is in fact welcome in order to sharpen one's focus; many students today find that their anxiety hinders their ability to perform on high-stakes tests.

   (C) While some measure of anxiety is to be expected and is, in fact, welcome in order to sharpen one's focus, many students today find that their anxiety hinders their ability to perform on high-stakes tests.

   (D) While some measure of anxiety is to be expected because it is in fact welcome in order to sharpen one's focus, the fact remains that many students today find that their anxiety hinders their ability to perform on high-stakes tests.

First, students should strive to have realistic expectations. It is becoming more and more competitive to earn admission to highly selective schools. ❸ Online applications and common essay prompts make it as easy to apply to ten schools as it once was to apply to only one. With the increased competition, students should set themselves up for success by striving to go to the school that is the best fit for them, ❹ rather than just chasing the most highly ranked school.

3. Which of the following statements, if inserted here, would provide the most specific and relevant support for the statement made in the previous sentence?

(A) College admission is a process that is carried out by teams of admissions representatives to ensure a thorough and reasonably objective process.

(B) In your application, be sure to state your grade point average, SAT and ACT test scores, and major extracurricular leadership positions.

(C) For example, at the University of Pennsylvania, an Ivy League institution, the admissions rate in 1991 was 47 percent—in 2015, it was less than 10 percent.

(D) Average salaries for those graduating in math and science programs can often be 30 percent higher than the salaries of those graduating from humanities programs.

4. Which statement provides the most precise and relevant contrast with what comes before in the sentence?

(A) NO CHANGE
(B) and doing what feels right.
(C) and struggling to achieve their childhood dreams of college acceptance.
(D) while bearing in mind the financial consequences of academic missteps.

Second, students can think through worst-case scenarios **5** to help calm their nerves and relieve internal tension. If the very worst outcome that could happen is not actually that bad, students' fears about mediocre test performance will decrease greatly. Suppose a major test doesn't go well. In all likelihood, there are many other times one can take the test to demonstrate one's knowledge and skills. Even with the all-important PSAT, which determines National Merit Scholarship eligibility, there are many more opportunities to take the SAT or ACT **6** , which play a major role in determining academic scholarships.

The bottom line is that if someone wants anything too badly, he or she will be **7** lesser in likelihood to obtain it. It is the same idea as when an overeager salesperson keeps pestering a customer in an attempt to make a deal—such desperation will turn him off, making him less likely to make a purchase. **8** To do the best on major tests, students should set reasonable expectations and think about worst case scenarios so that their minds are focused, not panicked.

5. (A) NO CHANGE
   (B) to calm their nerves.
   (C) to break free from the tension and anxiety that plagues them.
   (D) to achieve an internal equilibrium of peacefulness.

6. The author is considering deleting the underlined portion. Should it be kept or deleted?

   (A) Kept, because it provides a helpful elaboration.
   (B) Kept, because it details what the tests assess.
   (C) Deleted, because it contradicts information presented elsewhere in the paragraph.
   (D) Deleted, because it is irrelevant to the focus of the sentence.

7. (A) NO CHANGE
   (B) far, far less likely
   (C) for better or worse less expectedly
   (D) less likely

8. The author is considering inserting the following sentence at this point in the essay:

   "It is also similar to when somebody acts desperate in interpersonal relationships—no one wants to hang out with someone who is too intent on doing so."

   Should he do so?

   (A) Yes, because it continues the metaphorical discussion from the previous sentence.
   (B) Yes, because it introduces a new way of framing a topic critical to the argument of the essay.
   (C) No, because it repeats an idea already expressed in the previous sentence.
   (D) No, because it shifts the essay's focus away from the business practices of sales professionals.

Answers

1. **(B)** "Prevalent" is synonymous with "widespread," so it is repetitive to have both of these words. Choice B preserves the original meaning without adding extra words. Choices A and D are repetitive, and Choice C uses excessive and awkward reading to make the same point as Choice B.

2. **(C)** Choice C preserves the original meaning of the underlined sentences while joining them into a single complete sentence. Choice A has convoluted word order in the phrase "for the reason that it is in fact welcome," Choice B does not have a complete sentence before the semicolon, and Choice D is unnecessarily wordy.

3. **(C)** The statement in the previous sentence is that it is becoming increasingly difficult to earn admission to highly selective schools. Choice C provides the most specific support for this claim, since it gives relevant statistics that demonstrate just how much the selectivity of an elite school has increased over the years. Choice A is vague, and Choices B and D provide specific information that does not relate to the previous sentence.

4. **(A)** The first part of the sentence encourages students to pick a school based on what is the best fit for them. Based on the context of the passage, Choice A provides the most logical contrast because many students might instead focus unnecessarily on school rankings. Choice B is too vague, and Choices C and D do not provide a clear contrast.

5. **(B)** Choice B preserves the original meaning while deleting repetitive wording. Choices A, C, and D are all wordy and repetitive.

6. **(A)** Without the underlined portion, it would not be entirely clear as to why the statement about taking the SAT or ACT would be relevant. Having this portion clarifies their connectedness to scholarship opportunities. Thus, it provides a helpful elaboration. It is not Choice B because it mentions the tests very broadly and does not go into detail about what they assess. It is not Choice C or D because these advocate removing the selection.

7. **(D)** "Less likely" expresses the intended meaning without adding in unnecessary words. Choice A uses an awkward construction, and Choices B and C are clearly repetitive.

8. **(C)** The sentence that comes before this already makes this point using an analogy about a salesperson whose eagerness makes him seem desperate. It is not Choice D because the focus of the essay is not on the business practices of sales professionals. It is not Choice A or B because they advocate keeping a repetitive sentence.

SENTENCE STRUCTURE

Sentence Fragments and Run-On Questions

A **sentence** *expresses a complete thought with both a subject and predicate (i.e., a subject and a verb).* A subject will be a noun—a person, place, or thing. The predicate will have a verb—a word that expresses an *action*, such as "is," "were," "ate," "choose," or "eat." Here are some examples of complete sentences:

> What is this?
> He won the match.
> There is great trouble brewing in the town.

A **sentence fragment** *expresses an incomplete thought with only a subject or a predicate.* Here are some examples of sentence fragments:

> From my place.
> Homework for tomorrow's big test.
> Your neighbor's house, which is next to the spooky mansion on the hill.

A **run-on sentence** *consists of two or more complete sentences that are not joined together with appropriate punctuation or transitions.* Here are some examples of run-on sentences.

> Finish your meal it is really good for you to do so.
> I was excited to see the new show I stayed up really late to see it.
> The moon will be full tonight, let's stay up and enjoy its beauty.

TACTIC **11** **Evaluate whether a sentence is complete by determining if it has a subject and a verb—don't make assumptions based simply on the length of the sentence.**

A sentence can be complete while being quite short. For example, "I am" is a complete sentence. A selection can be a fragment even though it is rather long. For example, "For the benefit of the United States of America, today, tomorrow, and in the years to come" is a fragment. Consider each sentence on a case-by-case basis to make a determination.

SAMPLE QUESTION

We will need to get to the bottom of this news **8** story. Whether he is a winner in the hotly contested election.	8. (A) NO CHANGE (B) story. If (C) story. Whether or not (D) story as to whether

Choices A, B, and C all have a sentence fragment after the period. Choice D is the only option that joins the wording together in a way that provides one complete sentence.

SENTENCE STRUCTURE DRILL

Determine if the sentence is complete, a run-on, or a fragment.

1. To whom this letter may concern.

2. She wept.

3. I am looking forward to the movie I plan on standing in line for a couple of hours.

4. Whenever they leave the doors unlocked of their brand new automobile.

5. My best friend, whom I have known since childhood, will be visiting from out of town this upcoming weekend.

Answers

1. Fragment
2. Complete
3. Run-on
4. Fragment
5. Complete

Subordination and Coordination Questions

Coordinating conjunctions include words like "for," "and," and "but" to make compound sentences. Subordinating conjunctions include words like "if," "unless," and "whereas" to create sentence variety by making sentences more complex. For example, here is a sentence that does have an appropriate conjunction, "whereas," to illustrate a logical connection:

That politician is known for telling the truth, whereas his rival is known for deceit.

 TACTIC
12
When it comes to conjunctions, be careful that the word provides both a logical connection and a complete sentence.

SAMPLE QUESTION

I forgot to take my backpack **19** home, and I didn't have the materials I needed for my homework.	19. (A) NO CHANGE (B) home, also (C) home, so (D) home,

The part of the sentence before the comma and the part after the comma show a cause-and-effect relationship—it was because of not taking the backpack home that the narrator did not have the materials she needed. Choice C is the only option that uses a cause-and-effect conjunction, "so." Choices A and B use improper conjunctions, and Choice D results in a run-on sentence.

SUBORDINATION AND COORDINATION DRILL

Make changes, if needed, to correct any subordination/coordination issues in the sentences. There are multiple ways these sentences can be fixed.

1. Whenever I go out with my friends, I am certain to tell my parents where I will be.

2. I love running distance races, and I am excited about my upcoming marathon.

3. It is either going to be sunny and be bad weather tomorrow.

4. No matter the outcome, and play your very best and you should be satisfied.

5. I am extremely disappointed in your lack of truthfulness; and I am willing to give you a second chance.

Answers with Possible Corrections

1. Fine as is.
2. I love running distance races, **so** I am excited about my upcoming marathon.
3. It is either going to be sunny **or** be bad weather tomorrow.
4. No matter the outcome, ~~and~~ play your very best and you should be satisfied.
5. I am extremely disappointed in your lack of truthfulness; **however,** I am willing to give you a second chance.

Parallelism Questions

It is not just what you say, it is how you say it. To make one's writing flow as well as possible, having parallel structure is key. For an example of excellent parallelism, consider the Oath of Office for the President of the United States:

> "I do solemnly swear that I will faithfully execute the office of President of the United States, and will to the best of my ability, preserve, protect, and defend the Constitution of the United States."

Imagine if instead the oath read like this:

> I do solemnly swear that I will execute with faith the office of President of the United States, and to the best of my ability will preserving, to protect, and defense of the Constitution for United States.

If you had to momentarily pause while reading the second version, you intuitively recognized the lack of parallel structure.

TACTIC 13 — Consider the context around the underlined portion, and be certain that your choice is consistent with the phrasing surrounding it.

SAMPLE QUESTION

> Be sure to get a good night's sleep, ㊸ take your number 2 pencils, and arrive at the test site early.
>
> 41. (A) NO CHANGE
>   (B) taking your number 2 pencils
>   (C) your number 2 pencils take with you
>   (D) to take your number 2 pencils

The style of the phrasing in the other parts of the sentence is "Be sure . . . ," and "arrive . . . ," giving the reader direct advice. Choice A is the only option consistent with this style. The other options all use phrasing that does not match the other parts of the sentence.

PARALLEL STRUCTURE DRILL

Make corrections, if needed, to give the sentences parallel structure. There are multiple ways to fix these sentences.

1. Some of the best forms of exercise are running, swimming, and to go on a bike.

2. It is not whether you win or losing; it's how you play the game.

3. Her character garners the respect of colleagues and reporters alike.

4. Hard work and to persevere go hand in hand.

5. Lacking endorsements, donations, and media coverage, the candidate had little hope of winning.

Answers with Possible Corrections

1. Some of the best forms of exercise are running, swimming, and **biking.**
2. It is not whether you win or **lose**; it's how you play the game.
3. Fine as is.
4. Hard work and **perseverance** go hand in hand.
5. Fine as is.

Modifier Placement Questions

Consider these two improper sentences:

The fish loved its new aquarium, swimming quickly.

While reading the brand new book, many people were annoying.

These two sentences have confusing meaning. The first sentence literally expressed that the aquarium is swimming quickly. In the second sentence, it is unclear who is reading the new book. These sentences can be fixed by making sure the modifying words, like adjectives, and the words they modify, like nouns, are clearly stated and in a proper sequence. Here are proper versions of the two sentences:

The fish, swimming quickly, loved its new aquarium.

While I was reading the brand new book, many people annoyed me.

When it comes to modifier clarity and placement, remember this tip:

TACTIC

14 **Make sure that the *literal* meaning and the *intended* meaning are the same.**

SAMPLE QUESTION

My teacher asked me a question, but ❸❷ <u>too tired was I for giving</u> a prompt response.	32. (A) NO CHANGE (B) giving was too tired for me (C) I was giving too tired (D) I was too tired to give

To clearly express what is doing the action, "I" should follow the "but." Choices A and B have convoluted word order. Choice C has the correct placement of "I," but jumbles the wording later in the selection. Choice D has clarity of wording and a logical sequence throughout.

MODIFIER PLACEMENT DRILL

Make corrections, if needed, to give the sentences proper modifier placement and word order. There are multiple ways to fix these sentences.

1. While reading the book, forgot to leave a bookmark I did.

2. My car was unavailable for the road trip, which was in the repair shop.

3. The player's last game was rather abysmal, not practice very well leading up to it.

4. Route 1 was a beautiful stretch of freeway on our way to vacation, a six-lane superhighway.

5. Read all the way to the end of the book, and confusion will be replaced with clarity.

Answers with Possible Corrections

1. While reading the book, **I forgot to leave a bookmark.**
2. My car, **which was in the repair shop,** was unavailable for the road trip.
3. The player's last game was rather abysmal **since he did** not practice very well leading up to it.
4. Route 1, **a six-lane superhighway,** was a beautiful stretch of freeway on our way to vacation.
5. Fine as is. The sentence implies that the reader is being directly addressed.

Verb Use Questions

The PSAT requires you to be comfortable with the essentials of verb conjugation. Most students become familiar with the terminology for proper verb conjugation when they take a foreign language in high school—here is an overview of the key verb conjugation information that you may already know intuitively.

The following table is a summary of some of the basic conjugation patterns of verbs.

Past	Present	Future
He ate They were She ran We walked	He eats They are She runs We walk	He will eat They will She will run We will walk
Past Perfect	**Present Perfect**	**Future Perfect**
I had eaten They had been She had run We had walked	I have eaten They have been She has run We have walked	I will have eaten They will have been She will have run They will have walked

Although many verbs follow a simple pattern, quite a few verbs have irregular conjugations, particularly for the past and past perfect forms. These irregular verbs are often called "strong" verbs since they form a past tense without the aid of the "ed" ending as with "weak" verbs. Here is a sampling of some irregular verbs you might encounter.

Present Tense (*I am.*)	Past Tense (*I was.*)	Past Participle (What comes after "have" in the Present Perfect— "*I have been.*")
Become	Became	Become
Begin	Began	Begun
Bring	Brought	Brought
Choose	Chose	Chosen
Do	Did	Done
Draw	Drew	Drawn
Drink	Drank	Drunk
Drive	Drove	Driven
Fly	Flew	Flown
Get	Got	Gotten
Go	Went	Gone
Grow	Grew	Grown
Have	Had	Had
Hear	Heard	Heard
Know	Knew	Known
Lay (i.e., place)	Laid	Laid
Lead	Led	Led
Lie (i.e., recline)	Lay	Lain
Light	Lit	Lit

Present Tense (*I am.*)	Past Tense (*I was.*)	Past Participle (What comes after "have" in the Present Perfect— "*I have been.*")
Ride	Rode	Ridden
Ring	Rang	Rung
Rise	Rose	Risen
Run	Ran	Run
See	Saw	Seen
Shine	Shone	Shone
Show	Showed	Shown
Sing	Sang	Sung
Sink	Sank	Sunk
Swim	Swam	Swum
Swing	Swung	Swung
Take	Took	Taken
Wake	Woke	Woken
Wear	Wore	Worn

TACTIC

 15 **Look at the context surrounding the verb to see what verb tense, mood, or voice is appropriate.**

SAMPLE QUESTION

Three years ago on our trip to India, we visited Humayan's Tomb and **24** see the Siddhivinayak Temple.	24. (A) NO CHANGE (B) saw (C) seeing (D) shall see

The sentence refers to events that took place three years ago, making the entire sentence in the past tense. Choice B is the only option in the past tense. Choice A is in the present tense, Choice C uses the gerund form of the verb, and Choice D uses the future tense.

VERB USE DRILL

Make corrections, if needed, to give the sentences proper verb use. There are multiple ways to fix these sentences.

1. A decade ago, I decide to focus more intently on my studies.

2. The customer service message needs to be answered by you.

3. If you was able to find a job, you would not have the financial worries you currently did.

4. In 1992, Caitlin won the prize, but only after she practice for many months.

5. My teacher demands that I am quiet during the test.

Answers with Possible Corrections

1. A decade ago I **decided** to focus more intently on my studies. *Put it in the past tense since it was a decade ago.*

2. **You need to answer** the customer service message. *Avoid the passive voice—use the active voice instead.*

3. If you **were** able to find a job, you would not have the financial worries you currently **do**. *Use the subjunctive mood to express something contrary to fact, and use the present tense since the sentence says "currently."*

4. In 1992, Caitlin won the prize, but only after she **had practiced** for many months. *Use the past perfect tense to indicate that the practice was ongoing for a period in the past.*

5. My teacher demands that I **be** quiet during the test. *Since this is a demand, use "be" rather than "is."*

Pronoun Number Questions

Matching pronouns with the nouns they represent is easy when the words are close to each other. For example,

<u>Darnell</u> ate <u>her</u> entire lunch.

It becomes more challenging to match pronouns when the pronouns and the nouns are more separated. For example,

The <u>man</u> who left the calculator on top of the board games cabinet needs to pick up <u>his</u> property.

TACTIC

16 Match singular pronouns with singular nouns and plural pronouns with plural nouns.

Even though the pronouns and nouns may be separated from one another, be sure they are numerically consistent. These types of questions take a bit more focus because simply "mouthing them out" won't necessarily alert you to a grammatical problem; the separation between the pronouns and nouns makes the sentences sound pretty good as they are.

SAMPLE QUESTION

If only each respondent to the survey would have given ❸ <u>their</u> full name.	3. (A) NO CHANGE (B) they're (C) his or her (D) its

The full name is to be given by "each respondent," which is a singular person. Also, we do not know the gender of the respondents, so it is proper to refer to them individually as "his or her," making Choice C correct. Choice A uses the plural "their," Choice B means "they are," and Choice D would not be used when referring to people.

PRONOUN NUMBER DRILL

Make corrections, if needed, to give the sentences proper pronoun number. There are multiple ways to fix these sentences.

1. No matter your feelings on the vote, be sure that you are true to oneself.

2. Whenever I see someone struggling with math, I can't help but wonder if they missed some of the fundamentals earlier in school.

3. A sperm whale will probably have scars from deep-sea battles with giant squids all over their skin.

4. Members of the orchestra have to submit practice records before you are allowed to attend rehearsal.

5. A skilled surgeon will likely be quite proud of his rigorous training.

Answers with Possible Corrections

1. No matter your feelings on the vote, be sure that you are true to **yourself**. *Keep it consistent with "your" throughout.*

2. Whenever I see someone struggling with math, I can't help but wonder if **he or she** missed some of the fundamentals earlier in school. *This is referring to a singular person given the use of "someone."*

3. A sperm whale will probably have scars from deep-sea battles with giant squids all over **its** skin. *This refers to "a" sperm whale, so use the singular.*

4. Members of the orchestra have to submit practice records before **they** are allowed to attend rehearsal. *"They" will be consistent with "members of the orchestra."*

5. A skilled surgeon will likely be quite proud of **his or her** rigorous training. *It is unclear if this is a male or female, since it refers to skilled surgeons in general, so use "his or her."*

SENTENCE STRUCTURE PRACTICE

❶ The increased use of smartphones and Internet technology profoundly interaction with our friends and family. Class reunions and opening holiday

1. (A) NO CHANGE
   (B) The increased use of smartphones and Internet technology have profoundly influenced how we interact with our friends and family.
   (C) The increased using of smartphones and Internet technology had profoundly affected how we will interact with our friends and family.
   (D) The increased use of smartphones and Internet technology has profoundly affected how we interact with our friends and family.

greeting cards ❷ was once highly anticipated events that would offer updates on the goings-on of distant acquaintances. Now, a quick scan of a social media feed gives a real-time update. On the other hand, look at any group of people out for dinner or just hanging out, and you will inevitably find many of the group members buried in their phones, ❸ immersed in their own stimulation instead of meaningful interactions to be had with the people right in front of them. Is it possible to have both the blessings of instantaneous communication and the minimization of the effects of distraction and ❹ dehumanization?

It is possible to do so if we put ourselves on an "information diet." Instead of having your phone set to notify you every time there is a message or a new post, give ❺ oneself a reasonable schedule for updates. If you are working on a major project with other people, ❻ and you should probably check your phone more frequently. If you are on vacation, take advantage of "away" messages and ❼ as your gatekeeper let the computer serve, informing people that you will be available to respond upon your return. If you can take control of technology rather than letting it control you, you ❽ will be empowered to have the benefits of new technology while minimizing its pitfalls.

2. (A) NO CHANGE
   (B) has been the
   (C) were once
   (D) is now

3. (A) NO CHANGE
   (B) immersed in stimulation of their own instead of with the people right in front of them having meaningful interactions.
   (C) immersed in their own stimulation instead of having meaningful interactions with the people right in front of them.
   (D) immersed with the people right in front of them with meaningful interactions instead in their own stimulation.

4. (A) NO CHANGE
   (B) dehumanizing
   (C) to dehumanize
   (D) for the dehumanizing

5. (A) NO CHANGE
   (B) yourself
   (C) themselves
   (D) us

6. (A) NO CHANGE
   (B) but
   (C) because
   (D) DELETE the underlined portion.

7. (A) NO CHANGE
   (B) the computer you should let as your gatekeeper serve,
   (C) let the computer serve as your gatekeeper,
   (D) the computer should be served by you as the gatekeeper,

8. (A) NO CHANGE
   (B) shall
   (C) had been
   (D) have

Answers

1. **(D)** Choice D uses parallel structure and proper tense to make a clear, flowing sentence. It is not Choice A because it is a sentence fragment. It is not Choice B because it uses the plural "have" instead of "has" to match up with the singular "use." It is not Choice C because it improperly uses "using" instead of "use."

2. **(C)** Choice C uses a plural and past tense verb, "were," which is consistent with the fact that this refers to a past state of affairs, and that there is a compound subject of "reunions" and "cards." All of the other choices use singular verb forms.

3. **(C)** Choice C puts the words in the most logical and flowing order and leaves no words unclear. Choice A does not have a parallel structure, Choice B has jumbled word order with the phrase "instead of with the people right in front of them having," and Choice D changes the intended meaning.

4. **(A)** Choice A is the only option to use wording that parallels the "communication" and "distraction" that come before in the sentence. Choices B, C, and D all convey the same idea, but they do not do so in a way consistent with the rest of the sentence.

5. **(B)** The author is directly addressing the reader using the informal second person in this sentence, earlier stating "your phone" and "notify you." To be consistent with this wording, "yourself" is correct. The other options are inconsistent with the use of "you" elsewhere in the sentence.

6. **(D)** The "If" at the beginning of the sentence already serves to create an implied transition. Because of this, no transitional word is needed at this point.

7. **(C)** Choice C maintains the parallel structure established earlier in the sentence in which the narrator directly addresses the reader stating that he or she should "take advantage." The other options all lack this parallel structure.

8. **(A)** Choice A is the only option that properly uses the future tense. Choice B could work if it said "shall be," and Choices C and D both would be used to refer to past actions.

CONVENTIONS OF USAGE

Pronoun Clarity Questions

Pronouns can improve the flow of one's writing. Consider this sentence:

Bill went to Bill's house before Bill decided what Bill was going to have for Bill's dinner.

It would be far preferable to rewrite the sentence like this:

Bill went to his house before deciding what he was going to have for dinner.

The second version is far less choppy because it doesn't continually reintroduce the subject. If what a pronoun refers to is unclear, clarification is needed. For example:

Mark and Jason could not wait to see his new car.

There are two men mentioned—Mark and Jason—but we do not know whose car they cannot wait to see. If a PSAT question clarifies a vague pronoun with a noun, *do not worry about whether the replacement is true*—focus only on if the substitution is grammatically correct.

17 Pronouns are fine to use, as long as what they stand for is 100 percent clear.

If what the pronoun stands for is not 100 percent clear, choose an option that provides a clarification.

SAMPLE QUESTION

When I go to Susan and Marsha's hometown, I love to visit with **14** <u>her</u> family.	14. (A) NO CHANGE
	    (B) this
	    (C) Susan's
	    (D) they're

Susan and Marsha both live in the same town, but the narrator has not made clear which of the two families she wishes to visit. Choice C is the only option that clarifies which family the narrator will see. Choice A could refer to either Susan or Marsha. Choice B is also vague. Choice D means "they are" and is not a possessive pronoun.

PRONOUN CLARITY DRILL

Make corrections, if needed, to clarify vague pronouns. There are multiple ways to fix these sentences.

1. At the business, they do a nice job of making customers happy.

2. Whenever Kristen decides to take on a project, she always manages to do an excellent job.

3. Eloise laughed with her mother as she told the funny story.

4. Soon after the school contracted with the company, they were disappointed.

5. My brother enjoyed reading the book by the famous author that opened his mind to the new possibilities of space travel.

Answers with Possible Corrections

When a pronoun is vague, there are many possible ways it can be clarified. On the PSAT, as long as the substitution for a vague pronoun is grammatically appropriate, it is a valid choice.

1. At the business, **the sales associates** do a nice job of making customers happy.
2. Fine as is.
3. Eloise laughed with her mother as **Eloise** told the funny story.
4. Soon after the school contracted with the company, **the school officials** were disappointed.
5. My brother enjoyed reading the book by the famous author—**it opened my brother's** mind to the new possibilities of space travel.

Possession Questions

The PSAT will assess your understanding of possessive pronouns. Here is a table that summarizes what you need to know.

There vs. Their vs. They're	*there*: place *their*: possession *they're*: "they are"	They're excited to implement their new ideas when they travel over there.
Its vs. It's	*its*: possession *it's*: "it is" (*its'* is always incorrect)	It's a great day to take the car to be washed and vacuum all of its carpeting.
Your vs. You're	*your*: possession *you're*: "you are"	Your best friend tells you when you're not acting like yourself.
Whose vs. Who's	*whose*: possession *who's*: "who is"	Who's about to decide whose project wins the grand prize?

TACTIC

18

Pronouns that show possession do NOT have apostrophes, unlike most nouns.

Pronouns that use apostrophes are the contraction forms, like "they're" and "you're." Pronouns are different from most other words in that they show possession without apostrophes.

SAMPLE QUESTION

> When you try to turn on your computer, be sure that ❸ it's plugged into the wall outlet.

38. (A) NO CHANGE
    (B) its
    (C) its'
    (D) it is going to be

In the above sentence, the required meaning of the underlined portion is "it is," making Choice A correct. Choice B is used to show possession, Choice C is never correct, and Choice D is too wordy.

POSSESSION DRILL

Make corrections, if needed, to clarify possession. There are multiple ways to fix these sentences.

1. The chair was nonfunctional—its' legs no longer worked.

2. You're patience is appreciated as you wait for the next customer service representative.

3. I am confident that they're going to be on time.

4. Whose calculator needs new batteries?

5. While it's a nice day, please be sure to wash your car—it's windows are filthy.

Answers with Possible Corrections

1. The chair was nonfunctional—**its** legs no longer worked.
2. **Your** patience is appreciated as you wait for the next customer service representative.
3. Fine as is.
4. Fine as is.
5. While it's a nice day, please be sure to wash your car—**its** windows are filthy.

Subject-Verb Agreement Questions

Subject-verb agreement would be easy to determine if all sentences had the subject and verb close to one another. For example,

 Birds fly in the air.

When the subject and verb are separated from each other, creating agreement can be more challenging. For example,

 The movie about the terrifying monsters and evil ghosts were most frightening.

The subject "movie" and the verb "were" do not match numerically. Here is the corrected version:

 The movie about the terrifying monsters and evil ghosts <u>was</u> most frightening.

When you encounter subject-verb agreement questions remember this tip.

TACTIC 19 **Cut out the words between the subject and verb to see if the subject and verb are both singular or both plural.**

SAMPLE QUESTION

The general who led legions of soldiers ㉕ <u>were</u> triumphant in the battle.	25. (A) NO CHANGE (B) are (C) was (D) have been

The subject in the sentence is "general," which is singular. Choice C is the only option that has a singular verb. Choices A, B, and D are all plural, and thus incorrect. It would be easy to be confused about the subject and think that it was the plural "legions" or "soldiers."

NUMBER AGREEMENT DRILL

Make corrections, if needed, to a lack of number agreement. There are multiple ways to fix these sentences.

1. The company of actors do a wonderful production.

2. My teacher or his teaching assistant is in charge of grading the assignment.

3. Gender roles over the past century has evolved significantly.

4. My favorite summer diversion, reading and swimming, are quite enjoyable.

5. Each person on the train were glad to arrive at the destination.

Answers with Possible Corrections

1. The company of actors **does** a wonderful production.
2. Fine as is.
3. Gender roles over the past century **have** evolved significantly.
4. My favorite summer **diversions**, reading and swimming, are quite enjoyable.
5. Each person on the train **was** glad to arrive at the destination.

Frequently Confused Words Questions

There are many words in the English language that sound similar, yet have different meanings. Take a look at this table and memorize any rules about these commonly confused words that you do not already know.

Confused Words	General Rules	Examples of Proper Use
Accept vs. Except	*accept*: receive *except*: excluding	The college is eager to accept his application, except for the fact that he did not pay the application fee.
Affect vs. Effect	*affect*: typically a verb *effect*: typically a noun	The effect of the speaker's inspirational message on me was profound: it affected how I conducted myself in the years that followed.
Allude vs. Elude	*allude:* indirectly refer to *elude*: escape from	The newspaper report alluded to some interesting information: the criminal continued to elude the police.

Confused Words	General Rules	Examples of Proper Use
Amount vs. Number	*amount*: usually not countable *number*: usually countable	A <u>number</u> of my classmates told my teacher that the <u>amount</u> of homework was excessive.
Beside vs. Besides	*beside:* next to *besides:* in addition to	<u>Besides</u> being a beautiful building in and of itself, the skyscraper is made even more appealing since it stands <u>beside</u> another gorgeous building.
Between vs. Among	*between*: comparing one thing at a time, typically just two objects *among*: comparing non-distinct items, or three or more objects	<u>Among</u> all the people who applied for the prestigious scholarship, it came down to a choice <u>between</u> two incredible candidates.
Choose vs. Chose	*choose*: present tense *chose*: past tense	You do not have to <u>choose</u> the same thing off the menu as what you <u>chose</u> the last time you ate here.
Complement vs. Compliment	*complement*: complete something *compliment*: flattery	My friend <u>complimented</u> my fashion sense, noting how my choice of shoes <u>complemented</u> my outfit.
Elicit vs. Illicit	*elicit*: evoke or obtain *illicit*: illegal	It is difficult to <u>elicit</u> cooperation from those who engage in <u>illicit</u> activities.
Have vs. Of	*have*: verb (action word) *of*: preposition (connecting word)	I would <u>have</u> edited the paper. (Do not say "would of.")
I vs. Me	*I:* subject *me*: object	<u>I</u> love it when you give <u>me</u> a ride to school.
Less/much vs. Fewer/many	*less/much*: usually not countable *fewer/many*: usually countable	<u>Many</u> people believe that the candidate ahead in the polls is actually <u>less</u> qualified than his closest rival.
Lie vs. Lay	*lie*: recline *lay*: place	<u>Lay</u> your pillow on the mattress before you <u>lie</u> down to take a nap.
Lose vs. Loose	*lose*: suffer a loss *loose*: not tight-fitting	The jacket is so <u>loose</u> that I am afraid I may <u>lose</u> it in the wind.
Principal vs. Principle	*principal*: high-ranking person, or primary *principle*: rule or belief	The high school <u>principal</u> is known for her outstanding academic and disciplinary <u>principles</u>.

Confused Words	General Rules	Examples of Proper Use
Than vs. Then	*than*: for comparisons *then*: for time	It is a better time to find a job now <u>than</u> it was back <u>then</u> when I didn't have a high school diploma.
To vs. Too vs. Two	*to*: connecting preposition *two*: number *too*: comparisons	<u>Too</u> often students narrow their options <u>to</u> just <u>two</u> college choices, ignoring many schools that would potentially be excellent fits.
Which vs. That	*which*: nonrestrictive (extra information) *that*: restrictive (essential information)	The car <u>that</u> was driving quickly nearly ran over a pedestrian, <u>which</u> gave me major cause for concern.
Who vs. Whom	*who*: subject *whom*: object (Use "who" when you would use "he," and use "whom" when you would use "him.")	<u>Who</u> is going to finish the pizza? To <u>whom</u> will we give the leftover if no one eats the rest of it?

 TACTIC **20**

Practice the commonly confused words you don't know by making an effort to use them in your conversation and writing.

If you only have a rough feel for the proper use of the words in the table above, you will want to practice using them until you know them extremely well. The PSAT will present you with very tempting incorrect answers, so it is important to be very comfortable with proper word usage.

SAMPLE QUESTION

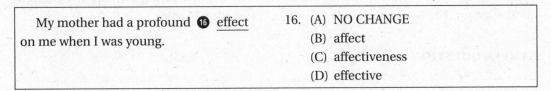

My mother had a profound **16** <u>effect</u> on me when I was young.

16. (A) NO CHANGE
　　(B) affect
　　(C) affectiveness
　　(D) effective

In this case, a noun is required for the underlined portion, since there is the adjective "profound" modifying it. Choice B is typically used as a verb; Choice C means "emotional character," which does not fit the context; and Choice D is an adjective. Choice A correctly uses a noun that fits the context.

CONFUSED WORDS DRILL

Make corrections, if needed, to the wording. There are multiple ways to fix these sentences.

1. I have far more clocks then watches in my apartment.

2. My friend was delighted to receive his exceptance letter to his favorite university.

3. I am sure you wish you would of practiced more for the big game.

4. Be sure to lay down your pencils at the end of the exam.

5. The emergency personnel will treat the car which is on fire.

Answers with Possible Corrections

1. I have far more clocks **than** watches in my apartment.
2. My friend was delighted to receive his **acceptance** letter to his favorite university.
3. I am sure you wish you would **have** practiced more for the big game.
4. Fine as is.
5. The emergency personnel will treat the car **that** is on fire.

Logical Comparison Questions

For these types of questions, it is important to be more formal in your approach. In a casual conversation, if someone made a statement like "The price of food in my cafeteria is far more than your cafeteria," you would reasonably conclude the person was comparing the price of food in one cafeteria to the price of food in the other. However, this is not what was literally said. The comparison as written was between "price" and "cafeteria," which would be illogical. When you encounter comparisons, keep this tip in mind:

TACTIC

Compare a part to a part, and a whole to a whole.

Logical comparison problems usually come from a writer comparing the part of a group to another group. The following sample question has an issue like this,

SAMPLE QUESTION

The principal of my high school is better than your ❶ high school.	17. (A) NO CHANGE (B) high school's. (C) high schools one is. (D) high schools' one.

In this question, the "part" is "principal," while the larger "group" is the "high school." To make this comparison logical, clarify that the sentence is comparing a principal to another principal. Choice B is the only option that does this, since writing "high school's" implies that the writer is referring to the principal of the high school. Choice A makes an illogical comparison, Choice C does not have an apostrophe in "schools" and is too wordy, and Choice D makes "school" plural instead of singular because of the apostrophe placement.

LOGICAL COMPARISON DRILL

Make corrections, if needed, to the wording. There are multiple ways to fix these sentences.

1. Susan's house is much more expensive than Mary.

2. My supervisor is nicer than anyone at my company.

3. Gas prices downtown are far greater than the countryside.

4. Hannah's car was messier than Caitlin's.

5. Among broccoli, cauliflower, and asparagus, which one do you like better?

Answers with Possible Corrections

1. Susan's house is much more expensive than **Mary's**.
2. My supervisor is nicer than **anyone else** at my company.
3. Gas prices downtown are far greater than **those in** the countryside.
4. Fine as is.
5. Among broccoli, cauliflower, and asparagus, which one do you like **the best**?

Conventional Expressions

These questions are the "wild card" of the PSAT Writing and Language section. The other types of issues you will encounter mostly come down to clear rules; however, these questions involve the proper use of common English phrases. For example, in casual conversation, people sometimes improperly use the word "irregardless." This is actually not a word— "regardless" should be used instead.

TACTIC 22

Trust your instincts when it comes to conventional expressions.

The more widely you read, the easier these sorts of questions will become—you will have greater familiarity with conventional expressions and you will be more confident in your intuition.

SAMPLE QUESTION

Many of the questions on the PSAT and the SAT are **30** <u>one in the same.</u>	30. (A) NO CHANGE (B) one of the same. (C) one and the same. (D) ones of the same.

The proper phrase based on common English practice is "one and the same," making Choice C correct. Choices A and B use incorrect prepositions ("in" and "of"), and Choice D uses the plural "ones," which does not conform to common English usage for this phrase.

CONVENTIONAL EXPRESSIONS DRILL

Make corrections, if needed, to the expressions. There are multiple ways to fix these sentences.

1. It is far less expensive to purchase the ingredients on bulk.

2. For lacking of a better idea, we opted for his suggestion.

3. The movie's duration was quite little—I was disappointed it was over so soon.

4. Will all those in favor for the motion raise their hands?

5. The criminal was not concerned about going to prison because the statue of limitations had passed.

Answers with Possible Corrections

1. It is far less expensive to purchase the ingredients **in** bulk.
2. For **lack** of a better idea, we opted for his suggestion.
3. The movie's duration was quite **short**—I was disappointed it was over so soon.
4. Will all those in favor **of** the motion raise their hands?
5. The criminal was not concerned about going to prison because the **statute** of limitations had passed.

CONVENTIONAL EXPRESSIONS PRACTICE

SAMPLE QUESTION

Picking a good birthday present for my friend Sarah is nearly impossible. ❶ <u>Irregardless</u> of what I buy her—be it new clothing, electronics, or even concert tickets—she never seems satisfied. Perhaps this is because Sarah is the girl ❷ <u>whom has</u> nearly everything already. She makes enough money from her job such that if ❸ <u>there is</u> an item

1. (A) NO CHANGE
   (B) Giving regarding to
   (C) Regardless
   (D) Regarding

2. (A) NO CHANGE
   (B) who has
   (C) whom have
   (D) who have

3. (A) NO CHANGE
   (B) their's
   (C) their is
   (D) they'res

she really wants, she will simply **4** <u>buy them</u> for herself. Even a gift card causes a hostile reaction from her—"why did you get **5** <u>her</u> something that I can only use at one store?"

    In the gift exchange this year, I could get Sarah, Bethany, or my Mother, but I **6** <u>was</u> worried I could have **7** <u>her</u>. Purchasing a present for Bethany is far easier **8** <u>than Sarah.</u>

4. (A) NO CHANGE
   (B) purchase those
   (C) exchange
   (D) buy it

5. (A) NO CHANGE
   (B) them
   (C) me
   (D) it

6. (A) NO CHANGE
   (B) had been
   (C) will be
   (D) am

7. (A) NO CHANGE
   (B) Sarah.
   (C) a gift for her.
   (D) an excellent present for her.

8. (A) NO CHANGE
   (B) then her.
   (C) then Sarah.
   (D) than doing so for Sarah.

Answers

1. **(C)** Choice C uses "regardless," which means *in spite of*. This makes sense given the context because the narrator is expressing that no matter what she tries to buy her friend, she is unsatisfied. Choice A is not a word, Choice B is too wordy and improperly uses "regarding," and Choice D, "regarding," means *concerning*.

2. **(B)** Choice B properly uses the subject form of "who" instead of the object form of "whom." Moreover, it uses the singular "has" instead of "have." The other options all either improperly use "whom," or use the plural "have."

3. **(A)** Choice A correctly uses "there is," which is used to make a statement about something. Choices B and C use "their," which is used for possession, and Choice D is not a word. ("They're" means "they are.")

4. **(D)** This part of the sentence is referring to purchasing a singular "item," so the singular pronoun "it" is needed. Choices A and B use plural pronouns, and Choice C lacks a needed pronoun while making a subtle change to the original meaning from "purchase" to "exchange."

5. **(C)** The sentence in quotation marks is from the first person point of view, making a reference to the speaker logical. So, "me" is appropriate in referring back to the speaker. The other options all do not refer to the speaker in the first person.

6. **(D)** Immediately after the underlined portion, it says "currently," indicating that this should be in the present tense. Choice D, "am," is the only option in the present tense.

7. **(B)** In the previous sentence, there are three females mentioned: Sarah, Bethany, and the narrator's mother. So, a pronoun would not be appropriate at this point because it is unclear to whom the pronoun refers. On the PSAT, you never need to worry about whether the word substituted for a vague pronoun is true—if the pronoun needs to be clarified, whatever logical noun they use will be fine. Choice A keeps the vague pronoun, and Choices C and D change the original meaning.

8. **(D)** Although it may seem a bit wordy, it is necessary to clarify this phrase by explicitly stating "doing so for Sarah" so that there can be a logical comparison. With the other options, the writer would be literally comparing the act of purchasing to a person, which does not make sense.

PUNCTUATION

Proper use of punctuation is a major area that is tested on the PSAT.

Commas

General Rule	Proper Use
Separate a phrase (dependent clause) from a complete sentence (independent clause).	When you open your birthday present, remember to whom you should send thank you notes.
Join two complete sentences when there is a transitional word, like the "FANBOYS": *for, and, nor, but, or, yet,* and *so.*	I am eager to receive my PSAT test scores online, but they will not come out for several weeks.
Separate extra information from the rest of the sentence.	The Hubble Telescope, which orbits our planet, has provided fantastic pictures of deep space.
Separate items in a list with commas.[1]	I will order a pizza topped with cheese, pepperoni, mushrooms, and green peppers.
Don't use commas to separate parts of a sentence if everything in the sentence is needed to make it clear and logical. (In this case, clarifying that the boat is sinking).	The boat that is sinking needs Coast Guard personnel to come rescue its passengers.
Just because a sentence is long doesn't mean that it needs a comma. Look more at the structure of the sentence than at its length.	The Great Barrier Reef off the coast of Australia offers some of the best snorkeling and scuba diving anywhere in the world.
A clarifying parenthetical phrase needs to be separated with commas. If the name is sufficient to know who the person is, commas are needed to separate the description. If the description is too vague to precisely narrow down the item, then no commas should separate descriptive phrases.	Eddie George, winner of the 1995 Heisman Trophy, had a successful professional football career after college.

[1]The PSAT has traditionally preferred the serial or "Oxford" comma (i.e., having a comma between the second-to-last and last items in a list), but since there is not a universally accepted rule about whether the serial comma should be used, it is extremely unlikely that the PSAT would include a test question about it.

COMMA DRILL

Make changes, if needed, to the comma usage.

1. Joe Montana winner of multiple Super Bowls, is undoubtedly one of the best to ever play football.

2. You are doing pretty well but you could be doing even better.

3. No I did not call the doctor.

4. *Gone With the Wind*, a nearly four-hour-long movie is so long that it has an intermission.

5. The horse currently winning the race will probably finish first.

Answers

1. Joe Montana**,** winner of multiple Super Bowls, is undoubtedly one of the best to ever play football.
2. You are doing pretty well**,** but you could be doing even better.
3. No**,** I did not call the doctor.
4. *Gone With the Wind*, a nearly four-hour-long movie**,** is so long that it has an intermission.
5. Fine as is.

Semicolons

General Rule	Proper Use
You can use a semicolon to separate two complete, related sentences.	My friend did most of the driving on our trip; she has much better stamina than I do.
Use a semicolon to separate items in a list when each item has a comma or commas within it.	On my European trip during college, I went to Paris, France; London, England; and Rome, Italy.

SEMICOLON DRILL

Make changes, if needed, to the semicolon usage.

1. Please clean up after yourself I don't want to find any messes.

2. My dad was convinced she was lying, however, I was not so sure.

3. Although my husband's snoring is quite annoying, I try my best to ignore it.

4. Cyber-bullying is a major problem, we need to do something to stop it.

5. On our "foundation of the nation" vacation we traveled to Boston, Massachusetts, Philadelphia, Pennsylvania, and Washington, D.C.

Answers

1. Please clean up after yourself; I don't want to find any messes.
2. My dad was convinced she was lying; however, I was not so sure.
3. Fine as is.
4. Cyber-bullying is a major problem; we need to do something to stop it.
5. On our "foundation of the nation" vacation we traveled to Boston, Massachusetts; Philadelphia, Pennsylvania; and Washington, D.C.

Colons

General Rule	Proper Use
Use a colon after a complete sentence to set off a list.	Whenever I go on a trip, I am certain to take the following items: my passport, a cell phone, and my wallet.
Use a colon after a complete sentence to set off a clarification. (A colon can work if it can be replaced by the word "namely.")	I was surprised at how my boyfriend proposed to me: he did so at the spot of our very first date.

COLON DRILL

Make changes, if needed, to the colon usage.

1. Be sure to do the following in the interview, make eye contact, listen carefully, and answer from the heart.

2. I whiffed something burning from downstairs it was the stove.

3. Lead paint should be avoided it can cause lower intelligence and delayed growth.

4. The player had a major announcement: he was retiring for good.

5. Both of the job candidates have major flaws, one candidate is inexperienced and the other is unprofessional.

Answers

1. Be sure to do the following in the interview: make eye contact, listen carefully, and answer from the heart.
2. I whiffed something burning from downstairs: it was the stove.
3. Lead paint should be avoided: it can cause lower intelligence and delayed growth.
4. Fine as is.
5. Both of the job candidates have major flaws: one candidate is inexperienced and the other is unprofessional.

Dashes

General Rule	Proper Use
While other punctuation can often work (in this case, a colon or semicolon could work instead of the dash), the dash can provide variety in your writing when you need to indicate an interruption or change of thought.	Shut the door behind you—it is freezing outside.
A dash can be used to interrupt a sentence and provide a change of voice.	She won the prize—this came as no surprise to me—and shared her prize money with all her friends.
Dashes can set off a parenthetical phrase. If you start with a dash on one end of the phrase, you need to use a dash on the other end of it for consistency.	Summer vacation—considered by many educators to be outdated—is probably my favorite time of year.

DASH DRILL

Make changes, if needed, to the dash usage.

1. Hold on a second please wait for me to finish.
2. Sam took just three things with him to class a laptop, reading glasses, and a ballpoint pen.
3. York City—home of the Statue of Liberty and the Empire State Building, is a major tourist attraction.
4. My brand new phone charger does not work nearly as well as my old one did.
5. My stomach was full I couldn't eat another bite.

Answers

1. Hold on a second—please wait for me to finish.
2. Sam took just three things with him to class—a laptop, reading glasses, and a ballpoint pen.
3. York City—home of the Statue of Liberty and the Empire State Building—is a major tourist attraction.
4. Fine as is.
5. My stomach was full—I couldn't eat another bite.

Apostrophes

General Rule	Proper Use
Use an apostrophe before the "s" to indicate that a singular entity possesses something.	The cat's claws needed to be trimmed.
Use an apostrophe after the "s" to indicate that a plural entity possesses something.	The class officers' retreat was extremely productive.
Use an apostrophe before the "s" to indicate possession after an already-plural noun.	Children's theater is often far more interesting than adults'.

APOSTROPHE DRILL

Make changes, if needed, to the apostrophe usage.

1. One dog's leash is sometimes just as expensive as two dog's leashes.

2. Womens restrooms frequently have longer lines than mens.

3. Your car's windows are so dirty I can write my name on them with my finger.

4. My one friends house is quite a bit more spacious than his.

5. Whale's skin is extremely thick in order to protect the animals from cold water.

Answers

1. One dog's leash is sometimes just as expensive as two **dogs'** leashes.
2. **Women's** restrooms frequently have longer lines than **men's**.
3. Fine as is.
4. My one **friend's** house is quite a bit more spacious than his.
5. **Whales'** skin is extremely thick in order to protect the animals from cold water.

FREQUENT TYPES OF PUNCTUATION QUESTIONS

End-of-Sentence Questions

It is unlikely that you will find an end-of-sentence punctuation question that asks you to identify the basic usage of a period or a question mark, since these concepts are typically mastered in elementary school.

 TACTIC

23 End-of-sentence punctuation questions will probably be about unusual situations.

SAMPLE QUESTION

My friend was wondering if it would be OK for me **6** <u>to take him home?</u>	6. (A) NO CHANGE (B) taking him home? (C) to take him home. (D) take him home!

Although the friend is asking a question, it is given indirectly. As a result, no question mark is needed, making Choice C the correct choice. Choices A and B both improperly make this into a direct question, and Choice D incorrectly makes this into an exclamation.

Items-in-a-Series Questions

As with end-of-sentence punctuation questions, items-in-a-series questions are unlikely to test basic concepts, such as knowing that a list of three or more items requires each item to be separated by punctuation of some kind. Be on the lookout for unusual situations with items in a series of questions, paying close attention to this tip.

 TACTIC

24 Make sure the punctuation separates one complete item from another.

SAMPLE QUESTION

When traveling in the Western United States, be sure to visit **29** <u>Yosemite National Park, Yellowstone National Park, and San Francisco.</u>	29. (A) NO CHANGE (B) Yosemite National Park Yellowstone National Park, and San Francisco. (C) Yosemite, National Park, Yellowstone National Park, and San Francisco. (D) Yosemite National Park Yellowstone National Park and San Francisco.

Choice A is the only option that correctly separates each destination from one another. Choices B and D jumble the destination names together, and Choice C breaks up "Yosemite National Park" unnecessarily.

Parenthetical Phrase Questions

A parenthetical phrase provides extra, clarifying information that can be removed and the sentence will still be complete. For example,

> My good friend Jen—a champion horseback rider—is one of the most talented people I have ever met.

Commas, dashes, and parentheses can all set off parenthetical phrases. Be sure of one thing:

TACTIC

25 **Start a parenthetical phrase in the same way that you end it.**

If the parenthetical phrase begins with a comma, end it with a comma; if it starts with a dash, end it with a dash. Do not mix and match punctuation types in these cases.

SAMPLE QUESTION

The widely respected **8** engineer, winner of numerous industry awards— was able to develop a solution to the seemingly intractable problem.	8. (A) NO CHANGE (B) engineer—winner of numerous industry awards—was (C) engineer, winner of numerous industry awards was (D) engineer winner of numerous industry awards was

The phrase "winner of numerous industry awards" is not essential to making this sentence complete, although it does provide helpful clarifying information. The only option that sets this phrase out of the way using consistent punctuation is Choice B. Choice A mixes a comma with a dash, and Choices C and D do not set the parenthetical phrase aside.

Unnecessary-Punctuation Questions

Some students tend to over-punctuate, feeling that PSAT answer choices with more elaborate punctuation are more sophisticated. Other students tend to under-punctuate, picking options that read like a stream of consciousness.

TACTIC
26
Find a balance between too much and too little punctuation. Use exactly what is needed, no more and no less.

SAMPLE QUESTION

In the ㉒ <u>summer months before, you start college,</u> be sure to enjoy time with your family and high school friends.

22. (A) NO CHANGE
    (B) summer months, before you start college be
    (C) summer months before you start college, be
    (D) summer months before you start college be

The introductory phrase of the sentence, "In the summer months before you start college," needs to be kept unified because it gives a precise description of the time period under discussion. Choices A and B interrupt this phrase. Choice D has no punctuation to separate the introductory clause from the complete sentence that follows. Choice C is the only option that correctly places a comma just after the introductory phrase.

PUNCTUATION PRACTICE

The extent of one's extracurricular ❶ <u>participation is a vital factor in college admissions decisions.</u> There are innumerable ways to become involved in your school and ❷ <u>community, running for</u> class office, starting a new club, and volunteering as a tutor or mentor.

1. (A) NO CHANGE
   (B) participation, is a vital factor in college admissions decisions.
   (C) participation is a vital factor, in college admissions decisions.
   (D) participation, is a vital factor in college, admissions decisions.

2. (A) NO CHANGE
   (B) community running, for class office starting
   (C) community running for class office; starting
   (D) community: running for class office, starting

Extracurricular participation should not be **❸** <u>burdensome you should find</u> activities that you find enjoyable and pursue them with passion. **❹** <u>Despite what many people think, selective</u> colleges are looking for a well-rounded class, not necessarily well-rounded students. What do we mean **❺** <u>by this!</u> <u>An</u> elite college would rather have a community of specialists than a group of generalists. **❻** <u>So in choosing your</u> <u>extracurricular activity; go</u> for in-depth involvement in one or two areas instead of superficial involvement in many areas.

3. (A) NO CHANGE
   (B) burdensome, you should
   (C) burdensome—you should
   (D) burdensome; you, should

4. (A) NO CHANGE
   (B) Despite what many people—think selective
   (C) Despite what many people think selective
   (D) Despite—what many people think—selective

5. (A) NO CHANGE
   (B) by this? An
   (C) by this. An
   (D) by this; an

6. (A) NO CHANGE
   (B) So, in choosing your extracurricular activity, go
   (C) So, in choosing your extracurricular activity; go
   (D) So, in choosing your extracurricular activity: go

Answers

1. **(A)** Even though this is a longer phrase, no commas are required. Choices B and D would separate the subject from the verb, and Choice C interrupts the phrase "factor in college admissions."

2. **(D)** A colon is appropriate here as it sets off a list of three different ways that one can become involved. Choices A and B do not provide a sufficient pause, and Choice C does not work because a semicolon must have a complete sentence both before and after.

3. **(C)** The dash provides an appropriately heavy pause to break up the two independent clauses. Choice A provides no break, Choice B makes this a run-on sentence, and Choice D has a comma inappropriately placed after "you."

4. **(A)** Choice A has a comma after the introductory dependent clause. Choice B places the pause too soon, Choice C has no breaks at all, and Choice D has too many breaks.

5. **(B)** This is the only option that correctly treats this as a question. Given the first part of the sentence, "What do we mean . . . ," it is clear that this should take the form of a question.

6. **(B)** This option correctly places commas around the parenthetical phrase. Choices A, C, and D are all incorrect because there must be a complete sentence before both a semicolon and a colon—"So, in choosing your extracurricular activity" is instead a fragment.

Questions 1–11 are based on the following passage and supplementary material.

The Boy Who Lived

The craze surrounding the *Harry Potter* series in the late 1990s and early 2000s was, in many ways, unprecedented. ❶ Developed into eight films and setting sales records that were nothing less than monumental. All of this established J. K. Rowling, a British author, as someone whose world of wizarding became a cornerstone of young adult fiction. Its achievements include the best-selling book series in history and the fastest-selling book ever; as of 2015, ❷ its film adaptations had grossed over $7 billion. So much was made of the young wizard Harry Potter and his friends, Ronald Weasley and Hermione Granger, as they endeavor to locate and destroy horcruxes ❸ for the purposes and reasons of the defeat the evil Lord Voldemort that the series gained a large adult audience and even had entire college-level courses devoted to it.

Certainly, fantasy is the genre that comes to mind when thinking of *Harry Potter*. ❹ Yet, adventure, romance, and coming-of-age all equally describe the series. In the first book, the

1. Which of the following provides the best combined version of the underlined sentences?

   (A) These eight films were developed into seven fantasy novels, making her world a cornerstone of young adult fiction.
   (B) The seven fantasy novels developed into eight films and set monumental records in sales, establishing British author J. K. Rowling's wizarding world as a cornerstone of young adult fiction.
   (C) With sales that were monumental, the development of J. K. Rowling's wizarding world became a young adult fiction cornerstone—additionally, she was a British author.
   (D) As the cornerstone of young adult fiction, J. K. Rowling, a British author, created a wizarding world that had eight films and set monumental sales records.

2. (A) NO CHANGE
   (B) it's
   (C) its'
   (D) much

3. (A) NO CHANGE
   (B) for
   (C) by
   (D) in order to

4. (A) NO CHANGE
   (B) Therefore
   (C) Coupled with these
   (D) So

Opening U.S. Domestic Weekend Box Office Totals

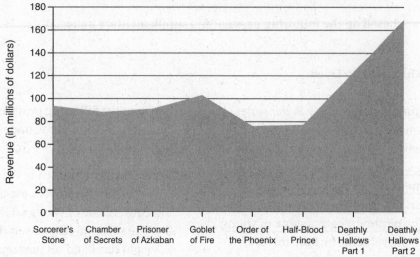

Source: *www.the-numbers.com*

young Harry, raised by his muggle (non-magical) aunt ❺ <u>and uncle learns his true identity, enrolls in Hogwarts School of Witchcraft and</u> Wizardry, and manages to keep Lord Voldemort from procuring immortality. During his next three years of grade school, Harry defeats Voldemort's murderous basilisk, rescues his godfather who is wrongly accused of betraying Harry's parents, and witnesses Voldemort's return to power during a wizarding tournament. In the fifth and sixth books, an order of wizards ❻ <u>reemerge to defeat</u> Voldemort and his followers, but suffers the deaths of Sirius Black (Harry's godfather) and Albus Dumbledore (headmaster of Hogwarts). And, in the ❼ <u>closing and last book</u> of the series, Harry secures the Deathly Hallows and, with the help of his friends, finally defeats the Dark Lord. The intricate plot to the final Harry Potter installment demanded not one, but two movies to portray it. Interest in the stories increased with the final installment, as the corresponding pair of movies grossed ❽ <u>nearly 300 million dollars combined in the United States on their opening weekends.</u>

5. (A) NO CHANGE
   (B) and uncle, learns his true identity, enrolls in Hogwarts School of Witchcraft and
   (C) and uncle, learns his true identity enrolls in Hogwarts School of Witchcraft and
   (D) and uncle learns his true identity enrolls in Hogwarts School of Witchcraft and

6. (A) NO CHANGE
   (B) reemerge for defeating
   (C) reemerges for defeat
   (D) reemerges to defeat

7. (A) NO CHANGE
   (B) ultimate ending finale text
   (C) final book
   (D) terminating wind-up tome

8. Which of the following provides a relevant, supporting detail consistent with the information in the graph?

   (A) NO CHANGE
   (B) an average of 100 million dollars per weekend during the first four installments.
   (C) 170 million dollars a piece.
   (D) slightly less than average for the *Order of the Phoenix* and the *Half-Blood Prince*.

(1) Though the series has been lauded for nearly two decades, controversy over its themes of witchcraft and politics ❾ have nearly equaled its acclaim. (2) Subject of school-wide bans and book burnings, *Harry Potter* has failed to be categorized with harmless fairy tales or even the works of C. S. Lewis like many supporters believe it should be. (3) Furthermore, illegal pre-releasing of content has resulted in legal controversy over copyrights. (4) Despite opposition and dissension, J. K. Rowling made history with her fantastical imaginings of "the boy who lived." (5) And for those muggles who aren't satisfied with visiting Harry via computer screen, Universal Studios Orlando hosts *The Wizarding World of Harry Potter*. (6) ❿ One thing is certain, there isn't a millennial out there who cannot recognize the lightning bolt scar etched into Harry's forehead. ⓫

9. (A) NO CHANGE
   (B) has
   (C) is
   (D) are

10. (A) NO CHANGE
    (B) One thing is certain there
    (C) One thing is certain: there
    (D) One thing, is certain there

11. The author would like to insert the following sentence into the preceding paragraph.

    Today, she continues the journey into the magical world on her interactive website, *Pottermore*.

    Where would this sentence most logically be placed?

    (A) Before sentence 2
    (B) Before sentence 3
    (C) Before sentence 5
    (D) Before sentence 6

Questions 12–22 are based on the following passage.

Up With the Rooster's Crow

(1) Depending on where you attend high school, your ⓬ teachers and peers might express confusion when you say you want to attend college to be a farmer. (2) Traditionally, we limit our conceptions of farming to the small family business portrayed in Hollywood movies. (3) A rooster crows long before the sunrise, and an exhausted adolescent clamors out of bed to join an already lively household. (4) Another misconception might involve the near extinction of farming. (5) Farming, largely a matter of the federal government or sizable corporations, simply doesn't exist for the public. (6) Despite these misconceptions and conspiratorial thinking, a college degree isn't the first thing you think about when imagining what it takes to be a successful farmer. (7) While these notions aren't completely artificial, they do limit our ⓭ sympathy of modern agriculture. ⓮

A rise in agricultural science degrees contradicts these widely held conceptions about farming. Students in agricultural science programs across the nation specialize in everything from forest to wildlife technologies, agricultural business to food science, and ⓯ biological engineering with veterinary medicine. The science behind planting, fertilizing, harvesting, and herding remains far from simple; often, it demands extensive education. However, if you enjoy working outdoors and using your hands, doing strenuous physical work, and have an

12. (A) NO CHANGE
    (B) teachers and peers, might express confusion when you say, you want to attend college to be a farmer.
    (C) teachers and peers might express confusion, when you say you want to attend, college to be a farmer.
    (D) teachers and peers might express, confusion when you say you want to attend college to be a farmer.

13. (A) NO CHANGE
    (B) wisdom
    (C) statistics
    (D) understanding

14. The author wishes to insert the following sentence into the previous paragraph.

    An elusive and unnamed stronghold somewhere steadily reduces the land dedicated to farming but still manages to increase food production—*it's a conspiracy.*

    Where should it be placed?

    (A) Before sentence 2
    (B) Before sentence 3
    (C) Before sentence 6
    (D) Before sentence 7

15. (A) NO CHANGE
    (B) biological engineering to veterinary medicine.
    (C) engineering of the biological variety and medicine of the veterinary type.
    (D) veterinarians doing medicine and biologists engineering.

interest in the chemical and biological aspects of food and livestock, farming might be the path for you. **16** Moreover, it can be an excellent choice for those interested in working hard for a living.

Food science, one specific path of the agricultural science degree, undertakes the study and inspection of food production, storage, and distribution. A food scientist is a **17** special type of farmer, one charged with the role of improving the productivity and sustainability of farms. By finding better ways to grow, process, and deliver foods to consumers, the food scientist concerns **18** themselves with the health and nutrition of the entire planet. In a time of increased food processing, the food scientist's job necessitates the break down and analysis of basic food content to forge processed foods that are both safe and nutritional. Generally, the career calls for **19** extensive university education that could entail four or five years of schooling.

16. The author is considering deleting the underlined sentence. Should this sentence be removed?

(A) Yes, because it shifts the essay's focus to the expected lifestyle of a farmer.

(B) Yes, because it repeats information already previously implied in the paragraph.

(C) No, because it provides a fitting conclusion to the paragraph.

(D) No, because it clarifies a claim made previously in the paragraph.

17. (A) NO CHANGE
    (B) special type, of farmer one
    (C) special type of farmer; one
    (D) special type of farmer one

18. (A) NO CHANGE
    (B) theirselves
    (C) yourself
    (D) himself or herself

19. Which of the following provides the most specific and relevant information to complete this sentence?

(A) NO CHANGE

(B) a college diploma in an area that relates to agriculture.

(C) a Bachelor's degree and yields an annual income of $60,000–65,000.

(D) further education beyond high school, with earnings in the five figures.

A closely related career path, animal science, unites food science with research on domestic farm animals. **20** An animal scientist studies animal nutrition, breeding, genetics, etc., to improve the production and processing of meat, poultry, eggs, and milk. This career differs from **21** those of a food scientists because it has the specific goal of increasing the quality and efficiency of livestock. Many times, the animal scientist pursues a graduate or doctoral degree in order to treat and care for farm animals, opening up doors for higher salaries.

22 Because of popular opinion, farms overflow with college degrees.

20. The author is considering removing the underlined sentence from the passage. Should it be kept or deleted?

(A) Kept, because it gives details to expand upon the general ideas of the previous sentence.

(B) Kept, because it explains the specific ways that the flavor of meat can be improved.

(C) Deleted, because it repeats information already expressed in the passage.

(D) Deleted, because it is only loosely related to the main focus of the passage.

21. (A) NO CHANGE
   (B) the food scientist's
   (C) the careers of food scientists'
   (D) food scientist

22. Which of the following provides an introductory phrase consistent with the overall message of the passage?

(A) NO CHANGE
   (B) Given
   (C) Despite
   (D) Coupled with

Questions 23–33 are based on the following passage.

Social Media: Good or Evil?

(1) I have ㉓ sweared off all social media on my phone, computer, and tablet. (2) While I am computer literate and I enjoy my family and friends, I would rather have a conversation with a live person sitting across from me than engage in frivolous texting and chatting. (3) ㉔ Yes, I do use e-mail in my work as an educator and will light up the search engines if I want to find something right away, but I have seen the harm that can be done by this new construct. (4) My pupils also hear my warning that an addicted social media adherent can never do any serious scholarship because there is just not enough time in the day. (5) I tell my classes about how I have seen students who had previously paid attention in class, only to have their participation plummet as soon as they had smartphones. ㉕

When I was in the classroom, I would ask my honors students how ㉖ much hours a day they spent with social media and video games, and these students always averaged between three and four hours a day. In my syllabus, I asked for one hour per day for outside work, and in my nine years working with these ㉗ terrible students, not a single student admitted at the end of the course that he or she had given the course one hour per day.

I have a number of professional friends and family members who manage businesses, and ㉘ they're number one challenge working

23. (A) NO CHANGE
    (B) swear
    (C) sworned
    (D) sworn

24. Which of the following options would provide the most logical introduction to this sentence?
    (A) NO CHANGE
    (B) Mildly,
    (C) Exceptionally,
    (D) Wrong,

25. What is the most logical placement of the sentence 5 in this paragraph?
    (A) Where it currently is
    (B) Before sentence 1
    (C) Before sentence 2
    (D) After sentence 3

26. (A) NO CHANGE
    (B) numbered
    (C) many
    (D) quantity

27. The author wishes to use wording at this point that will convey the narrator's mild sarcasm. Which of these choices would be most effective?
    (A) NO CHANGE
    (B) "advanced"
    (C) abysmal
    (D) "lazy"

28. (A) NO CHANGE
    (B) there
    (C) their
    (D) they are

with professional employees is dealing with social media in the workplace. **㉙** People will not have the action of staying away from this temptation, which is ever-present. The temptation is to experience some news, somewhere, in cyberspace. It is an ongoing issue in my brother's business with production employees and young engineers. He has actually fired several employees who could not **㉚** stay away from their phones.

I won't even go down the road of the connection of social media with **㉛** problems and issues around the globe or cyberbullying in our schools. Essentially, I see this as one more example of playing to the addictive tendencies of humans, and I believe it is as capable of diverting time and energy from productive uses as mildly powerful drugs. When you combine this with interactive video games, chat rooms, and phone apps for every diversionary interest, **㉜** it is a minor miracle that anything productive really happens in our daily lives. When was the last time you sat down and read an interesting book, or took out a sketchpad to record your visual observations? **㉝** Who has time, for quiet contemplation and creativity with the siren of the cellphone drawing you near for another glimpse of "reality"?

29. Which of the following provides the most effective combination of the underlined sentences?

(A) People will give into the new temptation of cyberspace.

(B) People will not stay away from this ever-present temptation to experience some news from somewhere in cyberspace.

(C) While people are interested in the act of avoiding temptation, this temptation of cyberspace (to find news somewhere) is present ever-more.

(D) Ever-present, the temptation to find out the news from somewhere provides cyberspace with an experience.

30. (A) NO CHANGE
(B) stay off from
(C) stay a grand and immense distance away from
(D) stay

31. (A) NO CHANGE
(B) complications and difficulties
(C) worries, snags, and hitches
(D) troubles

32. Which of the following options conveys that the narrator is amazed that productive endeavors can occur despite the widespread use of modern communications technology?

(A) NO CHANGE
(B) it comes as no surprise
(C) it is a cause for concern
(D) it is welcome news

33. (A) NO CHANGE
(B) Who has time for quiet contemplation and creativity
(C) Who has time, for quiet contemplation, and creativity
(D) Who has time? For quiet contemplation and creativity

Questions 34–44 are based on the following information and supplementary material.

Killer Cells

My mother brags that her children have **34** <u>especially resilient immune systems.</u> As an adolescent, I understood this only as a vague, obscure advantage **35** <u>of sorts my sister and I, pinnacles of robustness—defied infectious organisms.</u> I recall being sick only twice during my childhood; the two to three days of rest, cool baths, pungent medicines, and bland broths seemed destined to go on forever, and I couldn't fathom the somber lives of other students in my class who were ill several times each year. As I **36** <u>aging,</u> my apparent durability only increased; occasionally, I suffered from a runny nose or a sore throat, **37** <u>considering</u> nothing more.

I never felt a need to investigate my favorable strength further **38** <u>because</u> my father was diagnosed with Lupus. Lupus is a chronic autoimmune disorder in which the immune system—the source of my vigor—mistakenly attacks healthy cells causing muscle and joint pain and inflammation. In essence, his microscopic armor had gone rogue. Imagine that—the cells that freed me from routine sicknesses like the common cold to life-threatening diseases like cancer were murderous in my father, unable to differentiate allies from **39** <u>helpful cells.</u>

In a healthy immune system, white blood cells, or leukocytes, work closely with the circular system and lymphatic system to locate and destroy

34. Which of the following provides the most logical introduction to the paragraph?

(A) NO CHANGE
(B) overcome a plethora of lethal maladies.
(C) a tendency to be overly dramatic.
(D) unmatched aerobic endurance.

35. (A) NO CHANGE
(B) of sorts—my sister and I, pinnacles of robustness, defied infectious organisms.
(C) of sorts, my sister and I: pinnacles of robustness, defied infectious organisms.
(D) of sorts; my sister and I pinnacles of robustness defied infectious organisms.

36. (A) NO CHANGE
(B) had aging
(C) age
(D) aged

37. (A) NO CHANGE
(B) for
(C) but
(D) of

38. Which of the following provides the most logical transition at this point in the sentence?

(A) NO CHANGE
(B) until
(C) for
(D) when

39. Which phrase would create the most sensible contrast within the sentence?

(A) NO CHANGE
(B) neutral intermediaries.
(C) foreign invaders.
(D) wicked sorcery.

threatening pathogens. **40** Unlike other systems of the body the immune system, is relatively invisible with soldiers housed throughout the body in the spleen, lymph nodes, thymus, and bone marrow. These leukocytes produce antibodies to destroy disease-causing invaders called antigens. Some cells are responsible for sending messages, generating specific antibodies, destroying infected cells, or **41** remembering previous invaders so that the body is ready for them the next time. While the body fights, you often experience fever, fatigue, **42** having swelling, or runny nose—hence, my rare ailments. Immunity looks different for everyone: we are born with some immunity, acquire more as we grow, and obtain others through vaccination. Even then, each body defends differently and with varying degrees of efficiency.

A confused immune system, like that of my father, doesn't operate so. Instead, the leukocytes cannot determine friend from foe and attack healthy tissues in the same way they might attack virus and bacteria. Lupus can affect almost any organ in the body and varies in symptoms making it tough to diagnose and even more difficult to treat. My father experiences pain on a daily basis; his joints and muscles ache constantly, and he is often too tired to perform routine daily activities. His form of Lupus, Systemic Lupus Erythematosus, infects millions of people and **43** produces symptoms similar to Crohn's disease and Lyme disease. It is as if his troops simply turned against him. **44**

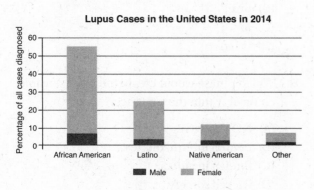

Lupus Cases in the United States in 2014

Source: *Lupus.org*

40. (A) NO CHANGE
    (B) Unlike other systems of the body, the immune system is relatively invisible with soldiers housed throughout the body in the spleen lymph nodes, thymus, and bone marrow.
    (C) Unlike, other systems of the body the immune system is, relatively, invisible with soldiers housed throughout the body in the spleen, lymph nodes, thymus, and bone marrow.
    (D) Unlike other systems of the body, the immune system is relatively invisible, with soldiers housed throughout the body in the spleen, lymph nodes, thymus, and bone marrow.

41. The author wishes to use a word that makes sense given the information that follows in the sentence. Which would best accomplish this goal?

    (A) NO CHANGE
    (B) trivializing
    (C) surrounding
    (D) approaching

42. (A) NO CHANGE
    (B) swelling
    (C) to swell
    (D) swellingness

43. (A) NO CHANGE
    (B) produced
    (C) producing
    (D) had produced

44. What new information about the narrator's father would make the statistics in the table most relevant in placing his illness in a greater societal context?

    (A) His age
    (B) His ethnicity
    (C) His gender
    (D) His salary

ANSWER KEY

1.	**B**	12.	**A**	23.	**D**	34.	**A**
2.	**A**	13.	**D**	24.	**A**	35.	**B**
3.	**D**	14.	**C**	25.	**D**	36.	**D**
4.	**A**	15.	**B**	26.	**C**	37.	**C**
5.	**B**	16.	**B**	27.	**B**	38.	**B**
6.	**D**	17.	**A**	28.	**C**	39.	**C**
7.	**C**	18.	**D**	29.	**B**	40.	**D**
8.	**A**	19.	**C**	30.	**A**	41.	**A**
9.	**B**	20.	**A**	31.	**D**	42.	**B**
10.	**C**	21.	**B**	32.	**A**	43.	**A**
11.	**C**	22.	**C**	33.	**B**	44.	**B**

ANSWERS EXPLAINED

1. **(B)** Choice A is flawed in that it eliminates the name of J. K. Rowling, thus leading to ambiguity. Choice D incorrectly identifies J. K. Rowling as the "cornerstone of young adult fiction," rather than her literature. Choice C, with its opening clause of, "With sales that were monumental," must refer to the Harry Potter series rather than the *development* of the series, as it does incorrectly. Choice B, however, is perfect—it maintains all relevant information while avoiding awkward word ordering.

2. **(A)** This is a good moment to review the various forms of "it." The first, "it's," is a contraction of *it is*. The second, "its," is the possessive form of *it*. The third, "its'," is always grammatically incorrect. We are looking for the possessive form, so "its" is the correct answer.

3. **(D)** Notice the context of what we're attempting to connect: it is cause and effect. When we paraphrase, it is, "Harry and his friends must defeat horcruxes *so that* Lord Voldemort can be defeated." The best cause-and-effect transition here (to substitute for *so that*) is "in order to." Choice A expresses our intended sentiment, but it does so in a manner that is far too wordy. Choices B and C neglect cause and effect entirely.

4. **(A)** This requires a *contrasting* transition. Paraphrased, the sentences are, "Fantasy is Harry Potter's genre, *but* there are aspects of adventure and romance, as well." "Yet," Choice A, is our best substitute for "but."

5. **(B)** The phrase, "raised by his muggle aunt and uncle" is a parenthetical phrase; we can eliminate those words and still have the sentence function perfectly well. Accordingly, we can surround the phrase with two commas or two dashes to separate it from our main clause. Eliminate Choices A and D as a result. Thereafter, we are listing actions. A comma is thus required between the actions of "learns his true identity" and "enrolls in Hogwarts . . . ." Choice C incorrectly omits that comma.

6. **(D)** The subject here was tricky: it was "order of wizards," with "order" being the operative word, not "wizards." "Order" is a singular noun, so we will need a singular verb to match. As "reemerge" is a plural verb, eliminate Choices A and B. Now, after "reemerges," the *infinitive* form of the verb is required: "to defeat." Choice D, "reemerges to defeat," therefore, is the correct answer.

7. **(C)** All four choices express the same sentiment of *last book*. However, while Choices A, B, and D achieve that in an overly verbose manner, Choice C manages to do so while maintaining concision.

8. **(A)** Analyze the graph, specifically looking at "Deathly Hallows: Part 1" and "Deathly Hallows: Part 2." Choice B is incorrect in that it doesn't answer the question, but instead refers to the wrong movies. Choice C is incorrect, as "Part 1" grossed only 120 million dollars. Choice D is incorrect, as the two grossed significantly more than "*Half-Blood Prince*" and "*Order of the Phoenix*." The correct answer is Choice A: the sum of the two movies was 280 million dollars, which is "nearly 300 million."

9. **(B)** The subject is "controversy," which is a singular noun. Eliminate Choices A and D as they are plural verbs, and thus can't be paired with a singular noun. Choice C is close to correct, but the passage would need to read as, "is nearly equaled *by* its acclaim." That requisite "by" is not there, however. Thus, "has equaled" is our best choice.

10. **(C)** Both "one thing is certain" and "there isn't a millennial out there who cannot recognize the lightning bolt scar etched into Harry's forehead" could be complete sentences independently. Therefore, proper punctuation is required to separate these two clauses. A colon is the best option here, as seen in Choice C. The colon serves as a sort of lead-in from clause 1 to clause 2. Choice A causes a run-on sentence while Choices B and D neglect punctuation entirely.

11. **(C)** Sentence 5 references a "computer screen," which is a perfect follow-up to our proposed insertion about Rowling's website. Otherwise, the proposed insertion isn't logical in the context of the other choices.

12. **(A)** Be careful not to confuse *length* with a *run-on sentence*. There is nothing in this clause that requires a comma to delineate it from something else, so be aware of avoiding unnecessary punctuation. Choices B, C, and D all include unnecessary commas that break with the flow of the sentence.

13. **(D)** In essence, the sentence is stating that we have little *knowledge* of modern agriculture. "Understanding" is the most apt synonym for "knowledge." "Wisdom" is similar to "knowledge," but it typically implies good decision making. As the old saying goes, "*Knowledge* is knowing that a tomato is a fruit. *Wisdom* is knowing not to put a tomato in a fruit salad."

14. **(C)** It makes the most sense to have this sentence connect sentences 5 and 6 because sentence 5 focuses on the idea of a big business and governmental conspiracy, and sentence 6 transitions away from the discussion of misconceptions and conspiracies. Placing this sentence any earlier would interrupt the introduction of the paragraph's topic, and placing it later would revert to conspiratorial thinking when that line of analysis had already stopped.

15. **(B)** Notice the parallelism of the sentence, specifically in the recurring reference of the word "to." Choice A breaks with that pattern by swapping "to" for "with." Choice D also breaks with the pattern by omitting "to." Choice C is wordy. Choice B, "biological engineering *to* veterinary medicine," maintains our desired parallelism.

16. **(B)** When deciding whether to delete the underlined sentence, ask two questions: *is it relevant, and is the information new?* If the answer is "no" to either of those questions,

then the sentence should be deleted. In this case, "interested in working hard for a living" is simply a restatement of "if you enjoy . . . doing strenuous physical work." Thus, the information is not new, and the sentence should be deleted.

17. **(A)** The main clause in our sentence is, "A food scientist is a special type of farmer . . . ." We must separate this from any information that comes after. In this case, that is, "one charged with the role of improving the productivity and sustainability of farms." Choices B and D neglect a pause between "farmer" and "one," so they can be eliminated accordingly. The problem with Choice C is that a semicolon requires the joining of two complete clauses. As the second clause is a fragment, the sentence therefore requires a comma as appropriately used in Choice A.

18. **(D)** We must choose the proper reflexive pronoun to match "the food scientist." "The food scientist" is a single person of indeterminate gender, so our reflexive pronoun should reflect that. "Theirselves" can be eliminated, as it is not a word. "Themselves" can be eliminated, as the food scientist is one person. "Yourself" can also be eliminated, as "the food scientist" is third person and "yourself" is second person. "Himself or herself" is the correct answer.

19. **(C)** The key to this question is the requirement for *specific* as all four choices are *relevant*. Choice C mentions a Bachelor's degree, which we can infer takes four or five years to complete. It also mentions a specific salary of $60,000–$65,000, which makes for three pieces of *specific* information—the degree, the required length of time, and the salary. Choice A gives us the length of the degree, Choice B only tells us that a degree is needed, and Choice D mentions that a degree is needed while mentioning that the salary could be between $10,000 and $99,999. It's clear to see the Choice C is most *specific*.

20. **(A)** When deciding whether to delete the underlined sentence, ask two questions: *is it relevant, and is the information new?* If the answer is "no" to either of those questions, then the sentence should be deleted. In this case, the information about the animal scientist is both relevant and new. In fact, without this sentence, the reader would be left with an incomplete picture of what animal science actually is. Choice B correctly insists on keeping the sentence, but its logic is flawed, as it doesn't actually "explain the specific ways that the flavor of meat can be improved."

21. **(B)** Remember to compare apples to apples, so to speak, in order to preserve parallelism. We are comparing "this career" to *the food scientist's career,* or simply "the food scientist's," as Choice B correctly states. Choice A is incorrect as "those" implies *multiple careers*, and Choice C is wrong for the same reason. Choice D is incorrect as we are comparing careers, not the people actually working in those careers.

22. **(C)** The point that the author is making is that it is assumed that higher education has no place in agriculture. However, as she has demonstrated and proceeds to state in this sentence, "farms overflow with college degrees." Thus, a contrasting transition is required. "Despite" is our only option that fulfills that need for contrast.

23. **(D)** The "have" indicates to us that our verb tense will be *present perfect*. The present perfect tense of "swore" is irregular—"sworn" is the correct answer.

24. **(A)** This is a question where it is probably easier to eliminate incorrect choices rather than zeroing in our correct answer immediately. "Wrong, I do use e-mail . . ." implies

that an incorrect assumption has been made, which is not the case. "Mildly, I do use e-mail . . ." is nonsensical. Similarly, "exceptionally, I use e-mail . . ." does not make sense, either. The correct choice was Choice A. Notice how the "yes" works in context: it is given as a concession that, even though the narrator is not terribly fond of technology, he still uses *some* technology.

25. **(D)** Sentence four references the pupils hearing the narrator's warning. Our proposed insertion is, in fact, that warning. Thus, the sentence must be placed before sentence 4, or "after sentence 3," as Choice D states.

26. **(C)** Recall that "many" and "few" are words used to describe concrete things that can be quantified. "Much" or "little" refer to more abstract concepts that are not easily quantifiable. In this case, *hours* are something that can be counted. Accordingly, we would say, "too *many* hours," which is Choice C.

27. **(B)** Read the question carefully. We need a choice that will use "mild sarcasm" to describe honors students who do not spend enough time studying. "Lazy" is an apt description of these students, but it conveys nothing of sarcasm or of sarcasm's cousin: irony. "Terrible" and "abysmal" aren't so much sarcastic as insulting. "Advanced" is a perfect choice here; it is ironic and certainly fits the definition of sarcasm.

28. **(C)** We need a possessive word to use as a stand-in for the "professional friends" and "family members" mentioned earlier in the sentence. Recall that "their" is a possessive word for multiple people, whereas "there" refers to *something over there*, for instance. "They're" is the contraction of *they are*. Thus, Choice C is the only adequate answer.

29. **(B)** The best way to combine the two sentences hinges on "temptation," as it was used once in each sentence. We can eliminate the need for two sentences by using "temptation" as the figurative fulcrum of the clause, as Choice B effectively executes. Choice A eliminates key information from our initial two sentences. Choice C changes the meaning, particularly in its statement of how "people are interested in the act of avoiding temptation." Nothing in the initial two sentences suggests that. Choice D's flaw is most apparent in its change of subject by omitting the word "people."

30. **(A)** Choice B is flawed in that it includes the extra preposition "from." Choice D, "stay their phones," is incorrect. Choices A and C both express the same sentiment, but Choice C is terribly wordy next to the concision of Choice A.

31. **(D)** We must strike the proper balance between the inclusion of relevant information and the exclusion of repetitive, unnecessary information. All four choices express the same sentiment, but Choices A, B, and C all do so by including multiple words that mean the exact same thing. For instance, we can say "complications and difficulties," but these two words are practically identical. In the interest of concision, simply say, "troubles."

32. **(A)** The operative word in the question is "amazed," and we will accordingly need a choice that indicates something of amazement. "It comes as no surprise" does not indicate amazement, just as "it is welcome news" does not. "It is a cause for concern" expresses a negative sentiment, which is certainly not amazement. People are amazed by miracles, however. "It is a minor miracle"—"NO CHANGE"—is the correct answer.

33. **(B)** Recall that length alone does not necessarily indicate a run-on sentence or a need for punctuation. In this case, "Who has time for quiet contemplation and creativity . . ."

is the core part of our main clause. Accordingly, it should not be dissected with commas but should instead be allowed to remain intact. Choices A, C, and D all insert unnecessary punctuation that breaks that main clause.

34. **(A)** In order to find the most logical introduction to the paragraph, we in fact need to *read* the entire paragraph. The theme is that the narrator and her siblings were rarely sick, whereas her peers were sick quite frequently. In this context, "especially resilient immune systems" would be most appropriate, as it was the immunity that prevented them from becoming sick in the first place. Choices C and D are off-topic. Choice B is incorrect in that the kids never became sick in the first place.

35. **(B)** This was a difficult one. Notice the first principal clause: "I understood this only as a vague, obscure advantage of sorts . . . ." That alone could be a full sentence, so we need an appropriate break between it and what follows. Choice A has no break, and Choice C, with its comma, provides too little of a break; Choice C is also flawed with its colon. With Choice D, a semicolon would be acceptable, but "pinnacles of robustness" is a parenthetical phrase that can use commas or dashes to surround it.

36. **(D)** Notice the use of "increased" later in the sentence. That verb is in past tense, so the verb we choose must be in past tense to maintain parallelism. Choice D is the only past tense verb. "Had aging" could be confused for past tense, but the correct form would have been "had *aged*."

37. **(C)** A contrast is needed here. "I suffered from a runny nose or sore throat, *but* nothing more." Paraphrased so that the contrast requirement is more apparent, the sentence is, "*although* I was sick with little things, nothing big ever affected me." Choices A, B, and D are not effective contrasting transitions.

38. **(B)** Choices A and C provide a cause-and-effect relationship that is *opposite* of our intentions, as if her father having lupus was the reason she never investigated. In actuality, she never investigated "until" her father had lupus, which is an inversion of Choices A and C. Choice D, similarly, provides an opposite meaning from our intended meaning.

39. **(C)** The sentence requires the most "sensible contrast," specifically with "allies." The opposite of an ally is an enemy. "Foreign invaders" would certainly be enemies.

40. **(D)** In a complex sentence such as this, it's probably easier to eliminate the three incorrect choices rather than initially diagnosing the correct one immediately. Choice A features an unnecessary comma separating the subject from the predicate. Choice B neglects a comma between "spleen" and "lymph nodes," and Choice C is incorrect from the very beginning with an unnecessary comma after "unlike." Upon eliminating those three, analyze the remaining choice, Choice D, and notice that it is faultless.

41. **(A)** The operative part of the question is "given the information that follows in this sentence"; what follows is, "previous invaders so that the body is ready for them next time." "Approaching" and "surrounding" are logical choices scientifically, but these words fail to take into account that stipulation about connecting with the second part of the sentence. In this case, "remembering" is the best match for an action that could connect with previous information or, more specifically, "previous invaders." To trivialize something is to make light of it, which isn't logical.

42. **(B)** "Swelling" operates as a noun in this case, as gerunds can do under certain circumstances. Having the word in noun form makes it parallel to the rest of the sentence, unlike Choices A and C. Choice D, "swellingness," is not a word.

43. **(A)** We want a verb that parallels "infects," which is a singular, present tense verb. "Produces" is also a singular, present tense verb. The other choices all sacrifice parallelism.

44. **(B)** Analyze the chart for this question. The only information listed in the chart pertains to gender and ethnicity. As we already know that it is his father, the only remaining piece of information unknown and potentially useful to us is his ethnicity.

WRITING AND LANGUAGE WRAP-UP

1. Use the full amount of time—take about 9 minutes per passage.

2. Write on the test booklet, as needed, to stay focused and organized.

3. Mouth out the passage as you read so you can intuitively pick up on grammar errors.

4. Make sure that the wording and style are consistent and logical throughout the passage.

5. Understand that there will not be grammar gimmicks—just grammar rules.

6. Be certain to answer the question that is asked; read the questions very carefully.

7. Remember that specific and relevant language is better than vague and off-topic language.

8. Carefully examine the axes and labels of the graphs to be clear on the data presented.

9. Understand that shorter is not necessarily sweeter. Consider which choice expresses the intended meaning while not being repetitive.

10. Look at enough context to determine how the writer is expressing him or herself.

11. Evaluate whether a sentence is complete by determining if it has a subject and a verb. Don't make assumptions simply based on the length of the sentence.

12. Make sure that the literal meaning and the intended meaning are the same.

13. Cut out the words between the subject and verb to see if the subject and verb are both singular or both plural.

14. Trust your instincts when it comes to conventional expressions.

15. Start a parenthetical phrase in the same way that you end it.

16. Find a balance between too much and too little punctuation. Use exactly what is needed, no more and no less.

PART FIVE
The Math Test

Introduction to the Math Test

4

Part Five consists of three chapters. This first brief chapter serves as an introduction to the mathematics part of the PSAT. Please do not skip it—take the few minutes necessary to carefully read everything in this chapter. It gives some valuable information about the organization of the math part of this book, as well as some important information about the test itself. It discusses the use of calculators on the test and explains the directions for both types of math questions.

Chapter 5 includes a discussion of all the essential tactics and strategies that good test takers need to know to do their best on the math part of the PSAT. The explanation of each tactic is followed by sample problems to solve using that particular tactic. The chapter ends with a set of exercises to test your understanding of the tactics discussed. If you master Chapter 5, you will be able to significantly improve your score on the math part of the PSAT.

Chapter 6 contains a review of the mathematics you need to know in order to do well on the PSAT, as well as hundreds of sample problems patterned on actual test questions. The chapter is conveniently divided into twenty short sections (Section A through Section T), each on a different topic—percents, ratios, averages, triangles, circles, and so on.

WHEN TO STUDY CHAPTERS 5 AND 6

How much time you initially devote to Chapter 6 should depend on your math skills. If you are an excellent student who consistently earns A's in math class, you can skip the instructional parts of Chapter 6 for now. If, while doing the practice tests in Part Six, you find that you keep making mistakes on certain types of problems (averages, percents, geometry, for example) or they take you too long, you should study the appropriate sections of Chapter 6. Even if your math skills are excellent and you don't need the review, you should do the sample questions in those sections; they are an excellent source of additional PSAT questions. If you know that your math skills are not very good, it is advisable to review the material in Chapter 6 and work out the problems before tackling the practice tests in Part Six.

No matter how good you are in math, you should carefully read Chapter 5. In that chapter you will learn techniques for (1) getting the correct answer to problems that you don't know how to solve and (2) getting the correct answer more quickly on those that you do know how to do.

AN IMPORTANT SYMBOL

Throughout the book, the symbol $\Rightarrow$ is used to indicate that one step in the solution of a problem follows immediately from the preceding one and that no explanation is necessary. You should read

$2x = 12 \Rightarrow x = 6$ as

$2x = 12$, which implies that $x = 6$, or, since $2x = 12$, then $x = 6$.

Here is a sample solution to the following problem using $\Rightarrow$:

What is the value of $3x^2 - 7$ when $x = -5$?

$x = -5 \Rightarrow x^2 = (-5)^2 = 25 \Rightarrow 3x^2 = 3(25) = 75 \Rightarrow 3x^2 - 7 = 75 - 7 = 68$

When the reason for a step is not obvious, $\Rightarrow$ is not used; rather, an explanation is given, often including a reference to a **KEY FACT** from Chapter 6. In many solutions, some steps are explained, while others are linked by the $\Rightarrow$ symbol, as in the following example:

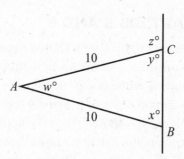

In the diagram above, if $w = 30$, what is the value of z?

- By **KEY FACT J1**, $w + x + y = 180$.
- Since $\triangle ABC$ is isosceles, $x = y$ [**KEY FACT J5**].
- Therefore, $w + 2y = 180 \Rightarrow 30 + 2y = 180 \Rightarrow 2y = 150 \Rightarrow y = 75$.
- Finally, since $y + z = 180$ [**KEY FACT I2**], $75 + z = 180 \Rightarrow z = 105$.

SIX IMPORTANT HEADINGS

In Chapters 5 and 6, you will see six headings that will appear either in the text or in the margins. They will indicate valuable information and will help to guide you as you study this book. Here is a brief explanation of each heading.

■ A useful strategy for attacking a certain type problem. Some TACTICS give you advice on how to handle multiple-choice questions, regardless of the subject matter. Others point out ways to handle specific subject matter, such as finding averages or solving equations, regardless of the type of problem.

■ **Key Fact Q2**

An important mathematical fact that you should commit to memory because it comes up often on the PSAT.

■ Math Reference Fact

A basic mathematical fact that is included in the "Reference Information" that appears on the first page of every math section.

■ Helpful Hint

A useful idea that will help you solve a problem more easily or avoid a pitfall.

■ Caution!

A warning of a potential danger. Often a Caution points out a common error or a source of careless mistakes.

■ Calculator

Possible or recommended calculator hints allow you to use your calculator to get answers to questions you would otherwise have to guess at.

You may *not* use the calculator on a cell phone. In fact, you may *not* have a phone on your desk at any time during the test.

USE OF THE CALCULATOR

Before doing any of the work in Part Five and the model tests in Part Six, you should reread the short discussion in Part One on the use of calculators on the SAT. As you do the sample problems in this book, always have available the calculator you intend to take to the SAT, and use it whenever you think it will be helpful. Throughout the rest of the book, whenever the use of a calculator is recommended, the icon has been placed next to the example or question. Remember:

- In the 25-minute math section, you may NOT use a calculator.
- In the 45-minute math section, many—but definitely not all—of the questions do require the use of a calculator.

Do not buy a new calculator right before you take the PSAT. The best advice is to use a calculator you are completely familiar with—the one you always use in your math class. If you don't have one or want to get a different one, buy it now and become familiar with it. Do all the practice exams in this book with the same calculator you intend to bring to the test.

In general, in the 45-minute math section you should do almost no arithmetic longhand. If you can't do a calculation mentally, use your calculator. In particular, avoid long division and multiplication in which the factors have two or more digits. If you know that $13^2 = 169$, terrific; if not, it's better to use your calculator than to multiply with paper and pencil.

Because students' mathematical knowledge and arithmetic skills vary considerably, the decision as to when to use a calculator is highly subjective. Consider the following rather easy problem. Would you use a calculator?

What is the average (arithmetic mean) of 301, 303, and 305?

Let's analyze the four possibilities:

1. Some students would use their calculators twice: first to add, $301 + 303 + 305 = 909$, and then to divide, $909 \div 3 = 303$.
2. Others would use their calculators just once: to add the numbers; these students would then divide mentally.
3. Others would not use their calculators at all, because they could add the three numbers mentally faster than they could on a calculator. (Just say to yourself: 300, 300, and 300 is 900; and $1 + 3 + 5$ is 9 more.)
4. Finally, others would do no calculations whatsoever. They would realize that the average of any three consecutive odd integers is the middle one: 301, **303**, 305.

NOTE: The more the calculator was used, the *longer* it took to solve the problem. Use your calculator only when it will really save you time or if you think you will make a mistake without it.

Here are three final comments on the use of calculators:

1. Don't pick up your calculator until you have analyzed the question and know exactly what has to be calculated. Remember that no calculator can *do* mathematics. *You* have to know the mathematics and the way to apply it. A calculator cannot tell you whether to multiply or divide or that on a particular question you should use the Pythagorean theorem.

2. PSAT questions don't require tedious calculations. However, if you don't see how to avoid calculating, just do it—*don't spend a lot of time looking for a shortcut that will save you a little time!*

3. Most students use calculators more than they should, but if you can solve a problem with a calculator that you might otherwise miss, use the calculator.

DIRECTIONS FOR MATHEMATICS SECTIONS

At the beginning of each math section, you will see the following directions and notes.

Directions: For each multiple-choice question, solve each problem and choose the best answer from the given choices. Fill in the corresponding circle on your answer sheet. For each grid-in question, solve the problem and enter your answer in the grid on the answer sheet.

Notes:
- Calculators **ARE NOT PERMITTED** in Section 3. Calculators **ARE PERMITTED** in Section 4.
- All variables and expressions represent real numbers unless indicated otherwise.
- All figures are drawn to scale unless indicated otherwise.
- All figures are in a plane unless indicated otherwise.
- Unless indicated otherwise, the domain of a given function is the set of all real numbers x for which the function has real values.

Immediately preceding Question 14 in Section 3 and Question 28 in Section 4, you will see the following set of instructions.

Grid-in Response Directions

First solve the problem, and then enter your answer on the grid provided on the answer sheet. The instructions for entering your answers follow.

- First, write your answer in the boxes at the top of the grid.
- Second, grid your answer in the columns below the boxes.
- Use the fraction bar in the first row or the decimal point in the second row to enter fractions and decimals.

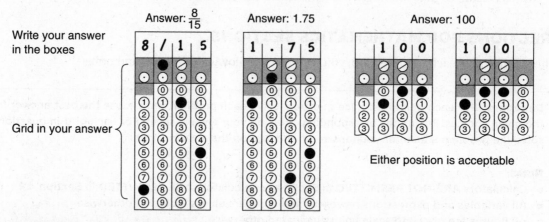

- Grid only one space in each column.
- Entering the answer in the boxes is recommended as an aid in gridding but is not required.
- The machine scoring your exam can read only what you grid, so you **must grid-in your answers correctly to get credit**.
- If a question has more than one correct answer, grid-in only one of them.
- The grid does not have a minus sign; so **no answer can be negative**.
- A mixed number *must* be converted to an improper fraction or a decimal before it is gridded.

  Enter $1\frac{1}{4}$ as 5/4 or 1.25; the machine will interpret 11/4 as $\frac{11}{4}$ and mark it wrong.

- **All decimals must be entered as accurately as possible.** Here are three acceptable ways of gridding

$$\frac{3}{11} = 0.272727\ldots$$

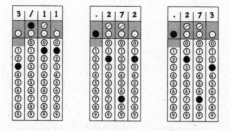

- Note that rounding to .273 is acceptable because you are using the full grid, but you would receive **no credit** for .3 or .27, because they are less accurate.

On the first page of every mathematics section of the PSAT is a box labeled "Reference Information" that contains several basic math facts and formulas. In each math section of every model test in this book, you will find the exact same information.

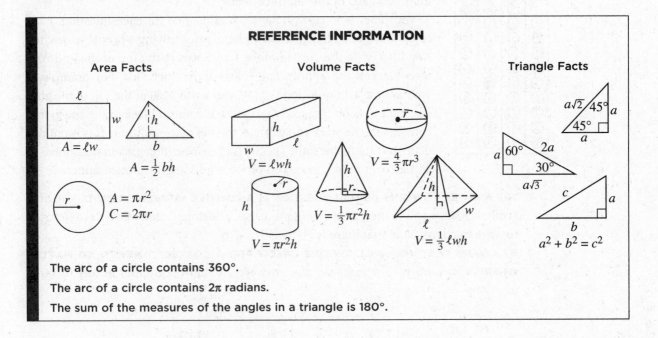

REFERENCE INFORMATION

The arc of a circle contains 360°.

The arc of a circle contains 2π radians.

The sum of the measures of the angles in a triangle is 180°.

Many books advise that since these formulas are printed in the exam booklet, students can always look them up as needed and, therefore, don't have to learn or review them. Even the College Board's official guide, SAT Preparation Booklet, states:

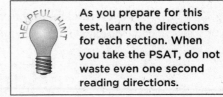

As you prepare for this test, learn the directions for each section. When you take the PSAT, do not waste even one second reading directions.

> The test doesn't require you to memorize formulas.
> Commonly used formulas are provided in the test
> booklet at the beginning of each mathematical section.

This is very poor advice. During the test, you don't want to spend any of your valuable time looking up facts that you can learn now. All of these "commonly used formulas" and other important facts are presented in Chapter 6, where each of them is highlighted and identified as a "Reference Fact." As you learn and review these facts, you should commit them to memory.

INSTRUCTIONS FOR GRID-IN QUESTIONS

Questions 14–17 in Section 3 and questions 28–31 in Section 4 are the student-produced response questions. This is the type of question that is most familiar—you solve a problem and then write the answer on your answer sheet. The only difference is that on the PSAT, *after* you write the answer on your answer sheet, you must then enter the answer on a special grid that can be read by a computer. For this reason, these questions are usually referred to as grid-ins.

To be sure you get credit for these questions, you need to know the guidelines for gridding-in your answers. Not all of this information is given in the directions printed in the exam booklet; so you should carefully read each of the ten rules below.

Your answer sheet will have ten grids, one for each question. Each one will look like the grid shown here. After solving a problem, the first step is to write the answer in the four boxes at the top of the grid. You then blacken the appropriate space under each box. For example, if your answer to a question is 2450, you write 2450 at the top of the grid, one digit in each box, and then in each column blacken the space that contains the number you wrote at the top of the column. This is not difficult, but there are some special rules concerning grid-in questions; so let's go over them before you practice gridding-in some numbers.

1. **THE ANSWER TO EVERY GRID-IN QUESTION IS A POSITIVE NUMBER OR ZERO.** The only symbols that appear in the grid are the digits 0 to 9, a decimal point, and a slash (/), used to write fractions. Note that there is no negative sign.

2. **BE AWARE THAT YOU WILL RECEIVE CREDIT FOR A CORRECT ANSWER NO MATTER WHERE YOU GRID IT.** For example, the answer 17 could be gridded in any of three positions:

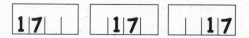

Neverthelesss, try to consistently *write all your answers* the way numbers are usually displayed—*to the right, with blank spaces at the left*.

$$\frac{1}{2} \qquad .4 \qquad .25 \qquad 6$$

3. **DO NOT ROUND OFF ANY ANSWER UNLESS YOU ARE SPECIFICALLY TOLD TO DO SO.**

   ■ For example, suppose the answer to a question is .148. If the question asks what is the value to the nearest hundredth, you must enter .15. You will receive no credit if you entered .148. On the other hand, if the question did not ask you to round off your answer, you will receive no credit for entering .15 since you could enter .148, which is more accurate.

   ■ If a decimal answer will not fit in the grid, enter a decimal point in the first column, followed by the first three digits. For example, if your answer is 0.454545..., enter it as .454. You would receive credit if you rounded it to .455, but don't. You might occasionally make a mistake in rounding, whereas you'll *never* make a mistake if you just copy the first three digits. *Note:* If the correct answer has more than two decimal digits, *you must use all four columns of the grid.* You will receive *no credit* for .4 or .5 or .45. (These answers are not accurate enough.)

4. **NEVER WRITE A 0 BEFORE THE DECIMAL POINT.** The first column of the grid doesn't even have a 0 in it. If the correct answer is 0.3333 . . ., you must grid it as .333. You can't grid 0.33, and 0.3 is not accurate enough.

5. **NEVER REDUCE FRACTIONS.**

- If your answer is a fraction that will fit in the grid, such as $\frac{2}{3}$ or $\frac{4}{18}$ or $\frac{6}{34}$, *just enter it.* Don't waste time reducing it or converting it to a decimal.

- If your answer is a fraction that won't fit in the grid, do not attempt to reduce it; use your calculator to *convert it to a decimal.* For example, $\frac{24}{65}$ won't fit in a grid— it would require five spaces: 2 4 / 6 5. Don't waste even a few seconds trying to reduce it; just divide on your calculator, and enter .369.

   Unlike $\frac{24}{65}$, the fraction $\frac{24}{64}$ can be reduced—to $\frac{12}{32}$, which doesn't help, or to $\frac{6}{16}$ or $\frac{3}{8}$, either of which could be entered. *Don't do it!* Reducing a fraction takes time, and you might make a mistake. You won't make a mistake if you just use your calculator: 24 ÷ 64 = .375.

6. **NEVER ENTER A MIXED NUMBER.** If your answer is $2\frac{1}{2}$, you *cannot* leave a space and enter your answer as 2 1/2. Also, if you enter $\boxed{2\,|\,1\,|\,/\,|\,2}$, the machine will read it as $\frac{21}{2}$ and mark it wrong. You *must* enter $2\frac{1}{2}$ as the improper fraction $\frac{5}{2}$ or as the decimal 2.5.

7. **FULL CREDIT IS GIVEN FOR ANY EQUIVALENT ANSWER. USE THESE GUIDELINES TO ENTER YOUR ANSWER IN THE SIMPLEST WAY.** If your answer is $\frac{6}{9}$, you should enter 6/9. (However, credit would be given for any of the following: 2/3, 4/6, 8/12, .666, .667.)

8. **IF A GRID-IN QUESTION HAS MORE THAN ONE CORRECT ANSWER, GRID IN ONLY ONE OF THE ACCEPTABLE ANSWERS.** For example, if a question asked for a positive number less than 100 that was divisible by both 5 and 7, you could enter *either* 35 *or* 70, but not both. Similarly, if a question asked for a number between $\frac{3}{7}$ and $\frac{5}{9}$, you could enter any *one* of more than 100 possibilities: fractions such as $\frac{1}{2}$ and $\frac{4}{9}$ or *any* decimal between .429 and .554—.43 or .499 or .52, for example.

9. **ENTER AN ANSWER FOR EVERY GRID-IN QUESTION.** Remember that since there is no penalty for an incorrect answer, *never* leave out any question on the SAT. If you are running out of time, just grid in any number, such as 1, in each grid when you have 10 seconds left.

10. **GRID EVERY ANSWER VERY CAREFULLY.** The computer does not read what you have written in the boxes; it reads only the answer in the grid. If the correct answer to a question is 100 and you write 100 in the boxes, but accidentally grid in 200, you get *no* credit.

11. **WRITE EACH ANSWER IN THE BOXES.** If you know that the answer to a question is 100, can you just grid it in and not bother writing it on top? Yes, you will get full credit, and so some SAT guides recommend that you don't waste time writing the answer. This is terrible advice. ***Write each answer in the boxes.*** It takes less than 2 seconds per answer to do this, and it definitely cuts down on careless errors in gridding. Equally important,

if you go back to check your work, it is much easier to read what's in the boxes on top than what's in the grid.

12. **NOTE THE LIMITATIONS OF THE GRID.** Be aware that the smallest number that can be gridded is 0; the largest is 9999. No number greater than 100 can have a decimal point. The largest number less than 100 that can be gridded is 99.9; the smallest number greater than 100 that can be gridded is 101.

Now check your understanding of these guidelines. Use the empty grids below to enter each of the following numbers.

1. 123

2. $\dfrac{7}{11}$

3. $2\dfrac{3}{4}$

4. $\dfrac{8}{30}$

5. 0

6. $\dfrac{48}{80}$

7. 1.1111 . . .

8. $\dfrac{19}{15}$

1. 2. 3. 4.

5. 6. 7. 8.

Solutions. Each grid shows the recommended answer. Other acceptable answers, if any, are written below each grid.

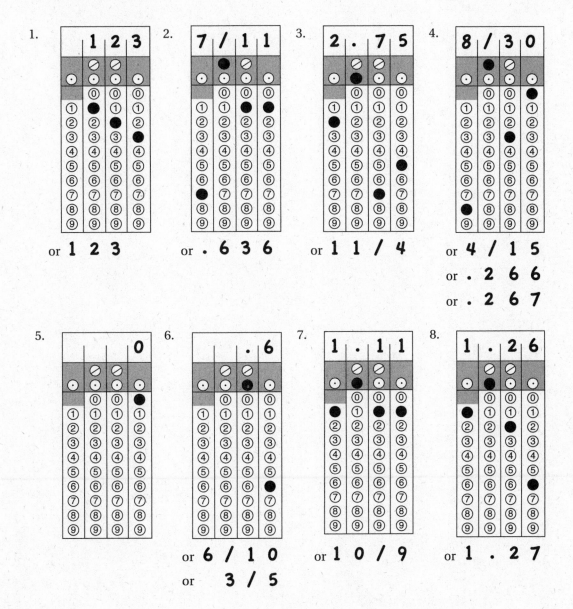

1. or **1 2 3**

2. or **. 6 3 6**

3. or **1 1 / 4**

4. or **4 / 1 5**
or **. 2 6 6**
or **. 2 6 7**

5.

6. or **6 / 1 0**
or **3 / 5**

7. or **1 0 / 9**

8. or **1 . 2 7**

If you missed even one of these, go back and reread the rules on gridding. *You never want to have a correct answer and get no credit because you didn't grid it properly.* When you do the grid-in problems on the practice PSATs in this book, actually grid in the answers. Make sure you understand all of these rules now. When you actually take the PSAT, don't even look at the gridding instructions.

Tactics and Strategies

5

In this chapter you will learn important strategies to help you answer both the multiple-choice and grid-in questions on the PSAT. However, as invaluable as these tactics are, use them only when you need them. *If you know how to solve a problem and are confident that you can do so accurately and reasonably quickly, JUST DO IT!*

TACTIC 5-1 Test the choices, starting with B or C

TACTIC 5-1, often called backsolving, is useful when you are asked to solve for an unknown and you understand what needs to be done to answer the question but you want to avoid doing the algebra. The idea is simple: Test the various choices to see which one is correct.

NOTE: On the PSAT the answers to virtually all numerical multiple-choice questions are listed in either increasing or decreasing order. Consequently, Choices B and C are the middle values, and in applying **TACTIC 5-1**, *you should always start with Choice B or C.* For example, assume that Choices A, B, C, and D are given in increasing order. Try Choice C. If it works, you've found the answer. If Choice C doesn't work, you should know whether you need to test a larger number or a smaller one, and that information permits you to eliminate some choices. If Choice C is too small, you need a larger number. So Choices A and B are out and the answer must be Choice D. If Choice C is too big, eliminate Choice D, which is even larger. The answer must be Choice A or B. So you should then test one of them.

Examples 1 and 2 illustrate the proper use of **TACTIC 5-1**.

➡ Example 1

If the average (arithmetic mean) of 5, 6, 7, and x is 10, what is the value of x?

(A) 13
(B) 18
(C) 22
(D) 28

Solution. Use **TACTIC 5-1**. Test Choice B: $x = 18$.

- Is the average of 5, 6, 7, and 18 equal to 10?

- No: $\dfrac{5+6+7+18}{4} = \dfrac{36}{4} = 9$, which is *too small*.

- Eliminate Choice B. For the average to be 10, x must be *greater* than 18. Eliminate Choice A, as well.
- The answer must be Choice C or D, so try one of them.
- Try Choice C: $x = 22$. Is the average of 5, 6, 7, and 22, equal to 10?
- Yes: $\frac{5+6+7+22}{4} = \frac{40}{4} = 10$. The answer is Choice C.

Remember that every problem that can be solved using **TACTIC 5-1** can be solved directly, usually in less time. Therefore, we again stress: *If you are confident that you can solve a problem quickly and accurately, just do so.*

Many students would find the following direct solution faster than backsolving:

$$\frac{5+6+7+x}{4} = 10 \Rightarrow 5 + 6 + 7 + x = 40 \Rightarrow$$
$$18 + x = 40 \Rightarrow x = 22$$

If you can quickly and accurately do the above algebra, then do so; if you are uncomfortable with the algebra, then just backsolve, and save **TACTIC 5-1** for those problems that you can't easily solve directly.

➡ Example 2 _____

Judy is now twice as old as Adam. Six years ago, though, she was five times as old as he was. How old is Judy now?

(A) 16
(B) 20
(C) 24
(D) 32

Solution. Use **TACTIC 5-1** and backsolve starting with Choice C. If Judy is now 24, Adam is 12, and six years ago, they would have been 18 and 4, respectively. Since Judy would have been less than five times as old as Adam, eliminate Choices C and D, and try Choice A or B. If Judy is now 16, Adam is 8; six years ago, they would have been 10 and 2. That's it; 10 *is* five times 2. The answer is Choice A. (See Example 1 in Section 6-H on word problems for the correct algebraic solution.)

Some tactics allow you to eliminate a few choices so that you can make an educated guess. On those problems where it can be used, **TACTIC 5-1** *always* gets you the right answer. The only reason not to use it on a particular problem is that you can *easily* solve the problem directly.

TACTIC
5-2 Replace variables with numbers

Mastery of **TACTIC 5-2** is critical for anyone developing good test-taking skills. This tactic can be used whenever the four choices involve the variables in the question. There are three steps:

1. Replace each letter with an easy-to-use number.
2. Solve the problem using those numbers.
3. Evaluate each of the five choices with the numbers you chose to see which choice is equal to the answer you obtained.

Examples 3 and 4 illustrate the proper use of **TACTIC 5-2**.

➡ Example 3 _____

If a is equal to the sum of b and c, which of the following is equal to the difference of b and c?

(A) $a - b - c$
(B) $a - b + c$
(C) $a - c$
(D) $a - 2c$

Solution.

- Choose three easy-to-use numbers that satisfy $a = b + c$: for example, $a = 5$, $b = 3$, $c = 2$.
- Then, solve the problem with these numbers: the difference of b and c is $3 - 2 = 1$.
- Finally, check each of the five choices to see which one is equal to 1:

(A) Does $a - b - c = 1$?	No.	$5 - 3 - 2 = 0$
(B) Does $a - b + c = 1$?	No.	$5 - 3 + 2 = 4$
(C) Does $a - c = 1$?	No.	$5 - 2 = 3$
(D) Does $a - 2c = 1$?	Yes!	$5 - 2(2) = 5 - 4 = 1$

- The answer is Choice D.

➡ Example 4 _____

If the sum of five consecutive even integers is t, then, in terms of t, what is the greatest of these integers?

(A) $\dfrac{t-20}{5}$

(B) $\dfrac{t-10}{5}$

(C) $\dfrac{t+10}{5}$

(D) $\dfrac{t+20}{5}$

 HELPFUL HINT Replace the letters with numbers that are easy to use, not necessarily ones that make sense. It is perfectly OK to ignore reality. A school can have 2 students, apples can cost 10 dollars each, trains can go 5 miles per hour or 1,000 miles per hour—it doesn't matter.

Solution.

- Choose five easy-to-use consecutive even integers: 2, 4, 6, 8, 10. Then their sum, t, is 30.
- Solve the problem with these numbers: the greatest of these integers is 10.
- When $t = 30$, the four choices are $\dfrac{10}{5}$, $\dfrac{20}{5}$, $\dfrac{40}{5}$, $\dfrac{50}{5}$.
- Only $\dfrac{50}{5}$, Choice D, is equal to 10.

Of course, if your algebra skills are good, Examples 3 and 4 can be solved without using **TACTIC 5-2**. The important point is that if you are uncomfortable with the correct algebraic solution, you don't have to omit these questions. You can use **TACTIC 5-2** and *always* get the correct answer.

Example 5 is somewhat different. You are asked to reason through a word problem involving only variables. Most students find problems like this one mind-boggling. Here, the use of **TACTIC 5-2** is essential. Without it, most students would find Example 5 very difficult, if not impossible.

➡ **Example 5** _____

A vendor sells h hot dogs and s sodas. If a hot dog costs twice as much as a soda, and if the vendor takes in a total of d dollars, how many *cents* does a soda cost?

(A) $\dfrac{100d}{s+2h}$

(B) $\dfrac{s+2h}{100d}$

(C) $\dfrac{100}{d(s+2h)}$

(D) $100d(s + 2h)$

Of course, when you check the choices, you should use your calculator whenever necessary. However, you do not need to determine the value of each choice; you only need to know if it is the correct choice. In Example 5, Choices B is a small fraction and could not possibly equal 50, and Choice D is clearly much greater than 50. So don't waste your time evaluating them. Only Choices A and C are even possible.

Solution.

- Replace h, s, and d with three easy-to-use numbers. Suppose a soda costs 50¢ and a hot dog $1.00. Then if he sold 2 sodas and 3 hot dogs, he took in $4.00.
- Which of the choices equals 50 when $s = 2$, $h = 3$, and $d = 4$?
- Only Choice A: $\dfrac{100(4)}{2+2(3)} = \dfrac{400}{8} = 50$.

TACTIC
5-3 **Choose an appropriate number**

TACTIC 5-3 is similar to **TACTIC 5-2**, in that we pick convenient numbers. However, no variable is given in the problem. **TACTIC 5-3** is especially useful in problems involving fractions, ratios, and percents.

➡ **Example 6** _____

On a certain college committee, $\dfrac{2}{3}$ of the members are female and $\dfrac{3}{8}$ of the females are varsity athletes. If $\dfrac{3}{5}$ of the committee members are not varsity athletes, what fraction of the members of the committee are male varsity athletes?

(A) $\dfrac{3}{20}$

(B) $\dfrac{1}{4}$

(C) $\dfrac{2}{5}$

(D) $\dfrac{5}{12}$

In problems involving fractions, the best number to use is the least common denominator of all the fractions. In problems involving percents, the easiest number to use is 100.

Solution. Since the lowest common denominator (LCD) of the three fractions is 120, assume that the committee has 120 members. Then there are $\frac{2}{3} \times 120 = 80$ females. Of the 80 females, $\frac{3}{8} \times 80 = 30$ are varsity athletes. Since $\frac{3}{5} \times 120 = 72$ committee members are not varsity athletes, then $120 - 72 = 48$ are varsity athletes; of these, 30 are female and the other 18 are male. Finally, the fraction of the members of the committee who are male varsity athletes is $\frac{18}{120} = \frac{3}{20}$ (Choice A).

➥ Example 7

From 1995 to 2000 the sales of a book decreased by 80 percent. If the sales in 2005 were the same as in 1995, by what percent did they increase from 2000 to 2005?

(A) 80 percent
(B) 100 percent
(C) 400 percent
(D) 500 percent

Solution. Since this problem involves percents, assume that 100 copies of the book were sold in 1995 (and 2005). Sales dropped by 80 (80 percent of 100) to 20 in 2000 and then increased by 80, from 20 back to 100, in 2005. By **KEY FACT C5**, the percent increase was

$$\frac{\text{the actual increase}}{\text{the original amount}} \times 100\% = \frac{80}{20} \times 100\% = 400\% \text{ (Choice C)}$$

TACTIC 5-4 Eliminate all absurd choices before you guess

When you have no idea how to solve a problem, eliminate all the absurd choices and guess from among the remaining ones.

During the course of a PSAT, you may very well find at least a few multiple-choice questions that you read but have no idea how to solve. *Do not just make a wild guess!* Often one or two of the answers are absurd. Eliminate them and then *guess*. Occasionally, three of the choices are absurd. When this occurs, your answer is no longer a guess.

What makes a choice absurd? Here are a few things to note. Even if you don't know how to solve a problem, you may realize that

- the answer must be positive, but some of the choices are negative.
- the answer must be even, but some of the choices are odd.
- a ratio must be less than 1, but some choices are greater than or equal to 1.

Let's look at five examples. In some of them the information given is intentionally insufficient to solve the problem, but you will still be able to determine that some of the answers are absurd. Even when there is enough information to solve the problem, don't. Rather, see if you can determine which choices are absurd and should therefore be eliminated.

➡ Example 8

A region inside a semicircle of radius *r* is shaded. What is its area?

(A) $\frac{1}{4}\pi r^2$

(B) $\frac{1}{3}\pi r^2$

(C) $\frac{1}{2}\pi r^2$

(D) $\frac{2}{3}\pi r^2$

Solution. Even if you have no idea how to find the area of the shaded region, you should know that since the area of a circle is πr^2, the area of a semicircle is $\frac{1}{2}\pi r^2$. So the area of the shaded region must be *less than* $\frac{1}{2}\pi r^2$. Eliminate Choices C and D. On an actual problem, if the diagram were drawn to scale, you may be able to make an educated guess between Choices A and B. If not, just choose one or the other.

➡ Example 9

The average of 5, 10, 15, and *x* is 20. What is *x*?

(A) 20

(B) 25

(C) 45

(D) 50

Solution. If the average of four numbers is 20, and three of them are less than 20, the other one must be greater than 20. Eliminate Choice A and guess. If you further realize that since 5 and 10 are *a lot* less than 20, *x* will be *a lot* more than 20, then eliminate Choice B, as well.

➡ Example 10

A prize of $27,000 is to be divided in some ratio among three people. What is the largest share?

(A) $18,900

(B) $13,500

(C) $ 8,100

(D) $ 5,400

Solution. If the prize were divided equally, each share would be worth $9,000. If it is divided unequally, the largest share must be *more than* $9,000; so eliminate Choices C and D. In an actual question, you would be told what the ratio is, and that information should enable you to eliminate Choice A or Choice B. If not, you would just guess.

➡ Example 11

A jar contains only red and blue marbles. The ratio of the number of red marbles to the number of blue marbles is 5 : 3. What percent of the marbles are blue?

(A) 37.5 percent
(B) 50 percent
(C) 60 percent
(D) 62.5 percent

Solution. Since there are 5 red marbles for every 3 blue ones, there are fewer blue ones than red ones. Therefore, *fewer than half* (50 percent) of the marbles are blue. Eliminate Choices B, C, and D. The answer is Choice A.

➡ Example 12

Square *WXYZ* is divided into two unequal regions. If *WX* = 4, which of the following could be the area of the larger region?

(A) 8π
(B) $8\pi - 32$
(C) $32 - 8\pi$
(D) $8\pi - 16$

Solution. Since the area of the square is 16, the area of the larger region must be more than 8. Since π is slightly more than 3, 8π (which appears in each choice) is somewhat more than 24, approximately 25. Check the choices:

- (A) $8\pi \approx 25$, which is more than the area of the whole square.
- (B) $8\pi - 32$ is negative. Clearly impossible!
- (C) $32 - 8\pi \approx 7$, which is too small.
- (D) $8\pi - 16 \approx 9$. The answer must be D.

TACTIC
5-5 Draw a diagram

On any geometry question for which a figure is not provided, draw one (as accurately as possible) in your test booklet. Often looking at the diagram will lead you to the correct method. Sometimes, as in Example 13, a careful examination of the diagram is sufficient to actually determine the correct answer.

➡ Example 13

A rectangle is 7 times as long as it is wide. If the width is *w*, what is the length of a diagonal?

(A) $5w\sqrt{2}$
(B) $7w$
(C) $8w$
(D) $50w$

Solution. First draw a rectangle that is 7 times as large as it is wide. (By marking off 7 widths, you should be able to do this quite accurately.) Then draw in a diagonal.

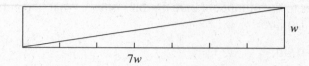

You probably realize that you can use the Pythagorean theorem to find the length of the diagonal, but by looking at the diagram, you should see that the diagonal is just slightly larger than the length, $7w$. Now check each answer choice using your calculator when necessary. Clearly, the answer is not $7w$, and $50w$ is way too big. Eliminate Choices B and D. Even Choice C, $8w$, is probably too big, but don't eliminate it until you use your calculator to test Choice A. $5\sqrt{2} \approx 7.07$, which looks just right. Choose Choice A.

 TACTIC

5-6 Use diagrams wisely. If a diagram is drawn to scale, trust it.

Remember that every diagram that appears on the PSAT has been drawn as accurately as possible, unless you see "Note: Figure not drawn to scale."

 On the PSAT, if you know how to solve a geometry problem, just do it. However, if you don't know how and if there is a diagram that has been drawn to scale, do not leave it out. Trusting the diagram to be accurate, you can always eliminate some of the choices and make an educated guess.

In figures that are drawn to scale, the following are true: line segments that appear to be the same length, are the same length; if an angle clearly looks obtuse, it is obtuse; and if one angle appears larger than another, you may assume that it is larger.

Examples 14, 15, and 16 below all contain diagrams that have been drawn to scale. Of course, each of these relatively easy examples has a correct mathematical solution, but for practice use **TACTIC 5-6** to eliminate as many choices as possible by simply looking at the given diagram.

➡ **Example 14** _____

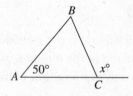

If in the figure above $AB = AC$, what is the value of x?

(A) 125
(B) 115
(C) 65
(D) 50

Solution. Clearly, the angle is obtuse; so x is greater than 90, and so you can immediately eliminate Choices C and D. You can "measure" x more accurately by drawing a couple of lines in the diagram. Draw in $\overline{DC}$ perpendicular to $\overline{AC}$.

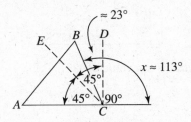

Then, $x = 90°$ plus the measure of $\angle DCB$. To estimate the measure of $\angle DCB$, draw in $\overline{EC}$, which bisects $\angle ACD$, a 90° angle. This creates angle ECD, a 45° angle, and it is clear that the measure of $\angle DCB$ is about half of that, say 23°. So, x is about $90 + 23 = 113$. The answer must be Choice B, 115.

⬥ **Example 15** _____

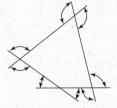

In the figure above, what is the sum of the measures of all the marked angles?

(A)   540°
(B)   720°
(C)   900°
(D)   1,080°

Solution. Make your best estimate of each angle and add them up. The five choices are so far apart that even if you're off by 15° or more on some of the angles, you'll get the right answer. The sum of the estimates shown is 690°; so the correct answer *must* be 720° (Choice B).

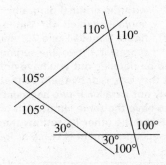

➡ **Example 16** _____

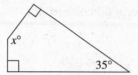

In the figure above, what is the value of *x*?

(A) 120
(B) 130
(C) 145
(D) 160

Solution. Since the diagram is drawn to scale, trust it. Look at *x*: it appears to be *about* 90 + 50 = 140; it is *definitely* less than 160.

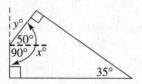

Also, *y* is clearly less than 45; so *x* is greater than 135. The answer must be 145 (Choice C).

 TACTIC
5-7   **Use diagrams wisely. If a diagram is not drawn to scale, redraw it to scale.**

In figures that are not drawn to scale, make *no* assumptions. Lines that look parallel might not be; an angle that appears to be obtuse, might, in fact, be acute; two line segments might have the same length even though one looks twice as long as the other.

In the examples illustrating **TACTIC 5-6**, all of the diagrams were drawn to scale, and we were able to use the diagrams to our advantage. When diagrams have not been drawn to scale, you must be more careful.

 In order to redraw a diagram to scale, ask yourself, "What is wrong with the original diagram?" If an angle is marked 45°, but in the figure it looks like a 75° angle, redraw it. If two line segments appear to be parallel, but you have not been told that they are, redraw them so that they are clearly not parallel. If two segments appear to have the same length, but one is marked 5 and the other 10, redraw them so that the second segment is twice as long as the first.

➡ **Example 17**

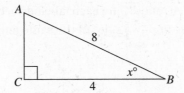

Note: Figure not drawn to scale

In △ABC, what is the value of x?

(A) 30
(B) 45
(C) 60
(D) 75

Solution. In what way is this figure not drawn to scale? $AB = 8$ and $BC = 4$, but in the figure, $\overline{AB}$ is not nearly twice as long as $\overline{BC}$. Although the figure is not drawn to scale, the square symbol at angle C indicates that angle C is a right angle. So draw a right triangle in which $\overline{AB}$ *is* twice as long as $\overline{BC}$. Now you can see that x is about 60 (Choice C).

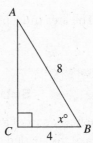

In fact, x is exactly 60. If the hypotenuse of a right triangle is twice the length of one of the legs, then the triangle is a 30-60-90 triangle, and the angle formed by the hypotenuse and that leg is 60° (see Section 6-J).

➡ **Example 18**

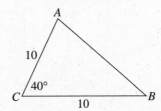

Note: Figure not drawn to scale

In the figure above, which of the following statements *could* be true?

  I. $\overline{AB} < \overline{AC}$
 II. $\overline{AB} > \overline{AC}$
III.   Area of △ABC = 50

(A) None
(B) I only
(C) II only
(D) I and III only

Solution. In the given diagram, $\overline{AB}$ is longer than $\overline{AC}$, which is 10. But, we know that we *cannot trust the diagram.* Actually, there are two things wrong: angle C is labeled 40° but looks much more like 60° or 70°, and $\overline{AC}$ and $\overline{BC}$ are each labeled 10, but $\overline{BC}$ is much longer. Redraw the triangle with a smaller angle and two sides of the same length.

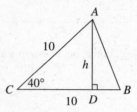

Now just look: $\overline{AB}$ is clearly shorter than $\overline{AC}$. So I is true and II is false. If you draw in altitude $\overline{AD}$, it is also clear that h is less than 10.

$$A = \frac{1}{2}\,bh = \frac{1}{2}\,(10)h = 5h < 5 \times 10 = 50$$

The area must be less than 50. III is false. Only I is true (Choice B).

TACTIC
5-8 Subtract to find shaded regions

Whenever part of a figure is shaded and part is unshaded, the straightforward way to find the area of the shaded portion is to find the area of the entire figure and subtract from it the area of the unshaded region. Occasionally, you may see an easy way to calculate the shaded area directly, but usually you should subtract.

➡ **Example 19** _____

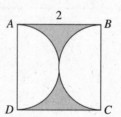

In the figure above, the shaded region is bounded by two semicircles and two sides of square $ABCD$. If $AB = 2$, what is the area of the shaded region?

(A) $4 - 2\pi$

(B) $4 - \pi$

(C) $4 + 2\pi$

(D) $16 - 4\pi$

Solution. The entire region is a square whose area is 4. Since each semicircle has a diameter of 2 (hence a radius of 1), together they form a circle of radius 1. The area of such a circle is $\pi(1)^2 = \pi$. So, the area of the shaded region is $4 - \pi$ (Choice B).

NOTE: Choices A and C are each absurd. Choice A is negative, and Choice C is greater than the area of the square.

TACTIC
5-9 Add equations

When a question involves two equations, often the best strategy is to add them or subtract them. If there are three or more equations, just add them.

➥ Example 20

If $4x + y = 23$ and $x - 2y = 8$, what is the average of x and y?

(A) 0
(B) 2.5
(C) 3
(D) 3.5

HELPFUL HINT Usually, answering a question that involves two or more equations does not require you to solve them.

Solution. Add the two equations:

$$\begin{array}{r} 4x + y = 23 \\ + \quad x - 2y = 8 \\ \hline 5x - y = 31 \end{array}$$

This does not appear to help, so try subtracting the two equations:

$$\begin{array}{r} 4x + y = 23 \\ - \quad x - 2y = 8 \\ \hline 3x + 3y = 15 \end{array}$$

Divide each side by 3:

$$x + y = 5$$

The average of x and y is their sum divided by 2:

$$\frac{x+y}{2} = \frac{5}{2} = 2.5$$

The answer is Choice B.

NOTE: You *could have* actually solved for x and y [$x = 6$, $y = -1$] and then taken their average. However, that method would have been more time-consuming and unnecessary.

➥ Example 21

If $a - b = 1$, $b - c = 2$, and $c - a = d$, what is the value of d?

(A) −3
(B) −1
(C) 1
(D) 3

Solution. Since there are more than two equations, add them:

$$\begin{array}{r} a - b = 1 \\ b - c = 2 \\ + \quad c - a = d \\ \hline 0 = 3 + d \Rightarrow d = -3 \end{array}$$

The answer is Choice A.

TACTIC
5-10   Systematically make lists

When a question asks "how many," often the best strategy is to make a list. If you do this, it is important that you make the list in a *systematic* fashion so that you don't inadvertently leave something out. Often, shortly after starting the list, you can see a pattern developing and can figure out how many more entries there will be without writing them all down.

Listing things systematically means writing them in numerical order (if the entries are numbers) or in alphabetical order (if the entries are letters). If the answer to "how many" is a small number (as in Example 22), just list all possibilities. If the answer is a large number (as in Example 23), start the list and write enough entries until you see a pattern.

➡ Example 22

The sum of three positive integers is 20. If one of them is 5, what is the greatest possible value of the product of the other two?

Solution. Since one of the integers is 5, the sum of the other two is 15. Systematically, list all possible pairs, (a, b), of positive integers whose sum is 15, and check their products. First let $a = 1$, then 2, and so on.

a	b	ab
1	14	14
2	13	26
3	12	36
4	11	44
5	10	50
6	9	54
7	8	56

The answer is 56.

➡ Example 23

A palindrome is a number, such as 74,947, that reads the same forward and backward. How many palindromes are there between 200 and 800?

Solution. First, write down the numbers in the 200s that end in 2:

202, 212, 222, 232, 242, 252, 262, 272, 282, 292

Now write the numbers beginning and ending in 3:

303, 313, 323, 333, 343, 353, 363, 373, 383, 393

HELPFUL HINT
Don't list *all* the possibilities. STOP as soon as you see the pattern.

By now you should see the pattern: there are ten numbers beginning with a 2, ten beginning with 3, and there will be ten beginning with 4, 5, 6, and 7 for a total of 6 × 10 = 60 palindromes.

None of these exercises *requires* the use of the tactics that you just learned. However, as you try each one, even if you know the correct mathematical solution, before solving it, think about which of the tactics could be used. An answer key follows the questions.

MULTIPLE-CHOICE QUESTIONS

1. If the average (arithmetic mean) of 10, 20, 30, 40, and a is 50, what is the value of a?

   (A) 50
   (B) 60
   (C) 100
   (D) 150

2. Larry has 250 marbles, all red, white, and blue, in the ratio of 1 : 3 : 6, respectively. How many blue marbles does he have?

   (A) 75
   (B) 100
   (C) 125
   (D) 150

3. If w whistles cost c cents, how many whistles can you get for d dollars?

   (A) $\dfrac{100dw}{c}$

   (B) $\dfrac{dw}{100c}$

   (C) $\dfrac{dw}{c}$

   (D) cdw

4. If x percent of w is 10, what is w?

   (A) $\dfrac{10}{x}$

   (B) $\dfrac{100}{x}$

   (C) $\dfrac{1,000}{x}$

   (D) $\dfrac{x}{100}$

5. If 8 percent of c is equal to 12 percent of d, which of the following is equal to $c + d$?

   (A) $1.5d$
   (B) $2d$
   (C) $2.5d$
   (D) $3d$

6. On a certain legislative committee consisting solely of Republicans and Democrats, $\dfrac{3}{8}$ of the members are Republicans. If $\dfrac{2}{3}$ of the committee members are men and $\dfrac{3}{5}$ of the men are Democrats, what fraction of the members are Democratic women?

   (A) $\dfrac{3}{20}$

   (B) $\dfrac{9}{40}$

   (C) $\dfrac{1}{4}$

   (D) $\dfrac{2}{5}$

7. Kim receives a commission of $25 for every $2,000 worth of merchandise she sells. What percent is her commission?

   (A) $1\dfrac{1}{4}$ percent

   (B) $2\dfrac{1}{2}$ percent

   (C) 5 percent

   (D) 25 percent

8. From 1990 to 1995, the value of one share of stock of *XYZ* corporation increased by 25 percent. If the value was *D* dollars in 1995, what was the value in 1990?

   (A) $1.25D$
   (B) $1.20D$
   (C) $0.80D$
   (D) $0.75D$

9. What is the value of p if p is positive and $p \times p \times p = p + p + p$?

(A) $\dfrac{1}{3}$

(B) $\sqrt{3}$

(C) 3

(D) $3\sqrt{3}$

10. What is 4 percent of 5 percent?

(A) 0.20 percent

(B) 2.0 percent

(C) 9 percent

(D) 20 percent

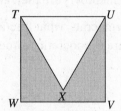

11. In the figure above, $TUVW$ is a square and TUX is an equilateral triangle. If $VW = 2$, what is the area of the shaded region?

(A) $4 - \sqrt{2}$

(B) $4 - \sqrt{3}$

(C) $4 - 2\sqrt{2}$

(D) $4 - 2\sqrt{3}$

12. If $12a + 3b = 1$ and $7b - 2a = 9$, what is the average (arithmetic mean) of a and b?

(A) 0.1

(B) 0.5

(C) 1

(D) 2.5

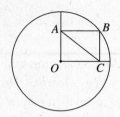

13. In the figure above, if the radius of circle O is 10, what is the length of diagonal AC of rectangle $OABC$?

(A) $\sqrt{10}$

(B) $5\sqrt{2}$

(C) 10

(D) $10\sqrt{2}$

GRID-IN QUESTIONS

14. What is the area of a rectangle whose length is twice its width and whose perimeter is equal to the perimeter of a square whose area is 1?

_____

15. For how many integers between 1 and 1000 is at least one of the digits a 9?

_____

Answer Key

Next to the answer for each question is the number of the tactic that would be most helpful in answering the question, in the event that you do not see the direct solution.

1. **D** (TACTIC 5-1)

2. **D** (TACTIC 5-1)

3. **A** (TACTIC 5-2)

4. **C** (TACTIC 5-2)

5. **C** (TACTIC 5-3)

6. **B** (TACTIC 5-3)

7. **A** (TACTIC 5-4)

8. **C** (TACTIC 5-4)

9. **B** (TACTIC 5-1)

10. **A** (TACTIC 5-4)

11. **B** (TACTIC 5-8)

12. **B** (TACTIC 5-9)

13. **C** (TACTIC 5-6)

14. $\dfrac{8}{9}$ (TACTIC 5-5)

15. **271** (TACTIC 5-10)

Review of PSAT Math

6

ARITHMETIC

> To do well on the PSAT, you need to feel comfortable with most topics of basic arithmetic. The first five sections of Chapter 6 provide you with a review of the basic arithmetic operations, signed numbers, fractions and decimals, ratios, percents, and averages. Because you will have a calculator with you at the test, you will not have to do long division, multiply three-digit numbers, or perform any other tedious calculations using paper and pencil. If you use a calculator with fraction capabilities, you can even avoid finding least common denominators and reducing fractions.
>
> The solutions to more than one-third of the math questions on the PSAT depend on your knowing the KEY FACTS in these sections. Be sure to review them all.

6-A BASIC ARITHMETIC CONCEPTS

A *set* is a collection of "things" that have been grouped together in some way. Those "things" are called the *elements* or *members*. For example:

If *A* is the set of states in the United States, then California is an element of *A*.

If *B* is the set of letters in the English alphabet, then *z* is a member of *B*.

If *C* is the set of even integers, then 46 is in *C*.

The *union* of two sets, *A* and *B*, is the set consisting of all the elements that are in *A* or *B* or both. Note that this includes those elements that are in *A* and *B*. The union is represented as $A \cup B$.

The *intersection* of two sets, *A* and *B*, is the set consisting only of those elements that are in both *A* and *B*. The intersection is represented as $A \cap B$.

In describing a set of numbers, we usually list the elements inside a pair of braces. For example, let A be the set of prime numbers less than 10, and let *B* be the set of even positive integers less than 10.

$$A = \{2, 3, 5, 7\} \qquad B = \{2, 4, 6, 8\}$$
$$A \cup B = \{2, 3, 4, 5, 6, 7, 8\}$$
$$A \cap B = \{2\}$$

The *solution set* of an equation is the set of all numbers that satisfy the equation.

➡️ Example 1 _____

If $C = \{-2, -1, 0, 1, 2\}$ and D is the set that consists of the squares of each of the elements of C, how many numbers are elements of D?

Solution. 0 is in D (since $0^2 = 0$); 1 is in D (since $1^2 = 1$); and 4 is in D (since $2^2 = 4$). These are the only elements of D; so D has 3 elements. Note that $(-1)^2 = 1$ and $(-2)^2 = 4$, but we have already listed 1 and 4. $D = \{0, 1, 4\}$.

Let's start our review of arithmetic by reviewing the most important sets of numbers and their properties. On the PSAT the word *number* always means *real number*, a number that can be represented by a point on the number line.

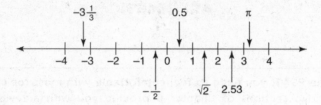

Signed Numbers

The numbers to the right of 0 on the number line are called **positive** and those to the left of 0 are called **negative**. Note that 0 is neither positive nor negative. Negative numbers must be written with a *negative sign* (-3); positive numbers can be written with a *plus sign* $(+3)$ but are usually written without a sign (3). All numbers can be called *signed numbers*.

The **absolute value** of a number a, denoted $|a|$, is the distance between a and 0 on the number line. Since 5 is 5 units to the right of 0 on the number line and -5 is 5 units to the left of 0, both have an absolute value of 5:

$$|5| = 5 \quad \text{and} \quad |-5| = 5$$

➡️ Example 2 _____

How many integers are solutions of the inequality $|x| < 5$?

(A) 4
(B) 8
(C) 9
(D) infinitely many

Solution. There are infinitely many *numbers* whose absolute value is less than 5, but only 9 of them are *integers*.

$$-4, -3, -2, -1, 0, 1, 2, 3, 4 \quad \text{(Choice C)}$$

In arithmetic we are basically concerned with the addition, subtraction, multiplication, and division of numbers. The table below gives the terms for the results of these operations.

Operation	Symbol	Result	Example	
Addition	$+$	**Sum**	16 is the sum of 12 and 4	$12 + 4 = 16$
Subtraction	$-$	**Difference**	8 is the difference of 12 and 4	$12 - 4 = 8$
Multiplication*	$\times$	**Product**	48 is the product of 12 and 4	$12 \times 4 = 48$
Division	$\div$	**Quotient**	3 is the quotient of 12 and 4	$12 \div 4 = 3$

*In certain situations, multiplication can also be indicated by a dot, parentheses, or the juxtaposition of symbols without any sign: $2^2 \cdot 2^4$, 3(4), 3(x + 2), 3a, 4abc.

Given any two numbers *a* and *b*, you can *always* find their sum, difference, product, and quotient (with a calculator, if necessary), but you can *never divide by zero*.

$$0 \div 7 = 0, \quad \text{but} \quad 7 \div 0 \text{ is meaningless}$$

➡ Example 3

What is the sum of the product and quotient of 8 and 8?

Solution. Product: $8 \times 8 = 64$. Quotient: $8 \div 8 = 1$. Sum: $64 + 1 = 65$.

Key Fact A1

For any number *a*: $a \times 0 = 0$. Conversely, if the product of two or more numbers is 0, *at least one* of them must be 0.

$$\text{If } ab = 0, \text{ then } a = 0 \text{ or } b = 0.$$
$$\text{If } rst = 0, \text{ then } r = 0 \text{ or } s = 0 \text{ or } t = 0.$$

➡ Example 4

What is the product of all the integers from -5 to 5, inclusive?

Solution. Before reaching for your calculator, look and think. You are asked for the product of eleven numbers, one of which is 0. So, by **KEY FACT A1**, the product is 0.

Key Fact A2

The product and quotient of two positive numbers or two negative numbers is positive; the product and quotient of a positive number and a negative number is negative.

$12 \times 2 = 24$	$12 \times (-2) = -24$	$(-12) \times 2 = -24$	$(-12) \times (-2) = 24$
$12 \div 2 = 6$	$12 \div (-2) = -6$	$(-12) \div 2 = -6$	$(-12) \div (-2) = 6$

To determine whether a product of more than two numbers is positive or negative, count the number of negative factors.

- The product of an *even* number of negative factors is positive.
- The product of an *odd* number of negative factors is negative.

➡ **Example 5**_____

Which of the following are equal to $(-1)^{25}$?

   I. $(-1)^{100}$
  II. $-(1)^{100}$
 III. $-(-1)^{100}$

(A) I only
(B) II only
(C) III only
(D) II and III only

Solution. Since 25 is odd and 100 is even, $(-1)^{25} = -1$, whereas $(-1)^{100} = 1$. (I is false.) Since $1^{100} = 1$, $-(1)^{100} = -1$. II is true. Since $(-1)^{100} = 1$, $-(-1)^{100} = -1$. III is true. Only II and III are true (Choice D).

- The sum of two positive numbers is positive.
- The sum of two negative numbers is negative.

$$6 + 2 = 8 \quad (-6) + (-2) = -8$$

- To find the sum of a positive and a negative number, find the difference of their absolute values and use the sign of the number with the larger absolute value.

To calculate $6 + (-2)$ or $(-6) + 2$, take the *difference*, $6 - 2 = 4$, and use the sign of the number whose absolute value is 6:

$$6 + (-2) = 4 \quad (-6) + 2 = -4$$

To subtract signed numbers, change the problem to an addition problem, by changing the sign of what is being subtracted, and use **KEY FACT A4**.

$$2 - 6 = 2 + (-6) = -4 \qquad 2 - (-6) = 2 + (6) = 8$$

$$(-2) - (-6) = (-2) + (6) = 4 \qquad (-2) - 6 = (-2) + (-6) = -8$$

In each case, the minus sign was changed to a plus sign, and either the 6 was changed to -6 or the -6 was changed to 6.

All arithmetic involving signed numbers can be accomplished on *any* calculator, but not all calculators handle negative numbers the same way. Be sure you know how to enter negative numbers and how to use them on *your* calculator. It is a good idea to always put negative numbers in parentheses.

Integers

The *integers* are $\{\ldots, -4, -3, -2, -1, 0, 1, 2, 3, 4, \ldots\}$
The *positive integers* are $\{1, 2, 3, 4, 5, \ldots\}$
The *negative integers* are $\{\ldots, -5, -4, -3, -2, -1\}$

Consecutive integers are two or more integers written in sequence in which each integer is 1 more than the preceding one. For example:

CAUTION: Never assume that *number* means *integer*: 3 is not the only number between 2 and 4—there are infinitely many.

$$22, 23 \qquad 6, 7, 8, 9$$

$$-2, -1, 0, 1 \qquad n, n+1, n+2, n+3, \ldots$$

➥ Example 6

If $0 < x < 3$ and $2 < y < 8$, what is the largest integer value of $x + y$?

Solution. If x and y are integers, the largest value of $x + y$ is $2 + 7 = 9$. However, even though $x + y$ is to be an integer, neither x nor y must be. If $x = 2.5$ and $y = 7.5$, then $x + y = 10$, which must be the largest integer value, since clearly $x + y < 11$.

The sum, difference, and product of two integers is *always* an integer; the quotient of two integers may be an integer, but not necessarily. The quotient $37 \div 10$ can be expressed as $\frac{37}{10}$ or $3\frac{7}{10}$ or 3.7. If the quotient is to be an integer, you can also say that the quotient is 3 and there is a *remainder* of 7. It depends upon your point of view. For example, if 37 pounds of rice is to be divided into 10 bags, each bag will hold 3.7 pounds; but if 37 books are to be divided among 10 people, each one will get 3 books and there will be 7 left over (the remainder).

To find the remainder when 100 is divided by 7, divide on your calculator: $100 \div 7 = 14.285714\ldots$ This tells you that the quotient is 14. Ignore everything to the right of the decimal point. To find the remainder, multiply: $14 \times 7 = 98$, and then subtract: $100 - 98 = 2$.

The standard way to find quotients and remainders is to use long division. But on the PSAT, you should *never* do long division; you should use your calculator.

➥ Example 7

If the remainder when a is divided by 7 is 2 and the remainder when b is divided by 7 is 4, what is the remainder when ab is divided by 7?

(A) 0
(B) 1
(C) 3
(D) 6

Solution. *a* can be any number that is 2 more than a multiple of 7: 9, 16, 23, ... *b* can be any number that is 4 more than a multiple of 7: 11, 18, 25, ...

For simplicity, let *a* = 9 and *b* = 11. Then *ab* = 99, and when 99 is divided by 7, the quotient is 14 and the remainder is 1 (Choice B).

If *a* and *b* are integers, the following four terms are synonymous:

a is a **divisor** of *b*	*a* is a **factor** of *b*
b is **divisible** by *a*	*b* is a **multiple** of *a*

All these statements mean that, when *b* is divided by *a*, there is no remainder (or, more precisely, the remainder is 0). For example:

3 is a divisor of 12.	3 is a factor of 12.
12 is divisible by 3.	12 is a multiple of 3.

The only positive divisor of 1 is 1. All other positive integers have at least two positive divisors: 1 and itself, and possibly many more. For example, 6 is divisible by 1 and 6, as well as 2 and 3, whereas 7 is divisible only by 1 and 7. Positive integers, such as 7, which have *exactly two* positive divisors are called **prime numbers** or **primes**. Here are the first few primes:

$$2, 3, 5, 7, 11, 13, 17, 19, 23$$

Memorize this list—it will come in handy. Note that 1 is *not* a prime.

➥ Example 8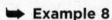

What is the sum of the largest prime factor of 26 and the largest prime factor of 28?

Solution.
The factors of 26 are 1, 2, 13, and 26. The largest *prime* factor is 13.
The factors of 28 are 1, 2, 4, 7, 14, and 28. The largest *prime* factor is 7.
The sum of 13 and 7 is 20.

The **even numbers** are all the integer multiples of 2: {. . . , −4, −2, 0, 2, 4, 6, . . .}
The **odd numbers** are the integers not divisible by 2: {. . . , −5, −3, −1, 1, 3, 5, . . .}

NOTE

0 is an even integer.

Key Fact A6

---

1. If two integers are both even or both odd, their sum and difference are even.
2. If one integer is even and the other odd, their sum and difference are both odd.
3. The product of two integers is even unless both of them are odd.

Exponents and Roots

Repeated addition of the same number is indicated by multiplication:

$$11 + 11 + 11 + 11 + 11 + 11 + 11 = 7 \times 11$$

Repeated multiplication of the same number is indicated by an exponent:

$$11 \times 11 \times 11 \times 11 \times 11 \times 11 \times 11 = 11^7$$

In the expression 11^7, 11 is called the **base** and 7 is the **exponent**.

Although most of the exponents you will encounter on the PSAT are positive integers, you may occasionally see 0, negative integers, and rational numbers used as exponents. All of these are defined in the next **KEY FACT**.

Key Fact A7

For any number b and positive integer n:

- $b^0 = 1$
- $b^1 = b$
- $b^n = b \times b \times \ldots \times b$, where b is used as a factor n times
- $b^{-n} = \dfrac{1}{b^n}$
- $b^{\frac{1}{n}} = \sqrt[n]{b}$

For example,

$$2^0 = 1 \qquad\qquad 2^1 = 2 \qquad\qquad 2^4 = 2 \times 2 \times 2 \times 2 = 16$$

$$2^{-4} = \dfrac{1}{2^4} = \dfrac{1}{16} \qquad\qquad 16^{\frac{1}{4}} = \sqrt[4]{16} = 2$$

Now consider the following four calculations.

(i) $\quad 5^4 \times 5^3 = (5 \times 5 \times 5 \times 5) \times (5 \times 5 \times 5) = 5^7 = 5^{4+3}$

(ii) $\quad \dfrac{5^6}{5^4} = \dfrac{\cancel{5} \times \cancel{5} \times \cancel{5} \times \cancel{5} \times 5 \times 5}{\cancel{5} \times \cancel{5} \times \cancel{5} \times \cancel{5}_1} = 5 \times 5 = 5^2 = 5^{6-4}$

(iii) $\quad (5^2)^3 = (5 \times 5)^3 = (5 \times 5) \times (5 \times 5) \times (5 \times 5) = 5^6 = 5^{2 \times 3}$

(iv) $\quad 5^3 \times 6^3 = (5 \times 5 \times 5) \times (6 \times 6 \times 6) = (5 \times 6)(5 \times 6)(5 \times 6) = (5 \times 6)^3$

These four examples illustrate the following important laws of exponents.

Key Fact A8

For any numbers b, c, m, and n:

(i) $b^m b^n = b^{m+n}$ $\qquad$ (ii) $\dfrac{b^m}{b^n} = b^{m-n}$ $\qquad$ (iii) $(b^m)^n = b^{mn}$ $\qquad$ (iv) $b^m c^m = (bc)^m$

➡ **Example 9**_____

If $5^a \times 5^b = 5^{50}$, what is the average (arithmetic mean) of a and b?

Solution. Since $5^a \times 5^b = 5^{a+b}$, we see that $a + b = 50 \Rightarrow \dfrac{a+b}{2} = 25$.

➡ Example 10

What is the value of $16^{\frac{3}{4}}$?

Solution. By **KEY FACT A8** (iii), $16^{\frac{3}{4}} = \left(16^{\frac{1}{4}}\right)^3 = \left(\sqrt[4]{16}\right)^3 = 2^3 = 8$.

Squares and Square Roots

The exponent that appears most often on the PSAT is 2. It is used to form the square of a number, as in πr^2 (the area of a circle), $a^2 + b^2 = c^2$ (Pythagorean theorem), or $x^2 - y^2$ (the difference of two squares). Therefore, it is helpful to recognize the **perfect squares**, numbers that are the squares of integers. The squares of the integers from 0 to 15 are as follows:

x	0	1	2	3	4	5	6	7	8	9	10	11	12	13	14	15
x^2	0	1	4	9	16	25	36	49	64	81	100	121	144	169	196	225

There are two numbers that satisfy the equation $x^2 = 4$: $x = 2$ and $x = -2$. The positive number, 2, is called the **principal square root** of 4 and is denoted by the symbol $\sqrt{4}$. Clearly, each perfect square has a square root: $\sqrt{0} = 0$, $\sqrt{16} = 4$, $\sqrt{49} = 7$, and $\sqrt{121} = 11$. It is an important fact, however, that *every* positive number has a square root.

Key Fact A9

For any positive number a, there is a positive number b that satisfies the equation $b^2 = a$. That number is called the principal square root of a and is written $b = \sqrt{a}$. Therefore, for any positive number a: $\sqrt{a} \times \sqrt{a} = (\sqrt{a})^2 = a$.

The only difference between $\sqrt{4}$ and $\sqrt{5}$ is that $\sqrt{4}$ is an integer, whereas $\sqrt{5}$ is not. Since 5 is greater than 4, we know that $\sqrt{5}$ is greater than $\sqrt{4} = 2$. In fact, $(2.2)^2 = 4.84$, which is close to 5, and $(2.23)^2 = 4.9729$, which is very close to 5. So, $\sqrt{5} \approx 2.23$. Using the square root key on your calculator, you can find the value of any square root to several decimal places of accuracy, much more than you need for the PSAT.

➡ Example 11

What is the circumference of a circle whose area is 10π?

(A) 10π

(B) $\pi\sqrt{10}$

(C) $2\pi\sqrt{10}$

(D) $\pi\sqrt{20}$

Solution. Since the area of a circle is given by the formula $A = \pi r^2$, we have

$$\pi r^2 = 10\pi \Rightarrow r^2 = 10 \Rightarrow r = \sqrt{10}$$

The circumference is given by the formula $C = 2\pi r$, so $C = 2\pi\sqrt{10}$ (Choice C).

(See Section 7-L on circles.)

PEMDAS

When a calculation requires performing more than one operation, it is important to carry out the operations in the correct order. For decades students have memorized the sentence, "Please Excuse My Dear Aunt Sally," or just the first letters, PEMDAS, to remember the proper order of operations. The letters stand for:

- **P**arentheses: First do whatever appears in parentheses, following PEMDAS within the parentheses also, if necessary.
- **E**xponents: Next evaluate all terms with exponents.
- **M**ultiplication and **D**ivision: Do all multiplications and divisions *in order from left to right*—do not necessarily multiply first and then divide.
- **A**ddition and **S**ubtraction: Finally, do all additions and subtractions *in order from left to right*—do not necessarily add first and then subtract.

Here are some worked-out examples.

1. $10 + 4 \times 2 = 10 + 8 = 18$ [Multiply before you add.]
    $(10 + 4) \times 2 = 14 \times 2 = 28$ [First add in the parentheses.]

2. $16 \div 2 \times 4 = 8 \times 4 = 32$ [Just go from left to right.]
    $16 \div (2 \times 4) = 16 \div 8 = 2$ [First multiply in the parentheses.]

3. $5 \times 2^3 = 5 \times 8 = 40$ [Do exponents first.]
    $(5 \times 2)^3 = 10^3 = 1,000$ [First multiply in the parentheses.]

4. $10 + 15 \div (2 + 3) = 10 + 15 \div 5 = 10 + 3 = 13$ [Do parentheses first, then divide.]

5. $100 - 2^2(3 + 4 \times 5) = 100 - 2^2(23) = 100 - 4(23) = 100 - 92 = 8$
    [Do parentheses first (using PEMDAS), then the exponent, then multiplication.]

Key Fact A10

(The distributive law) For any real numbers a, b, and c:

$$a(b + c) = ab + ac \qquad a(b - c) = ab - ac$$

and if $a \neq 0$

$$\frac{b+c}{a} = \frac{b}{a} + \frac{c}{a} \qquad \frac{b-c}{a} = \frac{b}{a} - \frac{c}{a}$$

➥ Example 12

Which of the following is equivalent to $\dfrac{x^5 + x^4}{x^4}$ for all nonzero numbers x?

(A) $x + 1$

(B) x^5

(C) $x^5 + 1$

(D) $x + x^4$

Solution. $\dfrac{x^5 + x^4}{x^4} = \dfrac{x^5}{x^4} + \dfrac{x^4}{x^4} = x + 1$ (Choice A).

PRACTICE EXERCISES

MULTIPLE-CHOICE QUESTIONS

1. For how many integers n, is it true that $n^2 = n^3$?

   (A) 1
   (B) 2
   (C) 4
   (D) More than 4

2. All of the students in Ms. Epstein's physics class earned a grade between 75 and 93, inclusive, on the midterm exam. For each integer, n, between 75 and 93, inclusive, at least one student earned a grade of n. Which of the following inequalities could be used to determine if any student earned a grade of G?

   (A) $|G - 93| \le 75$
   (B) $|G - 84| \le 9$
   (C) $|G - 75| \le 18$
   (D) $|G - 75| \le 93$

3. Which of the following is equal to $(5^5 \times 5^5)^5$?

   (A) 5^{15}
   (B) 5^{30}
   (C) 5^{50}
   (D) 5^{125}

4. If p and q are primes greater than 100, which of the following must be true?

   I. $p + q$ is even
   II. pq is odd
   III. $p^2 - q^2$ is even

   (A) I only
   (B) I and II only
   (C) I and III only
   (D) I, II, and III

5. If $(5^a)(5^b) = \dfrac{5^c}{5^d}$, what is d in terms of a, b, and c?

   (A) $\dfrac{c}{ab}$
   (B) $c - a - b$
   (C) $a + b - c$
   (D) $\dfrac{c}{a-b}$

GRID-IN QUESTIONS

6. What is the value of $\left(\dfrac{1}{2}\right)^{-4} \div \left(\dfrac{1}{2}\right)^4$?

7. If x satisfies the inequality $|x - 0.01| \le 0.001$, what is one possible value of x?

8. If the product of five consecutive even integers is equal to one of the integers, what is the largest possible value of one of the integers?

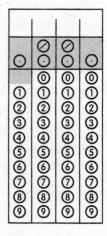

9. At Ben's Butcher Shop, 199 pounds of chopped meat being divided into packages, each weighing 2.5 pounds. How many pounds of meat are left when there isn't enough to make another whole package?

10. If a, b, and c are positive integers and $((19^a)^b)^c = 19^{19}$, what is the average (arithmetic mean) of a, b, and c?

Answer Key

1. **B**   2. **B**   3. **C**   4. **D**   5. **B**

6. **256**   7. **.01**

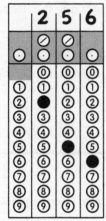

or any number satisfying $.009 \le x \le .011$

8. **8**   9. **1.5**   10. **7**

6-B FRACTIONS AND DECIMALS

Several questions on the PSAT involve fractions or decimals. In this section we will present all of the important facts you need to know for the PSAT. Remember that on one of the two math sections, you are not permitted to use a calculator. So, it is essential that you review all of this material thoroughly.

Comparing Fractions and Decimals

Key Fact B1

To compare two decimals, follow these rules:

- Whichever number has the greater number to the left of the decimal point is greater: since 10 > 9, 10.001 > 9.896 and since 1 > 0, 1.234 > 0.8.
- If the numbers to the left of the decimal point are equal (or if there are no numbers to the left of the decimal point), proceed as follows:

  1. If the numbers do not have the same number of digits to the right of the decimal point, add zeros to make the number of digits equal.
  2. Now, compare the numbers to the right of the decimal point (*ignoring* the decimal point itself).

For example, to compare 1.83 and 1.823, add a zero to the end of 1.83, forming 1.830. Now, thinking of them as whole numbers, compare the numbers to the right of the decimal point: $830 > 823 \Rightarrow 1.830 > 1.823$.

Key Fact B2

To compare two fractions, use one of the following two methods:

- **In section 4, use your calculator to convert the fractions to decimals. Then apply KEY FACT B2. This *always* works.**

  For example, to compare $\frac{1}{3}$ and $\frac{3}{8}$, write $\frac{1}{3} = 0.3333\ldots$ and $\frac{3}{8} = 0.375$.

  Since $0.375 > 0.333$, $\frac{3}{8} > \frac{1}{3}$.

- **In section 3, where you cannot use your calculator, use the fact that $\frac{a}{b} < \frac{c}{d}$ if and only if $ad < bc$.**

  For example, $\frac{1}{3} < \frac{3}{8}$ because $(1)(8) < (3)(3)$.

Key Fact B3

KEY FACTS B1 and **B2** apply to *positive* decimals and fractions. Clearly, any positive number is greater than any negative number. For negative decimals and fractions, note that if $a > b$, then $-a < -b$.

$$\frac{3}{8} > \frac{1}{3} \Rightarrow -\frac{1}{3} > -\frac{3}{8} \quad \text{and} \quad .83 > .829 \Rightarrow -.83 < -.829$$

Arithmetic Operations with Decimals and Fractions

Using a calculator saves time and avoids careless errors. If you know that $12 \times 12 = 144$ and that $1.2 \times 1.2 = 1.44$, fine, but if you're not sure, use your calculator rather than paper and pencil. You should even use your calculator to multiply $.2 \times .2$ if there's any chance that you would write 0.4 instead of 0.04 as the answer.

 HELPFUL HINT On the PSAT, all decimal arithmetic (including whole numbers) that you can't easily do mentally should be done on your calculator.

Key Fact B4

To multiply two fractions, multiply their numerators and multiply their denominators:

$$\frac{3}{5} \times \frac{4}{7} = \frac{3 \times 4}{5 \times 7} = \frac{12}{35}$$

Key Fact B5

To multiply a fraction by any other number, write that number as a fraction whose denominator is 1:

$$\frac{3}{5} \times 7 = \frac{3}{5} \times \frac{7}{1} = \frac{21}{5} \qquad \frac{3}{4} \times \pi = \frac{3}{4} \times \frac{\pi}{4} = \frac{3\pi}{4}$$

TACTIC B1   **Reduce fractions before multiplying (divide the numerator and the denominator by a common factor).**

➡ **Example 1**

Express the product, $\frac{3}{4} \times \frac{8}{9} \times \frac{15}{16}$, in lowest terms.

Solution. If you just multiply the numerators and denominators (with a calculator, of course), you get $\frac{360}{576}$, which is a nuisance to reduce. Also, dividing on your calculator won't help, since your answer is supposed to be a fraction in lowest terms. It is better to use **TACTIC B1** and reduce first:

$$\frac{\overset{1}{\cancel{3}}}{4} \times \frac{\overset{1}{\cancel{8}}}{\underset{1}{\cancel{9}}} \times \frac{\overset{5}{\cancel{15}}}{\underset{2}{\cancel{16}}} = \frac{1 \times 1 \times 5}{4 \times 1 \times 2} = \frac{5}{8}$$

When a problem requires you to find a fraction of a number, multiply.

➥ **Example 2**_____

If $\frac{5}{8}$ of the 320 seniors at Central High School are girls, and $\frac{4}{5}$ of the senior girls are taking a science course, how many senior girls are NOT taking a science course?

(A) 40

(B) 70

(C) 160

(D) 200

Solution. There are $\frac{5}{\cancel{8}_1} \times \cancel{320}^{40} = 200$ senior girls. Of these, $\frac{4}{\cancel{5}_1} \times \cancel{200}^{40} = 160$ are taking science. Then, $200 - 160 = 40$ are not taking science (Choice A).

CALCULATOR HINT

When you use your calculator, enter the numbers without reducing. Given the choice of multiplying $\frac{48}{128} \times 80$ or $\frac{3}{8} \times 80$, *you* would prefer the second option, but with *your calculator*, the first one is just as easy.

The ***reciprocal*** of any nonzero number x, is the number $\frac{1}{x}$. The reciprocal of the fraction $\frac{a}{b}$ is the fraction $\frac{b}{a}$.

Key Fact B6

To divide any number by a fraction, multiply that number by the reciprocal of the fraction:

$$20 \div \frac{2}{3} = \frac{20}{1} \times \frac{3}{2} = 30 \qquad \frac{3}{5} \div \frac{2}{3} = \frac{3}{5} \times \frac{3}{2} = \frac{9}{10}$$

➥ **Example 3**_____

A certain real estate course takes 36 hours to complete. If the course is divided into 40-minute classes, how many times does the class meet?

Solution. First, note that 40 minutes $= \frac{40}{60}$ hour $= \frac{2}{3}$ hour. Then, $36 \div \frac{2}{3} = \frac{36}{1} \times \frac{3}{2} = 54$.

   NOTE: In this problem, you could have changed 36 hours to $36 \times 60 = 2,160$ minutes and then divided: $2,160 \div 40 = 54$.

To add or subtract fractions with the same denominator, add or subtract the numerators and keep the denominator:

$$\frac{4}{9}+\frac{1}{9}=\frac{5}{9} \qquad \frac{4}{9}-\frac{1}{9}=\frac{3}{9}=\frac{1}{3}$$

To add or subtract fractions with different denominators, first rewrite the fractions as equivalent fractions with the same denominators:

$$\frac{1}{6}+\frac{3}{4}=\frac{2}{12}+\frac{9}{12}=\frac{11}{12}$$

NOTE: The *easiest* denominator to get is the product of the denominators ($6 \times 4 = 24$, in this example), but the *best* denominator to use is the *least common denominator*, which is the *least common multiple* (LCM) of the denominators (12 in this case). Using the least common denominator minimizes the amount of reducing that is necessary to express the answer in lowest terms.

➡ **Example 4**_____

Michael had a baseball card collection. Sally took $\frac{1}{3}$ of his cards and Heidi took $\frac{1}{4}$ of them. What fraction of his cards did Michael have left?

➡ **Example 5**_____

Michael had a baseball card collection. Sally took $\frac{1}{3}$ of his cards and Heidi took $\frac{1}{4}$ of what was left. What fraction of his cards did Michael have left?

Solution 4. $\frac{1}{3}+\frac{1}{4}=\frac{4}{12}+\frac{3}{13}=\frac{7}{12}$ of the cards were taken; so Michael had $\frac{5}{12}$ of them left.

Solution 5. $\frac{1}{3}+\frac{1}{4}\left(\frac{2}{3}\right)=\frac{1}{3}+\frac{1}{6}=\frac{2}{6}+\frac{1}{6}=\frac{3}{6}=\frac{1}{2}$ of the cards were taken; so Michael had $\frac{1}{2}$ of them left.

CAUTION: Be sure to read questions carefully.

In Example 4. Heidi took $\frac{1}{4}$ of the cards.

In Example 5, however, she took only $\frac{1}{4}$ of the $\frac{2}{3}$ that were left after Sally took her cards; she took

$\frac{1}{4} \times \frac{2}{3} = \frac{1}{6}$ of the cards.

MULTIPLE-CHOICE QUESTIONS

1. The school band has 24 boys and 16 girls. What fraction of the band members are girls?

   (A) $\dfrac{2}{5}$

   (B) $\dfrac{3}{5}$

   (C) $\dfrac{2}{3}$

   (D) $\dfrac{3}{4}$

2. Adam had a baseball card collection. One day he gave Noah $\dfrac{1}{5}$ of his cards. The following day Adam gave Pete $\dfrac{3}{8}$ of the cards he had left. What fraction of his original collection did Adam still have?

   (A) $\dfrac{3}{10}$

   (B) $\dfrac{17}{40}$

   (C) $\dfrac{1}{2}$

   (D) $\dfrac{23}{40}$

3. $\dfrac{1}{4}$ is the average (arithmetic mean) of $\dfrac{1}{5}$ and what number?

   (A) $\dfrac{1}{20}$

   (B) $\dfrac{3}{10}$

   (C) $\dfrac{1}{3}$

   (D) $\dfrac{9}{20}$

4. What fractional part of a week is 63 hours?

   (A) $\dfrac{7}{24}$

   (B) $\dfrac{3}{8}$

   (C) $\dfrac{24}{63}$

   (D) $\dfrac{4}{7}$

5. If $\dfrac{4}{9}$ of a number is 10, what is $\dfrac{8}{9}$ of that number?

   (A) 5

   (B) 10

   (C) 15

   (D) 20

GRID-IN QUESTIONS

6. $\dfrac{5}{8}$ of 24 is equal to $\dfrac{15}{7}$ of what number?

7. If $5x = 3$ and $3y = 5$, what is the value of $\dfrac{x}{y}$?

8. What is a possible value of w if $\dfrac{2}{3} < \dfrac{1}{w} < \dfrac{7}{9}$?

9. Michael gave $\dfrac{1}{12}$ of his money to Sally and $\dfrac{1}{5}$ of his remaining money to Heidi. If he still had $704, how much money did he have originally?

10. Let $A = \{1, 2, 3\}$ and $B = \{2, 3, 4\}$, and let C be the set consisting of the 9 fractions whose numerators are in A and whose denominators are in B. What is the product of all of the numbers in C?

Answer Key

1. **A**   2. **C**   3. **B**   4. **B**   5. **D**

6. 7

7. 9 / 2 5
or .36

8. 5 / 8
or any number satisfying
1.125 < x < 1.5

9. 9 6 0

10. 1 / 6 4

6-C PERCENTS

The word *percent* means hundredth. We use the symbol % to express the word "percent." For example, "15 percent" means "15 hundredths" and can be written with a % symbol, as a fraction, or as a decimal: $15\% = \frac{15}{100} = .15$.

Key Fact C1

To convert a percent to a decimal or a percent to a fraction, follow these rules:

1. To convert a percent to a decimal, drop the % symbol and move the decimal point two places to the left, adding zeros if necessary. (Remember that we assume that there is a decimal point to the right of any whole number.)
2. To convert a percent to a fraction, drop the % symbol, write the number over 100, and reduce.

$$25\% = .25 = \frac{25}{100} = \frac{1}{4} \qquad 100\% = 1.00 = \frac{100}{100}$$

$$12.5\% = .125 = \frac{12.5}{100} = \frac{125}{1000} = \frac{1}{8}$$

$$1\% = .01 = \frac{1}{100} \qquad \frac{1}{2}\% = .5\% = .005 = \frac{.5}{100} = \frac{1}{200}$$

$$250\% = 2.50 = \frac{250}{100} = \frac{5}{2}$$

Key Fact C2

To convert a decimal to a percent or a fraction to a percent, follow these rules:

1. To convert a decimal to a percent, move the decimal point two places to the right, adding zeros if necessary, and add the % symbol.
2. To convert a fraction to a percent, first convert the fraction to a decimal, and then complete step 1.

$$.375 = 37.5\% \quad .3 = 30\% \qquad 1.25 = 125\% \quad 10 = 1000\%$$

$$\frac{3}{4} = .75 = 75\% \qquad \frac{1}{3} = .33333\ldots = 33.333\ldots\% = 33\frac{1}{3}\%$$

You should be familiar with the following basic conversions.

$$\frac{1}{4} = 25\% \qquad \frac{1}{3} = 33\frac{1}{3}\% \qquad \frac{1}{2} = 50\% \qquad \frac{2}{3} = 66\frac{2}{3}\% \qquad \frac{3}{4} = 75\%$$

 In section 4, any question involving percents should be done on your calculator. To find 25 percent of 32, write 25 percent as a decimal and multiply: $32 \times .25 = 8$. Consider these three questions:

(i) What is 35 percent of 200?

(ii) 70 is 35 percent of what number?

(iii) 70 is what percent of 200?

Solving Percent Problems

Each question can be answered easily by using your calculator, but you must first set up the question properly so that you know what to multiply or divide. In each case, there is one unknown; call it x. Now, just translate each sentence, replacing "is" with "=" and the unknown by x.

(i) $x = 35$ percent of $200 \Rightarrow x = .35 \times 200 = 70$.

(ii) $70 = 35$ percent of $x \Rightarrow 70 = .35x \Rightarrow x = 70 \div .35 = 200$.

(iii) $70 = x$ percent of $200 \Rightarrow 70 = \dfrac{x}{100}(200) \Rightarrow x = 35$.

Another way to handle questions such as these is to set up the proportion $\dfrac{is}{of} = \dfrac{\%}{100}$. To use this method, think of "is," "of," and "%" or "percent" as variables.

In each percent problem you are given two of them and need to find the third, which you label x. Of course, you then solve such equations by cross-multiplying. For example, the three problems we just solved could be handled as follows:

(i) <u>What is</u> 35 percent of 200? (Let $x =$ the "is" number.)

$$\frac{x}{200} = \frac{35}{100} \Rightarrow 100x = 35(200) = 7,000 \Rightarrow x = 70$$

(ii) 70 <u>is 35 percent of what number?</u> (Let $x =$ the "of" number.)

$$\frac{70}{x} = \frac{35}{100} \Rightarrow 7,000 = 35x \Rightarrow x = 200$$

(iii) 70 is <u>what percent</u> of 200? (Let $x =$ the percent.)

$$\frac{70}{200} = \frac{x}{100} \Rightarrow 200x = 7,000 \Rightarrow x = 35$$

➡ **Example 1**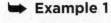

Justin gave 30 percent of his baseball cards to Judy and 25 percent to Lior. If he still had 540 cards, how many did he have originally?

Solution. Originally, Justin had 100 percent of the cards (all of them). Since he gave away 55 percent of them, he had $100\% - 55\% = 45\%$ of them left. So, 540 is 45 percent of what number? $540 = .45x \Rightarrow x = 540 \div .45 = 1,200$.

➡ **Example 2**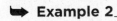

After Sharon gave 157 baseball cards to Zach and 95 to Samir, she still had 348 left. What percent of her cards did Sharon give away?

Solution. Sharon gave away a total of 252 cards and had 348 left. Therefore, she started with $252 + 348 = 600$ cards. So, 252 is what percent of 600?

$$252 = \frac{x}{1\cancel{0}0}(6\overset{6}{\cancel{0}0}) \Rightarrow 6x = 252 \Rightarrow x = 252 \div 6 = 42$$

Sharon gave away 42 percent of her cards.

For any positive number *a*: *a* percent of 100 is *a*. For example: 17.2 percent of 100 is 17.2; 600 percent of 100 is 600; and $\frac{1}{5}$ % of 100 = $\frac{1}{5}$.

In any problem involving percents, try to use the number 100.

➡ **Example 3**_____

In 1980 the populations of Madison and Monroe were the same. From 1980 to 1990, however, the population of Madison increased by 25 percent while the population of Monroe decreased by 25 percent. In 1990, the population of Monroe was what percent of the population of Madison?

(A) 25 percent

(B) 50 percent

(C) 60 percent

(D) $66\frac{2}{3}$ percent

Solution. Assume that in 1980 the population of each town was 100. Then, since 25 percent of 100 is 25, in 1990, the populations were 100 + 25 = 125 (Madison) and 100 − 25 = 75 (Monroe). Then, in 1990, Monroe's population was $\frac{75}{125}$ = $\frac{3}{5}$ = 60% of Madison's.

For any positive numbers *a* and *b*: *a*% of *b* = *b*% of *a*.

Percent Increase and Percent Decrease

The ***percent increase*** of a quantity is

$$\frac{\text{the actual increase}}{\text{the original amount}} \times 100\%$$

The ***percent decrease*** of a quantity is

$$\frac{\text{the actual decrease}}{\text{the original amount}} \times 100\%$$

For example:

- If the price of a radio goes from \$60 to \$75, the actual increase is \$15, and the percent increase is $\frac{15}{60} \times 100\% = \frac{1}{4} \times 100\% = 25\%$.

- If a \$75 radio is on sale for \$60, the actual decrease in price is \$15, and the percent decrease is $\frac{\overset{1}{\cancel{15}}}{\underset{5}{\cancel{75}}} \times 100\% = \frac{1}{5} \times 100\% = 20\%$.

Notice that the percent increase in going from 60 to 75 is *not* the same as the percent decrease in going from 75 to 60.

If the value of an investment rises from \$1,000 to \$5,000, the investment is now worth 5 times, or 500 percent, as much as it was originally, but there has been only a 400 percent increase in value:

$$\frac{\text{the actual increase}}{\text{the original amount}} \times 100\% =$$

$$\frac{4000}{1000} \times 100\% = 4 \times 100\% = 400\%$$

CAUTION: Percents over 100 percent, which come up most often on questions involving percent increases, are often confusing for many students. Be sure you understand that 100 percent of a particular number is that number, 200 percent of a number is 2 times the number, and 1,000 percent of a number is 10 times the number.

➡ Example 4

The value of an investment doubled every 5 years from 1980 to 1995. What was the percent increase in the value during this time?

Solution. The value doubled 3 times from, say, \$100 in 1980 to \$200 in 1985, to \$400 in 1990, and to \$800 in 1995. So the value in 1995 was 8 times the value in 1980, but this was an increase of \$700 or 700 percent.

PRACTICE EXERCISES

MULTIPLE-CHOICE QUESTIONS

1. What is 5% of 10% of 40%?

    (A) 0.002%
    (B) 0.2%
    (C) 2%
    (D) 20%

2. Ron bought a $60 sweater on sale at 10 percent off. How much did he pay, including 5 percent sales tax?

    (A) $53.50
    (B) $55.00
    (C) $56.70
    (D) $57.00

3. What percent of 25 is b?

    (A) $\dfrac{b}{25}$

    (B) $\dfrac{25}{b}$

    (C) $4b$

    (D) $25b$

4. 10 is $\dfrac{1}{10}$ percent of what number?

    (A)   1
    (B)   100
    (C)   1,000
    (D) 10,000

5. On a test consisting of 60 questions, Susan answered 90 percent of the first 50 questions correctly. What percent of the other 10 questions does she need to answer correctly for her grade on the entire exam to be exactly 80 percent?

    (A) 30 percent
    (B) 40 percent
    (C) 50 percent
    (D) 60 percent

GRID-IN QUESTIONS

6. A supermarket reduced the price per pound of whole chickens by 20 percent. How many pounds of chicken can now be purchased for the amount of money that used to buy 20 pounds of chicken?

7. If c is a positive number, 300 percent of c is what percent of $300c$?

8. If 25 students took an exam and 7 of them failed, what percent of them passed?

9. A college has 3,000 students. If 23.5 percent them are freshmen, 29.2 percent of them are sophomores, and 27 percent of them are juniors, how many are seniors?

10. There are twice as many girls as boys in a science class. If 30 percent of the girls and 45 percent of the boys have already completed their lab reports, what percent of the students have not yet finished their reports?

Answer Key

1. **B**   2. **C**   3. **C**   4. **D**   5. **A**

6. 2 5   7. 1   8. 7 2   9. 6 0 9   10. 6 5

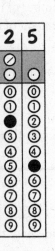

6-D RATIOS AND PROPORTIONS

A *ratio* is a fraction that compares two quantities that are measured in the *same* units. One quantity is the numerator of the fraction, and the other quantity is the denominator.

For example, if there are 6 boys and 16 girls in the chess club, we say that the ratio of the number of boys to the number of girls in the club is 6 to 16, or $\frac{6}{16}$, often written as 6:16. Since a ratio is just a fraction, it can be reduced or converted to a decimal or a percent. The following are all different ways to express the same ratio:

$$6 \text{ to } 16 \qquad 6{:}16 \qquad \frac{6}{16} \qquad 3 \text{ to } 8 \qquad 3{:}8 \qquad \frac{3}{8} \qquad .375 \qquad 37.5\%$$

Key Fact D1

If a set of objects is divided into two groups in the ratio of $a{:}b$, then the first group contains — $\frac{a}{a+b}$ of the objects and the second group contains $\frac{b}{a+b}$ of the objects.

➡ Example 1 _____

A jar contains only red and blue marbles. If the ratio of the number of blue marbles to the number of red marbles in the jar is 2:3, what percent of the marbles are red?

Solution. The red marbles constitute $\frac{2}{2+3} = \frac{3}{5} = 60$ percent of the total number.

➡ Example 2 _____

If 35 percent of the students in the honor society are male, what is the ratio of male students to female students in the society?

Solution. Assume that there are 100 students in the society; then 35 of them are male, and $100 - 35 = 65$ of them are female. So, the ratio of males to females is $\frac{35}{65} = \frac{7}{13}$.

 In problems involving percents, the best number to use is 100.

If we know a ratio, we *cannot* determine from that fact alone how many objects there are. In Example 1 above, since the ratio of blue marbles to red marbles is 2:3, there *might be* 2 blue marbles and 3 red ones, but *not necessarily*—there might be 200 blue marbles and 300 red ones, since the ratio 200:300 clearly reduces to 2:3. In the same way, all of the following are possibilities for the distribution of marbles.

Blue	4	6	8	20	400	8,000	**2x**
Red	6	9	12	30	600	12,000	**3x**

The important thing to observe is that the number of red marbles can be *any* multiple of 3, as long as the number of blue marbles is the *same* multiple of 2.

Key Fact D2

If two numbers are in the ratio of $a{:}b$, then for some number x, the first number is ax and the second number is bx.

TACTIC
D1
In any ratio problem, write the letter *x* after each number and use some given information to solve for *x*.

➡ **Example 3** _____

If the ratio of boys to girls at a pep rally is 4:5, which of the following CANNOT be the number of children at the pep rally?

(A) 27
(B) 108
(C) 120
(D) 360

Solution. If $4x$ and $5x$ are the number of boys and girls at the pep rally, respectively, then the number of children present is $4x + 5x = 9x$. Therefore, the number of children must be a multiple of 9. Only 120 (Choice C), is not divisible by 9.

Ratios can be extended to three or four or more terms. For example, we can say that the ratio of freshmen to sophomores to juniors to seniors in the school play is 2:3:5:3, which means that for every 2 freshmen in the play, there are 3 sophomores, 5 juniors, and 2 seniors.

➡ **Example 4** _____

If the measures of the three angles in a triangle are in the ratio of 5:6:7, what is the measure of the largest angle?

Solution. Let the measures of the three angles be $5x$, $6x$, and $7x$. Since in any triangle the sum of the measures of the three angles is 180° (**KEY FACT J1**):

$$5x + 6x + 7x = 180 \Rightarrow 18x = 180 \Rightarrow x = 10$$

Therefore, the measure of the largest angle is $7 \times 10 = 70°$.

A **proportion** is an equation that states that two ratios are equivalent. Since ratios are just fractions, any equation such as $\frac{4}{6} = \frac{10}{15}$, in which each side is a single fraction, is a proportion. Usually, the proportions you encounter on the PSAT involve one or more variables.

TACTIC
D2
Solve proportions by cross-multiplying: if $\frac{a}{b} = \frac{c}{d}$, then *ad* = *bc*.

➡ **Example 5** _____

If $\frac{2}{7} = \frac{x}{91}$, what is the value of *x*?

Solution. Cross-multiply: $2(91) = 7x \Rightarrow 182 = 7x \Rightarrow x = 26$.

A **rate** is a fraction that compares two quantities measured in *different* units. The word *per* often appears in rate problems: miles per hour, dollars per week, cents per ounce, children per classroom, and so on.

TACTIC
D3 Set up rate problems just like ratio problems.
Solve the proportions by cross-multiplying.

➡ **Example 6**_____

Susan completed 25 math exercises in 35 minutes. At this rate, how many exercises can she do in 42 minutes?

Solution. Handle this rate problem exactly like a ratio problem. Set up a proportion and cross-multiply:

$$\frac{\text{exercises}}{\text{minutes}} = \frac{25}{35} = \frac{x}{42} \Rightarrow 35x = 25 \times 42 = 1050 \Rightarrow x = 30$$

On the PSAT, some rate problems may involve only variables. These problems are handled in exactly the same way.

➡ **Example 7**_____

If a apples cost c cents, how many apples can be bought for d dollars?

(A) $\dfrac{100d}{ac}$

(B) $\dfrac{ad}{100c}$

(C) $\dfrac{c}{100ad}$

(D) $\dfrac{100ad}{c}$

Solution. First change d dollars to $100d$ cents, and set up a proportion:

$$\frac{\text{apples}}{\text{cents}} = \frac{a}{c} = \frac{x}{100d}$$

Now cross-multiply:

$$100ad = cx \Rightarrow x = \frac{100ad}{c} \quad \text{(Choice D)}$$

Rate problems are examples of **direct variation**. We say that one variable **varies directly** with a second variable or that the two variables are **directly proportional** if their quotient is a constant. So if y is directly proportional to x, there is a constant k, such that $\dfrac{y}{x} = k$. The constant is the rate of increase or decrease. In Example 6, the number of math exercises Susan does varies directly with the number of minutes she spends on them. Susan's rate of solving is $\dfrac{5}{7}$ exercises per minute.

The quotient $\dfrac{\text{exercises}}{\text{minutes}}$ is constant: $\dfrac{25}{35} = \dfrac{5}{7}$ and $\dfrac{30}{42} = \dfrac{5}{7}$

Notice that when two quantities vary directly, as the first quantity increases or decreases, so does the other. In Example 6, as the number of exercises increases, the number of minutes it takes Susan to do them also increases.

➥ **Example 8**_____

If x and y are directly proportional and $x = 12$ when $y = 3$, what is x when $y = 12$?

Solution. Since x and y are directly proportional, their quotient is a constant. So

$$\frac{12}{3} = 4 = \frac{x}{12} \Rightarrow x = 48$$

Occasionally on the PSAT you will encounter problems in which as one quantity increases, the other decreases. Problems such as these are usually examples of ***inverse variation***. We say that one variable ***varies inversely*** with a second variable or that the two variables are ***inversely proportional*** if their product is a constant. So if y is inversely proportional to x, there is a constant k such that $xy = k$.

➥ **Example 9**_____

If x and y are inversely proportional and $x = 12$ when $y = 3$, what is x when $y = 12$?

Solution. Since x and y are inversely proportional, their product is a constant. Since $xy = 12 \times 3 = 36$, if $y = 12$, then $x(12) = 36$, and so $x = 3$.

➥ **Example 10**_____

A landscaper has enough money on hand to hire six workers for ten days. Assuming each worker earns the same amount of money per day, for how many days could the landscaper meet his payroll if he hires fifteen workers?

(A) 4
(B) 6
(C) 12
(D) 15

Solution. As the number of workers increases, the number of days the money will last decreases. This is an example of inverse variation. The product, (workers) $\times$ (days), remains constant.

$$(6 \text{ workers}) \times (10 \text{ days}) = 60 \text{ worker-days} = (15 \text{ workers}) \times (d \text{ days}) \Rightarrow d = 4$$

MULTIPLE-CHOICE QUESTIONS

1. If the ratio of boys to girls in the French Club is 2:3, what percent of the club members are girls?

   (A) $33\frac{1}{3}$ percent
   (B) 40 percent
   (C) 60 percent
   (D) $66\frac{2}{3}$ percent

2. If $c + d = 180$ and $c:d = 5:7$, what is the value of $d - c$?

   (A) 15
   (B) 30
   (C) 75
   (D) 105

3. The measures of the three angles in a triangle are in the ratio of 1:2:3. Which of the following statements must be true?

   I. The length of the longest side is twice as long as the length of the shortest side.
   II. The length of the longest side is three times the length of the shortest side.
   III. The triangle is a right triangle.

   (A) I only
   (B) II only
   (C) III only
   (D) I and III only

4. Gilda can grade t tests in $\frac{1}{x}$ hours. At this rate, how many tests can she grade in x hours?

   (A) tx
   (B) tx^2
   (C) $\frac{x}{t}$
   (D) $\frac{1}{tx}$

5. Kerry can polish i inches of a railing in m minutes. At this rate, how many feet can he polish in h hours?

   (A) $\frac{5hi}{m}$
   (B) $\frac{60hi}{m}$
   (C) $\frac{hi}{12m}$
   (D) $\frac{5m}{hi}$

GRID-IN QUESTIONS

6. If $\frac{a}{9} = \frac{9}{2a}$, what is the value of a^2?

7. Roselle can read 36 pages per hour. At this rate, how many pages can she read in 36 minutes?

8. If $3a = 2b$ and $3b = 5c$, what is the ratio of a to c?

10. If a varies directly with b^2, and if $b = 4$ when $a = 3$, what is the value of a when $b = 8$?

9. In a quadrilateral, the ratio of the measures the four angles is 5:6:6:7. What is the degree measure of the largest angle?

Answer Key

1. **C**   2. **B**   3. **D**   4. **B**   5. **A**

6. 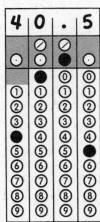 40.5   7. 21.6   8. 10/9   9. 105   10. 12

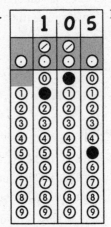

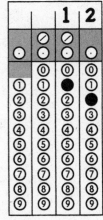

6-E AVERAGES

The *average* of a set of n numbers is the sum of those numbers divided by n.

$$\text{Average} = \frac{\text{the sum of the } n \text{ number}}{n} \quad \text{or simply} \quad A = \frac{\text{sum}}{n}$$

If you took three math tests so far this year and your grades were 81, 93, and 78, to calculate your average, you would add the three grades and divide by 3:

$$\frac{81+93+78}{3} = \frac{252}{3} = 84$$

The technical name for this is *arithmetic mean*, and on the PSAT those words always appear in parentheses—for example, "What is the average (arithmetic mean) of 81, 93, and 78?"

Often on the PSAT, you are *not* asked to find an average; rather, you are given the average of a set of numbers and asked to provide some other information. The key to solving all of these problems is to first find the sum of the numbers. Since $A = \frac{\text{sum}}{n}$, multiplying both sides by n yields this equation: sum $= nA$.

Key Fact E1

If the average of a set of n numbers is A, the sum of those numbers is nA.

TACTIC E1 **Whenever you know the average A of a set of n numbers, multiply A by n to get their sum.**

➡ Example 1

The average (arithmetic mean) of Carol's grades on the 6 French tests that she has taken this year is 86. If her average after the first 4 tests was 83, what was the average of her fifth and sixth tests?

(A) 87.5
(B) 89
(C) 90
(D) 92

Solution.

- Use **TACTIC E1**: Carol has earned a total of $6 \times 86 = 516$ points.
- Use **TACTIC E1** again: On her first 4 tests she earned $4 \times 83 = 332$ points.
- Subtract: On her last 2 tests Carol earned $516 - 332 = 184$ points.
- So, Carol's average on her last 2 tests is $\frac{184}{2} = 92$ (Choice D).

Example 2

In Mr. Walsh's biology class, the average (arithmetic mean) of the grades earned by the 15 girls was 90, and the average grade earned by the 10 boys was 80. What was the class average?

Solution.

- The 15 girls earned a total of $15 \times 90 = 1{,}350$ points.
- The 10 boys earned a total of $10 \times 80 = 800$ points.
- Together the 25 students earned a total of $1{,}350 + 800 = 2{,}150$ points.
- The class average was $2{,}150 \div 25 = 86$.

Notice that the answer to Example 2 is not 85. When we combine two or more averages to form a single average, we cannot take the average of the averages. We must assign each average its proper *weight*. In this case, more students earned 90 then 80, so the class average is closer to 90 than to 80. This is called a *weighted average*.

The solution to Example 2 can be expressed as a single fraction:

$$\frac{15(90)+10(80)}{25} = \frac{1{,}350+800}{25} = \frac{2{,}150}{25} = 86$$

Three other terms associated with averages are *median*, *mode*, and *range*.

- In a set of n numbers arranged in increasing order, the *median* is the middle number (if n is odd) or is the average of the two middle numbers (if n is even).
- In any set of numbers, the *mode* is the number that appears most often.
- In any set of numbers, the *range* is the difference between the greatest and least numbers.

Example 3

In 2015, Judith sold 9 paintings. The selling prices were: $500, $1,100, $1,200, $500, $1,200, $4,900, $700, $500, and $4,000. What is the average (arithmetic mean) of the median, the mode, and the range of this set of data?

Solution. The first step is to write the data in increasing order:

$$500, 500, 500, 700, \underline{1{,}100}, 1{,}200, 1{,}200, 4{,}000, 4{,}900$$

The median is 1,100, which is the middle number. The mode is 500, the number that appears more times than any other. The range in 4,400. It is the difference between 4,900 and 500. Finally, the average of the median, the mode, and the range is

$$\frac{1{,}100+500+4{,}400}{3} = \frac{6{,}000}{3} = 2{,}000$$

MULTIPLE-CHOICE QUESTIONS

1. If the average (arithmetic mean) of 15, 16, 17, and x is 18, what is the value of x?

   (A) 18
   (B) 24
   (C) 48
   (D) 72

2. Linda's average (arithmetic mean) on 3 tests is 80. What does she need on her fourth test to raise her average to 85?

   (A) 90
   (B) 95
   (C) 96
   (D) 100

3. If $x + y = 5$, $y + z = 8$, and $z + x = 9$, what is the average (arithmetic mean) of x, y, and z?

   (A) $\dfrac{11}{3}$
   (B) $\dfrac{11}{2}$
   (C) $\dfrac{22}{3}$
   (D) 11

4. If $x + y = 7(w + z)$, which of the following is the average (arithmetic mean) of w, x, y, and z in terms of w and z?

   (A) $\dfrac{w+z}{4}$
   (B) $\dfrac{w+z}{2}$
   (C) $w + z$
   (D) $2w + 2z$

5. Which of the following is the average (arithmetic mean) of $x^2 - 20$, $50 - x^2$, and $9x + 6$?

   (A) $2x + 3$
   (B) $2x + 30$
   (C) $3x + 12$
   (D) $4.5x + 10$

GRID-IN QUESTIONS

6. What is the average (arithmetic mean) of the positive integers from 1 to 50, inclusive?

7. If $20x + 20y = 70$, what is the average (arithmetic mean) of x and y?

8. What is the average (arithmetic mean), in degrees, of the measures of the eight angles in an octagon?

9. Jason's average (arithmetic mean) on 3 tests is 85. Assuming he can earn no more than 100 on any test, what is the least he can earn on his fourth test and still have a chance for a 90 average after 5 tests?

10. Let M be the median and m the mode of the following set of numbers: 20, 80, 30, 50, 80, 100. What is the average (arithmetic mean) of M and m?

Answer Key

For the PSAT you need to know only a small part of the algebra normally taught in high school. In Sections 6-F, 6-G, and 6-H, we will review only those topics that you absolutely need for the PSAT.

6-F POLYNOMIALS

Even though the terms monomial, binomial, trinomial, and polynomial are not used on the PSAT, you need to be able to work with simple polynomials, and these terms will make it easy to discuss the important concepts.

- A **monomial** is any number or variable or product of numbers and variables. Each of the following are monomials:

$$3 \qquad -4 \qquad x \qquad y \qquad 3x \qquad -4xyz \qquad 5x^3 \qquad 1.5xy^2 \qquad a^3b^4$$

The number that appears in front of the variables in a monomial is called the **coefficient**. The coefficient of $5x^3$ is 5. If there is no number, the coefficient is 1 or -1, because x means $1x$ and $-ab^2$ means $-1ab^2$.

- A **polynomial** is a monomial or the sum of two or more monomials. Each monomial that makes up the polynomial is called a **term** of the polynomial.

Polynomials that have two terms are called **binomials**, and polynomials that have three terms are called **trinomials**. The table below gives examples of each type.

Monomials	Binomials	Trinomials
x^2	$2x^2 + 3$	$x^2 + 5x - 1$
$3abc$	$3x^2 - 7$	$w^2 - 2w + 1$
$-a^2b^3$	$a^2b + b^2a$	$a^2 + 2ab + b^2$

Two terms are called *like terms* if they have exactly the same variables and exponents; they can differ only in their coefficients: $5a^2b$ and $-3a^2b$ are like terms, whereas a^2b and b^2a are not.

On the PSAT, you are often asked to evaluate a polynomial for specific values of the variables.

➡ **Example 1**_____

What is the value of $-2a^2b + ab$ when $a = -6$ and $b = 0.5$?

Solution. Rewrite the expression, replacing the letters a and b by the numbers -6 and 0.5, respectively. First, write each number in parentheses and then evaluate:

$$-2(-6)^2(0.5) + (-6)(0.5) =$$
$$-2(36)(0.5) + (-3) =$$
$$-36 - 3 = -39$$

 CAUTION: Be sure you follow PEMDAS: handle exponents before the other operations. In Example 1, you cannot multiply −2 by −6, get 12, and then square 12. You must first square −6, and then multiply by −2.

Key Fact F1

The only terms of a polynomial that can be combined are like terms.

Key Fact F2

To add two polynomials, put a plus sign between them, erase the parentheses, and combine like terms.

➡ **Example 2**_____

What is the sum of $5x^2 + 10x - 7$ and $3x^2 - 4x + 2$?

Solution.
$(5x^2 + 10x - 7) + (3x^2 - 4x + 2) =$
$5x^2 + 10x - 7 + 3x^2 - 4x + 2 =$
$(5x^2 + 3x^2) + (10x - 4x) + (-7 + 2) =$
$8x^2 + 6x - 5$

 HELPFUL HINT To add, subtract, multiply, and divide polynomials, use the usual laws of arithmetic. To avoid careless errors, write each polynomial in parentheses before performing any arithmetic operations.

Key Fact F3

To subtract two polynomials, change the minus sign between them to a plus sign and change the sign of every term in the second parentheses. Then use **KEY FACT F2** to add them: erase the parentheses and combine like terms.

➡️ **Example 3**

Subtract $3x^2 - 4x + 2$ from $5x^2 + 10x - 7$.

Solution. Be careful. Start with the second polynomial and subtract the first:

$$(5x^2 + 10x - 7) - (3x^2 - 4x + 2) =$$
$$(5x^2 + 10x - 7) + (-3x^2 + 4x - 2) =$$
$$2x^2 + 14x - 9$$

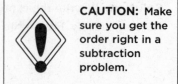

CAUTION: Make sure you get the order right in a subtraction problem.

Key Fact F4

To multiply monomials, first multiply their coefficients and then multiply their variables, by adding the exponents (see Section 6-A).

➡️ **Example 4**

What is the product of $5xy^3z^5$ and $-2x^3y$?

Solution. $(5xy^3z^5)(-2x^2y) = 5(-2)(x)(x^3)(y^3)(y)(z^5) = -10x^4y^4z^5$.

All other polynomials are multiplied by using the distributive property.

Key Fact F5

To multiply a monomial by any polynomial, just multiply each term of the polynomial by the monomial.

➡️ **Example 5**

What is the product of $2a$ and $3a^2 - 6ab + b^2$?

Solution. $2a(3a^2 - 6ab + b^2) = 6a^3 - 12a^2b + 2ab^2$.

On the PSAT, the only other polynomials that you could be asked to multiply are two binomials.

Key Fact F6

To multiply two binomials, use the so-called FOIL method, which is really nothing more than the distributive law. Multiply each term in the first parentheses by each term in the second parentheses and simplify by combining terms, if possible.

$$(2x - 7)(3x + 2) = \underbrace{(2x)(3x)}_{\text{First terms}} + \underbrace{(2x)(2)}_{\text{Outer terms}} + \underbrace{(-7)(3x)}_{\text{Inner terms}} + \underbrace{(-7)(2)}_{\text{Last terms}} = 6x^2 + 4x - 21x - 14 = 6x^2 - 17x - 14$$

➥ **Example 6**_____

What is the value of $(x - 3)(x + 4) - (x - 5)(x + 6)$?

Solution. First, multiply both pairs of binomials:

$(x - 3)(x + 4) = x^2 + 4x - 3x - 12 = x^2 + x - 12$

$(x - 5)(x + 6) = x^2 + 6x - 5x - 30 = x^2 + x - 30$

Now, subtract: $(x^2 + x - 12) - (x^2 + x - 30) = x^2 + x - 12 - x^2 - x + 30 = 18$.

Key Fact F7

The three most important binomial products on the PSAT are

- $(x - y)(x + y) = x^2 - y^2$
- $(x - y)^2 = x^2 - 2xy + y^2$
- $(x + y)^2 = x^2 + 2xy + y^2$

 HELPFUL HINT If you memorize the products, you won't have to multiply the binomials out each time you need them.

➥ **Example 7**_____

If $a - b = 9.2$ and $a + b = 5$, what is the value of $a^2 - b^2$?

Solution. The moment you see $a^2 - b^2$, you should think $(a - b)(a + b)$. So,

$$a^2 - b^2 = (a - b)(a + b) = (9.2)(5) = 46$$

On the PSAT, the only division of polynomials you will have to do is to divide a polynomial by a monomial. You will *not* have to do long division of polynomials.

Key Fact F8

To divide a polynomial by a monomial, use the distributive property.

➥ **Example 8**_____

What is the quotient when $24a^2b + 9ab^3c$ is divided by $6ab$?

Solution. By the distributive property, $\dfrac{24a^2b + 9ab^3c}{6ab} = \dfrac{24a^2b}{6ab} + \dfrac{9ab^3c}{6ab}$.

Now simplify each fraction: $4a + \dfrac{3}{2}b^2c$.

Occasionally on the PSAT you will be asked to simplify an algebraic expression. To do so, you will probably have to do some simple factoring.

Key Fact F9

To factor a polynomial, the first step is *always* to use the distributive property to remove the greatest common factor of all the terms.

For example:

$$6xy + 8yz = 2y(3x + 4z)$$
$$x^3 + x^2 + x = x(x^2 + x + 1)$$

To factor a trinomial, use trial and error to find the binomials whose product is that trinomial.

For example:

$$x^2 - 4x + 4 = (x - 2)(x - 2)$$
$$x^2 - 2x - 15 = (x - 5)(x + 3)$$
$$2x^2 + 12x + 16 = 2(x^2 + 6x + 8) = 2(x + 4)(x + 2)$$

➡ Example 9

Which of the following is equivalent to $\dfrac{2x^2 - 8}{x^2 - 4x + 4}$?

(A) $\dfrac{2(x+2)}{x-2}$

(B) $\dfrac{2(x+4)}{x-4}$

(C) $\dfrac{2x+2}{x-2}$

(D) $\dfrac{6}{4x-4}$

Solution.

$$\frac{2x^2 - 8}{x^2 - 4x + 4} = \frac{2(x^2 - 4)}{(x-2)(x-2)} = \frac{2(x-2)(x+2)}{(x-2)(x-2)} = \frac{2(x+2)}{(x-2)} \quad \text{(Choice B)}$$

In questions like Example 9, you can always just test a value. For example, when $x = 3$, the value of $\dfrac{2x^2 - 8}{x^2 - 4x + 4}$ is $\dfrac{2(3)^2 - 8}{3^2 - 4(3) + 4} = \dfrac{18 - 8}{9 - 12 + 4} = \dfrac{10}{1} = 10$.

Only Choice B is 10 when $x = 3$: $\dfrac{2(3+2)}{3-2} = \dfrac{2(5)}{1} = 10$

Note that this does not depend on the choice of x. You can verify, for example, that if $x = 6$, the original expression and the correct answer choice are both equal to 4. If $x = 10$, the original expression and the correct answer choice are both equal to 3. If $x = 0$, the original expression and the correct answer choice are both equal to –2.

HELPFUL HINT

If you ever get stuck trying to simplify an algebraic expression, you can plug in a number and test the answers.

MULTIPLE-CHOICE QUESTIONS

1. If $x^2 + y^2 = 36$ and $(x + y)^2 = 64$, what is the value of xy?

   (A)   7
   (B)   14
   (C)   28
   (D) 100

2. What is the value of $(500,001)^2 - (499,999)^2$?

   (A)   2
   (B)   4
   (C) 1,000,000
   (D) 2,000,000

3. If $\dfrac{1}{x} + \dfrac{1}{y} = \dfrac{1}{z}$ and $xy = z$, what is the average (arithmetic mean) of x and y?

   (A) 0
   (B) $\dfrac{1}{2}$
   (C) 1
   (D) $\dfrac{x+y}{2z}$

4. What is the average (arithmetic mean) of $x^2 + 2x - 3$, $3x^2 - 2x - 3$, and $30 - 4x^2$?

   (A) $\dfrac{8x^2 + 24}{3}$
   (B) $\dfrac{24 - 4x}{3}$
   (C) -12
   (D)   8

5. What is the value of $x^2 - 10x + 25$ when $x = 95$?

   (A)   90
   (B)   100
   (C)   950
   (D) 8,100

GRID-IN QUESTIONS

6. If $a^2 + b^2 = 4$ and $(a - b)^2 = 2$, what is the value of ab?

7. What is the value of $\dfrac{c^2 - d^2}{c - d}$ when $c = 23.4$ and $d = 34.5$?

8. If $a^2 - b^2 = 80$ and $a - b = 16$, what is the average (arithmetic mean) of a and b?

9. What is the value of $(2x + 3)(x + 6) - (2x - 5)(x + 10)?$

10. If $\left(\dfrac{1}{a} + a\right)^2 = 144$, what is the value of $\dfrac{1}{a^2} + a^2?$

Answer Key

6-G SOLVING EQUATIONS AND INEQUALITIES

Many of the equations and inequalities that you will have to solve on the PSAT have only one variable and no exponents. A simple six-step method, illustrated below, can be used on all of them.

➡ **Example 1** _____

If $\frac{1}{2}x + 3(x - 2) = 2(x + 1) + 1$, what is the value of x?

Solution. Follow the steps outlined in the following table.

Step	What to Do	Example
1	Remove fractions and decimals by multiplying both sides by the Lowest Common Denominator (LCD).	Multiply each term by 2: $x + 6(x - 2) = 4(x + 1) + 2$
2	Remove all parentheses by using the distributive property.	$x + 6x - 12 = 4x + 4 + 2$
3	Combine like terms on each side.	$7x - 12 = 4x + 6$
4	By adding or subtracting, get all the variables on one side.	Subtract $4x$ from each side: $3x - 12 = 6$
5	By adding or subtracting, get all the plain numbers on the other side.	Add 12 to each side: $3x = 18$
6	Divide both sides by the coefficient of the variable.	Divide both sides by 3: $x = 6$

Note: If you start with an inequality and in Step 6 you divide by a negative number, remember to reverse the inequality.

Example 1 *is actually much more difficult than any equation on the PSAT,* because it requires all six steps. This never happens on the PSAT. Think of the six steps as a list of questions that must be answered. Ask whether each step is necessary. If it isn't, move on to the next one; if it is, do it.

Let's look at Example 2, which does not require all six steps.

➡ Example 2

For what real number x is it true that $4(2x - 7) = x$?

(A) -4
(B) -1
(C) 1
(D) 4

Solution. Do whichever of the six steps are necessary.

Step	Question	Yes/No	Example
1	Are there any fractions or decimals?	No	
2	Are there any parentheses?	Yes	Get rid of them: $8x - 28 = x$
3	Are there any like terms to combine?	No	
4	Are there variables on both sides?	Yes	Subtract x from each side: $7x - 28 = 0$
5	Is there a plain number on the same side as the variable?	Yes	Add 28 to each side: $7x = 28$
6	Does the variable have a coefficient?	Yes	Divide both sides by 7: $x = 4$

 TACTIC G1 **Memorize these six steps in order, and use this method whenever you have to solve this type of equation or inequality.**

Sometimes on the PSAT, you are given an equation with several variables and asked to solve for one of them in terms of the others.

 TACTIC G2 **When you have to solve for one variable in terms of the others, treat all of the others as if they were numbers, and apply the six-step method.**

➡ Example 3

If $r = 5s - 2t$, what is the value of s in terms of r and t?

Solution. To solve for s, treat r and t as numbers, and use the six-step method with s as the only variable.

Step	Question	Yes/No	Example
1	Are there any fractions or decimals?	No	
2	Are there any parentheses?	No	
3	Are there any like terms to combine?	No	
4	Are there variables on both sides?	No	Remember: The only variable is s.
5	Is there a plain number on the same side as the variable?	Yes	Remember: We're considering t as a number, and it is on the same side as s, the variable. Add $2t$ to both sides: $r + 2t = 5s$
6	Does the variable have a coefficient?	Yes	Divide both sides by 5: $s = \dfrac{r+2t}{5}$

 In applying the six-step method, you should not actually make a table, as we did in Examples 1–3. Instead, use the method as a guideline and mentally go through each step, doing whichever ones are required.

The six-step method can also be used if a variable is in a denominator. Just be sure to start with Step 1 and get rid of the fraction.

➡ Example 4

If $\dfrac{1}{2x} + \dfrac{2}{3} = \dfrac{4}{3x}$, then $x =$

Solution. Multiply each term by $6x$, the LCD,

$$6x\left(\frac{1}{2x}\right) + 6x\left(\frac{2}{3}\right) = 6x\left(\frac{4}{3x}\right) \Rightarrow 3 + 4x = 8 \Rightarrow 4x = 5 \Rightarrow x = \frac{5}{4} \text{ (or 1.25)}$$

On the PSAT, you could have to solve an equation, such as $2\sqrt{x} - 7 = 5$, that involves a square root. Proceed normally, treating the square root as your variable, using whichever of the six steps are necessary until you have that square root equal to a number. Then square both sides.

➡ Example 5

If $2\sqrt{x} - 7 = 5$, then $x =$

Solution.

Add 7 to each side: $2\sqrt{x} = 12$

Divide each side by 2: $\sqrt{x} = 6$

Now square each side: $(\sqrt{x})^2 = 6^2 \Rightarrow x = 36$

On the PSAT, most of the equations that you will have to solve do not involve exponents. Of those equations that do have exponents, the ones you will see most often are quadratic equations. Quadratic equations are equations that can be written in the form $ax^2 + bx + c = 0$, where a, b, and c are real numbers and $a \neq 0$.

The easiest quadratic equations to solve are those that have no x-term, that is, those in which $b = 0$ as in the following three examples.

➡ Example 6

If x is a positive number and $x^2 + 4 = 29$, what is the value of x?

Solution. When there is an x^2-term but no x-term, just take the square root:

$$x^2 + 4 = 29 \Rightarrow x^2 = 25 \Rightarrow x = \sqrt{25} = 5$$

➡ Example 6a

If x is a positive number and $x^2 + 5 = 29$, what is the value of x?

Solution. This is exactly like Example 6, except now $x^2 = 24$. So $x = \sqrt{24}$. Even though 24 is not a perfect square, $\sqrt{24}$ can be simplified.

Since $24 = 4 \times 6$, we have that $x = \sqrt{24} = \sqrt{4} \times \sqrt{6} = 2\sqrt{6}$.

 CALCULATOR SHORTCUT

If you can easily simplify a square root, that's great; but in Section 4, you never have to. The answers to grid-in problems don't involve square roots. If the answer to a multiple-choice question turns out to be $\sqrt{24}$, which is approximately 4.9, you can use your calculator to see which of the four choices is closest to 4.9.

➡ Example 6b

If x is a positive number and $x^2 + 6 = 29$, what is the value of x?

Solution. Again, this is exactly like Example 6, except now $x^2 = 23$. Not only isn't 23 a perfect square, $\sqrt{23}$ can't be simplified. So $x = \sqrt{23}$.

The next easiest quadratic equations to solve are those that have no constant term, that is, those in which $c = 0$. In Example 7 below, $a = 5$, $b = -2$, and $c = 0$.

Example 7

What is the largest value of x that satisfies the equation $5x^2 - 2x = 0$?

Solution. When an equation has an x^2-term and an x-term but no constant term, solve it by factoring out the x. Then use the fact that if the product of two numbers is 0, one of them must be 0 (KEY FACT A3):

$$5x^2 - 2x = 0 \Rightarrow x(5x - 2) = 0$$

$$\text{So, } x = 0 \text{ or } 5x - 2 = 0 \Rightarrow$$

$$x = 0 \text{ or } 5x = 2 \Rightarrow$$

$$x = 0 \text{ or } x = \frac{2}{5} = .4$$

So the largest value of x that satisfies the given equation is **.4**.

Solving quadratic equations in which a, b, and c are all nonzero requires more sophisticated techniques. The two most common methods are factoring and using the quadratic formula. The easier method is factoring *if you immediately see how to factor the given expression.*

Example 8

If x is a positive number and $x^2 - 5x = 6$, what is the value of x?

Solution. First rewrite the given equation in the form $x^2 - 5x - 6 = 0$. See if you can factor $x^2 - 5x - 6$. Hopefully, you quickly realize that $x^2 - 5x - 6 = (x - 6)(x + 1)$. Then

$$(x - 6)(x + 1) = 0 \Rightarrow (x - 6) = 0 \text{ or } (x + 1) = 0 \Rightarrow x = 6 \text{ or } x = -1$$

So the positive number that satisfies the given equation is **6**.

Unfortunately, even if $ax^2 + bx + c$ can be factored, you may not immediately see how to do it. What's worse is that most quadratic expressions can't be factored. For example, even though $x^2 - 5x - 6$ can be factored, none of the following expressions can be factored:

$$x^2 - 5x - 7; \quad x^2 - 5x - 8; \quad x^2 - 5x - 9; \quad x^2 - 5x - 10$$

So how do you solve an equation such as $x^2 - 5x - 10 = 0$? Use the ***quadratic formula***.

Key Fact G1

Quadratic Formula

If a, b, and c are real numbers with $a \neq 0$ and if $ax^2 + bx + c = 0$, then

$$x = \frac{-b \pm \sqrt{b^2 - 4ac}}{2a}$$

Recall that the symbol $\pm$ is read "plus or minus" and that $x = \frac{-b \pm \sqrt{b^2 - 4ac}}{2a}$ is an abbreviation for $x = \frac{-b + \sqrt{b^2 - 4ac}}{2a}$ or $x = \frac{-b - \sqrt{b^2 - 4ac}}{2a}$.

As you can see, a quadratic equation has two solutions, usually referred to as **roots**, both of which are determined by the quadratic formula.

The expression $b^2 - 4ac$ that appears under the square root symbol is called the **discriminant** of the quadratic equation. As explained in KEY FACT G2, the discriminant provides valuable information about the nature of the roots of a quadratic equation. If we let D represent the discriminant, an alternative way to write the quadratic formula is

$x = \dfrac{-b \pm \sqrt{D}}{2a}$. The following examples illustrate the proper use of the quadratic formula.

First, let's look at a different solution to Example 8.

➥ Example 9

What are the roots of the equation $x^2 - 5x - 6 = 0$?

Solution. Here $a = 1$, $b = -5$, $c = -6$, and $D = b^2 - 4ac = (-5)^2 - 4(1)(-6) = 25 + 24 = 49$

$$\text{So } x = \frac{-(-5) \pm \sqrt{49}}{2} = \frac{5 \pm 7}{2} \Rightarrow$$

$$x = \frac{5+7}{2} = 6 \quad \text{or} \quad x = \frac{5-7}{2} = -1$$

➥ Example 10

What are the roots of the equation $x^2 = 10x - 25$?

Solution. First, rewrite the equation in the form $ax^2 + bx + c = 0$:

$$x^2 - 10x + 25 = 0$$

Then $a = 1$, $b = -10$, $c = 25$, and $D = b^2 - 4ac = (-10)^2 - 4(1)(25) = 100 - 100 = 0$

$$\text{So } x = \frac{-(-10) \pm \sqrt{0}}{2(1)} = \frac{10 \pm 0}{2} \Rightarrow$$

$$x = \frac{10+0}{2} = 5 \quad \text{or} \quad x = \frac{10-0}{2} = 5$$

Notice that since $10 + 0 = 10$ and $10 - 0 = 10$, the two roots are each equal to 5. Some people would say that the equation $x^2 - 10x + 25 = 0$ has only one root; it is better to say that the equation has two equal roots.

➥ Example 11

What are the roots of the equation $2x^2 - 4x - 1 = 0$?

Solution. $a = 2$, $b = -4$, $c = -1$, and $D = b^2 - 4ac = (-4)^2 - 4(2)(-1) = 16 + 8 = 24$

$$\text{So } x = \frac{-(-4) \pm \sqrt{24}}{2(2)} = \frac{4 \pm 2\sqrt{6}}{4} \Rightarrow$$

$$x = \frac{4 + 2\sqrt{6}}{4} = 1 + \frac{1}{2}\sqrt{6} \quad \text{or} \quad x = \frac{4 - 2\sqrt{6}}{4} = 1 - \frac{1}{2}\sqrt{6}$$

➡ Example 12 _____

What are the roots of equation $x^2 - 2x + 2 = 0$.

Solution. $a = 1$, $b = -2$, $c = 2$, and $D = b^2 - 4ac = (-2)^2 - 4(1)(2) = 4 - 8 = -4$

Since there is no real number whose square root is –4, we often say that this equation "has no solutions" or "has no roots." However, what we mean is that this equation "has no *real* roots." Continuing with the quadratic formula, we get:

$$x = \frac{-(-2) \pm \sqrt{-4}}{2(1)} = \frac{2 \pm 2i}{2} = 1 \pm i \Rightarrow$$

$$x = 1 + i \quad \text{or} \quad x = 1 - i$$

See Section 6-T for a discussion of the imaginary unit i and complex numbers.

Examples 9–12, illustrate the facts about the discriminant, D, that are summarized in Key Fact G2.

Key Fact G2

If a, b, and c are real numbers with $a \neq 0$, if $ax^2 + bx + c = 0$, and if $D = b^2 - 4ac$, then

Value of Discriminant	Nature of the Roots
$D = 0$	2 equal roots
$D > 0$	2 unequal real roots
$D < 0$	2 unequal complex roots that are conjugates of each other

Systems of Linear Equations

The equations $x + y = 10$ and $x - y = 2$ each have infinitely many solutions. However, there is only one pair of numbers, $x = 6$ and $y = 4$, which satisfy both equations simultaneously: $6 + 4 = 10$ and $6 - 4 = 2$. Since the graphs of $x + y = 10$ and $x - y = 2$ are both lines, this pair of equations is called a ***linear system of equations***.

A system of equations is a set of two or more equations involving two or more variables. To solve such a system, you must find values for each of the variables that will make each equation true. On the PSAT, the most useful method to solve a system of linear equations is to add or subtract the equations (usually add).

TACTIC

G3

To solve a system of equations, first try to add or subtract them. If there are more than two equations, add them.

➥ **Example 13** _____

If $2x + y = 10$ and $x - y = 2$, then what is the value of xy?

Solution. Add the two equations:

$$\begin{array}{r} 2x + y = 10 \\ + \quad x - y = \ 2 \\ \hline 3x \quad\ \ = 12 \end{array} \quad \text{so, } x = 4$$

Replacing x by 4 in $x - y = 2$ yields $y = 2$. So, $xy = (4)(2) = 8$.

➥ **Example 14** _____

If $3a + 5b = 10$ and $5a + 3b = 30$, what is the average (arithmetic mean) of a and b?

(A) 2.5
(B)   4
(C)   5
(D) 20

Solution. Add the two equations:

$$\begin{array}{r} 3a + 5b = 10 \\ + \quad 5a + 3b = 30 \\ \hline 8a + 8b = 40 \end{array}$$

Divide both sides by 8: $\qquad\qquad\qquad a + b = 5$

The average of a and b is: $\qquad\qquad \dfrac{a+b}{2} = \dfrac{5}{2} = 2.5$ (Choice A)

NOTE: It is not only unnecessary to first solve for a and b ($a = 7.5$ and $b = -2.5$), but because it is so much more time consuming, it would be foolish to do so.

Occasionally on the PSAT, it is as easy, or easier, to solve a system of equations by substitution.

TACTIC
G4

If one of the equations in a system of equations consists of a single variable equal to some expression, substitute that expression for the variable in the other equation.

➥ **Example 15** _____

If $2x + y = 10$ and $y = x - 2$, what is the value of xy?

Solution. This is essentially the same problem as Example 13. However, since here the second equation states that a single variable (y) is equal to some expression ($x - 2$), substitution is a more efficient method than adding. Replace y by $x - 2$ in the first equation: $2x + y = 10$ becomes $2x + (x - 2) = 10$. Then

$$3x - 2 = 10 \Rightarrow 3x = 12 \Rightarrow x = 4$$

To find the value of y, replace x by 4 in either of the original equations:

$$2(4) + y = 10 \Rightarrow y = 2 \text{ or } y = 4 - 2 = 2$$

Finally, $xy = (4)(2) = \mathbf{8}$.

Solving Linear-Quadratic Systems

A question on the PSAT could ask you to solve a system of equations in which one, or even both, of the equations are quadratic. The next example illustrates this.

➡ Example 16 _____

To solve the system $\begin{cases} y = 2x - 1 \\ y = x^2 - 2x + 2 \end{cases}$, use the substitution method. Replace the y in the second equation by $2x - 1$:

$$2x - 1 = x^2 - 2x + 2 \Rightarrow x^2 - 4x + 3 = 0 \Rightarrow$$

$$(x - 3)(x - 1) = 0 \Rightarrow x = 3 \text{ or } x = 1$$

If $x = 3$, then $y = 2(3) - 1 = 5$; and if $x = 1$, then $y = 2(1) - 1 = 1$.
So there are two solutions: $x = 3$, $y = 5$ and $x = 1$, $y = 1$.

Solving the system of equations in Example 16 is equivalent to determining the points of intersection of the line $y = 2x - 1$ and the parabola $y = x^2 - 2x + 2$. Those points are (1, 1) and (3, 5).

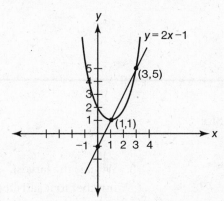

So an alternative method of solving the system of equations in Example 16 is to graph them. If you have a graphing calculator, you can graph the given line and parabola and then determine their points of intersection. Which solution is preferable? This is a personal decision. If your algebra skills are strong, solving the system graphically offers no advantage. If, on the other hand, your algebra skills are weak and your facility with the calculator is good, you could avoid the algebra and use your calculator.

PRACTICE EXERCISES

MULTIPLE-CHOICE QUESTIONS

1. If $5x + 12 = 5 - 2x$, what is the value of x?

   (A) $-\dfrac{17}{7}$

   (B) -1

   (C) 1

   (D) $\dfrac{17}{7}$

2. If $\dfrac{x}{x-y} = 4$, then $x =$

   (A) $\dfrac{3}{4}y$

   (B) $\dfrac{4}{3}y$

   (C) $\dfrac{4}{5}y$

   (D) $\dfrac{5}{4}y$

3. If $\dfrac{1}{3}w + \dfrac{1}{6}w + \dfrac{1}{9}w = 33$, what is the value of w?

   (A) 18

   (B) 27

   (C) 54

   (D) 72

4. If $ax - b = c - dx$, what is the value of x in terms of a, b, c, and d?

   (A) $\dfrac{b+c}{a+d}$

   (B) $\dfrac{c-b}{a-d}$

   (C) $\dfrac{b+c-d}{a}$

   (D) $\dfrac{c-b}{a-d}$

5. If $\dfrac{a+2b+3c}{3} = \dfrac{a+2b}{2}$, then $c =$

   (A) $\dfrac{a+2b}{6}$

   (B) $\dfrac{a+2b}{3}$

   (C) $\dfrac{a+2b}{2}$

   (D) $a + 2b$

GRID-IN QUESTIONS

6. If $9a + 11 = 32$, what is the value of $9a - 11$?

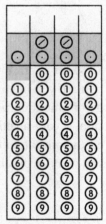

7. If $7n - 3 = 3$, what is the value of $(7n - 3)^3$?

8. What is the largest number that satisfies the equation $x^2 + 12 = 7x$?

9. If $7y - 5x = 3$, what is
    the smallest integer value
    of x for which $y > 75$?

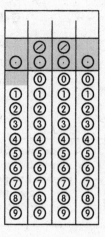

10. If $x^2 + 5 < 6$ and
    $2x^2 + 7 > 8$, what is
    one possible value of x?

Answer Key

1. **B**   2. **B**   3. **C**   4. **A**   5. **A**

6. 7. 8. 9. 10.

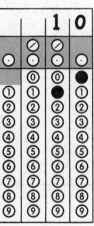

or any number
satisfying $.71 < x < 1$

6-H WORD PROBLEMS

A typical PSAT has several word problems. In this chapter you have already seen word problems on consecutive integers in Section 6-A, fractions in Section 6-B, percents in Section 6-C, ratios and proportions in Section 6-D, and averages in Section 6-E. Later in this chapter you will see word problems involving probability, circles, triangles, and other geometric figures. A few of these problems can be solved with just arithmetic, but most of them require basic algebra.

In problems involving ages, remember that "years ago" means you need to subtract, and "years from now" means you need to add.

Age Problems

Example 1 below is the same as Example 2 in Chapter 5. In Chapter 5 you were shown how to solve it by backsolving; now we will show you the correct algebraic solution.

➡️ **Example 1** _____

Judy is now twice as old as Adam, but six years ago, she was five times as old as he was. How old is Judy now?

(A) 16
(B) 20
(C) 24
(D) 32

Solution. Let x = Adam's age now, and fill in the table below.

It is often very useful to organize the data from a word problem in a table.

	Judy	**Adam**
Now	$2x$	x
6 years ago	$2x - 6$	$x - 6$

Now translate: Judy's age six years ago was five times Adam's age:

$$2x - 6 = 5(x - 6)$$
$$2x - 6 = 5x - 30 \Rightarrow 24 = 3x \Rightarrow x = 8$$

Adam is now 8. However, 8 is *not* the answer. The question could have asked for Adam's age now or six years ago or at any time. It could have asked for Judy's age at any time or for their combined ages. What it did ask for is Judy's age now, which is 16, twice Adam's age (Choice A).

In all word problems on the PSAT, circle what you're looking for in your exam booklet. Don't answer the wrong question!

Distance Problems

All distance problems involve one of three variations of the same formula:

$$\text{distance} = \text{rate} \times \text{time} \quad \text{rate} = \frac{\text{distance}}{\text{time}}$$

$$\text{time} = \frac{\text{distance}}{\text{rate}}$$

These are usually abbreviated, $d = rt$, $r = \dfrac{d}{t}$, and $t = \dfrac{d}{r}$.

➥ Example 2 _____

Justin drove 1 mile, from Exit 10 to Exit 11 on the thruway, at 50 miles per hour. Adam drove the same distance at 60 miles per hour. How many *seconds* longer did it take Justin than Adam to drive that mile?

Solution. The time to drive 1 mile at 50 miles per hour is given by

$$t = \frac{1 \text{ mile}}{50 \text{ miles per hour}} = \frac{1}{50} \text{ hour} = \frac{1}{50} \times 60 \text{ minutes} =$$

$$\frac{6}{5} \text{ minutes} = 1\frac{1}{5} \text{ minutes}$$

The time to drive 1 mile at 60 miles per hour is given by

$$t = \frac{1 \text{ mile}}{60 \text{ miles per hour}} = \frac{1}{60} \text{ hour} = 1 \text{ minute}$$

The difference is $\dfrac{1}{5}$ minute $= \dfrac{1}{5}$ (60 seconds) $= 12$ seconds.

Note that the solution to Example 2 used the time formula but required only arithmetic, not algebra. Example 3 requires an algebraic solution.

➥ Example 3 _____

Eve drove from her home to college at an average speed of 60 miles per hour. Returning over the same route, due to construction delays, she was able to average only 45 miles per hour. If the return trip took 30 minutes longer, how many miles did she drive each way?

(A)   1.5
(B)   2
(C)   90
(D) 180

Solution. Let $t =$ the number of hours it took to go. Then to return, it took $t + 0.5$ hours (*not* $t + 30$). Now make a table.

	Rate	Time	Distance
going	60	t	$60t$
returning	45	$t + 0.5$	$45(t + 0.5)$

Since she drove the same distance going and returning:

$$60t = 45(t + 0.5) \Rightarrow 60t = 45t + 22.5 \Rightarrow 15t = 22.5 \Rightarrow t = 1.5$$

Now be sure to answer the correct question. Choices A and B are the time, in hours, for going and returning. Choices C and D are the distances each way and round-trip. You could have been asked for any of the four. If you circled what you're looking for, you won't make a careless mistake. Eve drove 60(1.5) = 90 miles each way, and so the correct answer is Choice C.

The *d* in *d* = *rt* stands for "distance," but it could represent any type of work that is performed at a certain rate *r* for a certain amount of time *t*. Example 3 did not have to be about distance. Instead of driving 90 miles at 45 miles per hour for 2 hours, Eve could have read 90 pages at a rate of 45 pages per hour for 2 hours or planted 90 flowers at the rate of 45 flowers per hour for 2 hours or typed 90 words at a rate of 45 words per minute for 2 minutes.

 Most algebraic word problems on the PSAT are not too difficult. If you get stuck on one, however, don't despair. Use one or more of the tactics that you learned in Chapter 6, especially backsolving, to eliminate choices and, if necessary, guess.

MULTIPLE-CHOICE QUESTIONS

1. In 7 years Danielle will be twice as old as she was 8 years ago. How old is Danielle now?

   (A) 7
   (B) 15
   (C) 23
   (D) 30

2. One morning, Alan drove 100 miles at the rate of 60 miles per hour; that afternoon, he drove another 100 miles at the rate of 40 miles per hour. What was his average rate of speed, in miles per hour, for the day?

   (A) 45
   (B) 48
   (C) 50
   (D) 52

3. In a family of three, the father weighed 5 times as much as the child, and the mother weighed $\frac{3}{4}$ as much as the father. If the three of them weighed a total of 390 pounds, how much did the mother weigh?

   (A) 100
   (B) 125
   (C) 150
   (D) 200

4. At 7:00 P.M., the hostess of the party remarked that only $\frac{1}{4}$ of her guests had arrived so far but that as soon as 10 more showed up, $\frac{1}{3}$ of the guests would be there.

   How many people were invited?

   (A) 32
   (B) 80
   (C) 120
   (D) 144

5. If the sum of 5 consecutive integers is S, what is the largest of those integers in terms of S?

   (A) $\dfrac{S-10}{5}$

   (B) $\dfrac{S+4}{4}$

   (C) $\dfrac{S+5}{4}$

   (D) $\dfrac{S+10}{5}$

GRID-IN QUESTIONS

6. A box contains only red, yellow, and green jelly beans. The number of red jelly beans is $\frac{4}{5}$ the number of green ones, and the number of green ones is $\frac{3}{4}$ the number of yellow ones. If there are 470 jelly beans in all, how many of them are yellow?

7. On a certain project, the only grades awarded were 7 and 10. If 50 students completed the project and the average of their grades was 9.4, how many earned 10?

8. From 1953 to 2003, Frank gained two pounds every year. In 1983, he was 40 percent heavier than in 1953. What percent of his 1998 weight was his 1983 weight?

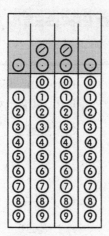

9. Neil has 80% as many baseball cards as Larry. If Neil has 80 fewer baseball cards than Larry, how many do they have altogether?

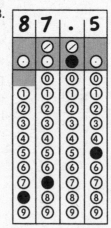

10. Let a and b be two positive numbers whose product is 750. If $a + b$ exceeds $a - b$ by 50, what is the value of a?

Answer Key

1. **C**   2. **B**   3. **C**   4. **C**   5. **D**

6. **200**   7. **40**   8. **87.5**   9. **720**   10. **30**

Although some of the math questions on the PSAT involve geometry, you need to know only a relatively small number of facts—far fewer than you would learn in a geometry course—and, of course, you don't need to provide proofs. In the next six sections we will review all of the geometry that you need to know to do well on the PSAT.

6-1 LINES AND ANGLES

On the PSAT, lines are usually referred to by lowercase letters, typically k, ℓ, and m. If P and Q are any points on line ℓ, we can also refer to ℓ as $\overleftrightarrow{PQ}$. In general, we have the following notations:

- $\overleftrightarrow{PQ}$ represents the **line** that goes through P and Q:

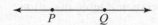

- $\overrightarrow{PQ}$ represents a **ray**; it consists of point P and all the points on $\overleftrightarrow{PQ}$ that are on the same side of P as Q:

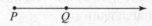

- $\overline{PQ}$ represents a **line segment** (often referred to simply as a **segment**); it consists of points P and Q and all the points on $\overleftrightarrow{PQ}$ that are between them:

- PQ represents the **length** of segment $\overline{PQ}$.

If $\overline{AB}$ and $\overline{PQ}$ have the same length, we say that $\overline{AB}$ and $\overline{PQ}$ are **congruent**, and write $\overline{AB} \cong \overline{PQ}$. We can also write $AB = PQ$.

> **NOTE**
>
> $\overline{AB} \cong \overline{PQ}$ means exactly the same thing as $AB = PQ$.

An **angle** is formed by the intersection of two line segments, rays, or lines. The point of intersection is called the **vertex**.

An angle can be named by three points: a point on one side, the vertex, and a point on the other side. When there is no possible ambiguity, the angle can be named just by its vertex. For example, in the diagram below we can refer to the angle on the left as $\angle B$ or $\angle ABC$. To talk about $\angle E$, on the right, however, would be ambiguous; $\angle E$ might mean $\angle DEF$ or $\angle FEG$ or $\angle DEG$.

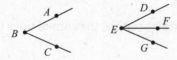

On geometry questions on the PSAT, angles are always measured in degrees. The degree measure of $\angle ABC$ is represented by $m\angle ABC$. If $\angle P$ and $\angle Q$ have the same measure, we say that they are ***congruent*** and write $\angle P \cong \angle Q$. In the diagram below, $\angle A$ and $\angle B$ are right angles. Therefore, $m\angle A = 90°$ and $m\angle B = 90°$, so $m\angle A = m\angle B$ and $\angle A \cong \angle B$. In equilateral triangle PQR, $m\angle P = m\angle Q = m\angle R = 60°$, and $\angle P \cong \angle Q \cong \angle R$.

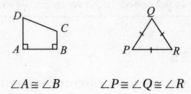

$$\angle A \cong \angle B \qquad \angle P \cong \angle Q \cong \angle R$$

Key Fact I1

Angles are classified according to their degree measures.

- An ***acute*** angle measures less than 90° (Figure 1).
- A ***right*** angle measures 90° (Figure 2).
- An ***obtuse*** angle measures more than 90° but less than 180° (Figure 3).
- A ***straight*** angle measures 180° (Figure 4).

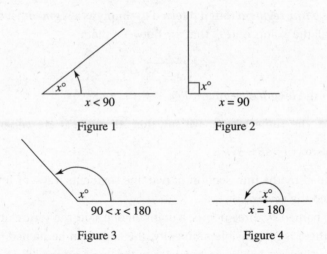

Key Fact I2

If two or more angles form a straight angle, the sum of their measures is 180°.

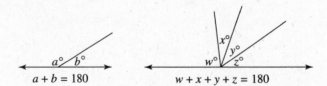

➡ Example 1 _____

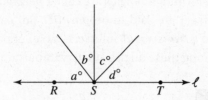

In the figure above, R, S, and T are all on line ℓ. What is the average of a, b, c, and d?

Solution. Since $\angle RST$ is a straight angle, by **KEY FACT I2**, $a + b + c + d = 180$, and so their average is $\frac{180}{4} = 45$.

Key Fact I3

The sum of the measures of all the angles around a point is 360°.

   NOTE: This fact is particularly important when the point is the center of a circle, as we shall see in Section 6-L.

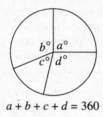

$$a + b + c + d = 360$$

When two lines intersect, four angles are formed. The two angles in each pair of opposite angles are called **vertical angles**.

Key Fact I4

Vertical angles are congruent.

NOTE

Key Fact I4 means that if $\angle A$ and $\angle B$ are vertical angles, then m$\angle A$ = m$\angle B$.

➡ Example 2 _____

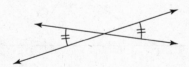

In the figure above, what is the value of a?

Solution. Because vertical angles are equal, $3a - 20 = 2a + 20 \Rightarrow a = 40$.

Two lines that intersect to form right angles are called ***perpendicular***.

Two lines that never intersect are said to be ***parallel***. So, parallel lines form no angles. However, if a third line, called a ***transversal***, intersects a pair of parallel lines, eight angles are formed; the relationships among these angles are very important.

Key Fact I5

If a pair of parallel lines is cut by a transversal that is not perpendicular to the parallel lines,

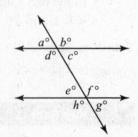

- Four of the angles are acute, and four are obtuse.
- All four acute angles are congruent: $a = c = e = g$.
- All four obtuse angles are congruent: $b = d = f = h$.
- The sum of the measures of any acute angle and any obtuse angle is 180°; for example, $d + e = 180$, $c + f = 180$, $b + g = 180, \ldots$

> **HELPFUL HINT**
>
> You must know Key Fact I5. However, you do *not* need to know the special terms you learned in your geometry class for these pairs of angles; those terms are not used on the PSAT.

➥ Example 3

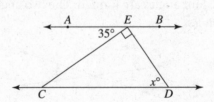

In the figure above, $\overline{AB}$ is parallel to $\overline{CD}$. What is the value of x?

Solution. Let y be the measure of $\angle BED$. Then, by **KEY FACT I2**,

$$35 + 90 + y = 180 \Rightarrow 125 + y = 180 \Rightarrow y = 55$$

Since $\overline{AB}$ and $\overline{CD}$ are parallel, by **KEY FACT I5**, $x = y \Rightarrow x = 55$.

MULTIPLE-CHOICE QUESTIONS

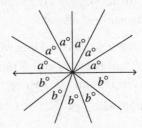

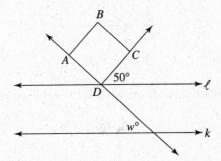

1. In the figure above, what is the value of $\frac{b+a}{b-a}$?

   (A) 6
   (B) 11
   (C) 30
   (D) 36

2. What is the measure of the smaller angle formed by the minute hand and the hour hand of a clock at 3:30?

   (A) 45°
   (B) 60°
   (C) 75°
   (D) 90°

4. In the figure above, lines k and ℓ are parallel, and line ℓ passes through D, one of the vertices of square $ABCD$. What is the value of w?

   (A) 30
   (B) 40
   (C) 45
   (D) 50

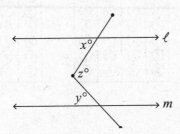

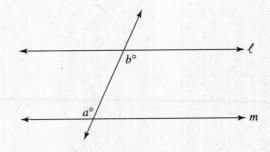

Note: Figure not drawn to scale

3. In the figure above, $\ell \parallel m$. Which of the following statements about x, y, and z is true?

   (A) $x + y = z$
   (B) $x + y = 180 - z$
   (C) $x + y = 90 - z$
   (D) It cannot be determined from the information given.

5. In the figure above, $\ell \parallel m$. Which of the following statements about $a + b$ is true?

   (A) $a + b = 180$
   (B) $180 < a + b \leq 270$
   (C) $270 < a + b \leq 360$
   (D) It cannot be determined from the information given.

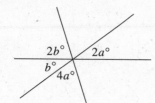

6. In the figure above, what is the value of b?

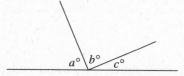

7. In the figure above, if a:b:c = 3:4:1, what is the value of a?

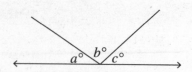

8. In the figure above, if a + c = b and a:c = 2:3, what is the value of a?

9. P, Q, and R are points on a line with Q between P and R. Let M and N be the midpoints of $\overline{PQ}$ and $\overline{QR}$, respectively. If PQ = 5QR, what is $\frac{PQ}{MN}$?

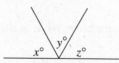

Note: Figure not drawn to scale

10. In the figure above, x:y = 3:5 and z:y = 2:1. What is the measure of the largest angle?

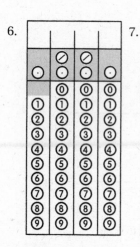
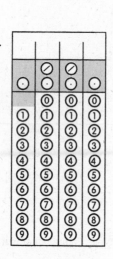
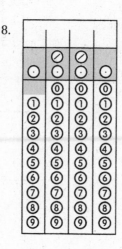
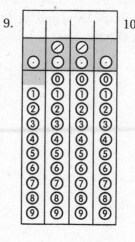

Answer Key

1. **B**   2. **C**   3. **A**   4. **B**   5. **D**

6. **36**   7. **67.5**   8. **36**   9. **5/3**   10. **100**

6-J TRIANGLES

More geometry questions on the PSAT pertain to triangles than to any other topic. To answer these questions correctly, you need to know several important facts about the angles and sides of triangles. The **KEY FACTS** in this section are extremely useful. Be sure you learn them all.

Key Fact J1

In any triangle, the sum of the measures of the three angles is 180°.

$$x + y + z = 180$$

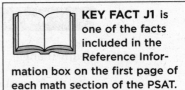

KEY FACT J1 is one of the facts included in the Reference Information box on the first page of each math section of the PSAT.

➡ Example 1

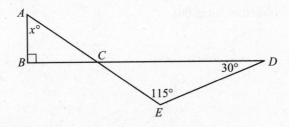

In the figure above, what is the value of x?

Solution. Use **KEY FACT J1** twice: first, in $\triangle CDE$ and then in $\triangle ABC$.

- $m\angle DCE + 115 + 30 = 180 \Rightarrow m\angle DCE + 145 = 180 \Rightarrow m\angle DCE = 35$
- Since vertical angles are congruent, $m\angle ACB = 35$ [**KEY FACT I4**]
- $x + 90 + 35 = 180 \Rightarrow x + 125 = 180 \Rightarrow x = 55$

An **exterior angle** of a triangle is an angle formed by one side of the triangle and the extension of another side.

Key Fact J2

The measure of an exterior angle of a triangle is equal to the sum of the measures of the two opposite interior angles.

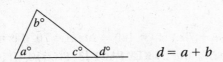

$$d = a + b$$

➡️ **Example 2**

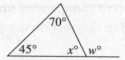

In the figure above, what is the value of w?

Solution. By **KEY FACT J2**: $w = 45 + 70 = 115$.

Key Fact J3

In any triangle

- the longest side is opposite the largest angle.
- the shortest side is opposite the smallest angle.
- sides with the same length are opposite angles with the same measure.

A triangle with two equal sides is called **isosceles**; the angles opposite the two equal sides have the same measure. A triangle with three equal sides is called **equilateral**; it has three equal angles, each of which measures 60°.

➡️ **Example 3**

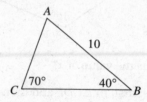

Note: Figure not drawn to scale

Which of the following statements about $\triangle ABC$ in the figure above must be true?

   I. $m\angle A = 70°$
  II. $BC = 10$
 III. Perimeter of $\triangle ABC = 30$

(A) I only
(B) II only
(C) I and II only
(D) I and III only

Solution.

- By **KEY FACT J1**, $m\angle A + 70 + 40 = 180 \Rightarrow m\angle A = 70$. (I is true.)
- Therefore, $m\angle A = m\angle C$, and by **KEY FACT J3**, $BC = 10$. (II is true.)
- Since $\angle B$ is the smallest angle, AC is the smallest side. In particular, it is less than 10.
- Therefore, the perimeter is less than 30. (III is false.)
- Only I and II are true (Choice C).

Right triangles are triangles that have one right angle and two acute ones. The side opposite the 90° angle is called the **hypotenuse**, and by **KEY FACT J3**, it is the longest side. The other two sides are called the *legs*.

➧ **Example 4** _____

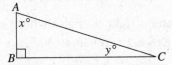

In the figure above, what is the average (arithmetic mean) of x and y?

Solution. Since the diagram indicates that $\triangle ABC$ is a right triangle, then, by **KEY FACT J1**, $90 + x + y = 180 \Rightarrow x + y = 90$. The average of x and y is $\dfrac{x+y}{2} = \dfrac{90}{2} = 45$.

The most important facts concerning right triangles are the **Pythagorean theorem** and its converse, which are given in **KEY FACT J4**.

Key Fact J4

If a, b, and c are the lengths of the sides of a triangle, with $a \le b \le c$, then the triangle is a right triangle if and only if $a^2 + b^2 = c^2$.

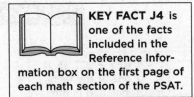

KEY FACT J4 is one of the facts included in the Reference Information box on the first page of each math section of the PSAT.

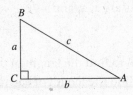

$$a^2 + b^2 = c^2$$

Consider the following two triangles.

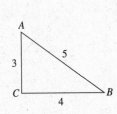

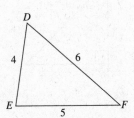

Since $3^2 + 4^2 = 5^2$, $\triangle ABC$ is a right triangle, whereas $\triangle DEF$ is not a right triangle, since $4^2 + 5^2 \ne 6^2$.

➧ **Example 5** _____

Which of the following are *not* the sides of a right triangle?

(A) $1, 1, \sqrt{2}$

(B) $1, \sqrt{3}, 2$

(C) $\sqrt{3}, \sqrt{4}, \sqrt{5}$

(D) $5, 12, 13$

Solution. Just check each of the choices.

- (A) $1^2 + 1^2 = 1 + 1 = 2 = (\sqrt{2})^2$ These *are* the sides of a right triangle.
- (B) $1^2 + (\sqrt{3})^2 = 1 + 3 = 4 = 2^2$ These *are* the sides of a right triangle.
- (C) $(\sqrt{3})^2 + (\sqrt{4})^2 = 3 + 4 = 7 \neq (\sqrt{5})^2$ These *are not* the sides of a right triangle.

Stop. The answer is Choice C. There is no need to check Choice D.

On the PSAT, the most common right triangles whose sides are *integers* are the 3-4-5 triangle and its multiples, such as 6-8-10 and 30-40-50.

Let x = length of each leg, and h = length of the hypotenuse, of an isosceles right triangle. By the Pythagorean theorem (**KEY FACT J4**).

$$x^2 + x^2 = h^2 \Rightarrow 2x^2 = h^2 \Rightarrow h = \sqrt{2x^2} = x\sqrt{2}$$

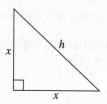

Key Fact J5

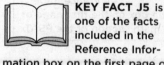

KEY FACT J5 is one of the facts included in the Reference Information box on the first page of each math section of the PSAT.

In a 45-45-90 right triangle, the sides are x, x, and $x\sqrt{2}$.

In a 45-45-90 right triangle:

- Multiply the length of a leg by $\sqrt{2}$ to find the length of the hypotenuse.
- Divide the hypotenuse by $\sqrt{2}$ to find the length of each leg.

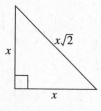 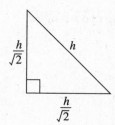

Key Fact J6

A diagonal of a square divides the square into two isosceles right triangles.

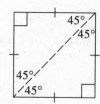

An *altitude* of a triangle is a line segment drawn from a vertex, perpendicular to the oppo-site side called the *base*. An altitude is often referred to as the *height* drawn to that base.

Key Fact J7

An altitude divides an equilateral triangle into two 30-60-90 right triangles.

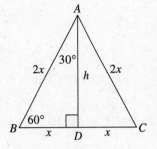

Let $2x$ be the length of each side of equilateral triangle ABC, in which altitude $\overline{AD}$ is drawn. Then $\triangle ABD$ is a 30-60-90 right triangle, and its sides are x, $2x$, and h. By the Pythagorean theorem,

$$x^2 + h^2 = (2x)^2 = 4x^2, \text{ so } h^2 = 3x^2,$$
$$\text{and } h = \sqrt{3x^2} = x\sqrt{3}.$$

Key Fact J8

In a 30-60-90 right triangle the sides are x, $x\sqrt{3}$, and $2x$.

In a 30-60-90 right triangle:

If you know the length of the shorter leg (x),

- multiply it by $\sqrt{3}$ to get the length of the longer leg, and
- multiply it by 2 to get the length of the hypotenuse.

KEY FACT J8 is one of the facts included in the Reference Information box on the first page of each math section of the PSAT.

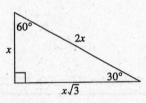

If you know the length of the longer leg (a),

- divide it by $\sqrt{3}$ to get the length of the shorter leg, and
- multiply the shorter leg by 2 to get the length of the hypotenuse.

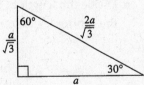

If you know the length of the hypotenuse (h),

- divide it by 2 to get the length of the shorter leg, and
- multiply the shorter leg by $\sqrt{3}$ to get the length of the longer leg.

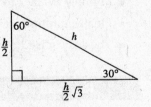

➡ **Example 6** _____

What is the area of a square whose diagonal is 4?

(A) 4
(B) 8
(C) 16
(D) $4\sqrt{3}$

Solution. Draw a diagonal in a square, creating two 45-45-90 right triangles. Label the diagonal 4 and each side s.

By **KEY FACT J6**, $s = \dfrac{4}{\sqrt{2}}$ and $A = s^2 = \left(\dfrac{4}{\sqrt{2}}\right)^2 = \dfrac{16}{2} = 8$. The answer is Choice B.

➡ **Example 7** _____

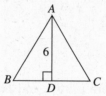

In equilateral triangle ABC, the length of altitude AD is 6. What is the perimeter of $\triangle ABC$?

(A) 18

(B) $6\sqrt{3}$

(C) $12\sqrt{3}$

(D) $18\sqrt{3}$

Solution. Use **KEY FACT J8**.

■ Divide the length of the longer leg, $\overline{AD}$, of right triangle ADB by $\sqrt{3}$ to get the length of the shorter leg, $\overline{BD}$:

$$\frac{6}{\sqrt{3}} = \frac{6}{\sqrt{3}} \times \frac{\sqrt{3}}{\sqrt{3}} = \frac{6\sqrt{3}}{3} = 2\sqrt{3}$$

■ Multiply BD by 2 to get BC. Then $BC = 2(2\sqrt{3}) = 4\sqrt{3}$.

■ Finally, multiply BC by 3 to get the perimeter of $\triangle ABC$: $3(4\sqrt{3}) = 12\sqrt{3}$.

■ The answer is Choice C.

Key Fact J9

(Triangle Inequality)

■ The sum of the lengths of any two sides of a triangle is greater than the length of the third side.

■ The difference of the lengths of any two sides of a triangle is less than the length of the third side.

■ The length of any side of a triangle is always greater than the difference and less than the sum of the lengths of the other two sides.

➡ **Example 8** _____

If the lengths of two of the sides of a triangle are 7 and 8, which of the following could be the length of the third side?

  I. 1
  II. 2
  III. 15

(A) None
(B) I only
(C) II only
(D) I and II only

Solution. Use **KEY FACT J9**.

- The length of the third side must be *less* than 7 + 8 = 15. So III is false.
- The length of the third side must be *greater* than 8 − 7 = 1. So I is false.
- *Any* number between 1 and 15 could be the length of the third side. So II is true.
- The answer is Choice C.

Key Fact J10

The area of a triangle is given by $A = \frac{1}{2} bh$, where b is the base and h is the height.

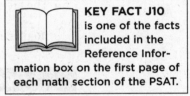

KEY FACT J10 is one of the facts included in the Reference Information box on the first page of each math section of the PSAT.

Note:

1. *Any* side of the triangle can be taken as the base.
2. The height is the altitude drawn to the base from the opposite vertex.
3. In a right triangle, either leg can be the base and the other the height.
4. The height may be outside the triangle. [See the figure below.]

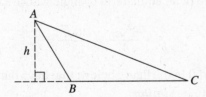

In the figure below:

If $\overline{AC}$ is the base, $\overline{BD}$ is the height. If AB is the base, $\overline{CE}$ is the height. If $\overline{BC}$ is the base, $\overline{AF}$ is the height.

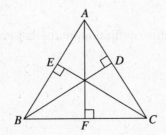

➡ **Example 9** _____

What is the area of an equilateral triangle whose sides are 10?

(A) 30

(B) $25\sqrt{3}$

(C) 50

(D) $50\sqrt{3}$

Solution. Draw an equilateral triangle and one of its altitudes.

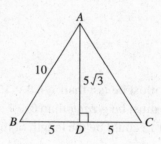

- By **KEY FACT J7**, $\triangle ABD$ is a 30-60-90 right triangle.
- By **KEY FACT J8**, $BD = 5$ and $AD = 5\sqrt{3}$.
- The area of $\triangle ABC = \frac{1}{2}(10)(5\sqrt{3}) = 25\sqrt{3}$ (Choice B).

Replacing 10 by s in Example 10 yields a very useful result.

Key Fact J11

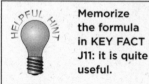

Memorize the formula in KEY FACT J11: it is quite useful.

If A represents the area of an equilateral triangle with side s, then $A = \frac{s^2\sqrt{3}}{4}$.

For example, the area of an equilateral triangle whose sides are each 6 is

$$A = \frac{6^2\sqrt{3}}{4} = \frac{36\sqrt{3}}{4} = 9\sqrt{3}$$

Two triangles, such as I and II in the figure below, that have the same shape, but not necessarily the same size, are said to be **similar**.

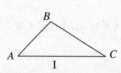
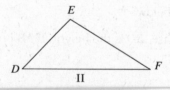

KEY FACT J12 makes this intuitive definition mathematically precise.

Two triangles are *similar* provided that the following two conditions are satisfied.

1. The three angles in the first triangle are congruent to the three angles in the second triangle:

$$m\angle A = m\angle D, \quad m\angle B = m\angle E, \quad m\angle C = m\angle F$$

2. The lengths of the corresponding sides of the two triangles are in proportion:

$$\frac{AB}{DE} = \frac{BC}{EF} = \frac{AC}{DF}$$

NOTE: Corresponding sides are sides opposite angles of the same measure.

An important theorem in geometry states that, if condition 1 in KEY FACT J12 is satisfied, then condition 2 is automatically satisfied. Therefore, to show that two triangles are similar, it is sufficient to show that their angles have the same measure. Furthermore, if the measures of two angles of one triangle are equal to the measures of two angles of a second triangle, then the measures of the third angles are also equal. This is summarized in KEY FACT J13.

Key Fact J13

If the measures of two angles of one triangle are equal to the measures of two angles of a second triangle, the triangles are similar.

➡ Example 10

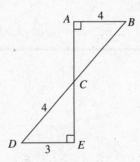

In the diagram above, what is *BC*?

Solution. Since vertical angles are congruent, $m\angle ECD = m\angle ACB$. Also, $m\angle A = m\angle E$ since both $\angle A$ and $\angle E$ are right angles. Then the measures of two angles of $\triangle CAB$ are equal to the measures of two angles of $\triangle CED$, and by KEY FACT J13, the two triangles are similar. Finally, by KEY FACT J12, corresponding sides are in proportion. Therefore:

$$\frac{DE}{AB} = \frac{DC}{BC} \Rightarrow \frac{3}{4} = \frac{4}{BC} \Rightarrow 3(BC) = 16 \Rightarrow BC = \frac{16}{3}$$

If two triangles are similar, the common ratio of their corresponding sides is called the *ratio of similitude.*

If two triangles are similar, and if k is the ratio of similitude, then:

- **The ratio of all the linear measurements of the triangles is k.**
- **The ratio of the areas of the triangles is k^2.**

In the figure below, $\triangle ABC$ and $\triangle PQR$ are similar with $m\angle C = m\angle R$.

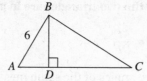

Then $\overline{AB}$ and $\overline{PQ}$ are corresponding sides, and the ratio of similitude is $\dfrac{6}{2} = 3$. Therefore,

- All the sides are in the ratio of 3:1:

$$BC = 3 \times QR \qquad AC = 3 \times PR$$

- The altitudes are in the ratio of 3:1:

$$BD = 3 \times QS$$

- The perimeters are in the ratio of 3:1:

$$\text{Perimeter of } \triangle ABC = 3 \times (\text{perimeter of } \triangle PQR)$$

- The areas are in the ratio of 9:1:

$$\text{Area of } \triangle ABC = 9 \times (\text{area of } \triangle PQR)$$

MULTIPLE-CHOICE QUESTIONS

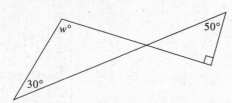

1. In the figure above, what is the value of *w*?

   (A) 90
   (B) 100
   (C) 110
   (D) 120

2. Two sides of a right triangle are 5 and 7. Which of the following could be the length of the third side?

   I. $\sqrt{24}$

   II. $\sqrt{54}$

   III. $\sqrt{74}$

   (A) I only
   (B) III only
   (C) I and II
   (D) I and III

Questions 3 and 4 refer to the following figure.

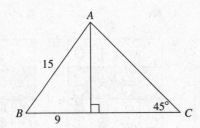

3. What is the perimeter of △*ABC*?

   (A) 36
   (B) $36 + 12\sqrt{2}$
   (C) $36 + 12\sqrt{3}$
   (D) $48 + 12\sqrt{3}$

4. What is the area of △*ABC*?

   (A) 126
   (B) $54 + 72\sqrt{2}$
   (C) $54 + 72\sqrt{3}$
   (D) 252

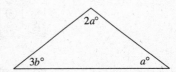

5. Which of the following expresses a true relationship between *a* and *b* in the figure above?

   (A) $b = 60 - a$
   (B) $b = a$
   (C) $b = 180 - 3a$
   (D) $a = 90 - 3b$

GRID-IN QUESTIONS

6. If the difference between the measures of the two acute angles of a right triangle is 6°, what is the measure, in degrees, of the smallest angle in the triangle?

7. In the figure below, what is the perimeter of △ABC?

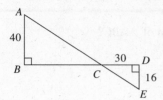

8. If the measures of the angles of a triangle are in the ratio of 1 : 2 : 3 and if the length of the smallest side is 10, what is the length of the longest side?

9. In the figure below, what is the value of AD?

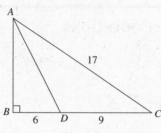

<u>Note</u>: Figure not drawn to scale

10. In the figure below, what is the value of w?

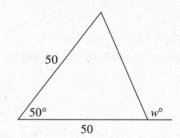

Answer Key

1. **C**   2. **D**   3. **C**   4. **A**   5. **A**

6. 4 2

7. 2 0 0

8. 2 0

9. 1 0

10. 1 1 5

6-K QUADRILATERALS

A *quadrilateral* is a polygon with four sides. In this section we will present the key facts you need to know about three special quadrilaterals.

Every quadrilateral has two diagonals. If you draw in either one, you will divide the quadrilateral into two triangles. Since the sum of the measures of the three angles in each of the triangles is 180°, the sum of the measures of the angles in the quadrilateral is 360°.

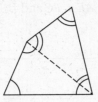

Key Fact K1

In any quadrilateral, the sum of the measures of the four angles is 360°.

➡ Example 1 _____

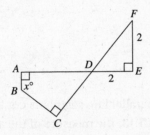

In the figure above, what is the value of x?

Solution. Since $\triangle DEF$ is an isosceles right triangle, $m\angle EDF = 45°$; also, since the two angles at vertex D are vertical angles, their measures are equal. Therefore, the measure of $\angle ADC$ is 45°. Finally, since the sum of the measures of all four angles of $ABCD$ is 360°:

$$45 + 90 + 90 + x = 360 \Rightarrow 225 + x = 360 \Rightarrow x = 135$$

A *parallelogram* is a quadrilateral in which both pairs of opposite sides are parallel.

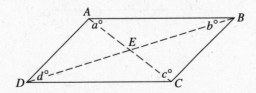

Parallelograms have the following properties:

- Opposite sides are congruent: $AB = CD$ and $AD = BC$.
- Opposite angles are congruent: $a = c$ and $b = d$.
- The measure of adjacent angles add up to 180°: $a + b = b + c = c + d = a + d = 180$.
- The diagonals bisect each other: $AE = EC$ and $DE = EB$.

➥ Example 2

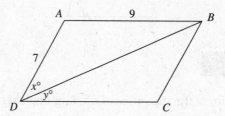

In the figure above, $ABCD$ is a parallelogram. Which of the following statements must be true?

(A) $x < y$
(B) $x = y$
(C) $x > y$
(D) $x + y < 90$

Solution. Since $\overline{AB}$ and $\overline{CD}$ are parallel line segments cut by transversal $\overline{BD}$, m$\angle ABD = y°$. In $\triangle ABD$ $AB > AD$, so by **KEY FACT J3**, the measure of the angle opposite $\overline{AB}$ is greater than the measure of the angle opposite $\overline{AD}$. Therefore, $x > y$ (Choice C).

A **_rectangle_** is a parallelogram in which all four angles are right angles. Two adjacent sides of a rectangle are usually called the **_length_** (l) and the **_width_** (w).

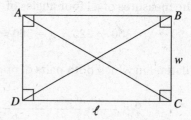

Since a rectangle is a parallelogram, all of the properties listed in **KEY FACT K2** hold for rectangles. In addition,

- The measure of each angle in a rectangle is 90°.
- The diagonals of a rectangle have the same length: $AC = BD$.

   A *square* is a rectangle in which all four sides have the same length.

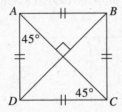

Since a square is a rectangle, all of the properties listed in **KEY FACTS K2** and **K3** hold for squares. In addition,

- All four sides have the same length.
- Each diagonal divides the square into two 45-45-90 right triangles.
- The diagonals are perpendicular to each other: $\overline{AC} \perp \overline{BD}$.

➡ Example 3

   What is the length of each side of a square if its diagonals are 8?

Solution. Draw a diagram. In square $ABCD$, diagonal $\overline{AC}$ is the hypotenuse of a 45-45-90 right triangle, and side $\overline{AB}$ is a leg of that triangle. By **KEY FACT J5**,

$$AB = \frac{AC}{\sqrt{2}} = \frac{8}{\sqrt{2}} \times \frac{\sqrt{2}}{\sqrt{2}} = \frac{8\sqrt{2}}{2} = 4\sqrt{2}$$

The *perimeter* (P) of any polygon is the sum of the lengths of all its sides.

In a rectangle, $P = 2(\ell + w)$, and in a square, $P = 4s$.

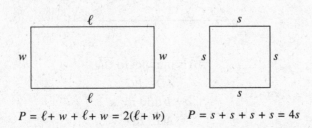

$$P = \ell + w + \ell + w = 2(\ell + w) \qquad P = s + s + s + s = 4s$$

⇒ Example 4 _____

A rectangle is divided into two squares, each with a perimeter of 10. What is the perimeter of the rectangle?

(A) 12.5
(B) 15
(C) 17.5
(D) 20

Solution. Don't do anything until you have drawn a diagram.

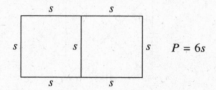

Since the perimeter of each square is 10, the length of each side is $10 \div 4 = 2.5$. Therefore, the perimeter of the rectangle is $6 \times 2.5 = 15$ (Choice B).

A *trapezoid* is a quadrilateral in which exactly one pair of opposite sides is parallel.

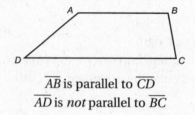

$\overline{AB}$ is parallel to $\overline{CD}$
$\overline{AD}$ is *not* parallel to $\overline{BC}$

The parallel sides are called the **bases** of the trapezoid, and the distance between the two bases is called the **height**.

If the two nonparallel sides are congruent, the trapezoid is called **isosceles**. In that case only, the diagonals are congruent.

Key Fact K6

Isosceles trapezoids have the following properties:

- **The base angles (the angles opposite the congruent sides) are congruent.**
- **The diagonals are congruent.**

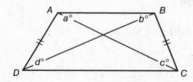

$\overline{AB}$ is parallel to $\overline{CD}$
$\overline{AD} \cong \overline{BC}$
$a = b$ and $c = d$
$\overline{AC} \cong \overline{BD}$

In Section 6-J we reviewed the formula for the **area** of a triangle. You also need to know the area formulas for a parallelogram, rectangle, square, and trapezoid.

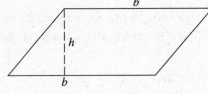

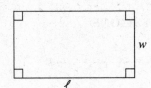

Here are the area formulas you need to know:

- For a parallelogram: $A = bh$
- For a rectangle: $A = \ell w$
- For a square: $A = s^2$ or $A = \frac{1}{2}d^2$
- For a trapezoid: $A = \frac{1}{2}h(b_1 + b_2)$

The formula for the area of a rectangle, given in **KEY FACT K7,** is one of the facts included in the Reference Information box on the first page of each math section of the PSAT.

➡ **Example 5** _____

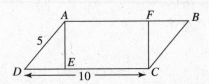

In the figure above, the area of parallelogram *ABCD* is 40. What is the area of rectangle *AFCE*?

(A) 20
(B) 24
(C) 28
(D) 32

Solution. Since the base *CD*, is 10 and the area of *ABCD* is 40, the height *AE* must be 4. Then △*AED* must be a 3-4-5 right triangle with *DE* = 3, which implies that *EC* = 7. The area of the rectangle is 7 × 4 = 28 (Choice C).

MULTIPLE-CHOICE QUESTIONS

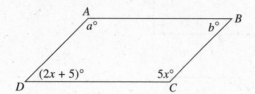

1. In the figure above, $ABCD$ is a parallelogram. What is the value of $a - b$?

   (A) 25
   (B) 55
   (C) 70
   (D) 90

2. What is the perimeter of a rectangle whose area is 21?

   (A) 10
   (B) 20
   (C) 21
   (D) It cannot be determined from the information given.

3. The area of square $ABCD$ is 125. In rectangle $PQRS$, PQ is 10 more than AB and QR is 10 less than AB. What is the area of rectangle $PQRS$?

   (A)   25
   (B) 115
   (C) 125
   (D) 225

4. What is the area of a square whose diagonals are 12?

   (A) $50\sqrt{2}$
   (B)   72
   (C) 144
   (D) $144\sqrt{2}$

5. If the length of a rectangle is 3 times its width and if its area is 108, what is its perimeter?

   (A) 24
   (B) 36
   (C) 48
   (D) 60

GRID-IN QUESTIONS

Questions 6 and 7 refer to the following figure, in which M, N, O, and P are the midpoints of the sides of rectangle $ABCD$.

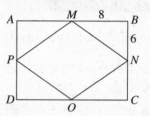

6. What is the perimeter of quadrilateral $MNOP$?

7. What is the area of quadrilateral $MNOP$?

8. If in the figures below, the area of rectangle *ABCD* is 100, what is the area of rectangle *EFGH*?

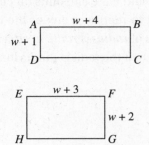

10. If in the figure below, *M* and *N* are the midpoints of two of the sides of square *PQRS*, what is the area of the shaded region?

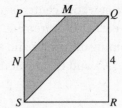

9. In quadrilateral *PQRS*, the measure of angle *S* is 20 more than the average of the measures of the other three. What is the measure of angle *S*?

Answer Key

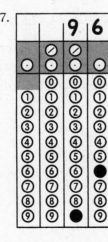

6-L CIRCLES

A *circle* consists of all the points in a plane that are the same distance from one fixed point called the *center*. That distance is called the *radius* of the circle. The figure below is a circle of radius 1 unit whose center is at the point O. Since A, B, C, D, and E are all points on circle O, they are each 1 unit from O. The word *radius* is also used to represent any of the line segments joining the center and a point on the circle. The plural of *radius* is *radii*. In circle O, $\overline{OA}$, $\overline{OB}$, $\overline{OC}$, $\overline{OD}$, and $\overline{OE}$ are all radii. If a circle has radius r, each of the radii is r units long.

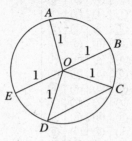

Key Fact L1

Any triangle, such as $\triangle COD$ in the figure above, formed by connecting the endpoints of two radii, is isosceles.

➥ Example 1 _____

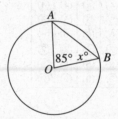

If A and B are points on circle O, what is the value of x?

Solution. Since $\triangle AOB$ is isosceles, angles A and B have the same measure. So

$$85 + x + x = 180 \Rightarrow 2x = 95 \Rightarrow x = 47.5$$

A line segment, such as $\overline{CD}$ in circle O at the beginning of this section, whose endpoints are on a circle, is called a *chord*. A chord such as $\overline{BE}$ in circle O that passes through the center is called a *diameter*. Since $\overline{BE}$ is made up of two radii, $\overline{OB}$ and $\overline{OE}$, a diameter is twice as long as a radius.

Key Fact L2

If d is the diameter and r the radius of a circle, then $d = 2r$.

Key Fact L3

A diameter is the longest chord that can be drawn in a circle.

➥ Example 2

A, B, and C, the three vertices of right triangle ABC, all lie on a circle whose radius is 4. Which of the following statements *could* be true?

   I. The hypotenuse of △ABC is 10
  II. The perimeter of △ABC is 25
 III. The area of △ABC is 35

(A) None
(B) I only
(C) II only
(D) III only

Solution. Since the radius is 4, the diameter is 8. Since each side of △ABC is a chord, none of the sides can be greater than 8; so AC cannot be 10 (I is false), and the perimeter can surely not exceed 24 (II is false). Since the area of a right triangle can be calculated using one of the legs as the base and the other as the height, the area cannot exceed $\frac{1}{2}$ (8)(8) = 32 and so cannot equal 35 (III is false). None of the statements is true (Choice A).

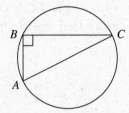

The total length around a circle is called the ***circumference*** of the circle. In every circle the ratio of the circumference to the diameter is exactly the same and is denoted by the symbol π (the Greek letter pi).

Key Fact L4

For every circle,

$$\pi = \frac{\text{circumference}}{\text{diameter}} = \frac{C}{d} \quad \text{or} \quad C = \pi d \quad \text{or} \quad C = 2\pi r$$

C = 2πr is one of the facts included in the Reference Information box on the first page of each math section of the PSAT.

Key Fact L5

The value of π is *approximately* 3.14.

➥ Example 3

If the circumference of a circle is equal to the perimeter of a square whose sides are π, what is the radius of the circle?

HELPFUL HINT

On almost every question on the PSAT that involves circles, you are expected to leave your answer in terms of π; so don't multiply by 3.14 unless you need to. If you need an approximation—to test a choice, for example—then use the π-key on your calculator.

Solution. If each side of the square is π, then its perimeter is 4π. Since the circumference of the circle is equal to the perimeter of the square, $C = 4\pi$. But $C = 2\pi r$, and so $2\pi r = 4\pi \Rightarrow r = 2$.

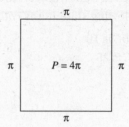

An **arc** consists of two points on a circle and all the points between them. If two points, such as P and Q in circle O, are the endpoints of a diameter, they divide the circle into two arcs called **semicircles**. On the PSAT, *arc AB* always refers to the small arc joining A and B.

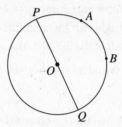

An angle whose vertex is at the center of a circle is called a **central angle**.

The degree measure of an arc equals the degree measure of the central angle that intercepts it.

CAUTION: Degree measure is *not* a measure of length. In these circles, arcs $\widehat{AB}$ and $\widehat{CD}$ each measure 72°, even though arc $\widehat{CD}$ is much longer.

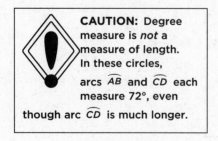

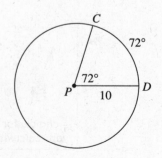

How long is arc *CD?* Since the radius of circle *P* is 10, its diameter is 20, and its circumference is 20π. Since there are 360° in a circle, arc *CD* is $\frac{72}{360}$, or $\frac{1}{5}$, of the circumference:

$$\frac{1}{5}(20\pi) = 4\pi$$

Key Fact L8

The formula for the area of a circle of radius *r* is $A = \pi r^2$

The area of circle *P*, based on KEY FACT L7, is $\pi(10)^2 = 100\pi$ square units. The area of sector *CPD* is $\frac{1}{5}$ of the area of the circle:

$$\frac{1}{5}(100\pi) = 20\pi$$

 KEY FACT L8 is one of the facts included in the Reference Information box on the first page of each math section of the PSAT.

Key Fact L9

If an arc measures $x°$, the length of the arc is $\frac{x}{360}(2\pi r)$, and the area of the sector formed by the arc and two radii is $\frac{x}{360}(\pi r^2)$.

Examples 4 and 5 refer to the figure below, in which the radius of the inner circle is 4 and the radius of the outer circle is 6.

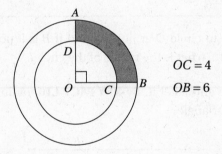

$OC = 4$
$OB = 6$

➡ Example 4 _____

What is the area of the shaded region, *ABCD?*

(A) 4π
(B) 5π
(C) 9π
(D) 16π

Solution. To find the area of *ABCD*, subtract the area of sector *DOC* from the area of sector *AOB*. Since m∠*AOB* is 90°, each sector is a quarter-circle.

The area of $AOB = \frac{1}{4}\pi(6)^2 = \frac{1}{4}(36\pi) = 9\pi$.

The area of $COD = \frac{1}{4}\pi(4)^2 = \frac{1}{4}(16\pi) = 4\pi$.

So the area of $ABCD = 9\pi - 4\pi = 5\pi$ (Choice B).

➧ Example 5 _____

What is the perimeter of the shaded region, *ABCD?*

(A) $2 + 5\pi$

(B) $4 + 5\pi$

(C) $4 + 20\pi$

(D) $4 + 24\pi$

Solution. Arcs $\overset{\frown}{AB}$ and $\overset{\frown}{CD}$ are each quarter-circles, and so their lengths are $\dfrac{1}{4}$ of the circumferences of circles whose diameters are 8 and 12.

$$AB = \frac{1}{4}(12\pi) = 3\pi \qquad CD = \frac{1}{4}(8\pi) = 2\pi$$

The lengths of line segments $\overline{AD}$ and $\overline{BC}$ are each $6 - 4 = 2$. So the perimeter is

$$2 + 2 + 3\pi + 2\pi = 4 + 5\pi \ \ \text{(Choice B)}$$

A line that touches a circle at exactly one point is called a ***tangent***. In example 6, line *l* is ***tangent*** to circle *O* at point *P*.

> **Key Fact L10**

A line tangent to a circle is perpendicular to the radius drawn to the point of contact.

➧ Example 6 _____

If line *l* is tangent to circle *O* at point *P* and if *B* is a point on *l* such that $PB = 8$ and $OB = 10$, what is the radius of the circle?

Solution. Draw a diagram and label it. By **KEY FACT L10**, radius $\overline{OP}$ is perpendicular to *l*. Therefore, $\triangle OPB$ is a right triangle.

You don't have to take the time to use the Pythagorean theorem if you recognize this as a multiple of a 3-4-5 triangle.

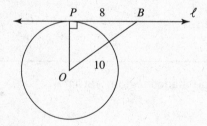

By the Pythagorean theorem,

$$OP^2 + 8^2 = 10^2 \Rightarrow OP^2 + 64 = 100 \Rightarrow OP^2 = 36 \Rightarrow OP = 6$$

PRACTICE EXERCISES

MULTIPLE-CHOICE QUESTIONS

Questions 1 and 2 refer to the following figure.

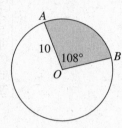

1. What is the length of arc *AB*?

   (A) 3π
   (B) 6π
   (C) 12π
   (D) 18π

2. What is the area of the shaded sector?

   (A) 6π
   (B) 12π
   (C) 18π
   (D) 30π

3. What is the circumference of a circle whose area is 100π?

   (A) 10
   (B) 10π
   (C) 20π
   (D) 25π

4. What is the area of a circle whose circumference is π?

   (A) $\frac{\pi}{4}$

   (B) $\frac{\pi}{2}$

   (C) π

   (D) 2π

5. In rectangle *ABCD*, *AB* = 3 and *BC* = 4. What is the area of the circle whose radius is $\overline{AC}$?

   (A) 5π
   (B) 9π
   (C) 16π
   (D) 25π

GRID-IN QUESTIONS

6. The circumferences of two circles are in the ratio of 3 : 5. What is the ratio of the area of the smaller circle to the area of the larger circle?

7. In the figure below, the ratio of the length of arc *CD* to the circumference of the circle is 2 : 9. What is the value of *w*?

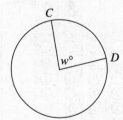

8. The circumference of a circle is x units, and the area of the circle is x square units. What is the radius of the circle?

9. In the figure below, the radius of circle O is 3, and the area of the shaded region is $a\pi$. What is the value of a?

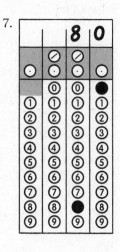

Note: Figure not drawn to scale.

10. If the area of a circle whose diameter is π, is written as $a\pi^b$, what is the value of ab?

Answer Key

6. 9/25   7. 80   8. 2   9. 13/2   10. 3/4

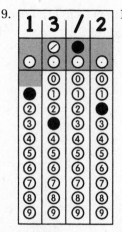

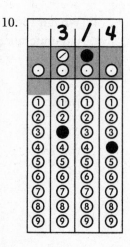

or **6.5**

6-M SOLID GEOMETRY

There is very little solid geometry on the PSAT. Basically, all you need to know are the formulas for the volume and surface areas of rectangular solids (including cubes) and cylinders.

A *rectangular solid* or *box* is a solid formed by six rectangles, called *faces*. The sides of the rectangles are called *edges*. As shown in the diagram below, the edges are called the *length*, *width*, and *height*. A *cube* is a rectangular solid in which the length, width, and height are equal, so all the edges are the same length.

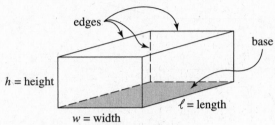

RECTANGULAR SOLID

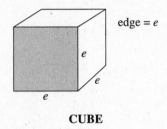

CUBE

KEY FACT M1 is one of the facts included in the Reference Information box on the first page of each math section of the PSAT.

| **Key Fact M1** |

- The formula for the volume of a rectangular solid is $V = \ell wh$.
- In a cube, all the edges are equal. Therefore, if e is the edge, the formula for the volume is $V = e^3$.

➡ **Example 1** _____

The base of a rectangular tank is 3 feet wide and 4 feet long; the height of the tank is 10 inches. If water is pouring into the tank at the rate of 3 cubic feet per hour, how many *minutes* will be required to fill the tank?

Solution. Draw a picture. Change all units to feet. Then the volume of the tank is $3 \times 4 \times \dfrac{5}{6} = 10$ cubic feet. At 3 cubic feet per hour, the required time is

$$\frac{10}{3} \text{ hours} = \frac{10}{3}(60) = 200 \text{ minutes.}$$

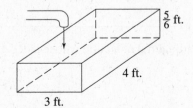

To find the **surface area** of a rectangular solid, add the area of the six rectangular faces. Since the top and bottom faces are equal, the front and back faces are equal, and the left and right faces are equal, we can calculate the area of one face from each pair and then double the sum. In a cube, each of the six faces has the same area.

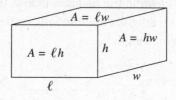

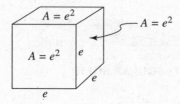

Key Fact M2

- The surface area of a rectangular solid is $A = 2(lw + \ell h + wh)$.
- The surface area of a cube is $A = 6e^2$.

➡ Example 2 _____

The volume of a cube is v cubic yards, and its surface area is a square feet.

If $v = a$, what is the length in inches of each edge?

Solution. Draw a diagram. If e is the length of the edge in yards, then $3e$ is the length in feet, and $36e$ is the length in inches. Therefore, $v = e^3$ and $a = 6(3e)^2 = 6(9e^2) = 54e^2$.

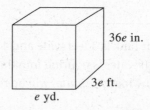

Since $v = a$, $e^3 = 54e^2 \Rightarrow e = 54$; the length of each edge is $36(54) = 1944$ inches.

A **diagonal** of a box is a line segment joining a vertex on the top of the box to the opposite vertex on the bottom.

➡ Example 3 _____

What is the length of a diagonal of a cube whose sides are 1?

Solution. Draw a diagram and label it. Since the base is a 1×1 square, the length of diagonal $\overline{AC}$ is $\sqrt{2}$. Then $\overline{AD}$, a diagonal of the cube, is the hypotenuse of right triangle ACD whose legs are 1 and $\sqrt{2}$; so

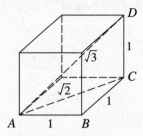

$$(AD)^2 = 1^2 + (\sqrt{2})^2 = 1 + 2 = 3, \text{ and } AD = \sqrt{3}$$

A *cylinder* is similar to a rectangular solid except that the base is a circle instead of a rectangle. The volume of a cylinder is the area of its circular base (πr^2) times its height (h).

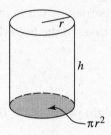

Key Fact M3

The formula for the volume, V, of a cylinder whose circular base has radius r and whose height is h is $V = \pi r^2 h$.

➡ Example 4

What is the height of a cylinder whose diameter is 10 and whose volume is 100π?

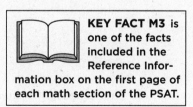

KEY FACT M3 is one of the facts included in the Reference Information box on the first page of each math section of the PSAT.

Solution. Since the diameter is 10, the radius is 5.

$$V = 100\pi = \pi r^2 h = \pi(5^2)h = 25\pi h \Rightarrow h = 4$$

Prisms

Rectangular solids and cylinders are special cases of geometric solids called prisms. A **prism** is a three-dimensional figure that has two congruent parallel **bases**. The (perpendicular) distance between the two bases is called the **height**. Three prisms are depicted in the figure below.

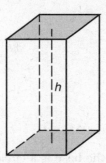 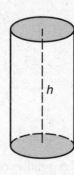 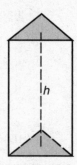

On the PSAT, all of the prisms are **right prisms**, which means that any line segment joining corresponding points on the bases is perpendicular to the bases. The volume formulas given in KEY FACTS M1 and M3 are special cases of the following formula.

Key Fact M4

The formula for the volume of any right prism is $V = Bh$, where B is the area of one of the bases and h is the height.

➡ Example 5

What is the volume of the triangular prism below?

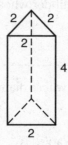

First calculate the area of a base, and then multiply it by the height. By KEY FACT J11, the area of an equilateral triangle whose sides are 2 is $\dfrac{2^2\sqrt{3}}{4} = \sqrt{3}$. So the volume of the prism is $(\sqrt{3})(4) = 4\sqrt{3}$.

Cones

Imagine taking a cylinder and shrinking the size of one of the circular bases.

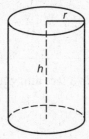 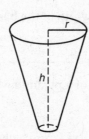 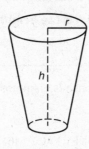 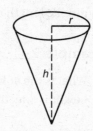

When it shrinks to a point, we call the resulting solid a cone. If you picture an ice cream cone (without the ice cream) or a dunce cap, you have the right idea. Notice that the radius of the circular base and the height of the cone are the same as in the original cylinder.

On the PSAT, cones are usually referred to as "right circular cones." This is done to emphasize that the base is a circle and that the height (the line segment joining the vertex and the center of the circular base) is perpendicular to the base.

Key Fact M5

The formula for the volume of a right circular cone is $V = \frac{1}{3}\pi r^2 h$.

➡ Example 6

Assume that the volumes of a right circular cone and a right circular cylinder are equal and that the radius of the cone is twice the radius of the cylinder. How do their heights compare?

> **KEY FACT M5** is one of the facts included in the Reference Information box on the first page of each math section of the PSAT.

Let r be the radius of the cylinder, $2r$ the radius of the cone, and h and H the heights of the cone and the cylinder, respectively. Then

$$\frac{1}{3}\pi(2r)^2 h = \pi r^2 H \Rightarrow \frac{1}{3}\pi 4r^2 h = \pi r^2 H \Rightarrow \frac{4}{3}h = H$$

Pyramids

A *pyramid* is very similar to a cone. The difference is that the base of a pyramid is a polygon, not a circle. If there is a question concerning a pyramid on the PSAT you take, the base will be a rectangle.

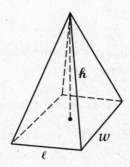

The formula for the volume of a pyramid with a rectangular base is $V = \frac{1}{3}\ell wh$, where ℓ *and* w are the length and width of the base and h is the height.

➡ **Example 7**_____

What is the volume of a pyramid whose base is a square of side 3 feet and whose height is 6 feet?

Sketch the pyramid and use the formula given in KEY FACT M6.

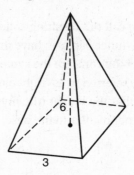

 KEY FACT M6 is one of the facts included in the Reference Information box on the first page of each math section of the PSAT.

The area of the square base is 9 square feet, and so $V = \frac{1}{3}(9)(6) = 18$ cubic feet.

Spheres

A sphere is the set of all points in space that are a fixed distance, r, from a given point, O. O is called the center of the sphere, and r is the radius.

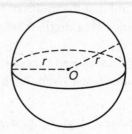

The formula for the volume of a sphere of radius r is $V = \frac{4}{3}\pi r^3$.

➡ **Example 8**_____

 KEY FACT M7 is one of the facts included in the Reference Information box on the first page of each math section of the PSAT.

What is the radius of a sphere whose volume is equal to the volume of a cube whose edges are 2?

By KEY FACT M1, the volume of the cube is $2^3 = 8$. Then by KEY FACT M7,

$$\frac{4}{3}\pi r^3 = 8 \Rightarrow \pi r^3 = 6 \Rightarrow r^3 = \frac{6}{\pi} \Rightarrow r = \sqrt[3]{\frac{6}{\pi}} \approx 1.24$$

MULTIPLE-CHOICE QUESTIONS

1. The volume of a cube is a cubic feet and its surface area is b square feet. If $a = b$, what is the length, in feet, of each edge?

    (A) 1
    (B) 2
    (C) 6
    (D) 12

2. The height and radius of a cylinder are each equal to the edge of a cube. What is the ratio of the volume of the cube to the volume of the cylinder?

    (A) $\dfrac{1}{\pi}$
    (B) π
    (C) π^2
    (D) π^3

3. What is the volume, in cubic centimeters, of a pyramid whose base is a square of area 144 square centimeters and whose four faces are equilateral triangles?

    (A) 288
    (B) $288\sqrt{2}$
    (C) 576
    (D) $576\sqrt{2}$

4. What is the volume, in cubic inches, of a cube whose surface area is 150 square inches?

    (A)   25
    (B)   100
    (C)   125
    (D) 1,000

5. What is the surface area, in square inches, of a cube whose volume is 64 cubic inches?

    (A)   16
    (B)   64
    (C)   96
    (D) 128

GRID-IN QUESTIONS

6. What is the number of cubic feet in one cubic yard? (1 yard = 3 feet)

7. What is the volume, in cubic feet, of a cube in which the sum of the lengths of all the edges is 12 feet?

8. A solid metal cube with sides of 3 inches is placed in a rectangular tank whose length, width, and height are 3, 4, and 5 inches, respectively. What is the volume, in cubic inches, of water that the tank can now hold?

9. The radius of sphere A is 2, and the radius of sphere B is 10. What is the ratio of the volume of sphere B to the volume of sphere A?

10. Two spherical balls fit snugly into a cylindrical can: the radius of each ball is equal to the radius of the can, and the balls just touch the bottom and the top of the can. What fraction of the volume of the can is taken up by the balls?

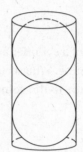

Answer Key

6-N COORDINATE GEOMETRY

The PSAT has very few questions on coordinate geometry. Most often they deal with the coordinates of points and with the slopes of lines.

In coordinate geometry, each point in the plane is assigned two numbers, an *x-coordinate* and a *y-coordinate*, which are written as an ordered pair, *(x, y)*.

- Points to the right of the *y*-axis have positive *x*-coordinates, and those to the left have negative *x*-coordinates.
- Points above the *x*-axis have positive *y*-coordinates, and those below it have negative *y*-coordinates.
- If a point is on the *x*-axis, its *y*-coordinate is 0.
- If a point is on the *y*-axis, its *x*-coordinate is 0.

For example, point *A* in the figure below is labeled (2, 3) since it is 2 units to the right of the *y*-axis and 3 units above the *x*-axis. Similarly, *B*(−3, −5) is 3 units to the left of the *y*-axis and 5 units below the *x*-axis.

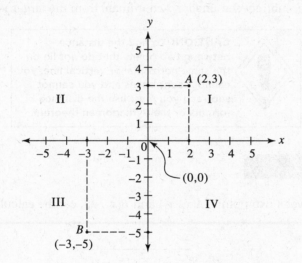

➡ **Example 1** _____

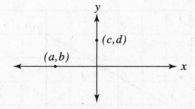

In the diagram above, which of the following must be true?

   I. $a + b < ab$
  II. $c + d < cd$
 III. $a + b < c + d$

(A) I only
(B) II only
(C) III only
(D) I and III only

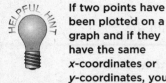
Solution. Since (a, b) is on the x-axis, $b = 0$. Therefore, $ab = 0$ and $a + b = a$, which is negative, since (a, b) is to the left of the y-axis. Since any negative number is less than 0, $a + b < ab$ (I is true). Since (c, d) is on the y-axis, $c = 0$. Therefore, $cd = 0$ and $c + d = d$, which is positive since (c, d) is above the x-axis. So $cd < c + d$ (II is false). Since $a + b$ is negative and $c + d$ is positive, $a + b < c + d$ (III is true). Only statements I and III are true (Choice D).

Occasionally, a question requires you to calculate the distance between two points. This is easiest when the points lie on the same horizontal or vertical line.

Key Fact N1

- All the points on a horizontal line have the same y-coordinate. To find the distance between any two of them, subtract the smaller x-coordinate from the larger x-coordinate.
- All the points on a vertical line have the same x-coordinate. To find the distance between any two of them, subtract the smaller y-coordinate from the larger y-coordinate.

CAUTION: To find the distance between two points that do *not* lie on the same horizontal or vertical line, you cannot count boxes and you cannot subtract; you *must* use the distance formula or the Pythagorean theorem.

Key Fact N2

The distance d, between two points, $A(x_1, y_1)$ and $B(x_2, y_2)$, can be calculated using the distance formula:

$$d = \sqrt{(x_2 - x_1)^2 + (y_2 - y_1)^2}$$

➡ **Example 2** _____

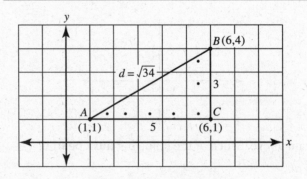

What is the perimeter of $\triangle ABC$, in the figure above?

(A) 13

(B) 16

(C) $8 + \sqrt{34}$

(D) $10 + \sqrt{34}$

Solution. By counting boxes or subtracting, you find that the distance from A to C is $6 - 1 = 5$, and the distance from B to C is $4 - 1 = 3$. To find the distance from A to B, use the distance formula:

$$AB = \sqrt{(6-1)^2 + (4-1)^2} = \sqrt{(5)^2 + (3)^2} = \sqrt{25+9} = \sqrt{34}$$

So the perimeter is $5 + 3 + \sqrt{34} = 8 + \sqrt{34}$ (Choice C).

Key Fact N3

If $P\,(x_1, y_1)$ and $Q\,(x_2, y_2)$ are any two points, then the midpoint, M, of segment $\overline{PQ}$ is the point whose coordinates are $\left(\dfrac{x_1 + x_2}{2}, \dfrac{y_1 + y_2}{2} \right)$.

➥ Example 3

ABCD is a rectangle whose vertices are at $A\,(2, 0)$, $B\,(0, 3)$, $C\,(6, 7)$, and $D\,(8, 4)$. If the diagonals intersect at E, what are the coordinates of E?

(A) $(2, 3.5)$
(B) $(3, 5)$
(C) $(4, 0.5)$
(D) $(4, 3.5)$

Solution. Since, by **KEY FACT K2**, the diagonals of a parallelogram (and, hence, a rectangle) bisect each other, E is the midpoint of diagonal AC:

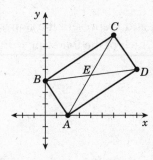

You should make a quick sketch. This often allows you to see the correct answer and always allows you to eliminate choices that are clearly wrong.

$$E = \left(\frac{2+6}{2}, \frac{7+0}{2} \right) = \left(\frac{8}{2}, \frac{7}{2} \right) = (4, 3.5) \text{ (Choice D)}$$

The *slope* of a line is a number that indicates how steep the line is.

Key Fact N4

- Vertical lines do not have slopes.
- To find the slope of any nonvertical line, proceed as follows:

  1. Choose any 2 points $A(x_1, y_1)$ and $B(x_2, y_2)$ on the line.
  2. Take the differences of the y-coordinates, $y_2 - y_1$, and the x-coordinates, $x_2 - x_1$.
  3. Divide. Slope $= \dfrac{y_1 - y_2}{x_1 - x_2}$.

➦ Example 4

What is the slope of the line that passes through $(0, 3)$ and $(4, 0)$?

Solution. Use the slope formula: $\dfrac{0-3}{4-0} = \dfrac{-3}{4} = -\dfrac{3}{4}$.

Key Fact N5

- The slope of any horizontal line is 0.
- The slope of any line that goes up as you move from left to right is positive.
- The slope of any line that goes down as you move from left to right is negative.

➦ Example 5

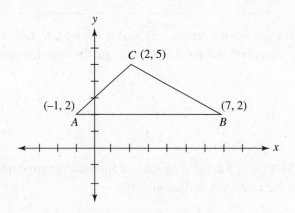

In the figure above, let r, s, and t represent the slopes of line segments $\overline{AB}$, $\overline{BC}$, and $\overline{AC}$, respectively. Which of the following is true?

(A) $r < s < t$
(B) $r < t < s$
(C) $s < r < t$
(D) $s < t < r$

Solution. Since $\overline{AB}$ is horizontal, its slope is 0: $r = 0$; since $\overline{BC}$ goes down as you move from left to right, its slope is negative: $s < 0$; and since $\overline{AC}$ goes up as you move from left to right, its slope is positive: $t > 0$. Therefore,

$$s < r < t \text{ (Choice C)}$$

Note that you *could have* calculated the slopes of $\overline{AC}$ and $\overline{BC}$, but it was unnecessary to do so.

- If two nonvertical lines are parallel, their slopes are equal.
- If two nonvertical lines are perpendicular, the product of their slopes is -1.

If the product of two numbers, a and b, is -1, then $ab = -1 \Rightarrow a = -\dfrac{1}{b}$. So another way to express the second part of **KEY FACT N6** is to say that *if two nonvertical lines are perpendicular, then the slope of one is the negative reciprocal of the slope of the other.*

➡ **Example 6**_____

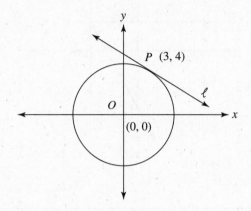

In the figure above, the center of circle O is at $(0, 0)$, and line l is tangent to the circle at $P(3, 4)$. What is the slope of l?

(A) $-\dfrac{4}{3}$

(B) $-\dfrac{3}{4}$

(C) $\dfrac{3}{4}$

(D) $\dfrac{4}{3}$

Solution. From the diagram, it is clear that the slope of l is negative; so the answer must be (A) or (B). In fact, the slope of radius $\overline{OP}$ is $\dfrac{4-0}{3-0} = \dfrac{3}{4}$. By **KEY FACT L10**, $\overline{OP} \perp l$, and so, by **KEY FACT N6**, the slope of l is the negative reciprocal of $\dfrac{4}{3}$. The slope of l is $-\dfrac{3}{4}$ (Choice B).

On the PSAT you won't have to graph a straight line (or anything else), but you should recognize the equations of straight lines.

For any real numbers a, b, m:

- The equation of the vertical line that crosses the x-axis at $(a, 0)$ is $x = a$.
- The equation of any nonvertical line can be written as $y = mx + b$.
- In the equation $y = mx + b$, m is the slope of the line, and b is the y-intercept.
- If $m = 0$, the line is horizontal, and its equation is $y = b$.

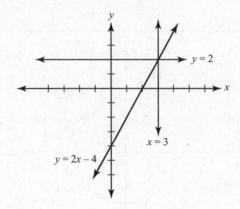

➡ Example 7

Which of the following is an equation of a line that is parallel to the line whose equation is $y = 2x - 3$?

(A) $y = 2x + 3$

(B) $y = -2x - 3$

(C) $y = -\dfrac{1}{2}x + 3$

(D) $y = -\dfrac{1}{2}x - 3$

Solution. By **KEY FACT N7**, the slope of the line $y = 2x - 3$ is 2. By **KEY FACT N6**, parallel lines have equal slopes. Only Choice A, $y = 2x + 3$, is also the equation of a line whose slope is 2.

On the PSAT, there could be a question concerning a linear inequality, such as $y > 2x + 1$. The graph of this inequality consists of all the points that are above the line $y = 2x + 1$. Note that the point $(2, 5)$ is on the line, whereas $(2, 6)$, $(2, 7)$, and $(2, 8)$ are all above the line. We indicate the set of all points satisfying the inequality by shading or striping the region above the line. To indicate that the points on the line itself do not satisfy the inequality, we draw a dotted line. To indicate that the points on a line are included in a graph, we draw a solid line. For example, $(2, 5)$ is not on the graph of $y > 2x + 1$, but it is on the graph of $y \geq 2x + 1$. Similarly, the graph of $y < 2x + 1$ and $y \leq 2x + 1$ are shaded or striped regions below the line $y = 2x + 1$. These inequalities are shown in the following graphs.

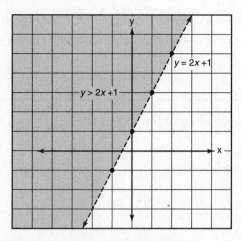 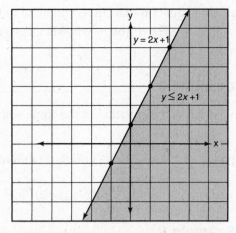

Besides the line, you need to know the equations for two other geometric shapes for the PSAT: the circle and the parabola.

Section 6-L discussed the facts you need to know about circles. In this section, we review the standard equation of a circle, which is given in KEY FACT N8.

Key Fact N8

- **The equation of the circle whose center is the point (h, k) and whose radius is r is $(x - h)^2 + (y - k)^2 = r^2$.**

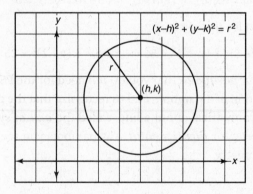

- **If the center is at the origin, (0, 0), then $h = k = 0$ and the equation reduces to $x^2 + y^2 = r^2$.**

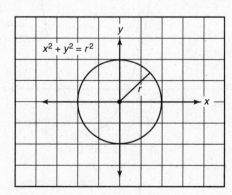

To write the equation of a circle, you need to know its center and its radius. Either they will be specifically given to you or you will be given some other information that will enable you to determine them.

➡ Example 8 _____

What is the equation of the circle whose center is at (–3, 2) and whose radius is 5?

Plug $h = -3$, $k = 2$, and $r = 5$ into the standard equation:

$$(x - (-3))^2 + (y - 2)^2 = 5^2 \Rightarrow (x + 3)^2 + (y - 2)^2 = 25$$

➡ Example 9 _____

Consider the circle in which $A(2, -3)$ and $B(8, 5)$ are the endpoints of a diameter. What is the equation of this circle?

The center of a circle is the midpoint of any diameter. The midpoint of $\overline{AB}$ is $\left(\frac{2+8}{2}, \frac{-3+5}{2}\right) = \left(\frac{10}{2}, \frac{2}{2}\right) = (5, 1)$. Now use the distance formula to get the radius. Either find the distance from the center, to A or B, or find the distance from A to B and divide that by 2.

$$OB = \sqrt{(8-5)^2 + (5-1)^2} = \sqrt{9+16} = \sqrt{25} = 5$$

Therefore, the equation for this circle is:

$$(x - 5)^2 + (y - 1)^2 = 5^2 \Rightarrow (x - 5)^2 + (y + 1)^2 = 25$$

There are many facts about **parabolas** that you do *not* need for the PSAT. Basically, you need to know the general equation of a parabola and to recognize that the graph of a parabola is a U-shaped curve that is symmetrical about a line, called the **axis of symmetry**, which passes through the parabola's **vertex**, or **turning point**. Any parabola you see on the PSAT will likely have a vertical axis of symmetry.

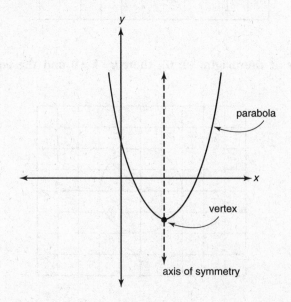

KEY FACT N9 lists the equations you need to know about parabolas.

For any real numbers *a*, *b*, *c* with $a \neq 0$:

- $y = ax^2 + bx + c$ is the equation of a parabola whose axis of symmetry is a vertical line.
- Conversely, the equation of any parabola with a vertical axis of symmetry has an equation of the form $y = ax^2 + bx + c$.
- The equation of the parabola's axis of symmetry is $x = \dfrac{-b}{2a}$.
- The vertex of the parabola is the point on the parabola whose *x*-coordinate is $\dfrac{-b}{2a}$.
- If $a > 0$, the parabola opens upward and the vertex is the lowest point on the parabola.
- If $a < 0$, the parabola opens downward and the vertex is the highest point on the parabola.

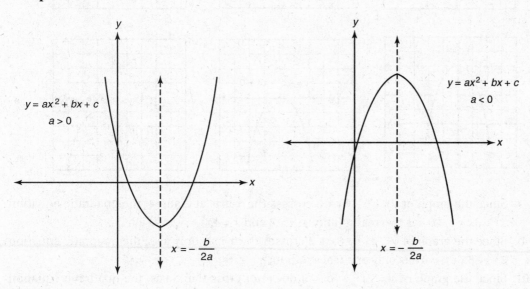

➥ Example 10

What is the vertex (turning point) of the parabola $y = 2x^2 - 4x + 5$?

First find its axis of symmetry. Since $a = 2$, $b = -4$, and $c = 5$, the equation of the axis of symmetry is $x = \dfrac{-b}{2a} = \dfrac{4}{4} = 1$. So the *x*-coordinate of the vertex is 1 and the *y*-coordinate is $2(1)^2 - 4(1) + 5 = 2 - 4 + 5 = 3$. The vertex is (1, 3).

An alternative solution would be to graph $y = 2x^2 - 4x + 5$ on a graphing calculator and to trace along the parabola until the cursor is at the vertex.

There is an important relationship between the parabola $y = ax^2 + bx + c$ and the quadratic equation $ax^2 + bx + c = 0$.

The *x*-intercepts of the graph of the parabola $y = ax^2 + bx + c$ are the (real) solutions of the equation $ax^2 + bx + c = 0$.

Consider the graphs of the following six parabolas.

(i)
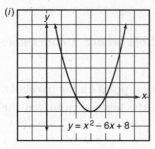
$y = x^2 - 6x + 8$

(ii)
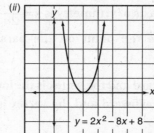
$y = 2x^2 - 8x + 8$

(iii)
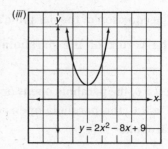
$y = 2x^2 - 8x + 9$

(iv)
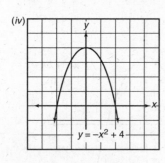
$y = -x^2 + 4$

(v)
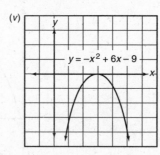
$y = -x^2 + 6x - 9$

(vi)
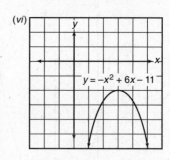
$y = -x^2 + 6x - 11$

  I. Since the graph of $y = x^2 - 6x + 8$ crosses the *x*-axis at 2 and 4, the quadratic equation $x^2 - 6x + 8 = 0$ has two real solutions: $x = 2$ and $x = 4$.

 II. Since the graph of $y = 2x^2 - 8x + 8$ crosses the *x*-axis only at 2, the quadratic equation $2x^2 - 8x + 8 = 0$ has only one real solution: $x = 2$.

III. Since the graph of $y = 2x^2 - 8x + 9$ does not cross the *x*-axis, the quadratic equation $2x^2 - 8x + 9 = 0$ has no real solutions.

Similarly, from graphs *(iv)*, *(v)*, and *(vi)*, you can see that the equation $-x^2 + 4 = 0$ has two real solutions; the equation $-x^2 + 6x - 9 = 0$ has only one real solution; and the equation $-x^2 + 6x - 11 = 0$ has no real solutions.

MULTIPLE-CHOICE QUESTIONS

1. What is the area of the rectangle, three of whose vertices are the points $A(2, 2)$, $B(7, 4)$, and $C(7, 2)$?

    (A) 10
    (B) 25
    (C) 40
    (D) 50

2. $B(7, -7)$ is a point on a circle whose center is at $(3, 5)$. If AB is a diameter of the circle, what is the slope of AB?

    (A) -3
    (B) $-\dfrac{1}{3}$
    (C) $\dfrac{1}{3}$
    (D) 3

3. What is the slope of the line that passes through $(0, a)$ and $(b, 0)$, where $b \neq 0$?

    (A) $\dfrac{a}{b}$
    (B) $-\dfrac{a}{b}$
    (C) $\dfrac{b}{a}$
    (D) $-\dfrac{b}{a}$

Questions 4 and 5 refer to circle O, in which $P(-2, 0)$ and $Q(6, 4)$ are the endpoints of a diameter.

4. What is the area of circle O?

    (A) 10π
    (B) 20π
    (C) 40π
    (D) 80π

5. Which of the following is the equation of circle O?

    (A) $(x + 2)^2 + (y - 2)^2 = \sqrt{20}$
    (B) $(x - 2)^2 + (y - 2)^2 = \sqrt{20}$
    (C) $(x + 2)^2 + (y - 2)^2 = 20$
    (D) $(x - 2)^2 + (y - 2)^2 = 20$

GRID-IN QUESTIONS

Questions 6 and 7 concern parallelogram $ABCD$, whose coordinates are $A(-6, 2)$, $B(-3, 6)$, $C(4, 6)$, $D(1, 2)$.

6. What is the area of parallelogram $ABCD$?

7. What is the perimeter of parallelogram $ABCD$?

8. If the coordinates of $\triangle JKL$ are $J(0, 0)$, $K(8, 0)$, and $L(2, 6)$, what is the sum of the slopes of the three sides of the triangle?

10. What is the absolute value of the sum of the x-coordinates of the points where the graph of the parabola crosses the x-axis?

<u>Questions 9–10</u> concern the parabola whose equation is $y = -x^2 - 20x + 69$.

9. Where does the graph of the parabola cross the y-axis?

Answer Key

1. **A**   2. **A**   3. **B**   4. **B**   5. **D**

6. **28**   7. **24**   8. **2**   9. **69**   10. **20**

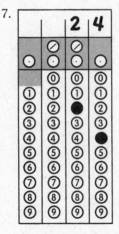

On the PSAT there are several questions that will require you to interpret the data that appear in some type of table or graph. Occasionally you will be asked two questions based on the same set of data. In this case, one of them is usually quite easy, requiring only that you *read* the information in the table or graph. The other question is usually a little more challenging and may ask you to *interpret* the data, *manipulate* them, or *make a prediction* based on them.

The data can be presented in the columns of a table or displayed graphically. The graphs that appear most often are circle graphs, bar graphs, line graphs, and scatterplot graphs. In this section, we will illustrate each of these and give examples of the types of questions that may be asked.

6-O INTERPRETATION OF DATA

Line Graphs

A **line graph** indicates how one or more quantities change over time. The horizontal axis is usually marked off in units of time; the units on the vertical axis can represent almost any type of numerical data: dollars, weights, exam grades, number of people, and so on.

Here is a typical line graph:

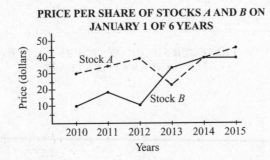

PRICE PER SHARE OF STOCKS *A* AND *B* ON JANUARY 1 OF 6 YEARS

Before reading even one of the questions based on the above graph, you should have acquired *at least* the following information: (i) the graph gives the values of two different stocks; (ii) the graph covers the period from January 1, 2010, to January 1, 2015; (iii) during that time, both stocks rose in value. There are several questions that could be asked about the data in this graph. Here are two examples.

➡ Example 1 _____

On January 1 of what year was the ratio of the value of a share of stock *A* to the value of a share of stock *B* the greatest?

(A) 2010
(B) 2011
(C) 2012
(D) 2015

Solution. From 2013 to 2015, the values of the two stocks were fairly close; so those years are not candidates. In 2012 the ratio was 40 : 10 or 4 : 1 or 4. In 2011 the ratio was 35 : 15 or 7 : 3 or 2.33. In 2010 the ratio was 30 : 10 or 3 : 1 or 3. The ratio was greatest in 2012 (Choice C).

➡ **Example 2** _____

What was the average yearly increase in the value of a share of stock *A* from 2010 to 2015?

Solution. Over the five-year period from January 1, 2010, to January 1, 2015, the value of a share of stock *A* rose from $30 to $45, an increase of $15. The average yearly increase was $15 ÷ 5 years, or $3 per year.

Tables and Bar Graphs

The same information that was given in the preceding line graph could have been presented in a *table* or in a *bar graph*.

In a bar graph, the taller the bar, the greater the value of the quantity. Bar graphs can also be drawn horizontally; in this case the longer the bar, the greater the quantity.

**PRICE PER SHARE OF STOCKS *A* AND *B*
ON JANUARY 1 OF 6 YEARS**

	Prices (dollars)					
Stock	2010	2011	2012	2013	2014	2015
Stock *A*	30	35	40	25	40	45
Stock *B*	10	20	15	35	40	40

**PRICE PER SHARE OF STOCKS *A* AND *B* ON
JANUARY 1 OF 6 YEARS**

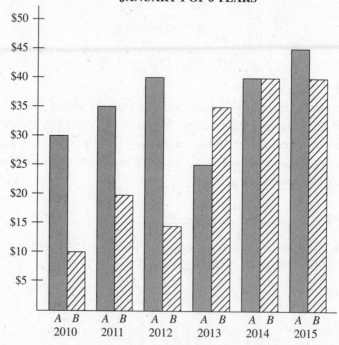

In a slight variation of the horizontal bar graph, the bars are replaced by a string of icons, or symbols. For example, the graph on the following page, in which each picture of a person represents 100 students, conveys information about the languages studied by the students at State College in 2016.

**NUMBERS OF STUDENTS ENROLLED IN
LANGUAGE COURSES AT STATE COLLEGE IN 2016**

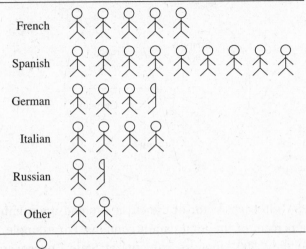

Each 👤 represents 100 students.

➥ Example 3

If the "Other" category includes five languages, what is the average
(arithmetic mean) number of students studying each language offered
at the college?

Solution. First determine the total number of students taking a language course. Either get
the number for each language and add or just count the number of icons: there are 24 full
icons and 2 half icons for a total of 25 icons, representing 2,500 students. The 2,500 students
are divided among 10 languages (the 5 languages listed plus the 5 in the "Other" category):
$2,500 \div 10 = 250$.

➥ Example 4

If the number of students studying Italian next year is the same as the
number taking Spanish this year, by what percent will the number of
students taking Italian increase?

Solution. The number of students taking Italian would increase by 500 from 400 to 900.
This represents a $\frac{500}{400} \times 100\% = 125\%$ increase.

Circle Graphs

A *circle graph* is another way to present data. In a circle graph, which is sometimes called a
pie chart, the circle is divided into sectors, with the size of each sector exactly proportional
to the quantity it represents. For example, the information included in the previous graph is
presented in the circle graph on page 450.

**NUMBERS OF STUDENTS ENROLLED IN
LANGUAGE COURSES AT STATE COLLEGE IN 2016**

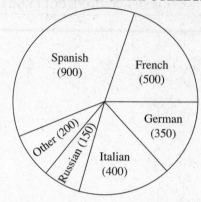

Usually on the PSAT, in each sector of the circle is noted the number of degrees of its central angle or the percent of the total data it contains. For example, in the circle graph above, since 500 of the 2,500 language students at State College are studying French, the sector representing French is exactly $\frac{1}{5}$ of the circle. On the PSAT this sector could be marked either $72°$ $\left(\frac{1}{5}\text{ of }360°\right)$ or 20% $\left(\frac{1}{5}\text{ of }100\%\right)$, as in the graphs below.

**DISTRIBUTION OF THE 2,500 STUDENTS
ENROLLED IN LANGUAGE COURSES**

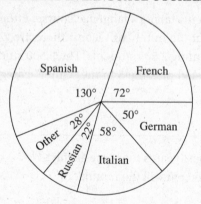

**DISTRIBUTION OF THE 2,500 STUDENTS
ENROLLED IN LANGUAGE COURSES**

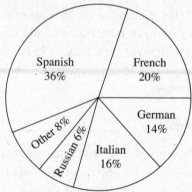

Often on the PSAT, some data are omitted from a circle graph, and it is your job to determine the missing item. Examples 5 and 6 are based on the following circle graph, which shows the distribution of marbles by color in a large jar.

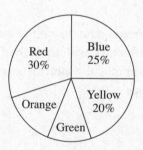

➡ Example 5

If the jar contains 1,200 marbles and there are twice as many orange marbles as there are green, how many green marbles are there?

Solution. Since the red, blue, and yellow marbles constitute 75 percent of the total (30% + 25% + 20%), the orange and green ones combined account for 25 percent of the total: 25 percent of 1,200 = 300. Then, since the ratio of orange marbles to green ones is 2:1, there are 200 orange marbles and 100 green ones.

➡ Example 6

Assume that the jar contains 1,200 marbles, and that all of the red ones are removed and replaced by an equal number of marbles, all of which are blue or yellow. If the ratio of blue to yellow marbles remains the same, how many additional yellow marbles are there?

Solution. Since 30 percent of 1,200 is 360, the 360 red marbles were replaced by 360 blue and yellow ones. To maintain the current blue to yellow ratio of 25 to 20, or 5 to 4, $\frac{5}{9}$ of the new marbles would be blue and $\frac{4}{9}$ would be yellow: $\frac{4}{9}$ of 360 = 160.

Scatterplots

A *scatterplot* is a graph that displays the relationship between two variables. It consists of a horizontal axis and a vertical axis (just like the first quadrant of the *xy*-coordinate plane) and a series of dots. Each dot represents an individual data point and is plotted the same way that points are plotted in the *xy*-plane. For example, in the scatterplot below, the horizontal axis represents the number of hours that a group of students studied for their final exam in math and the vertical axis represents the students' scores on the exam.

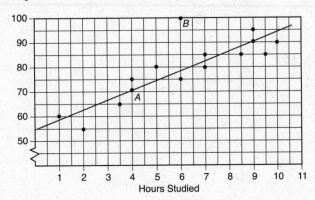

Look at Student *A*. He studied for 4 hours and earned a 70 on the final. Note that in this case, there is a fairly strong ***positive correlation*** between the two variables. The *general trend* is that more hours of study correlate to higher test scores. However, the correlation is clearly not perfect. Student *B*, for example, is an outlier. She studied for only 6 hours but had the highest score—higher than any of the students who studied 9 or 10 hours.

The line that is drawn on the scatterplot is called the ***line of best fit*** and can be used to predict the most likely value of one variable given the other. For example, from the line of best fit we see that a student who studies 8 hours would probably have a test score very close to 87. We also see that a student who earned a 60 on the final probably studied for about $1\frac{1}{2}$ hours.

Some scatterplots have a **negative correlation**, and some have no correlation at all. An example of two variables whose scatterplot would likely have a negative correlation is one where the variable along the horizontal axis is a person's weight and the variable on the vertical axis is the speed at which that person can run a 100-meters dash. The general trend would likely show that the heavier the person is, the slower he or she can run. An example of variables whose scatterplot would likely show no correlation is people's height and the number of times per month the people go to the movies.

Be very careful. A strong correlation *does not mean* that there is **causation**. Even if one variable increases whenever a second variable increases, there may be no cause and effect. For example, in 2015 in the town of Brest, there was a very high correlation between the number of gallons of ice cream consumed in a week and the number of people who drowned that week. Clearly eating ice cream didn't cause the drownings. Something else was going on. In fact, during the weeks that it was very hot, people ate lots of ice cream. During those same weeks, more people went to the pools and beaches. Hence, there were more drownings. The causative variable was the temperature.

On the PSAT, you will not be given a set of data and asked to create a scatterplot, nor will you have to calculate the line of best fit for a given scatterplot. However, you will have to recognize what type of correlation is exhibited. You may also have to make a prediction based on a line of best fit that has been drawn in a scatterplot graph.

MULTIPLE-CHOICE QUESTIONS

Questions 1 and 2 refer to the following graph.

BAKER FAMILY HOUSEHOLD BUDGET IN 2015

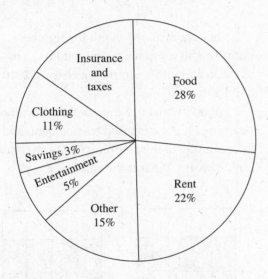

1. If the Baker's income in 2015 was $60,000, how much more did they spend on insurance and taxes than they did on clothing?

   (A) $3,000
   (B) $3,600
   (C) $4,000
   (D) $4,500

2. What is the degree measure of the central angle of the sector representing insurance and taxes?

   (A) 48.4
   (B) 54
   (C) 57.6
   (D) 60

Questions 3 and 4 refer to the following graph.

MATH PSAT SCORES OF SOPHOMORES
AT WESTSIDE HIGH SCHOOL IN 2015

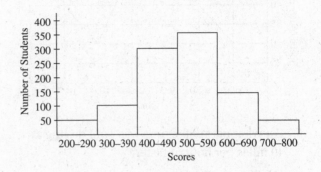

3. If there were 1,400 sophomores at Westside High School in 2015, how many of them did *not* take the PSAT?

   (A) 100
   (B) 200
   (C) 300
   (D) 400

4. To the nearest 5 percent, what percent of the sophomores who took the PSAT had Math scores of less than 500?

   (A) 40 percent
   (B) 45 percent
   (C) 50 percent
   (D) 55 percent

Questions 5 and 6 refer to the following graph.

SPEEDS AT WHICH TOM DROVE BETWEEN
8:00 A.M. AND 10:30 A.M. ON SUNDAY MORNING

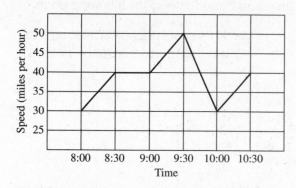

5. For what part of the time was Tom driving at
   40 miles per hour or faster?

   (A) 20 percent
   (B) 25 percent
   (C) 40 percent
   (D) 50 percent

6. How far, in miles, did Tom drive between
   8:30 and 9:00?

   (A) 0
   (B) 20
   (C) 30
   (D) 40

GRID-IN QUESTIONS

DISTRIBUTION OF GRADES ON
THE FINAL EXAM IN PHYSICS

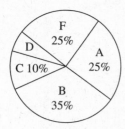

7. On the basis of the data in the graph above,
   if 300 students took the physics exam, how
   many earned a grade of D?

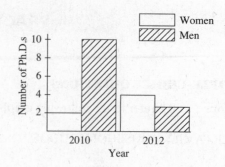

8. The bar graph above shows the number
   of men and women who earned Ph.D.s in
   French at Southwestern University in 2010
   and 2012.

   From 2010 to 2012 the number of women
   earning Ph.D.s increased by x percent, and
   the number of men earning Ph.D.s decreased
   by y percent. What is the value of $x - y$?

7.   8.

Answer Key

1. **A**   3. **D**   5. **D**
2. **C**   4. **B**   6. **B**

7.   8.

15   30

Most of the questions on the PSAT are on the topics already covered in sections A through O. The remaining questions are on miscellaneous topics covered in the last five sections of this chapter: probability, sequences, functions and their graphs, trigonometry, and both imaginary and complex numbers.

6-P BASIC PROBABILITY

The *probability* that an *event* will occur is a number between 0 and 1, usually written as a fraction, which indicates how likely it is that the event will happen. For example, if you spin the spinner below, there are four possible outcomes: it is equally likely that the spinner will stop in any of the four regions. There is one chance in four that it will stop in the region marked 2. So we say that the probability of spinning a 2 is one-fourth and write $P(2) = \dfrac{1}{4}$. Since 2 is the only even number on the spinner we could also say $P(\text{even}) = \dfrac{1}{4}$. There are three chances in four that the spinner will land in a region with an odd number in it, so $P(\text{odd}) = \dfrac{3}{4}$.

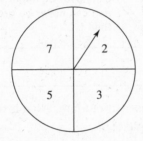

Key Fact P1

If E is any event, the probability that E will occur is given by

$$P(E) = \frac{\text{the number of favorable outcomes}}{\text{the total number of possible outcomes}}$$

assuming that all of the possible outcomes are equally likely, which is always the case on the PSAT.

In the preceding example, each of the four regions is the same size; so it is equally likely that the spinner will land on the 2, 3, 5, or 7. Therefore,

$$P(\text{odd}) = \frac{\text{the number of ways of getting an odd number}}{\text{the total number of possible outcomes}} = \frac{3}{4}$$

Let's look at some other probabilities associated with spinning this spinner once:

$$P(\text{number} > 8) = \frac{\text{the number of ways of getting a number} > 8}{\text{the total number of possible outcomes}} = \frac{0}{4} = 0$$

$$P(\text{prime number}) = \frac{\text{the number of ways of getting a prime number}}{\text{the total number of possible outcomes}} = \frac{4}{4} = 1$$

$$P(\text{number} < 5) = \frac{\text{the number of ways of getting a number} < 5}{\text{the total number of possible outcomes}} = \frac{2}{4} = \frac{1}{2}$$

Let E be an event and $P(E)$ the probability it will occur.

Then with reference to the example above:

- If E is *impossible* (such as getting a number greater than 8), $P(E) = 0$.
- If it is *certain* that E will occur (such as getting a prime number), $P(E) = 1$.
- In all cases $0 \leq P(E) \leq 1$.
- The probability that event E will *not* occur is $1 - P(E)$.
- If 2 or more events constitute all the outcomes, the sum of their probabilities is 1.

$$[\text{For example, } P(\text{even}) + P(\text{odd}) = \frac{1}{4} + \frac{3}{4} = 1]$$

- The more likely it is that an event will occur, the higher its probability (the closer to 1 it is); the less likely it is that an event will occur, the lower its probability (the closer to 0 it is).

CAUTION: The answer to a probability question can never be negative and can never be greater than 1.

➡ Example 1

A two-digit number is chosen at random. What is the probability that the number chosen is a multiple of 9?

Solution. There are 90 two-digit numbers (all of the integers between 10 and 99, inclusive). Of these 90 numbers, 10 of them (18, 27, 36, . . . , 99) are multiples of 9. Therefore,

$$\text{probability} = \frac{\text{the number of favorable outcomes}}{\text{the total number of possible outcomes}} = \frac{10}{90} = \frac{1}{9}$$

Key Fact P3

If an experiment is done two (or more) times, the probability that first one event will occur and then a second event will occur is the product of the probabilities.

➡ Example 2

The spinner shown at the beginning of this section is spun three times. What is the probability that it never lands on the 2?

(A) $\dfrac{1}{64}$

(B) $\dfrac{1}{4}$

(C) $\dfrac{27}{64}$

(D) $\dfrac{3}{4}$

Solution. We want the probability that on each of the three spins the spinner lands on one of the three odd numbers. Since $P(\text{odd}) = \frac{3}{4}$, by **KEY FACT P3**, the probability of three consecutive odd numbers is

$$P(\text{odd 1st time}) \times P(\text{odd 2nd time}) \times P(\text{odd 3rd time}) = \frac{3}{4} \times \frac{3}{4} \times \frac{3}{4} = \frac{27}{64}$$

Occasionally, on a PSAT there will be a question that relates to probability and geometry. The next **KEY FACT** will help you deal with that type of question.

Key Fact P4

If a point is chosen at random inside a geometrical figure, the probability that the chosen point lies in a particular region is

$$\frac{\text{the area of that region}}{\text{the area of the whole figure}}$$

➡ **Example 3**

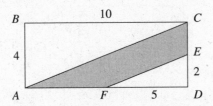

If a point is chosen at random inside rectangle *ABCD*, what is the probability that the point lies in the shaded region?

Solution. The area of rectangle *ABCD* is $4 \times 10 = 40$. The area of right triangle *ABC* is $\frac{1}{2}(4 \times 10) = 20$, and the area of right triangle *EDF* is $\frac{1}{2}(2 \times 5) = 5$. So the total area of the white region is $20 + 5 = 25$, and the area of the shaded region is $40 - 25 = 15$. The probability that the chosen point lies inside the shaded region is $\frac{15}{40} = \frac{3}{8}$.

PRACTICE EXERCISES

MULTIPLE-CHOICE QUESTIONS

Questions 1–3 refer to a jar that contains 5 marbles, 1 of each of the colors red, white, blue, green, and yellow.

1. If four marbles are removed from the jar, what is the probability that the yellow one was removed?

    (A) $\frac{1}{5}$

    (B) $\frac{1}{4}$

    (C) $\frac{4}{5}$

    (D) $\frac{5}{4}$

2. If one marble is removed from the jar, what is the probability that it is neither yellow nor green?

    (A) $\frac{1}{5}$

    (B) $\frac{2}{5}$

    (C) $\frac{3}{5}$

    (D) $\frac{5}{3}$

3. If two marbles are removed from the jar, what is the probability that each of them is red, white, or blue?

    (A) $\frac{6}{25}$

    (B) $\frac{3}{10}$

    (C) $\frac{9}{25}$

    (D) $\frac{2}{3}$

4. The Smiths have two children. If their older child is a boy, what is the probability that their younger child is also a boy?

    (A) $\frac{1}{4}$

    (B) $\frac{1}{3}$

    (C) $\frac{1}{2}$

    (D) $\frac{3}{4}$

5. The Kleins have two children. What is the probability that both of their children are boys?

    (A) $\frac{1}{4}$

    (B) $\frac{1}{3}$

    (C) $\frac{1}{2}$

    (D) $\frac{3}{4}$

GRID-IN QUESTIONS

6. If three coins are flipped, what is the probability that there are more heads than tails?

7. A box contains 10 slips of paper, each with a different number from 1 to 10 written on it. If one slip is removed at random, what is the probability that the number selected is a multiple of 2 or 3?

9. A number is a *palindrome* if it reads exactly the same from right to left as it does from left to right. For example, 66, 818, and 2,552 are all palindromes. If a three-digit number is chosen at random, what is the probability that it is a palindrome?

8. If two people are chosen at random, what is the probability that they were born on different days of the week?

10. In the diagram below, the radius of the large circle is 5 and the radius of the small circle is 3. If a point is chosen at random inside the large circle, what is the probability that the point lies inside the small white circle?

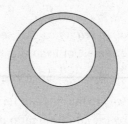

Answer Key

1. **C**   2. **C**   3. **B**   4. **C**   5. **A**

6. 1/2 or **.5**

7. 7/10 or **.7**

8. 6/7

9. 1/10

10. 9/25 or **.36**

6-Q SEQUENCES

There are three types of sequences that occasionally appear on the PSAT: *arithmetic sequences*, *geometric sequences*, and *repeating sequences*.

An **arithmetic sequence** is a sequence in which the *difference* between any two consecutive terms is the same. For example, the sequence 8, 11, 14, 17, 20, . . . is an arithmetic sequence in which the common difference is 3. An easy way to find the nth term of such a sequence is to start with the first term and add the common difference $n-1$ times. In this example, the fifth term is 20, which can be obtained by taking the first term, 8, and adding the common difference, 3, four times: $8 + 4(3) = 8 + 12 = 20$.

KEY FACT Q1 gives the formula for finding the nth term of any arithmetic sequence.

> ### Key Fact Q1

If a_1, a_2, a_3, . . . is an arithmetic sequence whose common difference is d, then

$$a_n = a_1 + (n-1)\, d$$

➥ **Example 1** _____

What is the 100th term of the sequence 8, 11, 14, 17, 20, . . . ?

Solution. This is an arithmetic sequence whose first term is 8 and whose comman difference is 3. So by **KEY FACT Q1**

$$a_{100} = a_1 + 99d = 8 + 99(3) = 8 + 297 = 305$$

A **geometric sequence** is a sequence in which the *ratio* between any two consecutive terms is the same. For example, the sequence 2, 8, 32, 128, 512, . . . is a geometric sequence: the ratios $\frac{8}{2}$, $\frac{32}{8}$, $\frac{128}{32}$ are all equal to 4.

An easy way to find the nth term of a geometric sequence is to start with the first term and multiply it by the common ratio $n-1$ times. For example, in the sequence 2, 8, 32, 128, 512, . . . the fourth term is 128, which can be obtained by taking the first term, 2, and multiplying it by the common ratio, 4, three times: $2 \times 4 \times 4 \times 4 = 2 \times 4^3 = 2 \times 64 = 128$. The next **KEY FACT** gives the formula for finding the nth term of a geometric sequence.

> ### Key Fact Q2

If a_1, a_2, a_3, . . . is a geometric sequence whose common ratio is r, then $a_n = a_1\,(r)^{n-1}$.

➥ **Example 2** _____

What is the 100th term of the sequence 2, 8, 32, 128, 512, . . . ?

(A) 2^{99}
(B) 2^{100}
(C) 2×4^{99}
(D) 2×4^{100}

Solution. This is a geometric series whose first term is 2 and whose common ratio is 4. So by **KEY FACT Q2**,

$$a_{100} = a_1(r)^{99} = 2 \times 4^{99} \text{ (Choice C)}$$

A *repeating sequence* is a sequence in which a certain number of terms repeat indefinitely. Each of the following is a repeating sequence

(i) $-1, 0, 1, -1, 0, 1, -1, 0, 1, \ldots$

(ii) $1, 4, 2, 8, 5, 7, 1, 4, 2, 8, 5, 7, \ldots$

(iii) red, white, blue, green, red, white, blue, green, $\ldots$

On the PSAT, questions concerning repeating sequences usually ask you to find a particular term of the sequence, such as the 100th term or 1,000th term. So you need to have a procedure for finding the term you want. For example, let's find the 500th term of the sequence 1, 4, 2, 8, 5, 7, 1, 4, 2, 8, 5, 7, . . . Think of this as a sequence in which the set {1, 4, 2, 8, 5, 7} of 6 numbers keeps repeating. Since the last number in the set is 7, if we write down 1 set or 2 sets or 3 sets or 10 sets, the last number will be 7. So the 6th, 12th, 18th, and 60th terms are all 7. In general, if *n* is a multiple of 6, the *n*th term is 7. So the 30th term, the 666th term, and the 6,000,000th terms are all 7. To answer the question, "What is the 500th term?" the first thing you should do is divide 500 by 6. If 500 is a multiple of 6, the answer will be 7. Using your calculator, you find that $500 \div 6 = 83.333$. So 500 is not a multiple of 6. When 500 is divided by 6, the *integer* quotient is 83 (ignore the decimal portion). This means that in the first 500 terms of the sequence, the set {1, 4, 2, 8, 5, 7} repeats 83 times. Since $83 \times 6 = 498$, the 498th term is 7. The 499th term starts the next set; it is 1 and the 500th term is 4.

TACTIC Q1 To find the *n*th term of a repeating sequence, divide *n* by the number of terms that repeat. If *r* is the integer remainder, then the *n*th term is the same as the *r*th term.

In the worked-out example preceding **TACTIC Q1**, we found the 500th term of the sequence 1, 4, 2, 8, 5, 7, 1, 4, 2, 8, 5, 7, . . . Using **TACTIC Q1**, we would proceed as follows:

$500 \div 6 = 83.333 \Rightarrow$ the quotient is 83. Then $83 \times 6 = 498$ and $500 - 498 = 2$.

The remainder is 2, and so the 500th term is the same as the 2nd term, namely 4.

PRACTICE EXERCISES

MULTIPLE-CHOICE QUESTIONS

1. What is the 100th term of the sequence 4, 9, 14, 19, 24, . . . ?

   (A) 494
   (B) 499
   (C) 504
   (D) 509

2. Consider the sequence 2, 6, 18, 54, 162, . . . What is the 25th term?

   (A) 3^{24}
   (B) 3^{25}
   (C) 2×3^{24}
   (D) 2×3^{25}

3. If today is Saturday, what day will it be 500 days from today?

   (A) Saturday
   (B) Sunday
   (C) Tuesday
   (D) Wednesday

4. If it is now September, what month will it be 555 months from now?

   (A) April
   (B) June
   (C) November
   (D) December

5. The first term of sequence I is 2 and each subsequent term is 2 more than the preceding term. The first term of sequence II is 2 and each subsequent term is 2 times the preceding term. What is the ratio of the 32nd term of sequence II to the 32nd term of sequence I?

   (A) 2
   (B) 2^{26}
   (C) 2^{27}
   (D) 2^{32}

GRID-IN QUESTIONS

6. The first term of a sequence is 1 and every term after the first one is 1 more than the square of the preceding term. What is the fifth term?

7. The first two terms of a sequence are 5 and 7. Each term after the second one is found by taking the average (arithmetic mean) of all the preceding terms. What is the 50th term of this sequence?

8. Consider the sequence 2, 6, 18, 54, 162, . . . If the 77th term is a and the 80th term is b, what is the value of $\dfrac{b}{a}$?

9. Consider the sequence
1, 2, 3, 1, 2, 3, 1, 2, 3, . . .
What is the sum of the
first 100 terms?

10. In a certain sequence,
each term is 4 greater
than the preceding term.
If the 20th term is 100,
what is the 2nd term?

Answer Key

1. **B** 2. **C** 3. **C** 4. **D** 5. **B**

6. 6 7 7
7.   6
8. 2 7
9. 1 9 9
10. 2 8

6-R FUNCTIONS AND THEIR GRAPHS

Very little of what is taught about functions in high school math classes is tested on the PSAT. In this section, we will review the basic facts about functions and their graphs that you need to know for the PSAT.

As used on the PSAT, a ***function*** is a rule that assigns to each number in one set a number in another set. The function is usually designated by the letter f, although other letters, such as g and h, are sometimes used. The numbers in the first set are labeled x, and the number in the second set to which x is assigned by the function is designated by the letter y or by $f(x)$.

For example, the function that assigns to each real number x, the number $2x + 3$, can be written $y = 2x + 3$ or $f(x) = 2x + 3$.

The number assigned to 5 is $2(5) + 3 = 10 + 3 = 13$, and the number assigned to –5 is $2(-5) + 3 = -10 + 3 = -7$.

To express these facts, we write

$f(5) = 13$ and $f(-5) = -7$

The proper way to think of the function $f(x) = 2x + 3$ is that f takes *anything* and assigns to it 2 times *that thing* plus 3:

$$f(anything) = 2(that\ thing) + 3$$

- $f(100) = 2(100) + 3 = 203$
- $f(a) = 2a + 3$
- $f(x^2) = 2x^2 + 3$

- $f(0) = 2(0) + 3 = 0 + 3 = 3$
- $f(a + b) = 2(a + b) + 3$
- $f(2x^2 + 3) = 2(2x^2 + 3) + 3 = 4x^2 + 9$

➡ Example 1 _____

If $f(x) = x^2 + 2x$, what is $f(3) + f(-3)$?

Solution.
$$f(3) = 3^2 + 2(3) = 9 + 6 = 15$$
$$f(-3) = (-3)^2 + 2(-3) = 9 - 6 = 3$$
Therefore,
$$f(3) + f(-3) = 15 + 3 = 18$$

➡ Example 2 _____

If $f(x) = x^2 + 2x$, what is $f(x + 2)$?

(A) $x^2 + 2x + 4$
(B) $x^2 + 2x + 8$
(C) $x^2 + 6x + 4$
(D) $x^2 + 6x + 8$

Solution. $f(x + 2) = (x + 2)^2 + 2(x + 2) = (x^2 + 4x + 4) + (2x + 4) = x^2 + 6x + 8$ (Choice D).

➡ Example 3 _____

Let $f(x) = x^2 + 2x$ and $g(x) = x^2 - 2x$. If $g(4) = a$ and $f(a) = b$, what is the value of b?

Solution. $g(4) = 4^2 - 2(4) = 16 - 8 = 8$; so $a = 8$. Then

$$f(a) = f(8) = 8^2 + 2(8) = 64 + 16 = 80.\ So\ b = 80$$

The *graph* of a function, f, is a certain set of points in the coordinate plane. The point (x, y) is on the graph of f if and only if $y = f(x)$. So, for example, the graph of $f(x) = 2x + 3$ consists of all points (x, y) such that $y = 2x + 3$. Since $f(5) = 13$ and $f(-5) = -7$, then $(5, 13)$ and $(-5, -7)$ are both points on the graph of $f(x) = 2x + 3$. On the PSAT you may have to know whether a certain point is on the graph of a given function, but you won't have to actually graph the function.

➡️ **Example 4** _____

Which of the following is NOT a point on the graph of $f(x) = x^2 + \dfrac{4}{x^2}$?

(A) $(-1, 5)$
(B) $(2, 5)$
(C) $(-2, -5)$
(D) $(4, 16.25)$

Solution.

$f(-1) = (-1)^2 + \dfrac{4}{(-1)^2} = 1 + 4 = 5 \Rightarrow (-1, 5)$ *is* a point on the graph.

$f(2) = 2^2 + \dfrac{4}{2^2} = 4 + 1 = 5 \Rightarrow (2, 5)$ *is* a point on the graph.

$f(-2) = (-2)^2 + \dfrac{4}{(-2)^2} = 4 + 1 = 5 \ne -5 \Rightarrow (-2, -5)$ is *NOT* a point on the graph.

The answer is Choice C.

➡️ **Example 5** _____

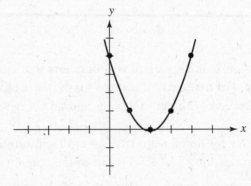

Which of the following could be the equation of the graph shown in the figure above?

(A) $y = -2x + 4$
(B) $y = 2x + 4$
(C) $y = x^2$
(D) $y = x^2 - 4x + 4$

Solution. Since the graph passes through (2, 0), $x = 2$ and $y = 0$ must satisfy the equation. Test each of the four choices in order.

- (A) Does $0 = -2(2) + 4$?   Yes
- (B) Does $0 = 2(2) + 4$?   No
- (C) Does $0 = 2^2$?   No
- (D) Does $0 = 2^2 - 4(2) + 4$?   Yes

The answer is (A) or (D). To break the tie, try another point on the graph, say (0, 4) and test choices (A) and (D).

- (A) Does $4 = -2(0) + 4$?   Yes
- (D) Does $4 = (0)^2 - 4(0) + 4$?   Yes

Unfortunately, that didn't help. Try one more, point (1, 1).

- (A) Does $1 = -2(1) + 4$?   No
- (D) Does $1 = 1^2 - 4(1) + 4$?   Yes

The answer is $y = x^2 - 4x + 4$ (D).

Of course, if you realized that the graphs of the equations in Choices A and B are straight lines, you could have immediately eliminated them and tested only Choices C and D.

You can think of a function as a machine. A washing machine performs a function. It cleans clothes: dirty clothes go in and clean clothes come out. In the same way you can think of $f(x) = 2x + 3$ as a machine. When 5 goes in, 13 comes out; when –5 goes in, –7 comes out.

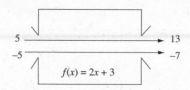

The **domain** of a function is the set of all real numbers that can go into the machine without causing a problem. The domain of $f(x) = 2x + 3$ is the set of all real numbers, because, for any real number whatsoever, you can double it and add 3. No number will cause the machine to jam.

If $f(x) = \sqrt{2x+3}$, however, the domain is not the set of all real numbers. Although 5 is in the domain of f, because $f(5) = \sqrt{2(5)+3} = \sqrt{13}$, –5 is not in the domain of f. The reason is that $\sqrt{2(-5)+3} = \sqrt{-10+3} = \sqrt{-7}$, which is not a real number. If you try to evaluate $\sqrt{2(-5)+3}$ on your calculator (a machine that evaluates many functions), you will get an error message.

Since the domain of a function is the set of all real numbers except those that cause problems, you need to know what can cause a problem. Many things can be troublesome, but for the PSAT you need to know about only two of them.

Key Fact R1

A number x is *not* in the domain of $y = f(x)$ if evaluating $f(x)$ would require you to divide by 0 or to take the square root of a negative number.

➡ **Example 6** _____

Which of the following numbers is NOT in the domain of $f(x) = \sqrt{4-x}$?

(A) −6
(B) −4
(C) 4
(D) 6

Solution. Since you cannot take the square root of a negative number, the domain of $f(x) = \sqrt{4-x}$ is the set of all real numbers x such that $4 - x \ge 0 \Rightarrow 4 \ge x$. Of the four choices, only 6 (D) is not in the domain.

Note that 4 is in the domain of $f(x) = \sqrt{4-x}$ because $f(4) = \sqrt{4-4} = \sqrt{0} = 0$. However, 4 is *not* in the domain of $g(x) = \dfrac{1}{\sqrt{4-x}}$ because $\dfrac{1}{\sqrt{4-4}} = \dfrac{1}{\sqrt{0}} = \dfrac{1}{0}$, which is undefined. Remember, you can *never* divide by 0.

Again, if a function is thought of as a machine, the ***range*** of a function is the set of all real numbers that can come out of the machine. Recall that, if $f(x) = 2x + 3$, then $f(5) = 13$ and $f(-5) = -7$, so 13 and −7 are both in the range of $f(x)$. In general, it is much harder to find the range of a function than to find its domain, but you will usually be able to test whether a particular number is in the range.

➡ **Example 7** _____

Which of the following is NOT in the range of $f(x) = x^2 - 3$?

(A) 6
(B) 1
(C −1
(D) −6

Solution. Since for any real number x, $x^2 \ge 0$, then $x^2 - 3 \ge -3$. Therefore, −6 (D) is not in the range of $f(x)$.

Note that in the solution to Example 7 you do not have to test each of the choices, but you can. To test whether 6 is in the range of $f(x)$, see whether there is a number x such that $f(x) = 6$: $x^2 - 3 = 6 \Rightarrow x^2 = 9 \Rightarrow x = 3$ or $x = -3$.

Then $f(3) = 6$, and 6 is in the range. Similarly, $f(2) = 1$ and $f(\sqrt{2}) = -1$, so 1 and −1 are also in the range. If you test −6, you see that $f(x) = -6 \Rightarrow x^2 - 3 = -6 \Rightarrow x^2 = -3$.

But there is no real number whose square is −3. Nothing that can go into the machine will cause −6 to come out.

On the PSAT, questions such as Examples 6 and 7 may be phrased without using the words "domain" and "range." For example, Example 6 may be expressed as follows:

The function $f(x) = \sqrt{4-x}$ is defined for each of the following numbers EXCEPT

(A) −6
(B) −4
(C)   4
(D)   6

Similarly, Example 7 may be expressed as follows:

For the function $f(x) = x^2 - 3$, which of the following numbers may NOT be the value of $f(x)$?

(A)   6
(B)   1
(C) −1
(D) −6

On the PSAT you take, it is possible that there will be a question that shows you a graph and asks you which of four other graphs is related to the original one in a certain way. To answer such a question, you can either test points or use the five facts listed in the following KEY FACT.

Key Fact R2

If $f(x)$ is a function and r is a positive number:

1. The graph of $y = f(x) + r$ is obtained by shifting the graph of $y = f(x)$ UP r units.
2. The graph of $y = f(x) - r$ is obtained by shifting the graph of $y = f(x)$ DOWN r units.
3. The graph of $y = f(x + r)$ is obtained by shifting the graph of $y = f(x)$ r units to the LEFT.
4. The graph of $y = f(x - r)$ is obtained by shifting the graph of $y = f(x)$ r units to the RIGHT.
5. The graph of $y = -f(x)$ is obtained by reflecting the graph of $y = f(x)$ in the x-axis.

Each part of **KEY FACT R2** is illustrated below.

Figure (a) is the graph of the absolute-value function: $y = f(x) = |x|$. Figures (b)–(f) are transformations of the original graph.

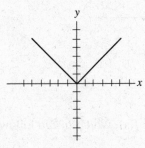

$y = f(x) = |x|$

(a)

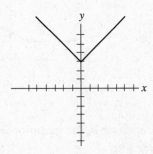

$y = f(x) + 3 = |x| + 3$

(b)

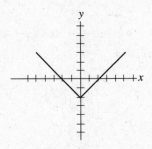

$y = f(x) - 2 = |x| - 2$

(c)

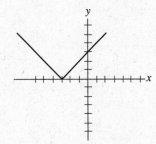

$y = f(x + 3) = |x + 3|$

(d)

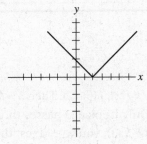

$y = f(x - 2) = |x - 2|$

(e)

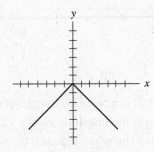

$y = -f(x) = -|x|$

(f)

➡ Example 8

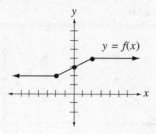

If the figure above is the graph of $y = f(x)$, which of the following is the graph of $y = f(x + 2)$?

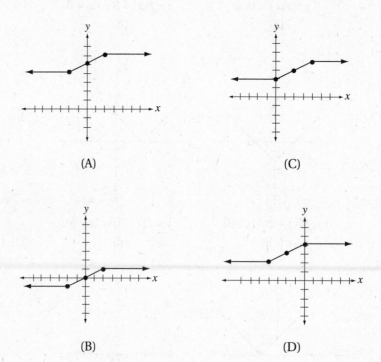

(A)

(C)

(B)

(D)

Solution 1. Since $(0, 3)$ is a point on the graph of $y = f(x)$, $f(0) = 3$. Then $3 = f(0) = f(-2 + 2)$ and so $(-2, 3)$ is a point on the graph of $y = f(x + 2)$. Only Choice D passes through $(-2, 3)$. Note that, if two or three of the graphs passed through $(-2, 3)$, you would test those graphs with a second point, say $(2, 4)$.

Solution 2. By **KEY FACT R2**, the graph of $y = f(x + 2)$ results from shifting the graph of $y = f(x)$ 2 units to the left. Only Choice D is 2 units to the left of the graph in question.

MULTIPLE-CHOICE QUESTIONS

1. If $f(x) = 3x + 5$ and $f(2) = a$, what is $f(a)$?

   (A) 11
   (B) 13
   (C) 25
   (D) 38

2. If $f(x) = 3x + 5$ and $g(x) = 5x + 3$, what is $g(6) - f(6)$?

   (A) 0
   (B) 6
   (C) 10
   (D) 56

3. Let $f(x) = 3x + 5$ and $g(x) = 5x + 3$. If $f(2) = a$ and $g(a) = b$, what is b?

   (A) 24
   (B) 44
   (C) 58
   (D) 143

4. If $f(x) = 3x - 5$ and $(2, b)$ is a point on the graph of $y = f(x)$, then $b =$

   (A) −1
   (B) 1
   (C) 3
   (D) 11

5. If $f(x) = |x|$, for what value of x does $f(x - 3) = f(x + 3)$?

   (A) −3
   (B) 0
   (C) 3
   (D) No value of x

GRID-IN QUESTIONS

6. If $f(x) = 3x + 5$ and $(a, 20)$ is a point on the graph of $y = f(x)$, then what is the value of a?

7. If $f(x) = 2^x + x^2$, what is $f(1)$?

8. Let $f(x) = x^2 + 1$ and $g(x) = 1 - x^2$. If $g(3) = a$ and $f(a) = b$, what is b?

9. If $f(x) = x^2 + 1$ and
$f(3) = a$, what is $f(a)$?

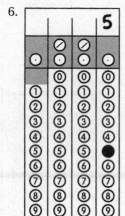

10. What is the largest integer
that is in the domain of
$g(x) = \sqrt{3\pi - x^2}$?

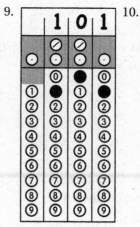

Answer Key

1. **D**   2. **C**   3. **C**   4. **B**   5. **B**

6. 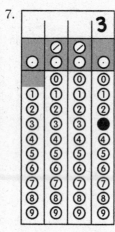 **5**

7. **3**

8. **6 5**

9. **1 0 1**

10. **3**

6-S TRIGONOMETRY

The SAT that you take will probably have a couple of questions on trigonometry. It is highly unlikely that the PSAT you take will have more than one such question. This section reviews the facts that you need to know in order to answer that question. If you have studied trigonometry in school, you surely have learned much more trigonometry than is required for either the PSAT or SAT. The question you see should present little or no difficulty. If, on the other hand, you are not familiar with trigonometry, you have two choices.

You can study this section carefully and learn what you need to know to answer that question. Alternatively, you can save the time and effort and just not worry about it. If you encounter a question involving a trigonometric ratio (sine, cosine, or tangent), just take a wild guess and move on. Remember that you don't need to attempt all of the questions to do really well. Correctly answering only 33 of the 48 math questions on the PSAT can earn you a score over 600. Correctly answering 41 of the 48 questions can earn you a score over 700! Certainly if you have a limited time to study, you are better off reviewing what you know rather than trying to learn a brand-new topic about which there will be only one question.

This section is rather short because it reviews very little of what is taught in a high school trigonometry course. It reviews only the trigonometry that could be the basis of a PSAT question. The most important things you need to know for the PSAT are the definitions of the trigonometric ratios. The one other thing to know is the definition of a radian and how to convert degree measure to radian measure.

Sine, Cosine, and Tangent

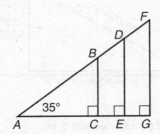

In the figure above, right triangles ABC, ADE, and AFG each have a 90° angle and a 35° angle, so they are all similar to one another. Therefore, their sides are in proportion:

$$\frac{BC}{AB} = \frac{DE}{AD} = \frac{FG}{AF} = \frac{\text{length of the side opposite the 35° angle}}{\text{length of the hypotenuse}}$$

This ratio is called the sine of 35° and is written sin 35°. To evaluate sin 35°, you could very carefully measure the lengths of $\overline{FG}$ and $\overline{AF}$ and divide. In the given figure, $FG \approx 1$ inch, $AF \approx 1.75$ inches, so $\frac{FG}{AF} \approx \frac{1}{1.75} = 0.57$.

Fortunately, you do not have to do this. You can use your calculator. Depending on what calculator you use, you would either enter 35 and then press the $\boxed{\text{sin}}$ button or press the $\boxed{\text{sin}}$ button and then enter 35. Regardless, in a fraction of a second, you will see the answer correct to several decimal places: sin 35° = 0.573576436, far greater accuracy than you need for the PSAT.

➡ Example 1

In the triangle below, what is the length of hypotenuse $\overline{AB}$?

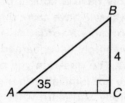

Solution. Use the sine ratio (and your calculator):

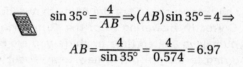

$$\sin 35° = \frac{4}{AB} \Rightarrow (AB)\sin 35° = 4 \Rightarrow$$

$$AB = \frac{4}{\sin 35°} = \frac{4}{0.574} = 6.97$$

The formal definitions of the three trigonometric ratios you need are given in **KEY FACT S1**.

Key Fact S1

Let θ be one of the acute angles in a right triangle.

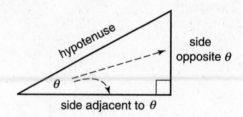

- **The formula for the sine of θ, denoted sin θ, is:**

$$\sin\theta = \frac{\text{the length of the side opposite } \theta}{\text{the length of the hypotenuse}}$$

$$= \frac{\text{opposite}}{\text{hypotenuse}}$$

- **The formula for the cosine of θ, denoted cos θ, is:**

$$\cos\theta = \frac{\text{the length of the side adjacent to } \theta}{\text{the length of the hypotenuse}}$$

$$= \frac{\text{adjacent}}{\text{hypotenuse}}$$

- The formula for the tangent of θ, denoted tan θ, is:

$$\tan \theta = \frac{\text{the length of the side opposite } \theta}{\text{the length of the side adjacent to } \theta}$$

$$= \frac{\text{opposite}}{\text{adjacent}}$$

- From the definitions of the three trigonometry ratios, it follows immediately that for any acute angle θ, $\tan \theta = \dfrac{\sin \theta}{\cos \theta}$.

For decades, students have remembered these definitions by memorizing the "word" SoHCaHToA. For example, the "S" in "SoH" stands for "sine" and the "oh" reminds you that sine is Opposite over Hypotenuse.

If you know the value of any one of sin θ, cos θ, or tan θ, you can always find the values of the other two.

Example 2

If $\sin \theta = \dfrac{15}{17}$, what are the values of cos θ and tan θ?

Solution. Draw right triangle ABC and label BC, the side opposite θ, as 15 and the hypotenuse as 17.

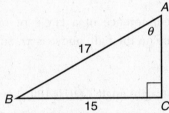

Now use the Pythagorean theorem to find AC:

$$(AC)^2 + 15^2 = 17^2 \Rightarrow AC^2 + 225 = 289 \Rightarrow$$
$$(AC)^2 = 64 \Rightarrow AC = 8$$

So, $\cos \theta = \dfrac{8}{17}$ and $\tan \theta = \dfrac{15}{8}$.

Example 3

What are the values of a and b in the triangle below?

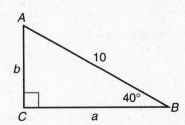

Solution. To find a and b, you can use the sine and cosine ratios:

$$\sin 40° = \frac{b}{10} \Rightarrow b = 10(\sin 40°) = 10(0.643) = 6.43$$

$$\cos 40° = \frac{a}{10} \Rightarrow a = 10(\cos 40°) = 10(0.766) = 7.66$$

Mathematicians sometimes use **radians** instead of degrees to measure angles. Since there will be at most one question on the PSAT involving radian measure, this is really a topic you can skip if you are not already familiar with the concept.

Recall that an arc of a circle consists of two points on the circle and all the points between them. On the PSAT, arc $\overset{\frown}{AB}$ always refers to the smaller arc joining A and B. The **radian measure** of a central angle of a circle is the ratio of the length of the arc cut off by the angle to the radius. In the figure on the left below, θ, measured in radians, is equal to the length of the arc, s, divided by the radius, r: $\theta = \dfrac{s}{r}$.

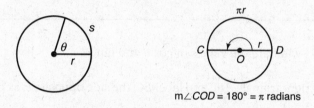

$$m\angle COD = 180° = \pi \text{ radians}$$

Since the length of the circumference of a circle of radius, r, is $2\pi r$, the length of semi-circular arc $\overset{\frown}{CD}$ in the figure on the right above is πr. So the radian measure of straight angle COD is $\dfrac{\pi r}{r} = \pi$.

Since the degree measure of straight angle COD is 180°, we have the following conversions between radians and degrees:

$$\pi \text{ radians} = 180° \qquad 2\pi \text{ radians} = 360° \qquad \frac{\pi}{2} \text{ radians} = 90° \qquad \frac{\pi}{4} \text{ radians} = 45°$$

$$1 \text{ radian} = \left(\frac{180}{\pi}\right)° \qquad 1° = \frac{\pi}{180} \text{ radians}$$

In the unlikely event that there is a question on the PSAT that involves radian measure and if you are determined to answer it, your best strategy would be to convert from radians to degrees.

For example, to evaluate $\sin \dfrac{\pi}{6}$, convert $\dfrac{\pi}{6}$ radians to $\dfrac{180}{6} = 30°$ and then use your calculator to evaluate $\sin 30°$: $\sin 30° = 0.5$.

➥ Example 4 _____

If $\sin \theta = a$, what is the value of $\sin(\pi - \theta)$?

(A) 0

(B) $-a$

(C) a

(D) $\dfrac{1}{a}$

Solution. The best way to answer a question like this on the PSAT is to pick a simple value for θ, measured in degrees, say $\theta = 30°$. Then $\pi - \theta$ radians = $180° - 30° = 150°$.

Now use your calculator to evaluate sin 30° and sin 150°. They are both equal to 0.5, so the answer is Choice C.

What You *Don't* Need To Know

We have just reviewed the ONLY trigonometry you need to know for the PSAT. Here is a list of several topics in trigonometry that you may have studied in school that are NOT included on the PSAT:

- Angles whose measures are negative
- Reference angles
- The reciprocal trigonometric functions: secant, cosecant, and cotangent
- Inverse trigonometric functions
- Graphs of the trigonometric and inverse trigonometric functions
- The law of sines and the law of cosines
- The trigonometric formula for the areas of a triangle and parallelogram
- Double-angle formulas and half-angle formulas
- Trigonometric identities

MULTIPLE-CHOICE QUESTIONS

1. In the triangle below, what is the ratio of c to b to the nearest hundredth?

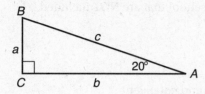

   (A) 0.34
   (B) 0.94
   (C) 1.06
   (D) 2.94

2. A ladder is leaning against a wall, forming an angle of 65° with the ground. If the foot of the ladder is 8 feet from the wall, what is the length of the ladder, in feet?

   (A) 7.25
   (B) 8.83
   (C) 17.15
   (D) 18.93

3. If $0° < \theta < 90°$ and $\tan \theta = \dfrac{5}{12}$, what is $\cos \theta - \sin \theta$?

   (A) $\dfrac{5}{13}$

   (B) $\dfrac{7}{13}$

   (C) $\dfrac{12}{13}$

   (D) $\dfrac{17}{13}$

4. If $\triangle PQR$ is isosceles and $m\angle R = 90°$, which of the following could be true?

   I. $\sin P = \cos P$
   II. $\sin P < \cos P$
   III. $\sin P > \cos P$

   (A) I only
   (B) I and II only
   (C) I and III only
   (D) I, II, and III

5. A kite string is tied to a peg in the ground. If the angle formed by the string and the ground is 70° and if there is 100 feet of string out, to the nearest foot, how high above the ground is the kite?

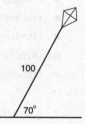

   (A) 34
   (B) 64
   (C) 74
   (D) 94

Answer Key

1. **C**   2. **D**   3. **B**   4. **A**   5. **D**

6-T IMAGINARY AND COMPLEX NUMBERS

> The SAT that you take will likely have one or two questions about imaginary or complex numbers. This is the only topic that is currently tested on the SAT that is *not* tested on the PSAT. *You should not expect to see any questions about imaginary or complex numbers on the PSAT.* However, since many students use their PSAT book when they begin their preparation for the SAT, we are including a few pages on this topic in this book in the interest of completeness. If you have studied complex numbers in school, the SAT questions on this topic should present no difficulty. If, on the other hand, you are not familiar with complex numbers, you have two choices.
>
> You can study this section carefully and learn what you need to know to answer those questions. Alternatively, you can save the time and effort and just not worry about this topic. Anytime you encounter a question involving the letter *i* (the imaginary unit), ignore it; *just take a wild guess and move on.* Remember that you don't need to attempt all of the questions to do really well. Correctly answering only 40 of the 58 math questions on the SAT can earn you a score over 600. Correctly answering 50 of the 58 questions can earn you a score over 700!

Imaginary Numbers

If x is a real number, then x is positive, negative, or zero. If $x = 0$, then $x^2 = 0$; and if x is either positive or negative, then x^2 is positive. So if x is a real number, x^2 CANNOT be negative.

In the set of real numbers, the equation $x^2 = -1$ has no solution. In order to solve such an equation, mathematicians defined a new number, i, called the **imaginary unit**, with the property that $i^2 = -1$. This number is often referred to as the square root of -1: $i = \sqrt{-1}$. Note that i is *not* a real number and *does not correspond to any point on the number line.*

All of the normal operations of mathematics—addition, subtraction, multiplication, and division—can be applied to the number i.

Addition:	$i + i = 2i$	$2i + 5i = 7i$
Subtraction:	$i - i = 0$	$2i - 5i = -3i$
Multiplication:	$(i)(i) = i^2 = -1$	$(2i)(5i) = 10i^2 = 10(-1) = -10$
Division:	$\dfrac{i}{i} = 1$	$\dfrac{2i}{5i} = \dfrac{2}{5}$

Key Fact T1

If x is a positive number, then $\sqrt{-x} = \sqrt{-1}\sqrt{x} = i\sqrt{x}$.

➡ **Example 1** _____

$$\sqrt{-16} = \sqrt{16}\sqrt{-1} = 4i \text{ and}$$
$$\sqrt{-12} = \sqrt{-1}\sqrt{12} = \sqrt{-1}\sqrt{4}\sqrt{3} = i \cdot 2 \cdot \sqrt{3} = 2i\sqrt{3}$$

CAUTION

$(\sqrt{-4})(\sqrt{-4}) =$
$(2i)(2i) = 4i^2 = -4$

$(\sqrt{-4})(\sqrt{-4})$ is
not equal to
$\sqrt{(-4)(-4)} = \sqrt{16} = 4$

➡️ **Example 2** _____

What is $5\sqrt{-25}-3\sqrt{-64}$?

Solution.

$$5\sqrt{-25}=5\sqrt{-1}\sqrt{25}=(5i)(5)=25i \text{ and}$$
$$3\sqrt{-64}=3\sqrt{-1}\sqrt{64}=(3i)(8)=24i$$
$$\text{Therefore, } 5\sqrt{-25}-3\sqrt{-64}=25i-24i=i$$

On the SAT, you could be asked to raise i to some positive integer power. In particular, note:

$i^1 = i$ ($a^1 = a$ for *any* number)

$i^2 = -1$ (by definition)

$i^3 = -i$ $i \cdot i \cdot i = (i \cdot i)(i) = i^2 \cdot i = -1(i) = -i$

$i^4 = 1$ $i^4 = i \cdot i \cdot i \cdot i = (i \cdot i)(i \cdot i) = (-1)(-1) = 1$

$i^5 = i$ $i^5 = i^4 \cdot i = 1 \cdot i = i$

$i^6 = -1$ $i^6 = i^5 \cdot i = i \cdot i = i^2 = -1$

$i^7 = -i$ $i^7 = i^6 \cdot i = (-1)i = -i$

$i^8 = 1$ $i^8 = i^7 \cdot i = (-i)(i) = -i^2 = -(-1) = 1$

Note that the powers of i form a repeating sequence in which the four terms, i, -1, $-i$, 1 repeat in that order indefinitely.

As you will see in **KEY FACT T2**, this means that to find the value of i^n for any positive integer n, you should divide n by 4 and calculate the remainder.

Key Fact T2

For any positive integer n:

- If n is a multiple of 4, $i^n = 1$.
- If n is not a multiple of 4, $i^n = i^r$, where r is the remainder when n is divided by 4.

➡️ **Example 3** _____

To evaluate i^{375}, use your calculator to divide 375 by 4:

$$375 \div 4 = 93.75 \Rightarrow \text{the quotient is } 93$$

Then multiply 93 by 4:

$$93 \times 4 = 372 \Rightarrow \text{the remainder is } 375 - 372 = 3$$

So $i^{375} = i^3 = -i$.

NOTE: The concepts of *positive* and *negative* apply only to real numbers. If a is positive, a is to the right of 0 on the number line. Since imaginary numbers do not lie on the number line, you cannot compare them. It is meaningless even to ask whether i is positive or negative or whether $12i$ is greater than or less than $7i$.

Complex Numbers

The imaginary unit can be added to and multiplied by real numbers to form **complex numbers**. Every complex number can be written in the form $a + bi$, where a and b are real numbers. a is called the **real part** and bi the **imaginary part** of the complex number $a + bi$. Two complex numbers are equal if, and only if, their real parts are equal and their imaginary parts are equal.

Key Fact T3

If $a + bi = c + di$, then $a = c$ and $b = d$.

➡ **Example 4** _____

If $2(3 + yi) = x + 8i$, what are the values of x and y?

Solution.

$$x + 8i = 2(3 + yi) \Rightarrow x + 8i = 6 + 2yi$$

So, $x = 6$ and $8 = 2y \Rightarrow x = 6$ and $y = 4$

The **conjugate** of the complex number $a + bi$ is the complex number $a - bi$.

The arithmetic of complex numbers follows all the rules you are familiar with for real numbers. **KEY FACT T4**, below, gives you these rules and demonstrates each one using the complex numbers $3 + 5i$ and $2 + 3i$.

Key Fact T4

- **To add complex numbers, add their real parts and add their imaginary parts. For example:**

$$(3 + 5i) + (2 + 3i) = 5 + 8i$$

- **To subtract complex numbers, subtract their real parts and subtract their imaginary parts. For example:**

$$(3 + 5i) - (2 + 3i) = 1 + 2i$$

- **To multiply complex numbers, "FOIL" them as if they were binomials and then replace i^2 by -1. For example:**

$$(3 + 5i)(2 + 3i) = 6 + 9i + 10i + 15i^2$$
$$= 6 + 19i + 15(-1)$$
$$= 6 + 19i - 15$$
$$= -9 + 19i$$

- The product of the complex number $(a + bi)$ and its conjugate $(a - bi)$ is the real number $a^2 + b^2$:

$$(a + bi)(a - bi) = a^2 - (bi)^2 = a^2 - b^2(-1) = a^2 + b^2$$

For example: $(2 + 3i)(2 - 3i) = 2^2 + 3^2 = 4 + 9 = 13$

- To divide two complex numbers, write the quotient as a fraction, and multiply the numerator and the denominator by the conjugate of the denominator. For example:

$$(3 + 5i) \div (2 + 3i) = \frac{3 + 5i}{2 + 3i} = \frac{3 + 5i}{2 + 3i} \cdot \frac{2 - 3i}{2 - 3i} = \frac{6 - 9i + 10i - 15i^2}{4 + 9} = \frac{21 + i}{13} = \frac{21}{13} + \frac{1}{13}i$$

PRACTICE EXERCISES

MULTIPLE-CHOICE QUESTIONS

1. If a and b are real numbers and if $ai^2 = bi^4$, which of the following must be true?

 I. $a = b$
 II. $a = -b$
 III. $|a| = |b|$

 (A) I only
 (B) II only
 (C) III only
 (D) II and III only

2. Which of the following is a negative real number?

 (A) i^{25}
 (B) i^{50}
 (C) i^{75}
 (D) i^{100}

3. Which of the following is equal to $(2 + 3i)(3 + 2i)$?

 (A) 12
 (B) $13i$
 (C) $12 + 13i$
 (D) $12 - 13i$

4. If a and b are real numbers, which of the following is equal to $(a + bi)^2 - (a - bi)^2$?

 (A) 0
 (B) $a^2 - b^2$
 (C) $4abi$
 (D) $-4abi$

5. If $(a + bi)(c + di)$ is a real number, which of the following statements must be true?

 (A) $ac = bd$
 (B) $ac = -bd$
 (C) $ad = bc$
 (D) $ad = -bc$

Answer Key

1. **D** 2. **B** 3. **D** 4. **C** 5. **D**

PART SIX
Test Yourself

Two Practice Tests

Two Practice Tests

A two-hour and forty-five–minute test can be exhausting. Here are some tips that will help you cope on the day of the test:

- Build up your stamina. You have to get used to answering tough questions for more than two hours straight. Take these two practice tests under timed conditions. Try to stay focused the entire time. This practice will pay off when you take the actual test.
- Be well rested on the day of the test. Last-minute cramming will only tire you out. Try to organize your study plan so that you can quit prepping a few days before you take the test. Above all, get a good night's sleep the night before the test.
- Bring a timepiece, preferably the same one you have been using while you have been taking your practice exams. Remember, no beeps or rings! You are not allowed to use a watch or timer with an audible alarm.
- Wear layers. You don't want to be too hot or too cold.
- As you take the test, use the short breaks to stretch and get out the kinks. Breathe in deeply, and let go of the tension as you breathe out. You've done a good job preparing, so think positive, and relax.

Additional tests are available online at
http://barronsbooks.com/tp/psat19/

ANSWER SHEET
Practice Test 1

Section 1: Reading

1. Ⓐ Ⓑ Ⓒ Ⓓ	14. Ⓐ Ⓑ Ⓒ Ⓓ	27. Ⓐ Ⓑ Ⓒ Ⓓ	40. Ⓐ Ⓑ Ⓒ Ⓓ
2. Ⓐ Ⓑ Ⓒ Ⓓ	15. Ⓐ Ⓑ Ⓒ Ⓓ	28. Ⓐ Ⓑ Ⓒ Ⓓ	41. Ⓐ Ⓑ Ⓒ Ⓓ
3. Ⓐ Ⓑ Ⓒ Ⓓ	16. Ⓐ Ⓑ Ⓒ Ⓓ	29. Ⓐ Ⓑ Ⓒ Ⓓ	42. Ⓐ Ⓑ Ⓒ Ⓓ
4. Ⓐ Ⓑ Ⓒ Ⓓ	17. Ⓐ Ⓑ Ⓒ Ⓓ	30. Ⓐ Ⓑ Ⓒ Ⓓ	43. Ⓐ Ⓑ Ⓒ Ⓓ
5. Ⓐ Ⓑ Ⓒ Ⓓ	18. Ⓐ Ⓑ Ⓒ Ⓓ	31. Ⓐ Ⓑ Ⓒ Ⓓ	44. Ⓐ Ⓑ Ⓒ Ⓓ
6. Ⓐ Ⓑ Ⓒ Ⓓ	19. Ⓐ Ⓑ Ⓒ Ⓓ	32. Ⓐ Ⓑ Ⓒ Ⓓ	45. Ⓐ Ⓑ Ⓒ Ⓓ
7. Ⓐ Ⓑ Ⓒ Ⓓ	20. Ⓐ Ⓑ Ⓒ Ⓓ	33. Ⓐ Ⓑ Ⓒ Ⓓ	46. Ⓐ Ⓑ Ⓒ Ⓓ
8. Ⓐ Ⓑ Ⓒ Ⓓ	21. Ⓐ Ⓑ Ⓒ Ⓓ	34. Ⓐ Ⓑ Ⓒ Ⓓ	47. Ⓐ Ⓑ Ⓒ Ⓓ
9. Ⓐ Ⓑ Ⓒ Ⓓ	22. Ⓐ Ⓑ Ⓒ Ⓓ	35. Ⓐ Ⓑ Ⓒ Ⓓ	
10. Ⓐ Ⓑ Ⓒ Ⓓ	23. Ⓐ Ⓑ Ⓒ Ⓓ	36. Ⓐ Ⓑ Ⓒ Ⓓ	
11. Ⓐ Ⓑ Ⓒ Ⓓ	24. Ⓐ Ⓑ Ⓒ Ⓓ	37. Ⓐ Ⓑ Ⓒ Ⓓ	
12. Ⓐ Ⓑ Ⓒ Ⓓ	25. Ⓐ Ⓑ Ⓒ Ⓓ	38. Ⓐ Ⓑ Ⓒ Ⓓ	
13. Ⓐ Ⓑ Ⓒ Ⓓ	26. Ⓐ Ⓑ Ⓒ Ⓓ	39. Ⓐ Ⓑ Ⓒ Ⓓ	

Section 2: Writing and Language

1. Ⓐ Ⓑ Ⓒ Ⓓ	12. Ⓐ Ⓑ Ⓒ Ⓓ	23. Ⓐ Ⓑ Ⓒ Ⓓ	34. Ⓐ Ⓑ Ⓒ Ⓓ
2. Ⓐ Ⓑ Ⓒ Ⓓ	13. Ⓐ Ⓑ Ⓒ Ⓓ	24. Ⓐ Ⓑ Ⓒ Ⓓ	35. Ⓐ Ⓑ Ⓒ Ⓓ
3. Ⓐ Ⓑ Ⓒ Ⓓ	14. Ⓐ Ⓑ Ⓒ Ⓓ	25. Ⓐ Ⓑ Ⓒ Ⓓ	36. Ⓐ Ⓑ Ⓒ Ⓓ
4. Ⓐ Ⓑ Ⓒ Ⓓ	15. Ⓐ Ⓑ Ⓒ Ⓓ	26. Ⓐ Ⓑ Ⓒ Ⓓ	37. Ⓐ Ⓑ Ⓒ Ⓓ
5. Ⓐ Ⓑ Ⓒ Ⓓ	16. Ⓐ Ⓑ Ⓒ Ⓓ	27. Ⓐ Ⓑ Ⓒ Ⓓ	38. Ⓐ Ⓑ Ⓒ Ⓓ
6. Ⓐ Ⓑ Ⓒ Ⓓ	17. Ⓐ Ⓑ Ⓒ Ⓓ	28. Ⓐ Ⓑ Ⓒ Ⓓ	39. Ⓐ Ⓑ Ⓒ Ⓓ
7. Ⓐ Ⓑ Ⓒ Ⓓ	18. Ⓐ Ⓑ Ⓒ Ⓓ	29. Ⓐ Ⓑ Ⓒ Ⓓ	40. Ⓐ Ⓑ Ⓒ Ⓓ
8. Ⓐ Ⓑ Ⓒ Ⓓ	19. Ⓐ Ⓑ Ⓒ Ⓓ	30. Ⓐ Ⓑ Ⓒ Ⓓ	41. Ⓐ Ⓑ Ⓒ Ⓓ
9. Ⓐ Ⓑ Ⓒ Ⓓ	20. Ⓐ Ⓑ Ⓒ Ⓓ	31. Ⓐ Ⓑ Ⓒ Ⓓ	42. Ⓐ Ⓑ Ⓒ Ⓓ
10. Ⓐ Ⓑ Ⓒ Ⓓ	21. Ⓐ Ⓑ Ⓒ Ⓓ	32. Ⓐ Ⓑ Ⓒ Ⓓ	43. Ⓐ Ⓑ Ⓒ Ⓓ
11. Ⓐ Ⓑ Ⓒ Ⓓ	22. Ⓐ Ⓑ Ⓒ Ⓓ	33. Ⓐ Ⓑ Ⓒ Ⓓ	44. Ⓐ Ⓑ Ⓒ Ⓓ

ANSWER SHEET
Practice Test 1

Section 3: Math (No Calculator)

1. Ⓐ Ⓑ Ⓒ Ⓓ
2. Ⓐ Ⓑ Ⓒ Ⓓ
3. Ⓐ Ⓑ Ⓒ Ⓓ
4. Ⓐ Ⓑ Ⓒ Ⓓ

5. Ⓐ Ⓑ Ⓒ Ⓓ
6. Ⓐ Ⓑ Ⓒ Ⓓ
7. Ⓐ Ⓑ Ⓒ Ⓓ
8. Ⓐ Ⓑ Ⓒ Ⓓ

9. Ⓐ Ⓑ Ⓒ Ⓓ
10. Ⓐ Ⓑ Ⓒ Ⓓ
11. Ⓐ Ⓑ Ⓒ Ⓓ
12. Ⓐ Ⓑ Ⓒ Ⓓ

13. Ⓐ Ⓑ Ⓒ Ⓓ

14.

15.

16.

17.

ANSWER SHEET
Practice Test 1

Section 4: Math (Calculator)

1. Ⓐ Ⓑ Ⓒ Ⓓ
2. Ⓐ Ⓑ Ⓒ Ⓓ
3. Ⓐ Ⓑ Ⓒ Ⓓ
4. Ⓐ Ⓑ Ⓒ Ⓓ
5. Ⓐ Ⓑ Ⓒ Ⓓ
6. Ⓐ Ⓑ Ⓒ Ⓓ
7. Ⓐ Ⓑ Ⓒ Ⓓ
8. Ⓐ Ⓑ Ⓒ Ⓓ

9. Ⓐ Ⓑ Ⓒ Ⓓ
10. Ⓐ Ⓑ Ⓒ Ⓓ
11. Ⓐ Ⓑ Ⓒ Ⓓ
12. Ⓐ Ⓑ Ⓒ Ⓓ
13. Ⓐ Ⓑ Ⓒ Ⓓ
14. Ⓐ Ⓑ Ⓒ Ⓓ
15. Ⓐ Ⓑ Ⓒ Ⓓ
16. Ⓐ Ⓑ Ⓒ Ⓓ

17. Ⓐ Ⓑ Ⓒ Ⓓ
18. Ⓐ Ⓑ Ⓒ Ⓓ
19. Ⓐ Ⓑ Ⓒ Ⓓ
20. Ⓐ Ⓑ Ⓒ Ⓓ
21. Ⓐ Ⓑ Ⓒ Ⓓ
22. Ⓐ Ⓑ Ⓒ Ⓓ
23. Ⓐ Ⓑ Ⓒ Ⓓ
24. Ⓐ Ⓑ Ⓒ Ⓓ

25. Ⓐ Ⓑ Ⓒ Ⓓ
26. Ⓐ Ⓑ Ⓒ Ⓓ
27. Ⓐ Ⓑ Ⓒ Ⓓ

28.

29.

30.

31.

READING TEST

60 MINUTES, 47 QUESTIONS

Turn to Section 1 of your answer sheet to answer the questions in this section.

Directions: Following each of the passages (or pairs of passages) below are questions about the passage (or passages). Read each passage carefully. Then, select the best answer for each question based on what is stated in the passage (or passages) and in any graphics that may accompany the passage.

Questions 1–9 are based on the following passage.

This excerpt from the novel Hard Times *by Charles Dickens focuses on Thomas Gradgrind, headmaster of a so-called model school.*

Thomas Gradgrind, sir. A man of realities. A man of facts and calculations. A man who proceeds upon the principle that two and
Line two are four, and nothing over, and who is
(5) not to be talked into allowing for anything over. Thomas Gradgrind, sir—peremptorily Thomas—Thomas Gradgrind. With a rule and a pair of scales, and the multiplication table always in his pocket, sir, ready to weigh
(10) and measure any parcel of human nature, and tell you exactly what it comes to. It is a mere question of figures, a case of simple arithmetic. You might hope to get some other nonsensical belief into the head of
(15) George Gradgrind, or Augustus Gradgrind, or John Gradgrind, or Joseph Gradgrind (all suppositions, non-existent persons), but into the head of Thomas Gradgrind—no, sir!

Mr. Gradgrind walked homeward from the
(20) school in a state of considerable satisfaction. It was his school, and he intended it to be a model. He intended every child in it to be a model—just as the young Gradgrinds were all models.
(25) There were five young Gradgrinds, and they were models every one. They had

been lectured at from their tenderest years: coursed, like little hares. Almost as soon as they could run alone, they had been made
(30) to run to the lecture-room. The first object with which they had an association, or of which they had a remembrance, was a large blackboard with a dry Ogre chalking ghastly white figures on it.

(35) Not that they knew, by name or nature, anything about an Ogre. Fact forbid! I only use the word to express a monster in a lecturing castle, with Heaven knows how many heads manipulated into one, taking
(40) childhood captive, and dragging it into gloomy statistical dens by the hair.

No little Gradgrind had ever seen a face in the moon: it was up in the moon before it could speak distinctly. No little Gradgrind
(45) had ever learnt the silly jingle, Twinkle, twinkle, little star; how I wonder what you are! No little Gradgrind had ever known wonder on the subject of the stars, each little Gradgrind having at five years old dissected
(50) the Great Bear like a Professor Owen, and driven Charles's Wain like a locomotive engine-driver. No little Gradgrind had ever associated a cow in a field with that famous cow with the crumpled horn who tossed
(55) the dog who worried the cat who killed the rat who ate the malt, or with that yet more famous cow who swallowed Tom Thumb: it had never heard of those celebrities, and

GO ON TO THE NEXT PAGE

had only been introduced to a cow as a
(60) graminivorous ruminating quadruped with
several stomachs.

Their father walked on in a hopeful
and satisfied frame of mind. He was an
affectionate father, after his manner; but
(65) he would probably have described himself
as 'an eminently practical' father. He had
a particular pride in the phrase eminently
practical, which was considered to have
a special application to him. Whatsoever
(70) the public meeting held in Coketown, and
whatsoever the subject of such meeting,
some Coketowner was sure to seize the
occasion of alluding to his eminently
practical friend Gradgrind. This always
(75) pleased the eminently practical friend.
He knew it to be his due, but his due was
acceptable.

1. The primary purpose of the passage is to

(A) introduce the reader to a positive role
model.
(B) present a broadly satirical portrait of a
character.
(C) demonstrate the academic advantages of
a model school.
(D) persuade the reader to adopt a particular
pedagogical method.

2. The phrase "peremptorily Thomas" (lines 6–7)
emphasizes Gradgrind's

(A) absolute insistence upon facts.
(B) dislike of the name Augustus.
(C) need to remind himself of the simplest
details.
(D) desire to be on a first-name basis with
others.

3. As used in line 20, "state" most nearly means

(A) territory.
(B) ceremony.
(C) government.
(D) condition.

4. Gradgrind's mood as he marches homeward
can best be characterized as one of

(A) uncertainty.
(B) complacency.
(C) relief.
(D) hopefulness.

5. Which choice provides the best evidence for
the answer to the previous question?

(A) Lines 7–11 ("With a rule . . . comes to")
(B) Lines 13–18 ("You might hope . . . no,
sir!")
(C) Lines 19–22 ("Mr. Gradgrind . . . model")
(D) Lines 22–24 ("He intended . . . models")

6. The passage suggests that Gradgrind rejects
from his curriculum anything that is in the
least

(A) analytical.
(B) mechanical.
(C) fanciful.
(D) didactic.

7. Which choice provides the best evidence for
the answer to the previous question?

(A) Lines 2–6 ("A man who . . . over")
(B) Lines 21–24 ("It was his . . . models")
(C) Lines 26–30 ("They had been . . .
lecture-room")
(D) Lines 44–47 ("No little . . . what you are")

GO ON TO THE NEXT PAGE

8. The passage is narrated from the point of view of

    (A) an observer who does not know Gradgrind at first but who comes to know about him in the course of the passage.

    (B) an observer whose understanding of Gradgrind is necessarily incomplete.

    (C) an observer who knows all about Gradgrind's thoughts and feelings.

    (D) a newly employed instructor at Gradgrind's model school.

9. As used in line 69, "application" most nearly means

    (A) formal request.

    (B) implementation.

    (C) relevance.

    (D) hard work.

Questions 10–19 are based on the following passage.

African elephants now are an endangered species. The following passage, taken from a newspaper article written in 1989, discusses the potential ecological disaster that might occur if the elephant were to become extinct.

The African elephant—mythic symbol of a continent, keystone of its ecology and the largest land animal remaining on earth—has
Line become the object of one of the biggest,
(5) broadest international efforts yet mounted to turn a threatened species off the road to extinction. But it is not only the elephant's survival that is at stake, conservationists say. Unlike the endangered tiger, unlike even the
(10) great whales, the African elephant is in great measure the architect of its environment. As a voracious eater of vegetation, it largely shapes the forest-and-savanna surroundings in which it lives, thereby setting the terms
(15) of existence for millions of other storied animals—from zebras to gazelles to giraffes and wildebeests—that share its habitat. And as the elephant disappears, scientists and conservationists say, many other species
(20) will also disappear from vast stretches of forest and savanna, drastically altering and impoverishing whole ecosystems.

Just as the American buffalo was hunted almost to extinction a century ago, so the
(25) African elephant is now the victim of an onslaught of commercial killing, stimulated in this case by soaring global demand for ivory. Most of the killing is illegal, and conservationists say that although
(30) the pressure of human population and development contributes to the elephants' decline, poaching is by far the greatest threat. The elephant may or may not be on the way

GO ON TO THE NEXT PAGE

to becoming a mere zoological curiosity like
(35) the buffalo, but the trend is clear.

In an atmosphere of mounting alarm among conservationists, a new international coordinating group backed by 21 ivory-producing and ivory-consuming countries
(40) has met and adopted an ambitious plan of action. Against admittedly long odds, the multinational rescue effort is aimed both at stopping the slaughter of the elephants in the short term and at nurturing them as a vital
(45) "keystone species" in the long run.

It is the elephant's metabolism and appetite that make it a disturber of the environment and therefore an important creator of habitat. In a constant search for
(50) the 300 pounds of vegetation it must have every day, it kills small trees and underbrush and pulls branches off big trees as high as its trunk will reach. This creates innumerable open spaces in both deep tropical forests
(55) and in the woodlands that cover part of the African savannas. The resulting patchwork, a mosaic of vegetation in various stages of regeneration, in turn creates a greater variety of forage that attracts a greater variety of
(60) other vegetation-eaters than would otherwise be the case.

In studies over the last 20 years in southern Kenya near Mount Kilimanjaro, Dr. David Western has found that when
(65) elephants are allowed to roam the savannas naturally and normally, they spread out at "intermediate densities." Their foraging creates a mixture of savanna woodlands (what the Africans call bush) and grassland.
(70) The result is a highly diverse array of other plant-eating species: those like the zebra, wildebeest and gazelle, that graze; those like the giraffe, bushbuck and lesser kudu, that browse on tender shoots, buds, twigs and

(75) leaves: and plant-eating primates like the baboon and vervet monkey. These herbivores attract carnivores like the lion and cheetah.

When the elephant population thins out. Dr. Western said, the woodlands become
(80) denser and the grazers are squeezed out. When pressure from poachers forces elephants to crowd more densely onto reservations, the woodlands there are knocked out and the browsers and primates
(85) disappear.

Something similar appears to happen in dense tropical rain forests. In their natural state, because the overhead forest canopy shuts out sunlight and prevents growth on
(90) the forest floor, rain forests provide slim pickings for large, hoofed plant-eaters. By pulling down trees and eating new growth, elephants enlarge natural openings in the canopy, allowing plants to regenerate on the
(95) forest floor and bringing down vegetation from the canopy so that smaller species can get at it.

In such situations, the rain forest becomes hospitable to large plant-eating mammals
(100) such as bongos, bush pigs, duikers, forest hogs, swamp antelopes, forest buffaloes, okapis, sometimes gorillas and always a host of smaller animals that thrive on secondary growth. When elephants disappear and the
(105) forest reverts, the larger animals give way to smaller, nimbler animals like monkeys, squirrels and rodents.

GO ON TO THE NEXT PAGE

10. The passage is primarily concerned with

   (A) clarifying why elephants are facing the threat of extinction.
   (B) explaining how the elephant's impact on its surroundings affects other species.
   (C) distinguishing between savannas and rain forests as habitats for elephants.
   (D) contrasting elephants with members of other endangered species.

11. As used in line 5, "mounted" most nearly means

   (A) ascended.
   (B) increased.
   (C) launched.
   (D) attached.

12. In the opening paragraph, the author mentions tigers and whales in order to emphasize which point about the elephant?

   (A) Like them, the elephant faces the threat of extinction.
   (B) It is herbivorous rather than carnivorous.
   (C) Unlike them, it physically alters its environment.
   (D) It is the largest extant land mammal.

13. A necessary component of the elephant's ability to transform the landscape is its

   (A) massive intelligence.
   (B) ravenous hunger.
   (C) lack of grace.
   (D) ability to regenerate.

14. It can be inferred from the passage that

   (A) the elephant is dependent upon the existence of smaller plant-eating mammals for its survival.
   (B) elephants have an indirect effect on the hunting patterns of certain carnivores.
   (C) the floor of the tropical rain forest is too overgrown to accommodate larger plant-eating species.
   (D) the natural tendency of elephants is to crowd together in packs.

15. Which choice provides the best evidence for the answer to the previous question?

   (A) Lines 9–11 ("Unlike . . . environment")
   (B) Lines 56–61 ("The resulting . . . case")
   (C) Lines 76–77 ("These . . . cheetah")
   (D) Lines 98–104 ("In such situations . . . growth")

16. In line 45, the quotation marks around the phrase "keystone species" serve to

   (A) emphasize the triteness of the timeworn phrase.
   (B) contradict the literal meaning of the term.
   (C) imply the phrase has ironic connotations.
   (D) indicate the phrase is being used in a special or technical sense.

17. As used in line 102, "host" most nearly means

   (A) food source for parasites.
   (B) very large number.
   (C) provider of hospitality.
   (D) military force.

GO ON TO THE NEXT PAGE

18. Which of the following statements best expresses the author's attitude toward the damage to vegetation caused by foraging elephants?

(A) It is a regrettable by-product of the feeding process.
(B) It is a necessary but undesirable aspect of elephant population growth.
(C) It fortuitously leads to the creation of environments suited to diverse species.
(D) It proves that the impact of elephants on the environment is more detrimental than beneficial.

19. Which choice provides the best evidence for the answer to the previous question?

(A) Lines 23–28 ("Just as . . . ivory")
(B) Lines 36–41 ("In an atmosphere . . . action")
(C) Lines 46–49 ("It is . . . habitat")
(D) Lines 70–76 ("The result . . . monkey")

Questions 20–28 are based on the following passage.

In 1873, three years after the passage of the 15th Amendment had granted African American men the right to vote, Susan B. Anthony was fined $100 for casting an illegal ballot in the 1872 presidential election. In response, she set out on a speaking tour in support of female voting rights, during which she gave this speech.

Friends and fellow citizens: I stand before you tonight under indictment for the alleged crime of having voted at the last presidential
Line election, without having a lawful right to
(5) vote. It shall be my work this evening to prove to you that in thus voting, I not only committed no crime, but, instead, simply exercised my citizen's rights, guaranteed to me and all United States citizens by the
(10) National Constitution, beyond the power of any state to deny.
The preamble of the Federal Constitution says:
"We, the people of the United States, in
(15) order to form a more perfect union, establish justice, insure domestic tranquility, provide for the common defense, promote the general welfare, and secure the blessings of liberty to ourselves and our posterity, do
(20) ordain and establish this Constitution for the United States of America."
It was we, the people; not we, the white male citizens; nor yet we, the male citizens; but we, the whole people, who formed the
(25) Union. And we formed it, not to give the blessings of liberty, but to secure them; not to the half of ourselves and the half of our posterity, but to the whole people—women as well as men. And it is a downright mockery
(30) to talk to women of their enjoyment of the

GO ON TO THE NEXT PAGE

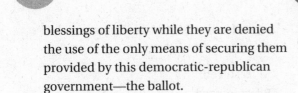

blessings of liberty while they are denied the use of the only means of securing them provided by this democratic-republican government—the ballot.

(35)   For any state to make sex a qualification that must ever result in the disfranchisement of one entire half of the people, is to pass a bill of attainder[1], or, an ex post facto law, and is therefore a violation of the supreme
(40) law of the land. By it the blessings of liberty are forever withheld from women and their female posterity.

To them this government has no just powers derived from the consent of the
(45) governed. To them this government is not a democracy. It is not a republic. It is an odious aristocracy; a hateful oligarchy of sex; the most hateful aristocracy ever established on the face of the globe; an oligarchy of wealth,
(50) where the rich govern the poor. An oligarchy of learning, where the educated govern the ignorant, or even an oligarchy of race, where the Saxon rules the African, might be endured; but this oligarchy of sex, which
(55) makes father, brothers, husband, sons, the oligarchs over the mother and sisters, the wife and daughters, of every household— which ordains all men sovereigns, all women subjects, carries dissension, discord, and
(60) rebellion into every home of the nation.

Webster, Worcester, and Bouvier all define a citizen to be a person in the United States, entitled to vote and hold office.

The only question left to be settled now is:
(65) Are women persons? And I hardly believe any of our opponents will have the hardihood to say they are not. Being persons, then, women are citizens; and no state has a right to make any law, or to enforce any old law, that
(70) shall abridge their privileges or immunities. Hence, every discrimination against women

in the constitutions and laws of the several states is today null and void, precisely as is every one against Negroes.

_____

[1]An item of legislation (prohibited by the U.S. Constitution) that inflicts the forfeiture of civil rights without judicial process.

20. The primary purpose of the passage is to

(A) propose an approach to gaining a political goal.
(B) contrast venerated moral principles with political reality.
(C) challenge the power of the federal government.
(D) establish the lawfulness of an action.

21. Anthony indicates that talking to women about their enjoyment of the blessings of liberty is

(A) intimidating to those who must secure these blessings.
(B) essential for them to understand the importance of voting.
(C) both ironic and upsetting given their lack of the franchise.
(D) pointless in the light of their inability to value such blessings.

22. Anthony makes which point about the right of states to deny women the right to vote?

(A) It is comparable to the right of states to deny the poor the vote.
(B) It is based upon the preamble to the Federal Constitution.
(C) It is in conflict with constitutional law.
(D) It fails to reflect contemporary social ideals.

GO ON TO THE NEXT PAGE

23. Which choice provides the best evidence for the answer to the previous question?

    (A) Lines 12–21 ("The preamble . . . America")
    (B) Lines 35–40 ("For any . . . land")
    (C) Lines 46–50 ("It is an odious ... poor")
    (D) Lines 64–67 ("The only . . . not")

24. Anthony contends that the situation she describes in the passage is so divisive that

    (A) only the passage of a bill of attainder can correct it.
    (B) the governed will refuse to grant powers to the government.
    (C) it almost equals the wickedness of the Saxons' enslavement of Negroes.
    (D) it pits members of the same family against one another.

25. Which choice provides the best evidence for the answer to the previous question?

    (A) Lines 22–29 ("It was we . . . as men")
    (B) Lines 35–40 ("For any state . . . the land")
    (C) Lines 43–50 ("To them . . . the poor")
    (D) Lines 50–60 ("An oligarchy . . . the nation")

26. As used in line 59, "carries" most nearly means

    (A) holds.
    (B) brings.
    (C) stocks.
    (D) is approved.

27. As used in line 64, "settled" most nearly means

    (A) resolved.
    (B) colonized.
    (C) quieted.
    (D) paid.

28. In the context of the final paragraph, the word "precisely" serves primarily to

    (A) demonstrate Anthony's desire to make the logic of her argument clear to her audience.
    (B) emphasize that a strong precedent for granting the right to vote to a disfranchised group now exists.
    (C) encourage women to imitate the strategies used by African American men in gaining the right to vote.
    (D) question the accuracy of the 15th Amendment that gave African American men the vote.

GO ON TO THE NEXT PAGE

Questions 29–37 are based on the following passage and supplementary material.

This passage is taken from Thomas Sumner, "Changing Climate." ©2016 by Society for Science & the Public.

In August 2005, Hurricane Katrina slammed into the Gulf Coast. Floodwaters covered roughly 80 percent of New Orleans,
Line 1,836 people died, hundreds of thousands
(5) became homeless and the most active Atlantic hurricane season on record was far from over. As the last storm fizzled, damages had reached $160 billion, meteorologists had run through the alphabet of preselected
(10) storm names and many people, including former Vice-President Al Gore, were indicting global warming as a probable culprit.

"Hurricanes were the poster child of global warming," says Christopher Landsea,
(15) a meteorologist at the National Oceanic and Atmospheric Administration's National Hurricane Center in Miami. "In reality, it's a lot more subtle than that."

Tropical cyclones, such as Atlantic
(20) hurricanes, are stirred up where seawater is warmer than the overlying air. Because climate change raises ocean temperatures, it made sense that such storms could strike more often and with more ferocity. A closer
(25) look at hurricanes past and future suggests, however, that the relationship between warming and hurricanes is less clear-cut.

Several studies in the mid-2000s examining the history of Atlantic hurricanes
(30) pointed to an overall rise in the number of 20th century storms in step with warming sea surface temperatures. Scrutinizing those numbers, Landsea uncovered a problem: Hurricane-spotting satellites date back only
(35) to 1961's Hurricane Esther. Before then, storm watchers probably missed many weaker, shorter-lived storms. Taking this into account, Landsea and colleagues reported in 2010 that the number of annual storms has
(40) actually decreased somewhat over the last century.

That decrease could be explained by climate factors other than rising sea surface

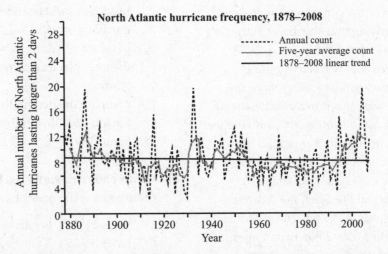

North Atlantic hurricane frequency, 1878–2008

------- Annual count
     Five-year average count
     1878–2008 linear trend

Annual number of North Atlantic hurricanes lasting longer than 2 days

Year

Steady storms The record-smashing 2005 hurricane season raised concerns that storms were becoming stronger and more frequent. Yet, a closer look at the long-term trends revealed that Atlantic hurricane frequency has not significantly changed since 1878.

Source: C. Landsea/NHC/NOAA

GO ON TO THE NEXT PAGE

temperatures. Changes in atmospheric
(45) heating can increase the variation in wind
speed at different elevations, known as
wind shear. The shearing winds rip apart
burgeoning storms and decrease the number
of fully formed hurricanes, researchers
(50) reported in 2007 in *Geophysical Research
Letters.*

The overall frequency of storms, however,
is less important than the number of
Katrina-scale events, says Gabriel Vecchi,
(55) an oceanographer at NOAA's Geophysical
Fluid Dynamics Laboratory in Princeton, N.J.
Category 4 and 5 storms, the most violent,
make up only 6 percent of U.S. hurricane
landfalls, but they cause nearly half of all
(60) damage. Vecchi and colleagues used the
latest understanding of how hurricanes form
and intensify to forecast how the storms will
behave under future climate conditions.

The work, published in 2010 in *Science,*
(65) predicted that the frequency of Category 4
and 5 storms could nearly double by 2100
due to ocean warming, even if the overall
number of hurricanes doesn't rise. At
present, however, climate change's influence
(70) on hurricanes is probably too small to detect,
Vecchi says, adding that Katrina's wrath can't
be blamed on global warming.

Future hurricanes will cause more
damage, Landsea predicts, whether or not
(75) there's any change in storm intensity. Rising
sea levels mean floodwaters will climb higher
and reach farther inland. Hurricane Sandy,
which stormed over New Jersey and New
York in October 2012, had weakened by
(80) the time it reached the coast. But it drove a
catastrophic storm surge into the coastline
that caused about $50 billion in damages.
If sea levels were higher, Sandy's surge
would have reached even farther inland and
(85) damage could have been much worse.

Many vulnerable areas such as St.
Petersburg, Fla., are woefully underprepared

for threats posed by storms at current sea
levels, Landsea warns. Higher sea levels
(90) won't help. "We don't need to invoke climate
change decades down the line—we've got a
big problem now," he says.

www.sciencenews.org I April 16, 2016 23

29. The passage is written from the perspective of
someone who is

(A) actively engaged as a hurricane spotter.
(B) a participant in an ongoing study of
atmospheric phenomena.
(C) well-informed about the ongoing debate
on climate change.
(D) a victim of 2005's devastating hurricane
in the Gulf Coast.

30. It is reasonable to conclude that the primary
purpose of the passage is to

(A) provide perspective on the possible
effects of global warming on storm
intensity.
(B) refute the argument that future
hurricanes will be more destructive than
current storms.
(C) determine actions to be taken to harness
the energy released by more intense
storms.
(D) compare the destructiveness of Hurricane
Katrina (2005) with that of Hurricane
Sandy (2012).

31. Which choice provides the best evidence for
the answer to the previous question?

(A) Lines 21–24 ("Because . . . ferocity")
(B) Lines 24–27 ("A closer . . . clear-cut")
(C) Lines 32–35 ("Scrutinizing . . . Esther")
(D) Lines 44–47 ("Changes . . . shear")

GO ON TO THE NEXT PAGE

32. What is the Vecchi study's main point about the incidence of Category 4 and 5 storms?

(A) The overall frequency of Category 4 and 5 hurricanes will diminish over time.
(B) As global warming increases, more tropical storms will fall under these categories.
(C) If the overall number of hurricanes fails to rise, the number of Category 4 and 5 storms will correspondingly decrease.
(D) The most violent storms become less destructive once they have reached landfall.

33. Which choice provides the best evidence for the answer to the previous question?

(A) Lines 57–60 ("Category . . . damage")
(B) Lines 60–63 ("Vecchi . . . conditions")
(C) Lines 64–68 ("The work . . . rise")
(D) Lines 68–72 ("At present . . . warming")

34. As used in line 61, "form" most nearly means

(A) produce.
(B) arrange.
(C) take shape.
(D) serve as.

35. As used in line 88, "posed" most nearly means

(A) pretended.
(B) presented.
(C) suggested.
(D) mystified.

36. What information discussed in paragraph 4 (lines 28–41) is represented by the graph?

(A) The information in lines 28–32 ("Several . . . temperatures")
(B) The information in lines 32–33 ("Scrutinizing . . . problem")
(C) The information in lines 34–35 ("Hurricane-spotting . . . Esther")
(D) The information in lines 37–41 ("Taking . . . century")

37. Which statement about North Atlantic hurricanes in the period from 1878 to 2008 is best supported by the graph?

(A) The annual number of North Atlantic hurricanes (1878 to 2008) ranged from two per year to twenty per year.
(B) No North Atlantic hurricanes (1878–2008) lasted longer than two days.
(C) The five-year average count of hurricanes seldom exceeded twelve per year.
(D) The number of South Atlantic hurricanes was greater than the number of North Atlantic hurricanes.

GO ON TO THE NEXT PAGE

Questions 38–47 are based on the following passages.

The following passages are excerpts from Web posts about the decline of print journalism in America today.

Passage 1

The term "seismic shift" is overused, but it applies to what's happened to American newspapers. In 2007, there were
Line 55,000 full-time journalists at nearly 1,400
(5) daily papers; in 2015, there were 32,900, according to a census by the American Society of News Editors and the School of Journalism and Mass Communication at Florida International University. That
(10) doesn't include the buyouts and layoffs last fall, like those at the *Los Angeles Times*, the *Philadelphia Inquirer* and the *New York Daily News*, among others, and weeklies and magazines like *National Geographic.*
(15) For most of the past century, journalists could rely on career stability. Newspapers were an intermediary between advertisers and the public; it was as if their presses printed money. The benefit of this near-
(20) monopoly was that newsrooms were heavily stocked with reporters and editors, most of them passionate about creating journalism that made a difference in their communities. It often meant union protection, lifetime
(25) employment and pensions. Papers like the *Sacramento Bee* bragged to new hires in the 1980s that even during the Great Depression, the paper had never laid off journalists.

All of that is now yesterday's birdcage
(30) lining. The sprawling lattice of local newsrooms is shrinking—105 newspapers closed in 2009 alone—whittled away by the rise of the Internet and decline of display ads, with the migration of classified advertising to
(35) Craigslist hitting particularly hard. Between 2000 and 2007, a thousand newspapers lost $5 billion to the free site, according to a 2013 study by Robert Seamans of New York University's Stern School of Business and
(40) Feng Zhu of the Harvard Business School. Falling circulation numbers have also taken their toll.

And things may get a lot worse, according to former *Los Angeles Times* executive Nicco
(45) Mele. "If the next three years look like the last three years, I think we're going to look at the 50 largest metropolitan papers in the country and expect somewhere between a third to a half of them to go out of business," said Mele,
(50) now a professor at USC's Annenberg School of Journalism.

But the shift is also deeper and more systemic. Like the story of Willy Loman, cast aside in his creeping middle age, the tale of
(55) today's discarded journalists is, at its core, a parable of the way our economy sucks people dry and throws them away as their cultural and economic currency wanes. Many older workers, not just journalists, are hurting.
(60) Amid the so-called recovery, some 45 percent of those seeking jobs over the age of 55 have been looking six months or longer, according to the Bureau of Labor Statistics.

But there's one major difference between
(65) other workers and journalists—when the latter are laid off, the commonweal suffers. "You know who loves this new day of the lack of journalism? Politicians. Businessmen. Nobody's watching them anymore," says
(70) Russ Kendall, a lifelong photojournalist and editor who is now self-employed as a pizza maker.

There are still print newspapers—and news websites—producing heroic local

GO ON TO THE NEXT PAGE

Newspaper	Average Print Circulation (March 2013)	Individual Paid Print Circulation (September 2015)
Wall Street Journal	1,481,000	1,064,000
New York Times	731,000	528,000
Washington Post	431,000	330,000
Los Angeles Times	433,000	328,000
USA Today	1,424,000	299,000
Chicago Tribune	368,000	266,000
New York Post	300,000	245,000
New York Daily News	360,000	228,000
Newsday	266,000	217,000
Minneapolis Star-Tribune	228,000	184,000
Houston Chronicle	231,000	169,000
Arizona Republic	286,000	164,000
Denver Post	214,000	156,000 (3/15)
Cleveland Plain Dealer	216,000	153,000 (2 days)
Tampa Bay Times	241,000	141,000
Dallas Morning News	191,000	140,000
Boston Globe	172,000	140,000
Philadelphia Inquirer	185,000	138,000
Chicago Sun-Times	185,000	118,000
San Diego Union-Tribune	193,000	117,000
Newark Star-Ledger	180,000	114,000
Orange County Register	159,000	110,000
Honolulu Star-Advertiser	126,000	94,000
Atlanta Journal-Constitution	150,000	92,000
Las Vegas Review-Journal	126,000	90,000

(75) journalism. But it's clear that the loss of a combined several hundred thousand years of experience from newsrooms across the country is hurting American democracy.

Passage 2

Last October, a McKinsey report declared,
(80) "We believe that many of the people likely to abandon print newspapers and print consumer magazines have already done so . . . We believe most of this core audience— households that have retained their print

(85) subscriptions despite having access to broadband—will continue to do so for now, effectively putting a floor on the print markets."

Wow. Just because of inertia? Is the only
(90) medium-term threat to print the fact that most of its current audience will gradually die over the next 30 years? That would be great news, especially because nearly all newspapers still get most of their revenue
(95) from print advertising. But it doesn't feel

GO ON TO THE NEXT PAGE

right in a world in which even mature adults' media consumption habits seem to be quickly evolving.

(100) The simple chart above lays out the numbers for "total average print circulation" of the nation's 25 largest newspapers as of March 2013, which is the last time print newspaper circulation figures were widely reported. These are the basis for the figures (105) you get if you Google search the issue or look for a list on Wikipedia. Then the chart compares these with the number of copies most recently reported to the Alliance for Audited Media (in September 2015) for (110) "individually paid print circulation," that is, the number of copies being bought by subscription or at newsstands. This is the best indication of consumer demand for the product. In both cases, the figures are (115) for weekday average circulation. Sunday numbers are generally higher.

38. The author most likely uses the examples in lines 1–14 of Passage 1 ("The term . . . *Geographic*") to highlight the

   (A) anxiety encountered by newcomers to the profession.
   (B) extensive news coverage provided by the institutions cited.
   (C) need to find competent replacements for missing personnel.
   (D) severity of problems facing a once-stable industry.

39. As used in line 31, "shrinking" most nearly means

   (A) becoming withdrawn.
   (B) contracting.
   (C) quailing.
   (D) growing shorter.

40. Which choice does the author of Passage 1 explicitly cite as an advantage of the position of newspapers in the twentieth century?

   (A) Speed of communications
   (B) Economic security
   (C) Convenience
   (D) Buyouts

41. Which choice provides the best evidence for the answer to the previous question?

   (A) Lines 16–19 ("Newspapers . . . money")
   (B) Lines 30–35 (" The sprawling . . . hard")
   (C) Lines 43–51 ("And things . . . Journalism")
   (D) Lines 58–63 ("Many older . . . Statistics")

42. What function does the sixth paragraph of Passage 1 (lines 64–72, "But there's . . . maker") serve in the passage as a whole?

   (A) It presents an overview of an aspect of the problem that has not been addressed by the experts previously quoted in the passage.
   (B) It acknowledges the extreme impact that the advent of the Internet has had on the finances of the newspaper industry.
   (C) It advocates for revitalizing an industry that has undergone a severe but reversible decline in recent years.
   (D) It proposes the adoption of alternative career paths by journalists laid off in the course of the seismic shift experienced by American newspapers.

43. As used in line 69, "watching" most nearly means

   (A) staying awake.
   (B) awaiting expectantly.
   (C) protecting.
   (D) monitoring.

GO ON TO THE NEXT PAGE

44. According to the author of Passage 2, the decline of print journalism in America today

   (A) has recently reached a plateau.
   (B) will not be complete until its audience dies off in 30 years.
   (C) is coming about even more rapidly than expected.
   (D) is a byproduct of inertia.

45. Which choice provides the best evidence for the answer to the previous question?

   (A) Lines 79–82 ("Last October . . . done so")
   (B) Lines 89–92 ("Is the only . . . years?")
   (C) Lines 106–114 ("Then the chart . . . product")
   (D) Lines 114–116 ("In both cases . . . higher")

46. According to the chart, which of the following major newspapers experienced the most extreme decline in circulation between the years 2013 and 2015?

   (A) *New York Times*
   (B) *Wall Street Journal*
   (C) *USA Today*
   (D) *Las Vegas Review-Journal*

47. Which best describes the overall relationship between Passage 1 and Passage 2?

   (A) Passage 1 focuses on a contemporary view of an industry undergoing transition, whereas Passage 2 attempts to provide historical perspective on that industry's troubles.
   (B) Passage 1 discusses both the economic and sociopolitical impact of a change, whereas Passage 2 concentrates on its financial aspects.
   (C) Passage 1 presents a hypothesis regarding the importance of advertising revenue to the economy, whereas Passage 2 proposes an alternative to that hypothesis.
   (D) Passage 1 questions the feasibility of the survival of an institution, whereas Passage 2 acknowledges its ongoing influence.

STOP

If there is still time remaining, you may review your answers.

WRITING AND LANGUAGE TEST

35 MINUTES, 44 QUESTIONS

Turn to Section 2 of your answer sheet to answer the questions in this section.

Directions: Questions follow each of the passages below. Some questions ask you how the passage might be changed to improve the expression of ideas. Other questions ask you how the passage might be altered to correct errors in grammar, usage, and punctuation. One or more graphics accompany some passages. You will be required to consider these graphics as you answer questions about editing the passage.

There are three types of questions. In the first type, a part of the passage is underlined. The second type is based on a certain part of the passage. The third type is based on the entire passage.

Read each passage. Then, choose the answer to each question that changes the passage so that it is consistent with the conventions of standard written English. One of the answer choices for many questions is "NO CHANGE." Choosing this answer means that you believe the best answer is to make no change in the passage.

Questions 1–11 are based on the following passage and supplementary material.

The Unexpected Shake

I had just turned nine when I experienced my first (and only) earthquake. We had left home the day after my birthday party for San Diego, California, where my Uncle Jesse lived. ❶ My twin cousins Jake and Jillian, were taller than I, but a year younger, and rarely stopped talking. They had lived in warm, sunny California for almost two years now—two years without ❷ snow, sledding, ice skating, or hot cocoa.

1. (A) NO CHANGE
   (B) My twin cousins, Jake and Jillian were taller
   (C) My twin cousins Jake and Jillian were taller
   (D) My twin cousins, Jake and Jillian, were taller

2. Which of the following would most vividly express that the climate in California was quite a bit different from that in the narrator's part of the country?

   (A) NO CHANGE
   (B) massive earthquakes that could topple skyscrapers.
   (C) the cold temperatures to which I was accustomed.
   (D) much contact from their family, other than via the Internet.

GO ON TO THE NEXT PAGE

❸ A great shaking of the ground then came about. It provided an interruption on the third day of our vacation to our shopping trip that day. Earthquakes happen when tectonic plates scrape, drag against, or crash into one another, but I didn't know that then. The shelves in Powell's Bookstore jolted slightly, and I held onto my mother's pant leg, glancing up into her alarmed face. From beginning to end, the earthquake lasted only around seven seconds, ❹ and seven seconds seems a lot longer when nobody speaks, moves, or laughs.

Mr. Wilbert, the store manager, reassured everyone that we were safe when the shaking stopped—his slightly apprehensive speech marked the first time I'd heard the word "earthquake." Before we left the bookstore, I begged my mother for three books on earthquakes; she acquiesced. I found out that Earth is ❺ composed of layers: the inner and outer cores, mantle, and crust. The crust is the most interesting of all the layers because it is like a floating puzzle made of tectonic plates. Sometimes, these plates get stuck or shift onto one another and release energy, creating seismic waves. The largest wave, called the mainshock, ❻ was often preceded by foreshocks and followed by aftershocks, which contribute to the unpredictability of earthquakes and, perhaps, explain Mr. Wilbert's nervous demeanor.

The earthquake that day had a magnitude ❼ on a 4.0, which means that almost everybody felt the ground shaking, but little damage occurred. Jake and Jillian said

3. Which of the following gives the best combination of the two sentences?

 (A) An interruption by the shaking of the ground to our trip of shopping occurred on the third day.
 (B) On the third day of vacation, a great shaking of the ground interrupted our shopping trip.
 (C) That day, an interruption was experienced by us when the shaking of the ground occurred during the third day of our shopping trip.
 (D) A great shaking, interruption of our vacation, occurred on the third day of our trip while we were shopping.

4. (A) NO CHANGE
 (B) with
 (C) but
 (D) since

5. (A) NO CHANGE
 (B) composed of layers; the inner and outer cores,
 (C) composed of layers, the inner and outer cores
 (D) composed of layers. The inner and outer cores,

6. (A) NO CHANGE
 (B) is
 (C) have
 (D) had

7. (A) NO CHANGE
 (B) in
 (C) with
 (D) of

GO ON TO THE NEXT PAGE

Notable Earthquakes

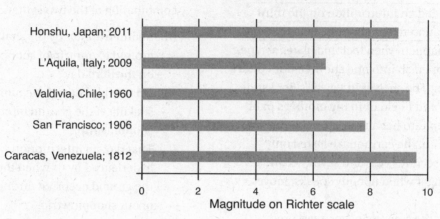

they'd felt one other earthquake before, also of slight to moderate magnitude. I informed them, ❽ however, that they'd most likely experienced many more but hadn't noticed them. According to *National Geographic*, earthquakes aren't felt until a magnitude of 3.0 or 4.0 and aren't very dangerous until they reach a 6.0 or 7.0; the most dangerous recorded earthquakes in history were approximately ❾ 6.5 in magnitude. The Richter Scale is logarithmic, meaning that an earthquake with a magnitude of 7.0 is 10 times as strong as an earthquake with a magnitude of 6.0; an earthquake with a magnitude of 8.0 is 100 times as strong as an earthquake with a magnitude of 6.0. So, the highly destructive Honshu earthquake in 2011 was about ❿ 1,000 times as powerful as the earthquake I experienced.

Although I'm not a fan of California's disregard of winter, I have often ⑪ wishing for a return and feel the dizzying shake of the earth beneath my feet.

8. (A) NO CHANGE
    (B) and
    (C) thus,
    (D) to alleviate the ignorance I encountered,

9. Which of the following is consistent with the information in the accompanying chart?

    (A) NO CHANGE
    (B) 7.0
    (C) 8.5
    (D) 9.5

10. Which of the following is consistent with the information in the accompanying chart and the anecdote in the passage?

    (A) NO CHANGE
    (B) 10,000
    (C) 100,000
    (D) 1,000,000

11. (A) NO CHANGE
    (B) wished to return
    (C) wished for return
    (D) wishing to returning

GO ON TO THE NEXT PAGE

Questions 12–22 are based on the following passage.

More Than His Other Half

Zelda Sayre Fitzgerald enjoyed iconic status in both life and death. **12** Yet she remains most widely known as the wife, of F. Scott Fitzgerald, a narrow label she endeavored her entire adult life to escape. Recognized as a symbol of the excess of the 1920s, Zelda exemplifies the beautifully emancipated, careless flapper who would try anything once. **13** Zelda lived in the time of the early twentieth century. Independent, artistic, passionate, and destructively reckless, Zelda seems to walk off the page of one of her **14** husband's short stories. It is erroneous, **15** consequently, to conceive of Zelda as arising from Scott's wild imagination rather than to understand her as the very inspiration to his remarkable imaginings—a mistake to perceive her as symbol but not creator.

Zelda was indeed more than just an alluring wife. As a writer, dancer, and painter, **16** in far more than physical beauty did Zelda excel. She was born to a prominent Southern family in Montgomery, Alabama, in 1900, the youngest of five children. Her affluent father and indulgent mother boasted of the Confederacy and of their daughters' talents and beauty. Zelda, the spoiled baby, grew up untended and overly pampered. When she met F. Scott Fitzgerald in 1918, she was already the most coveted young woman in all of Alabama. They married in 1920, beginning one of the most famously impassioned and foolishly wasteful **17** marriage in literary history.

12. (A) NO CHANGE
    (B) Yet, she remains most widely known as the wife of F. Scott Fitzgerald a narrow
    (C) Yet, she remains most widely known as the wife of F. Scott Fitzgerald, a narrow
    (D) Yet she remains most widely known as the wife of F. Scott Fitzgerald a narrow

13. The writer is considering removing the underlined sentence from the passage. Should it be removed?
    (A) Yes, because it shifts the focus to a different time period.
    (B) Yes, because it repeats information from the earlier part of the paragraph.
    (C) No, because it clarifies information stated earlier in the paragraph.
    (D) No, because it is critical to understanding the argument later in the essay.

14. (A) NO CHANGE
    (B) husbands
    (C) husband
    (D) husbands'

15. (A) NO CHANGE
    (B) in addition
    (C) because of this
    (D) though

16. (A) NO CHANGE
    (B) Zelda, with her physical beauty, was excelled by nobody at all.
    (C) Zelda excelled in far more than physical beauty.
    (D) the physical beauty of Zelda was excelled by no one else.

17. (A) NO CHANGE
    (B) marriages in
    (C) marriage for
    (D) marriages on

GO ON TO THE NEXT PAGE

18 The two people had a daughter in the year of 1921. However, the child was not successful in stopping their recklessness. Considered the emblematic couple of the Jazz Age, Zelda and Scott kept constant company with fashionably wealthy socialites. They knew everyone, partied everywhere. Zelda, though, became restless with her overlooked role as the silly, gorgeous wife of a rising author. She wrote; she painted; she danced. As with all things in her life, Zelda devoted herself to her work excessively, destroying her health and mental state as she flocked from one obsession to the next. When she became **19** obstinately consumed by ballet, she fell into psychological breakdowns and was committed to several mental hospitals.

Despite her ailing health, Zelda accomplished more than her **20** "doomed and beautiful," as Fitzgerald scholar Matthew J. Bruccoli calls it,

18. Which of the following provides the most logical and effective combination of the underlined sentences?

(A) The two, in the year 1921, had a daughter; the child, on the other hand, was not able to do anything to stop their reckless behavior.

(B) The two had a daughter in 1921, but the child failed to quell their recklessness.

(C) They had a daughter, unfortunately, the child did not help them stop being reckless.

(D) While the having of the daughter by the two was important, this act alone did not stand in the way of their continued recklessness.

19. (A) NO CHANGE
(B) stubbornly and inflexibly obsessed with
(C) passionately gripped and fixated on
(D) open to the possibility of the consideration of

20. The author is considering deleting the quotation marks around the underlined phrase. Should this deletion be made?

(A) Yes, because it is not a quotation from Zelda.

(B) Yes, because it is inconsistent with the style of the essay as a whole.

(C) No, because it denotes a scholar's opinion.

(D) No, because it allows the author to share his personal views.

GO ON TO THE NEXT PAGE

reputation divulges. She wrote a novel, *Save Me the Waltz*; a play, *Scandalabra*; and several successful short stories. **㉑** Additionally, her literary career, furthermore, pales in comparison to her talent as a painter—her work embellished the walls of several New York City galleries. As a dancer, Zelda was offered a solo in an Italian ballet that would **㉒** have begun a rewarding professional career, but she declined the offer when she suffered a nervous breakdown. Zelda's tragic flaw, it seems, was only that her artistic talents were too extensive to manage sensibly.

21. (A) NO CHANGE
    (B) Also
    (C) However
    (D) DELETE the underlined portion and start the sentence with "Her"

22. (A) NO CHANGE
    (B) had begun
    (C) began
    (D) begun

GO ON TO THE NEXT PAGE

Questions 23–33 are based on the following passage.

The Devil at Work

The year 1692 is a year of American history that can be described in three words: bigotry, paranoia, and hysteria. **㉓** More than two hundred people were accused of witchcraft in Salem Village—now Danvers, Massachusetts. Nineteen were hanged. One man was pressed to death with heavy stones. Several others died hungry, cold, and alone in jail. **㉔** In contrast, the Salem witch trials have captured the attention of historians, politicians, social activists, novelists, playwrights, and film producers, signifying **㉕** the depths of cruelty, that stem from intolerance and mistrust.

Many historical renderings of the events hold responsible the village's population of displaced refugees and the subsequent strain on resources. Certainly, the severe Reverend Samuel Parris and his constant greed **㉖** are entirely to blame for this tragedy. The preceding European witch craze accompanied by a puritanical obsession with Satan and a general distrust of difference encouraged the stream of accusations and scapegoating that characterized the yearlong prosecutions. Regardless of which factors contributed more significantly, when Elizabeth **㉗** and Abigail, the young daughter and niece of Reverend Parris, began having fits of temper in 1692, the village was desperate to point a finger. Under pressure to place blame, the two girls chose three easy targets: Tituba, their family's Caribbean slave; Sarah Good, a homeless beggar;

23. Which of the following would provide the most specific language at this point in the sentence?

(A) NO CHANGE
(B) Many people of the town
(C) Quite a few men and women
(D) Several persons

24. (A) NO CHANGE
(B) On top of this,
(C) Since then,
(D) From those,

25. (A) NO CHANGE
(B) the depths, of cruelty, that stem from intolerance and mistrust.
(C) the depths of cruelty, that stem from intolerance, and mistrust.
(D) the depths of cruelty that stem from intolerance and mistrust.

26. Which of the following would best express that the author believes that Parris is somewhat to blame for these events?

(A) NO CHANGE
(B) are rightly assigned some responsibility.
(C) had no role to play in the horrific events.
(D) were noted by historians as unexpected.

27. (A) NO CHANGE
(B) and Abigail the young daughter and niece of Reverend Parris began
(C) and Abigail, the young daughter, and niece of Reverend Parris, began
(D) and Abigail, the young daughter and niece of Reverend Parris began

GO ON TO THE NEXT PAGE

and Sarah Osbourne, a generally disliked elderly woman. The three women were jailed, marking the beginning of a period of rampant accusations of witchcraft among the **28** towns inhabitants.

Puritans believed—were consumed by the idea—that the Devil recruited people and gave them evil powers **29** to cause harm and hardship upon those who professed the religion of Christianity. A constant preoccupation with the Devil's intrusion into their daily lives manifested in dangerous and unpredictable suspicions. On June 10, Bridget Bishop was hanged on the aptly named Gallows Hill. Eighteen others—mostly women— met the same fate. A four-year-old girl trembled alone in jail as one of the accused. And several of the town's other children, eager to be part of the scandal, began screaming, throwing themselves on the ground, distorting their bodies, and **30** listing off names of the "witches" who had cursed them.

In May 1693, Governor Phip pardoned those of the accused who remained alive, but it wasn't until 1702 that the trials were declared unlawful. The descendants of the victims **31** are granted restitution in 1711. The tragedy of the Salem witch trials has inspired numerous historical and sociological texts, novels by authors from Nathaniel Hawthorne to Ann Petry, and Arthur

28. (A) NO CHANGE
    (B) towns'
    (C) town's
    (D) town is

29. (A) NO CHANGE
    (B) to inflict harm onto Christians
    (C) to do bad things
    (D) DELETE the underlined portion.

30. (A) NO CHANGE
    (B) to make a list of the names
    (C) a list of the names
    (D) give a name list

31. (A) NO CHANGE
    (B) is
    (C) was
    (D) were

GO ON TO THE NEXT PAGE

Miller's lauded play *The Crucible*. Although these works take a unique approach to the seventeenth-century prosecutions, they all seem to culminate in a similar moral lesson: a ㉜ terrifying and horrifying lesson against suspicion of difference and the perilous tendency to assign blame to others. ㉝

32. (A) NO CHANGE
      (B) dire warning
      (C) momentous happening
      (D) fact of inspiration

Question 33 is about the passage as a whole.

33.

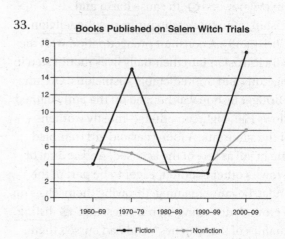

Books Published on Salem Witch Trials

An independent publishing company reports the above publications for books published that focus on or are motivated by the 1692 witch trials.

The author is considering adding the above chart to accompany the passage. Should it be added?

(A) Yes, because it gives the first mention of the historical impact of the witch trials on the modern publishing industry.

(B) Yes, because it provides concrete statistics to support an assertion in the final paragraph.

(C) No, because it does not focus on the late seventeenth century, focusing instead on modern events.

(D) No, because it diverges from the primary argument laid out in the introductory paragraph.

GO ON TO THE NEXT PAGE

Questions 34–44 are based on the following passage.

How to Interview

There is a common misconception that a college degree from ③④ you're dream school will land you that illustrious job that you've always wanted. Similarly, others are under the impression that a sparkling GPA is the golden key that will unlock any door you come up against. Certainly, each of these is an important criterion in the hiring process, and you would be wise to go to a great school and do as well as possible there. ③⑤ But, what if I told you ③⑥ that—more than academic credentials—interviewing skills might actually be the single biggest determinant of job application success or failure? Fret not, however; in this essay, I will cover how to excel in your next interview, and I will include a few deal-breaking mistakes to avoid in the name ③⑦ with thoroughly.

First, research the company at which you are interviewing, and the specific position for which you are interviewing. This demonstrates both ③⑧ hard-working diligence and a real and genuine interest, signaling to the interviewer that you would be thrilled to land the job. ③⑨ Moreover, it shows self-awareness: it is important to know how you will fit in at the company and what role you will fulfill.

34. (A) NO CHANGE
   (B) you are
   (C) your
   (D) there

35. The author is considering inserting the following sentence at this point in the paragraph:

"Attendance at a prestigious school will be a most advisable course of action."

Should the author make this addition?

   (A) Yes, because it elaborates on the thesis of the essay.
   (B) Yes, because it provides details related to the preceding sentence.
   (C) No, because it repeats an assertion already made in the paragraph.
   (D) No, because it diverges from the focus of the paragraph.

36. (A) NO CHANGE
   (B) that, more than academic credentials— interviewing
   (C) that, more than academic, credentials interviewing
   (D) that more than academic credentials interviewing

37. (A) NO CHANGE
   (B) in through.
   (C) of thoroughness.
   (D) for being thorough.

38. (A) NO CHANGE
   (B) diligence and genuine interest,
   (C) a positive attitude,
   (D) DELETE the underlined portion.

39. (A) NO CHANGE
   (B) Surprisingly,
   (C) However,
   (D) Because of this,

GO ON TO THE NEXT PAGE

Second, if you are interviewing at a larger company, there will be information readily available on the Internet on various job websites from applicants ㊵ who has interviewed at the company before. Listed on the site will often be questions that were asked, and it would be wise to study these as they are often repeated!

(1) Third, prepare a handful of questions that *you* would like to ask your interviewer. (2) Plus, an interview should not ㊶ be a stressful experience. (3) Keep in mind that an interview is also an opportunity to assess whether the position would be a good fit for you, and not just the other way around! ㊷

Now, as for *do-not's,* remember that standard social conventions still apply. Under no circumstances should you show up late! It is rude outside of the corporate world, and it is rude inside it, as well. Also, under no circumstances should you interrupt or talk over your ㊸ interviewer; be involved, but never domineering, in the conversation. And, of course, leave the chewing gum at home. It can wait!

Now, armed with these tips, you should be ready to ace that next interview. ㊹ With the economy undergoing precipitous decline, have the prescience to seize auspicious opportunities.

40. (A) NO CHANGE
    (B) that has
    (C) whom have
    (D) who have

41. Which of the following, if inserted for the underlined portion, would best express that an interview should be an interactive process?

    (A) NO CHANGE
    (B) have to be a one-way conversation.
    (C) be the only means to career success.
    (D) monopolize most of your day.

42. The author wishes to insert this sentence into the preceding paragraph.

    "Again, this shows initiative and interest."

    Where is the best placement?

    (A) Before sentence 1
    (B) After sentence 1
    (C) After sentence 2
    (D) After sentence 3

43. (A) NO CHANGE
    (B) interviewer, be involved but
    (C) interviewer, be involved, but
    (D) interviewer be: involved but

44. Which sentence best concludes the essay by being focused on the essay's topic and consistent with its tone?

    (A) NO CHANGE
    (B) Whatever you do, make things happen.
    (C) Try to schedule your interview within one business day of the initial communication from the potential employer.
    (D) Keep calm, trust yourself, and go win the job you've always dreamed about!

STOP

If there is still time remaining, you may review your answers.

MATH TEST (NO CALCULATOR)

25 MINUTES, 17 QUESTIONS

Turn to Section 3 of your answer sheet to answer the questions in this section.

Directions: For questions 1–13, solve each problem and choose the best answer from the given choices. Fill in the corresponding circle on your answer sheet. For questions 14–17, solve each problem and enter your answer in the grid on your answer sheet.

Notes:
- Calculators are **NOT PERMITTED** in this section.
- All variables and expressions represent real numbers unless indicated otherwise.
- All figures are drawn to scale unless indicated otherwise.
- All figures are in a plane unless indicated otherwise.
- Unless indicated otherwise, the domain of a given function is the set of all real numbers x for which the function has real values.

REFERENCE INFORMATION

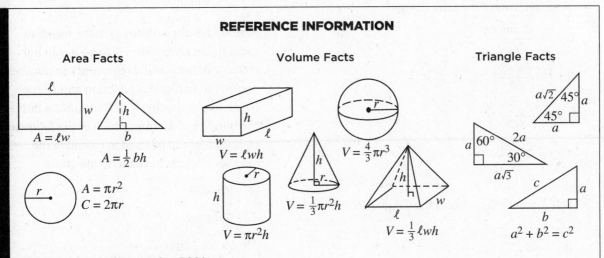

The arc of a circle contains 360°.

The arc of a circle contains 2π radians.

The sum of the measures of the angles in a triangle is 180°.

GO ON TO THE NEXT PAGE

1. Which of the following statements is true concerning the equation below?

$$8(x-4) = 8x - 4$$

(A) The equation has no solutions.
(B) The equation has one positive solution.
(C) The equation has one negative solution.
(D) The equation has infinitely many solutions.

$$C = 85 + (t-1)60$$

2. The equation above expresses the relationship between C, the total charge, in dollars, for a house call by a plumber and t, the time in hours that the plumber is in a customer's home. Which of the following expresses the time in terms of the total charge?

(A) $t = \dfrac{C-85}{60}$

(B) $t = \dfrac{C+85}{60}$

(C) $t = \dfrac{C-25}{60}$

(C) $t = \dfrac{C+25}{60}$

3. If $17 - 2\sqrt[3]{x} = 21$, what is the value of x?

(A) −8
(B) −2
(C) 8
(D) There is no value of x that satisfies the equation.

4. For all real numbers x, $h(5-x) = x^2 + x + 1$. What is the value of $h(9)$?

(A) 11
(B) 13
(C) 21
(D) 91

5. What is the value of a if a is positive and $(a)(a)(a) = a + a + a$?

(A) $\dfrac{1}{3}$

(B) $\sqrt{3}$

(C) 3

(D) $3\sqrt{3}$

6. In the xy-plane, line l intersects the parabola whose equation is $y = 2x^2 + 6x + 1$ at the point $(1, 9)$. Which of the following could be the equation of line l?

(A) $y = 4x^3 + 5$
(B) $y = 5x^2 + 4$
(C) $y = 4x + 5$
(D) $-y = 4 - 5x$

7. Barbara has three times as many baseball cards in her collection as Diane has in her collection. Let b and d represent the number of cards in Barbara's collection and Diane's collection, respectively. If Barbara has 864 cards in her collection, which of the following equations could be used to calculate the number of cards in Diane's collection?

(A) $3d = 864$

(B) $\dfrac{1}{3}d = 864$

(C) $b + 3d = 864$

(D) $864d = b$

GO ON TO THE NEXT PAGE

$$a = \frac{bc^2}{4de}$$

8. The equation above expresses the variable a in terms of the variables b, c, d, and e. Which of the following expresses c in terms of a, b, d, and e?

   (A) $c = 2\sqrt{\dfrac{ade}{b}}$

   (B) $c = 4\sqrt{\dfrac{ade}{b}}$

   (C) $c = \dfrac{1}{2}\sqrt{\dfrac{ab}{de}}$

   (D) $c = 2\sqrt{\dfrac{ab}{de}}$

9. Central County's Chamber of Commerce sponsors a Young Executive's Club that is open only to men and women between the ages of 21 and 29, inclusive, who own their own businesses. Which of the following inequalities can be used to determine if a business owner who is y years old is eligible to be a member of the Young Executive's Club?

   (A) $|y - 21| \le 8$
   (B) $|y - 21| \le 29$
   (C) $|y - 29| \le 21$
   (D) $|y - 25| \le 4$

10. What is the circumference of the circle whose center is the point (3, 5) and that passes through (–3, 5)?

    (A) 3π
    (B) 6π
    (C) 9π
    (D) 12π

$$\frac{4x^2}{2x-1} = \frac{8x-3}{2x-1} + A$$

11. Which of the following expressions is equal to A in the equation above?

    (A) $2x - 3$
    (B) $2x + 3$
    (C) $\dfrac{2x-3}{2x-1}$
    (D) $\dfrac{2x+3}{2x-1}$

12. Because her test turned out to be more difficult than she intended it to be, a teacher decided to adjust the grades by deducting only half the number of points a student missed. For example, if a student missed 20 points, she received a 90 instead of an 80. Before the grades were adjusted, Mary's grade was G. What was her grade after the adjustment?

    (A) $50 + \dfrac{G}{2}$

    (B) $\dfrac{1}{2}(100 - G)$

    (C) $100 - \dfrac{G}{2}$

    (D) $\dfrac{100 - G}{2}$

$$2x + 3y = 7$$
$$x - 3y = 17$$

13. If (x, y) is the solution of the system of equations shown above, what is the value of x?

    (A) –3
    (B) 0
    (C) 8
    (D) 10

GO ON TO THE NEXT PAGE

Grid-in Response Directions

In questions 14–17, first solve the problem, and then enter your answer on the grid provided on the answer sheet. The instructions for entering your answers follow.

- First, write your answer in the boxes at the top of the grid.
- Second, grid your answer in the columns below the boxes.
- Use the fraction bar in the first row or the decimal point in the second row to enter fractions and decimals.

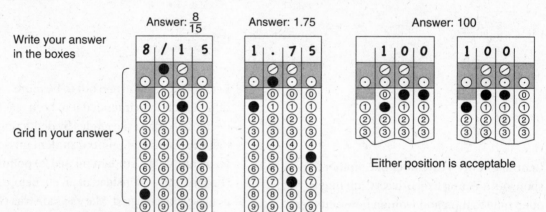

- Grid only one space in each column.
- Entering the answer in the boxes is recommended as an aid in gridding but is not required.
- The machine scoring your exam can read only what you grid, so you **must grid-in your answers correctly to get credit**.
- If a question has more than one correct answer, grid-in only one of them.
- The grid does not have a minus sign; so no answer can be negative.
- A mixed number *must* be converted to an improper fraction or a decimal before it is gridded.

  Enter $1\frac{1}{4}$ as 5/4 or 1.25; the machine will interpret 11/4 as $\frac{11}{4}$ and mark it wrong.

- **All decimals must be entered as accurately as possible.** Here are three acceptable ways of gridding

$$\frac{3}{11} = 0.272727\ldots$$

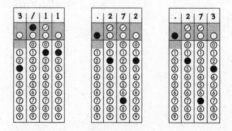

- Note that rounding to .273 is acceptable because you are using the full grid, but you would receive **no credit** for .3 or .27, because they are less accurate.

GO ON TO THE NEXT PAGE

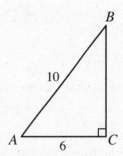

14. If 25 percent of x equals 35 percent of x, what is 45 percent of x?

15. For what value of x is $\dfrac{2}{x} + \dfrac{3}{4} = \dfrac{4}{5}$?

16. Since 2000, the population, P, of Star City has been declining steadily at a rate of 7 percent per year. Demographers studying this trend use the formula $P_{2000+t} = P_{2000}r^t$, where t is the number of years since 2000 and where P_{2000} and P_{2000+t} are the populations of Star City in the year 2000 and the year $2000+t$, respectively. What is the value of r in the formula?

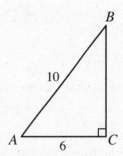

17. In the figure above, what is the value of the sine of angle A?

If there is still time remaining, you may review your answers.

MATH TEST (CALCULATOR)

45 MINUTES, 31 QUESTIONS

Turn to Section 4 of your answer sheet to answer the questions in this section.

Directions: For questions 1–27, solve each problem and choose the best answer from the given choices. Fill in the corresponding circle on your answer sheet. For questions 28–31, solve each problem and enter your answer in the grid on your answer sheet.

Notes:

- Calculators **ARE PERMITTED** in this section.
- All variables and expressions represent real numbers unless indicated otherwise.
- All figures are drawn to scale unless indicated otherwise.
- All figures are in a plane unless indicated otherwise.
- Unless indicated otherwise, the domain of a given function is the set of all real numbers x for which the function has real values.

REFERENCE INFORMATION

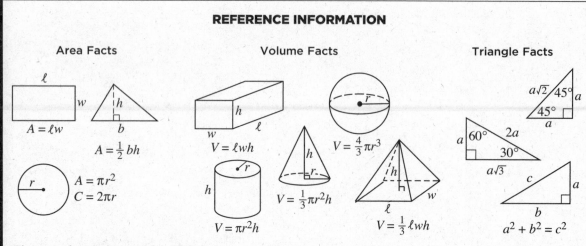

Area Facts

$A = \ell w$

$A = \frac{1}{2} bh$

$A = \pi r^2$
$C = 2\pi r$

Volume Facts

$V = \ell wh$

$V = \pi r^2 h$

$V = \frac{4}{3} \pi r^3$

$V = \frac{1}{3} \pi r^2 h$

$V = \frac{1}{3} \ell wh$

Triangle Facts

$a^2 + b^2 = c^2$

The arc of a circle contains 360°.

The arc of a circle contains 2π radians.

The sum of the measures of the angles in a triangle is 180°.

GO ON TO THE NEXT PAGE

1. If a basket of fruit contains 5 pounds of apples, 3 pounds of oranges, and 1 pound of pears, by weight, what fraction of the fruit is oranges?

   (A) $\frac{1}{9}$

   (B) $\frac{1}{5}$

   (C) $\frac{1}{3}$

   (D) $\frac{3}{8}$

Results of the Sale of Two Stocks Ed Purchased in 2014 and Sold in 2015

	Cost	Selling Price	Outcome
Stock 1	x	$4,000	20% Profit
Stock 2	y	$4,000	20% Loss

2. As indicated in the chart above, in 2014 Ed purchased two stocks that he sold in 2015. On the first stock, he made a 20 percent profit. On the second stock, he had a 20 percent loss. Which of the following statements is true about his net profit or loss on the sale of both stocks?

   (A) He had a loss of less than $300.
   (B) He had a loss of more than $300.
   (C) He had a profit of less than $300.
   (D) He had a profit of more than $300.

3. Eli deposited D dollars in a non-interest-bearing bank account and then made weekly deposits of d dollars. After four weeks, Eli had $60 in his account. After eight weeks, he had $85. What is the smallest number of weekly deposits that Eli has to make for the total dollar amount of his account to be at least $500?

   (A) 72
   (B) 73
   (C) 74
   (D) 75

4. On a recent exam in Ms. Bouvier's French honors course, the mean grade of the b boys in the class was 91, and the mean grade of the g girls in the class was 95. If $b \neq g$, which of the following must be true about the mean grade, m, of all the students in the class?

   (A) $m = 93$
   (B) $m \neq 93$
   (C) $m < 93$
   (D) $m > 93$

5. Twenty workers were sharing equally the cost of a present for their supervisor. When 4 of the workers decided not to contribute, each of the others had to pay $1.50 more. How much, in dollars, did the present cost?

   (A) 80
   (B) 100
   (C) 120
   (D) 150

GO ON TO THE NEXT PAGE

6. In 2014, Sandy's Sandwich shop sold 20 percent more sandwiches than in 2013. In 2014 the price of each sandwich the shop sold was 10 percent more than in 2013. The total income from the sale of sandwiches was what percent greater in 2014 than in 2013?

(A) 20 percent
(B) 22 percent
(C) 30 percent
(D) 32 percent

	Studied Abroad	Did Not Study Abroad
Males	70	160
Females	130	140

7. The table above shows how many of the male and female students who graduated from Harts College in 2015 had studied abroad for at least one semester of their college career. If one of the graduating seniors who studied abroad was chosen at random, what is the probability that the student was male?

(A) $\dfrac{14}{100}$

(B) $\dfrac{35}{100}$

(C) $\dfrac{40}{100}$

(D) $\dfrac{60}{100}$

8. The lines whose equations are $\dfrac{1}{2}x - y = 2$ and $3x - y = 5$ intersect at the point (a, b). What is the value of $a + b$?

(A) $-\dfrac{7}{5}$

(B) $-\dfrac{1}{5}$

(C) $\dfrac{1}{5}$

(D) $\dfrac{6}{5}$

9. The formula for the volume of a sphere of radius r is $V = \dfrac{4}{3}\pi r^3$. Which of the following equations correctly expresses r in terms of V?

(A) $r = \sqrt[3]{\dfrac{3V}{4\pi}}$

(B) $r = \sqrt[3]{\dfrac{4\pi V}{3}}$

(C) $r = \dfrac{4\pi}{3}\sqrt[3]{V}$

(D) $r = \dfrac{3}{4\pi}\sqrt[3]{V}$

GO ON TO THE NEXT PAGE

10. A secretary can type 24 words in 18 seconds. At this rate, how many words can he type in one and a half hours?

(A) 3,600
(B) 4,050
(C) 6,400
(D) 7,200

11. Neil purchased a suit that was on sale for 20 percent off the regular retail price. He was charged 5 percent sales tax and an additional charge of $20 for alterations, which was not subject to tax. If Neil's total expense was $377.00, what was the regular retail price of the suit?

(A) $272.00
(B) $340.00
(C) $400.00
(D) $425.00

12. The estate of a wealthy man was distributed as follows: 10 percent to his wife, 5 percent divided equally among his 3 children, 5 percent divided equally among his 5 grandchildren, and the balance to a charitable trust. If the trust received $1,000,000, how much did each grandchild inherit?

(A) $10,000
(B) $12,500
(C) $20,000
(D) $62,500

Questions 13 and 14 refer to the following information.

The guidance department of the local high school released data concerning how many of the school's 400 seniors were on the school's honor roll and how many played a varsity sport. That information is summarized in the chart below.

	Honor Roll	Not on Honor Roll	Totals
On a varsity team	50	110	160
Not on a varsity team	40	200	240
Totals	90	310	400

13. If a senior is chosen at random from those who are not on a varsity team, which of the following is closest to the probability that the student chosen is on the honor roll?

(A) 0.167
(B) 0.208
(C) 0.458
(D) 0.833

14. What percent of the school's seniors were on the honor roll or on a varsity team?

(A) 37.5 percent
(B) 40 percent
(C) 50 percent
(D) 87.5 percent

GO ON TO THE NEXT PAGE

PRACTICE TEST 1

15. On Daniel's map of Massachusetts, 1 inch represents a distance of 40 miles. One day, Daniel drove from Goshen to Deerfield, which are 0.6 inches apart on his map, at an average speed of 40 miles per hour. How many minutes did his drive take?

(A) 24
(B) 28
(C) 30
(D) 36

16. What is the sum of all the *positive* solutions of the equation $x^6 - 10x^4 + 9x^2 = 0$?

(A) 2
(B) 4
(C) 8
(D) 10

17. Line l is the reflection of line k in the x-axis, and line m is perpendicular to line l. If the slope of line k is $\frac{2}{3}$, what is the slope of line m?

(A) $\frac{2}{3}$

(B) $-\frac{2}{3}$

(C) $\frac{3}{2}$

(D) $-\frac{3}{2}$

18. If $\frac{5}{8}$ of the members of a chess club are boys, what is the ratio of girls to boys in the club?

(A) $\frac{3}{13}$

(B) $\frac{5}{13}$

(C) $\frac{3}{5}$

(D) $\frac{5}{3}$

19. Of the 450 boys who attend Maple Hill School, 360 are eligible for free lunch. The percentage of girls who receive free lunches is exactly the same as the percentage of boys who receive them. If 336 girls get free lunches, how many students attend the school?

(A) 850
(B) 870
(C) 890
(D) 920

$$\frac{30}{x+6} = \frac{5}{x+1} + 2$$

20. There are two values of x that satisfy the equation above. What is their sum?

(A) −2.5
(B) 2.5
(C) 4
(D) 5.5

GO ON TO THE NEXT PAGE

21. An office supply store sells ballpoint pens in 3 packs and in 10 packs. Last week, the store sold exactly 100 packs of pens that had a total of 615 pens in them. If the store sold each 3 pack for $2.88 and each 10 pack for $7.59, how much did the store receive for the sale of all 100 packs?

    (A) $475.45
    (B) $499.95
    (C) $523.50
    (D) $547.05

22. Which of the following expressions is equivalent to $a^8 - b^8$?

    (A) $(a^4 - b^4)^2$
    (B) $(a^2 - b^2)^2(a^2 + b^2)^2$
    (C) $[(a - b)^2(a + b)^2]^2$
    (D) $(a - b)(a + b)(a^2 + b^2)(a^4 + b^4)$

23. The base of pyramid 1 is a rectangle whose length is 3 and whose width is 4. The base of pyramid 2 is a square whose sides are 5. If the volumes of the pyramids are equal, what is the ratio of the height of pyramid 1 to the height of pyramid 2?

    (A) $\dfrac{12}{25}$

    (B) $\dfrac{3}{5}$

    (C) $\dfrac{4}{5}$

    (D) $\dfrac{25}{12}$

24. Mr. Brandler has scheduled eight tests for his Algebra I course this semester, all of which are graded on a scale from 0 to 100. After the first four tests, Brian's average (arithmetic mean) is 82. What is the least Brian can earn on his fifth test and still have the possibility of ending the semester with an average of 85 or more?

    (A) 52
    (B) 62
    (C) 72
    (D) 82

25. A lottery prize worth d dollars was to be divided equally among 4 winners. It was subsequently discovered that there were 2 additional winners, and the prize would now be divided equally among all the winners. How much more money, in dollars, would each original winner have received if the additional winners had not been discovered?

    (A) $\dfrac{d}{12}$

    (B) $\dfrac{d}{6}$

    (C) $\dfrac{12}{d}$

    (D) $\dfrac{6}{d}$

GO ON TO THE NEXT PAGE

Questions 26 and 27 refer to the data in the following chart.

In a survey of 1,855 adults that asked about their travel preferences, the respondents indicated which of five continents they would most like to visit on their next vacation: Europe, Asia, North America, South America, and Africa.

Age	Europe	Asia	Another Continent	Total
Less than 30	130	170	210	510
30–49	100	110	80	290
50–69	105	185	265	555
70 and over	195	180	125	500
Total	530	645	680	1,855

26. According to the table, for which age group did the highest percentage of people prefer a continent other than Europe or Asia?

(A) Less than 30
(B) 30–49
(C) 50–69
(D) 70 and over

27. In a random sampling of 100 of the respondents who preferred a continent other than Europe or Asia, 48 preferred North America, 24 preferred South America, and the rest preferred Africa. Which of the following is likely to be closest to the percentage of all the respondents in the survey who preferred Africa?

(A)   4 percent
(B)   6 percent
(C)   8 percent
(D) 10 percent

GO ON TO THE NEXT PAGE

Grid-in Response Directions

In questions 28–31, first solve the problem, and then enter your answer on the grid provided on the answer sheet. The instructions for entering your answers follow.

- First, write your answer in the boxes at the top of the grid.
- Second, grid your answer in the columns below the boxes.
- Use the fraction bar in the first row or the decimal point in the second row to enter fractions and decimals.

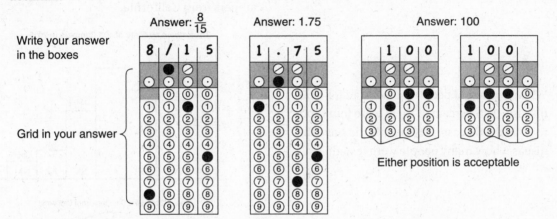

- Grid only one space in each column.
- Entering the answer in the boxes is recommended as an aid in gridding but is not required.
- The machine scoring your exam can read only what you grid, so you **must grid-in your answers correctly to get credit**.
- If a question has more than one correct answer, grid-in only one of them.
- The grid does not have a minus sign; so no answer can be negative.
- A mixed number *must* be converted to an improper fraction or a decimal before it is gridded.

  Enter $1\frac{1}{4}$ as 5/4 or 1.25; the machine will interpret 11/4 as $\frac{11}{4}$ and mark it wrong.

- **All decimals must be entered as accurately as possible.** Here are three acceptable ways of gridding

$$\frac{3}{11} = 0.272727\ldots$$

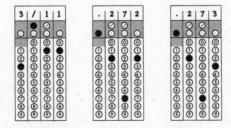

- Note that rounding to .273 is acceptable because you are using the full grid, but you would receive **no credit** for .3 or .27, because they are less accurate.

28. Jim, Kim, Ben, and Len divided $1000 as follows: Kim got twice as much as Jim, Ben got 3 times as much as Jim, and Len got $100. How much, in dollars, did Jim get?

29. When a group of people were tested for a rare disease, 99.6 percent of them were found not to have the disease. If 10 people did have the disease, how many people were tested?

Questions 30 and 31 are based on the information and graphs below.

The data in the following charts give information about the 400 campers who attended the Western States Sports Academy in 2015. The bar graph gives the breakdown by home state of the participants. The circle graph shows the sports specialties of the campers from California.

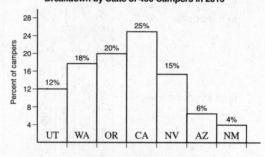

Breakdown by State of 400 Campers in 2015

Specialties of the Campers from California

30. How many of the campers were basketball players from California?

31. In 2015, 12 of the campers from Utah (UT), 18 of the campers from Washington (WA), and 15 percent of the campers from Oregon (OR), Nevada (NV), Arizona (AZ), and New Mexico (NM) played basketball. In total, how many campers played a sport other than basketball?

If there is still time remaining, you may review your answers.

ANSWER KEY
Practice Test 1

Section 1: Reading

1.	**B**	14.	**B**	27.	**A**	40.	**B**
2.	**A**	15.	**C**	28.	**B**	41.	**A**
3.	**D**	16.	**D**	29.	**C**	42.	**A**
4.	**B**	17.	**B**	30.	**A**	43.	**D**
5.	**C**	18.	**C**	31.	**B**	44.	**C**
6.	**C**	19.	**D**	32.	**B**	45.	**C**
7.	**D**	20.	**D**	33.	**C**	46.	**C**
8.	**C**	21.	**C**	34.	**C**	47.	**B**
9.	**C**	22.	**C**	35.	**B**		
10.	**B**	23.	**B**	36.	**D**		
11.	**C**	24.	**D**	37.	**C**		
12.	**C**	25.	**D**	38.	**D**		
13.	**B**	26.	**B**	39.	**B**		

Number Correct _____

Number Incorrect _____

Section 2: Writing and Language

1.	**D**	12.	**C**	23.	**A**	34.	**C**
2.	**A**	13.	**B**	24.	**C**	35.	**C**
3.	**B**	14.	**A**	25.	**D**	36.	**A**
4.	**C**	15.	**D**	26.	**B**	37.	**C**
5.	**A**	16.	**C**	27.	**A**	38.	**B**
6.	**B**	17.	**B**	28.	**C**	39.	**A**
7.	**D**	18.	**B**	29.	**B**	40.	**D**
8.	**A**	19.	**A**	30.	**A**	41.	**B**
9.	**D**	20.	**C**	31.	**D**	42.	**B**
10.	**C**	21.	**D**	32.	**B**	43.	**A**
11.	**B**	22.	**A**	33.	**B**	44.	**D**

Number Correct _____

Number Incorrect _____

ANSWER KEY
Practice Test 1

Section 3: Math (No Calculator)

1. **A**	5. **B**	9. **D**	13. **C**
2. **C**	6. **C**	10. **D**	
3. **A**	7. **A**	11. **A**	
4. **B**	8. **A**	12. **A**	

14. **0**   15. **40**   16. **.93**   17. **.8**

Number Correct _____

Number Incorrect _____

ANSWER KEY
Practice Test 1

Section 4: Math (Calculator)

1.	**C**	7.	**B**	13.	**A**	19.	**B**	25.	**A**
2.	**B**	8.	**B**	14.	**C**	20.	**D**	26.	**C**
3.	**D**	9.	**A**	15.	**D**	21.	**B**	27.	**D**
4.	**B**	10.	**D**	16.	**B**	22.	**D**		
5.	**C**	11.	**D**	17.	**C**	23.	**D**		
6.	**D**	12.	**B**	18.	**C**	24.	**A**		

28. **150**   29. **2500**   30. **20**   31. **323**

Number Correct _____

Number Incorrect _____

SCORE ANALYSIS

Reading and Writing Test

Section 1: Reading   _____ = _____ (A)
                         # correct   raw score

Section 2: Writing   _____ = _____ (B)
                         # correct   raw score

To find your Reading and Writing test scores, consult the chart below: find the ranges in which your raw scores lie and read across to find the ranges of your test scores.

_____ + _____ = _____ (C)
range of reading   range of writing   range of reading + writing
test scores   test scores   test scores

To find the range of your Reading and Writing Scaled Score, multiply (C) by 10.

Test Scores for the Reading and Writing Sections

Reading Raw Score	Writing Raw Score	Test Score
39–47	39–44	33–38
33–38	33–38	30–32
28–32	28–32	27–29
21–27	22–27	23–27
15–20	17–21	20–23
11–14	13–16	17–20
8–10	9–12	15–17
4–7	5–8	13–15
less than 4	less than 5	8–12

Math Test

Section 3:   _____ = _____ (D)
                 # correct   raw score

Section 4:   _____ = _____ (E)
                 # correct   raw score

Total Math raw score: (D) + (E) = _____

To find your Math Scaled Score, consult the chart below: find the range in which your raw score lies and read across to find the range for your scaled score.

Scaled Scores for the Math Test

Raw Score	Scaled Score	Raw Score	Scaled Score
39–48	700–760	16–19	450–490
35–38	650–690	12–15	400–440
31–34	600–640	9–11	350–390
25–30	550–590	6–9	300–340
20–24	500–540	less than 6	160–290

ANSWERS EXPLAINED

Section 1: Reading Test

1. **(B)** Throughout the passage, Dickens is poking fun at Gradgrind's teaching methods and philosophy. His intent is to present the reader with *a broadly satirical portrait of a character.*

      Choice A is incorrect. Dickens does not praise Gradgrind or argue that the reader should look up to him. He definitely does not present Gradgrind as a positive role model. Choices C and D are incorrect. Nothing in the passage suggests either possibility.

2. **(A)** Dickens implies that Gradgrind is so peremptory (absolute; dogmatic) that he would make a point of insisting upon the fact that his given name was, in fact, Thomas.

3. **(D)** Gradgrind's state of satisfaction is his emotional *condition* or mood. Although "state" can mean territory ("driving across several Western states"), ceremony ("seated on her throne in state"), or government ("a state-run agency"), that is not how the word is used in this particular context.

4. **(B)** As he walks home, Gradgrind is "in a state of considerable satisfaction." He is pleased with himself and with the school he has created; his mood is clearly one of *complacency* or smugness.

5. **(C)** When you answered the previous question, did you make a mark in your book next to the sentence about Mr. Gradgrind's walk homeward? If so, you managed to find the answers to both Questions 4 and 5 at the same time. It pays to look ahead at the questions and locate each command-of-evidence question in advance, so that you can pay special attention when you answer the question immediately preceding it and note the place in the passage that best supports your answer.

6. **(C)** Gradgrind never introduces his pupils to nursery rhymes or to fantasy creatures such as ogres. This suggests that he rejects from his curriculum anything that is in the least *fanciful* or imaginative.

7. **(D)** When they look at the moon, the little Gradgrinds never fancy they see a face looking back at them. They never wonder what the stars are. This evidence supports the claim that Gradgrind, who wishes his pupils to be models, just as his children are models, has rejected from his curriculum anything that is the least bit fanciful.

8. **(C)** Look at what the narrator tells you. The narrator tells you what Gradgrind thinks: Gradgrind is a "man who proceeds upon the principle that two and two are four, and nothing over, and who is not to be talked into allowing for anything over"; Gradgrind intended his school "to be a model." Likewise, the narrator tells you what Gradgrind feels: "Mr. Gradgrind walked homeward from the school in a state of considerable satisfaction"; he "walked on in a hopeful and satisfied frame of mind." Thus, the narrator clearly is *an observer who knows all about Gradgrind's thoughts and feelings.*

9. **(C)** The phrase "eminently practical" supposedly has a special *relevance* or aptness as a description of Thomas Gradgrind; it is an apt way to describe this most factual and pragmatic of men. Although "application" can mean *formal request* ("my application for a transfer"), *implementation* ("strict application of the rules"), or *hard work* ("years of hard work and application"), that is not how the word is used here.

10. **(B)** The author's emphasis is on the elephant as an important "creator of habitat" for other creatures. Thus, he is concerned with *explaining how the elephant's impact on its surroundings affects other species.*

11. **(C)** To mount an effort to rescue an endangered species is to *launch* or initiate a campaign. Although "mounted" can mean *ascended* ("she mounted the steps"), *increased* ("his debts mounted over the years"), or *attached* ("we mounted the poster on the wall"), that is not the way in which it is used in the present context.

12. **(C)** The passage indicates that tigers and whales are not the architects of their environment. The elephant, however, is. It is the architect of its environment in that *it physically alters its environment*, transforming the landscape around it.

13. **(B)** The author states that it is the elephant's metabolism and appetite—in other words, its voracity or *ravenous hunger*—that leads to its creating open spaces in the woodland and transforming the landscape.

14. **(B)** Since the foraging of elephants creates a varied landscape that attracts a diverse group of plant-eating animals and since the presence of these plant-eaters in turn attracts carnivores, it follows that elephants have an indirect effect on the hunting patterns of carnivores.

15. **(C)** The author has just stated that the elephants' foraging creates a mixture of bush and grassland that attracts plant-eating species. In lines 76–77, he goes on to state that the presence of the herbivores attracts carnivores. (The carnivores move to areas in which the herbivores live.) The elephants have created those areas. Thus, the *elephants have an indirect effect on the hunting patterns of those carnivores.*

16. **(D)** Here the phrase "keystone species" is being used in a special or technical sense to mean a species whose very presence contributes to a diversity of life and whose extinction would consequently lead to the extinction of other forms of life.

17. **(B)** The author is listing the many species that depend on the elephant as a creator of habitat. Thus, the host of smaller animals is the *very large number* of these creatures that thrive in the elephant's wake. Although "host" can mean a *food source for parasites* ("tapeworms live in the gut of their host"), a *provider of hospitality* ("the host of the banquet"), or a *military force* ("drive off the hosts of Mordor"), that is not the way in which it is used here.

18. **(C)** Choices A, B, and D all indicate that the author's attitude toward the damage to vegetation caused by elephants is negative. However, throughout the passage the author has described the importance of the elephant as a creator of habitat and has warned that the elephant's extinction would have an adverse impact on plant-eating species that now live in open spaces created by elephant foraging. He is objective about the damage to vegetation but sees that it has some positive effects, for it *fortuitously* (accidentally, but perhaps fortunately) results in the creation of *environments suited to diverse species.*

19. **(D)** The elephants' foraging creates a landscape that meets the needs of many species. This sentence provides evidence to support this assertion, for it lists a wide variety of plant-eating species ranging from grazers to browsers to plant-eating primates.

20. **(D)** In the opening paragraph, Anthony explicitly states her purpose in writing this speech. She is "under indictment" for a crime, that is, formally accused of having committed a crime. It is her task to prove that her action was *not* a crime, but a lawful act. In other words, her purpose is to *establish the lawfulness of an action.*

21. **(C)** The key words in this sentence are "enjoyment" and "liberty." Scan the passage to find them. In the second paragraph, Anthony quotes the preamble to the Constitution, emphasizing the founding fathers' intent to "secure the blessings of liberty." She concludes the paragraph with the statement that "it is a downright mockery to talk to women of their *enjoyment* of the blessings of *liberty* while they are denied the use of the only means of securing them provided by this democratic-republican government—the ballot." It is a mockery, it is a farce, to pretend that women are enjoying the blessings of liberty when they lack the right to vote. And to talk to women about their enjoyment of these blessings is *both ironic and upsetting given their lack of* that right.

22. **(C)** Anthony states plainly that the states have no such right. Why do the states have no such right? The states have no right to deny women the right to vote because, Anthony argues, the Federal Constitution guarantees women that right, and, when state law *is in conflict with constitutional law*, constitutional law takes precedence.

23. **(B)** Making women forfeit their civil rights without going through any judicial process is "a violation of the supreme law of the land." In other words, it is in conflict with constitutional law, the supreme law of these United States.

24. **(D)** Anthony sees the current situation as dividing every home in the nation, pitting wives against husbands, brothers against sisters, fathers against daughters, mothers against sons. Choice A is incorrect. The passage of a bill of attainder, which would deprive citizens of their civil rights without recourse to judicial process, would not correct the situation. Choices B and C are incorrect. Anthony makes neither argument.

25. **(D)** "(E)very home in the nation" is affected by this oligarchy (small ruling group having control of a government or institution) of sex.

26. **(B)** To carry dissension into every home is to *bring* the quarrel about women's rights into every home. Although "carries" may mean *holds* ("she carries herself gracefully"), *stocks* ("the bridal shop carries the latest fashions"), or *is approved* ("the motion carries"), that is not how the word is used here.

27. **(A)** A question that is left to be settled is one that needs to be *resolved* (straightened out; set right). Although "settled" may mean *colonized* ("The English settled much of Australia"), *quieted* ("The baby finally settled down"), or *paid* ("They settled the bill"), that is not how the word is used here.

28. **(B)** In 1870, the passage of the 15th Amendment granted African American men the right to vote. The amendment asserted that no state had a right to make any new law or enforce any old law that prevented African American men from exercising their right to vote. Thus, in 1873 there was *a strong precedent for granting the right to vote to a disfranchised group*. Anthony states that any laws preventing women from exercising their right to vote are null and void "*precisely* as is every one against Negroes." The use here of *precisely* emphasizes the importance of this precedent.

29. **(C)** The author reports on several studies examining the history of mid-Atlantic hurricanes. He cites articles in *Geophysical Research Letters* on the relationship between atmospheric heating and hurricanes and in the magazine *Science* on the relationship between ocean warming and hurricanes. Clearly he is *well-informed about the ongoing debate about climate change.*

30. **(A)** Note how throughout the article the author keeps on qualifying his statements. First he says that it makes sense that if ocean temperatures go up, storms would become more frequent and more intense; then he says the situation isn't that unambiguous. You can't simply say that global warming explains all the phenomena that researchers observe. His aim apparently is to *provide perspective on the possible effects of global warming on storm intensity.*

31. **(B)** During Hurricane Katrina, many people were quick to blame the extremely intense hurricane season on global warming. By stating that the relationship between warming and hurricanes is less clear-cut (unambiguous) than it seemed in 2005, the passage gives readers a better understanding of the importance of the effects of global warming on storm intensity. In other words, it gives them some perspective on the degree to which raised ocean temperatures affect the ferocity of tropical storms.

32. **(B)** Scan the passage looking for the terms "Vecchi" and "Category 4 and 5." They appear in the sixth and seventh paragraphs. If the frequency of Category 4 and 5 storms per year could nearly double over the next 90 years, despite the total number of storms per year staying the same, that would mean that more storms per year would belong to Categories 4 and 5. Instead of making up only 6 percent of U.S. hurricane landfalls, these monster storms could make up 10 to 12 percent of U.S. hurricane landfalls, with a corresponding increase in destruction.

33. **(C)** Vecchi and his colleagues are forecasting how the storms will behave. The *specific point* they make is a prediction that the *incidence* or "frequency" of Category 4 and 5 storms could nearly double by 2100. In other words, *As global warming increases, more tropical storms will fall under these categories.*

34. **(C)** In studying how hurricanes *form*, Vecchi and his colleagues are examining how hurricanes come into being and *take shape.* Although "form" can mean *conceive* ("form an idea"), *arrange* ("form the recruits into lines"), or *enter into* ("form close friendships"), that is not how the word is used in this context.

35. **(B)** The storms that posed threats to low-lying coastal regions *presented* threats to these regions. Although "posed" can mean *pretended* ("the con men posed as police officers"), *suggested* ("posed a topic for discussion"), or *modeled* ("she posed for a photographer"), that is not how the word is used in this context.

36. **(D)** Look at the almost horizontal line running straight across the graph. Note that it is slightly lower on its right-hand side than on the left. This slight incline represents the minor decrease in the number of annual storms that Landsea and his colleagues found had taken place over the last century.

37. **(C)** The vertical axis of this graph represents the number of hurricanes in a given year that lasted longer than two days. These typically are more intense, destructive storms. Look at the jagged line representing the annual hurricane count. Now look at the less

jagged line representing the five-year average count of hurricanes. Note the high points along both lines. Although some individual years may have as many as twenty intense storms, when you average the number of hurricanes per year for a five-year period, the line smooths out. The graph shows that *(t)he five-year average count of hurricanes seldom exceeded 12 per year.*

Choice A is incorrect. In the period from 1878 to 2008, the annual number of North Atlantic hurricanes never fell as low as two. Choice B is incorrect. The graph conveys no information about how much longer than two days any hurricane may have lasted. Choice D is incorrect. The graph contains no information about South Atlantic hurricanes.

38. **(D)** All the examples cited in lines 1–14 illustrate *problems facing a once-stable industry.* These problems range from the declining number of journalists employed in the industry to the disruption caused in the industry both by buyouts of newspapers and magazines and by layoffs of employees.

39. **(B)** The loosely connected, though spread out, framework of newspaper offices has been shrinking or *contracting* (growing smaller) as the number of newspapers has decreased. Although "shrinking" can mean *becoming withdrawn* ("shrinking into oneself"), *quailing* ("shrinking from danger") or *growing shorter* ("shrinking in height"), that is not how the word is used in this context.

40. **(B)** "Career stability" or *economic security* was an advantage that newspapers could provide for their employees during the greater part of the twentieth century.

41. **(A)** The fact that in the twentieth century newspapers received so much money from advertisers that "it was as if their presses printed money" is strong evidence that they were in a position to provide their fortunate employees with *economic security.*

42. **(A)** The experts quoted earlier in Passage 1—business school professors Robert Seamans and Feng Zhu, journalism professor Nicco Mele—address the issues of falling print advertising revenues and of failing newspapers. They are concerned with the financial troubles that have marked the decline of print journalism. The sixth paragraph, however, deals with a different aspect of the problem. It discusses the loss of journalism's watchdog function and the impact of this loss on America's democratic commonweal. Thus, the sixth paragraph *presents an overview of an aspect of the problem that has not been addressed by the experts previously quoted in the passage.*

43. **(D)** By saying that nobody is watching the politicians and businessmen anymore, Kendall is asserting that too few journalists are still engaged in *monitoring* the activities of these powerful figures to safeguard the public from any unethical or criminal acts on their parts. Although watching can mean *staying awake* ("watching through the night"), *awaiting expectantly* ("watching one's opportunity"), or *protecting* ("watching over someone like a mother"), that is not how the word is used in this context.

44. **(C)** Passage 2 begins with its author's quoting a McKinsey report indicating that the rapid decline of print journalism has bottomed out, that is, reached its lowest point before stabilizing or improving. However, the author disagrees strongly with the McKinsey report's conclusion. "Wow," he says. It would be nice to think that, but there's evidence to refute that conclusion.

45. **(C)** The author presents his evidence in a chart comparing 2013 average circulation figures with analogous paid circulation figures for 2015 and states that the paid circulation figures are "the best indication of consumer demand for the product." From the chart, it is clear that the demand for this product has continued to fall since 2013, and far more rapidly that the McKinsey report would have predicted.

46. **(C)** Although between 2013 and 2015 both the *Wall Street Journal* and the *New York Times* experienced sharp drops in circulation, the most extreme decline in circulation was experienced by *USA Today*, with a drop from an average print circulation of 1,424,000 in 2013 to an individually paid circulation of 299,000 in 2015.

47. **(B)** Both Passage 1 and Passage 2 discuss the financial impact of the change in the public's news-reading habits from print journalism to electronic media. However, in addition to analyzing the financial aspects of this change, Passage 1 goes into its sociopolitical impact in some detail.

Section 2: Writing and Language Test

1. **(D)** The phrase "Jake and Jillian" is unnecessary in that it could be eliminated and the sentence would still function effectively. In such an instance, the unnecessary phrase must be outlined with both a comma before and a comma after to separate it from the principal clause. Choice D is the only choice that places a necessary comma before "Jake" and another necessary comma after "Jillian."

2. **(A)** We need to find the most vivid option to contrast with California's "warm, sunny climate." Choices B and D are irrelevant and can be eliminated. Choice C mentions cold, but it isn't terribly descriptive. Choice A, on the other hand, is quite vivid and is, therefore, the correct answer.

3. **(B)** We must find the most concise and fluid option that combines the two sentences. In Choice A, the word ordering is unwieldy; also, "trip of shopping" is wordy. In Choice C, it is unnecessary to say both "that day" and "the third day." In Choice D, it reads as if what shook was the vacation interruption instead of the ground. Choice B, on the other hand, is both concise and fluid. It is the correct answer.

4. **(C)** A contrasting transition is needed to express the difference between how short the earthquake actually was, as expressed before the underlined portion, and how long the earthquake actually felt, as expressed after the underlined portion. "But" is the only choice that expresses a contrast.

5. **(A)** In this sentence, we are listing. And, when we list items, realize that a colon is a valid way to start a list. A colon is only one way to introduce a list. ("Rocks may be classified as metamorphic, igneous, or sedimentary.") That is what is required here. A dash, perhaps, would also have been acceptable. None of Choices B, C, or D places acceptable punctuation after "layers."

6. **(B)** Notice the other verb tenses in the preceding sentences: "the crust is . . ." and "because it is like," for instance. "Is" is a present tense verb, so we must use a present tense verb here, as well. We can discount Choice A and Choice D, accordingly. The subject is "the largest wave," which is a single thing and, therefore, requires a singular verb. "Have" is a plural verb. So, "is," Choice B, is the only option.

7. **(D)** The proper preposition to follow "magnitude" is "of," so "magnitude of 4.0" is the only proper choice. The others all use prepositions not used typically with "magnitude."

8. **(A)** We must examine how this sentence relates to the previous. Paraphrasing, it says, "they said they had experienced few earthquakes, but I informed them that they had experienced many more." A contrasting transition, therefore, is needed. Choice A, "however," is the only choice denoting the "but" in our paraphrasing.

9. **(D)** We must analyze the chart. The question asks for the highest recorded earthquakes in history. In our chart, we can see that those were Caracas and Valdivia, which were between 9 and 10, or about 9.5.

10. **(C)** The earthquake that the narrator experienced was 4.0 on the Richter scale. Honshu, according to our chart, was 9.0. Per the given logarithmic explanation of the Richter Scale, we could calculate the difference by subtracting 4.0 from 9.0, which equals 5.0. Since the passage indicates that an increase in one digit of Richter Scale value results in 10 times greater magnitude (i.e., a 5.0 on the scale is 10 times greater in magnitude than a 4.0), an increase of 5 digits on the scale will result in a magnitude that is $10 \times 10 \times 10 \times 10 \times 10 = 10^5$ greater. Thus, Honshu was 1 with five zeroes behind it, or "100,000" times stronger.

11. **(B)** The passage provides "have" for us already in our verb conjugation, and that is something we cannot change. What we are looking for here is the perfect tense, which is "have wished." Since we have conjugated "wish," we must then follow it with the infinitive tense, which is "to return." Combine all that, and we have Choice B.

12. **(C)** The main clause is "she remains most widely known as the wife of F. Scott Fitzgerald." A comma is required after "yet," as it is separate from the main clause. Eliminate Choices A and D accordingly. Similarly, a comma is required to separate the main clause from what comes after, beginning with "a narrow." Choice C, then, is the correct answer.

13. **(B)** Notice the previous sentence discussing how Zelda was alive during the 1920s, which is the "early twentieth century." Thus, it is not necessary to restate "early twentieth century" as that is already apparent from the mention of the 1920s. Choice B, therefore, is the correct answer.

14. **(A)** The idea we are attempting to express in possessive form is the short stories of her husband. An apostrophe and "s" after "husband" is required to demonstrate said possession. Choice D is flawed in that it reads as if she had multiple husbands.

15. **(D)** Notice how this sentence contrasts with the previous one. Essentially, though Zelda fits the personality of her husband's characters, she was actually the inspiration for—rather than the product of—his fiction. "Though" is the only choice that fulfills that contrasting transition role. Choices A and C read as cause and effect, whereas Choice B incorrectly reads as an elaboration on the previous statement, rather than a qualification used to negate it, as it should.

16. **(C)** Beginning the sentence with, "As a writer, dancer, and painter," the main clause must then immediately address who played those roles. Zelda, then, should be the subject. Eliminate Choice D for incorrect subject usage, accordingly. Choice A incorrectly employs the passive voice. Choice B, particularly with its usage of "excelled by nobody

at all," isn't logical. Choice C, however, correctly uses the active voice, addresses Zelda as the subject, and manages to avoid awkward word ordering.

17. **(B)** "Marriages" must be plural, as we are discussing "one of the most famously impassioned . . . marriages." Though we are referring to just this one marriage, we are establishing a comparison among many marriages. Eliminate Choices A and C. Second, the correct phrase is "in history," rather than "on history." Choice B is correct.

18. **(B)** Choice A employs various pauses and reads with a lack of fluidity. Choice C is a comma splice. Choice D eliminates the information of 1921, which is relevant and useful. Choice B, in contrast with the other three, is both concise and thorough in capturing the initial information in the two sentences.

19. **(A)** In Choice B, using both "stubbornly" and "inflexibly" is unnecessary, as the two convey the same meaning. Choice C similarly lacks concision by employing two phrases with similar meanings. Choice D does not strongly enough emphasize Zelda's passion with ballet strongly enough. "Obstinately consumed" is both concise and effectively descriptive. It is our correct answer.

20. **(C)** "Doomed and beautiful" is a direct quote by Matthew Bruccoli describing Zelda. Because it is a direct quote, the quotation marks must be maintained to denote it as such.

21. **(D)** Notice how "furthermore" is used later in the sentence. It would be unnecessary to use both "additionally" and "furthermore" as they both represent the same idea. It is best, then, to delete "furthermore," which is Choice D.

22. **(A)** This is a difficult verb tense known as the perfect conditional. As the word "would" is already provided in the passage, we must find a choice that maintains concordance with "would." "Would had begun," "would began," and "would begun" are all improper verb conjugations, and there is no instance in which one would encounter those as acceptable phrases. "Would have begun," however, is perfectly acceptable.

23. **(A)** We are searching for the answer that provides the most specific information. In Choices B, C, and D, we have references that are imprecise, whereas Choice A gives us a numerical representation of 200.

24. **(C)** We are not contrasting the previous sentence with this one, so Choice A is incorrect. The idea that we are trying to express is, essentially, from the past until now. Choice C, "since then," is our best option. Choices B and D imply that one is building on the last sentence with the next one, which is not our purpose.

25. **(D)** If punctuation is not necessary, avoid it. Such is the case in this question where no comma is necessary, as we see in Choice D. Choices A, B, and C all have unnecessary commas. Be careful not to assume that a lengthy clause is automatically a run-on sentence.

26. **(B)** It is imperative to read the question carefully. We must find an answer that expresses some measure of culpability for Parris, without assigning him too much blame. It is *The Goldilocks Zone* of blame that we require. Choice A assigns too much blame, whereas Choice C assigns no blame. Choice D is unrelated to blame. Choice B, however, expresses that concept of "somewhat to blame," as quoted in the question.

27. **(A)** The clause, "the young daughter and niece of Reverend Parris," is unnecessary: we can remove it, and the sentence still functions properly. In order to do this grammatically, we must insert a comma both before and after the clause to set it apart. Choice A is the only one that properly inserts a comma both before and after the clause, while also avoiding an unnecessary comma within, as in Choice C. Choice B lacks both necessary commas, while Choice D neglects to insert the second comma.

28. **(C)** The inhabitants belong to the town, illustrating possession. We must then insert an apostrophe between "town" and the "s," as executed properly in Choice C. Choice A omits the necessary apostrophe. Choice B incorrectly places the apostrophe after "towns," which would signify inhabitants of multiple towns, as opposed to only Salem, as is intended.

29. **(B)** Choice B is concise while still managing to communicate the intended message effectively. Contrast this with Choice C, which is simple, but too much so; we swap wordiness for ambiguity, and that isn't our aim. Choice D eliminates relevant information. Choice A is far too wordy. Case in point: do not say, "those who professed the religion of Christianity" when it is far simpler to say "Christians."

30. **(A)** We must maintain verb parallelism. Notice the other verbs in this sequence: "screaming," "throwing," and "distorting." We need another -ing verb to maintain that parallelism, and "listing" is the only valid option, as in Choice A.

31. **(D)** There are two aspects to this question: subject-verb agreement and verb tense. The subject is "descendants," which is plural. We therefore need a plural verb and can eliminate "is" and "was" based on this. The second aspect is verb tense. The action occurred in 1711, which is the past. Choice A, "are," can thus be eliminated. "Were" is the correct choice here.

32. **(B)** The idea expressed here is a cautionary tale, and "dire warning"—Choice B—fits that. Choice A is wordy; it is unnecessary to say both "terrifying" and "horrifying" because they mean the same thing. Choices C and D are irrelevant to our desired meaning.

33. **(B)** The preceding paragraph makes the following statement: "The tragedy of the Salem witch trials has inspired numerous historical and sociological texts." This graph supports this assertion because it shows how there have been quite a few texts written about this topic. It is not Choice A because this is not the first mention of this relationship. Choices C and D would prevent this helpful graph from being inserted.

34. **(C)** The possessive form of "you" is "your," and that is what is required here. Recall that Choice A is the contraction of "you are," which is not what is intended here. Choice D is equally a misinterpretation of the possessive "their."

35. **(C)** Whenever dealing with questions of "should the author insert . . . ," ask yourself, first, is it relevant? Second, ask, does it provide new information or simply restate something already given? In this case, the proposed insertion—though relevant—is just repeating previous information expressed in "you would be wise to go to a great school." Thus, it is unnecessary, and Choice C is our correct answer.

36. **(A)** In this sentence, "more than academic credentials" is unnecessary to the overall functioning of the sentence; eliminate it, and the sentence will still function grammatically. Thus, per our grammatical rules, we must set it aside with dashes or

commas (one before the phrase and one after). Choices C and D fail to do this properly. Choice B does outline the clause, but notice that the first pause is a comma whereas the second is a dash. This contrasts with our requirement for parallelism (i.e., we must select one or the other (dash or comma) and stick with it). Choice A is the only option that executes this correctly by using two dashes.

37. **(C)** A common English phrase is "in the name of *blank*" where the *blank* is always a noun. For example, think in the name of love. Choice C successfully follows that pattern with "thoroughness" being our valid noun. Choices A, B, and D do not effectively fit into the sentence.

38. **(B)** "Real" and "genuine" are synonyms, making Choice A a flawed, wordy version of our correct option, Choice B. Choice C is flawed because the sentence says "both," implying that it is about to list two things; a positive attitude is only one. Choice D is wrong for the same reason, except there we list nothing at all after "both," which leads to confusion about what was being discussed in the first place.

39. **(A)** In questions requiring the proper transition, we must analyze the previous sentence in conjunction with the next to determine the relationship between the two. In this case, our second sentence effectively is building on the first, making "Moreover" the desired choice. Choice D, "because of this," would express a cause-and-effect relationship, which is not the intention. "However" is a contrasting word and is the opposite of our intention. "Surprisingly" is not sensible in this context.

40. **(D)** The first aspect of this is subject-verb agreement. The subject is "applicants," and we accordingly require the verb "have" in this sentence. Thus, we can eliminate Choices A and B. The second aspect is "who" versus "whom." Rewrite the sentence using "he" or "him." In this case, you would say "he interviewed." Recall that if "he" fits, use "who," and if "him" fits, use "whom."

41. **(B)** In these rhetorical questions, read the question closely and react accordingly. We are searching for the choice that best expresses that an interview should be interactive—meaning, a back-and-forth discussion, as opposed to a monologue. Choices A, C, and D are unrelated to our purpose of expressing that the interview should be interactive. Choice B is the only valid option.

42. **(B)** The initiative and interest refers to the action of preparing a handful of questions for the interviewer, and thus the sentence would best be placed after sentence 1—Choice B. With Choices A, C, and D, the chronology is faulty.

43. **(A)** Recall that a semicolon is used to connect two complete, independent sentences. "Also, under no circumstances should you interrupt or talk over your interviewer" is a full sentence, just as "be involved, but never domineering, in the conversation" is a full sentence as well. So, it is best to join them with a semicolon. The other choices are all variations of run-on sentences.

44. **(D)** Focus carefully on what the question demands. We need a conclusion to the essay that maintains its tone and focuses on its topic. The essay gives encouraging advice on how to best conduct oneself in an interview, and Choice D maintains this positive attitude and continues the emphasis on this topic. Choice A is too negative and uses an overly formal tone. Choice B is too vague. Choice C is too focused on a narrow piece of advice to serve as a conclusion to the essay as a whole.

Section 3: Math Test (No Calculator)

1. **(A)** $8(x-4) = 8x - 4 \Rightarrow 8x - 32 = 8x - 4 \Rightarrow -32 = -4$

    Since there is no value of x for which $-32 = -4$, the equation has no solutions.

    **A solution to the equation $8(x-4) = 8x - 4$ would be the x-coordinate of the point of intersection of the straight lines $y = 8(x-4)$ and $y = 8x - 4$. However, since these lines are parallel (they both have a slope of 8), they do not intersect.

2. **(C)** Solve the given equation for t:

    $C = 85 + (t-1)60 \Rightarrow$

    $C - 85 = (t-1)60 \Rightarrow$

    $\dfrac{C-85}{60} = t - 1 \Rightarrow$

    $t = \dfrac{C-85}{60} + 1 = \dfrac{C-85}{60} + \dfrac{60}{60} = \dfrac{C-25}{60}$

3. **(A)** $17 - 2\sqrt[3]{x} = 21 \Rightarrow -2\sqrt[3]{x} = 4 \Rightarrow \sqrt[3]{x} = -2 \Rightarrow x = -8$

4. **(B)** If $9 = 5 - x$, then $x = -4$. So $h(9) = h(5-(-4)) = (-4)^2 + (-4) + 1 = 16 - 4 + 1 = 13$

5. **(B)** Write the given equation as $a^3 = 3a$. Since a is positive, you can divide both sides by a, getting $a^2 = 3$. Now take the square root of each side: $a = \sqrt{3}$.

6. **(C)** The equation of the parabola is irrelevant. You just need to see which of the four answer choices is the equation of a line that passes through $(1, 9)$. First note that Choices A and B are not the equations of a line. So they can be eliminated right away, even though each of them is the equation of a curve that does pass through $(1, 9)$. Choices C and D are each the equation of a line. So you just have to test each of them by replacing x by 1 and y by 9. Choice C works: $9 = 4(1) + 5$. Choice D doesn't work.

7. **(A)** From the given information we know two things: $b = 3d$ and $b = 864$. So $3d = 864$.

8. **(A)** $a = \dfrac{bc^2}{4de} \Rightarrow 4ade = bc^2 \Rightarrow c^2 = \dfrac{4ade}{b} \Rightarrow c = \sqrt{\dfrac{4ade}{b}} = 2\sqrt{\dfrac{ade}{b}}$

9. **(D)** In questions such as these, first find the midpoint of the eligible values. Here, a value for y is acceptable only if $21 \le y \le 29$; the midpoint of this interval is 25. All of the acceptable ages are within 4 years of 25—anywhere from 4 years less than 25 to 4 years greater than 25. The inequality that expresses this is $|y - 25| \le 4$.

10. **(D)** Since the distance between $(-3, 5)$ and $(3, 5)$ is 6, the radius of the circle is 6. So the diameter is 12, and the circumference is 12π.

11. **(A)** $\dfrac{4x^2}{2x-1} = \dfrac{8x-3}{2x-1} + A \Rightarrow \dfrac{4x^2 - (8x-3)}{2x-1} = A \Rightarrow \dfrac{4x^2 - 8x + 3}{2x-1} = A$

    At this point, you have two choices: either factor and reduce or divide.

    Factor and reduce: $A = \dfrac{4x^2 - 8x + 3}{2x-1} = \dfrac{(2x-1)(2x-3)}{2x-1} = 2x - 3$

    Divide:

    $$2x-1 \overline{\big)\, 4x^2 - 8x + 3}$$
    $$\begin{array}{r} 2x \quad -3 \\ \underline{4x^2 - 2x} \\ -6x + 3 \\ \underline{-6x + 3} \\ 0 \end{array}$$

12. **(A)** If Mary earned a grade of G on the test, she missed $(100 - G)$ points. In adjusting the grades, the teacher decided to deduct only half that number: $\dfrac{100 - G}{2}$.

So Mary's new grade was $100 - \left(\dfrac{100 - G}{2}\right) = 100 - 50 + \dfrac{G}{2} = 50 + \dfrac{G}{2}$.

**Pick a number for G. For example, if G is 80, as explained in the question, Mary's adjusted grade would be 90. Only Choice A is equal to 90 when G is 80.

13. **(C)** There are three ways to attack this question. First, you can add the two equations. You immediately get that $3x = 24$. So $x = 8$. Second, you can rewrite the second equation as $x = 3y + 17$. Then replace x by $3y + 17$ in the first equation:

$$2(3y + 17) + 3y = 7 \Rightarrow 6y + 34 + 3y = 7 \Rightarrow 9y = -27 \Rightarrow y = -3$$

Then plug in that value for y into the second equation:

$$x - 3(-3) = 17 \Rightarrow x + 9 = 17 \Rightarrow x = 8$$

Third, you can multiply the second equation by 2, which results in $2x - 6y = 34$. Then subtract that from the first equation, resulting in $9y = -27$ and $y = -3$.

Replace y by -3 in the second equation to get $x = 8$.

14. **(0)** For any numbers a and b, if $a \neq b$ and $ax = bx$, then x must be 0.

Therefore, 25% of x = 35% of $x \Rightarrow x = 0 \Rightarrow$ 45% of $x = 0$.

15. **(40)** To solve the equation $\dfrac{2}{x} + \dfrac{3}{4} = \dfrac{4}{5}$, first subtract $\dfrac{3}{4}$ from each side:

$$\dfrac{2}{x} + \dfrac{3}{4} = \dfrac{4}{5} \Rightarrow \dfrac{2}{x} = \dfrac{1}{20}$$

Then cross multiply to get $x = 40$.

****Note:** Do not waste time getting a common denominator; just use your calculator.

16. **(.93)** $P_{2001} = P_{2000} - .07(P_{2000}) = .93(P_{2000})$. Similarly,

$P_{2002} = P_{2001} - .07(P_{2001}) = .93(P_{2001}) = .93(.93)(P_{2000}) = P_{2000}(.93)^2$.

In general, $P_{2000 + t} = P_{2000}(.93)^t$. So in the given formula, $r = .93$.

Note that if a quantity decreases by 7 percent per year, then each year it retains 93 percent of its value. If a quantity decreases by x percent per year, each year it retains $(100 - x)$ percent of its value.

17. **(.8)** Since triangle ABC is a right triangle, we can use the Pythagorean theorem to find BC: $6^2 + (BC)^2 = 10^2 \Rightarrow (BC)^2 = 100 - 36 = 64 \Rightarrow BC = 8$

(Of course, if you immediately realize that triangle ABC is a 6-8-10 right triangle, then you don't have to use the Pythagorean theorem.)

So, $\sin A = \dfrac{\text{opposite}}{\text{hypotenuse}} = \dfrac{8}{10} = 0.8$.

Section 4: Math Test (With Calculator)

1. **(C)** The weight of the fruit is $5 + 3 + 1 = 9$ pounds, of which 3 pounds are oranges. Hence, the desired fraction is $\frac{3}{9} = \frac{1}{3}$.

2. **(B)** On Stock 1, Ed made a 20 percent profit; so if he bought Stock 1 for x, he sold it for $x + .20x = 1.20x$. Then, $1.20x = 4{,}000 \Rightarrow x = 4{,}000 \div 1.2 = 3{,}333.33$. His profit was \$666.67.

   On Stock 2, Ed lost 20 percent. If he bought Stock 2 for y, he sold it for $y - .20y = .80y$. Then, $.80x = 4{,}000 \Rightarrow x = 4{,}000 \div .80 = 5{,}000$. His loss was \$1,000.

   So Ed had a net loss of $\$1{,}000 - \$666.67 = \$333.33$.

3. **(D)** From the given information, we have that $D + 4d = 60$ and $D + 8d = 85$. Subtracting the first equation from the second gives $4d = 25$, and so $d = 6.25$. Replacing $4d$ by 25 in the first equation gives $D + 25 = 60 \Rightarrow D = 35$. So, Eli's initial deposit was \$35. Each week, he deposited \$6.25 into his account. After w weeks, the value of the account was $35 + 6.25w$ dollars. So the question is what is the smallest value of w for which $35 + 6.25w \geq 500$.

$$35 + 6.25w \geq 500 \Rightarrow 6.25w \geq 465 \Rightarrow w \geq 465 \div 6.25 = 74.4$$

   Since w must be a whole number, the smallest value of w is 75.

4. **(B)** Since the average of 91 and 95 is 93, the only way that the mean grade, m, of all the students in the class could be 93 is if $b = g$. Since it is given that $b \neq g$, m cannot be 93.

   **The weighted average, m, of all the students in the class is $\dfrac{91b + 95g}{b + g}$. If m were 93, then $\dfrac{91b + 95g}{b + g} = 93 \Rightarrow 91b + 95g = 93b + 93g \Rightarrow 2b = 2g \Rightarrow b = g$. Since it is given that $b \neq g$, m cannot be 93.

   **Note that the answer could not possibly be Choices C or D. If $m < 93$ or if $m > 93$ were true statements, then Choice B ($m \neq 93$) would also be true. So the answer has to be Choice A or B.

5. **(C)** Let x be the amount in dollars that each of the 20 workers was going to contribute. Then $20x$ represents the cost of the present. When 4 workers dropped out, the remaining 16 each had to pay $(x + 1.50)$ dollars, so

$$16(x + 1.5) = 20x \Rightarrow 16x + 24 = 20x \Rightarrow 24 = 4x \Rightarrow x = 6$$

   So the cost of the present was $20 \times 6 = \$120$.

6. **(D)** Assume that in 2013 the shop sold x sandwiches at a price of y dollars each. Then in 2014, it sold $x + 0.20x = 1.2x$ sandwiches at a price of $y + 0.10y = 1.1y$ dollars each. So the total income in 2013 was xy. In 2014, it was $(1.2x)(1.1y) = 1.32xy$, an increase of 32 percent.

   **Do exactly what was done above except replace x and y with 100. Assume that in 2013, the shop sold 100 sandwiches for \$100 each for a total of \$10,000. Then in 2014, the shop sold 120 sandwiches for \$110 each, for a total of \$13,200.

   Finally, \$13,200 is \$3,200 more than \$10,000, an increase of $\dfrac{3{,}200}{10{,}000} = 0.32 = 32$ percent.

7. **(B)** Of the $70 + 130 = 200$ Harts College graduating seniors who studied abroad, 70 were male. So the probability that the student chosen was male is $\frac{70}{200} = \frac{35}{100}$.

8. **(B)** The given equations are equivalent to $y = \frac{1}{2}x - 2$ and $y = 3x - 5$. Solve the equation $\frac{1}{2}x - 2 = 3x - 5$. Multiplying both sides by 2 gives $x - 4 = 6x - 10$. So $5x = 6$ and $x = \frac{6}{5}$. Then $y = \frac{1}{2}\left(\frac{6}{5}\right) - 2 = \frac{3}{5} - \frac{10}{5} = -\frac{7}{5}$. So, (a, b), the point of intersection of the two lines, is $\left(\frac{6}{5}, -\frac{7}{5}\right)$ and $a + b = \frac{6}{5} + \left(-\frac{7}{5}\right) = -\frac{1}{5}$.

9. **(A)** Multiplying both sides of the equation $V = \frac{4}{3}\pi r^3$ by 3 gives $3V = 4\pi r^3$. Divide both sides by 4π to get $\frac{3V}{4\pi} = r^3$. Finally, taking the cube root of each side results in: $r = \sqrt[3]{\frac{3V}{4\pi}}$.

10. **(D)** Set up a proportion, being sure to keep your units straight. First convert seconds to minutes: $\frac{24 \text{ words}}{18 \text{ seconds}} = \frac{x \text{ words}}{60 \text{ seconds}} \Rightarrow 18x = 1{,}440 \Rightarrow x = 80$. So the secretary can type 80 words in 60 seconds or 1 minute. One and a half hours equals $60 + 30 = 90$ minutes. In 90 minutes, he can type $90 \times 80 = 7{,}200$ words.

11. **(D)** \$20 of the \$377 that Neil paid was for alterations. The remaining \$357 was what he paid for the suit, including the 5 percent sales tax. If P represents the pretax price of the suit, then $\$357 = 1.05P \Rightarrow P = \$357 \div 1.05 = \$340$. Since Neil bought the suit on sale at 20 percent off the regular retail price, R, $\$340 = 80\%(R)$. So $R = \$340 \div 0.8 = \$425$.

12. **(B)** The trust received 80 percent of the estate (10 percent went to the man's wife, 5 percent to his children, and 5 percent to his grandchildren). If E represents the value of the estate, then $0.80E = 1{,}000{,}000$. Therefore,

$$E = 1{,}000{,}000 \div 0.80 = 1{,}250{,}000$$

Each grandchild received 1 percent of \$1,250,000, or \$12,500.

13. **(A)** There are 240 seniors who are not on a varsity team. Of these, 40 are on the honor roll. Therefore, the desired probability is $\frac{40}{240} = \frac{1}{6} = 0.1666 \approx 0.167$.

14. **(C)** Remember that in mathematics, "A or B" means "A or B, possibly both." The number of students who were on the honor roll or on a varsity team includes those students who were on both the honor roll and on a varsity team. The only students who do not satisfy the condition of being on the honor roll or on a varsity team are the 200 students who are on neither the honor roll nor a varsity team. The other 200 students do satisfy the condition. Finally, 200 is 50 percent of 400.

15. **(D)** First set up a proportion to determine the actual distance between Goshen and Deerfield: $\frac{1 \text{ inch}}{40 \text{ miles}} = \frac{0.6 \text{ inches}}{x \text{ miles}}$. So $x = (0.6)(40) = 24$. When traveling at 40 miles

per hour, it takes $\frac{24}{40} = \frac{6}{10}$ of an hour to drive 24 miles. Finally, $\frac{6}{10}$ of an hour is equal to $\frac{6}{10}$ (60 minutes) = 36 minutes.

16. **(B)** Clearly 0 is a solution to the equation. Since we are looking only for positive solutions, we can divide each term by x^2, reducing the equation to $x^4 - 10x^2 + 9 = 0$. As a general rule, we have no procedures for solving 4th-degree equations. However, $x^4 - 10x^2 + 9 = 0$ factors rather easily: $x^4 - 10x^2 + 9 = (x^2 - 9)(x^2 - 1)$. So,

$$x^4 - 10x^2 + 9 = 0 \Rightarrow (x^2 - 9)(x^2 - 1) = 0 \Rightarrow (x - 3)(x + 3)(x - 1)(x + 1) = 0$$

The solutions to the original equation, besides 0, are 3, –3, 1, and –1. The positive solutions are 3 and 1, and their sum is 4.

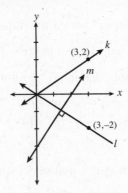

17. **(C)** You might be able to reason this out easily. However, the safest method is to sketch quickly lines k, l, and m that satisfy the given conditions. Let k, whose slope is $\frac{2}{3}$, be the line that goes through $(0, 0)$ and $(3, 2)$. Then line l, the reflection of line k in the x-axis, goes through $(0, 0)$ and $(3, -2)$. So line k has a slope of $-\frac{2}{3}$.

Since line m is perpendicular to line l, its slope is $\frac{3}{2}$, the negative reciprocal of $-\frac{2}{3}$.

One possibility for m is shown in the graph.

18. **(C)** Choose easy-to-use numbers. Since $\frac{5}{8}$ of the members are boys, assume there are 8 members, 5 of whom are boys. Then the other 3 members are girls. The ratio of girls to boys is 3 to 5, or $\frac{3}{5}$.

19. **(B)** Since $360 \div 450 = 0.8$, 80 percent of the boys receive free lunches. So, 80 percent of the girls also get them. If x represents the number of girls in the school,

$$.8x = 336 \Rightarrow x = 420$$

So the total number of students in the school is $450 + 420 = 870$.

20. **(D)** Eliminate the fractions in the given equation by multiplying both sides by $(x + 6)(x + 1)$:

$$(x + 6)(x + 1)\left(\frac{30}{x + 6}\right) = (x + 6)(x + 1)\left(\frac{5}{x + 1}\right) + 2(x + 6)(x + 1)$$

Then $30x + 30 = 5x + 30 + 2(x^2 + 7x + 6) \Rightarrow 2x^2 - 11x + 12 = 0$

The simplest thing to do now is to factor: $0 = 2x^2 - 11x + 12 = (2x - 3)(x - 4)$

So, $2x - 3 = 0$ or $x - 4 = 0$. Therefore, $x = 1.5$ or $x = 4$. Finally, the sum of the two roots is $1.5 + 4 = 5.5$.

**If you couldn't or didn't want to factor $2x^2 - 11x + 12$, you could have used the quadratic formula to solve the equation.

21. **(B)** Let x represent the number of 3 packs and let y represent the number of 10 packs the store sold last week. Then $x + y = 100$ and $3x + 10y = 615$. Multiplying the first equation by 3 gives $3x + 3y = 300$. Subtracting that equation from $3x + 10y = 615$ results in $7y = 315$. So, $y = 45$ and $x = 100 - 45 = 55$. Finally, the store received $55(\$2.88) + 45(\$7.59) = \$499.95$.

22. **(D)** You just have to recognize that $a^8 - b^8$ is the difference of two squares:

$$a^8 - b^8 = (a^4)^2 - (b^4)^2 = (a^4 - b^4)(a^4 + b^4)$$

$(a^4 + b^4)$ can't be simplified, but $(a^4 - b^4)$ is the difference of two squares:

$$(a^4 - b^4)(a^4 + b^4) = (a^2 - b^2)(a^2 + b^2)(a^4 + b^4)$$

Finally, $(a^2 + b^2)$ can't be simplified, but $(a^2 - b^2)$ is the difference of two squares:

$$\begin{aligned} a^8 - b^8 &= (a^4 - b^4)(a^4 + b^4) \\ &= (a^2 - b^2)(a^2 + b^2)(a^4 + b^4) \\ &= (a - b)(a + b)(a^2 + b^2)(a^4 + b^4) \end{aligned}$$

23. **(D)** The formula for the volume of a pyramid with a rectangular base is $V = \frac{1}{3} lwh$, where l and w are the length and width of the rectangle and where h is the height of the pyramid. (Remember that this fact is given to you on the first page of each math section.)

The base of pyramid 1 is a 3 by 4 rectangle whose area is $(3)(4) = 12$.

The base of pyramid 2 is a square of side 5 whose area is $5^2 = 25$. If h_1 and h_2 represent the two heights, then:

$$\frac{1}{3}(12)h_1 = \frac{1}{3}(25)h_2 \Rightarrow 12h_1 = 25h_2 \Rightarrow \frac{h_1}{h_2} = \frac{25}{12}$$

24. **(A)** Since Brian's average after 4 tests is 82, so far he has earned a total of $4 \times 82 = 328$ points. For his average after all 8 tests during the semester to be 85 or more, he will need a total of at least $8 \times 85 = 680$ points. So, on the last 4 tests he needs at least $680 - 328 = 352$ more points. Since the most he can earn on the last 3 tests is a total of 300 points, he must earn at least 52 points on the fifth test.

25. **(A)** Originally, the fund of d dollars was to be divided among 4 winners, in which case each of them would have received $\frac{d}{4}$ dollars. Instead, the fund was divided among 6 winners, and each received $\frac{d}{6}$ dollars. This represents a loss to each of the original winners of $\frac{d}{4} - \frac{d}{6} = \frac{3d}{12} - \frac{2d}{12} = \frac{d}{12}$ dollars.

**Unless you are comfortable with the algebra, plug in a number for d; say $d = 24$. Then the 4 winners would have received $24 \div 4 = 6$ dollars each. Now the 6 winners will receive $24 \div 6 = 4$ dollars each, a difference of $2. Which of the choices is equal to 2 when $d = 24$? Only $\frac{d}{12}$.

26. **(C)** For each of the four age groups, you can just divide the number in the column headed "Another Continent" by the number in the column headed "Total." You may immediately notice that for the 30–49 and for the 70 and over groups that quotient will be well less than one-third. You may also notice that for the less than 30 and for the 50–69 groups the quotient is much greater than one-third. So you can just do the division for two groups.

Less than 30: $210 \div 510 = 0.412 = 41.2\%$

50–69: $265 \div 555 = 0.477 = 47.7\%$

So the answer is Choice C, 50–69.

27. **(D)** Of the 100 people in the sample, $48 + 24 = 72$ of them preferred North America or South America. The other $100 - 72 = 28$ people preferred Africa. So, 28 percent of the 100 people in the sample preferred Africa. Thus, approximately 190 respondents (28 percent of the 680 people who chose "another continent") preferred Africa. Finally, Africa was the choice of $190 \div 1855 = 0.102$, or 10.2 percent of all the students.

**Since 36.7 percent of all the people preferred a continent other than Europe or Asia ($680 \div 1855 = 0.367$) and, from the explanation above, 28 percent of those people preferred Africa, we have 28 percent of 36.7 percent = $0.28 \times 0.367 = 0.103 = 10.3$ percent.

28. **(150)** Since Len got $100, the other three shared the remaining $900. If x represents Jim's share, then Kim got $2x$ and Ben got $3x$. Then $900 = x + 2x + 3x = 6x \Rightarrow x = 150$.

29. **(2500)** If 99.6 percent of the people tested did not have the disease, then 0.4 percent of them did have the disease. If $x =$ the number or people tested, then

$$10 = 0.004x \Rightarrow x = 10 \div 0.004 = 2,500$$

30. **(20)** From the bar graph, we see that 25 percent of the 400 campers were from California. Since 25 percent of 400 is 100, there were 100 Californians at the camp. From the circle graph, we see that 20 percent of the campers from California played basketball. So the number of basketball players from California at the camp in 2015 was 20 percent of 100, which equals 20.

31. **(323)** We are told that 12 of the campers from Utah and 18 of the campers from Washington played basketball. From the solution to question 30, we know that 20 of the campers from California played basketball. Finally, from the bar graph we know that $20\% + 15\% + 6\% + 4\% = 45\%$ of the 400 campers, or 180, collectively, were from Oregon, Nevada, Arizona, and New Mexico. Since 15 percent of those 180 campers played basketball, that accounts for 27 more basketball players. Finally, the total number of basketball players was $12 + 18 + 20 + 27 = 77$; so $400 - 77 = 323$ campers played a sport other than basketball.

ANSWER SHEET
Practice Test 2

Section 1: Reading

1. Ⓐ Ⓑ Ⓒ Ⓓ
2. Ⓐ Ⓑ Ⓒ Ⓓ
3. Ⓐ Ⓑ Ⓒ Ⓓ
4. Ⓐ Ⓑ Ⓒ Ⓓ
5. Ⓐ Ⓑ Ⓒ Ⓓ
6. Ⓐ Ⓑ Ⓒ Ⓓ
7. Ⓐ Ⓑ Ⓒ Ⓓ
8. Ⓐ Ⓑ Ⓒ Ⓓ
9. Ⓐ Ⓑ Ⓒ Ⓓ
10. Ⓐ Ⓑ Ⓒ Ⓓ
11. Ⓐ Ⓑ Ⓒ Ⓓ
12. Ⓐ Ⓑ Ⓒ Ⓓ
13. Ⓐ Ⓑ Ⓒ Ⓓ

14. Ⓐ Ⓑ Ⓒ Ⓓ
15. Ⓐ Ⓑ Ⓒ Ⓓ
16. Ⓐ Ⓑ Ⓒ Ⓓ
17. Ⓐ Ⓑ Ⓒ Ⓓ
18. Ⓐ Ⓑ Ⓒ Ⓓ
19. Ⓐ Ⓑ Ⓒ Ⓓ
20. Ⓐ Ⓑ Ⓒ Ⓓ
21. Ⓐ Ⓑ Ⓒ Ⓓ
22. Ⓐ Ⓑ Ⓒ Ⓓ
23. Ⓐ Ⓑ Ⓒ Ⓓ
24. Ⓐ Ⓑ Ⓒ Ⓓ
25. Ⓐ Ⓑ Ⓒ Ⓓ
26. Ⓐ Ⓑ Ⓒ Ⓓ

27. Ⓐ Ⓑ Ⓒ Ⓓ
28. Ⓐ Ⓑ Ⓒ Ⓓ
29. Ⓐ Ⓑ Ⓒ Ⓓ
30. Ⓐ Ⓑ Ⓒ Ⓓ
31. Ⓐ Ⓑ Ⓒ Ⓓ
32. Ⓐ Ⓑ Ⓒ Ⓓ
33. Ⓐ Ⓑ Ⓒ Ⓓ
34. Ⓐ Ⓑ Ⓒ Ⓓ
35. Ⓐ Ⓑ Ⓒ Ⓓ
36. Ⓐ Ⓑ Ⓒ Ⓓ
37. Ⓐ Ⓑ Ⓒ Ⓓ
38. Ⓐ Ⓑ Ⓒ Ⓓ
39. Ⓐ Ⓑ Ⓒ Ⓓ

40. Ⓐ Ⓑ Ⓒ Ⓓ
41. Ⓐ Ⓑ Ⓒ Ⓓ
42. Ⓐ Ⓑ Ⓒ Ⓓ
43. Ⓐ Ⓑ Ⓒ Ⓓ
44. Ⓐ Ⓑ Ⓒ Ⓓ
45. Ⓐ Ⓑ Ⓒ Ⓓ
46. Ⓐ Ⓑ Ⓒ Ⓓ
47. Ⓐ Ⓑ Ⓒ Ⓓ

Section 2: Writing and Language

1. Ⓐ Ⓑ Ⓒ Ⓓ
2. Ⓐ Ⓑ Ⓒ Ⓓ
3. Ⓐ Ⓑ Ⓒ Ⓓ
4. Ⓐ Ⓑ Ⓒ Ⓓ
5. Ⓐ Ⓑ Ⓒ Ⓓ
6. Ⓐ Ⓑ Ⓒ Ⓓ
7. Ⓐ Ⓑ Ⓒ Ⓓ
8. Ⓐ Ⓑ Ⓒ Ⓓ
9. Ⓐ Ⓑ Ⓒ Ⓓ
10. Ⓐ Ⓑ Ⓒ Ⓓ
11. Ⓐ Ⓑ Ⓒ Ⓓ

12. Ⓐ Ⓑ Ⓒ Ⓓ
13. Ⓐ Ⓑ Ⓒ Ⓓ
14. Ⓐ Ⓑ Ⓒ Ⓓ
15. Ⓐ Ⓑ Ⓒ Ⓓ
16. Ⓐ Ⓑ Ⓒ Ⓓ
17. Ⓐ Ⓑ Ⓒ Ⓓ
18. Ⓐ Ⓑ Ⓒ Ⓓ
19. Ⓐ Ⓑ Ⓒ Ⓓ
20. Ⓐ Ⓑ Ⓒ Ⓓ
21. Ⓐ Ⓑ Ⓒ Ⓓ
22. Ⓐ Ⓑ Ⓒ Ⓓ

23. Ⓐ Ⓑ Ⓒ Ⓓ
24. Ⓐ Ⓑ Ⓒ Ⓓ
25. Ⓐ Ⓑ Ⓒ Ⓓ
26. Ⓐ Ⓑ Ⓒ Ⓓ
27. Ⓐ Ⓑ Ⓒ Ⓓ
28. Ⓐ Ⓑ Ⓒ Ⓓ
29. Ⓐ Ⓑ Ⓒ Ⓓ
30. Ⓐ Ⓑ Ⓒ Ⓓ
31. Ⓐ Ⓑ Ⓒ Ⓓ
32. Ⓐ Ⓑ Ⓒ Ⓓ
33. Ⓐ Ⓑ Ⓒ Ⓓ

34. Ⓐ Ⓑ Ⓒ Ⓓ
35. Ⓐ Ⓑ Ⓒ Ⓓ
36. Ⓐ Ⓑ Ⓒ Ⓓ
37. Ⓐ Ⓑ Ⓒ Ⓓ
38. Ⓐ Ⓑ Ⓒ Ⓓ
39. Ⓐ Ⓑ Ⓒ Ⓓ
40. Ⓐ Ⓑ Ⓒ Ⓓ
41. Ⓐ Ⓑ Ⓒ Ⓓ
42. Ⓐ Ⓑ Ⓒ Ⓓ
43. Ⓐ Ⓑ Ⓒ Ⓓ
44. Ⓐ Ⓑ Ⓒ Ⓓ

ANSWER SHEET
Practice Test 2

Section 3: Math (No Calculator)

1. Ⓐ Ⓑ Ⓒ Ⓓ
2. Ⓐ Ⓑ Ⓒ Ⓓ
3. Ⓐ Ⓑ Ⓒ Ⓓ
4. Ⓐ Ⓑ Ⓒ Ⓓ

5. Ⓐ Ⓑ Ⓒ Ⓓ
6. Ⓐ Ⓑ Ⓒ Ⓓ
7. Ⓐ Ⓑ Ⓒ Ⓓ
8. Ⓐ Ⓑ Ⓒ Ⓓ

9. Ⓐ Ⓑ Ⓒ Ⓓ
10. Ⓐ Ⓑ Ⓒ Ⓓ
11. Ⓐ Ⓑ Ⓒ Ⓓ
12. Ⓐ Ⓑ Ⓒ Ⓓ

13. Ⓐ Ⓑ Ⓒ Ⓓ

14.

15.

16.

17.

ANSWER SHEET
Practice Test 2

Section 4: Math (Calculator)

1. Ⓐ Ⓑ Ⓒ Ⓓ
2. Ⓐ Ⓑ Ⓒ Ⓓ
3. Ⓐ Ⓑ Ⓒ Ⓓ
4. Ⓐ Ⓑ Ⓒ Ⓓ
5. Ⓐ Ⓑ Ⓒ Ⓓ
6. Ⓐ Ⓑ Ⓒ Ⓓ
7. Ⓐ Ⓑ Ⓒ Ⓓ
8. Ⓐ Ⓑ Ⓒ Ⓓ

9. Ⓐ Ⓑ Ⓒ Ⓓ
10. Ⓐ Ⓑ Ⓒ Ⓓ
11. Ⓐ Ⓑ Ⓒ Ⓓ
12. Ⓐ Ⓑ Ⓒ Ⓓ
13. Ⓐ Ⓑ Ⓒ Ⓓ
14. Ⓐ Ⓑ Ⓒ Ⓓ
15. Ⓐ Ⓑ Ⓒ Ⓓ
16. Ⓐ Ⓑ Ⓒ Ⓓ

17. Ⓐ Ⓑ Ⓒ Ⓓ
18. Ⓐ Ⓑ Ⓒ Ⓓ
19. Ⓐ Ⓑ Ⓒ Ⓓ
20. Ⓐ Ⓑ Ⓒ Ⓓ
21. Ⓐ Ⓑ Ⓒ Ⓓ
22. Ⓐ Ⓑ Ⓒ Ⓓ
23. Ⓐ Ⓑ Ⓒ Ⓓ
24. Ⓐ Ⓑ Ⓒ Ⓓ

25. Ⓐ Ⓑ Ⓒ Ⓓ
26. Ⓐ Ⓑ Ⓒ Ⓓ
27. Ⓐ Ⓑ Ⓒ Ⓓ

28.

29.

30.

31.

READING TEST

60 MINUTES, 47 QUESTIONS

Turn to Section 1 of your answer sheet to answer the questions in this section.

> **Directions:** Following each of the passages (or pairs of passages) below are questions about the passage (or passages). Read each passage carefully. Then, select the best answer for each question based on what is stated in the passage (or passages) and in any graphics that may accompany the passage.

Questions 1–10 are based on the following passage.

In the following excerpt from Jane Austen's Pride and Prejudice, *the members of the Bennet family react to news of the impending marriage of Lydia, the youngest Bennet daughter, to Mr. Wickham, with whom she had run away, to her family's shock and distress. Elizabeth, second of the Bennet daughters and the novel's heroine, is in love with Mr. Darcy and worries how this unexpected marriage may affect her relationship with him.*

A long dispute followed this declaration;
but Mr. Bennet was firm: it soon led to
another; and Mrs. Bennet found, with
Line amazement and horror, that her husband
(5) would not advance a guinea[1] to buy clothes
for his daughter. He protested that she
should receive from him no mark of affection
whatever, on the occasion of her marriage.
Mrs. Bennet could hardly comprehend it.
(10) That his anger could be carried to such a
point of inconceivable resentment, as to
refuse his daughter a privilege, without
which her marriage would scarcely seem
valid, exceeded all that she could believe
(15) possible. She was more alive to the disgrace,
which the want of new clothes must reflect
on her daughters nuptials, than to any sense
of shame at her eloping and living with
Wickham, a fortnight before they took place.

(20) Elizabeth was now most heartily sorry that
she had, from the distress of the moment,
been led to make Mr. Darcy acquainted
with their fears for her sister, for since her
marriage would so shortly give the proper
(25) termination to the elopement, they might
hope to conceal its unfavorable beginning
from all those who were not immediately on
the spot.
She had no fear of its spreading farther,
(30) through his means. There were few people
on whose secrecy she would have more
confidently depended; but at the same
time, there was no one, whose knowledge
of a sister's frailty would have mortified
(35) her so much. Not, however, from any fear
of disadvantage from it, individually to
herself, for at any rate, there seemed a gulf
impassable between them. Had Lydia's
marriage been concluded on the most
(40) honorable terms, it was not to be supposed
that Mr. Darcy would connect himself with a
family, where to every other objection would
now be added, an alliance and relationship
of the nearest kind with the man whom he so
(45) justly scorned.
From such a connection she could not
wonder that he should shrink. The wish of
procuring her regard, which she had assured
herself of his feeling in Derbyshire, could
(50) not in rational expectation survive such
a blow as this. She was humbled, she was

GO ON TO THE NEXT PAGE

grieved; she repented, though she hardly knew of what. She became jealous of his esteem, when she could no longer hope to
(55) be benefitted by it. She wanted to hear of him, when there seemed the least chance of gaining intelligence. She was convinced that she could have been happy with him, when it was no longer likely they should meet.

(60)   What a triumph for him, as she often thought, that the proposals which she had proudly spurned only four months ago would now have been gladly and gratefully received! He was as generous, she doubted not, as the
(65) most generous of his sex. But while he was mortal, there must be a triumph.

  She began now to comprehend that he was exactly the man who, in disposition and talents, would most suit her. His
(70) understanding and temper, though unlike her own, would have answered all her wishes. It was an union that must have been to the advantage of both—by her ease and liveliness, his mind might have been
(75) softened, his manners improved; and from his judgment, information, and knowledge of the world, she must have received benefit of greater importance.

  But no such happy marriage could
(80) now teach the admiring multitude what connubial felicity really was. An union of different tendency, and precluding the possibility of the other, was soon to be formed in their family.

(85)   How Wickham and Lydia were to be supported in tolerable independence, she could not imagine. But how little of permanent happiness could belong to a couple who were only brought together
(90) because their passions were stronger than their virtue, she could easily conjecture.

---

[1] A British coin.

1. Which choice best describes what takes place in the opening paragraph?

(A) One character acquiesces readily to a decision made by another character.
(B) Two characters reach a compromise about how to treat a third character.
(C) One character expresses dismay over another character's proposed course of action.
(D) Two characters agree to disagree about the resolution of a crisis involving them both.

2. The "privilege" that Mr. Bennet refuses to grant his daughter (line 12) is the privilege of

(A) marrying Mr. Wickham.
(B) buying a new wardrobe.
(C) running away from home.
(D) seeing her mother and sisters.

3. As used in line 15, "alive" most nearly means

(A) living.
(B) in existence.
(C) aware.
(D) animated.

4. Which outcome does Mrs. Bennet most fear from her husband's decision?

(A) It will legally invalidate their daughter's wedding.
(B) It will place a financial burden on the newlyweds.
(C) It will reflect badly upon the family's reputation.
(D) It will disrupt the nuptial arrangements.

5. Which choice provides the best evidence for the answer to the previous question?

   (A) Lines 1–6 ("A long . . . daughter")
   (B) Lines 6–8 ("He protested . . . marriage")
   (C) Lines 10–15 ("That his anger . . . possible")
   (D) Lines 15–19 ("She was . . . place")

6. The expression "a sister's frailty" (line 34) refers to Elizabeth's sister's

   (A) delicate health since birth.
   (B) reluctance to marry a man whom others disdain.
   (C) fear of being considered an old maid.
   (D) moral weakness in running away with a man.

7. According to the passage, Mr. Darcy feels contempt for

   (A) the hastiness of Lydia's marriage.
   (B) secrets that are entrusted to him.
   (C) Elizabeth's confession to him.
   (D) Lydia's future husband.

8. Which choice provides the best evidence for the answer to the previous question?

   (A) Lines 20–23 ("Elizabeth was now . . . sister")
   (B) Lines 30–32 ("There were . . . depended")
   (C) Lines 35–38 ("Not, however . . . between them")
   (D) Lines 38–45 ("Had Lydia's . . . scorned")

9. As used in line 57, "intelligence" most nearly means

   (A) intellect.
   (B) news.
   (C) comprehension.
   (D) espionage.

Questions 10–18 are based on the following passage.

The following passage is taken from Cosmosapiens: Human Evolution from the Origin of the Universe *by John Hands. Published in 2015, the book is an interdisciplinary study of current theories about the origin and evolution of matter, life, consciousness, and humankind.*

According to the Big Bang model, if you run back the clock of the universe's expansion it produces a singularity.

Line
(5)
singularity: a hypothetical region in space-time where gravitational forces cause a finite mass to be compressed into an infinitely small volume and therefore to have infinite density, and where space-time becomes infinitely distorted.

(10) In 1970 Stephen Hawking and Roger Penrose published a mathematical proof that there must have been a Big Bang singularity provided only that the General Theory of Relativity is correct and that the universe (15) contains as much matter as we observe. This became the orthodox theory.

Hawking, however, has since changed his mind and maintains that the singularity disappears once quantum effects are taken (20) into account.

Hence, was there a singularity at the Big Bang, and if there was, what do we know about the universe at this point?

Orthodox theory about the origin of (25) matter invokes the Standard Theory of Particle Physics to explain how matter was created from the energy explosively released at the Big Bang.

According to the Standard Theory (30) an elementary particle of matter can spontaneously materialize from an energy

GO ON TO THE NEXT PAGE

PRACTICE TEST 2

field together with its symmetrically opposite particle of antimatter, which has the same mass and spin but opposite charge. Thus

(35) an electron (negatively charged) appears with a positron (positively charged), and a proton (positively charged) with an antiproton (negatively charged). In laboratory conditions these particles and

(40) antiparticles can be separated and "bottled" by electromagnetic fields. However, without externally applied fields the lifetime of such elementary particles and antiparticles is minute, typically 10^{-21} seconds, after which

(45) they annihilate each other in an explosive burst of energy—a reverse of the process by which they are made.

Hence the Inflationary Big Bang model needed to explain the following: (a) since any

(50) particle-antiparticle pairs produced were pressed next to each other in the extremely high density following the Big Bang, why did all the particles and antiparticles not annihilate each other; and (b) since we know

(55) that an enormous amount of matter exists in the universe, where is the corresponding amount of antimatter?

Speculations about anti-galaxies gave way to observational estimates of the ratio

(60) of photons to protons in the universe, which is roughly two billion to one. Hence, theorists concluded, for every one billion antiparticles—antiprotons and positrons— that materialized from the Big Bang energy

(65) release, one billion and one corresponding particles—protons and electrons—must have materialized. Each billion particles and antiparticles annihilated one another in an explosive burst of energy producing

(70) two billion photons, which are quanta of electromagnetic energy. According to the Big Bang model it is this energy, now expanded

and cooled, that forms the cosmic microwave background radiation energy we see today.

(75) The billionth-and-one orphan protons and electrons survived and subsequently combined to make all the matter—all the planets, solar systems, galaxies, and galactic clusters—of the universe.

(80) However, this conflicted with the Standard Theory of Particle Physics, which said that, according to the law of symmetry, only pairs of particles and antiparticles could materialize.

(85) The reason for this conflict remained a problem for theoretical physicists until the mid-1970s, when they conjectured that at the extremely high temperatures of the Big Bang three fundamental forces of nature—

(90) electromagnetic, weak nuclear, and strong nuclear—are just different aspects of the same force. The theorists devised different mathematical models, which they called grand unified theories (GUTs), although

(95) experimental data has disproved the original GUT and so far has failed to validate any others. These conjectures allow every type of elementary particle to interact with, and transmute into, every other particle. As a

(100) consequence, theoretical physicists believed that the symmetry between matter and antimatter need not be conserved. They adjusted the Standard Model to provide for asymmetry. This adjustment doesn't predict

(105) the amount of asymmetry but, like the charge of an electron, requires observational measurements that are then inserted into the model so that the model becomes consistent with observation.

(110) Despite the hopes expressed in the 1970s, matter-antimatter asymmetry in the laboratory wasn't detected and measured until 2001, when B mesons and anti-B

GO ON TO THE NEXT PAGE

mesons were produced and survived for
(115) 10^{-21} seconds. However, the asymmetry
observed was not large enough to explain
the estimated ratio of energy to matter in the
universe.

10. Details in the passage indicate that scientists
attempt to prove theories in particle physics
using **all** of the following methods EXCEPT

(A) ignoring nontheoretical observations.
(B) devising mathematical models.
(C) describing laboratory findings.
(D) testing conjectures and hypotheses.

11. As used in line 25, "invokes" most nearly
means

(A) declares in effect.
(B) entreats.
(C) cites.
(D) summons.

12. It can most reasonably be inferred that
outside of a physics laboratory, electrons and
positrons are **not**

(A) magnetically attracted to one another.
(B) naturally contained and kept apart.
(C) an important part of the Big Bang model.
(D) annihilated in bursts of energy.

13. Which choice provides the best evidence for
the answer to the previous question?

(A) Lines 1–3 ("According . . . singularity")
(B) Lines 34–38 ("Thus an electron . . .
(negatively charged)")
(C) Lines 38–41 ("In laboratory . . . fields")
(D) Lines 71–74 ("According . . . we see
today")

14. According to the passage, physicists adjusted
the Standard Theory of Particle Physics to
explain how

(A) the Big Bang could occur at lower
temperatures than previously believed.
(B) the universe was formed when particles
and antiparticles annihilated one
another.
(C) protons and positrons need each other in
order to exist.
(D) matter and antimatter with asymmetrical
mass can survive.

15. It can most reasonably be inferred that the
production of matter-antimatter asymmetry
in a physics laboratory

(A) furnished scientists with an estimated
ratio of energy to matter in the universe.
(B) supported scientists' adjustment of the
Standard Model to allow for asymmetry.
(C) encouraged scientists in the U.S. to
definitively discount the Big Bang theory.
(D) prevented scientists from measuring
symmetry in the same physics laboratory.

16. Which choice provides the best evidence for
the answer to the previous question?

(A) Lines 80–84 ("However, . . . materialize")
(B) Lines 97–99 ("These conjectures . . .
particle")
(C) Lines 110–113 ("Despite the hope . . . until
2001")
(D) Lines 115–118 ("However, . . . universe")

GO ON TO THE NEXT PAGE

17. As used in line 103, "provide" most nearly means

(A) allow.
(B) support.
(C) equip.
(D) offer.

18. As described in the passage, the relationship between measurements made through observation and theoretical models is best described by which of the following statements?

(A) Observational measurements can support, prove, or disprove theoretical models.
(B) Observational measurements require theoretical models to make them valid.
(C) Theoretical models cannot be proven or disproven by observational measurements.
(D) Theoretical models can be inserted into observational measurements to support them.

Questions 19–28 are based on the following passage.

The following passage is taken from How Soccer Explains the World: An Unlikely Theory of Globalization *by Franklin Foer.*

Pundits have employed many devices to sum up America's cultural divisions. During the 1980s they talked about the
Line "culture war"—the battle over textbooks,
(5) abortion, prayer in school, affirmative action, and funding of the arts. This war pitted conservative defenders of tradition and morality against liberal defenders of modernity and pluralism. More recently
(10) this debate has been described as the split between "red and blue America"—the two colors used to distinguish partisan preference in maps charting presidential election voting. But another explanatory
(15) device has yet to penetrate political science departments and the national desks of newspapers. There exists an important cleavage between the parts of the country that have adopted soccer as its pastime and
(20) the places that haven't. And this distinction lays bare an underrated source of American cultural cleavage: globalization.

Other countries have greeted soccer with relative indifference. The Indian
(25) subcontinent and Australia come to mind. But the United States is perhaps the only place where a loud portion of the population actively disdains the game, even campaigns against it. This anti-soccer lobby believes, in
(30) the words of *USA Today*'s Tom Weir, "that hating soccer is more American than apple pie, driving a pickup, or spending Saturday afternoons channel surfing with the remote control." Weir exaggerates the pervasiveness

GO ON TO THE NEXT PAGE

(35) of this sentiment. But the cadre of soccer haters has considerable sway.

Not just pundits buried in the C Section of the paper, but people with actual power believe that soccer represents a genuine
(40) threat to the American way of life. The former Buffalo Bills quarterback Jack Kemp, one of the most influential conservatives of the 1980s, a man once mentioned in the same breath as the presidency, holds this view. In
(45) 1986, he took to the floor of the United States Congress to orate against a resolution in support of an American bid to host the World Cup. Kemp intoned, "I think it is important for all those young out there, who someday
(50) hope to play real football, where you throw it and kick it and run with it and put it in your hands, a distinction should be made that football is democratic, capitalism, whereas soccer is a European socialist [sport]."
(55) Allen Barra, a sports writer for the *Wall Street Journal*, argues, "Americans are such suckers when it comes to something with a European label that many who have resisted thus far would give in to trendiness and push
(60) their kids into youth soccer programs." And more than that, he worries that the soccer enthusiasts want the U.S. to "get with the rest of the world's program."

As Barra makes clear, the anti-soccer
(65) lobby really articulates a phobia of globalization.

It's not surprising that Americans should split like this over soccer. Globalization increasingly provides the subtext for the
(70) American cultural split. This isn't to say America violently or even knowingly divides over globalization. But after September 11 opened new debates over foreign policy, two camps in American politics have
(75) clearly emerged. One camp believes in the essential tenets of the globalization religion as preached by European politicians, that national governments should defer to institutions like the UN and WTO. These
(80) tend to be people who opposed the war in Iraq. And this opinion reflects a worldview. These Americans share cultural values with Europeans—an aggressive secularism, a more relaxed set of cultural mores that
(85) tolerates gays and pot smoking—which isn't surprising, considering that these Americans have jobs and tourist interests that put them in regular contact with the other side of the Atlantic. They consider themselves to be part
(90) of a cosmopolitan culture that transcends national boundaries.

On the other side, there is a group that believes in American exceptionalism, an idea that America's history and singular
(95) form of government has given the nation a unique role to play in the world; that the US should be above submitting to international laws and bodies. They view Europeans as degraded by their lax attitudes, and
(100) worry about the threat to American culture posed by secular tolerance. With so much relativism seeping into the American way of life, they fret that the country has lost the self-confidence to make basic moral
(105) judgments, to condemn evil. Soccer isn't exactly pernicious, but it's a symbol of the US junking its tradition to "get with the rest of the world's program."

There are many conservatives who hate
(110) relativism and still adore soccer. But it's not a coincidence that the game has become a small touchstone in this culture war.

GO ON TO THE NEXT PAGE

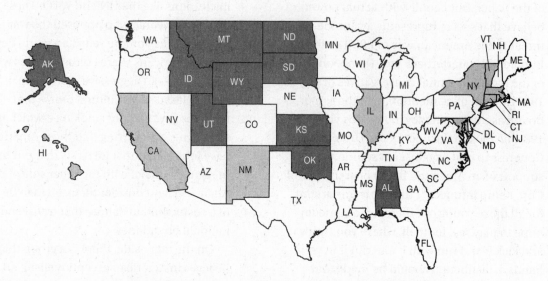

Figure 1. Map of the 10 most strongly Democratic (Blue)
and Republican (Red) states in 2015 (based on data from Gallup)

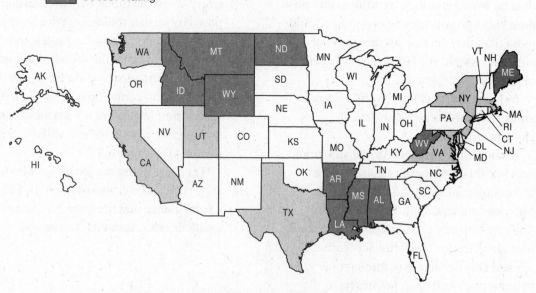

Figure 2. Map of the 10 most strongly soccer loving
and hating states in 2014 (based on data from Estately)

GO ON TO THE NEXT PAGE

19. The main purpose of the passage is to

(A) explain why some people do not like soccer.
(B) use attitudes toward soccer as a framework for understanding the cultural conflict over globalization.
(C) argue that the increasing popularity of soccer in the U.S. demonstrates that the country is growing more cosmopolitan.
(D) predict whether soccer will be able to surpass other major league sports in popularity in the U.S.

20. In the passage, the author anticipates which of the following objections to his argument?

(A) Some conservatives are fans of soccer.
(B) Soccer is growing in popularity in the U.S.
(C) Soccer is more popular in the U.S. than it is in India and Australia.
(D) The author has confused causation and correlation.

21. Which choice provides the best evidence for the answer to the previous question?

(A) Lines 14–17 ("But another . . . newspapers")
(B) Lines 70–72 ("This isn't . . . globalization")
(C) Lines 89–91 ("They consider . . . boundaries")
(D) Lines 109–112 ("There are . . . war")

22. As used in line 1, "employed" most nearly means

(A) occupied themselves with.
(B) provided work to.
(C) devoted time to.
(D) made use of.

23. The main purpose of the third paragraph (lines 37–54) is to

(A) demonstrate that some political leaders view soccer as a threat to American values.
(B) prove that critics of soccer are extremist pundits motivated by the desire to sell newspapers.
(C) convince readers that soccer is a threat to American values.
(D) explain why Americans like football better than soccer.

24. As used in line 96, "play" most nearly means

(A) take part in.
(B) tamper with.
(C) perform.
(D) compete against.

25. Which choice best supports the author's claim that soccer represents, to some, America's capitulation to globalization?

(A) Lines 3–9 ("During the . . . pluralism")
(B) Lines 9–14 ("More recently . . . voting")
(C) Lines 37–40 ("Not just . . . life")
(D) Lines 60–63 ("And more . . . program")

26. The main idea of the final full paragraph is that

(A) soccer is a threat to traditional American values.
(B) soccer symbolizes acceptance of European influence and values.
(C) rejecting soccer will restore the U.S.'s self-confidence and moral authority.
(D) the U.S. should embrace soccer and become more cosmopolitan in its outlook.

GO ON TO THE NEXT PAGE

27. The map of the strongest Red and Blue states indicates what about the distribution of political beliefs in the U.S.?

(A) Strongly Republican states are distributed evenly throughout the U.S.
(B) Strongly Republican states tend to be clustered in the South.
(C) Strongly Republican states tend to be located away from the coasts.
(D) There are no strongly Democratic states in the Northeast.

28. Considered together, the two maps support which of the following conclusions?

(A) All of the most Democratic-leaning states love soccer.
(B) None of the most Republican-leaning states are interested in soccer.
(C) Some correlation exists between interest in soccer and political beliefs.
(D) No correlation exists between interest in soccer and political beliefs.

Questions 29–37 are based on the following passage.

The following passage is taken from a 2015 National Institute of Environmental Health Sciences study of flavoring chemicals in e-cigarettes.

The World Health Organization (WHO) reports that $3 billion was spent on electronic cigarettes (e-cigarettes) in 2013 in the United
Line States alone, with sales expected to increase
(5) 17-fold in 15 years. Centers for Disease Control (CDC) estimates that 1.78 million children tried e-cigarettes as of 2012, with 160,000 of them reporting that they had not used tobacco cigarettes. E-cigarettes are not
(10) currently regulated; the U.S. Food and Drug Administration (FDA), which has the authority to regulate certain tobacco and nicotine-containing products under the Food, Drug, and Cosmetic Act, has issued a proposed rule
(15) to include e-cigarettes under this Act (FDA 2014). Although the popularity and use of e-cigarettes continues to increase, there is a lack of data on the exposures and potential human health effects of the use of e-cigarettes.
(20) Concerns regarding e-cigarettes primarily focus on nicotine exposure, second-hand exposure, the potential for e-cigarettes to be a gateway to cigarette use, and renormalization/social acceptance
(25) of smoking. Other recent investigations have focused on the chemical content of the e-cigarettes beyond nicotine, with researchers finding that users of e-cigarettes are exposed to carbonyl compounds,
(30) aldehydes, fine particulate matter, metals, propylene glycol, glycerol, formaldehyde, and other additives. However, despite over 7,000 flavors of e-cigarettes currently marketed, there have only been three
(35) published papers that focus on exposure

GO ON TO THE NEXT PAGE

to flavoring chemicals specifically, and one opinion piece in *JAMA* that highlights the potential respiratory health effects from using flavored e-cigarettes. The use of (40) flavorings in food products gained public attention in the early 2000s because of reports of serious lung disease in microwave popcorn workers. The flavoring chemicals involved were on the Generally Recognized (45) As Safe (GRAS) list that applies only to ingestion, but exposures were occurring via inhalation and very little was known about potential inhalation hazards of these chemicals at that time. In May 2000, eight (50) persons who had previously worked at a microwave-popcorn processing plant were reported to have severe bronchiolitis obliterans, an irreversible loss of pulmonary function that can become so severe that (55) the only treatment option may be a lung transplant. Researchers from the National Institute of Occupational Safety and Health (NIOSH) Division of Respiratory Disease Studies conducted an investigation at the (60) facility where the impacted workers were employed. NIOSH determined that workers at this plant had greater than two times the expected rates of chronic cough, shortness of breath, asthma, and chronic bronchitis, (65) and non-smokers had over 10 times the expected prevalence of airway obstruction. A strong association was found between this excess of lung disease, including bronchiolitis obliterans, and airborne (70) exposures to butter-flavoring chemicals in the facility. Diacetyl was the most prominent chemical in the butter flavorings. Workers in the area where diacetyl-containing butter-flavoring was added into heated (75) mixing vats were exposed to volatilized flavor chemicals and a significant, positive dose response relationship was identified. Based on its occurrence in microwave

popcorn manufacturing plants, bronchiolitis (80) obliterans (and some related respiratory diseases of the small airways) became commonly known as "Popcorn Lung."

Diacetyl is contained in a variety of flavors in addition to butter-flavor (Table (85) 1; OSHA 2010), and its use is not limited to microwave popcorn facilities or food flavoring production facilities. Diacetyl, 2,3-pentanedione (a structurally related replacement for diacetyl), and acetoin are (90) used in the manufacture of many other foods for a wide range of flavors beyond butter flavorings (e.g., caramel, butterscotch, pina colada, strawberry). Many of these same flavors are common in e-cigarette flavor (95) cartridges, and are often sold with names that we consider to be potentially appealing to children, teenagers, and young adults: Cupcake, Fruit Squirts, Waikiki Watermelon, Cotton Candy, Tutti Frutti, Double Apple (100) Hookah, Blue Water Punch, Oatmeal Cookie and Alien Blood. Further, e-cigarettes utilize a battery-driven nicotine delivery system in which an atomizer produces an aerosol (and vapors of evaporated liquids) through the (105) heating of e-cigarette liquids contained in replaceable cartridges or refillable wells.

Based on the widespread use of these food flavors across many industries and knowledge that specific chemicals/ (110) artificial flavors were developed to mimic certain natural flavors commonly used in e-cigarettes, we hypothesized that these compounds are likely used in the manufacturing of flavored e-cigarettes. We (115) sought to expand the state of knowledge on flavoring chemicals in e-cigarettes with a particular focus on e-cigarettes sold by the largest cigarette companies and also on those flavors that we deemed would be appealing (120) to children, teenagers, and young adults.

GO ON TO THE NEXT PAGE

Table 1. Flavors that contain diacetyl according to OSHA*

Flavor Type	Flavors in This Group
Dairy flavorings	butter, cheese, cream cheese, cheesecake, milk, yogurt, ice cream, egg, ranch dressing, sour cream, buttermilk
Brown flavorings	butterscotch, caramel, vanilla, coffee, tea, toffee, chocolate, cocoa, cocoa butter, maple, brown sugar, marshmallow, peanut butter, praline, hazelnut, other nut flavors
Fruit flavorings	strawberry, cranberry, raspberry, boysenberry, other berry flavors, fruit flavors—nearly any kind (e.g., banana, apple, grape, pear), cider, tomato
Alcohol flavorings	brandy, rum, whiskey, tequila, piña colada
Miscellaneous flavorings	nutmeg, honey, graham cracker, vinegar, meat flavors

*OSHA, 2010

29. The primary purpose of the passage is to

   (A) evaluate the research that led to the manufacture of a product.
   (B) present the reasons for the creation of a data-gathering project.
   (C) document the background of a medical discovery.
   (D) explain the methods scientists use to evaluate environmental hazards.

30. The authors' attitude toward e-cigarettes is best described as one of

   (A) amazement at their surging popularity.
   (B) concern over their possible deleterious effects.
   (C) appreciation of their increasing financial impact
   (D) dismay at their forthcoming governmental regulation.

31. Which choice provides the best evidence for the answer to the previous question?

   (A) Lines 1–5 ("The World Health . . . years")
   (B) Lines 5–9 ("Centers . . . cigarettes")
   (C) Lines 9–16 ("E-cigarettes . . . (FDA 2014)")
   (D) Lines 16–19 ("Although . . . e-cigarettes")

32. As used in line 30, "fine" most nearly means

   (A) superior.
   (B) in good health.
   (C) powdery.
   (D) bright and clear.

33. In the second paragraph (lines 20–82), the authors most likely refer to current research papers in order to

   (A) suggest a need.
   (B) challenge a hypothesis.
   (C) explain an outcome.
   (D) describe a phenomenon.

34. The authors most likely use the account of the discovery of serious lung disease in microwave popcorn workers to call attention to the

   (A) potential dangers involved in the inhalation of supposedly harmless chemicals.
   (B) progress made by NIOSH's Division of Respiratory Disease Studies in identifying environmental hazards.
   (C) increased usefulness of the Generally Recognized As Safe list of food ingredients.
   (D) necessity for the regulation of working conditions in microwave-popcorn processing plants.

35. Which choice provides the best evidence for the answer to the previous question?

   (A) Lines 39–43 ("The use . . . workers")
   (B) Lines 43–49 ("The flavoring . . . time")
   (C) Lines 71–72 ("Diacetyl . . . flavorings")
   (D) Lines 83–87 ("Diacetyl . . . facilities")

36. As used in line 67, "association" most nearly means

   (A) organization.
   (B) connection.
   (C) cooperation.
   (D) friendship.

37. The chart following the passage offers evidence that the flavoring chemical diacetyl

   (A) is the most prominent chemical in butter flavorings.
   (B) becomes volatilized when added into heated mixing vats.
   (C) contributes to the spread of the respiratory disease bronchiolitis obliterans.
   (D) is used in the manufacture of a wide range of flavored products.

GO ON TO THE NEXT PAGE

Questions 38–47 are based on the following passages.

The following passages are taken from the writings of two of America's most eminent black leaders. The first comes from a speech delivered by Booker T. Washington at the Cotton States and International Exposition in Atlanta in 1895; the second, from The Souls of Black Folk *by W.E.B. du Bois, published in 1903.*

Passage 1

To those of the white race who look to the incoming of those of foreign birth and strange tongue and habits for the prosperity
Line of the South, were I permitted I would
(5) repeat what I say to my own race, "Cast down your bucket where you are." Cast it down among the eight millions of Negroes whose habits you know, whose fidelity and love you have tested in days when to have
(10) proved treacherous meant the ruin of your firesides. Cast down your bucket among these people who have, without strikes and labor wars, tilled your fields, cleared your forests, builded your railroads and cities,
(15) and brought forth treasures from the bowels of the earth, and helped make possible this magnificent representation of the progress of the South. Casting down your bucket among my people, helping and encouraging them
(20) as you are doing on these grounds, and to education of head, hand, and heart, you will find that they will buy your surplus land, make blossom the waste places in your fields, and run your factories. While doing this, you
(25) can be sure in the future, as in the past, that you and your families will be surrounded by the most patient, faithful, law-abiding, and unresentful people that the world has seen. As we have proved our loyalty to you in the
(30) past, in nursing your children, watching by

the sick-bed of your mothers and fathers, and often following them with tear-dimmed eyes to their graves, so in the future, in our humble way, we shall stand by you with a
(35) devotion that no foreigner can approach, ready to lay down our lives, if need be, in defense of yours, interlacing our industrial, commercial, civil, and religious life with yours in a way that shall make the interests
(40) of both races one. In all things that are purely social we can be as separate as the fingers, yet one as the hand in all things essential to mutual progress.

Passage 2

Mr. Washington represents in Negro
(45) thought the old attitude of adjustment and submission; but adjustment at such a peculiar time as to make his programme unique. This is an age of unusual economic development, and Mr. Washington's
(50) programme naturally takes an economic cast, becoming a gospel of Work and Money to such an extent as apparently almost completely to overshadow the higher aims of life. Moreover, this is an age when the more
(55) advanced races are coming in closer contact with the less developed races, and the race-feeling is therefore intensified; and Mr. Washington's programme practically accepts the alleged inferiority of the Negro races.
(60) Again, in our own land, the reaction from the sentiment of war time has given impetus to race-prejudice against Negroes, and Mr. Washington withdraws many of the high demands of Negroes as men and American
(65) citizens. In other periods of intensified prejudice, all the Negro's tendency to self-assertion has been called forth; at this period a policy of submission is advocated. In the history of nearly all other races and peoples
(70) the doctrine preached at such crises has been

GO ON TO THE NEXT PAGE

that manly self-respect is worth more than lands and houses, and that a people who voluntarily surrender such respect, or cease striving for it, are not worth civilizing.

(75)   In answer to this, it has been claimed that the Negro can survive only through submission. Mr. Washington distinctly asks that black people give up, at least for the present, three things,—

(80)   First, political power,
        Second, insistence on civil rights,
        Third, higher education of Negro youth,
        —and concentrate all their energies on industrial education, the accumulation of
(85) wealth, and the conciliation of the South. This policy has been courageously and insistently advocated for over fifteen years, and has been triumphant for perhaps ten years. As a result of this tender of the palm-
(90) branch, what has been the return? In these years there have occurred:

    1. The disfranchisement of the Negro.
    2. The legal creation of a distinct status of civil inferiority for the Negro.
(95) 3. The steady withdrawal of aid from institutions for the higher training of the Negro.

        These movements are not, to be sure, direct results of Mr. Washington's
(100) teachings; but his propaganda has, without a shadow of doubt, helped their speedier accomplishment. The question then comes: Is it possible, and probable, that nine millions of men can make effective progress
(105) in economic lines if they are deprived of political rights, made a servile caste, and allowed only the most meager chance for developing their exceptional men? If history and reason give any distinct answer to these
(110) questions, it is an emphatic No.

38. The author of Passage 1 argues that Southern whites should prefer black workers to "those of foreign birth" because

(A) they were owed compensation for having been enslaved.
(B) they were more numerous.
(C) they would be more loyal and self-sacrificing.
(D) they would be better educated.

39. Which choice provides the best evidence for the answer to the previous question?

(A) Lines 1–6 ("To those . . . you are")
(B) Lines 11–18 ("Cast down . . . the South")
(C) Lines 24–28 ("While doing . . . has seen")
(D) Lines 29–40 ("As we . . . one")

40. The author of Passage 1 uses the phrase, "Cast down your bucket where you are," as a

(A) metaphor for white Southerners' employing and doing business with black people.
(B) literal reference to the types of physical labor performed by black Americans.
(C) figure of speech demonstrating that progress results from hard work.
(D) symbol of the hard work that would be required to improve the status of blacks.

41. As used in line 44, "represents" most nearly means

(A) exemplifies.
(B) appears for.
(C) depicts as.
(D) constitutes.

GO ON TO THE NEXT PAGE

PRACTICE TEST 2

42. As used in line 51, "cast" most nearly means

(A) company.
(B) throw.
(C) character.
(D) mold.

43. The author of Passage 2 argues that black Americans are unlikely to make economic progress

(A) without Mr. Washington's "programme."
(B) as a result of racial prejudice.
(C) if they are denied political rights and education.
(D) if they are too assertive in demanding their rights.

44. Which choice provides the best evidence for the answer to the previous question?

(A) Lines 48–54 ("This is . . . of life")
(B) Lines 68–74 ("In the history . . . civilizing")
(C) Lines 89–97 ("As a result . . .of the Negro")
(D) Lines 102–110 ("The question . . . emphatic No")

45. Which choice best describes the structure of the second paragraph of Passage 2?

(A) A problem is described, its causes are analyzed, and a solution is suggested.
(B) A position is summarized, its consequences are described, and the position is repudiated.
(C) A principle is stated, opposing principles are offered, and a consensus is reached.
(D) A historical period is described, and its influence is evaluated.

46. Which choice best states the relationship between the two passages?

(A) Passage 2 attacks a strategy that Passage 1 strongly advocates.
(B) Passage 2 urges caution regarding a strategy that Passage 1 describes in favorable terms.
(C) Passage 2 provides additional examples in support of an argument made in Passage 1.
(D) Passage 2 explains the reasons for the effectiveness of the strategy advocated in Passage 1.

47. The authors of both passages would most likely agree with which of the following statements about the position of blacks in the South at the turn of the twentieth century?

(A) They were making rapid progress in achieving economic equality.
(B) They needed education in order to achieve progress.
(C) They could improve their position most rapidly by prioritizing economic advancement over civil rights.
(D) They could improve their position most rapidly by prioritizing civil rights over economic advancement.

STOP

If there is still time remaining, you may review your answers.

PRACTICE TEST 2

WRITING AND LANGUAGE TEST

35 MINUTES, 44 QUESTIONS

Turn to Section 2 of your answer sheet to answer the questions in this section.

> **Directions:** Questions follow each of the passages below. Some questions ask you how the passage might be changed to improve the expression of ideas. Other questions ask you how the passage might be altered to correct errors in grammar, usage, and punctuation. One or more graphics accompany some passages. You will be required to consider these graphics as you answer questions about editing the passage.
>
> There are three types of questions. In the first type, a part of the passage is underlined. The second type is based on a certain part of the passage. The third type is based on the entire passage.
>
> Read each passage. Then, choose the answer to each question that changes the passage so that it is consistent with the conventions of standard written English. One of the answer choices for many questions is "NO CHANGE." Choosing this answer means that you believe the best answer is to make no change in the passage.

Questions 1–11 are based on the following passage and supplementary material.

Investing

Most workers today are responsible for their own retirement savings. Because of the general lack of financial education, many feel over their head and decide to avoid taking chances with their investments. There are certainly merits to a risk-averse approach in personal finance. **❶** As Warren Buffett one of the greatest investors of all time once said, "The first rule is not to lose. The second rule is not to forget the first rule." Nonetheless, Buffett did not become famous for *not* risking money; every day, he puts tens of billions of his own dollars on the line in the stock market (**❷** because after countless hours of research), and the average worker would be wise to follow a similar approach.

1. (A) NO CHANGE
   (B) As Warren Buffett—one of the greatest investors of all time once
   (C) As Warren Buffett—one of the greatest investors of all time—once
   (D) As Warren Buffett, one of the greatest investors of all time: once

2. (A) NO CHANGE
   (B) albeit
   (C) since
   (D) consequently

GO ON TO THE NEXT PAGE

For Deposits in U.S. Accounts in January, 2016, with Less than $100,000

Type of Account	Average U.S. Financial Institution Interest Rate (%)
Savings	0.06
Interest Checking	0.04
Money Market	0.08
1 month CD	0.06
3 month CD	0.08
6 month CD	0.12
12 month CD	0.21
36 month CD	0.49
60 month CD	0.80

Source: *FDIC.gov*

A common place to store money is a standard bank savings account, and it pains me dearly to see so many people err on the side of caution. Consider that a common annual interest rate on such an account is **3** 0.04 percent, which means that an account with several hundred dollars will accrue only a few cents over the course of an entire year! **4** It seems that the whole world is content to surrender, hard-earned money, to organizations unwilling to compensate them fairly for the privilege.

What I advocate, **5** instead, is to invest that money in relatively low-risk mutual funds, which are compilations of often upwards of one

3. Which of the following is consistent with the information in the accompanying table?

(A) NO CHANGE
(B) 0.06 percent
(C) 0.08 percent
(D) 0.12 percent

4. (A) NO CHANGE
(B) It seems that the whole world is content to surrender hard-earned money to organizations unwilling to compensate them fairly for the privilege.
(C) It seems that the whole world is content to surrender hard-earned money, to organizations unwilling to compensate them fairly for the privilege.
(D) It seems that the whole world is content to surrender hard-earned money to organizations, unwilling to compensate, them fairly for the privilege.

5. (A) NO CHANGE
(B) likewise
(C) replacingly
(D) furthermore

GO ON TO THE NEXT PAGE

hundred stocks run by qualified professionals. The reasoning for this is simple: it ❻ had incorporated Warren Buffett's credo of loss avoidance with a healthy opportunity for capital gains. With a large cross-section of the overall stock market, an investor insulates herself against unwelcome market volatility. And, unlike in a savings account, she stands to earn wholesome gains over the long run. ❼ Her gains could be large as long as she invests for a great period of time.

Contrary to the old naysayer's warning that the stock market is "nothing but legalized gambling," ❽ casino gambling is in fact legal in only a handful of states. To wit, from the one-hundred-year period from December 31, 1914, until January 2, 2015, the Dow Jones Industrial Average has had an average annual growth rate of 5.95 percent. That is 119 times greater than an investor would receive in a standard savings account, and that includes the market meltdowns of 1929, the dot-com bubble, and the 2008 housing crisis! Moreover, that 5.95 percent is just an average, which is akin to selecting stocks completely at random. ❾ Avid, educated investors have been known to attain gains more than twice that over the long run with thorough research and diligent decision-making.

❿ For the many different reasons I have heretofore provided, I propose to you today that the average investor isn't so much risk-averse as he is *profit-averse*. The opportunity is there, so stop throwing away money and ⓫ seizing the bull market by its horns!

6. (A) NO CHANGE
(B) incorporated
(C) incorporate
(D) incorporates

7. The author is considering deleting the underlined sentence. Should it be removed?
(A) Yes, because it repeats the idea expressed in the preceding sentence.
(B) Yes, because it distracts from the general idea of the paragraph.
(C) No, because it provides helpful supporting details to the author's argument.
(D) No, because it outlines a key reason for long-term investing.

8. Which of the following would provide the most effective and specific contrast in the sentence while being consistent with the paragraph as a whole?
(A) NO CHANGE
(B) wise investors realize that optimism is a more useful attitude.
(C) decades of double-digit losses in many stocks prove otherwise.
(D) the stock market has posted consistent profits since its inception.

9. (A) NO CHANGE
(B) Avid educated investors
(C) Avid, educated, investors
(D) Avid; educated; investors

10. (A) NO CHANGE
(B) While this all may be important
(C) Thus
(D) To the large corporations and to middle-sized companies

11. (A) NO CHANGE
(B) seize
(C) seized
(D) had seized

GO ON TO THE NEXT PAGE

Questions 12–22 are based on the following passage.

Folktales

The first African slaves to arrive in the United States **⓬** was captured and brung to Virginia in 1619, beginning a nearly two-hundred-fifty-year era of American slavery. The inhumane imprisonment, callous trade, and cruel forced labor of human beings peaked in the early nineteenth century after the invention of the cotton gin in 1793. Then, finally, in **⓭** 1865, two years after President Lincoln declared slaves free in his Emancipation Proclamation, the Thirteenth Amendment officially abolished slavery. The barbaric treatment and squalid conditions under institutionalized slavery are now well documented in a myriad of historical texts, slave narratives, films, and literary sources. **⓮** Moreover, they are found in a plethora of written works. What begets less attention are the oral records of enslavement and of those enslaved—the African American folktales told in Black communities during plantation times or after emancipation.

⓯ Folktales have a long history of oral renderings. Oral performances, most often, rely on call-and-response dynamics, involving the audience in the very storytelling itself, and are characterized by repetitions, hesitations, and a

12. (A) NO CHANGE
    (B) was captured and brought
    (C) were captured and brung
    (D) were captured and brought

13. (A) NO CHANGE
    (B) 1865, two years after President Lincoln declares slaves free in his Emancipation Proclamation the
    (C) 1865 two years after President Lincoln declared slaves free in his Emancipation Proclamation the
    (D) 1865 two years after President Lincoln declared slaves free, in his Emancipation Proclamation, the

14. The author is considering deleting the underlined sentence. Should the author make this deletion?

    (A) Yes, because it is irrelevant to the focus of the paragraph.
    (B) Yes, because it repeats ideas already stated in the paragraph.
    (C) No, because it gives details to elaborate on the previous sentence.
    (D) No, because it explains the main point of the essay.

15. Which of the following would best introduce this paragraph and provide a transition from the previous paragraph?

    (A) NO CHANGE
    (B) An oral performance involves the audience quite a bit.
    (C) Emancipation was a key moment in American history.
    (D) Slavery was the original sin of the United States.

GO ON TO THE NEXT PAGE

range of voices. The griot, or storyteller, might scream, **16** shout, speak with a lisp sing, or dance while encouraging spontaneous improvisation by active listeners. The audience's participation cannot be undervalued. Folktales are often told multiple times in multiple ways on a variety of occasions and, in this way, are created and recreated to the audience's preferences. Thus, the community decides which storytelling devices stick: which communal references become parts of the tale, **17** . It is easy to imagine, then, how folktales are constantly changing and being revised to fit the needs of the current generation. The very language of African American folktales evolves as Creoles and dialects change over time and space.

18 Because of this, some things remain constant. African American folktales transcend mere entertainment, acting, instead, as a vital response to the exploitation and deprivation of an uprooted people. The stories do not rely on the traditional beginning, middle, and end structure, but **19** evokes a sense of continuity, of remaining unfinished, resembling a series rather than a single presentation. In this way, the very structure of folktales **20** reflects the perseverance

16. (A) NO CHANGE
    (B) shout speak with a lisp, sing,
    (C) shout, speak with a lisp, sing,
    (D) shout speak, with a lisp, sing

17. Which of the following, if inserted here, would provide the most relevant logical contrast to conclude the sentence?

    (A) and which interesting ideas are included
    (B) and which stylistic effects get left behind
    (C) and which parts of the story are added
    (D) and which scientific descriptions are omitted

18. (A) NO CHANGE
    (B) Additionally,
    (C) Consequently,
    (D) Yet,

19. (A) NO CHANGE
    (B) evoke
    (C) evoking
    (D) to evoke

20. (A) NO CHANGE
    (B) reflect
    (C) for reflecting
    (D) reflection

GO ON TO THE NEXT PAGE

of African peoples and traditions despite centuries of colonialism. **㉑** These rambunctious tales reveal much more than the nonsensical and fictive exaggerations of the culture in which they originate. **㉒** On the other hand, African American folktales teach crucial lessons about being Black in a system of White supremacy, and give breath to expressive resilience and creativity.

21. The author is considering inserting the following wording to begin the sentence that immediately follows (adjusting the capitalization accordingly):

"From *Brer Rabbit* to *Anancy*, the trickster spider,"

Should the author make this insertion?

(A) Yes, because it provides an elaboration by giving specific examples of the "tales."
(B) Yes, because it gives scholarly analysis of the plots of famous African stories.
(C) No, because the paragraph has already provided the names of several African folktales.
(D) No, because stories with these titles clearly have no place in modern literature.

22. (A) NO CHANGE
(B) In fact,
(C) While,
(D) For the sake of emphasis,

GO ON TO THE NEXT PAGE

Questions 23–33 are based on the following passage and supplementary material.

Gulag

If the title of this passage is unfamiliar and unrecognizable to you, you are, sadly, not alone. Gulag refers to a system of mass forced labor across the Soviet Union that lasted from 1918 until 1953, subjecting an estimated 18 million people to slave labor in concentration camps— **㉓** a number a little more than twice as much as the number of German deaths during all of World War II. That number is almost as unbelievable as the absence of the Gulag in Western popular consciousness. While the Holocaust and Adolf Hitler occupy a notoriety that reflect their atrocities, the Gulag and names like Vladimir Lenin, Leonid Brezhnev, and Joseph Stalin are rarely discussed, sometimes utterly unknown—a phenomenon made more appalling by the fact that Stalin's death toll exceeds **㉔** Hitler.

㉕ Since the network of labor camps traces its origins to Czarist Russia, the camps truly evolved after the Russian Revolution. In the early twentieth century, Lenin began imprisoning potential opponents, naming and subsequently arresting "enemies" of the state. **㉖** The camps, expanded rapidly, with the rise of Joseph Stalin in the 1920s. Stalin embraced the camps as a means of speeding up industrialization within the Soviet Union, establishing them as central to the economy. In almost five hundred camps **㉗** where people were forced to be against their will, the Gulag's millions of victims worked in logging, mining, manufacturing, farming, and all other aspects of labor. Millions of others were exiled—usually because of their political affiliation or ethnicity— into remote, unlivable areas of the Soviet Union where they perished from starvation and extreme climates.

23. Which of the following statements is supported by the information in the accompanying graphs?

(A) NO CHANGE
(B) a number substantially more than triple the number of German deaths
(C) a number roughly equivalent to the number of U.S. deaths
(D) a number that is about half of the total number of civilian and military deaths in the Soviet Union

24. (A) NO CHANGE
(B) that of Hitler.
(C) Hitlers.
(D) Hitler's dying.

25. (A) NO CHANGE
(B) While
(C) Because
(D) For

26. (A) NO CHANGE
(B) The camps, expanded rapidly with the rise, of Joseph Stalin in the 1920s.
(C) The camps expanded rapidly, with the rise of Joseph Stalin in the 1920s.
(D) The camps expanded rapidly with the rise of Joseph Stalin in the 1920s.

27. The author is considering deleting the underlined portion from the sentence. Should it be deleted?

(A) Yes, because it mischaracterizes the nature of the camps.
(B) Yes, because it restates an already implicit idea.
(C) No, because it provides details in support of the topic sentence of the paragraph.
(D) No, because it considers a likely objection from the reader.

GO ON TO THE NEXT PAGE

Anne Applebaum, columnist and scholar, argues that the widespread ignorance and the general dismissal of the Gulag's crimes against humanity **28** result from a hesitation to condemn communist ideologies that sound good on paper. In contrast to Nazi ideals of racial supremacy, communism's emphasis on equality and its alignment to Marxism **29** seems desirable. Despite the fact that Soviet Union communism *looked* a lot different than it *sounded* in the 1930s and 1940s, many found it difficult to rebuke a system founded on principles that they themselves supported. Moreover, to acknowledge Stalin's crimes would be to accept that our World War II ally, a country that suffered approximately **30** 3,000,000 total deaths during the conflict, was perhaps just as evil.

28. (A) NO CHANGE
    (B) results from
    (C) resulting
    (D) result

29. (A) NO CHANGE
    (B) seeming
    (C) seem
    (D) to seem

30. Which of the following is an accurate statement based on the information in the graphs?

    (A) NO CHANGE
    (B) 8,000,000
    (C) 11,000,000
    (D) 23,000,000

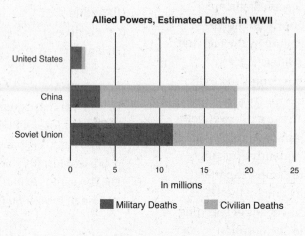

Allied Powers, Estimated Deaths in WWII

In millions

■ Military Deaths   ■ Civilian Deaths

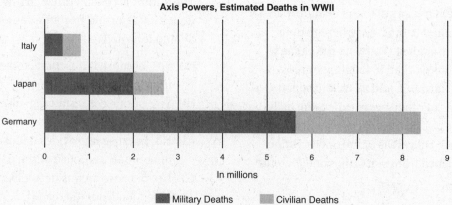

Axis Powers, Estimated Deaths in WWII

In millions

■ Military Deaths   ■ Civilian Deaths

GO ON TO THE NEXT PAGE

The camps supposedly disappeared with Stalin's death **31** in 1953 instead, they evolved into political camps that existed well into the 1970s—smaller, less harsh, and not nearly as integral to the economy, **32** but still reminiscent of their antecedent. With their actual extinction at the end of the 1970s, information about the Gulag administration and slave system became more widely accessible. **33** The lessons of history are difficult to ignore.

31. (A) NO CHANGE
    (B) in 1953: instead they,
    (C) in 1953; instead, they
    (D) in 1953, instead they

32. (A) NO CHANGE
    (B) and
    (C) thus
    (D) effectively

33. Which of the following provides the most effective, specific, and relevant conclusion to the essay?

    (A) NO CHANGE
    (B) Why is it, then, that we all know Nazi Germany but shrug cluelessly at the Gulag?
    (C) The deaths from the Gulag were difficult to fathom.
    (D) Who are we to suppose that we could know what actually transpired in the past?

GO ON TO THE NEXT PAGE

Questions 34–44 are based on the following passage.

Everyday Physics

(1)

One morning, I was walking along the side of the road in a residential district when I saw a car going down the middle of the street. **34** It was tossing newspapers out of both sides of his car onto all the driveways in the subdivision. I made sure that I avoided the car (and newspapers) as he passed.

(2)

As I continued along the road, I began to notice the newspapers **35** lying on the driveways. In every case, the papers were located in the exact center of the driveway. This guy was the Michael Jordan of newspaper delivery. All the way down the road this centered landing spot was replicated. **36** Newspapers, although being rapidly replaced by tablets and computers, still are widely read.

(3)

I teach physics in high school and I use this newspaper delivery problem every year when we begin the module on the Laws of Motion or Kinematics. I provide rolled newspapers and we go down to the football field. **37** The football field is where our high school team won its last district championship. The faster athletes run down the center of the field and toss them between two orange cones, which represent the entrances to the driveways. **38** Nobody, is able to replicate the newspaper persons precision.

34. (A) NO CHANGE
    (B) He
    (C) They
    (D) The driver

35. (A) NO CHANGE
    (B) laying
    (C) lied
    (D) had lain

36. Which of the following would provide the best conclusion to this paragraph?

    (A) NO CHANGE
    (B) It was as if a walking delivery person had neatly dropped them right in the middle.
    (C) The road was only two lanes wide, much smaller than the highway I traveled on later that day.
    (D) It was interesting to see all of this take place.

37. The author is considering deleting the underlined sentence from the passage. Should it be removed?

    (A) Yes, because it is irrelevant to the focus of the paragraph.
    (B) Yes, because it repeats information already stated earlier in the essay.
    (C) No, because it provides helpful details to support the essay's primary argument.
    (D) No, because it explains why the class was on the football field.

38. (A) NO CHANGE
    (B) Nobody is able to replicate, the newspaper persons precision.
    (C) Nobody is able, to replicate, the newspaper person's precision.
    (D) Nobody is able to replicate the newspaper person's precision.

GO ON TO THE NEXT PAGE

(4)

During the next few weeks, **39** and we discuss the mathematics of projectile motion and return to the question of newspapers after some experience in problem solving. Some of the more astute and curious students begin to see that as long as the newspapers are tossed out horizontally and perpendicular to the motion of the car, **40** it will all hit the pavement at the same time, no matter how hard they throw them. **41** Thus, for the papers to hit the middle of the driveway each and every time, all the newspaper delivery person has to do is **42** annihilate his toss at a distance from the driveway so that the time it takes for the car to move forward along the road to the center of the driveway will exactly match the time it takes for the paper to fall from the release height to the pavement. Knowing that athletes in a **43** variety of sports, baseball, basketball, football, lacrosse, etc.; develop this sort of hand-eye-distance-motion coordination, it soon becomes clear to all that this was just another example of the ability of a human to perform difficult tasks with objects in motion. **44**

STOP

If there is still time remaining, you may review your answers.

39. (A) NO CHANGE
    (B) but
    (C) while
    (D) DELETE the underlined portion

40. (A) NO CHANGE
    (B) they
    (C) you
    (D) one

41. (A) NO CHANGE
    (B) However
    (C) Nevertheless
    (D) Notwithstanding

42. (A) NO CHANGE
    (B) destroy
    (C) execute
    (D) crush

43. (A) NO CHANGE
    (B) variety of sports—baseball, basketball, football, lacrosse, etc.—develop this
    (C) variety of sports: baseball, basketball, football, lacrosse etc. develop this
    (D) variety of sports baseball, basketball, football, lacrosse, etc.—develop this

44. The author wishes to place the following paragraph in the passage.

    "I discussed this observation from my stroll at breakfast, and nobody really shared my puzzlement about what I had seen. Perhaps the driver was just lucky that day. Or had he incorporated the laws of physics in a very practical way into his daily task?"

    Where would it most logically be placed?

    (A) Before paragraph 1
    (B) Before paragraph 2
    (C) Before paragraph 3
    (D) Before paragraph 4

MATH TEST (NO CALCULATOR)

25 MINUTES, 17 QUESTIONS

Turn to Section 3 of your answer sheet to answer the questions in this section.

Directions: For questions 1–13, solve each problem and choose the best answer from the given choices. Fill in the corresponding circle on your answer sheet. For questions 14–17, solve each problem and enter your answer in the grid on your answer sheet.

Notes:

- Calculators are **NOT PERMITTED** in this section.
- All variables and expressions represent real numbers unless indicated otherwise.
- All figures are drawn to scale unless indicated otherwise.
- All figures are in a plane unless indicated otherwise.
- Unless indicated otherwise, the domain of a given function is the set of all real numbers x for which the function has real values.

REFERENCE INFORMATION

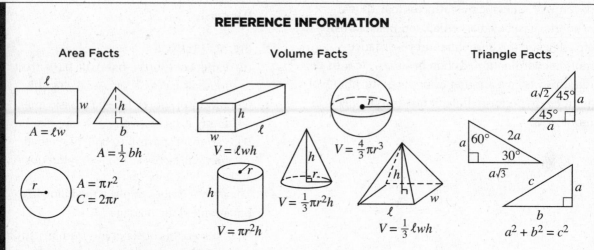

The arc of a circle contains 360°.
The arc of a circle contains 2π radians.
The sum of the measures of the angles in a triangle is 180°.

GO ON TO THE NEXT PAGE

1. If $7d + 5 = 5d + 7$, what is the value of d?

   (A) -1
   (B) 1
   (C) 5
   (D) 7

$$|2x - 3| < 5$$

2. Which of the following inequalities is equivalent to the inequality above?

   (A) $x < 1$
   (B) $x < 4$
   (C) $-4 < x < 2$
   (D) $-1 < x < 4$

3. If the lines whose equations are $ax + by = c$ and $dx + ey = f$ are parallel, which of the following statements must be true?

   (A) $a = d$
   (B) $b = e$
   (C) $ad = be$
   (D) $ae = bd$

4. Stuart deposited D dollars in a non-interest-bearing bank account. If Stuart withdrew d dollars from the account every week and made no additional deposits, how much money, in dollars, was in the account w weeks after it was opened?

   (A) $D - wd$
   (B) $(D - w)d$
   (C) $D - \dfrac{w}{d}$
   (D) $D - \dfrac{d}{w}$

$$[(3x + y) + (x + 3y)]^2$$

5. Which of the following expressions is equivalent to the expression above?

   (A) $4(x^2 + y^2)$
   (B) $16(x^2 + y^2)$
   (C) $4(x + y)^2$
   (D) $16(x + y)^2$

6. Newton's Law of Universal Gravitation states that any two bodies in the universe attract each other with a force (F), measured in newtons, that is directly proportional to the product of their masses (m_1 and m_2), measured in kilograms, and inversely proportional to the square of the distance between them (r), measured in meters. The equation that expresses this is $F = G\dfrac{m_1 m_2}{r^2}$, where G is a constant. Which of the following expresses r in terms of F, G, m_1, and m_2?

   (A) $r = \sqrt{F}Gm_1m_2$
   (B) $r = \sqrt{FGm_1m_2}$
   (C) $r = \dfrac{Gm_1m_2}{\sqrt{F}}$
   (D) $r = \sqrt{\dfrac{Gm_1m_2}{F}}$

7. Which of the following statements is true concerning the equation below?

$$2(7 - 3x) = 6(3 - x) - 4$$

   (A) The equation has no solutions.
   (B) The equation has one positive solution.
   (C) The equation has one negative solution.
   (D) The equation has infinitely many solutions.

GO ON TO THE NEXT PAGE

8. If $f(x) = x^{\frac{1}{2}} + x^{\frac{1}{4}}$, what is the value of $f(16)$?

   (A) 6
   (B) 8
   (C) 12
   (D) 32

9. If a and b are positive numbers, which of the following is equivalent to $\left(\dfrac{a^{-2}}{b^{-2}}\right)^{-\frac{1}{2}}$?

   (A) $-\dfrac{a}{b}$

   (B) $\dfrac{a}{b}$

   (C) $-\sqrt{\dfrac{a}{b}}$

   (D) $\sqrt{\dfrac{a}{b}}$

10. At Rinaldo's Record Shop, Rinaldo sells used CDs for \$5.00 and used DVDs for \$11.00. One day from 9:00 A.M. to 6:00 P.M., Rinaldo sold a total of 65 CDs and DVDs and took in \$475. Which of the following systems of equations could be used to determine the number of CDs, c, and the number of DVDs, d, that Rinaldo sold during that 9-hour period?

   (A) $c + d = 475$
        $5c + 11d = 65$

   (B) $c + d = 65$
        $5c + 11d = \dfrac{475}{8}$

   (C) $c + d = 65$
        $5c + 11d = 475$

   (D) $c + d = 65$
        $5c + 11d = 475 \times 8$

11. Which of the following are the solutions of the equation $x^2 + 2x = 4$?

   (A) $1 + \sqrt{5}$ and $1 - \sqrt{5}$
   (B) $-1 + \sqrt{5}$ and $-1 - \sqrt{5}$
   (C) $1 + \sqrt{5}$ and $-1 - \sqrt{5}$
   (D) $-1 + \sqrt{5}$ and $1 - \sqrt{5}$

12. An insurance company is offering a Supplemental Retirement Account (SRA) that has a guaranteed compounded annual rate of return of 4 percent per year. What type of relationship is there between the value of a client's account and the number of years from the time the client purchased the SRA?

   (A) A linear relationship whose graph has a slope of 0.04.
   (B) A linear relationship whose graph has a slope of 4.
   (C) An exponential relationship in which greater account values correspond to a greater number of years.
   (D) A quadratic relationship in which lower account values correspond to a lesser number of years.

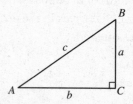

13. In right triangle ABC above, which of the following is equal to $(\sin A)(\cos A)(\tan A)$?

   (A) abc

   (B) $\dfrac{ab}{c^2}$

   (C) $\dfrac{a^2}{c^2}$

   (D) $\dfrac{b^2}{c^2}$

GO ON TO THE NEXT PAGE

Grid-in Response Directions

In questions 14–17, first solve the problem, and then enter your answer on the grid provided on the answer sheet. The instructions for entering your answers follow.

- First, write your answer in the boxes at the top of the grid.
- Second, grid your answer in the columns below the boxes.
- Use the fraction bar in the first row or the decimal point in the second row to enter fractions and decimals.

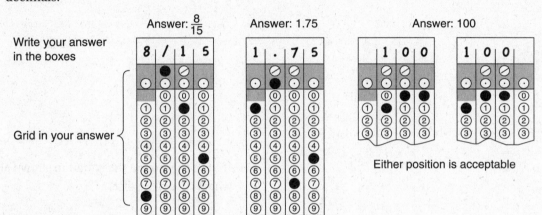

Write your answer in the boxes

Grid in your answer

Answer: $\frac{8}{15}$ Answer: 1.75   Answer: 100

Either position is acceptable

- Grid only one space in each column.
- Entering the answer in the boxes is recommended as an aid in gridding but is not required.
- The machine scoring your exam can read only what you grid, so you **must grid-in your answers correctly to get credit**.
- If a question has more than one correct answer, grid-in only one of them.
- The grid does not have a minus sign; so no answer can be negative.
- A mixed number *must* be converted to an improper fraction or a decimal before it is gridded.

  Enter $1\frac{1}{4}$ as 5/4 or 1.25; the machine will interpret 11/4 as $\frac{11}{4}$ and mark it wrong.

- **All decimals must be entered as accurately as possible.** Here are three acceptable ways of gridding

$$\frac{3}{11} = 0.272727\ldots$$

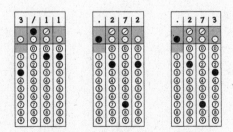

- Note that rounding to .273 is acceptable because you are using the full grid, but you would receive **no credit** for .3 or .27, because they are less accurate.

14. Consider the graph whose equation is $(x-4)^2 + (y-2)^2 = 4$. If m represents the number of times the graph intersects the y-axis and if n represents the number of times the graph intersects the x-axis, what is the value of $m + n$?

$$2y \geq x - 10$$
$$3y \leq x + 18$$

16. If $(9, b)$ is a solution of the system of inequalities shown above, what is the greatest possible value of b?

15. If $5\sqrt{x} + 1 = 46$, what is the value of x?

$$12(3x - 4) = 15(4 - 3x)$$

17. If x is a solution of the equation shown above, what is the value of x?

STOP

If there is still time remaining, you may review your answers.

MATH TEST (CALCULATOR)

45 MINUTES, 31 QUESTIONS

Turn to Section 4 of your answer sheet to answer the questions in this section.

Directions: For questions 1–27, solve each problem and choose the best answer from the given choices. Fill in the corresponding circle on your answer sheet. For questions 28–31, solve each problem and enter your answer in the grid on your answer sheet.

Notes:

■ Calculators **ARE PERMITTED** in this section.
■ All variables and expressions represent real numbers unless indicated otherwise.
■ All figures are drawn to scale unless indicated otherwise.
■ All figures are in a plane unless indicated otherwise.
■ Unless indicated otherwise, the domain of a given function is the set of all real numbers x for which the function has real values.

REFERENCE INFORMATION

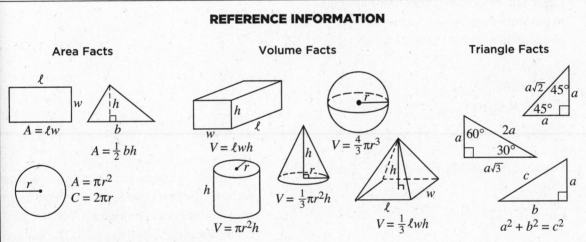

Area Facts

Volume Facts

Triangle Facts

The arc of a circle contains 360°.

The arc of a circle contains 2π radians.

The sum of the measures of the angles in a triangle is 180°.

GO ON TO THE NEXT PAGE

$$C = 2x + 3y$$

1. The equation above expresses the total cost C, in dollars, to purchase x hot dogs and y hamburgers at a snack bar. In the equation, what does the 3 represent?

   (A) The number of hot dogs purchased
   (B) The cost, in dollars, of each hot dog
   (C) The number of hamburgers purchased
   (D) The cost, in dollars, of each hamburger

2. According to a survey taken in 2015 of 5,000 family doctors chosen at random throughout the United States, 1,200 of them had a policy of recommending that all of their patients over the age of 40 have a chest X-ray as part of their annual physical examination. Given that in 2015 there were 209,000 family physicians in the United States, approximately how many of them did not have such a policy?

   (A) 50,000
   (B) 79,000
   (C) 109,000
   (D) 159,000

3. For what value of a is $\frac{3}{5}a - 5 = 11 - \frac{11}{15}a$?

   (A) 12
   (B) 15
   (C) $\frac{9}{12}$
   (D) $\frac{120}{7}$

4. At Twin Pines Camp, the campers are divided into three groups: lions, tigers, and bears. One afternoon, each of the campers chose to participate in one of three activities: baseball, tennis, and swimming. The table below shows the choices, broken down by group, that were made that afternoon.

	Lions	Tigers	Bears	Total
Baseball	17	22	30	69
Tennis	15	26	37	78
Swimming	32	38	10	80
Totals	64	86	77	227

What fraction of the lions and tigers chose an activity other than swimming?

   (A) $\frac{1}{3}$
   (B) $\frac{2}{5}$
   (C) $\frac{1}{2}$
   (D) $\frac{8}{15}$

5. To fix a customer's air conditioner, a repairman charges a flat fee of f dollars, which includes the first hour of his time. For his time in excess of 1 hour, he charges h dollars per hour. One day, he had two jobs. The first job took 2.5 hours, for which his charge was \$238. The second job took 3.25 hours, for which his charge was \$292. What is the value of $f + h$?

   (A) 130
   (B) 152
   (C) 172
   (D) 202

GO ON TO THE NEXT PAGE

6. If y is inversely proportional to x, and $y = 8$ when $x = 4$, what is the value of y when $x = 5$?

    (A) 0.4
    (B) 2.5
    (C) 6.4
    (D) 10

7. On January 12, 2016, the official rate of exchange for 1 United States dollar was 7.81 Egyptian pounds and 0.657 British pounds. On that date, to the nearest hundredth, how many Egyptian pounds could be exchanged for 1 British pound?

    (A) 0.08
    (B) 5.13
    (C) 8.81
    (D) 11.89

8. How many positive integers, n, satisfy the inequality $\frac{1}{5}(7n - 10) < n$?

    (A) 0
    (B) 4
    (C) 5
    (D) Infinitely many

9. There are 12 men on a basketball team. In a game, 5 of them play at any one time. If the game is one hour long and if each man plays exactly the same amount of time, how many minutes does each man play?

    (A) 12
    (B) 24
    (C) 25
    (D) 30

Questions 10 and 11 are based on the following information.

In January 2016, surveys were conducted at each of two colleges—Leeds, which has 1,600 students, and Bryce, which has 2,500 students. In the fall of 2015, each college's football team played eight games, four at home and four away. Each survey asked 200 students how many of their college's home games they had attended. The results of those surveys are tabulated below.

Number of Games	Leeds	Bryce
0	40	80
1	60	50
2	40	40
3	40	30
4	20	0

10. What is the average (arithmetic mean) number of games attended by all of the students in the two surveys?

    (A) 1.0
    (B) 1.3
    (C) 1.4
    (D) 2.0

GO ON TO THE NEXT PAGE

11. Assume that the results of each survey are representative of the total student body at each college. Which of the following statements is most probably true?

(A) More students at Leeds than at Bryce attended at least one game.
(B) Approximately 200 more students at Bryce than at Leeds attended at least one game.
(C) Approximately the same number of students at Bryce and at Leeds attended exactly two games.
(D) The number of students at Leeds who attended three games is approximately equal to the number of students at Bryce who attended two games.

12. On January 1, 2000, Jana opened a retirement savings account with an initial deposit of $2,500. On January 15 and on the 15th of every month thereafter, she deposited $75 into the account. As of July 31, 2005, what was the total amount of money that Jana had deposited into the account?

(A) $5,950
(B) $6,025
(C) $6,625
(D) $7,525

13. In a list of four numbers, each number is 50 percent greater than the preceding number. If the sum of all four numbers is 325, what is the smallest number in the list?

(A) 20
(B) 30
(C) 40
(D) 50

14. In the year 2000, the populations of New York, New Jersey, and Connecticut were approximately 19,000,000, 9,000,000, and 3,450,000, respectively. Their population densities, in people per square mile of land area, were approximately 400, 1,200, and 750, respectively. Which of the following is closest to the total land area, in square miles, of the three states?

(A) 60,000
(B) 65,000
(C) 70,000
(D) 75,000

15. Which of the following expressions is equivalent to $(x + y + 3)(x + y + 3)$?

(A) $(x + y)^2 + 9$
(B) $(x + y)^2 + 6(x + y)$
(C) $(x + y)^2 + 6(x + y) + 9$
(D) $(x + y)^2 + 9(x + y) + 9$

16. If $2.3 - 4.4n \leq 6.7$, what is the least possible value of $2.3 + 4.4n$?

(A) -6.7
(B) -4.4
(C) -2.3
(D) -2.1

GO ON TO THE NEXT PAGE

PRACTICE TEST 2

Year	Number
2009	4
2010	5
2011	10
2012	6
2013	9
2014	12

17. The table above shows the number of races that Nicholas entered each year from 2009 to 2014. In what year did he enter 50 percent more races than the year before?

    (A) 2011
    (B) 2012
    (C) 2013
    (D) 2014

18. A school has 100 varsity athletes: 40 boys and 60 girls, of whom 30 are juniors and 70 are seniors. If 15 junior girls are varsity athletes, how many senior boys are varsity athletes?

    (A) 10
    (B) 15
    (C) 20
    (D) 25

19. If Elaine drove 190 kilometers between 12:00 noon and 3:20 P.M., what was her average speed in kilometers per hour?

    (A) 50
    (B) 54
    (C) 57
    (D) 60

20. Last year at South Hadley High School, 572 students played on at least one varsity team. If the ratio of boys to girls on the teams was 7 to 4, how many of the varsity athletes were girls?

    (A) 143
    (B) 208
    (C) 364
    (D) 429

21. Peter and Robert share an apartment whose rent is $600 a month. Of that amount, Peter pays p dollars and Robert pays r dollars, with $p > r$ since Peter has the larger bedroom. Which of the following expressions represents the percent of the monthly rent that Peter pays?

    (A) $\dfrac{p}{p+r}$

    (B) $\dfrac{100p}{p+r}$

    (C) $\dfrac{600p}{p+r}$

    (D) $\dfrac{p}{600}$

GO ON TO THE NEXT PAGE

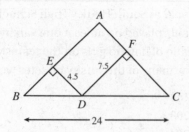

Note: Figure not drawn to scale

22. In triangle ABC in the figure above, $AB = AC$. D is a point on side $\overline{BC}$, and segments $\overline{DE}$ and $\overline{DF}$ are perpendicular to sides $\overline{AB}$ and $\overline{AC}$, respectively. If $DE = 4.5$, $DF = 7.5$, and $BC = 24$, what is CF, rounded to the nearest whole number?

(A) 8
(B) 10
(C) 12
(D) 13

23. If the parabola whose equation is $y = 4x^2 - 8x + 3$ crosses the x-axis at p and q, what is the value of $p + q$?

(A) 0.5
(B) 1
(C) 1.5
(D) 2

24. What is the value of $\dfrac{\left(5^{-\frac{1}{3}}\right)\left(10^{\frac{1}{2}}\right)}{\left(5^{\frac{2}{3}}\right)\left(10^{-\frac{1}{2}}\right)}$?

(A) $\dfrac{1}{50}$

(B) $\dfrac{1}{10}$

(C) $\dfrac{1}{2}$

(D) 2

25. If $y = mx + b$ is the equation of a line that passes through all of the quadrants except Quadrant II, which of the following statements could be true?

I. $m < b$
II. $mb < 0$
III. $m + b = 0$

(A) I and II only
(B) I and III only
(C) II and III only
(D) I, II, and III

26. The graph of line l intersects the y-axis at 12 and passes through the point $(9, 9)$. Which of the following is an equation of a line that is perpendicular to l?

(A) $y = -3x + \dfrac{1}{3}$

(B) $y = -\dfrac{1}{3}x + 3$

(C) $y = \dfrac{1}{3}x - 3$

(D) $y = 3x - \dfrac{1}{3}$

27. Ariella knits sweaters and scarves, and then she sells them online. She sells her scarves for $18 and her sweaters for $75. In December 2015, she sold 40 items for a total of $1,461. How many more scarves than sweaters did Ariella sell that month?

(A) 13
(B) 14
(C) 15
(D) 16

GO ON TO THE NEXT PAGE

Grid-in Response Directions

In questions 28–31, first solve the problem, and then enter your answer on the grid provided on the answer sheet. The instructions for entering your answers follow.

- First, write your answer in the boxes at the top of the grid.
- Second, grid your answer in the columns below the boxes.
- Use the fraction bar in the first row or the decimal point in the second row to enter fractions and decimals.

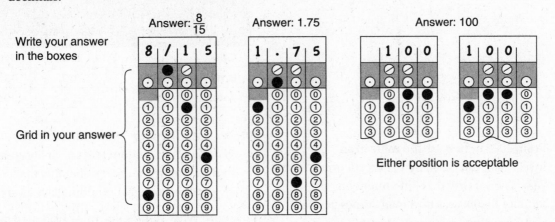

- Grid only one space in each column.
- Entering the answer in the boxes is recommended as an aid in gridding but is not required.
- The machine scoring your exam can read only what you grid, so you **must grid-in your answers correctly to get credit**.
- If a question has more than one correct answer, grid-in only one of them.
- The grid does not have a minus sign; so no answer can be negative.
- A mixed number *must* be converted to an improper fraction or a decimal before it is gridded.

  Enter $1\frac{1}{4}$ as 5/4 or 1.25; the machine will interpret 11/4 as $\frac{11}{4}$ and mark it wrong.

- **All decimals must be entered as accurately as possible.** Here are three acceptable ways of gridding

$$\frac{3}{11} = 0.272727\ldots$$

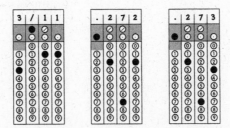

- Note that rounding to .273 is acceptable because you are using the full grid, but you would receive **no credit** for .3 or .27, because they are less accurate.

28. On an architectural blueprint of a house, 0.4 inches represents 3 feet. The shape of the living room of the house is a rectangle whose length and width on the blueprint are 4 inches and 2.4 inches, respectively. What is the actual area, in square feet, of the living room's floor?

Questions 30 and 31 are based on the information below.

A survey of 800 randomly selected high school seniors in Texas asked whether or not the student plays a varsity sport. The results of the survey are tabulated below.

	Plays a Varsity Sport	Does Not Play a Varsity Sport	Total
Girls	136	234	370
Boys	140	290	430
Total	276	524	800

29. From 2000 until 2010, the value of an investment increased by 10 percent every year. The value of that investment on January 1, 2006 was how many times greater than the value on January 1, 2004?

30. Let p represent the probability that a senior girl chosen at random plays a varsity sport, and let q represent the probability that a senior boy chosen at random plays a varsity sport. What is the value of $\frac{p}{q}$, rounded to the nearest hundredth?

31. Assume there are 480,000 high school seniors in Texas and the results of the survey are representative of all seniors in Texas. To the nearest whole number, how many thousands of seniors in Texas play a varsity sport? (For example, if you believe that 50,000 seniors in Texas play a varsity sport, you should grid in 50.)

If there is still time remaining, you may review your answers.

ANSWER KEY
Practice Test 2

Section 1: Reading

1.	C	14.	D	27.	C	40.	A
2.	B	15.	B	28.	C	41.	A
3.	C	16.	B	29.	B	42.	C
4.	C	17.	A	30.	B	43.	C
5.	D	18.	A	31.	D	44.	D
6.	D	19.	B	32.	C	45.	B
7.	D	20.	A	33.	A	46.	A
8.	D	21.	D	34.	A	47.	B
9.	B	22.	D	35.	B		
10.	A	23.	A	36.	B		
11.	C	24.	C	37.	D		
12.	B	25.	D	38.	C		
13.	C	26.	B	39.	D		

Number Correct   _____

Number Incorrect   _____

Section 2: Writing and Language

1.	C	12.	D	23.	A	34.	D
2.	B	13.	A	24.	B	35.	A
3.	B	14.	B	25.	B	36.	B
4.	B	15.	A	26.	D	37.	A
5.	A	16.	C	27.	B	38.	D
6.	D	17.	B	28.	A	39.	D
7.	A	18.	D	29.	C	40.	B
8.	D	19.	B	30.	D	41.	A
9.	A	20.	A	31.	C	42.	C
10.	C	21.	A	32.	A	43.	B
11.	B	22.	B	33.	B	44.	C

Number Correct   _____

Number Incorrect   _____

Section 3: Math (No Calculator)

1. **B**   5. **D**   9. **B**   13. **C**
2. **D**   6. **D**   10. **C**
3. **D**   7. **D**   11. **B**
4. **A**   8. **A**   12. **C**

14. **1**   15. **81**   16. **9**

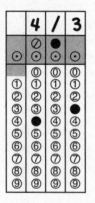

17. **4/3** or **1.33**

or

Number Correct _____

Number Incorrect _____

Section 4: Math (Calculator)

1. **D**	7. **D**	13. **C**	19. **C**	25. **C**
2. **D**	8. **B**	14. **A**	20. **B**	26. **D**
3. **A**	9. **C**	15. **C**	21. **B**	27. **B**
4. **D**	10. **C**	16. **D**	22. **D**	
5. **D**	11. **B**	17. **C**	23. **D**	
6. **C**	12. **D**	18. **D**	24. **D**	

28. **540**   29. **1.21**   30. **1.13**   31. **166**

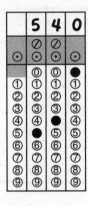   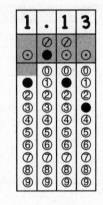

Number Correct _____

Number Incorrect _____

SCORE ANALYSIS

Reading and Writing Test

Section 1: Reading _____ = _____ (A)
　　　　　　　　　　　　　　# correct　　　raw score

Section 2: Writing _____ = _____ (B)
　　　　　　　　　　　　　　# correct　　　raw score

To find your Reading and Writing test scores, consult the chart below: find the ranges in which your raw scores lie and read across to find the ranges of your test scores.

_____ + _____ = _____ (C)
range of reading　　　　range of writing　　　range of reading + writing
test scores　　　　　　　test scores　　　　　　test scores

To find the range of your Reading and Writing Scaled Score, multiply (C) by 10.

Test Scores for the Reading and Writing Sections

Reading Raw Score	Writing Raw Score	Test Score
39–47	39–44	33–38
33–38	33–38	30–32
28–32	28–32	27–29
21–27	22–27	23–27
15–20	17–21	20–23
11–14	13–16	17–20
8–10	9–12	15–17
4–7	5–8	13–15
less than 4	less than 5	8–12

Math Test

Section 3: _____ = _____ (D)
　　　　　　　　　# correct　　　raw score

Section 4: _____ = _____ (E)
　　　　　　　　　# correct　　　raw score

Total Math raw score: (D) + (E) = _____

To find your Math Scaled Score, consult the chart below: find the range in which your raw score lies and read across to find the range for your scaled score.

Scaled Scores for the Math Test

Raw Score	Scaled Score	Raw Score	Scaled Score
39–48	700–760	16–19	450–490
35–38	650–690	12–15	400–440
31–34	600–640	9–11	350–390
25–30	550–590	6–9	300–340
20–24	500–540	less than 6	160–290

ANSWERS EXPLAINED

Section 1: Reading Test

1. **(C)** Mr. Bennet informs his wife that he would not advance any money to enable his daughter to buy new clothes for her wedding. His proposed course of action is to take *no* action; he refuses to give any sign of approval of this elopement. Mrs. Bennet is amazed and horrified by his decision and expresses her dismay at great length.

   Choice A is incorrect. Mrs. Bennet does not acquiesce readily to Mr. Bennet's decision; she protests it vehemently. Choice B is incorrect. The Bennets do not reach a compromise about how to treat their runaway daughter; they remain at odds. Choice D is incorrect. When parties agree to disagree, they resolve their argument by tolerating the other party's position without accepting it. Mrs. Bennet is not reconciled to Mr. Bennet's decision; she continues to be amazed and shocked by it.

2. **(B)** The "privilege" Mr. Bennet refuses his daughter is buying a new wardrobe. In the opening sentence, we learn that Mr. Bennet would not come up with any money ("would not advance a guinea") to buy his daughter new clothes. To Mrs. Bennet, the purchase of new clothes on the occasion of a wedding was a privilege automatically granted the bride.

3. **(C)** Mrs. Bennet was alive to the disgrace that the absence of new wedding garments would bring upon the newlyweds and their family. In other words, she was very *aware* how people would view this slight to the bride. Although "alive" can mean *living* ("kept alive by a respirator"), *in existence* ("Michael Jackson's memory is still alive"), or *animated* ("I come alive when I dance"), that is not the way the word is used in the present context.

4. **(C)** Mrs. Bennet is far more concerned about what the neighbors will think than she is about the virtuousness or sinfulness of Lydia and Wickham's conduct. She worries that, by not providing the customary wedding perks that the neighbors expect brides to receive, her husband is exposing the family to gossip and criticism. In other words, she fears her husband's decision *will reflect badly upon the family's reputation.*

5. **(D)** The final sentence of the opening paragraph makes it clear how little Mrs. Bennet is concerned about her daughter's actual morals and how much she is concerned about keeping up appearances.

6. **(D)** Frailty here is the moral weakness of giving way to temptation and running off to "live in sin" with a man.

7. **(D)** Use the process of elimination to answer this question. Does Mr. Darcy feel contempt for the hastiness of Lydia's marriage? Nothing in the passage indicates that he is even aware yet that Lydia and Wickham are about to be married. You can eliminate Choice A. Does Mr. Darcy feel contempt for secrets that have been entrusted to him? Given Elizabeth's certainty that Darcy would keep the secret she had entrusted to him, it is most unlikely that he would regard those secrets with contempt. You can eliminate Choice B. Does Mr. Darcy feel contempt for Elizabeth's confession to him? There is nothing in the passage to suggest it.

Only Choice D is left. It is the correct answer. Mr. Darcy feels contempt for Lydia's future husband. He has such a negative view of Wickham (deservedly so) that Elizabeth is sure he would never marry into a family to which Wickham belonged.

8. **(D)** The concluding sentence of the third paragraph indicates that Darcy scorned or felt contempt for Lydia's new husband.

9. **(B)** Elizabeth wants to hear of Darcy. What she wants is *news* of the man she has come to love. Although "intelligence" can mean *intellect* ("a scholar of high intelligence"), *comprehension* ("to read with intelligence"), or *espionage* ("military intelligence"), that is not how the word is used in the present context.

10. **(A)** Choice A is correct. Nothing in the passage indicates that scientists attempting to prove theories in particle physics ignore actual ("nontheoretical") observations. Rather, they use observational measurements to prove or disprove their theories.

    Choice B is incorrect. Scientists typically devise mathematical models that they call grand unified theories (GUTs). Therefore, you can eliminate Choice B. Choice C is incorrect. Scientists describe their laboratory findings; see the reference to the 2001 lab findings about matter-antimatter asymmetry. Therefore, you can eliminate Choice C. Choice D is incorrect. The passage as a whole describes how particle physicists constantly test conjectures and hypotheses regarding the Big Bang. Therefore, you can eliminate Choice D. Only Choice A is left. It is the correct answer.

11. **(C)** To say that orthodox theory "invokes" the Standard Theory of Particle Physics to explain things is to say that it cites or refers to the Standard Theory as an authority. Although "invokes" can mean *declares in effect* ("the plaintiff invokes the law of negligence"), *entreats* ("the poet invokes his muse"), or *summons* ("the shaman's chant invokes the spirits") that is not how the word is used in this particular context.

12. **(B)** The passage states that particles and antiparticles "can be separated and 'bottled' by electromagnetic fields" (lines 40–41) in a laboratory setting, but outside of that setting, that is, "without externally applied fields" (line 41–42), the particles annihilate each other within a very short period of time. Choice B is correct because it describes the process of separating and "bottling" the particles.

    Choice A is incorrect. These particles maintain the same relationship to each other whether they are inside or outside of a physics laboratory. Choice C is incorrect. It is the interaction of symmetrical particles that is at the heart of the Big Bang model, which describes a process that occurred outside of a physics laboratory. Choice D is incorrect. Nothing in the passage suggests that electrons and positrons could be annihilated in bursts of energy only in the setting of a physics laboratory. In fact, the passage states that electrons and their corresponding antiparticles (the positrons) annihilated one another in the Big Bang, which definitely did not take place inside a physics laboratory.

13. **(C)** Only Choice C describes the process of separating and containing electrons and positrons, which can occur within a laboratory. Choice A is an introduction to the subject of singularities. Choice B describes the relationship between particles and antiparticles but says nothing about where these relationships are true. Choice D describes the energy that comprises background radiation energy in the universe; it does not focus on what can occur only within a laboratory.

14. **(D)** The Standard Theory of Particle Physics supported the belief that only pairs of particles and antiparticles could materialize, according to the law of symmetry. The energy created by the annihilation of corresponding particles "forms the cosmic microwave background radiation energy we see today" (lines 74–75). However, the author states, "The billionth-and-one orphan protons and electrons survived and subsequently combined to make all the matter—all the planets, solar systems, galaxies, and galactic clusters—of the universe" (lines 75–79), and it is the possibility of these asymmetric protons and electrons that conflicted with the law of symmetry. Physicists therefore adjusted the theory to allow for asymmetry, as stated in Choice D.

15. **(B)** The Big Bang model posits that the energy resulting from the annihilation of symmetrical particles and antiparticles formed the background radiation energy present today, while the "billionth-and-one orphan protons and electrons survived and subsequently combined to make all the matter—all the planets, solar systems, galaxies, and galactic clusters—of the universe" (lines 75–79). This meant that the Standard Theory of Particle Physics, which until that time allowed only for the existence of symmetrical pairs of particles and antiparticles, needed to be adjusted. Choice B describes this result. It is the correct answer. Choice A is contradicted by the last sentence of the passage. There is no support in the passage for the claims made in Choices C and D.

16. **(B)** Choice B describes the hypotheses presented in grand unified theories (GUTs) devised by theorists to explain the conflict resulting from the laboratory findings, which led the theorists to believe that symmetry "need not be conserved" (line 102). In that case, the Standard Theory of Particle Physics had to be adjusted to allow for asymmetry.

Choice A describes the problem presented by the production of matter-antimatter asymmetry in a physics laboratory but not what followed, which was an adjustment to the Standard Theory of Particle Physics. Choice C describes the timeline of the measurement of matter-antimatter asymmetry, and Choice D comments on the laboratory observation of asymmetry, which occurred 30 years after the adjustment of the Standard Theory of Particle Physics.

17. **(A)** The theoretical physicists adjusted the Standard Model to provide or *allow for* asymmetry. Although "provide" can mean *support* ("Bob's life insurance will provide for his family"), *equip* ("provide me with an umbrella") or *offer* ("many websites provide useful information"), that is not how the word is used in the present context.

18. **(A)** The adjustment to the Standard Theory of Particle Physics did not predict the amount of asymmetry between particles and antiparticles, but it established a model that "requires observational measurements that are then inserted into the model so that the model becomes consistent with observation" (lines 106–109). Only Choice A describes this relationship of measurements and models.

19. **(B)** Choice B is correct. In the opening paragraph, the author describes soccer as an "explanatory device" for understanding America's cultural divisions. Choice A is incorrect. Though the passage does propose reasons why some people dislike soccer, it does this in service to another goal—enlightening the reader about other deeper and more significant cultural divisions. Choice C is incorrect. Though the passage associates the love of soccer with a cosmopolitan outlook, it does not claim that soccer is growing

more popular. Choice D is incorrect. The passage does not include any predictions about the future.

20. **(A)** Choice A is correct. At the end of the passage the author anticipates and grants the objection that the correlation between attitudes toward soccer and beliefs about globalization is not perfect—some conservatives (who fear globalization) do appreciate soccer.

   Choice B is incorrect. As noted above, the passage does not include any predictions about the future. Choice C is incorrect. Though the author notes that neither India nor Australia has experienced a backlash against soccer similar to the one in the United States, the passage does not include any comparison of the popularity of soccer in those countries and the United States. Choice D is incorrect. The passage illustrates a correlation but does not go so far as to claim causation. As a result, there is no need for the author to anticipate this objection.

21. **(D)** Choice D is correct. These two sentences anticipate and grant the objection that not all conservatives dislike soccer, while going on to conclude that soccer is still a good standard (or touchstone) by which to measure conservatism. The author would probably say that conservative soccer fans are the exception to the rule.

   Choice A is incorrect. This sentence argues that political scientists and news writers have not yet noticed the connection between soccer and political beliefs. It does not, however, imply that they would object to this theory. Choice B is incorrect. This sentence clarifies the author's claim by explaining that the cultural conflict over globalization may be unconscious. Though this clarification could be an answer to an objection (that there is no cultural conflict over globalization), this cannot be the correct answer because this objection is not included in the list of possibilities in question 20. Choice C is incorrect. This sentence simply describes the beliefs of the liberal side of the cultural battle. It supports the central argument of the passage and does not mention any objection to that argument.

22. **(D)** Choice D is correct. The author of the passage describes how pundits use various devices to explain "America's cultural divisions." Although "employ" can mean to keep *occupied* ("volunteering was a productive way to employ my time"), to *provide work to* ("two cake decorators were employed by the bakery"), or to *devote time to* ("he employed himself with the task of mastering French"), that is not how the word is used in this particular context.

23. **(A)** Choice A is correct. Though the quotation from Jack Kemp is certainly over the top, he is presented as an example of a powerful person who is strongly anti-soccer. Kemp, a former Congressman and presidential candidate, is used to demonstrate that hatred of soccer is espoused by very respectable people, and not just, "pundits buried in the C Section of the paper."

   Choice B is incorrect. Though it begins with a mention of these pundits, the bulk of the paragraph is devoted to demonstrating that more mainstream and powerful people "share these views." Choice C is incorrect. Though the quotation from Jack Kemp argues that soccer undermines traditional American values, it is employed to demonstrate that there are respectable people who have this belief. It is not employed to persuade readers that this is the correct belief. Choice D is incorrect. Though this paragraph, and the passage as a whole, includes arguments against soccer, football is not mentioned.

24. **(C)** Choice C is correct. The passage describes the unique role played or *performed* by America. Although "play" can mean *take part in* ("she plays club soccer most weekends"), *tamper* ("the alarm did not go off because someone had played with the settings"), or *compete against* ("France played Germany in the final round of the international competition"), that is not how the word is used in this particular context.

25. **(D)** Choice D is correct. This quotation from Barra demonstrates that some see the acceptance of soccer, and international sport, as "get(ting) with" (agreeing to) the world's program rather than our own. Soccer is, for people like Barra, a capitulation to globalization.

    Choice A is incorrect. It makes no mention of soccer. Choice B is incorrect. It too makes no mention of soccer. Choice C is incorrect. This sentence argues that some see soccer as a threat to the "American way of life," but it does not identify globalization as the threat. Additionally, it does not frame liking soccer as a capitulation.

26. **(B)** Choice B is correct. This paragraph describes soccer as a symbol of acceptance of or giving in to European values. Saying that the United States is "junking" its tradition and "get(ting) with" the world's program is a colloquial way of describing capitulating to international influence. Additionally, the final sentence of the paragraph states that soccer is a "symbol" of this capitulation.

    Choice A is incorrect. This paragraph argues that conservatives believe that soccer is a threat to traditional American values, but it does not argue that it is an actual threat to those values. Choice C is incorrect. Though it argues that some believe that soccer is a threat to traditional American values, it does not make the reverse causal claim—that rejecting soccer will restore those values. Choice D is incorrect for two reasons. First, this paragraph is about why conservatives dislike soccer, not why liberals like it. Second, this paragraph, and the entire passage in which it is found, is descriptive rather than normative. It describes how people think and feel, but it does not say how they should feel or recommend any action.

27. **(C)** Choice C is correct. The map of Red and Blue leaning states shows the Red (Republican) states clustered in the Midwest and Northwest. With the exception of Alaska (and a small part of Alabama), none of these states could be considered coastal.

    Choice A is incorrect. The map shows the Red (Republican) states to be clustered together rather than distributed evenly across the country. Choice B is incorrect. The map illustrates that the majority of strongly Red (Republican) states are located in the North. Choice D is incorrect. According to the map, the majority of the strongly Blue (Democratic) states are located in the Northeast.

28. **(C)** Choice C is correct. Though the correlation is not perfect, there appears to be some correlation between political attitudes and feelings about soccer. Fully half (5 out of 10) of the most Republican-leaning states are also among the top 10 soccer-hating states. Additionally, 4 of the 10 most Democratic-leaning states are also among the top 10 most soccer-loving states. Finally, only one state, Utah, is both strongly Republican and soccer loving, and no strongly Democratic states are found among the soccer-hating states.

    Choice A is incorrect. Though some strongly Democratic states like California love soccer, the two maps show exceptions to this rule. For example, Illinois and New Mexico are strongly Democratic, but neither appears to be passionate about soccer.

Choice B is incorrect. Though many of the most Republican states are not interested in soccer, Utah is an exception to this rule. According to the maps, Utah is one of the 10 most strongly Republican states and also one of the top 10 soccer-loving states. Choice D is incorrect. Choice D is incorrect for the same reason that Choice C is correct.

29. **(B)** Choice B is correct. The authors are engaged in gathering data about the effects on health of the flavoring chemicals that are most likely being used in electronic cigarettes. They cite their reasons for being concerned about the use of such chemicals in e-cigarettes.

    Choice A is incorrect. The research they discuss is not research that led to a product's manufacture; it is research that led to a product's being identified as hazardous. Choice C is incorrect. The authors are not making a record of a medical discovery; they are advocating an investigation of a potential public health problem. Choice D is incorrect. The authors are not explaining the methods scientists use to evaluate environmental hazards. Instead, they are encouraging scientists to apply these methods to the flavoring chemicals used in e-cigarettes.

30. **(B)** The authors describe the long search that eventually led to the identification of the flavoring chemicals used in the manufacture of microwave popcorn as the cause of the condition that came to be known as popcorn lung. They are concerned that the presence of some of these same chemicals in e-cigarettes may also prove harmful to the public.

31. **(D)** The authors explicitly state that "there is a lack of data on the exposures and potential human health effects of the use of e-cigarettes." When people comment on the lack of data about the potential human health effects of using e-cigarettes, it takes no great stretch of the imagination to realize that they are concerned about the potential *negative* human health effects of e-cigarette use.

32. **(C)** The fine particulate matter mentioned here consists of fine-grained, *powdery*, tiny particles of matter. Although "fine" can mean *superior* ("fine wines"), *in good health* ("I'm feeling fine. And you?"), or *bright and clear* ("what fine weather we're having!"), that is not how the word is used in the present context.

33. **(A)** The authors remark there are *only* three research papers and one journal opinion piece that suggest that e-cigarettes may become a serious problem. The fact that there are so few studies of what may become a significant public health problem strongly suggests a need for further research.

34. **(A)** The authors tell the story of the discovery that the inhalation of supposedly harmless flavoring chemicals in microwave popcorn had exposed factory workers to a severe, potentially life-threatening disease. They do so because they want to call people's attention to an analogous situation in which the inhalation of harmless-seeming flavoring chemicals may prove dangerous to the public.

35. **(B)** Because the flavoring chemicals had been declared safe for ingestion, people had difficulty realizing that they were far from safe when volatilized and inhaled.

36. **(B)** The investigation found a strong association or *connection* between the airborne exposure to butter-flavoring chemicals and the development of severe lung disease. Although "association" can mean *organization* ("National Association for the

Advancement of Colored People"), *cooperation* ("in association with the Department of Music"), or *friendship* ("a close association that began in college"), that is not how the word is used in the present context.

37. **(D)** The function of the chart is to show the great variety of flavors that contain diacetyl. Choice A is incorrect. The chart provides no evidence that diacetyl *is the most prominent chemical in butter flavorings*. Choices B and C are incorrect. Although the passage contains evidence that both statements are correct, there is nothing in the chart to support either of them.

38. **(C)** Choice C is correct. The passage begins by observing that white Southerners are looking to immigrants (those of foreign birth) to bring prosperity to the South. It suggests that they should instead turn to black Southerners with whom they are familiar and who have worked for them for generations. It supports this argument by reminding white Southerners of the patience and loyalty of black workers.

   Choice A is incorrect. Though the black workers to whom Washington refers are in fact former slaves who could justifiably claim compensation, Washington does not employ this argument. His claim is that hiring black workers will benefit the South, not that it will benefit southern blacks. Choice B is incorrect. Washington gives many reasons why Southern whites should prefer black workers to foreign workers but the greater numbers of black workers is not one of the reasons. Choice D is incorrect. Though Washington encourages Southern whites to provide education for blacks, he makes no claims about their level of education, either absolute or in comparison to the education of foreign workers.

39. **(D)** Choice D is correct. This long sentence begins by reminding Southern whites of the past loyalty of blacks during slavery, when they served as nursemaids and cared for Southern whites from cradle to grave. It goes on to promise the same loyalty in the future, and insists that "no foreigner" could match this level of devotion.

   Choice A is incorrect. Though this sentence does mention workers of "foreign birth" and goes on to urge Southern whites to favor blacks over immigrants, it does not give a reason why they should do this. Choice B is incorrect. This sentence lists a number of contributions made by blacks in the past, but it does not make an explicit comparison to foreign workers. The mention of "labor wars" may be a veiled reference to immigrants and their role in the union movement, but it is not explicit. Choice C is incorrect. This sentence promises the loyalty of black workers in the future, but like the previous sentence, it makes no comparison to immigrant workers.

40. **(A)** Choice A is correct. "Cast down your bucket where you are" is a metaphorical command to seek help close to home, rather than looking elsewhere (by seeking workers from foreign lands). The help close to home that Washington suggests is the free black population of the South.

   Choice B is incorrect. The bucket is a metaphor. It is not a literal representation of anything. Choice C is incorrect. Though the quoted phrase is a figure of speech, it does not represent laborious work. Casting down a bucket where you are would actually be quite easy. In fact, the ease of casting down a bucket further supports Washington's argument by underscoring how simple it would be for Southern whites to hire black workers. Choice D is incorrect for the same reason as Choice C. Casting down a bucket is easy; it is not a symbol of hard work.

41. **(A)** Choice A is correct. Du Bois accuses Washington of being an *example* of the old submissive attitude. Although "represents" can mean *appears for* ("the attorney represents small businesses in bankruptcy proceedings"), *depicts as* ("the media represents the candidate as a wild-eyed radical"), or *constitutes* ("the amount represents only 5% of the projected market"), that is not how the word is used in this particular context.

42. **(C)** By saying that Mr. Washington's program takes an economic cast, Du Bois is asserting that Washington's program has an economic *character*. Although "cast" can mean *company* ("cast of characters"), *throw* ("a mighty cast of his spear"), or *mold* ("plaster cast"), that is not how the word is used in the present context.

43. **(C)** Choice C is correct. Du Bois strongly implies that blacks will not achieve economic progress if they are denied political rights and education.

Choice A is incorrect. Washington's "programme" focuses on making economic progress rather than demanding equal rights. Du Bois argues that political rights and education are needed for economic progress. Choice B is incorrect. Though Du Bois would almost certainly agree that racial prejudice would make it difficult for blacks to progress economically, he does not make this argument. The main thrust of his argument is that as Washington's conciliatory strategy of focusing on economic progress without demanding rights took hold, rights for black Americans were rolled back disastrously. His focus is on Washington's failure to demand rights, rather than racism. Choice D is incorrect. Washington was concerned about being too aggressive in demanding rights, but Du Bois felt that it was important to insist on political power, civil rights, and education.

44. **(D)** Choice D is correct. Through the use of a rhetorical question, Du Bois argues that economic progress for blacks is dependent upon having political rights and education.

Choice A is incorrect. Here Du Bois decries the focus on wealth at the expense of the higher aims of life, but he does not claim that to have a singular focus on wealth might prevent economic progress. Choice B is incorrect. In this sentence, Du Bois argues that historically, other oppressed groups have prized self-respect over wealth. He does not, however, make a claim about how this prioritization affects the achievement of economic progress. Choice C is incorrect. In this section, Du Bois outlines the disastrous rollback in civil rights that occurred in the years after Washington's advice to prioritize economic advancement over civil rights was followed. As in choice B, no claim is made about the effect of this prioritization on the achievement of economic progress.

45. **(B)** Choice B is correct. The second paragraph of Passage 2 opens by summarizing Mr. Washington's position. It goes on to enumerate three consequences of the adoption of Mr. Washington's position. Finally, it rejects Washington's position with an emphatic No.

Choice A is incorrect. It begins by summarizing a position rather than stating a problem. Additionally, it proposes no action or solution. Choice C is incorrect. Even though the summary of Washington's position could be described as a principle being stated, no opposing principle is offered. Additionally, Du Bois disagrees with Washington, so no consensus or middle position is reached. Choice D is incorrect. Though this paragraph describes the events of a historical period, it does not evaluate that period's influence.

46. **(A)** Choice A is correct. Booker T. Washington's strategy was to focus on economic progress at the expense of advocating for civil rights. W.E.B. Du Bois rejected that strategy because he felt that self-respect was more important than wealth, and that economic progress could not be achieved without political power, civil rights, and education.

Choice B is incorrect. Du Bois is more than just cautious about Washington's strategy. He sees it as disastrous and rejects it outright. Choice C is incorrect. Though Du Bois does provide examples, his examples all undermine Washington's argument. Choice D is incorrect. Passage 2 demonstrates the *ineffectiveness* of the strategy advocated in Passage 1. It does not concede the strategy's effectiveness, nor does it give a reason for its (contested) effectiveness.

47. **(B)** Choice B is correct. In Passage 1, Washington exhorts white Southerners to assist blacks with, among other things, the "education of head." In Passage 2, Du Bois focuses on the need for higher education for "developing their exceptional men." Choice A is incorrect. Though Washington does not make a claim about the pace of progress, Du Bois is emphatic in arguing that there was a significant rollback in the rights of black Americans in the years surrounding the turn of the twentieth century. Choice C is incorrect. This is Washington's position, but Du Bois vehemently disagrees with it. Choice D is incorrect. This is the opposite of Washington's position. Additionally, Du Bois does not make a claim about the fastest way to achieve progress.

Section 2: Writing and Language Test

1. **(C)** Recall that any information that is superfluous to the functioning of a sentence must be outlined by commas or dashes—one before and one after the phrase. In this case, "one of the greatest investors of all time" is unnecessary to the overall functioning of the sentence; it can be removed and the sentence is still complete and grammatically acceptable. Thus, those words must be outlined as mentioned. Only Choice C executes this properly. Choice D does add punctuation in the necessary places, but notice that the second mark is a colon instead of a comma.

2. **(B)** "Albeit" is a word most similar to "although." It is used to indicate a contrast of some sort. Notice the contrast in the sentence: in essence, Buffett is willing to risk money, *although* only after countless hours of research. "Because," "since," and "consequently" are cause-and-effect words (think: *if this* then *that*). They do not suit our purpose.

3. **(B)** We must examine the table for this question. The sentence in the passage mentions "savings accounts," and our table lists the interest rate for those as 0.06 percent, which is Choice B.

4. **(B)** A common misconception is that a lengthy clause must automatically be a run-on sentence. However, there simply is nothing in here that requires punctuation in order to achieve grammatical validity. Though long, we have only one clause here, so avoid punctuation. Choice B is correct.

5. **(A)** With these transition words, it is important to diagnose context, specifically in how this sentence relates to previous sentences. In the last paragraph, the author spoke of savings accounts. In this new paragraph, he is referring to a contrasting course of action

of stock market investment. "Instead" is the only contrasting option listed. "Likewise" and "furthermore" are words used to continue along the same line of thinking, rather than veering to a new topic as we are doing here. "Replacingly" is an archaic adverb that is no longer used in standard American English.

6. **(D)** We need to diagnose both our proper verb tense and our subject on which the verb is acting. For verb tense, notice context: the other verbs in this paragraph are written in the present tense, so this verb must be, as well. We can accordingly eliminate Choices A and B. The subject is "it," which requires a singular verb. Therefore, it "incorporates" is the correct answer.

7. **(A)** When deciding whether to delete a sentence, ask two things: is it relevant, and has the information already been previously stated or could be readily inferred? "Wholesome gains over the long run," as previously stated in the passage, perfectly encompass any information that would be added. Therefore, the addition is unnecessary—Choice A.

8. **(D)** The question is asking us for "the most effective and specific contrast" against the earlier information in the sentence stating that the market is nothing but "legalized gambling." Choice A is on-topic in that it refers to gambling, but it is off-topic in every other sense. Choice B is off-topic, as optimism is irrelevant to the sentence. Choice C is the opposite of what we are looking for. In fact, it supports the legalized gambling claim instead of contrasting with it. Choice D is our best option, as it declares that the stock market isn't actually such a gamble after all.

9. **(A)** When placing two adjectives side by side, recall that a comma must separate them. "Avid, educated investors . . ." is our best option. Choice B neglects the comma, and Choice D incorrectly uses a semicolon. Choice C adds an additional comma; one after "educated" is unnecessary.

10. **(C)** Choices C and A both are logical, but Choice A is far too wordy, and "thus" is simpler while still being effective. Choice D refers to an irrelevant audience, and Choice B would imply that we were about to contradict ourselves.

11. **(B)** We must diagnose both required verb tense and the subject on which the verb acts. The other sentences in this paragraph are written in present tense, so maintain parallelism and select a present tense verb (eliminate Choices C and D, accordingly). Choice A reads as if we should *stop* seizing the bull by the horns, which isn't what is desired. Choice B, "seize," is our correct answer.

12. **(D)** There is both a subject-verb agreement and verb tense aspect to consider here. First, we must identify the subject. In this case, it is "African slaves." Accordingly, we must use the plural verb "were" and can thus eliminate Choices A and B. Second, we are speaking about an event in 1619—the past. A past tense verb fits, and we thus select "brought" instead of "brung," which is a dialectical variant not generally accepted in standard American English.

13. **(A)** "Two years after President Lincoln declared slaves free in his Emancipation Proclamation" is a parenthetical phrase; it can be removed from the sentence and the sentence would still function acceptably. Accordingly, we can place a set of commas/dashes surrounding the phrase to isolate it from the principal clause. Choice A is the only option that correctly employs this device.

14. **(B)** When evaluating whether to delete a sentence, ask first, is it relevant to the topic? Ask second, does it repeat previously stated information or information that can be readily inferred? The phrase, "plethora of written works" is a restatement of "myriad historical texts" and is, therefore, unnecessary. Choice B is the correct answer. Choice A is incorrect, as it is indeed relevant, but is unfortunately not adding any unique information.

15. **(A)** When evaluating the best sentence to transition from one paragraph to the next, attempt to discern the main idea of each paragraph, and then select a sentence that encompasses part of each. At the end of our first paragraph, we have what is essentially our thesis statement referring to folktales. The next paragraph continues to elaborate on folktales. Therefore, it is only sensible that our correct answer would make a reference to folktales, and Choice A is the only choice that does. Choices B, C, and D neglect to include anything about folktales.

16. **(C)** We are listing a series of actions: to shout, to speak with a lisp, and to sing. Each of these actions must be separated from the others by a comma, and Choice C effectively accomplishes this. Choice A, on the other hand, omits a necessary comma after "lisp." Choices B and D both omit a comma after "shout."

17. **(B)** Pay scrutinizing attention to what the question requires: "the most relevant, logical contrast to conclude the sentence." In order to find a contrast, it is necessary to understand with what we are contrasting. The first part is about which "devices stick," or are maintained. A logical contrast, therefore, would be which are lost. Choices B and D both address that loss, but Choice D is about "scientific descriptions," which are not "relevant" to a sentence on folktales. Choices A and C, instead of focusing on losing elements, misinterpret the desired contrast by actually mentioning adding more elements—the opposite of our intent.

18. **(D)** Transition words to begin sentences are often difficult, as the intended meaning can be subtle. Notice the contrast between the previous sentence talking about folktales evolving and this one that talks about folktales remaining the same. Our only applicable contrasting option is "yet," Choice D. "Additionally," "consequently," and "because of this" do not express an appropriate contrasting relationship.

19. **(B)** Find the subject first. It is "stories," a plural word that requires a plural verb. "Evoke" is the correct answer. Choice A, "evokes," is a singular verb, which is not our desire. Similarly, the infinitive "to evoke" is not acceptable, just as using "evoking" is not applicable in this context.

20. **(A)** Find the subject first. In this case, it is "structure," a singular noun that will require a singular verb. "Reflect" is a plural verb and can be eliminated. "Reflection" is a noun, and "for reflecting" is a more complicated way of saying to reflect. The infinitive would not function here.

21. **(A)** When deciding to insert content, first ask, is it relevant? Second, ask, does it add meaning that hasn't been already expressed? In this instance, the answer is yes in both cases, so we can eliminate Choices C and D. Choice B is incorrect as it has no pertinence to "scholarly analysis."

22. **(B)** We need a transition here that reflects the second sentence building upon the first. "On the other hand" and "while" reflect contradictory transitions. Equally incorrect is Choice D, as the second sentence isn't for "emphasis." Choice B, "In fact," is the desired transition.

23. **(A)** We must examine the graphs in this question. Let us examine each choice one by one to analyze its validity (or lack thereof). Choice A refers to German deaths, so we must use the Axis graph to see if 18 million is more than twice the number of German deaths. German deaths are roughly 8.5 million, so Choice A is correct. Choice B is incorrect as 3 times 8.5 is 25.5, which is more than 18. For Choice C, we must analyze the Allies graph. U.S. deaths were roughly only 1 million, so that is far less than 18 million. Choice D is incorrect because about half of the 23 million Soviet deaths would come to about 11.5 million, not 18 million.

24. **(B)** We must make a parallel, logical comparison here; the comparison is between Stalin's death toll and Hitler's death toll, not between Stalin and Hitler, as Choices A and C incorrectly state. Equally, "Hitler's dying" is not apt in the comparison. Choice B, "that of Hitler," is an acceptable stand-in for "Hitler's death toll."

25. **(B)** "While" in this instance is a stand in for "although" or "even though." It is a qualifying statement affixed to another in order to modify the meaning. "Since" expresses cause and effect, which isn't our desired intention, and "because" acts in the same way. So Choices A and C can be eliminated accordingly. Choice D, "for," isn't compatible with the desired meaning of "although."

26. **(D)** In this sentence, everything functions acceptably grammatically without a comma, so there's no reason to insert one. Thus, Choice D is the correct answer. Choices A, B, and C all insert superfluous commas that unnecessarily interrupt the flow of the sentence.

27. **(B)** When deciding whether to delete, consider our two determining criteria: is it relevant, and has this information already been stated elsewhere, or can it be comfortably inferred? In this case, though relevant, the information is implied. It's a labor camp; of course, people are there "against their will" so there's no need to state that. Thus, Choice B is the correct answer. Choices C and D state false assumptions, and Choice A has flawed logic; it isn't a mischaracterization at all.

28. **(A)** Subject-verb agreement is difficult to discern here. Our subject is "widespread ignorance and general dismissal," which are two separate things. Thus, a plural verb is required to match our plural subject. Neither Choice B nor Choice C fits our requirement for a plural verb, so they can be eliminated. Choice D does have the proper verb "result," but it lacks the preposition "from" to logically tie the sentence together. Choice A, therefore, is the answer.

29. **(C)** Subject-verb agreement is difficult to discern here, as well. Again, there are two items named in the subject: "Communism's emphasis on quality" is the first. "And its alignment to Marxism" is the second. So, we need a plural verb to match the plural subject. Choice A—"seems"—is a singular verb, and neither "seeming" nor "to seem" fits appropriately. "Seem"—Choice C—is the best option.

30. **(D)** We must analyze the graphs for this question. The question asks how many total deaths Stalin (read: the Soviet Union) suffered during the war. The bar in the Allies graph falls somewhere between 20 and 25 million. It's difficult to say with any real precision whether that is 22 or 23, but Choices A, B, and C are so far off that we are left only with Choice D: 23 million.

31. **(C)** Recall that a semicolon is used to separate two distinct, complete clauses that could otherwise be full sentences. "The camps supposedly disappeared with Stalin's death in 1953" could be a full sentence, just as "instead, they evolved into political camps that existed well into the 1970s" could be a full sentence. It is best to combine these with a semicolon, as seen in Choice C. Choices A and D are run-on sentences, and Choice B incorrectly employs a colon in place of a semicolon.

32. **(A)** We need a transition here that will illustrate the contrast between the first half and the second half of the sentence. "But" is that effective transition to contrast/qualify. "And," "effectively," and "thus" communicate the opposite, as if the clauses built on one another, which is not our intention.

33. **(B)** Pay close attention to what the question asks of you: find "the most effective, specific, and relevant conclusion." Those words are important and should not be discounted lightly. Choice A is far too general, whereas Choice C is perhaps not as effective of a conclusion as we would like. Choice D, like Choice A, lacks information specific to our topic of the Gulag. This leaves us with Choice B, which is *effective, specific,* and *relevant* to our purpose.

34. **(D)** Simpler is often better, but with the caveat that we don't want to eliminate too much information in our search for concision; otherwise, the subject matter can become ambiguous. Both Choices B and D are logical grammatically, but Choice B leaves the reader asking, but who is he? We need to specify the driver. "They was" is grammatically incorrect. "It was tossing newspapers out of his car" would be equally illogical.

35. **(A)** Recall the difference between "lay" and "lie": "lay" means *to set something down* (i.e., placing), while "lie" signifies *the physical act of being prone or resting in a horizontal position* (i.e., reclining). "Lying" suits our purpose better, as the newspaper is in that aforementioned resting position. Choice A, then, is our correct answer. Choice D is a conjugation of "lay," which—again—is not the correct verb. Choice C, a past tense verb, does not function as well as a gerund.

36. **(B)** The best conclusion would be a combination of relevance and specificity. Choice A isn't terribly relevant; even though it mentions newspapers, this fact isn't terribly apt in context of throwing newspapers. Choice C is wholly irrelevant. Choice D is relevant, but it lacks specificity; no new, useful information is added. Choice B, though, is both relevant and specific.

37. **(A)** Ultimately, the discussion of the football field and the accomplishments of the football team are not relevant to the content of the essay, which focuses on the physics of throwing newspapers. So, the sentence should be deleted due to a lack of relevance, as Choice A states. The logic behind Choices B, C, and D is either flawed or wholly incorrect depending on the choice.

38. **(D)** In this sentence, "nobody" is the subject, and "is able to replicate the newspaper person's precision" is the predicate. Granted, the predicate is lengthy, but length, in and of itself, is not indicative of requiring punctuation. In fact, we do not want to splice the subject or the predicate in any form, so no punctuation is required. Choice D is the best answer. Choices A, B, and C all include commas that are superfluous to grammatical needs.

39. **(D)** Ultimately, no conjunction is required, as "during the next few weeks" is a dependent clause, and the rest of the sentence is an independent clause. Thus, they fit together perfectly acceptably without any additions whatsoever, so "delete the underlined portion."

40. **(B)** First, we must address the word that our proposed pronoun will represent. In this case, the question regards the proper pronoun to use as a substitute for "newspapers," which are the items that "will all hit the pavement at the same time." "Newspapers" is plural, so "it" doesn't function here. Similarly, neither "you" nor "one" is logical. "They," however, is an acceptable substitute for "newspapers."

41. **(A)** "Notwithstanding," "however," and "nevertheless" all mean the exact same thing. That should have been our first indication that none of these is the correct answer. Moreover, they are all contrasting transitions, whereas the relationship between our two sentences is more causal than contrasting. "Thus" is a causal transition.

42. **(C)** "Execute," of course, can have a very violent meaning, but it can also mean *to carry out or put into effect*. In this case, the delivery person was carrying out his toss. "Destroy," "crush," and "annihilate" are words that *only* have violent or destructive connotations that do not fit in this sentence.

43. **(B)** "Baseball, basketball, football, lacrosse, etc." are words that are inconsequential to the main clause; eliminate them, and the sentence still functions perfectly well. Those words, therefore, form a parenthetical phrase that can be surrounded by two dashes or two commas to separate them from the main clause. Choice B is the only option that effectively executes this.

44. **(C)** The proposed insertion takes place during breakfast, which would chronologically be after the narrator's walk. Paragraph 2 is still discussing the walk, while paragraph 3 transitions to the present time. Our insertion would be best between these two paragraphs, which is Choice C.

Section 3: Math Test (No Calculator)

1. **(B)** $7d + 5 = 5d + 7 \Rightarrow 2d + 5 = 7 \Rightarrow 2d = 2 \Rightarrow d = 1$

2. **(D)** $|2x - 3| < 5 \Rightarrow -5 < 2x - 3 < 5 \Rightarrow -2 < 2x < 8 \Rightarrow -1 < x < 4$

3. **(D)** First write the equations of each line in slope-intercept form:

$$ax + by = c \Rightarrow by = -ax + c \Rightarrow y = -\frac{a}{b}x + \frac{c}{b}$$

$$dx + ey = f \Rightarrow ey = -dx + f \Rightarrow y = -\frac{d}{e}x + \frac{f}{e}$$

The slopes of the two lines are the coefficients of x: $-\frac{a}{b}$ and $-\frac{d}{e}$. Since the slopes of parallel lines are equal: $-\frac{a}{b} = -\frac{d}{e} \Rightarrow ae = bd$.

4. **(A)** If Stuart withdrew d dollars every week, the total amount he withdrew in w weeks was wd dollars. So the amount remaining in the account at that time was $D - wd$ dollars.

   **Plug in easy-to-use numbers. Assume Stuart's initial deposit was \$100 and that he withdrew \$10 each week. After 6 weeks, he would have withdrawn \$60 and would still have had \$40 in the account. Which answer choice is equal to 40, when $D = 100$, $d = 10$, and $w = 6$? Only Choice A works.

5. **(D)** $[(3x + y) + (x + 3y)]^2 = [4x + 4y]^2 = [4(x + y)]^2 = 16(x + y)^2$

   **Questions such as this can always be answered by plugging in numbers. For example, if x and y were each 1, the given expression would be equal to $(4 + 4)^2 = 8^2 = 64$. Of the four choices, only $16(x + y)^2$, Choice D, is equal to 64 when x and y are each equal to 1.

6. **(D)** $F = G\dfrac{m_1 m_2}{r^2} \Rightarrow Fr^2 = Gm_1 m_2 \Rightarrow r^2 = \dfrac{Gm_1 m_2}{F} \Rightarrow r = \sqrt{\dfrac{Gm_1 m_2}{F}}$

7. **(D)** $2(7 - 3x) = 6(3 - x) - 4 \Rightarrow 14 - 6x = 18 - 6x - 4 = 14 - 6x$

   Since every real number is a solution of the equation $14 - 6x = 14 - 6x$, the original equation has infinitely many solutions.

   **A solution to the equation $2(7 - 3x) = 6(3 - x) - 4$ would be the x-coordinate of the point of intersection of the straight lines $y = 2(7 - 3x)$ and $y = 6(3 - x) - 4$. However, since these lines are the same line (they both have the equation $y = 14 - 6x$), every point on one line is a point on the other.

8. **(A)** $f(16) = f(16)^{\frac{1}{2}} + (16)^{\frac{1}{4}} = \sqrt{16} + \sqrt[4]{16} = 4 + 2 = 6$

9. **(B)** For any positive number n, $n^{-2} = \dfrac{1}{n^2}$ and $\dfrac{1}{n^{-2}} = n^2$. So $\dfrac{a^{-2}}{b^{-2}} = \dfrac{b^2}{a^2}$.

   For any positive number n, $n^{\frac{1}{2}} = \sqrt{n}$ and $n^{-\frac{1}{2}} = \dfrac{1}{\sqrt{n}}$.

   So $\left(\dfrac{a^{-2}}{b^{-2}}\right)^{-\frac{1}{2}} = \dfrac{1}{\sqrt{\dfrac{b^2}{a^2}}} = \dfrac{1}{\left(\dfrac{b}{a}\right)} = \dfrac{a}{b}$.

10. **(C)** Since c represents the number of CDs Rinaldo sold during that 9-hour period and since d represents the number of DVDs he sold during that same period, $c + d$ is the total number of items sold. So $c + d$ must equal 65. Since each CD costs 5 dollars and each DVD costs 11 dollars, $5c + 11d$ is the total number of dollars Rinaldo took in. So, $5c + 11d$ must equal 475.

11. **(B)** Subtract 4 from both sides of the given equation to put it in the standard form for a quadratic equation: $x^2 + 2x - 4 = 0$. Looking at the answer choices should make it clear that this equation cannot be solved by factoring. So, use the quadratic formula:

   $$x = \frac{-2 \pm \sqrt{4 - (-16)}}{2} = \frac{-2 \pm \sqrt{20}}{2} = \frac{-2 \pm 2\sqrt{5}}{2} = -1 \pm \sqrt{5}$$

   The two solutions are $-1 + \sqrt{5}$ and $-1 - \sqrt{5}$.

12. **(C)** A basic fact that you need to know is that compound interest rates always result in exponential growth. Assume a client invests D dollars in an SRA that has an annual rate

of return of 4 percent and that $V(n)$ represents the SRA's value after n years. Then at the end of the first year, the SRA's value, $V(1)$, is $1.04D$. During the second year, the SRA earns 4 percent of $1.04D$. So at the end of the year, $V(2) = (1.04)(1.04D) = 1.04^2 D$. After n years, the value of the SRA will be $V(n) = 1.04^n D$, which is an increasing exponential function.

13. **(C)** $(\sin A)(\cos A)(\tan A) = \left(\dfrac{a}{c}\right)\left(\dfrac{b}{c}\right)\left(\dfrac{a}{b}\right) = \dfrac{a^2}{c^2}$

Alternatively, $(\sin A)(\cos A)(\tan A) = (\sin A)(\cos A)\left(\dfrac{\sin A}{\cos A}\right) = (\sin A)^2 = \left(\dfrac{a}{c}\right)^2 = \dfrac{a^2}{c^2}$.

14. **(1)** If you recognize the given equation as the equation of a circle whose center is the point $(4, 2)$ and whose radius is 2, make a quick sketch (see below) to answer the question immediately.

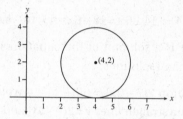

The circle never intersects the y-axis and intersects the x-axis at only 1 point. So $m + n = 1$.

However, you don't need to know that the graph is a circle to answer this question easily. Since the x-coordinate of each point on the y-axis is 0, the graph intersects the y-axis when $x = 0$. Replacing x by 0 in the given equation results in:

$$(0-4)^2 + (y-2)^2 = 4 \Rightarrow 16 + (y-2)^2 = 4 \Rightarrow (y-2)^2 = -12$$

However, $(y-2)^2$ cannot be negative. So the graph does not touch the y-axis, and $m = 0$.

Since the y-coordinate of each point on the x-axis is 0, the graph intersects the x-axis when $y = 0$. Replacing y by 0 in the given equation results in:

$$(x-4)^2 + (0-2)^2 = 4 \Rightarrow (x-4)^2 + 4 = 4 \Rightarrow (x-4)^2 = 0 \Rightarrow x-4 = 0 \Rightarrow x = 4$$

So, the only point where the graph intersects the x-axis is the point $(4, 0)$, and so $n = 1$. Therefore, $m + n = 0 + 1 = 1$.

15. **(81)** If $5\sqrt{x} + 1 = 46$, then $5\sqrt{x} = 45$. So, $\sqrt{x} = 9$ and $x = 81$.

16. **(9)** First, divide the top inequality by 2 and the bottom inequality by 3. This yields

$$y \geq \frac{1}{2}x - 5 \text{ and } y \leq \frac{1}{3}x + 6$$

So, (a, b) is a solution of this system of inequalities if and only if (a, b) lies above the line whose equation is $y = \frac{1}{2}x - 5$ and below the line whose equation is $y = \frac{1}{3}x + 6$.

The point $(9, -\frac{1}{2})$ lies on the first line, and the point $(9, 9)$ lies on the second line.

For all b such that $-\frac{1}{2} \leq b \leq 9$, the point $(9, b)$ is a solution of the given system of inequalities. So the greatest possible value of b is 9.

17. $\left(\frac{4}{3}\ \text{or}\ 1.33\right)$ Even though you can't use your calculator in Section 3, the arithmetic isn't that bad. You could simply distribute and solve:

$$12(3x-4) = 15(4-3x) \Rightarrow 36x-48 = 60-45x \Rightarrow 81x=108 \Rightarrow 9x=12 \Rightarrow 3x=4 \Rightarrow x=\frac{4}{3}$$

However, you can answer this question without doing any calculations. If you take a second to look at the given equation, you should realize that $4-3x$ is the negative of $3x-4$. So the original equation can be written as $12(3x-4) = -15(3x-4)$. The only way that 12 times some quantity can be equal to -15 times that same quantity is if the quantity is 0. So, $3x-4=0$ and $x=\frac{4}{3}$. Of course, you will also get credit if you bubble in 1.33.

Section 4: Math Test (With Calculator)

1. **(D)** To find the total cost, C, of purchasing x hot dogs and y hamburgers, we need to multiply x by the cost, in dollars, of each hot dog and y by the cost, in dollars, of each hamburger. Since the given equation is $C = 2x + 3y$, hot dogs cost 2 dollars apiece and hamburgers cost 3 dollars apiece.

2. **(D)** Since $\frac{1,200}{5,000} = 0.24$, 24 percent of the family doctors surveyed recommended routine chest X-rays as part of an annual physical; the other 76 percent of the doctors did not do so. Since the survey participants were randomly selected throughout the country, it is likely that approximately 76 percent of all family doctors in the United States did not routinely recommend the chest X-rays:

$$76\ \text{percent of } 209,000 = 0.76 \times 209,000 \approx 159,000$$

3. **(A)** $\frac{3}{5}a-5=11-\frac{11}{15}a \Rightarrow \frac{3}{5}a+\frac{11}{15}a=16 \Rightarrow \frac{20}{15}a=16 \Rightarrow \frac{4}{3}a=16 \Rightarrow a=\frac{3}{4}(16)=12$

4. **(D)** There were 150 lions and tigers (64 lions and 86 tigers). Of those, 70 chose swimming ($32 + 38 = 70$). So, $150 - 70 = 80$ of the lions and tigers chose an activity other than swimming. The desired fraction is $\frac{80}{150} = \frac{8}{15}$.

5. **(D)** The second job cost $292 - $238 = $54 dollars more than the first because it took $3.25 - 2.5 = 0.75$ hours longer. So his hourly rate, h, is $54 \div 0.75$ hours = $72 per hour. His charge of $238 for the first job consisted of his flat fee of f dollars plus $72 per hour for the 1.5 additional hours:

$$238 = f + 1.5(72) = f + 108 \Rightarrow f = 130$$

So, $f + h = 130 + 72 = 202$.

**Alternatively, to get the values of f and h, we could have solved the following system of equations:

$$292 = f + 2.25h \quad \text{and} \quad 238 = f + 1.5h$$

By subtracting the second equation from the first, we get $54 = 0.75h$. Now proceed as above: $h = 54 \div 0.75 = 72$. Replacing h by 72 in either of the equations gives $f = 130$.

6. **(C)** If y is inversely proportional to x, there is a constant k that $xy = k$: so $k = (8)(4) = 32$. Thus, $32 = 5y$ and $y = \frac{32}{5}$ or 6.4.

7. **(D)** 7.81 Egyptian pounds and 0.657 British pounds have the same value (namely, 1 U.S. dollar). Set up a proportion:

$$\frac{\text{Egyptian pounds}}{\text{British pounds}} = \frac{7.81}{0.657} = \frac{x}{1} \Rightarrow x = 11.887,$$

or 11.89 rounded to the nearest hundredth.

8. **(B)** $\frac{1}{5}(7n - 10) < n \Rightarrow 7n - 10 < 5n \Rightarrow 2n < 10 \Rightarrow n < 5$

There are 4 positive integers less than 5: 1, 2, 3, and 4.

9. **(C)** Since the game takes one hour, or 60 minutes, and there are always 5 men playing, the game consists of $5 \times 60 = 300$ player-minutes. If that is evenly divided among the 12 players, each one plays $300 \div 12 = 25$ minutes.

**If you get stuck, test the choices. Eliminate the choices that can't be right, and guess. If 5 men played the first 12 minutes and 5 other men played the next 12 minutes, there wouldn't be 5 men available to play the rest of the game.

So 12 is much too small. Eliminate Choice A. If 5 men played for 30 minutes and 5 other men played the next 30 minutes, the game would be over. So 2 men wouldn't have played at all. So eliminate Choice D. The answer must be 24 or 25.

10. **(C)** At the two schools combined, the number of students attending 0, 1, 2, 3, and 4 games was 120, 110, 80, 70, and 20, respectively. Now just calculate the weighted average:

$$\frac{(120 \times 0) + (110 \times 1) + (80 \times 2) + (70 \times 3) + (20 \times 4)}{400} = \frac{0 + 110 + 160 + 210 + 80}{400} = \frac{560}{400} = 1.4$$

11. **(B)** At Leeds, 20 percent (40 out of 200) of the students surveyed attended no games and the other 80 percent attended at least one game. So we should expect that about 1,280 students at Leeds (80 percent of the 1,600 students) attended at least one game.

Similarly at Bryce, 40 percent of the students surveyed attended no games and the other 60 percent attended at least one game. So we should expect that about 1,500 students at Bryce (60 percent of the 2,500 students) attended at least one game.

Choice A is clearly wrong and Choice B appears to be true. At this point, you could just choose Choice B, but you could also check Choices C and D to make sure they are false. At both colleges, 20 percent of the students surveyed (40 out of 200) attended exactly two games. Since Bryce has 900 more students than Leeds, far more students at Bryce attended two games than at Leeds.

Choice D is like Choice C. 20 percent of the students at Leeds attended three games and 20 percent of the students at Bryce attended two games. Because Bryce has so many more students, far more students at Bryce attended two games than students at Leeds attended three games.

12. **(D)** After making n monthly deposits, the total amount of money that Jana had deposited into her account was $2{,}500 + 75n$ dollars. She made 12 deposits in each of the 5 years from 2000 to 2004, inclusive, and then made 7 monthly deposits in 2005. Therefore, as of July 31, 2005, she had made a total of $(12 \times 5) + 7 = 67$ monthly deposits of $75 each. So the total amount of money she had deposited was $\$2{,}500 + (67 \times \$75) = \$7{,}525$.

13. **(C)** Let n be the smallest number in the list. Each of the other three numbers is 1.5 times the preceding number.

So the numbers are n, $1.5n$; $1.5(1.5n) = 2.25n$, and $1.5(2.25n) = 3.375n$.

The sum of the four numbers is $n + 1.5n + 2.25n + 3.375n = 8.125n$.

Finally, $8.125n = 325 \Rightarrow n = 325 \div 8.125 = 40$.

****Alternatively, you could backsolve. Try Choice B: 30. Then the four numbers would be 30, 45, 67.5, 101.25. Clearly, their sum is not 325 (it's not even a whole number). Try Choice C: 40. It works: $40 + 60 + 90 + 135 = 325$.

14. **(A)** Use the formula (population) $\div$ (population per square mile) = area, in square miles, to find the approximate area of each state.

For NY, 19,000,000 people $\div$ 400 people per square mile $\approx$ 47,500 square miles.

For NJ, 9,000,000 people $\div$ 1,200 people per square mile $\approx$ 7,500 square miles.

For CT, 3,450,000 people $\div$ 750 people per square mile $\approx$ 4,600 square miles.

The total area of the three states is approximately:

$$47,500 + 7,500 + 4,600 = 59,600 \text{ square miles}$$

Choice A is the best approximation.

15. **(C)** The presence of $(x + y)^2$ in some of the answer choices suggests that rather than multiplying each term in the first parentheses by each term in the second parentheses and then rearranging terms, it would be more efficient to rewrite the given expression as $\big((x + y) + 3\big)\big((x + y) + 3\big)$ and treat this as the square of a binomial. Just as $(a + 3)^2 = a^2 + 6a + 9$, $\big((x + y) + 3\big)^2 = (x + y)^2 + 6(x + y) + 9$, Choice C.

16. **(D)** $2.3 - 4.4n \le 6.7 \Rightarrow -4.4n \le 4.4$. Multiply both sides of $-4.4n \le 4.4$ by -1, remembering to reverse the inequality sign: $4.4n \ge -4.4$. So the least possible value of $2.3 + 4.4n$ is $2.3 + -4.4 = 2.3 - 4.4 = -2.1$.

17. **(C)** Check the answers, starting with Choice D. In 2014, he entered 3 more races than 2013, an increase of $\frac{3}{9} = \frac{1}{3}$, which is less than 50 percent. Now check Choice C. In 2013, he entered 3 more races than in 2012, an increase of $\frac{3}{6} = \frac{1}{2} = 50$ percent.

(Note: From 2010 to 2011, the increase was 100 percent, and from 2011 to 2012 there was a decrease.)

18. **(D)** Draw a Venn diagram, and label each region. Since there are 15 junior girls, there are $30 - 15 = 15$ junior boys and $60 - 15 = 45$ senior girls. Therefore, the number of senior boys is $100 - (15 + 15 + 45) = 100 - 75 = 25$.

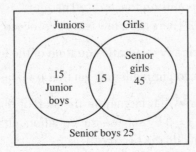

19. **(C)** To find Elaine's average speed in kilometers per hour, divide the distance she went, in kilometers (190), by the time it took, in hours. Elaine drove for 3 hours and 20 minutes, which is

$$3\frac{1}{3} \text{ hours } (20 \text{ minutes} = \frac{20}{60} \text{ hour} = \frac{1}{3} \text{ hour})$$

Elaine's average speed is

$$190 \div 3\frac{1}{3} = 190 \div \frac{10}{3} = \overset{19}{\cancel{190}} \times \frac{3}{\cancel{10}} = 57$$

20. **(B)** Since the ratio of boys to girls was 7 to 4, there were 7 boys for every 4 girls. This means that of every 11 students on a varsity team, 7 were boys and 4 were girls.

So the girls made up $\frac{4}{11}$ of the varsity athletes, and $\frac{4}{11} \times 572 = 208$.

21. **(B)** Both the total monthly rent ($600) and the fact that Peter pays more than Robert ($p > r$) are irrelevant. The total rent is $p + r$ dollars, of which Peter pays p dollars.

So the fraction of the rent that Peter pays is $\frac{p}{p+r}$, which is Choice A. Since $p + r = 600$, Choice D is also the fraction of the rent that Peter pays. However, the question asks for the percent of the monthly rent that Peter pays. To get that, you have to multiply the fraction by 100. So the answer is Choice B.

**Note that if Peter pays $400 and Robert pays $200, then the fraction of the rent that Peter pays was $\frac{400}{600} = \frac{2}{3}$. However, Peter pays $\frac{2}{3} \times 100 = 66\frac{2}{3}$ percent of the rent.

22. **(D)** Since $AB = AC$, m$\angle B$ = m$\angle C$. Since $\angle BED$ and $\angle CFD$ are right angles, their measures are equal. So, triangles BED and CFD are similar. Since $DE = 4.5$ and $DF = 7.5$, the ratio of BD to DC is

$$4.5 \text{ to } 7.5 = \frac{4.5}{7.5} = 0.6 = \frac{3}{5}$$

Represent BD and DC by $3x$ and $5x$, respectively. Since $BC = 24$, we have

$$3x + 5x = 24 \Rightarrow 8x = 24 \Rightarrow x = 3 \Rightarrow DC = 5x = 15$$

At this point, you could proceed in either of the following two ways: First, since $\triangle CFD$ is a right triangle, you can use the Pythagorean theorem:

$(7.5)^2 + (CF)^2 = (15)^2 \Rightarrow (CF)^2 = 225 - 56.25 = 168.75$

$CF = \sqrt{168.75} = 12.99$.

Second, you could notice that since leg $\overline{DF}$ is half of hypotenuse $\overline{DC}$, $\triangle CFD$ is a 30-60-90 right triangle. So, $CF = 7.5\sqrt{3} = 12.99$.

Finally, to the nearest whole number, $CF = 13$.

23. **(D)** If the graph of a function crosses the x-axis at n, then $(n, 0)$ is a point on the graph. So, $(p, 0)$ and $(q, 0)$ are points on the graph. Therefore, p and q are the solutions of the equation $4x^2 - 8x + 3 = 0$. There are a few ways to proceed.

First, if you know that for any quadratic equation of the form $ax^2 + bx + c = 0$, the sum of the roots is $-\frac{b}{a}$, then you immediately get that $p + q = -\frac{-8}{4} = 2$.

Second, if you don't know that fact about the sum of the roots, you have to find the two roots of $4x^2 - 8x + 3 = 0$ by solving the equation, either by factoring or using the quadratic formula. Then add the two roots.

Solution by factoring:

$$4x^2 - 8x + 3 = (2x - 3)(2x - 1)$$

$$2x - 3 = 0 \text{ or } 2x - 1 = 0 \Rightarrow x = \frac{3}{2} \text{ or } x = \frac{1}{2}$$

So, p and q are $\frac{3}{2}$ and $\frac{1}{2}$, and $p + q = \frac{3}{2} + \frac{1}{2} = 2$.

Solution using the quadratic formula:

$$x = \frac{8 \pm \sqrt{(-8)^2 - 4(4)(3)}}{2(4)} = \frac{8 \pm \sqrt{64 - 48}}{8} = \frac{8 \pm \sqrt{16}}{8} = \frac{8 \pm 4}{8}$$

So, $x = \frac{12}{8} = \frac{3}{2}$ or $x = \frac{4}{8} = \frac{1}{2}$. Again their sum is $\frac{3}{2} + \frac{1}{2} = 2$.

24. **(D)** You can use your calculator if you are incredibly careful with your use of parentheses and the way in which you enter negative fractional exponents on your calculator. It is probably much safer to use the laws of exponents to simplify the given expression.

$$\frac{5^{-\frac{1}{3}}}{5^{\frac{2}{3}}} = 5^{-\frac{1}{3} - \frac{2}{3}} = 5^{-1} = \frac{1}{5}$$

$$\frac{10^{\frac{1}{2}}}{10^{-\frac{1}{2}}} = 10^{\frac{1}{2} - \left(-\frac{1}{2}\right)} = 10^{\frac{1}{2} + \frac{1}{2}} = 10^1 = 10$$

$$\frac{\left(5^{-\frac{1}{3}}\right)\left(10^{\frac{1}{2}}\right)}{\left(5^{\frac{2}{3}}\right)\left(10^{-\frac{1}{2}}\right)} = \left(\frac{1}{5}\right)(10) = 2$$

25. **(C)** Any line that passes through Quadrants I, III, and IV has a positive slope and a negative y-intercept. Since m is positive and b is negative, m cannot be less than b (I is false), and the product mb must be negative (II is true). Statement III certainly does not have to be true, but it could be true.

For example, if $m = 1$ and $b = -1$, $m + b = 0$.

So, statements II and III only could be true.

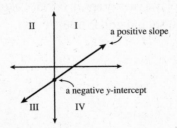

26. **(D)** Since the line l crosses the y-axis at 12, it passes through the point $(0, 12)$.

Since it also passes through $(9, 9)$, its slope is $\frac{9 - 12}{9 - 0} = \frac{-3}{9} = -\frac{1}{3}$. If two lines are perpendicular, the product of their slopes is -1. So the slope of every line that is perpendicular to l is 3. Each of the four answer choices is the equation of a line in slope-intercept form. So in each choice, the slope is the coefficient of x. Only Choice D is the equation of a line whose slope is 3. Note that it was not necessary to get the equation of *l*. The only thing we needed to know about *l* was its slope.

27. **(B)** Let x and y represent the number of scarves and sweaters Ariella sold, respectively. Set up two equations:

$$x + y = 40 \quad \text{and} \quad 18x + 75y = 1{,}461$$

By multiplying the first equation by 18, we get that $18x + 18y = 720$. Subtracting $18x + 18y = 720$ from $18x + 75y = 1{,}461$ gives $57y = 741$. So $y = 741 \div 57 = 13$. So in December 2015, Ariella sold 13 sweaters and $40 - 13 = 27$ scarves. Finally, she sold $27 - 13 = 14$ more scarves than sweaters.

28. **(540)** Since a blueprint is a scale drawing, the units are directly proportional to one another. Let *l* and *w* represent the actual length and the actual width of the living room, respectively. Set up two proportions:

$$\frac{\text{inches on blueprint}}{\text{actual distances}} = \frac{0.4 \text{ inches}}{3 \text{ feet}} = \frac{4 \text{ inches}}{l \text{ feet}} \Rightarrow 0.4l = 12 \Rightarrow l = 30$$

$$\frac{\text{inches on blueprint}}{\text{actual distances}} = \frac{0.4 \text{ inches}}{3 \text{ feet}} = \frac{2.4 \text{ inches}}{w \text{ feet}} \Rightarrow 0.4w = 7.2 \Rightarrow l = 18$$

The living room is a rectangle whose area is $30 \times 18 = 540$ square feet.

29. **(1.21)** Since this is a percent problem, assume the value of the investment on January 1, 2004 was \$100. Since 10 percent of 100 is 10, one year later the value of the investment had increased by \$10 to \$110. Now, 10 percent of 110 is 11, so in the next year the value increased by \$11 to \$121. Finally, 121 is 1.21×100.

30. **(1.13)** The probability, p, that a senior girl chosen at random plays a varsity sport is $136 \div 370 = 0.3676$. The probability, q, that a senior boy chosen at random plays a varsity sport is $140 \div 430 = 0.3256$. Then $\dfrac{p}{q} = \dfrac{0.3676}{0.3256} = 1.1289$, which to the nearest hundredth is 1.13. Be careful not to round off too soon. If you rounded off the value of p as 0.37 and the value of q as 0.33, when you divide, you would have $0.37 \div 0.33 = 1.1212$. So you would incorrectly think the answer is 1.12.

31. **(166)** From the survey, we know that 276 of the 800 seniors in the survey, or 34.5 percent of them, are playing a varsity sport, so it is likely that approximately 34.5 percent of the 480,000 seniors in Texas play a varsity sport: $0.345 \times 480{,}000 = 165{,}600$, or to the nearest thousand, 166,000. So you should grid in 166.

After the PSAT/NMSQT

After the scores of the PSAT/NMSQT are received, you, your parents, and your guidance counselor can begin to make plans for college. Here are some Barron's reference books that will be very helpful to you.

Barron's *SAT* by Sharon Weiner Green, Ira K. Wolf, and Brian W. Stewart (2017, 29th Edition). This classic includes a diagnostic test and four additional practice tests that enable you to practice under exact SAT format and test conditions; all tests have answer keys and answer explanations. Extensive review and practice is provided for each type of test question. The Reading review includes graph analysis and the Master Word List, with definitions and parts of speech. The Writing and Language review includes common grammar and usage errors, quantitative graph analysis, and writing strategies. The Math review covers basic arithmetic through high school algebra and geometry. Testing tactics and strategies are featured. Two additional practice tests are provided online, along with the master vocabulary list in a flash card format.

Reading Workbook for the New SAT by Brian W. Stewart (2016), ***Math Workbook for the New SAT*** by Lawrence Leff (2016, 6th Edition), ***Writing Workbook for the New SAT*** by George Ehrenhaft (2016, 4th Edition). These workbooks provide the detailed review you may need for specific sections of the test. Each book contains hundreds of practice questions with answers and extensive review specific to the topic.

The SAT and ACT Grammar Workbook by George Ehrenhaft (2016, 4th Edition). This workbook provides a review of the grammatical issues you are most likely to be asked about on the SAT and ACT. You'll learn terms you need to know and how to avoid the grammar pitfalls that give almost everyone a headache. And you will learn how to write a proper exam essay. The book includes plenty of practice questions with complete answer explanations.

Hot Words for the SAT by Linda Carnevale (2016, 6th Edition). This book includes hundreds of words, grouped by concept, with definitions, sample sentences, and quizzes.

SAT 1600 by Linda Carnevale and Roselyn Teukolsky (2017). Written for the student who is aiming for that perfect score, this book breaks down the toughest questions and analyzes why they are tough. Practice questions are provided for each of the three SAT sections: reading, writing and language, and math. A complete practice test is provided at the end of the book. An additional complete practice SAT test with automatic scoring and explained answers can be found online.

New SAT Flash Cards by Sharon Weiner Green and Ira K. Wolf (2016, 3rd Edition). This handy boxed set includes 200 math cards with 75 important math facts, strategies, and sample multiple-choice and grid-in questions; 200 grammar cards covering parts of speech, sentence construction, and more; and 100 vocabulary cards with definitions and sample sentences.

Essays That Will Get You Into College by Daniel Kaufman, Chris Dowhan, and Adrienne Dowhan (2014, 4th Edition). More than fifty model essays that have worked for applicants, with advice, discussion, and commentary, reveal the secrets of successful essay writing.

Barron's Profiles of American Colleges (2017, 34th Edition). Profiles of more than 1,600 regionally accredited four-year American colleges and universities give the prospective student a preview of his or her relationship to a particular college—based on its facilities, outstanding features and programs, admission requirements, costs, available financial aid, extracurricular activities, programs and major offerings, degrees awarded, enrollment, religious affiliation, housing facilities, and social and honorary societies. Includes online access.

Index

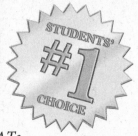